P9-BHY-269

Amenity Resource Valuation:
Integrating Economics with Other Disciplines

Amenity Resource Valuation: Integrating Economics with Other Disciplines

Edited by
George L. Peterson
B. L. Driver
Robin Gregory

Venture Publishing, Inc.
State College, PA 16803

Copyright 1988
Venture Publishing, Inc.
1640 Oxford Circle,
State College, PA 16803
All rights reserved

No part of this material protected by this copyright notice may be reproduced or utilized in any form by
any means, electronic or mechanical, including photocoping, recording, or by any information storage
and retrieval system, without written permission from the copyright owner.

Production Supervision by Bonnie Godbey
Cover Design by Sandra Sikorski
Design by Marilyn Shobaken
Editorial and Production Assistance by Bob Winokur, USDA Forest Service
Library of Congress Catalogue Card Nubmer 88-50862
ISBN 0-910251-27-4

Contents

AUGUSTANA UNIVERSITY COLLEGE
LIBRARY

Part 5: Methodological Issues in Economic Valuation 179

Part 6: Critique and Response 219

Concluding Remarks 253

Preface

Our goal in preparing this text is captured in rich imagery by Ken Boulding and Sven Lundstedt at the conclusion of their paper:

> Economics and psychology . . . are continents of the mind separated by a very wide ocean, no doubt produced by academic continental drift. Furthermore, they seem to be continents without any good harbors. However, we have tried to send our little boats from one to the other. Some of them may have gotten wrecked on the way, but we are more convinced than ever that this is a valuable exercise and that these two continents do belong to the same planet. It is a fundamental principle of economics that specialization without trade is worthless. Unfortunately, in the continents of the mind, specialization seems to feed on itself, and there are large, invisible tariff barriers against the interchange of ideas. We are both grateful to the Forest Service . . . for providing an island in the middle of the ocean . . . where these different disciplines can meet on a practical problem.

We have brought together creative minds from apparently disparate disciplines, hoping to generate new ideas and new working relationships, and hoping thereby to improve concepts and methods for valuation of unpriced amenity goods and services.

Decisions about such amenities are continually being made by individual consumers and by resource managers. Some of these decisions are intuitive, where valuation is an implicit outcome of the decision itself and can only be discovered by examining the choices people make. Some are reasoned institutional choices, and explicit valuation is needed before the decision can be made. It is in this latter category of decision that our interest lies -- in the problem of explicit valuation as an information system for public policy choices by agents of the public trust.

Such valuation has long been studied by economists within the elegantly but narrowly defined neoclassical microeconomic theory of human behavior and as part of the general problem of efficient allocation of scare resources. Valuation has also been studied by psychologists and other behavioral scientists in their quest to describe, explain, and improve individual and social behavior. Each of these disciplines has accumulated storehouses full of knowledge and skills with great potential for trade, but with a few notable exceptions, their continents have drifted apart, and there is little intercontinental commerce. Viewed from the perspective of one's own discipline, as it were through nationalistic eyes, the doings of other academic continents may seem aimed at building churches with no doors and trains with no tracks. But do we not have stored in our own locked closets a few useless church doors, or perhaps some tracks on which trains mightrun?

In 1956 Kenneth Boulding wrote, "One wonders sometimes if science will not grind to a stop in an assemblage of walled-in hermits, each mumbling to himself in a private language that only he can understand." Another author (unknown) describes a group of people who attempted to build a tower to Heaven in order to make themselves equal to God and to protect themselves from another flood. God's response was to confound their languages. Unable to communicate with each other, they were unable to cooperate in combining their skills and energies, and the Tower of Babel was left unfinished. One wonders if their science was not highly developed and if the babel that defeated them was not the babel of many private languages of walled-in scientific hermits.

Unfortunately, exchanges between disciplines are sometimes reminiscent of Gulliver's encounter with two nations warring over which end of an egg to crack. At other times the conversations sound like two carpenters who are arguing about whether hammers or screwdrivers are better without realizing that the job of one of the carpenters is to drive nails while that of the other is to drive screws. One of the most interesting and frustrating of such exchanges is between two draftsmen who disagree about whether an object they are drawing is a circle or a rectangle, when their object actually is a three dimensional cylinder being drawn from different two dimensional points of view. Out of this chaos must come order through communication if there is to be meaningful progress. The answer does not lie in withdrawal into separate monasteries carefully defended at the tops of remote mountain peaks.

Specialization within the disciplines is necessary and important. Sharp blades cut quickly and deeply, and bright flashlights with narrow beams illuminate well those things that fall within their circles of light. But, someone needs to draw the lines that guide the cutting blades, and this requires integration of the narrow beams of many searching lights. Inbreeding must be guided toward strength, not recessive weakness, while cross-breeding must aim at robust diversity and powerful mutants, not sterile mules. We must also resist the temptation to search under a street lamp for keys that were lost in a dark alley.

The disciplines must reach out beyond themselves to find greater strength and usefulness. Nowhere is this more apparent than in economics. Debates rage as to whether economic theory attempts to describe and predict human behavior, whether (like religion) it is a normative model of how people ought to behave, or whether (like mathematics) it is simply a logical structure derived from positive axioms and definitions. Apparently speaking from the descriptive philosophy, Hirschleifer (1985) had this to say:

> There is always something to be said for modesty. But the scientific enterprise demands more. When the phenomenon of radioactive decay refuted the principle of conservation of mass, it would have been modest but unproductive for physicists to decide henceforth to limit their investigations to

those processes for which mass was indeed conserved. And similarly, if the hypothesis of economic man fails in any field of application, the correct scientific response is not modest retreat but an aggressive attempt to produce a better theory. (p. 59)

Anomalies in human behavior that appear to question economic theory have begun to appear in the literature. While economists cling to theory and argue that the fault lies in experimental method or misinterpretation of data, psychologists are not surprised by the anomalies and tend to see them as believable findings about human behavior. We need to get together so we can profit from each other's knowledge.

Economics offers a powerful paradigm and an applied perspective from which to develop and question valuation theories and methods. Psychology and other behavioral sciences offer a detailed collection of findings about human behavior as well as proven experimental methods and measurement technology. While economists have been developing theoretical structures and exploring their logical implications, psychologists have been observing human behavior and measuring human responses. A wedding, it seems, would combine the best of the two. It is difficult to understand how they could wish to remain celibate when the opposite sex is so attractive.

There have been a few notable cases of successful collaboration, e.g., Bishop and Heberlein, Kahneman and Knetsch, and McClellan and Schulze. An attempt was made to follow the tracks of such pioneers in producing this book. The aim was to bring unlikely partners together to write about common interests that both have pursued separately from different points of view. Playing the role of matchmaker, we hoped to facilitate new ways of thinking and new working relationships among the participants. It has been a planned exercise in the creation of creativity. Time, the participants themselves, and our readers must decide whether it was worth the trouble.

However history may judge the effort, it has been a smashing success in at least one respect. The process by which the book was produced included a 3-day meeting of the authors at the Stanley Hotel in Estes Park, Colorado. At that meeting, the Navies of the separate nations of Academia sent forth their "little boats" in search of commerce and conquest. Shots were fired and treaties were signed, and in the midst of the fray, Mr. Boulding was struck by the Spirit of the Muse. True to tradition, he offered a benediction at the close of the meeting in an original bit of verse.

References

Boulding, K. E. (1956). General systems theory--the skeleton of science. Management Science, 2, 197-208. Reprinted in Buckley, Walter (Ed.). 1968. *Modern systems research for the behavioral scientist* (pp. 3-10). Chicago: Aldine Publishing Co.

Hirshleifer, J. (1985). The expanding domain of economics. *The American Economic Review*, 75, 53-68.

Introduction

As demands on publicly administered natural resources grow, the need for improved knowledge of the beneficial and detrimental consequences of alternative resource allocations also increases. Monetary valuation of the gains and losses is an important part of this needed information. These monetary values include marginal prices for products exchanged in reasonably competitive markets and for amenity goods and services (for which efficient market prices are not available). Because public actions affecting the allocation of natural resource sometimes cause prices to change, there is also a need for nonmarginal valuation of market and nonmarket natural resource products.

Economists have made good progress in developing techniques (e.g., the travel cost method (TCM), the contingent valuation method (CVM), and hedonic pricing (HP)) for estimating willingness to pay (WTP) for marginal and nonmarginal changes in amenity goods and services. These techniques are widely accepted and applied by natural resource economists, but the methods are not without controversy. Many so-called "noneconomists" criticize the neoclassical microeconomic theory that is the foundation of these methods. It is too narrow, they say, and too dependent on restrictive and unrealistic assumptions about human behavior. Even among the resource economists who advocate the methods, there remain important theoretical disagreements and empirical debates.

But perhaps of greatest practical concern are the policymakers, some of whom are pretty good economists, who often appear unwilling to accept or to act on the results of valuation studies, including those they have commissioned. To be sure, some of their reasons are political and, therefore, at least in part, outside the scientific domain. However, some of their hesitation stems from well-founded technical concerns, and simply reflects the fact that credibility has not yet been firmly established.

The technical issues that are the focus of controversy include concerns about (1) consistency between economic theory and human behavior, (2) validity of methodological assumptions, (3) adequacy of experimental design, (4) clarity and validity of interpretation, (5) appropriateness of generalization, and (6) adequacy of economic measures to include and represent all relevant dimensions of human concern. Economists who use these methods tend to respond by arguing that their theories and methods are designed for specific purposes, and that criticisms too often are based on the results of misapplication or illogical complaints (i.e., tools will not do things they were not designed to do).

This book was designed to help resolve some of these issues by attempting to integrate the perspective and methods of economics with other behavioral sciences, such as sociology and psychology, in the valuation of nonpriced amenity goods and services. Our starting point is the premise that people who study economics and people who study other behavioral sciences generally work within similar domains and come to some common conclusions. For example, whether they are viewed as normative or descriptive, both economics and psychology are behavioral sciences. That is, both disciplines focus on particular kinds of behavior undertaken by individuals, groups, and their institutions.

The particular behavioral domain of economics is the allocation of scarce resources. In pursuing this domain, thoughtful people have developed the powerful framework of neoclassical microeconomic consumer theory as a basis from which to describe, predict, and evaluate individual and social choices. It is from and within this framework of theory that resource economists have derived their nonmarket valuation methods. Application of these methods requires important assumptions about individual behavior. Application also involves the design of experiments and observations involving human behavior, and at least where contingent valuation methods are concerned, the measurement of human responses to hypothetical situations.

Although scientists from other behavioral disciplines usually are not specifically interested in the allocation of scarce resources as a domain of scientific study, they also study human behavior. They have accumulated observations and propositions about how and why people make decisions, including economic decisions. They also have a good deal of knowledge about the behavioral properties and characteristics of human beings, and some of this information pertains to the assumptions and propositions of economic theory.

Cognitive and social psychologists, for example, have further made it their business to measure such human phenomena as intelligence, aptitude, personality, attitude, and perception, and for these purposes they have developed powerful measurement approaches. Because people are their objects of study, psychologists also have invested much effort in designing experiments that can adequately isolate and describe behavior and its determinants.

To the casual observer, it is surprising that economists have not been more diligent in looking to psychology for models of human behavior, and that psychologists have not more diligently included economic behavior as part of their domain. It is to this interdisciplinary end that our book is directed. Economists and scholars from other domains of behavioral science were pulled together in teams of two and three to write papers on subjects of common interest. We chose the topics to illustrate the interface of theory and practice, and selected participants who are active contributors to both worlds. We then designed the teams to facilitate stress and integration between different points of view, in the hope of stimulating creative new ideas, new working relationships, and new ways of looking at old problems.

When first drafts of the assigned papers were completed, the authors were brought together in a 3-day workshop in Estes Park, Colorado. The papers were grouped in sections, and each module was discussed in two independent sessions. One of the sessions was led by an economist, and the other was led by a noneconomist. At least one author of each of the papers under discussion was in attendance at each session. Authors of other papers not under discussion were assigned to the two groups so as to maximize heterogeneity and, the editor hoped, creative conflict. Two people were assigned to lead each discussion, and together they wrote a joint summary and critique of the papers and discussions in their section. Following the Estes Park meeting, all authors then were asked to revise and resubmit their manuscripts, based on what they had learned from other presentations and from the discussions of their own papers. Also present at the workshop were five people assigned to critique the overall critiquers process, products, and objectives. These five people attended the general presentations and participated in one of the two discussion sessions on each module of papers.

The book is organized according to the workshop structure, although it is certainly not a conference proceedings in the usual sense. The papers, the discussion summaries, and the overall critiques were commissioned for the purpose of solving problems, stimulating creativity, and producing a book. The workshop, which was attended only by invited authors, was simply a tool for enhancing the achievement of these goals by providing feedback on the papers and encouraging interaction among the participants.

In addition to the introduction, the overview chapter by the editors, and the five critiques, the book contains 17 principal chapters that are organized into five sections. Each of the five sections is introduced and reviewed by the respective session leaders. The first section, introduced by John Stoll and Robin Gregory, explains the valuation problem and develops the concepts and paradigms needed to fully understand economic and noneconomic value measurement. In their lead-off paper, Fred Kaiser, Perry Brown, and Robert Davis explain why economic values are needed in resource management and how they typically are used. Ken Boulding and Sven Lundstedt review valuation from a philosophical point of view, and trace the historical roots of economic and psychological value concepts. Tom Brown and Paul Slovic examine the relativity of assigned values to the context in which the valuation task is framed. The last paper in this section, by Bev Driver and Bill Burch, offers a comprehensive paradigm for valuation of nonpriced amenity goods and services in the public policy arena.

The second section is introduced by Perry Brown and Al Dyer. This section offers a general description of economic and psychological approaches to valuation. The paper by Robert Mendelsohn and George Peterson explains monetary valuation as derived from economic theory. In a second paper, Icek Ajzen and George Peterson discuss psychological concepts of value and show how lessons learned in psychology can improve the definition and measurement of economic value, particularly in hypothetical market situations. Paul Kleindorfer and Howard Kunreuther then examine economic behavior and economic valuation in the presence of risk and uncertainty. In the last paper in this section, Roger Ulrich describes ways that physiological measurement approaches can help explain the process by which nonpriced benefits and costs are produced, and he raises important questions about the adequacy of assigned values based on verbal responses and conscious choices.

Herb Schroeder and John Dwyer introduce the third section, which examines several specific concerns about economic valuation. In the first paper, Baruch Fischoff addresses specification problems arising from the definition and perception of the object to which value is to be assigned. Doug MacLean and Claudia Mills discuss the relationship between economic value and the real and perceived framework of property rights. Ann Fisher, Gary McClelland, and Bill Schulze review the controversial disparity between willingness to pay and compensation demanded approaches to value measurement. The last paper in this section, by Robin Gregory and Richard Bishop, asks when and how these two measures of economic worth should be used in policy decisions.

The fourth section, introduced by Tom Brown and Richard Walsh, addresses the use of hypothetical or simulated market methods for estimating economic value. John Hoehn and Cindy Sorg Swanson review important concerns about the contingent valuation method. In the second paper, Robert Mendelsohn and Don Markstrom discuss methods (such as travel cost analysis and hedonic pricing) that can be used to derive values for nonpriced goods and services indirectly from market transactions. In the last paper of this section, David Brookshire, Don Coursey, and Karen Radosevich report on the use of simulated auctions as a tool for exploring disparities in willingness to pay and compensation demanded measures of value.

The fifth section, introduced by Terry Daniel and Cindy Sorg Swanson, addresses some specific methodological issues in economic valuation. Robert Mitchell and Richard Carson review potential sources of bias, particularly where hypothetical market methods are used. Charles Harris, Howard Tinsley, and Dennis Donnelly then offer a critique of economic valuation in general, emphasizing issues of validity, reliability, sampling, and generalizability.

Following these principal chapters, each of the five reviewers present their response to the overall effort. In a final chapter, the editors strive to integrate the different points of view expressed by conference participants and point out some of the most promising directions for future research.

Part 1: The Amenity Valuation Problem

Overview

John R. Stoll
Department of Agricultural Economics
Texas A&M University

Robin Gregory
Decision Research
Eugene, Oregon

Value, as used in economics, is the worth of some set of changed circumstances as judged by the sovereign individual. The concept is more broadly defined by many outside the field of economics, as "an enduring belief ... [concerning] desirable modes of conduct or desirable end-states of existence" (Rokeach, 1973, p. 3), or in terms of perceived gains and losses (constituting beneficial or adverse changes in welfare). Economic value also is thought about in these terms, but generally defined more narrowly as the monetary measure of that subset of gains and losses capable of being represented by the monetary metric.

This distinction is directly related to the purposes of the papers on value concepts and justifications in this section. The authors of these papers are cognizant of the fact that value, as commonly considered, is a broader concept than the monetary metric widely used to represent value. Therefore, the questions addressed in the papers, as well as in the 3-day workshop at which they were discussed, are two-fold: "What components are generally omitted from the monetary representation of value due to incommensurability?" and "What measurement problems are likely to occur when attempting to estimate values for more tangible components of observed environmental changes."

Clearly, values are readily and, for the most part, accurately reflected for many items in the marketplace. The trading of items for money, which occurs in conventional markets, helps to establish a forum for determining at least relative values through trial and error decision making, and provides a forgiving environment where learning can occur over time. The papers in this section are most directly concerned with items often referred to as nonmarket goods, because they are not traded in conventional markets. Some of these nonmarket goods are reasonably well defined by social scientists, but their use for decision purposes--as part of a framework whereby tradeoffs are made between competing sources of value--too often is neglected. When this occurs, decisions about the allocation or value of all goods will be skewed, and public policy decisions may poorly reflect the nation's objectives.

One thing is clear: Social scientists, who often work within the more narrow confines of their own disciplines, have much to gain by pooling their insights and making shared contributions to public decisionmaking. In the context of developing a better representation of the public's amenity resource values, the papers in this section encourage this shared contribution to amenity valuation.

An Integrative Overview

The process of arriving at values and their use in decisions regarding public amenity resources can be schematically represented, as in Figure 1. Individuals have initial sets of social values, beliefs, knowledge, and endowments that are, in part, the product of their particular institutional setting (Box 2, Figure 1). Alterations in amenity resources could involve either a small change in resource endowments or the threat of a total loss of the resource. When these individuals are confronted with such alterations (Box 2, Figure 1), they must combine the information

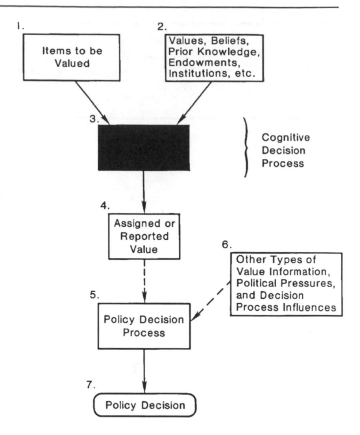

FIGURE 1. Policy decision process.

they are given with the information they already possess, and use their prior beliefs, knowledge, and endowments to arrive at a valuation of the change. That is, they must arrive at a recognition of the gain or loss in welfare associated with the proposed or reported change. This gain or loss is then translated into the assigned or reported value obtained by the researcher who has attempted to measure values for such amenity resource changes (Box 4, Figure 1). If this researcher is an economist, the reported value likely will be in terms of a monetary metric; those from other disciplines may prefer to obtain noneconomic measures (e.g., importance) or a combination of different measures. In either case, the change in amenity resource conditions is an input into the cognitive valuation process (Box 3, Figure 1), and the measures of gain or loss reported by an individual are the output of that process.

At best, our understanding of this cognitive valuation process is incomplete; at worst, it is sufficiently misleading that we may count as a value something that is a product of the elicitation process itself (see Brown & Slovic, this volume). For this reason, we have represented it as a black box. We know, in general terms, what goes in (although not how it is perceived) and we can observe what comes out (but not necessarily how it is translated from the actual results of the cognitive process). The authors of the papers in this section recognize this void and attempt to illuminate portions of it.

Once observed measures of value, monetary or otherwise, are obtained as output from the cognitive processes of individuals, they are entered into the policy decision process (Box 5, Figure

1) and begin to influence the choice of alternative amenity resource policies. This policy decision process also considers a variety of other information, which may include participants' perceptions of other social goals as well as assorted forms of political lobbying and pressures from vested interest groups (Box 6, Figure 1). The economist's monetary, or other social scientists' nonmonetary, measures of value are therefore only one input to this decision process that ultimately will determine the fate of the amenity resources under consideration (Box 7, Figure 1).

Each of the four papers presented in this section can be cast in the context of this seven-part representation of the amenity resource valuation process.

Kaiser, Brown, and Davis address the question of resource policy decisions and the types of inputs needed to create a more effective decision process. They recognize that information about values is needed as part of any decision for which conflicts may occur, and they recognize that in recent decades decisions concerning amenity resources have become increasingly controversial (in part because many such resources are becoming more scarce). Whereas the policy decision process could proceed somewhat haphazardly in the past, recent decreases in supply, coupled with increases in demand, have led to a decision-making environment in which one must proceed more carefully. Amenity resource values, which according to Kaiser et al. are not often reflected effectively in markets, are needed for decisions involving tradeoffs between commercial and noncommercial uses of the resource base that supports amenity values.

Although monetary measures of amenity resource values are most often sought by administrative agencies for use in the policy decision process, these same value estimates are obtained by techniques that many administrators judge with skepticism. The values are needed as indicators of the relative importance of amenity resource uses. But to be effective inputs to this decision process, Kaiser et al. argue that more attention needs to be paid to justification or defense of the methods used to obtain value estimates of nonmarket goods.

Two questions are of particular concern. First, what are the conceptual bases of each of the methods used to obtain nonmarket values, and do these methods lead to value estimates consistent with the outcomes of market processes? Second, why do individuals place values on the amenity services of natural resources? It is these questions, Kaiser et al. argue, that must be answered to assure a greater acceptance of the outputs of nonmarket valuation techniques as part of the policy decision process. In concluding, the authors recognize the role that other influences (Box 6, Figure 1) play in the policy decision process when they state "analysis will not replace resource decision making, but refinements in theory and application will continue to enhance the usefulness of analysis." We wholeheartedly agree.

The second paper, by Boulding and Lundstedt, logically follows Kaiser et al. by addressing the concept of value and its justifications. Boulding and Lundstedt perceive economists to be in possession of a few simplistic, yet extremely useful, insights to offer to the valuation process. Individuals are continuously confronted with the need to make choices regarding alternative "images of the future." The study of choices leads to a recognition of the alternative future images, which must be

forgone to obtain the outcomes of the choices one makes. Thus, Boulding and Lundstedt explicitly recognize the importance of opportunity cost. Further, the use of money as a metric leads to a common measure of this opportunity cost, which is useful to decisionmakers despite its unidimensional nature.

Although the structure of economics has much to offer in examining values, Boulding and Lundstedt stress that it is also overly simplistic in several key regards: The paradigm largely ignores uncertainty, assumes individuals are mentally healthy, grants legitimacy to existing distributions of power and wealth, and pays insufficient heed to social taboos (i.e., social constraints upon behavior). They propose that a more robust conception of values requires both an economic and psychological perspective. In their presentation, Boulding and Lundstedt make special note of their belief that many of the building blocks for developing an integrated view of value for amenity resources already have been laid by the two disciplines--there is no need to reinvent the wheel. They stress that what is needed is closer cooperation between the disciplines and a more rigorous examination of the behavioral assumptions of each discipline. In this sense, their message is simple but well taken: Start with building bridges between the disciplines and removing artificial linguistic barriers, so that the communalities between disciplinary researchers can be acknowledged, and together researchers can explore improved methods for assessing amenity resource values.

Brown and Slovic consider the role of context and the circumstances that surround and condition the individual in the valuation process. Thus, their presentation comes closest to addressing the actual cognitive decision process (Box 3, Figure 1) through which individuals must traverse. Initially they discuss the role of held values, beliefs, and endowments as things affecting the value of objects. Some of these beliefs are relevant in any particular context and are intermixed with perception of the objects for which values are to be assigned by the individual.

Brown and Slovic include a relatively detailed discussion of the existing research on those contextual factors that may affect the values assigned to objects by individuals. These factors involve the choice of response modes, relative magnitudes, order affects, stimulus mixture, informational clues, constituency affected by valuation outcomes, repetition in soliciting responses, and the definition of social settings. Although not all evidence leads to consistent results, their conclusion is that substantial support exists for the notion that contextual factors often significantly influence the assigned values expressed by respondents.

Although context is argued to affect values, Brown and Slovic acknowledge that an understanding of exactly why this occurs is not yet forthcoming. Thus, the contents of the black box representing the cognitive decision process are becoming slightly more visible but remain far from clear. They suggest that context may serve to "fill in" when decision situations call for greater degrees of cognitive effort, when personal values conflict, or when attitudes are not well defined. Further, it is possible that the context itself is an integral part of the valuation, that is, values are meaningless without context because they do not exist in its absence. Thus, any significant change in context could necessarily lead to alterations in values. If this model is appropriate, then such a shift is not only to be expected but it may be perfectly legitimate. For this reason, increasing attention should be paid to the context from which values are collected, the consistency of results across varying contexts, and the legitimacy of chosen contexts.

Driver and Burch recognize the legislative necessity to assess changes in resource uses. This mandate clearly includes the U.S. Forest Service and, in part, prompted the papers on amenity value assessment in this section. Administrative procedures for considering these values have been promulgated as a series of rules that lay out the basic structure of the evaluation process. The thrust of Driver and Burch's paper is that they are uncomfortable with the usual tact taken by economists, involving the assignment of an economic value for amenity resource alterations in the form of a monetary metric. Their concern is that much is lost in the process of translating the multidimensional amenity resource services to a single monetary metric. Instead, Driver and Burch argue for the adoption of an approach wherein the amenity resource service changes are described in terms of their altered conditions, inclusive of the effects that these altered conditions can have on individuals. Driver and Burch believe that this procedure will encourage a better understanding of the changes being considered to be reflected in the decision process.

Driver and Burch's concern boils down to skepticism regarding what is actually done as part of a project assessment with information regarding changes that cannot be monetized. As such, their paper does not address the cognitive decision process directly. Rather, their concern is with the outputs of that process (Box 4, Figure 1), the forms of that output, and the other types of information (Box 6, Figure 1) that legitimately have a bearing upon the overall policy decision process (Box 5, Figure 1) to ensure that "good" policy decisions are achieved (Box 7, Figure 1). Their argument raises legitimate concerns, but their solution, involving a multiple-accounts evaluation approach, raises two sets of questions for the present authors. First, few would dispute that not all changed conditions can be represented with a monetary metric; however, tradeoffs involving monetary implications still must be considered in any properly performed evaluation of altered resource conditions. Moreover, if the output of an evaluation is information about the expected project impacts displayed in the form of multiple accounts, how the package is put together may prove as important as its content. Second, how will decisions about the choice of response units be

made? Driver and Burch's focus is on a new approach for valuation of amenity goods and services; the earliest steps in that assessment process, involving the identification and measurement of gains and losses, ultimately may prove to be the most troublesome.

Summary

Until amenity values can be presented as inputs to the decision process and defended as compatible with market-generated values in terms of their perceived accuracy, their usefulness will be limited. There are a variety of reasons for this, many of which have been discussed above. Clearly, various constituent groups will have vested interests and particular concerns related to specific costs and benefits or the secondary impacts of decisions upon local and regional areas. Often amenity values will be viewed as a constraint upon the achievement of more tangible products for particular sectors of the public (e.g., interest groups). None of the above are necessarily illegitimate. However, the legitimate role of amenity values associated with particular resource uses will be enhanced by the development of a more coherent set of procedures for their measurement. This will necessarily entail a greater degree of attention to the contents of the black box (Box 3, Figure 1) representing the cognitive decision process (about which we, too, have been skirting). The papers in this section, and some of these authors' recent work in economics and psychology, make significant inroads in this direction. Yet considerable progress remains to be made. Creation of an added stimulus for researchers, and perhaps the identification of others wanting to walk the same path, could well be the most significant outcome of this workshop and volume.

Reference

Rokeach, M. (1973). *The nature of human values*. New York: Free Press, Inc.

The Need for Values of Amenity Resources Public Natural Resources Management

H. Fred Kaiser
USDA Forest Service
Forest Inventory and Economics Research Staff

Perry J. Brown
Department of Resource Recreation Management
Oregon State University

Robert K. Davis
USDI Bureau of Land Management
Division of Wildlife

Public resource management is a complex phenomenon, which requires many kinds of information. It is based on the simple notion that through management of natural resources, people can derive benefits; however, actually deriving the benefits is not simple. Effective resource management requires that one know the benefits desired by relevant constituents and the means to produce those benefits.

In the Workshop on Integrating Economic and Psychological Knowledge in Valuations of Public Amenity Resources, we examined the question "How can we best estimate the worth of amenity resources?" Only a small part of amenity valuation focuses on information useful for program and budget justification, policy formulation and analysis, and investment decisions.

Resources viewed as commodities (e.g., timber, forage) usually have their worth established through market transactions. Amenity resources (e.g., recreation, wildlife, aesthetics), on the other hand, usually are not exchanged in established markets and thus their worth must be established by extra-market procedures. While the workshop focused on how to improve these extra-market procedures for valuing amenity resources, the purposes of this paper are to explore why it is necessary to establish the value of amenity resources, and to identify some of the approaches now being used.

Within the realm of valuation, we have carved out a relatively specific niche for this workshop. In a broad sense, we can identify two basic kinds of value: held values and assigned values (Brown, 1981). Held values concern the goodness and badness of objects, ideas, etc., whereas assigned values represent the worth of objects. Thus, worth of objects is dependent upon the held values about the objects.

We focus on the subset of social values recognized as economic values (Brown and Manfredo, in press), primarily those concerned with extra-market values necessary for economic efficiency analysis. Extra-market values for amenity resources are most problematic for natural resource administrators doing policy and investment analysis. Cooperation between behavioral scientists and economists is needed for two issues regarding these extra-market values: "What are the products we want to value?" and "How best can we measure their economic worth?"

Need for Amenity Resource Valuation

Anticipated increases in human population and needs for economic development will continue to exert pressures to exploit the forest and range lands for timber, livestock, and other industrial products. At the same time, needs for forests to provide recreation and other amenity services will increase. Balancing the competing demand for commodities and amenities will require thoughtful and rigorous evaluation of alternatives.

In the past, application of evaluation concepts by land managers has been primarily informal and intuitive, particularly where conflicts over resource allocations have not been intense. For many years, the success of judgmental planning methods was measured by continuing political support and relative lack of controversy over land use policies. Recently, the situation has changed as pressures have mounted for maximizing net public

benefits. The environmental movement of the 1960's and early 1970's led to federal legislation, regulations, and executive orders that required increased attention to economic and environmental consequences of federal natural resource management actions. For example, the 1974 Forest and Range Land Renewable Resources Planning Act (RPA) directs the Forest Service to identify management needs, opportunities, and alternative programs and to analyze their long-term costs and benefits. The 1976 Federal Land Policy and Management Act requires the Bureau of Land Management to develop multiple-use management plans for lands under its administration and to inventory the resource values of these lands to identify changes and emerging resource needs. The Principles and Guidelines for Water Resources Development direct the U. S. Army Corps of Engineers, Bureau of Reclamation, and Soil Conservation Service to identify the national economic development benefits of their projects.

These legislative and administrative guidelines have stimulated a major need for recreation, wildlife, and other amenity resource values. For example, the National Forest System is now guided by Section 6 of the Forest and Range Land Renewable Resource Act, which requires formulation of a detailed planning system for program coordination. Some key characteristics of this system are (a) allocation of resource production targets based on resource capability of each administrative unit and on relative efficiency of production; (b) regional foresters use assessment findings and the National RPA Program to prepare regional plans, which show how targets are distributed among national forests within each region; and (c) using the assigned target range and local information on capabilities to prepare a multiresource plan for each national forest. Specific aspects of this plan are:

1. A 4-decade program is developed for each national forest based on the RPA Recommended Program.
2. Land units are identified at the national forest level, and appropriate activities and investments necessary for production of resulting outputs are identified. This identification will come from the inventory information base for each national forest.
3. Benefit-cost analysis of the relative efficiency of production from each resource unit or group of resource units with similar characteristics are performed.
4. Major issues and program responsiveness to these issues are identified.

As the Forest Service and other agencies have found out, however, resource planning and evaluation are complex processes. Public land management covers a wide range of activities and the use of diverse combinations of natural resource management facilities. Identification and measurement of benefits from forest and range lands can create major challenges because some of the outputs from these lands lack a conventional pricing mechanism.

Although it can be tempting for public resource administrators and analysts to ignore amenity resource values, the values must be considered in making adequate resource evaluations and in justifying programs. Simply, amenity resources are important to too many people to ignore their worth when justifying programs and budgets, formulating and analyzing policies, and making investment decisions. If amenity resource values are ignored, interested publics will take the administrators to task and challenge their decisions, sometimes in court.

We find that in dealing with Congress, administrators can use amenity resource values to communicate how they view the worth of these resources, and legislators can respond based on their perception of values. At a minimum, stating the worth of amenity resources enables the opening of a dialogue about these resources relative to other resources. Such a dialogue has proven valuable when legislators are interested in how resource administrators justify their program and budget requests.

The issue of below cost timber sales on national forests is a case where amenity values are proving to be an important part of the debate. Concern is expressed by conservation and forest industry groups, forest and economic professionals, and Congress about whether or not some national forest timber sales fail to recover the costs of offering them, or involve expenditures that are not cost effective. This interest has intensified the discussion of amenity values currently being used by the Forest Service to justify these sales. Questions concern whether or not these values are properly defined and if proper measurement techniques have been used to establish them.

The same kinds of issues arise when administrators propose programs and budgets to Office of Management and Budget (OMB) staff. The reasonableness and precision of value estimates are often important issues because OMB staffers want to know precisely what benefits will be produced for what costs. The OMB, like Congress, is interested in the tradeoffs among programs between and within agencies. Reliable value estimates enable assessment of such tradeoffs.

Currently, the OMB is questioning if the Forest Service is using proper amenity values for their national and regional planning. The Forest Service is using the consumers' willingness to pay for such activities as camping, picknicking, wilderness visits, and hiking. The conceptual basis for valuing these benefits is the simulated market price for access times quantity of the output. The use of willingness to pay and the value of these goods is assumed to be the benefit to society. The difference between the estimated access price of the output and the actual fee collected by the Forest Service for the output is defined as a consumer benefit. The OMB questions if proper techniques are being used to identify these values and, in some instances, if these values actually exist.

Because both the Forest Service and Bureau of Land Management (BLM) are responsible for multiple outputs from the lands they administer, presenting value estimates for each multiple output is important when they speak with Congress and the OMB. For example, it has been customary for the Forest Service to have value estimates for timber and for the BLM to have value estimates for livestock grazing, but with their multiple-use responsibilities they need value estimates for all outputs, including wildlife, fish, recreation opportunities, clean water, and scenery. Without such value estimates, there is little basis for comparing outputs of commodity and amenity resources.

Reliable estimates of the value of amenity resources also are needed for decisions within public resource management organizations. They also are useful for program and budget justification and are needed for budget allocation, land management planning, resolution of policy conflicts, and project investment analysis. In making administrative decisions, value estimates

can be used to conduct tradeoff and benefit-cost analyses, and build the value of management outputs into estimates of present net worth. Without value estimates for amenity resources, the resources become constraints in the analysis and limit the production of other outputs. In this case, we usually have a difficult time transmitting the meaning of these constraints to all decisionmakers and we do not know what these constraints are worth; we just impose them.

Habitat for the spotted owl is such an issue currently being analyzed by the Forest Service. This species exists in old growth stands of Douglas-fir in Oregon and Washington. Questions are being raised on how to properly analyze this issue. The Forest Service has developed estimates from 1 to 5 billion dollars in timber harvest revenues foregone if it is unable to harvest the timber where the species exists. However, the Forest Service has not been able to value the preservation of spotted owls for future generations.

Value estimates for amenity resources, similar to those of commodity resources, are needed for investment analysis. If one is considering wildlife habitat management, construction of a trail, or forest preservation for scenic and wildlife maintenance, one needs value estimates of the outputs, to assess whether the projects are financially sound. For example, the BLM has developed an investment analysis program (SAGERAM) that uses a file of prices for various market and extra-market outputs. The prices for forage are provided by an annual U. S. Department of Agriculture (USDA) survey supported by both the Forest Service and BLM. Prices for hunting, fishing, and other types of outdoor recreation are obtained from Forest Service resource planning act studies. This could change as more western states complete travel cost and contingent value studies of fishing and hunting prices (as Idaho has done and Montana and Nevada are doing) because each state office in the BLM can use the source of its choosing when selecting amenity prices.

Finally, value assessments for amenity resources also are useful for dealing with the public. They communicate to the public how agencies value different amenity resources, provide a reference so that the public can counter agency values, and make it clear that the value of amenity resources is neither zero nor infinity. For example, when agencies display to the public the worth of flat water recreation with a dam and the worth of wild river recreation without the dam, tradeoffs become readily apparent. Also, if the worth of recreation opportunities is used to justify below cost timber sales or any other management activity, the public can assess the reasonableness of the justification if explicit amenity values are given.

We can assign values to amenity resources, and we certainly need these values. The question is, can we do a better job in assigning value to amenity resources? Can we improve the credibility, validity, and reliability of our estimates?

Assigning Economic Values to Amenity Resource Values

Identification and measurement of recreation, wildlife, and other amenity values continue to be major challenges for most resource analysts, although the idea for the use of extra-market values goes back at least to the 17th century. In 1844, a French engineer named Dupuit argued that public transportation facilities should be determined by what the potential users would be willing to pay for using them. Although a number of innovative approaches have been developed to infer quantitative prices for service outputs, four primary approaches are currently used: (1) intrinsic value, (2) opportunity cost, (3) consumer cost, and (4) transaction evidence.

The intrinsic value approach provides a baseline for comparing alternative forest investments. In Czechoslovakia, Papanek (1984) developed a method using this approach, which employs both quantitative and qualitative characteristics. Considering the resource productivity, suitability, and demands of a forest site, he analyzed the factors that influenced production of timber, recreation, and other forest products. Factors considered included production costs as well as those accepted by the visitors to reach the site. From these factors, a monetary value was awarded for each product and the forest site classified. Other researchers, such as Hills in Canada and McHarg in the United States, have developed similar analytical approaches (Belknap & Furtado, 1967).

The opportunity cost approach has been used to value production opportunities. The opportunity cost is the return that the capital or resources could produce if invested in the alternative endeavor producing the best financial return. The Federal Republic of Germany and Switzerland have most actively used this approach (Gundermann, 1981). In these countries, an attempt has been made to evaluate the additional costs and returns to timber, recreational, and protective functions of forests. Although the method does not indicate a value for benefits, it does provide a baseline for comparing alternative investments.

The consumer cost method measures the value to the participant in dollars spent, not the costs of development but rather the costs incurred in travel to and use of the site. These estimates are often the first evidence that managers seek when they need to show the importance of a recreation activity. The consumer cost method was used for hunting and fishing in the 1940's, and is presently used to derive costs of nonconsumptive uses and nongame species. For example, hundreds of millions of dollars are spent on birdseed, binoculars, bird books, and other items for nonconsumptive use of wildlife (DeGraaf & Payne, 1975). The 1980 National Survey of Hunting and Fishing is now providing a data base for analyzing the determinants of demand for wildlife watching (Hay & McConnell, 1979).

Economists disapprove of the gross consumer cost approach because of two major weaknesses of the method. First, the gross consumer cost method does not measure the value of an additional opportunity to the consumer. Public expenditures involve tradeoffs among different resources; therefore, when determining value of an additional recreation site, net value from the added opportunity rather than the gross value, must be measured. Measuring only the gross change in expenditures gives no indication of how much the consumer is willing to pay. A second weakness of the gross consumer cost method is that many expenditures cannot be attributed solely to the site--expenditures may be ancillary to the actual use of the site.

To overcome some of these problems, a method was developed by several researchers in North America using travel cost as a surrogate for price (Clawson & Knetsch, 1966). This method derives a demand function from differences in travel costs from different origins, and assumes that people coming from different distances experience about the same benefits on site. Therefore, the difference in their travel costs will reflect the net benefits they receive. For each origin, travel costs are incrementally increased, and use estimated at each increment. A site demand curve is plotted using these estimates. Willingness to pay for the site is estimated by the area under this demand curve. A strength of this method is the use of actual behavior to place a value on benefits. Also, the method accounts for spatial differences in the market.

Certain circumstances lend themselves to the use of the travel cost method, while other situations present difficulties (Dwyer, Kelly, & Bowes, 1977). First, to estimate demand accurately, sufficient variation in travel costs must exist among users; thus, users must generally travel from a wide range of distances. Second, the method works for a single purpose visit, but can be biased on multiple purpose trips. If visitors travel to multiple sites in a market area, analysts find it difficult to decide how much of the costs to allocate to the site being evaluated. The problem is most acute for sites in a market area with several recreation alternatives. Third, a travel cost demand curve implicitly assumes that recreational quality remains constant over the range from zero use to the full use at the present admission fee. Finally, the method assumes that no benefits are derived from the travel itself; thus, travel costs and travel time can be used to represent the price paid to visit the recreation site (Rosenthal, Loomis, & Peterson, 1984).

A method receiving increasing attention from researchers is transaction evidence. This method attempts to estimate value by comparing a public recreation site with a comparable recreation site operated by private entrepreneurs where a price is charged. Conceptually, the method is appealing because it measures the actual amount a user pays for an opportunity in the market. The method is useful primarily in those situations where similar prices are charged for similar recreational sites. The price charged for the opportunity can then be used as a comparable value for the unpriced or administratively priced recreation opportunity.

In practice, however, finding similar sites and conditions is often difficult or impossible. This is especially true for opportunities such as primitive recreation sites where a large number of public activities is provided. In those cases where comparable market price opportunities are not available, weaknesses arise in the method. First, the price determined often cannot be applied to a different site because a market value is associated with a particular product. Each site that has a different market must be valued at a different price. Second, because of the many different types of environments, a standardized value is likely to be inaccurate.

Currently, contingent or simulated markets are often used as proxies for actual markets, which allow analysts to predict quantity demanded at different price levels (Davis, 1964). Surveys are used to estimate site values by asking users a series of questions to determine their willingness to pay (or willingness to accept compensation) for use of a site. Surveys are most useful in instances when the sites being evaluated are part of multiple trip destinations or when changes in travel cost or number of visits occur because of a small change in site quality.

This method assumes that consumers can assign accurate values and that a series of questions can accurately elicit value.

The structure of the method may, in fact, not meet these assumptions for several reasons. First, the consumer may not be able to assign values on the basis of descriptions of hypothetical circumstances (Dwyer et al., 1977). For the model to be useful, the dollar value assigned by the user must reflect his or her actual behavior in the market. This assignment is difficult because market prices for the opportunity generally do not exist. When people buy items in a market, they consider alternatives for a long time, consult with knowledgeable people, shop around for the best buy, and base their decision on past experience in the market. The short time spent with an interviewer may not discern actual market behavior when market prices have not actually been paid.

Second, the interviewer must be certain that the respondent clearly understands the scale of the question. The survey seeks to elicit only values that apply to specific opportunities affected by a project. Therefore, a respondent must clearly understand whether a question refers to a specific opportunity, such as fishing at a particular lake, or a general activity, such as hunting. Values for the general availability of an activity cannot be used to determine the value of the same activity for a specific site. Thus, it should be clear to a respondent whether a question is evaluating a specific site or the general availability of an opportunity over time. Otherwise, errors in value estimates result.

Even with these problems, contingent valuation is gaining increasing credibility. Market and contingent values have been found to be consistent with derived market prices (Brookshire, 1982; Coursey, 1985). Comparison with travel cost evaluations produced similar results (Bishop, 1982; Desvousges, Smith, & McGivney, 1983; Sellar, Stoll, & Chavas, 1985). Although contingent value might or might not be totally accurate, it produces values that can be useful in resource evaluation.

Relevance of Extra-market Values

Although application of extra-market values has some shortcomings, the advancement in extra-market valuation theory and methods has improved multiple-use management and forest analysis. Multiresource analysis provides (1) a reasonably consistent framework for examining resource management options, (2) an overview of development opportunities, and (3) some indicators of market interactions even when formal markets do not exist. The travel cost method, for example, provides information on spatial relationships as well as value estimates. Also, notable applications of research methods to valuation problems have also been made by analysts in a number of studies over the past 10 years (Charbonneau & Hay, 1978; Gum & Martin, 1975; Hammack & Brown, 1974; Miller & Hay, 1981). Not only have some usable results been obtained, but the work has resulted in refinement and verification of travel cost methods.

Two issues need to be addressed, however, before extra-market valuation can be fully integrated into resource analysis: (1) developing extra-market values that share the same theoretical and philosophical foundation with market values and (2) understanding why individuals establish values for social services involving natural resources.

The first issue concerns developing resource values that are commensurate or show the same theoretical and philosophical foundation, so that the value of one resource output is directly comparable to the value of another resource output. This would enable tradeoff analysis to be made between resources based on value estimates. Without these commensurate values, extra-market values are often not used in resource evaluation or investment decisions.

The market-based theory for the travel cost method is accepted by econometricians who have worked on the method over the past 20 years. The behavioral theory of contingent valuation is less well accepted, but the method has received equivalent acceptance for simulating markets where none exist. Both methods find more acceptance among social scientists than among officials of the public land managing agencies. These officials, accustomed to dealing with commodity prices, prefer that prices for the extra-market resources be based on market transactions. If we cannot find market-based data, then more effort is needed to validate the results of simulation methods.

An example of the type of research needed has been done by Bishop, Heberlein, and Kealy (1983) at the University of Wisconsin. They determined what price hunters were willing to accept for selling their public land hunting permits by using actual cost transactions. The study determined market clearing prices for goose and deer hunting. They also compared these values to other value estimates derived through travel cost and contingent value approaches.

The second issue involves clarification of why and how resource benefits are valued. Clarification of the value of products and attributes is needed to improve resource decision making. For example, researchers have already contributed two other ideas that are often useful when resource investments are discussed: option value and existence or bequest value. Option value is when users of a good or service are willing to pay something to retain the prospect or option to use it at some time in the future. Existence value is when nonusers might be willing to pay something to assure the continued existence of an asset during their lifetime or for the benefit of future generations. Several researchers have argued that most forms of wildlife that possess option and or existence values have indeed been rewarded with positive responses (Brookshire, Eubanks, & Randall, 1978; Stoll & Johnson, 1983). Wilderness values have received more attention in this regard. Recent discussion about option values leads to caution about concluding that the value can be consistently measured or that it is necessarily always positive (Freeman, 1984). A total willingness to pay that includes use value as well as option value is the quantity that will probably be measured in the foreseeable future (Bishop, 1982). Ambiguities may be present in existence values as well, but such information collected from well-run studies can be useful in making choices where resources might be irreversibly destroyed (Brookshire, Eubanks, & Randall, 1983).

Another area receiving increasing attention is hedonic pricing. This pricing method focuses on consumer satisfaction derived from attributes associated with the particular goods, rather than the goods themselves. By concentrating on these attributes, analysts are able to identify variation in key characteristics and thereby estimate the willingness to pay for marginal changes in those characteristics (Brookshire, 1982).

Conclusion

Significant progress has been made in theoretical and applied aspects of the economics of multiple-use management. Simple economic applications have been replaced by more complex ones. However, much work remains to be done.

Empirical work is needed to define relevant products, estimate production possibilities, and define social values. Studies on the various relationships between resource inputs and outputs are needed. These dynamic interactions are presently only partially understood. In addition, studies involving different accounting stances should be pursued. Analysis will not replace resource decision making, but refinements in theory and application will continue to enhance the usefulness of analysis.

Values of amenity resources need to be estimated. They are useful for program and budget justification at congressional, OMB, department, and agency levels; policy formulation and analysis; and investment decisions at all levels. The task before us is to develop valuation methods to the point of acceptability by land managers, who must be convinced both of the credibility of a method for valuing extra-market resources and of its practicality. We have made much progress with theory and method in recent years; the challenge is for development and application to proceed. We must know when and when not to use economic valuation in resource analysis and we must know how to improve our techniques to ensure meeting tests of credibility, validity, reliability, and practicality.

References

Belknap, R. K., & Furtado, J. G. (1967). *Three approaches to environment resource analysis*. Washington, DC: Conservation Foundation.

Bishop, R. C. (1982). Option value: An exposition and extension. *Land Economics, 58*, 1-15.

Bishop, R. C., Heberlein, T. A., & Kealy, M. S. (1983). Contingent valuation of environmental assets. *Natural Resources Journal, 23*, 619-633.

Brookshire, D. S. (1982). Valuing public goods: A Comparison of survey and hedonic approaches. *American Economics Review, 72*, 165-177.

Brookshire, D. S., Eubanks, L. S., & Randall, A. (1978). Valuing wildlife resources: An experiment. *Transactions of the North American Wildlife and Natural Resources Conference, 43*, 302-310.

Brookshire, D. S., Eubanks, L. S., & Randall, A. (1983). Estimating option prices and existence values for wildlife resources. *Land Economics, 59*, 1-15.

Brown, P. J., & Manfredo, M. J. (1987). Social values of wildlife. In D. Decker & G. Goff (Eds.), *Valuing wildlife resources* (pp. 12-23). Boulder, CO: Westview Press.

Brown, T. C. (1981). *Tradeoff analysis in local land management planning* (General Technical Report RM-82). Fort Collins, CO: Rocky Mountain Forest and Range Experiment Station, U.S. Department of Agriculture, Forest Service.

Charbonneau, J., & Hay, M. J. (1978). Determinants and economic values of hunting and fishing. *Transactions of the North American Wildlife and Natural Resources Conference, 43*, 391-403.

Clawson, M., & Knetsch, J. L. (1966). *Economics of outdoor recreation*. Baltimore, MD: Johns Hopkins Press.

Coursey, D. (1985). *Experimental methods for assigning environmental benefits*. Washington, DC: U.S. Environmental Protection Agency.

Davis, R. K. (1964). The value of big game hunting in a private forest. *Transactions of the North American Wildlife and Natural Resources Conference, 29*, 393-403.

DeGraaf, R. M., & Payne, B. R. (1975). Economic values of nongame birds and some urban wildlife research needs. *Transactions of the North American Wildlife and Natural Resources Conference, 40*, 281-287.

Desvousges, W. H., Smith, V. K., & McGivney, M. P. (1983). *Comparison of alternative approaches for estimating recreation and related benefits of water quality improvements* (Report No. EPA 230-05-83-001). Washington, DC: U.S. Environmental Protection Agency.

Dwyer, J. F., Kelly, J. R., & Bowes, M. D. (1977). *Improved procedures for valuation of the contribution of recreation to national economic development* (Research Report No. 128). Champaign, IL: University of Illinois Water Resources Center.

Freeman, A., III. (1984). The sign and size of option value. *Land Economics, 60*, 1-13.

Gum, R. L., & Martin, W. E. (1975). Problems and solutions in estimating the demand for and value of rural outdoor recreation. *American Journal of Agricultural Economics, 57*(4), 558-566.

Gundermann, E. (1981). Evaluation of the recreation evaluation methods used in western Europe. *XVII IUFRO World Congress Proceeding, Division 4*, 513-518.

Hammack, J., & Brown, G. M., Jr. (1974). *Waterfowl and wetlands: Toward bioeconomic analysis*. Baltimore, MD: Johns Hopkins University Press.

Hay, M. J., & McConnell, K. E. (1979). An analysis of participation in nonconsumptive wildlife recreation. *Land Economics, 55*, 460-471.

Miller, J. R., & Hay, M. J. (1981). Determinants of hunter participation: Duck hunting in the Mississippi Flyway. *American Journal of Agricultural Economics, 64*, 677-684.

Papanek, F. (1984). Use of economic values of forest functions in decisionmaking. In *IUFRO Proceedings of the International Conference, Thessalonica, Greece, Forest Research Institute of Thessalonica (Vol. 1)* (pp. 263-271).

Rosenthal, D. H., Loomis, J. B., & Peterson, G. L. (1984). *The travel cost model, concepts and applications* (Report No. 109). Fort Collins, CO: U.S. Department of Agriculture, Forest Service, Rocky Mountain Forest and Range Experiment Station.

Sellar, C., Stoll, J. R., & Chavas, S. P. (1985). Validation of empirical measures of welfare change: A comparison of nonmarket techniques. *Land Economics, 61*, 156-175.

Stoll, J. R., & Johnson, L. A. (1983). *Concepts of value, nonmarket valuation, and the case of the whooping crane*. Unpublished manuscript, Natural Resource Working Paper Series, Department of Agricultural Economics, Texas A & M University, College Station, TX.

Value Concepts and Justifications

Kenneth E. Boulding
Institute of Behavioral Science
University of Colorado, Boulder

Sven B. Lundstedt
School of Public Administration
The Ohio State University

Valuations appear to be essential for three important aspects of human behavior. The first aspect is choice or decision, a continuing and fundamental aspect of human history, action, and events. The economist thinks of choice as involving an agenda consisting of a number of images of alternative futures that the chooser believes are all possible and can be chosen, and will always result from the decision taken. All items on the agenda are evaluated and ranked on a scale from better to worse. In economic language, each is given a "utility ordering." The first item on the list is chosen as the expected alternative future. This process is the basis of the "theory of maximizing behavior," which can be described as a set of mathematical variations on the theme that "everybody does what they think is best at the time," which few will deny.

The second aspect of human activity that involves valuation in a fundamental way can be described as "conversation." Although conversation can refer to discussions we have with ourselves, it mainly involves mutual communication among persons. The most casual chat and table talk is full of valuations--"It's a nice day"; "Have a nice day"; "What an improvement over yesterday." We continuously evaluate the weather, people, events, news, and politics and we compare our valuations with those of other people, a sort of social comparison process, even though no decisions to act are involved. In this enduring conversation about values, we learn to form our own values, which form the basis for choice and decision. The study of this process is perhaps more in the domain of psychology, although also highly relevant for anthropology, sociology, and philosophy.

A third aspect of human life connected intimately with evaluative thought processes consists of conditioning and learning, emotion, perception, and their aberrations, beloved by the psychologist, but completely neglected by the economist. The abstraction known as "economic man" (or woman) is singularly devoid of passion.

The Economist's View of Choice in Exchange

The economist's view of choice and decision seems at first very simple, but the apparent simplicity is but a cap on a considerable "can of worms." The simple case of decisions about exchange where something bought or sold does not affect its price, can be expressed in the familiar indifference curve diagram (Figure 1). Two commodities, A and B, can be measured; commodity A along OA and B along OB (Figure 1). We can visualize above this field a utility surface, the height of which is the value of each point on the field. The indifference curves are the contours of this utility surface. We do not, however, need to postulate a cardinal utility. All that is required is the assumption that each contour represents all points of equal value in the field and that we know which contours are higher and lower. In Figure 1 we assume that each of the commodities has a positive value, so that utility increases from left to right or from bottom to top. We also assume that the chooser (decisionmaker) has an initial amount of each commodity as represented by the point Q, the point of intersection of OB_q along line B and OA_q along line A. The "opportunity function," illustrated in Figure 1 is denoted by the straight line AB; the ratio of exchange of commodities A

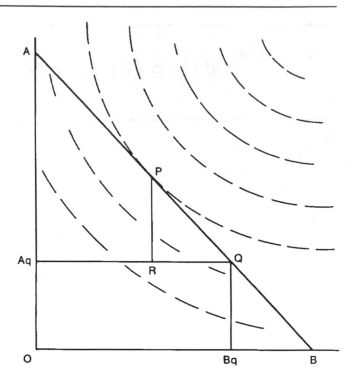

FIGURE 1. Indifference curve.

and B is the slope of this line. If the chooser has the power to give or throw away a commodity, then his or her field of choice is represented by the points on the triangle AOB. If both commodities have a positive value, however, the chooser will prefer to be on the line AB and will move from Q to P. P is the point that touches the highest indifference curve within the field of choice. In this case, the chooser will sell RQ of B and will buy RP of A.

This choice pattern can be easily extended to two parties, as in the famous Edgeworth-Bowley box diagram, or to n parties and n commodities, similar to the Walrasian general equilibrium, an ecological equilibrium of commodities.

Limitations on the Economist's View

Exchange is a special case of choice. The scope of the choice can be widened by adding other noneconomic variables. However, agendas of most decisions are much more complex than a numerical field of bushels of wheat and dollars of money. A great many social and philosophical dimensions and complexities are involved even in economic choices. For example, virtually all finished goods purchased by households come in an immense variety of qualities and forms. How much automobile is there, for instance, in an automobile? To answer this question would involve taking each component part of a car and evaluating it separately on a cardinal scale and then adding up the results to give some sort of bottom line conclusion. A price, or more a ratio of exchange, is a ratio not only of the quantities exchanged, but of qualities as well. If the quantities and qualities cannot be calculated except by a set of uncertain estimates, the whole concept of a ratio of exchange becomes extremely vague and tenuous.

Beyond determining simple economic choice, economists generally have a limited view of negative commodities (i.e., those things valued "bad," which when increased decreases our utility). This is complicated by the seeming paradox that every good becomes a bad if we have too much of it, thus revealing the disutility of such things as greed, avarice, gluttony, and extremes of all kinds--reminding us of Aristotle's theory that moral virtues are a mean between doing too much and too little. This can be illustrated as the "parabola principle" (Figure 2). We can measure the quantity of any good along line OA and its utility along line OU, assuming we use some kind of cardinal scale. Increasing A increases utility, which after reaching a maximum at M, declines and even becomes negative beyond the point N, where what used to be a desired commodity is now an undesired "discommodity." The shape of the utility line (its position) depends on what other commodities we desire or have in hand, complicating our choices because having or wanting more of some things causes us to have less of others. This principle also applies to more abstract goods like virtues. Courage becomes foolhardiness, kindliness becomes sentimentality, thrift becomes miserliness, proper pride becomes arrogance, and so on as the quantity increases. This implies that every utility surface is a mountain with a top, on the far side of which we get pollution. Economists still debate whether bads can be priced satisfactorily.

Economists often also have a limited view of benevolence and malevolence. Our utility depends on the image that we have of other people's utility or welfare. If person A is benevolent toward person B, then if A perceives that B is relatively better off, A feels better off too. Malevolence is the opposite of this attitude. A will become malevolent toward B if A's image is that B becoming better off makes A worse off in his or her own estima-

tion. Including these concepts into a economic model is not difficult; however, they are frequently neglected. Selfishness actually is a rare case and represents the zero point on the scale between benevolence and malevolence. Malevolence can interfere with exchange. For exchange to flourish, some benevolence must reflect a sense of community and a reasonable amount of trust.

A dilemma of choice that economists rarely consider is that they nearly always assume, first, that choice is virtually costless, and second, that all value orderings are strong and that we always know whether one point on the choice agenda is better or worse than another. As a matter of fact, dilemmas of choice are common and nearly all ordering rather weak. For example, people often do not care about which particular dish they order in a restaurant or where they go for a vacation. Choices are made often by using some kind of subjective probability. At other times choices may be impulsively made.

Another aspect of valuation neglected by economists is the issue of the legitimacy of choice. Legitimacy is concerned about the quality of the possibility boundary (e.g., line AB in Figure 1). Economists often assume that the question of legitimacy is not an issue to be concerned about. But, actually the possibility boundary is often seen as imposed by some person or event that is an externality. So one may well experience images of injustice or exploitation concerning certain kinds of choices made. It seems odd that the concept of exploitation is not included in standard economic theory, perhaps as a reaction to the exploiting of exploitation by the Marxists.

An economist may determine that point P in Figure 1 is equilibrium, where economic man placidly and happily succeeds in finding highest welfare on the possibility boundary; however, a psychologist might interpret this point as frustration. Economic man recognizes that the possibility boundary is a fence on the utility mountain and climbs to the highest point of it. Psychological man, yet another simplistic concept like economic man, screams, "there's the fence, there's the fence .... I can't get over it" and experiences frustration. One of the curious things about the abstraction "economic man" is that it seems to have none of the seven deadly sins. This is likely to be an unrealistic guide to behavior.

Another important problem economists neglect is the human learning process. Many economists see utility functions and indifference curves simply as handed from heaven. They are strangely monotheistic about the idea of utility; "there is only one value and its name is utility." Utility is to be taken as a given of the universe. But as we know, values are largely learned in the process of socialization. Learning undoubtedly reflects a genetic influence, but we know relatively little about it. If there is such a thing as basic human needs, which economists tend to deny because they concentrate entirely on wants, some valuations will be linked to physiological drives such as hunger or thirst. The desire for food, drink, warmth, housing, and sex all have physiological bases that are ultimately genetic.

But, the unique and varied expressive forms of basic needs are learned. These become the demand characteristics of consumer markets and economic exchanges as, for example, in the many exploitive ways that the various forms taken by the sex drive is a basis in the United States culture of advertising and marketing, and ultimately sales. The cosmetic, clothing, and entertainment industries are examples. The capacity of the human race for

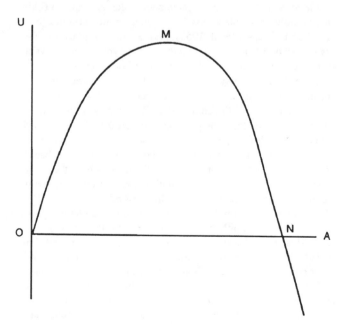

FIGURE 2. Parabola principle.

unhealthful diets, smoking, drugs, sexual deviation, absurd display, and even war are learned ways to deal with needs that have physiological and genetic roots. The distinction between a want and a need is not just a matter of semantics. Although the potential for human desires and wants originate in basic needs, what parts of this large and diverse potential are realized depend on learning experiences throughout the whole of life.

One of the most important concepts that economists can contribute to our understanding of the learning process and motivation is alternative cost--the idea that all choice is limited and that the more of one thing that is chosen always means less of something else can be chosen. Sigmund Freud once suggested that alternative cost plays a role in the "psychic economy" within the personality. The neurotic person, for example, is "blind" to alternative costs, thus leading to the familiar inefficiencies of neurotic behavior. If this principle is applied to learning, it is easy to see that if one uses one's energies to learn one subject well, it will be at the relative expense of some others (thus, limiting the possibility boundary).

The economist also tends to reason that the basis of costs are goods foregone rather than bads incurred. This kind of thinking may not always be realistic because both bads and goods are in the opportunity field inside the possibility boundary. But, this economic bias is a useful idea because it provides a counterweight to those who think of cost only as an increase in bads.

Valuation from an Historic Perspective in Psychology

Psychologists, like others who study human behavior, accept valuation, choice, and preference as basic human attributes. The precise differences among psychologists come from the way in which they locate and define values in the individual, and to what they say causes these values to form. Unlike economics, over the years there has been a basic controversy between the "centralists" and the "peripheralists" among the psychologists. These terms differentiate those who lean toward phenomenology and systems theory and those who prefer the logical positive empiricist approach. The former would have quite different contributions to make to economic theory than would the latter.

For example, behaviorists B. F. Skinner, E. L. Thorndike, John Watson, Clark Hull, O. Hobart Mowrer, and, of course, Pavlov would prefer very stringent theories derived from experimental and empirical studies of behavior. By contrast, Koffka and Kohler, Henry Murray, Gordon Allport, Kurt Lewin, and other systems-oriented theorists prefer to create hypothetical constructs and intervening variables to explain the stark emptiness of the familiar "black box." Economists should not be uncomfortable with either group. Each has something useful to offer economics as purely empirical studies or new concepts and terminology to help explain complex economic behavior.

Because the peripheralists do not accept the necessity of many intervening variables and hypothetical constructs, their research illustrates the economic concept of alternative costs at work. Their devotion to one point of view and reductionism makes it hard for them to accept other views open-mindedly. The central-

ists are also more willing to accept the existence of an inner life of consciousness, awareness, selfhood, identity, and personality processes that constitute a "mind" of which we are aware through consciousness--the various states of which we communicate about with others through language. Values for them are internal mental structures that organize thinking, choice, and action.

Psychologists seem to be more eclectic today, but the underlying philosophical differences, the "deep structures," still remain. Although the two schools of thought might accept the same facts and observations, their philosophical positions would cause them to interpret them quite differently. But, there have been those who have tried to reconcile the two paradigms, for example, Tolman (1952) and, of course, Simon (1963) who has attempted a partial reconciliation of economics and psychology. This difference among psychologists may have some approximate parallel in economics that separates some of its theoretical debates along such lines as represented by the institutionalists and those who favor mathematics; an example of logical positivism as contrasted with phenomenology. And the reductionism of neoclassical economic theory, with its assumption of economic man, is similar in some ways to the psychological behaviorists who have a tendency to oversimplify the psychological interpretations of human behavior by a kind of "least cost" use of theory. In the future, hopefully, these disparate elements will be put together in imaginative ways to form a more realistic picture of economic processes.[1]

According to Gordon Allport (1961), well known for his pioneering work on values, "A value is a belief upon which [one] acts by preference. It is thus a cognitive, a motor and above all deeply propriate disposition." This psychological terminology simply means that values and valuing behavior always involves thinking of some kind, a tendency to respond or to act in a certain way reflecting a particular value, and that the value is "deeply propriate" because it is one's own and personal. Above all, valuation is preferential behavior involving choice and judgement even if one does not act upon the choice.

Tolman's (1952) creative systems approach attempts to fill in the psychological "black box" with intervening variables (cf. MacCorquodale & Meehl, 1951), giving a central place to values as part of a "belief-value matrix." Its dynamic is that valuation occurs in response to "conditions of drive arousal or satiation," another way of saying it activates a "need system" eventually resulting in "restructured behavior," which is learned and adaptive (Tolman, 1952). The need system contains intervening variables to help account in part for why an individual chooses to hold a particular value or engage in valuation. A need stands for a requirement in the body and mind, the absence of which creates a state of tension. If the need is met, the inner tension is reduced or eliminated until the next arousal by some stimulus in the environment or in the person.

Imagine how this might work in the case of a commodity like a durable or nondurable good. As the need for the good is aroused, a state of desire or wanting is created by the need. The object is then evaluated both during and after the search for it in the market. If it fits the evaluation of pricing, functional quality, and durability (and other less tangible criteria like tastes, decor, etc.), it is purchased. Price alone is not the only determining criteria. The "belief-value matrix" is a heuristic concept that helps locate the particular evaluation relative to a need. A product may also have a positive or negative force of attraction, or a valence (Lewin, 1951), which explains part of the motivation to buy it. That force is embodied in an evaluation of the product.[2]

By contrast, the arch "peripheralist" Edward L. Thorndike (1936) stated: Judgements of value are simply one sort of judgement of fact, distinguished from the rest by two characteristics: They concern consequences. These are consequences to the wants of sentient beings. Values, positive and negative, reside in the annoyance felt by animals, person or deities. If the occurrence X can have no influence on the satisfaction of or discomfort of any one present or future, X has no value, is neither good nor bad, desirable nor undesirable. Values are functions of preferences. Judgements about values--statements that A is good, B is bad, C is right, D is useful--refer ultimately to satisfactions or annoyance in sentient creatures and depend upon their preferences. Competent students judge the existence of things by observations of them: They judge the values of things by observations of their consequences.

Thorndike was one of the first to provide a taxonomy of needs (Murray, 1938). Examples from the taxonomy, called variables of personality, include: achievement, aggression, affiliation, autonomy, deference, dominance, exhibition, harm-avoidance, nurturing, order, rejection, acquisition, retention, sentience, and succorance.

The late George Katona (1951), a "psychological economist," used the intervening variable of "expectation" or "expectancy" to bridge economics and psychology. Expectation means that one "anticipates" having a need satisfied by certain economic actions and this serves as an economic incentive to plan, buy, save, etc. Each expectation is paired with a value or set of values about a preference in the future. Expectancies can have either positive or negative valences and as such always involve positive or negative valuation. Simon (1963) also used the construct of values in his linking of economics and psychology. Subjective (expected) utility with its subjectively assessed (value) probabilities goes beyond the idea of "rational man" (Edwards, 1954, 1961). Other examples of the use of values as constructs in decision theory bridging psychology and economics are Tversky and Kahneman (1981) and Slovic, Lichtenstein, and Fischhoff (1977).

The fractionalization of psychology into subspecialties (e.g., a job for everyone and a full employment policy) creates yet another problem. With the exception of psychologists like Herbert Simon, few seem to have either the interest, curiosity, or courage to wander too far from their particular research specialty. There are few incentives to branch out into other specialties. Intellectual curiosity does not seem to be one of them. But, eventually an integration of theory has to occur so that deeper and more encompassing research questions can be asked as were in the earlier Harvard personality studies (Murray, 1938) and in the "Theory of Action" (Parsons & Shils, 1951). Seeing the whole person in a larger social and cultural context is necessary to make any sense of the complexity of economic behavior.

Personality, the social system, and culture form levels of analysis in the study of values. Cultural values embody language and, through language, provide meaning for economic choices and decisions. Needs when aroused activate and express thoughts (cognitions), perception, and emotion as encoded and decoded by values embodied in language. Parsons and Smelser (1956), discussing the sociology of economics, said:

The value system of any social system controls system processes via the motivation of individuals. In general, the value system operates through two channels: (1) the internalization of the value system (and its appropriate sub-systems) in the personalities of individual members of the system; and (2) the sanctions administered by other system members which, in a changing situation, tend to stabilize the internalized orientations and adapt specific behavior to the changing exigencies. (p. 178)

Intermediate Goods as Coaptation of Economics and Psychology

As we noted earlier, the economist's theory of value is highly monotheistic. Utility is the economist's ultimate value; that is, the good for which all other things are good. Psychologists, on the other hand, have a variety of value typologies.

A possible resolution of this difference is to postulate a "goodness function" expressed as $G = (A, B, C, ... N)$, where G is simply that which goes up when we estimate things are getting better and what goes down when things are getting worse. G is close to the economist's concept of utility, and A, B, C, ... N are the intermediate values, which may, of course, be either positive or negative. A positive value is something an increase in which makes G go up; a negative value is something an increase in which makes G go down. The function is a good deal complicated by the fact that A, B, C ... N are interrelated. If A (which is freedom) goes up, B (which is riches) may go up too, but then C (which is equality) may go down, and so on for endless combinations of values. The overall increase in G as a result, say, of a unit increase in A, depends on the changes in all other intermediate goods (positive values) that result, and on the effect that each of these changes has on G. The determination of all these relationships is extremely difficult.

The intermediate values A, B, C, ... N form the taxonomies used in studies of values within psychology, anthropology, and sociology. If coaptation of these disciplines is to be valued for economics and have "utility," economics needs to consider them in answering questions about the various substantive meanings of G, or utility, for any individual economic actor, group, organization, institution, nation, state, or culture. This would be especially important in an area like international trade where intermediate values express cultural differences and the cross-cultural meaning of G varies. However, it would be important in any economic transaction. The economic term "utility" is analogous to the term functional adaptation in psychology. Human behavior, if it is to enhance positive survival and growth in all forms, must be utilitarian and functional to these ends. Intermediate values constitute the variety of ways this can be done in different cultures.

Valuation and Value Consensus

We are all aware of the comparative problem of understanding the different valuations of people. In the academic community there is less consensus in images of values than in images of facts, although most have serious doubts that this is true. In any event, research has rarely dealt with this problem. However, research has confirmed that a single cohesive group and subculture tends toward a consensus of values and norms among its members. Experimental studies have shown that anyone who chooses to be a nonconformist and not to accept the value consensus of a group will first be the object of educational efforts to increase conformity, and if that does not work, will be rejected by the group (cf. examples of this research in Cartwright and Zander [1960]).

For example, the Jesuits, or Mormons, who publicly lose the faith which unites their organization or subculture will leave or be expelled. The larger society also criticizes and sometimes tries to expel subcultures, as the existence of criminal justice organizations testifies. Nevertheless, we are left with an enormous variety of subcultures, national cultures, and supranational cultures, each of which has a distinct set of commonly held structures of valuation. It is important to recognize that valuation is a process of judgement and as such is a form of thought in action, not an object.

A remarkable thing about the human race is its aesthetic value consensus. Even though different cultures produce different forms of art and music, there is an increasing amount of cross-cultural appreciation and a remarkable consensus across cultures (as well as within them) as to what constitutes the aesthetic value of different works of art and the quality of different artists and composers. Many people experience a shock when a new form of art is introduced, like the impressionists or the Bauhaus or atonal music. Once the shock has died down, there is usually remarkable consensus as to who are the best artists, composers, and writers, and even what are their best works. For example, there probably is no anti-Beethoven society anywhere in the world. With the enormous contact now between different world cultures, concerts of European music are given in Asia and Africa, and African and Asian music have penetrated Europe and the Americas.

Consensus on political, religious, and economic values is much less, but may be increasing in economics for reasons given earlier. There is little consensus among the world religions. The Koran rarely is read or observed outside the Islamic communities. The Jewish or the Christian bibles have not had much impact on Buddhism or Shinto. Political values seem even more irreconcilable. The ideological conflicts between Capitalism and Communism still threaten the survival of the human race, even though the instrumental values and ultimate values of both are unclear. Even here, ultimate values may have more in common than the instrumental ones. However, some economic instrumental values in the socialist economies are changing, and market-oriented activity is evident and growing.

People agree more about what they ultimately want than about how to get it. Even within the world religions, the diversity is curiously uniform. Perhaps the Bahai's are right after all that underneath everything is a value similarity. Even fundamentalists in all cultures are much alike. Every great religion has its liberal wing. This suggests that the comparative value systems and structures, even of religious and political values, may reflect more consensus than people think.

The size and scope of agendas, the "field" over which evaluations are made, vary immensely. At one end of the various

orders of magnitude is the totally self-centered autistic person who places no values at all on any part of the field outside of his or her own person. Next in sequence is the ethnocentric family-centered person who has an agenda that includes kin and perhaps close friends. Third is the organization centered person who places little value on the environment outside of the organization. Fourth is the chauvinistic nationalist who values only the people belonging to his or her own nation and who values people outside negatively or not at all. Fifth, and finally, is the Universalist who values the whole planet, even the solar system and beyond. Placing values on the state of the universe is still an idea beyond most people, but an intriguing one to contemplate.

Just what it is in people that causes widening of value agendas is something about which we know relatively little. Those with wider cognitive styles may look upon those with narrower intellectual agendas as being parochial. An endless conversation goes on to this effect, often not much listened to by those with the narrower, and often dogmatically held, value ranges. This cognitive difference in the scope of mind and values represents a significant source of value conflict and for this reason would be a subject for research on intellectual and cognitive styles especially such things as public economic decision making. As in the case of learning, economists have tended to neglect cognitive style perhaps because from their narrower viewpoints they see no problem to study, or are captives of their own kind of reductionist thinking.

The problem of public choice and values, for example, is a particularly difficult one, and highly relevant to the theme of this book. Economists James Buchanan, now a Nobel Laureate, and Gordon Tullock, for example, have made a considerable number of attempts to solve this problem but along the line of the conventional assumptions of a narrow range of quantitative method and economic libertarianism. This point of view is open to question. Any purely economic cost-benefit approach in the context of neoclassic economic theory is at best a crude approximation of reality.

As earlier suggested, it is certainly useful to specify in reasonable detail the larger social system changes going on as a result of public decisions. For example, those changes embodied in a decision to establish a wilderness area or to increase, or not increase, armaments. Even the alternative cost idea has to be used carefully here because we cannot assume, narrowly, that zero-sum games dominate everything. If there are many unemployed resources, any decision that leads to diminution of them by some method of cost allocation and distribution is a positive-sum game. A public decision that leads to diversion of public resources into means of destruction and insecurity may easily create wars and can be a negative-sum game.

There is an inherent danger in using a narrowly quantitative cost-benefit analysis. That danger is greatest when the quantitative accounting for such a game is zero sum. Conversely, in any choice among economic and social alternatives there has to be some "socioeconomic" bottom line. A summation of anticipated value in socioeconomic terms, even if approximate at the beginning, would help decision making because it would bring into the social balance sheet psycho-social and philosophical agenda items now of growing interest in the social indicator field. All evaluations involve some kind of conclusion, objective function, or "bottom line." But, that bottom line does not have to be expressed as a number, or even a number of dollars. It is usually true that a qualitative valuation of some choice is sharpened by a comparison of its qualitatively different alternatives, not only quantitative ones.

Suppose we have four alternatives, A, B, C, and D. At first, A may seem very good, B as good, C as moderately good, and D as not very good. Naturally, we tend to reject those at the bottom of the list and concentrate at the top. Further elimination may lead to a change in the relative position of A and B so that B is preferred to A. It is important to recognize that all data, especially scientific data, consists of evidence and not absolute truth. Evidence always has to be weighed as preferences in someone's mind. This is especially true in the travel cost method and similar value assessing techniques in economics. We should be careful to note that any research evidence, however quantitative, is incomplete without qualitative evidence to support it. Actual public use of national forests and other such amenities would be poorly understood without studying intrinsic valuation behavior in people. For example, a person's inclination to engage in contemplative thought about nature might be important to know about. People may take satisfaction in contemplating the image of a wilderness even though they may not have the slightest intention of visiting one.

We may also experience guilt, shame, and pride about events remote from our lives. If one's government supports oppressive regimes abroad, increases poverty, behaves belligerently, and permits spread of acid rain and the irreversible "green house" effect of a damaged ozone layer, we may experience shame even though remote from centers of decision and power. If one's government supports policies of benevolence, generosity, and conservation to promote the dignity and beauty of the earth and its people, we experience pride although still remote from centers of decision.

Benevolent public goods, like improvements in the wilderness and similar national treasures, come out of government budgets strongly affected by the willingness of people to pay taxes or suffer inflation. Wildernesses are rewards of the "grants economy." When we pay taxes, we diminish our personal net worth and presumably increase the net worth of government and its ability to accomplish cherished values.

We may increase our net worth of pleasurable valuation as we contemplate the positive things taxes can buy. Taxes, by the way, do not always involve a large and obvious conscious sense of reciprocity. The motives and the values that underlie willingness to pay taxes are different from those that determine willingness to buy and sell things in the marketplace. We pay taxes partly out of fear, but a curiously legitimated fear, in the sense that we are willing to be threatened by the consequences of not paying taxes, provided everyone else is threatened similarly and taxes are used for purposes we approve. Taxes increase our pride or reduce our shame as we contemplate the positive values of our society with which we presumably identify.

The Measurement of Values: An Historical Perspective

Whatever we may choose to believe about the philosophical meaning of values, it should be obvious at this point that as humans we are valuing beings. To sustain functional relationships with others in space and time, people attribute, appraise, ascribe, arrogate, rate, assess, assay, estimate, analyze, evaluate, and above all, judge people and events constantly to survive and grow. Judging that which is good and bad, beautiful and ugly, harmful and safe, a cause for joy or sorrow, and just or unjust is complex and difficult to reflect upon. It is also hard to measure.

A key sentence in Aristotle's well-known treatise on values, the Nicomachean Ethics, is that "every art and every inquiry, and similarly every action and pursuit, is thought to aim at some good." Simply replace the word "good" with the general word "utility" and one moves ahead centuries to the present and immediately modernizes Aristotle's passage not only in economic terms [Aristotle (GBWW), 1952]. We are as troubled now about identifying, as he was then, which "utilities" are to receive the highest and lowest value; which is to be called the "summum bonum." This kind of search for "the values" comes uncomfortably to a halt at the precipice of philosophical complexity. We could probably agree that a principal good, or utility, of economics seems to be understanding the universal rules governing wealth. But what is the highest good in politics, science, literature, poetry, art, and music?

The highest good in politics is good government. In science it is knowledge, understanding, and truth. In literature, poetry, art, and music it is something elusively called beauty in the aesthetic sense. Where does wealth fit in this order of values? At least in some walks of American life, the mistake is not asking if wealth alone should be a highest good, or whether other goods should be even higher priorities. They may be our value "lost horizons" to the extent that we allow them to be left off the main agenda. Every now and then a voice within tells us something profound about our value priorities. For those who recognize wilderness as a form of higher "utility," aesthetically speaking, John Muir's (1973) writings seem to offer one example of eloquent prioritizing. Muir said that it is:

> Wonderful how completely everything in wild nature fits into us, as if truly part and parent of us. The sun shines not on but in us. The rivers flow not past, but through us, thrilling, tingling, vibrating every fiber and cell of the substance of our bodies, making them glide and sing. The trees wave and the flowers bloom in our bodies as well as our souls, and every bird song, wind song, and tremendous storm song of the rocks in the heart of the mountains is our song, our very own, and sings our love .... So pure and sure and universal is the harmony ... as soon as we are absorbed in the harmony, plain, mountain, calm, storm, lilies and sequoias, forests and meads are only different strands of many-colored light--are on the sunbeam?

John Muir expressed as his supreme good the relationship between nature which, given that "utility" ordered all other intermediate values, defined rather clearly what he at least considered to be vulgar as opposed to sublime.[3]

Valuation in literature, poetry, music, and art, a focus of aesthetics, differs from the so-called "scientific" measurement of values illustrated later on because in the definition of beauty the interesting philosophical issues of subjectivism and objectivism still influence thought. Subjectivism and objectivism are the philosophical doctrines that state that the truth of an aesthetic valuation is found only in the mind itself as it perceives the object as opposed to only in the object itself. The psychological measurement of values is an interesting example of efforts to "objectify the subjective." Benedetto Croce once said that "... the basis of all poetry is moral consciousness," thus placing aesthetic values at the very center of judgement. The previous passage by John Muir (1973) illustrates this point.

The formal scientific measurement of values came after the birth of psychology and sociology in the late 19th century. Philosophy, in contrast, has assessed and studied values and their bases for centuries. Scientific measurement of values is relatively recent. The polling industry has often carried this to an extreme, giving value research a commercial aspect.

In sociology, for example, the earlier Yankee City studies led by W. Lloyd Warner at The University of Chicago are examples of social class value analysis (Warner, Meeker, & Ealls, 1949). Warner's group used two systems of measurement. In the method of evaluated participation, values were measured indirectly by six measurement techniques: (1) matched agreement by several informants of a person's social class, (2) rating by symbolic placement using identification with cultural symbols, (3) rating by status reputation by informants (reputational method), (4) rating by comparison with others, (5) rating by simple class assignment, and (6) rating by institutional membership. The index of status characteristics method was based on the idea that economic and related prestige factors were important value indicators of status. The four characteristics of occupation, source of income, house type, and dwelling area indirectly measured values. The social area method created by Tryon (1959) is another approach to social class value analysis.

Self ratings, projective techniques, objective tests and scales, expressive behavior ratings, and analysis of documents are used as methods of value measurement in psychology. The best known early study using objective scales is by Vernon and Allport (1931); Allport, Vernon, and Lindzey, (1951).

Political Process and Values

Whenever public institutions become involved in economic choices, the question of political values and influence on allocation of public goods becomes salient and important. In the United States the forum for considering which values shall prevail and which shall not is the Congress, where values are translated into policy in the form of legislation. The executive branch of government is concerned with implementation of these value policies and the courts with adjudication over conflicts created by them. But, this rather efficient arrangement in theory is undermined by the influence of powerful special interests in the form of lobbies and Political Action Groups (PACS).

Issue creation and agenda content is the battleground over both instrumental and substantive values between contending groups who want a share of the economic and political pie. Administrators of an agency, such as the USDA Forest Service, and the public at large acting as consumers of government services, are often caught in the middle of value conflicts as they try to implement mandated programs such as care of wilderness areas. Consequently, being clear about one's value agenda in the policy formation process in this politically turbulent environment is important. It is not an arena for "weak hearts" or ambivalent people. This "political" process has been summarized by Cobb and Elder (1983).

In managing the dynamics of issue creation and expansion by all players on the political playing field, including elected officials, citizens, and administrators, it is critical to understand the symbolic role of political, economic, and cultural value systems. Three symbolic levels are important to know about: (1) government and personalities (e.g., powerful congressmen or senators); (2) the regime in power with its formal and informal value and procedural structures; and (3) the political community, or those who attempt through common means to satisfy their needs through a shared political structure (Easton & Hess, 1962). Without clear understanding of the underlying values of the system, the management of policies and agencies is placed in jeopardy by misrepresentation or by the ambivalence and lack of administrative action that comes from de-energizing value confusion.

Moreover, in the participative democracy of the United States, fullest citizen representation is the critical factor in guiding societal values about use of natural resources. Control of such value agendas by powerful interest groups creates a setting for a perverse conflict of value interests, protracted political conflict, and thus ultimately an erosion of decision making competence in implementation of public policy and in meeting the public interest. Therefore, in this complex political process there must be opportunities for preserving common values rather to guard against their cynical manipulation by shortsighted and selfish interest groups. The Congress is one such place and the Supreme Court the other, although now that very court has undergone a change in leadership that may affect its ability to safeguard environmental values.

The mind and heart of the average citizen are ultimately the most important loci of common values about the environment. It is there that values associated with stewardship and care of natural resources have to take root and grow, and become expressed in political process. This is why value education, as well as education in the political process in the form of knowing that one's political responsibility is to vote and communicating effectively with one's congressional representatives, is essential. Professional stewards such as the administrative agencies and special interest groups (e.g., the Sierra Club and National Audubon Society) sustain values about conservation through education to counter public indifference and ignorance. In all of this, recurring value clarification is essential. Conflicts will never disappear in the political system and should not. But, disputes can be resolved in better ways with more equity in outcomes of such disputes and perhaps even outcomes with greater public awareness of overriding values that represent the diverse bases of life in the United States, rather than certain narrow special interest values that represent uncritical exploitation of natural resources.

The Bridge Between Economics and Other Social Science Disciplines

The main point of this entire discussion, aside from our modest effort to critique some shortcomings of economic theory, is to draw attention to the importance of adopting an enlarged framework of analysis of the psychological and social context of economic behavior. Traditional neoclassical economic theory is much too limited by its adherence to utilitarianism as well as notion of economic man and pure rationality. If we start with a consideration of the pure phenomenology of economic behavior using empirical methods of research rather than defending presuppositions about it based on an ideological or special theory, we see that more than one point of view is needed to understand its complexity.

For example, in the case of contingency valuation measurement, the travel cost method, and the hedonic model, the basic variables that form the conceptual framework in these methods can be helped by being supplemented by others that enlarge the social psychological analytic potential of these measurements. Valuation measurement is enhanced by introducing variables, such as attitudes, needs, expectations, levels of aspiration and motivation, perception, and cognition, that describe psychological processes.

Radical changes in professional identities of either economists or psychologists, or others, is not usually necessary or even wise. Interdisciplinary and transdisciplinary cooperation cannot be a zero-sum game and be productive. The fear that one loses something of one's professional identity, and one's "ownership" over an idea or method, in this form of cooperation has no basis in reality. Rather what happens is everyone gains and becomes enriched by exchanges leading to new questions and research alternatives. This hardly describes a major threat to one's core professional identify.

Vested interests are always strong. At best, progress, what there is to be of it, can be slow. Yet, over the last few decades, there has been encouraging progress. The disciplinary trenches may be filling with the debris of "inert ideas" and many are looking out over the disciplinary parapet with more hope and confidence of finding new interesting patterns and questions.

It is clear from the experience we have had in writing this paper that economics and psychology (or, for example, sociology, anthropology, and political science) are continents of the mind separated by a very wide ocean, no doubt produced by academic continental drift. Furthermore, they seem to be continents without any good harbors. However, we have tried to send our little boats from one to the other. Some of them may have gotten wrecked on the way, but we are more convinced than ever that this is a valuable exercise and that these two continents do belong to the same planet. It is a fundamental principle of economics that specialization without trade is worthless. Unfortunately, in the continents of the mind, specialization seems to feed on itself, and there are large, invisible tariff barriers against the interchange of ideas. We are both grateful to the USDA Forest Service for providing an island in the middle of the ocean that separates us where these different disciplines can meet on a practical problem.[4]

References

Adorno, T. W., Frenkel-Brunswick. E., Levinson, D. J., & Sanford, R. N. (1950) *The authoritarian personality*. New York: Harper and Row.

Allport, G. W. (1961). *Pattern and growth in personality*. Cambridge: Harvard University Press.

Allport, G. W., Vernon, P. E., & Lindzey, G. (1951). *A study of values* (Revised ed.). Boston, MA: Houston.

Aristotle (GBWW, 1952). *The Works of Aristotle Volume II*, Great Books of the Western World, Number 9, (Translated by W.D. Ross). Chicago: Encyclopedia Brittannica, 1952, p. 339.

Barton, A. (1962). Measuring the values of individuals. *Religious Education*, 57, 4.

Cartwright, D., & Zander, A. (1960). *Group dynamics* (2nd ed.). New York: Harper and Row.

Cobb, R. W., & Elder, C. D. (1983). *Participation in American politics* (2nd ed.). Baltimore, MD: Johns Hopkins Press.

Easton, D., & Hess. R. (1962). The child's political world. *Midwest Journal of Political Science, 6*. p. 124.

Edwards, W. (1954). The theory of decisionmaking. *Psychology Bulletin, 51*, 380-417

Edwards, W. (1961). Behavioral decision theory. In P. R. Farnsworth (Ed.), *Annual review of psychology*. Palo Alto, CA: Annual Reviews.

Hughes, T. P. (1982). Conservative and radical technologies. In S. B. Lundstedt, & W. C. Colglazier, Jr. (Eds.). *Managing innovation: The social dimensions of creativity, invention and technology*. New York: Pergamon Press.

Katona, G. (1951). *Psychological analysis of consumer behavior*. New York: McGraw-Hill.

Krech, D., Crutchfield, R. S., & Ballachey, E. L. (1962). *Individual in society*. New York: McGraw-Hill.

Lewin, K. (1951). *Field theory in social science*. New York: Harper and Row.

Likert, R. A. (1932). A technique for the measurement of attitudes. *Archives of Psychology*, No. 140.

Lundstedt, S. B. (1956). Some aspects of change in the personality of the learner. *School Review, 9*, 402-408.

MacCorquodale, K., & Meehl, P. E. (1951). On a distinction between hypothetical constructs and intervening variables. *Psychology Review, 55*, 95-107.

Muir, J. (1973). *The American wilderness in the words of John Muir*. Waukehasa, WI: Country Beautiful.

Murray, H. A. (1938). *Explorations in Personality*. New York: Oxford.

Parsons, T., & Shils, E. A. (Eds.). (1951). *Toward a general theory of action*. Cambridge, MA: Harvard University Press.

Parsons, T., & Smelser, H. J. (1956). *Economy and society*. New York: Free Press.

Simon, H. A. (1963). Economics and psychology. In S. Kocj (Ed.). *Psychology: A study of a science*, pp. 685-723. New York: McGraw-Hill.

Slovic, P., Lichtenstein, S., & Fischhoff, B. (1977). Behavior decision-theory. *Annual Review of Psychology, 28*, 1-39.

Steele, E. D., & Redding, W. C. (1962). The American value system: Premises for persuasion. *Western Speech, 26*, 83-91.

Stern, G. A., Stein, M. I., & Bloom, B. S. (1956). *Methods in Personality Assessment*. Glencoe, IL: Free Press.

Thorndike, E. E. (1936). Presidential address to the American Association for the Advancement of Science. *Science, 86*, 1-8.

Thurstone, L. L. (1931). The measurement of social attitudes. *Journal of Abnormal and Social Psychology, 26*, 249-269.

Tolman, E. C. (1952). A psychological model. In T. Parson, & E. A. Shils (Eds.). *Toward a general theory of action*. Cambridge: Harvard University Press.

Tryon, R. C. (1959). *The social dimensions of modern man*. Paper presented at the American Psychological Association.

Tversky, A., & Kahneman, D. (1981). The framing of decisions and the psychology of choice. *Science, 211*, 453-458.

Vernon, P. E., & Allport, G. W. (1931). A test for personal values. *Journal of Abnormal and Social Psychology, 26*, 233-248.

Warner, W. L., Meeker, M., & Ealls, K. (1960). *Social class in America*. New York: Harper and Row.

White, R. K. (1951). *Value-analysis: The nature and use of the method*. Ann Arbor, MI: The Psychological Study of Social Issues.

Footnotes

[1]In 1974, the term "quality of life" was just beginning to appear in the technical language. It achieved a peak during the Carter administration and has not been in use much since then. It has become somewhat of a cliche. Quality of life values were heavily debated and studied because they reflected a new concern for how we thought and felt about the physical and psychological basis of our life styles across the country. The environment was the chief focus of attention, but the concept also spread elsewhere. Today the issues of acid rain and ozone depletion once again focuses attention upon what may happen to our quality of life in the future.

One case example of the concern within government for quality of life was the report of Task Force Number 4 (*Values and the Public Works Investment Policy*), of the Science Advisory Panel of the Committee on Public Works in The U. S. House of Representatives, which appeared in November, 1974. The Task Force recognized the changing value structure of American life and government and recommended the guiding vision of the future should be quality of life within the framework of the American democratic process.

[2]We did not introduce axiology into our discussion because our focus was on the social and behavioral sciences, but the field of Axiology, a branch of philosophy, is another analytic methodology for value analysis. The implication that values can be measured suggests to some philosophers that there can be a science of values. Axiology is the systematic study of the conceptual qualities of values. Starting from this axiom, a science of value can be constructed in three stages: (a) study of the implications of this basic axiom, (b) considerations of the categories of value that follow from the axiom, and (c) study of the logic and the calculus of value that comes out of the various substantive combinations of the categories of value. See Hartman, R. S. (1959).The science of value. In Maslow, A. H. (Ed.), *New knowledge in human values* (pp. 13-37). New York: Harper and Row.

[3]We said that philosophy has considered the problem of values for centuries. The following are illustrative references about that long history and contrast the more recent social and behavioral science material we have discussed. This is not a representative list:

Ross, E. A. (1939). *Foundations of ethics*. London: Oxford.

Ross, E. A. (1931). *The right and the good*. London: Oxford.

Mill, J. S. (1952). *Utilitarianism*. Chicago, IL: The Great Books of the Western World.

Moore, G. E. (1903). *Principia ethica*. Cambridge: Cambridge University Press.

Moore, G. E. (1922). *Philosophical studies*. London: Kegan-Paul.

Dewey, J. (1922). *Human nature and conduct*. New York: Holt.

Dewey, J. (1939). *The theory of valuation*. Chicago, IL: University of Chicago Press.

Hume, D. (1957). *Inquiry concerning the principles of morals*. New York: Liberal Arts Press.

Russell, B. (1955). *Human society in ethics and politics*. New York: Simon and Schuster.

Ogden, C. K., & Richards, I. S. (1923). *The meaning of meaning*. London: Kegan-Paul.

Aristotle, (1915). Ethics. In J. A. Smith & W. D. Ross (Eds.), *Aristotle's works: Vol. IX*. New York: Oxford.

Plato. (1952). *The republic. Vol I and II*. Chicago, IL: The Great Books of the Western World.

Kant, I. (1952). *Fundamental principles of the metaphysics of morals*. Chicago, IL: Great Books of the Western World.

Effects of Context on Economic Measures of Value

Thomas C. Brown
USDA Forest Service
Rocky Mountain Forest and Range Experiment Station
Fort Collins, Colorado

Paul Slovic
Decision Research
Eugene, Oregon

Human judgment and choice is an important area of study among decision theorists, cognitive psychologists, and economists. Much recent study has focused on testing the axioms of expected utility theory as proposed by von Neumann and Morgenstern (1944). Concurrently, psychologists, survey researchers, and economists have studied the ability of people to provide consistent and well-founded responses to questions regarding preferences and values (including estimates of willingness to pay for environmental changes). These efforts have important implications for economics.

The principal focus in examining the descriptive adequacy of expected utility theory has been on the extent to which people act in accordance with the axioms of expected utility theory (i.e., "rationally"). Experiments have shown that in some circumstances a significant proportion of people do not act, or at least do not respond verbally, in accordance with the axioms. Often these experiments show that decisions differ as a result of seemingly minor differences in the way decision situations are described and questions are posed.

Meanwhile, a principal focus of preference research, including willingness to pay studies, has been on determining the extent to which people have attitudes or values that they can accurately and consistently report upon request. Again, this has been tested by systematically examining the effect of seemingly trivial variations in factors like question wording, availability of auxiliary information, and response format.

With both choices among risky alternatives and statements of preference, the details of the decision situation (e.g., the social setting, the mix of goods, their labels, and the mode in which preference is expressed) constitute the "context" of the decision situation. Thus, the method employed in both cases has been one of examining actions or responses in the face of changes in contextual factors.

In this paper, we consider choices among defined alternatives and expressions of attitudes as expressions or "assignments" of value. That is, both choice and attitudes involve expressions of preference, and indicate the relative importance or worth of an object or event in a given context (Brown, 1984). While obvious differences exist between choice among well-defined alternatives and more general statements of attitudes, both are the result of preference expressed within a given context. The effect of the context on expressed preferences is the focus of this paper.

Sensitivity of preferences to changes in social setting, response mode, labels, and other contextual factors would of course raise questions about people's "rationality" in choice and judgment situations (Schoemaker, 1982). However, such sensitivity would also raise questions about the cognitive processes that allow context to play such a prominent role (Slovic, Fischhoff, & Lichtenstein, 1982).

SOME DETERMINANTS OF ASSIGNED VALUE

Factors that affect a person's assignment of value to an object (e.g., a good, situation, or possible outcome) can be grouped into those factors that the person brings to the valuation situation and those that characterize the valuation situation itself.

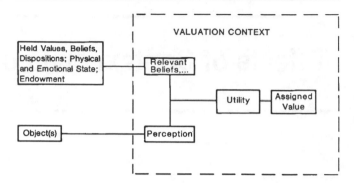

FIGURE 1. Framework for assignment of value to objects.

Although the latter are the primary focus of this paper, the distinction between the two is probably more easily communicated by first describing the former.

Factors that the person brings to the valuation include (1) a collection of held values (Brown, 1984; Rokeach, 1973), beliefs, and dispositions; (2) a physical and emotional state; and (3) an endowment of current and expected assets (Figure 1). The first factor is a complex set of rather general proclivities, including "tastes and preferences," that are assumed to be relatively stable over the time during which distinct valuations occur. Regarding these proclivities, people may differ in a nonrandom way with respect to their association with social groups. The second factor may be expected to vary among individuals in a random manner, and therefore be of little but academic interest if we are interested in group, as opposed to individual, values. If individuals differ in some nonrandom way regarding the third factor (their endowment), the appropriate variables typically are modeled as demand shifters.

The context of a valuation is the set of circumstances that characterizes both the situation in which the person interacts with the object(s) and the mode in which the assigned value is expressed (Figure 1). This interaction involves perception of the objects at issue and a process whereby the relevant held values, beliefs, and dispositions come to the forefront. Of course, perception may affect which beliefs play a role, and beliefs may affect which characteristics of the object are perceived. In any case, the interaction results in an unobservable sense of value, called utility, which may through some mode of expression yield an assigned value.

The conceptual framework presented in Figure 1 is obviously a simplification of the complex process by which humans express value. For example, feedback loops, by which valuation of objects may alter one's held values, beliefs, etc., are lacking. However, Figure 1 helps depict the salient point that we wish to make--the valuation context may affect how objects are perceived, the beliefs that become relevant, the utility experienced, and the value assigned.

The physical and emotional state that the individual brings to a valuation situation may interact with his or her values, affecting the relevancy of beliefs and causing different valuations of the same object or event at different times. Schelling (1984) listed numerous examples of such differences in discussing "self command," where the individual is aware of the difference, and attempts in one state to influence the seemingly uncontrollable valuations and actions expected to occur in the other state. For example, knowing from experience of the difficulty in rising from bed on time, one may, the night before, place the alarm clock out of reach. Obviously, by choosing to ignore factors that the person brings to the valuation, we are bypassing some interesting issues.

FACTORS THAT CHARACTERIZE THE CONTEXT

The numerous factors that characterize the context of the valuation include response mode, relative magnitudes, order effects, stimulus mixture, informational cues, constituency, iterations of valuation, and social setting.

Response Mode

Possible response modes include choice among available options, ratings, rankings, expressions of willingness to pay, and willingness to donate time. Response mode has been shown to affect valuation in numerous situations. The so-called "preference reversals" in evaluations of gambles are an important example of this (Slovic & Lichtenstein, 1983). Lichtenstein and Slovic (1971, 1973) presented people with pairs of gambles, one featuring a high probability of winning a modest sum of money (the P bet) and the other featuring a low probability of winning a larger amount of money (the $ bet). The gambles of each pair were of similar but usually not identical expected value. They found that people tended to choose the P bet as the one they would prefer to play, but when stating the maximum amount of money they would be willing to pay to play the gambles or the minimum amount for which they would be willing to sell the chance to play the gambles, they tended to assign a higher monetary value to the $ bets. Lichtenstein and Slovic concluded that choices appeared to be influenced primarily by probabilities of winning or losing, while monetary bids were primarily determined by the dollar amounts that could be won or lost. These findings have been replicated in numerous studies (e.g., Grether & Plott, 1979; Lindman, 1971; Mowen & Gentry, 1980; Pommerehne, Schneider, & Zweifel, 1982; Reilly, 1982).

Tversky and Slovic (1984) compared choices, monetary bids, and ratings of attractiveness for gambles with potential gain but no loss dimension. For example, one pair of gambles was a 27/36 chance to win $2.50 and a 6/36 chance to win $8.50. They found that the rating responses were even more different from the dollar bids than were the choices. Across their two groups of subjects, high probability/low payoff bets were chosen over low probability/ high payoff bets 65% of the time, rated higher 87% of the time, and were given higher bids only 20% of the time. Eighty-three percent of the subjects who provided both rating and dollar responses reversed themselves in their preferences, and all high probability/low payoff bets received higher mean attractiveness ratings than any of the low probability/high payoff bets. Across the 12 gambles, mean bid prices correlated .92 with payoffs and -.58 with probabilities, while mean ratings correlated -.57 with payoffs and .95 with probabilities.

In a related study, Hershey, Kunreuther, and Schoemaker (1982) compared two types of responses regarding indifference judgments between a sure monetary outcome (S) and a two-outcome gamble. The gambles included a probability (P) of a monetary gain (G) along with a probability (1-P) of a monetary loss (L). Of course, $O < P < 1$, and $L < S < G$. Subjects given the three characteristics of the gamble (P, G, L) and asked to state an indifference level in terms of the dollar amount of the sure outcome tended to be more risk seeking than subjects given the amounts of the sure outcome, the gain, and the loss and asked to state an indifference level in terms of the probability. The effect was strongest for gambles with a relatively high probability of losing.

Brown (1984) examined dollar and rating responses of subject's willingness to pay for environmental amenities (air quality and forest scenic quality) and commodities (cameras, cars, stereos, and bicycles). Most subjects were willing to pay more for the commodities than for the amenities when giving their answers in dollars, but most rated their willingness to pay for the amenities higher than their willingness to pay for the commodities.

A finding related to response mode is the dichotomy sometimes found between people's willingness to pay verses their willingness to accept compensation. Several studies have found that the compensation measure significantly exceeded the willingness to pay measure (e.g., Gregory, in press; Hammack & Brown, 1974; Knetsch & Sinden, 1984; Rowe, d'Arge, & Brookshire, 1980). It is tempting to attribute this dichotomy to some type of response mode bias. However, the difference between buying and selling is probably more fundamental than a mere response mode difference. Experiments comparing relative evaluations of gains and losses indicate that gains and losses are usually evaluated from the reference point of current endowment, and that gains and losses are evaluated quite differently (Kahneman & Tversky, 1979). Thus, a change in endowment, part of what the person brings to the valuation, distinguishes the two responses. Kahneman and Tversky (1982) concluded that a loss apparently has a greater subjective effect than an equivalent gain.

Relative Magnitudes

The relative magnitudes of the quantities involved in an evaluation often affect the outcome. Tversky and Kahneman (1981) provided an interesting example of this. Sixty-eight percent of their respondents stated that they would be willing to drive to another store 20 minutes away to save $5 on a $15 calculator, but only 29% thought they would be willing to make the trip to save $5 on a $125 jacket. This finding is reminiscent of the Weber-Fechner law of psychophysics, that the just noticeable difference in any stimulus is proportional to the log of the stimulus (Stigler, 1965). Although in both cases, 20 minutes (and associated travel costs) are given up for a gain of $5.00, the savings apparently seems like a better deal with a smaller purchase.

Order Effects

Order effects have long been a concern in survey research (Cantril, 1944). For example, Ferber (1952) found that the order of presentation of a list of occupations biased responses to questions about those occupations. Carpenter and Blackwood (1979) found that question order affected attitudes toward wild and domestic animals. Fischhoff et al. (1978) found that people judged the risks associated with various technologies to be more acceptable following a judgment task about the benefits of those technologies than following a task about their risks.

Stimulus Mixture

The range and relative mixture of items being evaluated may also affect expressed values. For example, Brown and Daniel (in press) found that people rated the scenic beauty of a common set of average forest scenes significantly lower when they were shown with a set of more attractive scenes than when they were shown with a set of less attractive scenes.

Informational Clues

In the broadest sense, all contextual factors are information. For example, the response mode conveys information to the evaluator. However, by "informational cues" we mean the nonessential, ancillary information that may accompany a valuation.

Informational cues are most often communicated verbally. First of all, the labels used to describe objects can affect the valuation, for example in the four following studies. Anderson (1981) found that the land use designations attached to forest scenes significantly affected judgments of scenic quality of the scenes, with "wilderness area" and "national park" consistently elevating perceived scenic quality and "commercial timber stand" and "leased grazing range" consistently reducing it. Hodgson and Thayer (1980) found that labels implying a natural as opposed to an artificial origin of landscape features, such as "lake" versus "reservoir," led to increased judgments of attractiveness. Schoemaker and Kunreuther (1979) found that people were more likely to incur a small loss to avoid a much larger one when the sure loss was called an insurance premium. Tversky and Kahneman (1981) presented people with a situation of the United States preparing for an outbreak of an unusual disease that was expected to kill 600 people. They found that people's evaluations of programs to combat the disease differed depending on whether the programs were described in terms of numbers of lives saved or numbers of deaths, relative to the 600-person estimate.

Information suggesting judgment criteria can be significant. For example, Buhyoff and Leuschner (1978) asked subjects to choose preferred forest scenes from among pairs differing in numerous characteristics, including level of insect damage. Degree of insect damage correlated about .85 with the scaled responses of those subjects who were informed of the insect damage, but only about .33 with the judgments of uninformed subjects.

Ancillary information about the judgments of others can also be significant. For example, Rowe et al. (1980) found that respondent's bids of willingness to pay for improved air quality were affected by information provided about previous mean bids. In a second example, White (1975) surveyed college students regarding either the number of hours per week that they would be willing to donate to a language tutoring program or the maximum amount that a student should have to pay for books for a three-unit, upper-division class. Subjects were individually surveyed on campus by another student whom they did not know. After agreeing to participate, subjects read the appropriate question and signed their name and response. Each control subject responded on the top of the survey sheet. Each experimental subject received a sheet containing eight signatures and judgments, which had been planted by the experimenters. In different experiments, these "anchors" accounted for 24-48% of the variance in responses. White concluded that judgments were "massively influenced across wide social anchoring ranges" (p. 1047) for both issues, although no rewards were promised and the surveyor and hypothetical others were nonthreatening strangers. This is strong support for Crano and Messe's (1982) conclusion that, "Under conditions of poor resolution...people will attempt to decrease ambiguity by using the responses of others in coming to a decision about their own thoughts and behavior" (p. 79). The experiment is all the more significant because the questions dealt with topics about which one would expect students to have relatively well-formed opinions.

Other types of information can also serve as anchors to potential responses. A common example in contingent valuation is the starting point for iterative bidding. Rowe et al. (1980) found that the starting point significantly affected the final bid of willingness to pay, with higher starting points raising final bids.

Constituency

The explicit or implied constituency of a valuation might also affect expressed value (Brown, 1984). As Arrow (1963) suggested, "In general, there will ... be a difference between the ordering of social states according to the direct consumption of the individual and the ordering when the individual adds his general standards of equity..." (p. 18). The constituency may be obvious in a valuation; one might make one purchase if spending one's own money, but another when administering a trust, or a public health official may make a personal decision to drive his or her car to work rather than the bus, yet urge people to do the opposite for the good of society. More subtly, the nature of the good being evaluated may suggest a constituency; a rival and exclusive good (Randall, 1983) may engender a private constituency while a "public" good may incite a social constituency.

Knetsch and Sinden (1984) found evidence of the importance of constituency on valuation in their experiments comparing willingness to pay with willingness to accept compensation. While the compensation measure significantly exceeded the willingness-to-pay measure for people managing their own endowments, no significant difference between the measures was found for those advising others about payment and compensation decisions. Thus, when acting as agents for others, people considered losses and gains equal in importance but, when acting in their own behalf, they considered a loss to have greater subjective impact than an equivalent gain.

Iterations of Valuation

Some valuation contexts call for iterative valuations, where respondents repetitively indicate the value they assign to an object. The repetitions may influence the responses. For example, in the Vickrey auctions used by Coursey, Hovis, and Schulze (1987) and Brookshire, Coursey, and Radosevich (this volume), individual subjects, in a group setting, repetitively recorded their willingness to pay or willingness to accept compensation in a sealed bid regarding an unfamiliar object. In both experiments, the willingness to accept compensation responses gradually decreased. While this trend may have been influenced by the group interaction, another plausible explanation is that the gradual familiarity with the good created via the repetitions changed the valuations.

Social Setting

A final contextual factor in valuation is the social setting of the valuation situation. Who will be aware of an expressed value may be important, especially if strong notions of social desirability are associated with the object being evaluated. This is a common area of study in social psychology (see Crano & Messe, 1982).

Explanations

The studies cited above indicate that, in many choice and judgment situations, the assigned values of a significant portion of people are influenced by the context of the valuation. Of course, experiments where context was found to be unimportant are rarely reported, so the ones in the literature may not present a well-rounded picture of the importance of contextual factors. However, sufficient evidence warrants speculation about the cause of these context effects and their implications for economic analysis.

One explanation for the importance of some contextual factors in valuations is that the cost of information relevant to the valuation may be perceived by the valuator to be greater than the benefit the information would provide. The cost may be in the form of time and effort to acquire objective information about the alternatives and their outcomes, or in the form of cognitive effort to either analyze the alternatives or carefully reflect on one's values and attitudes (i.e., cognitively generate information

pertinent to the valuation). Without the costly information, choices or judgments may be more easily influenced by contextual factors. For example, some people's apparent lack of interest in or ability to compute expected values of gambles may result from their assessment that the added accuracy is not worth the mathematical effort, or people's susceptibility to informational cues may result from their assessment that the benefits of careful analyses and reflection about the question posed are not worth the cognitive effort. In this sense, individuals can still be considered optimizers, and indeed even more sophisticated optimizers than if they had not considered the cost of information.

Some evidence, however, indicates that even when information is readily available, it is often not used, for example, several studies that have dealt with preference reversals. Lichtenstein, Slovic, and Zink (1969) found that subjects were disinclined to maximize expected value when choosing among bets, even when they were given expected values along with a rationale stressing their importance. Other criteria, such as risk aversion or desire to achieve a high payoff, took precedence. Similarly, when Grether and Plott (1979) showed subjects the expected values of the gambles and described the expected value concept, preference reversals remained frequent.

These examples suggest that information cost is not necessarily an adequate explanation of context effects. Further research, specifically designed to test the hypothesis that the cost of thought explains the importance of context in valuation, is needed.

A second and closely related explanation for context effects is that question and answer sessions and other experimental situations do not provide enough incentive to induce well-considered responses. Thus, participants will be easily influenced by contextual cues, implying that their choices will be less likely to be influenced when their actions produce significant, real consequences. In essence, this approach suggests that when the benefits of making a good decision are obviously small, because the choice is hypothetical, the benefits are less likely to outweigh the costs of cognitive effort.

Ample "evidence" has shown that attitudes are often poor indicators of behavior when the context of the attitudinal response differed from (usually was less specific than) the context of the specific behavior being evaluated. Attitudes about specific behaviors are often good predictors of behavior (Ajzen & Fishbein, 1980). When the only difference between the hypothetical and actual situations is whether or not the person must live with the consequences of the choice, lack of incentive appears not to be a pervasive problem. For example, several studies have shown that adding incentive to choice of gambles does not alter the results. Lichtenstein and Slovic (1973) found that gamblers in a Las Vagas casino, playing with their own money, exhibited the same "preference reversals" as college students in purely hypothetical circumstances. Grether and Plott (1979) also found that introducing real money into the situation had little effect on preference reversals. Schoemaker (1982) concluded, "I know of no evidence that suboptimal laboratory behavior improves when committing subjects financially to their decisions... The failure to optimize appears to be cognitive...rather than motivational" (p. 553).

A more comprehensive and satisfying explanation for the importance of context was offered by Thaler (1980), who suggested that these "systematic, predictable differences between normative models of behavior and actual behavior" (p. 40) occur because of what Herbert Simon called "bounded rationality." According to Simon (1957):

> The capacity of the human mind for formulating and solving complex problems is very small compared with the size of the problems whose solution is required, for objectively rational behavior in the real world--or even for a reasonable approximation to such objective rationality." (p. 198)

Kahneman and Tversky (1979) presented a model of choice that illustrates bounded rationality in action. They distinguished between two phases of the choice process: a preliminary "framing" of the problem where the alternatives and possible outcomes are represented, and a subsequent evaluation phase where the choice is made. The frame is affected by the person's beliefs, values, etc., but is also influenced by the context of the valuation. For example, Slovic (1985) suggested that the ease of coding or mapping a stimulus component into the response may influence the evaluation process. He proposed that the easier it is to execute such a mapping, the greater the weight given to the stimulus component.

While context appears to be important in valuations, what exactly is its role? We suggest two possible roles. The first is that contextual factors "fill in" where cognitive abilities or effort (in using decision rules, in integrating and utilizing information, in memory, etc.) are lacking or where values conflict or attitudes are not well-founded. Here, context takes up the slack, helping people to choose and respond in the situations in which they find themselves.

People may have relatively few basic values (Rokeach, 1973) or stable beliefs (Ajzen & Fishbein, 1980). Rarely will a decision situation elicit a response that is a direct expression of such a value or belief. Furthermore, it is well known that most people, when asked for their cooperation, will come up with a reasoned response. Even when people do not have an opinion about the issue, they will usually respond with one. When a choice or judgment situation does not call upon a well-formed belief, it is likely to be more easily influenced by the contextual cues present in the situation. The lower the resolution (i.e., degree of clarity or focus) of the relevant beliefs, the more important the context. As Crano and Messe (1982) concluded, opinion-consistent behavior is more likely in situations where the actor's belief system is at a high level of resolution and where the social context is at a low level of resolution. Thus, filling in may play an important role in situations of low value or belief resolution.

Filling in may also be important when values conflict. People have conflicting values about many issues, particularly those of social relevance. As Fischhoff, Slovic, and Lichtenstein (1980) noted, "when conflicting values are relevant to a particular issue, the priming or evocation of one will tend to suppress the accessibility of its counterpart" (p. 127). For example, the very act of asking people for their own personal values may suppress social values. Thus, people may be more likely to use contextual cues to help frame a choice situation where values conflict.

The other role that contextual factors may play is more fundamental. In this role, contextual factors are viewed as integral to valuation--as indispensable aspects of any assigned value. This understanding of the role of context is apparently gaining accep-

tance. Einhorn and Hogarth (1981) stated in their review of behavioral decision theory that:

> The most important empirical results in the period under review have shown the sensitivity of judgment and choice to seemingly minor changes in tasks. Such results illustrate the importance of context in understanding behavior in the same way that the context of a passage affects the meaning of individual words and phrases. We consider context to refer to both the formal structure and the content of a task...normative models gain their generality and power by ignoring content in favor of structure and thus treat problems out of context. However, content gives meaning to tasks and thus should not be ignored in trying to predict and evaluate behavior. (p. 61)

Hershey et al. (1982), in summarizing their experiments of bias in assessments of von Neumann-Morgenstern utility functions, stated that "It is difficult to speak of the utility function for an individual" (p. 944), and that "people do not hold preferences free of context....Indeed, without context, the choice is not likely to be very meaningful" (p. 951). Fischhoff et al. (1980) agreed that the strong effects of contextual factors, acting on ill-defined preferences, can make elicitation procedures major forces in shaping the expression of values. In such cases, they concluded, "the method becomes the message" (p. 117). Similarly, Brown (1984) observed, "There is no such thing as the value of an object" (p. 244) because assigned value is a function of context.

This view can be seen as following from the explanation of human nature expounded in Kant's Critique of Pure Reason. Kant argued that we interpret sensory data via our *a priori* concepts, which allow us to filter information in a manner that seems appropriate to us at the time. We build these *a priori* concepts through repeated encounters with sensory data, across many situations. These *a priori* concepts are, however, independent of what we sense at any given time. They screen the available information and give form and meaning to what we take in. Following Kant's argument, we make two points. First, these *a priori* concepts are developed in specific contexts. As Ajzen and Fishbein (1980) stated, "a single action is always performed with respect to a given target, in a given context, and at a given point in time" (p. 34). Second, any specific valuation context is likely to call upon certain *a priori* concepts, which will affect how the information contained in the context is used. As the evidence summarized above suggests, the *a priori* concepts do not always lead people to behave with the clarity and singlemindedness that expected utility theory or some valuation studies would suggest.

In summary, the rapidly accumulating evidence of the past few years increasingly suggests that contextual factors play an important role in valuation. That role is unavoidable to some extent. Furthermore, the role of seemingly trivial contextual factors probably increases in situations where people's belief systems and dispositions are in conflict or are not highly relevant to the specific valuation.

IMPLICATIONS FOR ECONOMICS

The evidence on context effects, first of all, has implications for expected utility theory. The importance of response mode in valuation of risky alternatives have shown that people do not always act in accordance with the axioms of the theory. The descriptive, and possibly the positive, importance of the theory is in question, and some changes seem warranted. Regarding the theory's normative role, two positions arise. On the one hand, the biases and inconsistencies found in individual choices support the normative importance of standard utility theory. If people are unable to process information and evaluate alternatives to the extent that seems advantageous, the model may steer them in the right direction. However, this approach requires a "leap of faith" that may be more than many are willing to make. On the other hand, the experimental evidence can be interpreted to indicate that people's preferences differ fundamentally from the axioms of the model. (See Schoemaker's [1982] review of expected utility theory for a detailed treatment of these concerns.)

Research on people's ability or inclination to act in accordance with the axioms of expected utility theory has focused on gambles and other chances to win or lose money. In these cases, people's attitudes and behavior tend to bring utility theory into question. Thus, the question arises about the applicability of the findings to other types of choices. Research that strenuously tests utility theory in other situations is obviously needed.

A second application of the importance of contextual factors in valuation is that an economic measure of value (e.g., demand function) is but one context-specific measure of assigned value. Economic measures of value arise from a context of given response mode (e.g., transfer of money for goods), constituency (usually private, not social), and social setting (exchange, which may or may not include bargaining or auction behavior). The use of money implies a set of rules, customs, and concepts about the nature and meaning of money. The measure of value that arises from such a context may be quite different from that of another context. We stress this rather self-evident fact for two reasons. First, it is useful to be reminded that the competitive market paradigm is but one approach to valuation. Second, it raises the issue of comparability among value measures, which is of particular concern in the use of the contingent valuation method (CVM) to estimate market price for nonmarket goods.

Contingent valuation involves asking individuals, in survey or experimental settings, to reveal their personal valuations, in monetary terms, of increments or decrements of in unpriced goods by using contingent markets (Randall, Hoehn, & Brookshire, 1983). The importance of the valuation context has two obvious implications for CVM. First, the hypothetical nature of CVM may be more of a problem than is generally recognized. As mentioned earlier, where people's values and attitudes are not at a high level of resolution, their responses tend to be more heavily influenced by contextual cues. As shown in White's (1975) research on the susceptibility of student's estimates of the money they should be expected to pay for books or the time they would be willing to donate, such judgments are highly labile even when concerned with familiar goods. People are much less accustomed to paying for the type of goods (nonexclusive or nonrival goods) that are typically the object in CVM surveys than students are for books.

CVM is used because such goods are not privately purchased. Although the appropriate context is the market, the goods involved are not traded. Because people are not familiar with paying for goods they cannot privately own, they are likely to be particularly susceptible to unintended contextual cues, such as the social acceptability of paying a lot (to create a favorable impression), labels, order effects, and implied constituencies.

This hypothetical problem should not be confused with the bias introduced simply by the use of an experiment (verses observing actual behavior) to obtain indications of assigned value. As mentioned earlier, the mere fact that the response is about a hypothetical situation does not seem to introduce much bias. Rather, the point is that, because real life experiences of paying for public goods rarely exist (not even taxes are paid for specific environmental goods, and taxes are involuntary in any case), people do not have a well-established context to which to relate, and may therefore be heavily influenced by the artificial context of the evaluation process.

A related problem for CVM flows from the difficulty of accurately specifying the good. Because the type of goods typically evaluated using CVM are not specifically valued in monetary terms in real life situations, it is apparently difficult for people to consider these goods in a payment context. As a result, the specific good at issue often serves as a symbol for a whole class of goods. Kahneman (1986) recently reported evidence of this in people's willingness to pay to maintain fishing by cleaning up lakes in Canada. Willingness to pay to clean up the lakes in one region was nearly as large as willingness to pay to clean up the lakes in a whole province containing numerous such regions. Respondents were apparently providing evidence of their general attitudes about cleaning up lakes for fish.

The other implication for CVM deals with the context of payment. Specifying a payment vehicle may significantly affect bids. For example, people may object to paying outright for something that they value highly, but they consider to be rightfully theirs. They may think that the government should pay for it, which suggests that their willingness to pay in taxes would be higher than their willingness to pay outright. (However, they may have biases against taxes.) They may also think that industry (for example, in the case of industrial air pollution) should pay, rather than themselves. Furthermore, for nonrival goods in particular, the perceived fairness of the payment vehicle may affect people's willingness to pay. The importance of context in the numerous studies cited above suggests that so called "payment vehicle bias" should receive more study.

CONCLUSION

The evidence reviewed in this paper indicates that seemingly minor contextual factors often significantly affect assigned values. Whether context merely "fills in" for ambiguity or whether it is essential to assigning value, it is potentially important to valuation. Its importance suggests that it is misleading to speak of a person's "true preferences" or of the "real value" of an object. Because assigned value depends on the established context, the context determines the relevant bounds of the valuation. Experiments to elicit assigned values must be carefully designed to represent the context to which the results are to be generalized.

If contingent valuation is to produce monetary estimates of value comparable to values arising in actual markets, both used in benefit-cost analysis, much effort is needed to demonstrate that comparability. The hurdles to obtaining comparable values are significant for nonexcludable and nonrival goods, not simply because contingent markets are merely surveys, but because of the difficulties in structuring realistic payment situations for such goods. Because of the potential ambiguities in contingent valuation of goods that cannot by their nature be exchanged in competitive markets, contextual factors are likely to play a significant role in determining the outcome. The validity of any contingent valuation measure of value is called into question unless the context of the valuation is clearly appropriate for the intended application of the resulting value, or unless the value is found to be robust under several related contexts.

References

Anderson, L. M. (1981). Land use designations affect perception of scenic beauty in forest landscapes. *Forest Science, 27,* 392-400.

Ajzen, I., & Fishbein, M. (1980). *Understanding attitudes and predicting social behavior.* Englewood Cliffs, NJ: Prentice-Hall.

Arrow, K. J. (1963). *Social choice and individual values* (2nd ed.). New York: John Wiley & Sons.

Brown, T. C. (1984). The concept of value in resource allocation. *Land Economics, 60,* 231-246.

Brown, T. C., & Daniel, T. C. (in press). Context effects in perceived environmental quality assessments: Scene selection and landscape quality ratings. *Journal of Environmental Psychology.*

Buhyoff, G. J., & Leuschner, W. A. (1978). Estimating psychological disutility from damaged forest stands. *Forest Science, 24,* 424-432.

Cantril, H. (1944). *Gauging public opinion.* Princeton, NJ: Princeton University Press.

Carpenter, E. H., & Blackwood, L. G. (1979). The effect of question position on responses to attitudinal questions. *Rural Sociology, 44,* 56-72.

Coursey, D. L., Hovis, J. J., & Schulze, W. D. (1987). The disparity between willingness to accept and willingness to pay measures of value. *Quarterly Journal of Economics, 102,* 679-690.

Crano, W. D., & Messe, L. A. (1982). *Social psychology.* Homewood, IL: Dorsey Press.

Einhorn, H. J., & Hogarth, R. M. (1981). Behavioral decision theory: Processes of judgement and choice. *Annual Review of Psychology, 32,* 53-88.

Ferber, R. (1952) Order bias in a mail survey. *Journal of Marketing, 17,* 171-178.

Fischoff, B., Slovic, P., Lichtenstein, S., Read, S., & Combs, B. (1978). How safe is safe enough? *Policy Sciences, 8,* 127-152.

Fischhoff, B., Slovic, P., & Lichtenstein, S. (1980). Knowing what you want: Measuring labile values. In T. S. Wallsten (Ed.), *Cognitive processes in choice and decision behavior* (pp. 117-141). Hillsdale, NJ: Erlbaum.

Gregory, R. (in press). Interpreting measures of economic loss: Evidence from contingent valuation and experimental studies. *Journal of Environmental Economics and Management.*

Grether, D. M., & Plott, C. R. (1979). Economic theory of choice and the preference reversal phenomenon. *American Economic Review, 69,* 623-638.

Hammack, J., & Brown, G. M. (1974). *Waterfowl and wetlands: Toward bioeconomic analysis.* Baltimore, MD: Johns Hopkins Press.

Hershey, J. C., Kunreuther, H. C., & Schoemaker, P. J. H. (1982). Sources of bias in assessment procedures for utility functions. *Management Science, 28,* 936-954.

Hodgson, R. W., & Thayer, R. L., Jr. (1980). Implied human influence reduces landscape beauty. *Landscape Planning, 7,* 171-179.

Kahneman, D. (1986). Comments by Professor Daniel Kahneman. In R. G. Cummings, D. S. Brookshire, & W. D. Schultze (Eds.). *Valuing Environmental Goods: An Assessment of the Contingent Valuation Method* (pp. 185-194). Totowa, NJ: Rowman & Allanheld.

Kahneman, D., & Tversky, A. (1979). Prospect theory: An analysis of decision under risk. *Econometrica, 47,* 262-291.

Kahneman, D., & Tversky, A. (1982). The psychology of preferences. *Scientific American, 246,* 160-173.

Knetsch, J. L., & Sinden, J. A. (1984). Willingness to pay and compensation demanded: Experimental evidence of an unexpected disparity in measures of value. *Quarterly Journal of Economics, 99,* 507-521.

Lichtenstein, S., & Slovic, P. (1971). Reversals of preference between bids and choices in gambling decisions. *Journal of Experimental Psychology, 89,* 390-397.

Lichtenstein, S., & Slovic, P. (1973). Response-induced reversal of preference in gambling: An extended replication in Las Vegas. *Journal of Experimental Psychology, 101,* 16-20.

Lichtenstein, S., Slovic, P., & Zink, D. (1969). Effect of instruction in expected value on optimality of gambling decisions. *Journal of Experimental Psychology, 79,* 236-240.

Lindman, H. R. (1971). Inconsistent preferences among gambles. *Journal of Experimental Psychology, 89,* 390-397.

Mowen, J. C., & Gentry, J. W. (1980). Investigation of the preference-reversal phenomenon in a new product introduction task. *Journal of Applied Psychology, 65,* 715-722.

Pommerehne, W. W., Schneider, F., & Zweifel, P. (1982). Economic theory of choice and the preference reversal phenomenon: A re-examination. *American Economic Review, 72,* 569-574.

Randall, A. (1983). The problem of market failure. *Natural Resources Journal, 23,* 131-148.

Randall, A., Hoehn, J. P., & Brookshire, D. S. (1983). Contingent valuation surveys for evaluating environmental assets. *Natural Resources Journal, 23,* 635-648.

Reilly, R. J. (1982). Preference reversal: Further evidence and some suggested modifications in experimental design. *American Economic Review, 72,* 576-584.

Rokeach, M. (1973). *The nature of human values.* New York: Free Press.

Rowe, R. D., d'Arge, R. C., & Brookshire, D. S. (1980). An experiment on the economic value of visibility. *Journal of Environmental Economics and Management, 7,* 1-19.

Schelling, T. C. (1984). Self-command in practice, in policy, and in theory of rational choice. *AEA Papers and Proceedings, 74,* 1-11.

Schoemaker, P. J. H. (1982). The expected utility model: Its variants, purposes, evidence and limitations. *Journal of Economic Literature, 20,* 529-563.

Schoemaker, P. J. H., & Kunreuther, H. C. (1979). An experimental study of insurance decisions. *Journal of Risk and Insurance, 46,* 603-618.

Simon, H. (1957). *Models of man.* New York: Wiley.

Slovic, P. (1985). *Violations of dominance in the rated attractiveness of playing bets* (Report 85-6). Eugene, OR: Decision Research.

Slovic, P., & Lichtenstein, S. (1983). Preference reversals: A broader perspective. *American Economic Review, 73,* 596-605.

Slovic, P., Fischhoff, B., & Lichtenstein, S. (1982). Response mode, framing, and information processing effects in risk assessment. In R. M. Hogarth (Ed.), *New directions for methodology of social and behavioral science: The framing of questions and the consistency of response* (pp. 21-36). San Francisco, CA: Jossey-Bass.

Stigler, G. J. (1965). *Essays in the history of economics.* Chicago: University of Chicago Press.

Thaler, R. (1980). Toward a positive theory of consumer choice. *Journal of Economic Behavior for Organization,* 1, 39-60.

Tverksy, A., & Kahneman, D. (1981). The framing of decisions and the psychology of choice. *Science, 211,* 453-458.

Tversky, A., & Slovic, P. (1984). *Compatibility effects and preference reversals.* Unpublished manuscript. Eugene, Oregon, Decision Research.

von Neumann, J., & Morgenstern, O. (1944). *Theory of games and economic behavior* (2nd ed.). Princeton, NJ: Princeton University Press.

White, G. M. (1975). Contextual determinants of opinion judgements: Field experimental probes of judgmental relativity boundary conditions. *Journal of Personality and Social Psychology, 32,* 1047-1054.

A Framework for More Comprehensive Valuations of Public Amenity Goods and Services

B. L. Driver
USDA Forest Service
Rocky Mountain Forest and Range Experiment Station
Fort Collins, Colorado

William R. Burch, Jr.
School of Forestry and Environmental Studies
Yale University

In this paper, we bridge the gap between the three preceding introductory papers and those following, which focus on "nonmarket" techniques for estimating the willingness to pay or compensation demanded for amenity goods and services. We first review why the diffuse public amenity resource policy and managerial (i.e., allocation) decision processes require information on many types of values and, therefore, need input from technical experts representing many disciplines. We then offer a framework identifying the components that must be considered and types of analyses that must be accomplished to attain more comprehensive and integrated valuations of public amenity goods and services. Specifically, we recommend that much additional attention be given to identifying and quantifying the gains and losses associated with provision and use of public amenity goods and services--not just to improve benefit-cost analyses (BCAs) but to provide information about other types of value for consideration in the allocation decision processes.[1] Finally, we briefly describe the research needed to implement the proposed framework for valuation.

We describe the public decision processes and their informational needs as we see them and do not try to develop any normative theories about social welfare. Our view of those processes follows that of Freeman and Frey (1986) who proposed two levels of valuation: "a technical level ... where the analyst specifies and justifies value criteria and a political/administrative level ... where decisionmakers make tradeoffs among competing value criteria" (p. 230). Because of insufficient information, those decisionmakers must rely on some personal (highly subjective) system for defining and weighing the relevant values associated with suspected but ill-defined and inadequately measured impacts (later defined as gains and losses). Within this highly information-deficient situation, the decisionmaker is expected to make value judgments that reflect a "miraculous" jump to the best decision possible, despite the lack of good information. Because those types of decisions are not only miraculous, but almost magical, the decisionmaker has commonly been pictured as pulling the necessary information from a black box--the contents of which remain mystical.

We see the "miraculous decisionmakers" as being reasonable (Ajzen & Fishbein, 1980) and thus receptive to factual information about the many values they must consider, while still promoting particular ideologies with which some technical analysts do not agree. We also subscribe to the concepts of consumer and voter sovereignty as "good" rules, but we see much plasticity in individual preferences, considerable impulse and whim guiding decisions, and many people behaving in ways that they will readily admit are probably not "good" for them, which we feel is their right. We argue for better information on the impacts of alternative decisions and for both monetary and nonmonetary measures of the values assigned those impacts.

NEED FOR MULTIDISCIPLINARY INPUT

To understand why public amenity resource allocation decision processes need input from many disciplines, consider the following nonmutually exclusive and frequently conflicting multiple goals that must be weighed by policymakers and managers

of most public resource agencies (words indicating specific values are underlined):[2]

1. Promote national economic "development" through efficient allocations and operations.
2. Sustain the productive capacities of basic natural resources over time.
3. Promote regional and local economic development.
4. Maintain community stability.
5. Make fair or equitable allocations regarding subcultures (e.g., the indigent and those with lower incomes).
6. Protect what have become accepted as basic rights (e.g., civil and equal rights, rights to reasonably clean air and water, rights of future generations, and even the "right" for plant and animal species to live).
7. Maintain established cultural values (e.g., ethnic diversity and pride in country and community through maintenance of national historic and heritage parks and monuments, and promotion of national holidays).
8. Recognize (usually by subsidy in the form of lower user fees) the contributions to society of special groups (e.g., the elderly and veterans).
9. Promote freedom of religion (e.g., designating particular areas as sacred grounds).
10. Provide for special values related to special-use areas (e.g., those designed as Class I Air Visibility Areas, national recreational trails and rivers, scenic areas, wilderness and natural areas, and areas having unique geologic formations).
11. Maintain genetic diversity and preserve representative ecosystems for utilitarian reasons (e.g., new medicines and crop species, scientific laboratories, stewardship).
12. Protect the general health, safety, and welfare, which frequently means limiting use opportunities despite high willingness to pay (e.g., preventing skiing in high-risk avalanche areas).
13. Reduce conflicts by making compromise allocations that try to give a little to all major interest groups (including dipping into the "pork barrel"), even if normative criteria exist to indicate these allocations might not produce socially optimal results if tested using a particular disciplinary perspective.
14. Create social infrastructure to capture external economies (i.e., meritorious spin-off benefits) of particular uses and to prevent external diseconomies.
15. Help balance the budget through administration of user fees.

This list is not intended to be inclusive; there are no doubt other goals and values we may have overlooked.

Officials responsible for allocating public natural resources must mentally balance incommensurate information related to these multiple and competing goals, each of which can constitute a separate decision criterion. No one valuation method exists now, or is likely to exist in the near future, that provides both commensurate and sufficiently comprehensive measures; important information is left out of all methods. Thus, no one evaluation paradigm can do more than provide partial information about the gains and losses associated with the diffuse values and goals, most of which are established in law or by strong historical precedence. For example, BCAs now can provide useful information to evaluate some of these goals; with contin-

TABLE 1. Weighing Results of Benefit-cost Analyses Under Conditions of Different Availability of Information

Situation	Amount of efficiency-related gains and losses that can be:			Role of economic analyst	Role of decisionmaker
	Identified	Quantified	Monetized		
I	All	All	All	Make BCAs and rank the alternatives according to their contributions to potential Pareto improvements (PPIs).	Judge whether other nonmonetary values are large or important enough to alter the recommendation made by the economic analyst.
II	All	All	Some	Make BCAs using available information, list and describe nonmonetized gains and losses, make judgment about the influence of the nonmonetized gains and losses on the BCAs, and rank the alternatives.	Make a separate judgment about the influence of the nonmonetized gains and losses on the BCAs, then proceed as for Situation I.
III	All	Some	Some	As for Situation II, but also list identified but unquantified gains and losses and make judgment about their influence on the BCAs before ranking the alternatives.	As for Situation II, but include separate judgment by decisionmaker about influence of identified but unquantified gains and losses on the BCAs.
IV	Some	Some	Some	As for Situation III, but specify that unidentified gains and losses probably exist.	As for Situation III, but explicitly recognize that unidentified gains and losses probably exist.

ued improvement in methodology, they may provide even wider coverage. Pursuit of several other values, however, can conflict with the being-economically-efficient value. In some of those instances, tests of cost-effectiveness can at least disclose the least costly ways, or the opportunity costs, of pursuing particular goals for which the benefits cannot be monetized. But in most decisions, the results of the "efficiency analyses" must be weighed by the decisionmaker against the other multiple decision criteria listed (Randall, 1984a). This is true for all single index measures made for any one criterion. However, that situation does not diminish the importance of each of the large number of single-index measures needed. We wish fewer were needed and that commensurate measures could be made of all the relevant values, but we do not see decisions being made that way, or ever likely to be.

Fisher (1986, personal communication) agrees that public policy and managerial decisions are diffuse and that BCAs represent one important input. She reflects on the many types of value that must be considered by decisionmakers and recommends "organizing information by the different dimensions of value." We have extended her sketch of how the decisionmaker should weigh economic efficiency values against other values

(Table 1) by adding the column "Role of Economic Analysts."

Table 1 indicates the roles of the economist (as technical advisor) and the decisionmaker regarding the use of BCAs when the relevant gains and losses (called benefits and costs in Fisher [1986], but gains and losses in her personal communication) can be "identified," "quantified," and "monetized" to different degrees--ranging from complete knowledge (Situation I) to much uncertainty (Situation IV). In all four situations, the recommended role of the decisionmaker is to weigh the BCA (efficiency) values against the other values in the black box. The technical analysts can provide information that will help establish the weights, but the final weighing will be by the decisionmaker. In moving from Situation I to IV, the decisionmaker must rely increasingly on subjective judgment to establish the weights. It is our view that Situation IV best describes the current valuation condition for publicly provided amenity goods and services, with the caveat that the systems for inputting information on the nonmonetized values are generally less quantitatively advanced than those for making the BCAs. The task then is to improve all value analysis systems to reduce the size of the black box.

A FRAMEWORK FOR EXAMINING MULTIPLE VALUES

Although it is easy to say that all relevant values should be considered by public decisionmakers, it is difficult to define some of those values, for example, those covered under the rubric of ''health, safety, and welfare.'' Other, more easily defined values, for example, equity, are difficult to analyze within any normative theory of social welfare and are commonly ''handled'' through voter sovereignty and the political-democratic process.

This section offers a framework for better defining and integrating all relevant values into the decision process. It emphasizes the need for better information on the gains and losses associated with a proposed policy or management alternative as the key for opening the black box, and for improving BCAs. Although the framework might not help ''reduce the number of dimensions of value that have to be considered by the decisionmakers'' (another of Fishers objectives) it should help clarify those dimensions and provide better information about them.[3]

Basic Components

The basic parts of the proposed framework are identified as the types of information that need to be provided to decisionmakers by technical analysts (Figure 1). Many of those components are

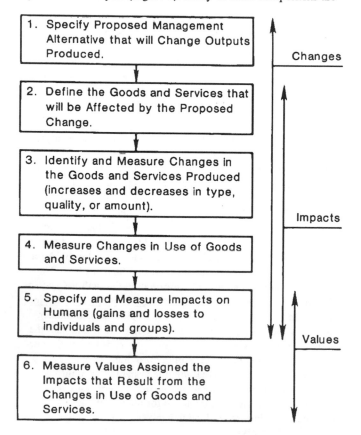

FIGURE 1. Technical analyses needed for impact assessment and valuation.

common in the literature on proposed project evaluation and impact assessment. Some reflect a departure from convention (Driver & Rosenthal, 1982; Driver, Brown, & Burch, 1987).

The logic of the framework is derived from production economics. It is based on the notion that implementation of any non-status quo allocation will affect the flow of goods and services currently being provided. The production and use of these goods and services create desirable and undesirable impacts, to which values are assigned.

Box 1 (Figure 1) indicates that the first task of a technical analyst who is evaluating a proposed management alternative is to specify clearly what that proposed action is. Will it call for more resources to be allocated to the production of so-called ''commodities'' than to amenities? Will dispersed forms of recreation be emphasized more than concentrated forms? Will roads be built? Such questions must be clarified to understand how the proposed management action would change the type, quantity, or quality of the outputs, or goods and services, that would be produced.

Once the proposed management action has been specified, the goods and services that would be affected by that action must be defined clearly (Box 2) before the impacts and values associated with production and use of those goods and services can be measured. Those goods and services include the full range of outputs--from marketed timber to recreation opportunities, to acres preserved as wilderness. Such specification remains a serious analytical problem for the amenity goods and services (Driver 1985; Driver et al. 1985; Fischhoff, this volume). Recreation sites--even one as large as Grand Canyon National Park--that provide many goods and services are entered as the object demanded in many economic studies without adequate definition of whether the demand is for access or for a particular good or service. Among other things, this muddles application of the ''with and without principle.'' The units (e.g., recreation visitor days, trips, visits) employed to measure demand also remain problematic, with different units disclosing different economic demands in analyses of the same area and recreation opportunity.

Changes in goods and services produced under the allocation being evaluated must be identified and measured (Box 3, Figure 1)--not an easy task. The changes of concern are the differences between the type (or mix), quality, and quantity of goods and services currently being produced (i.e., the status quo alternative) and those that would be produced under the proposed alternative. Or, changes in the goods and services produced by several proposed alternatives--rather than a proposed alternative and the current situation--can be evaluated. These changes can result directly or indirectly from the proposed management action. A proposed alternative might recommend increasing the sale of timber outputs from a particular area. If implemented, that action might cause stream siltation, which would reduce the number and quality of fishing opportunities. In that case, the proposed alternative would directly change output levels (i.e., increase the timber products) and indirectly cause secondary impacts (siltation), which change outputs (decreased fishing opportunities). Those impacts, in turn, might cause canoe and boat liveries to close, resulting in indirect tertiary reductions in opportunities for river use by recreationists who do not fish. Tracking all these changes can be difficult, but it should be done for comprehensiveness.

Although projected demand and supply should be in close agreement, the estimated changes in amenity goods and services that would be produced under a proposed allocation often differ substantially from the actual changes in the use of those goods and services. For example, it is frequently necessary to provide what can be called excess recreation capacity at most times to meet peak demands at particular times.[4] All probable changes in the use of goods and services must be quantified to the extent possible (Box 4, Figure 1). This use ranges from consumptive (e.g., board-feet of timber) to on-site nonconsumptive (e.g., recreation visitor days of hiking) to off-site nonconsumptive (e.g., an area preserved as wilderness). Changes in use--possibly decreasing for some goods and increasing for others--might result from direct or indirect impacts of a change in management. In addition to measuring the changes in use, the users affected must be identified.

Changes in the use of the goods and services cause desirable and undesirable impacts (Box 5, Figure 1). Although some researchers (Callicott, 1985; Rolston, 1981) propose that greater attention be given to impacts on species other than humans, attention here is limited to impacts on humans. These impacts can be viewed as gains or losses to individuals or groups of individuals. As elaborated under "The Newer Dimensions,", a gain is defined as an improvement in the condition or state of an individual, group, or society. A loss reflects a worsened condition.

The evaluation tasks (Box 5) involved in assessing impacts are to identify the gains and losses associated with the changes in use of the amenity goods and services, measure their magnitudes, and determine the distribution of those gains and losses across different social units. In question form those tasks are "What are the gains and losses? How large are they? and Who are the gainers and losers?" Very little systematic research has addressed these three questions; most of what we know is intuitive. The analyses necessary to answer the questions must consider the preferences of the gainers and losers to determine their "held values" or the ranking, by preferential judgments, of one thing or condition as being above or below (i.e., more or less preferred than) another (T. C. Brown, 1984). These held values constitute the belief structures that define the multiple values the allocation decisionmakers must weigh.

Once the impacts have been identified and quantified, the values assigned those gains and losses must be measured (Box 6, Figure 1). These "assigned values" can be measured in monetary or nonmonetary units (P. J. Brown, 1984; Peterson, Driver, & Brown, in press). Measures of willingness to pay or compensations demanded are the most common metrics used (see Mendelsohn & Peterson, this volume).

Definition and measurement of changes, impacts, and assigned values overlap in valuation (see vertical lines on the right side of Figure 1). Much of the literature about evaluation procedures tend to ignore this overlap, and confusion is created by different disciplines using the same term to mean different things. Most economists, for example, use the word "benefit" as a measure of the monetary worth of a good or service, while other analysts may use that word to denote a specific type of gain or improved condition. These semantic differences impede communication and discourage the more comprehensive and integrated approach needed.[5]

5A. Define the impacts of the changes in goods and services
 1. Specify gains
 2. Specify losses
5B. Quantify the magnitude of the impacts
 1. Measure gains
 2. Measure losses
6. Measure the values assigned the impacts (or the goods and services)
 1. Using monetary metrics
  a. Measure worth of the gains by measuring willingness to pay (or compensation demanded) for the changes in the goods and services
  b. Measure monetary costs of the losses caused by the changes in the goods and services
 2. Using nonmonetary metrics
  a. Measure the worth of the benefits
  b. Measure the costs of the losses
7. Summarize the gains and losses and the worths and costs associated with the proposed management alternative

FIGURE 2. Specifying, measuring, and valuing impacts (elaboration of Boxes 5 and 6 in Figure 1).

The Newer Dimensions

The newer dimensions of the framework sometimes use words not common to the impact assessment and valuation literature. To help establish definitions for those dimensions, Figure 2 elaborates on specifying and measuring the impacts and valuing those impacts (Boxes 5 and 6, Figure 1).

Defining the Impacts of Changes in Goods and Services (Item 5A, Figure 2)

If not the most difficult, certainly the most fundamental task of any analysis is defining clearly the variables to be measured. Perhaps the most difficult variables to specify are the desirable and undesirable impacts that are to be measured and valued. We defined these impacts as either gains or losses to individuals or groups of individuals (Box 5, Figure 1). We prefer to think of the gains as benefits, which Randall (1986) defined as arising from the "provision of anything that generates positive utility and from the removal of anything that generates disutility." Because we are advocating better quantification of specific types of gains (and losses), we will not use the aggregating abstraction "utility."

The first task is to define the gains and losses (i.e., impacts in conventional parlance) associated with changes in use of the goods and services that would result from implementation of the proposed allocation. To answer the question "What are the gains and losses that will occur?" we need to know who gains and who loses and how. Qualitative analyses (Peterson et al., in press) are needed to help answer these questions, because saying that an impact is a gain or a loss involves a valuation by the gainers and losers or by those who represent them. Those judgments reflect the gainers' and losers' held values (or preferential judgments), and they vary from one context to another (T. C. Brown, 1984). Various impacts of adding a new area to the Wilderness Preservation System would be considered as gains by members of the Wilderness Society, but that allocation might be perceived as mostly causing losses to a party interested in commodity uses of the same area. Of course, either party might understand the perspectives of the other, but still differ in its preferential judgments about wilderness. Also, what is considered a gain at one point in time may be considered a loss at another by the same party. An avid jogger might later suffer knee injury caused by the jogging. The ex ante and ex post values assigned opportunities for jogging might differ.

At some stage, gainers and losers should be involved in defining the gains and losses to protect the sovereignty of those whom the proposed allocation will impact. Those impacted must definitely be involved directly in defining any gains and losses that are not yet well specified. Such involvement might, for example, include members of an Indian tribe claiming sacred significance of a land area, recreationists desiring use of the same area, or a mining company seeking profit from mineral extraction. On the other hand, less involvement is now needed where good definitions exist for certain impacts, such as the cardiovascular benefits of using an area for exercise (Buccola & Stone, 1975) or the losses associated with wildfire caused by recreationists.

Past research along with new studies must be used to achieve comprehensive definitions of the gains and losses associated with use of particular amenity goods and services. Involving the gainers and losers in both survey research and public involvement exercises should yield a clearer understanding of whether the conditions that would accompany a proposed change in allocation are beneficial or not. Over time, the actual existence of the gains and losses will be tested by the Item 5A research. In this way, a body of knowledge will be built from which generalizations can be made about probable gains and losses, just as some can now be made from past research.

Quantifying the Magnitude of the Impacts (Item 5B, Figure 2)

Measurement of the magnitudes of the gains and losses accomplishes two objectives: (1) it documents the level of the gains and losses, and (2) it validates the extent to which the gains and losses have been specified accurately. Regarding the first objective, it must be recognized that the gains and losses affect either individuals or groups of individuals. At both levels, the magnitudes of the impacts are measurable in two distinct ways, by observation and by questionnaire. Changes in an individual's behavior (e.g., choices made, performance, physiological responses, and other observable changes defined as beneficial or detrimental) may be objectively measured by someone other than the user of the good or service. Ulrich (this volume) elaborates some of these measures. Alternatively, introspective measures of levels of gains or losses can be reported by the user through survey research and other methods. Similarly, changes in social conditions may be observed by the analysts or indicated by survey. These impacts include changes that affect resource stocks for future generations, community stability, conditions that facilitate developing a sense of place and belonging, and opportunities for social bonding and for promoting cooperative, altruistic, and patriotic behaviors.

Observed changes of individual behavior or social conditions would be of greatest value to decisionmakers, but responses

about perceived changes will also be useful, especially until the "harder" measures are available. Here too, sufficient studies must be undertaken until a body of knowledge is developed from which generalizations to similar situations can be made.

Once the magnitudes of the perceived gains or losses have been estimated, that information can be used to validate the definition of those impacts. Assume for example, that some people express the belief that use of particular recreation opportunities helped them to relax mentally. Suppose too that empirical evidence showed that while those people were engaged in those activities, they registered higher alpha (brain wave) amplitude (on an EEG), showing increased wakeful relaxation. In this case, the perceived gains are at least partially confirmed, so this measure of the magnitude of the "mental health" benefits helps define that impact or gain. This ex post factor validation is needed simply because so little is known about the impacts of using amenity goods and services.

Measuring the Values Assigned the Impacts of the Changes in the Goods and Services (Item 6, Figure 2)

Probably our greatest departure from conventional terminology is in use of the term "assigned values" to denote the worth of the gains and the costs of the losses in Figure 2. These measures reflect the relative importances of the gains and losses to the gainers and losers. They are measured using two basic types of metrics: monetary and nonmonetary. With two semantic exceptions, the monetary measures (Item 6A) are identical to those made within the conventional BCA paradigm, which needs no elaboration. The first exception is that we employ the word "worth" rather than benefit, because of our belief that not all benefits (gains) can or should be monetized. Second, we prefer conceptually to hold the view that the impacts are being monetized rather than the goods and services that provide them (which is consistent with consumer utility theory). We accept the practical need to "price" the goods and services--while still urging the broader mind set that we feel is necessary to understand the proposed framework.

Measurement of the worth of the gains and the costs of the losses in nonmonetary units (Item 6B) can be used both to supplement the monetary measures and to provide information on assigned values when monetary measures cannot be made at all or made as accurately as desired. Because these nonmonetary measures are supplemental and are used for different purposes by the decisionmaker than are the monetary measures (see Table 1), we see little problem of double counting. Recall the multiple goals and values that must be weighed by the miraculous decisionmakers.

The nonmonetary measures of assigned value are of two types: nonmonetary economic and nonmonetary noneconomic. The "nonmonetary economic" measures index the assigned values in terms of personal economic resources (time, space, other goods and services) that people are willing to exchange to realize the gains or to prevent the losses. Most, if not all of these units will have direct correspondence to monetary units of value even though those conversions might be difficult to make, as indicated by the debate on the monetary value that should be assigned time in the travel-cost method. The "nonmonetary noneconomic" measures are more abstract and might or might not have correspondence to monetary measures. When such correspondence is evident, it is indirect. Although these indices are much more difficult to conceptualize and measure--or even to fit systematically into the miraculous decisionmaker's black box--they are important and must be considered for comprehensiveness. They frequently relate to perceptions of rights and reflect particular ethical and moral postures. Because they usually involve measurement of opinion and sentiment, they generally are based on self-reports that indicate relative importance based on an ordinal scale, like those commonly employed in opinion polls. For example, one role of public involvement is to gain ordinal information about the relative importance different user groups place on the likely impacts of proposed developments. Sometimes the introspective measures have correspondence to behavioral measures, as reflected by protests, demonstrations (including civil disobedience, strikes, and boycotts), letter writing, contributions, memberships, hiring of lobbyists, and litigation--each of which attempts to display the relative importance of the perceived magnitudes of probable gains and losses.[6]

The assigned values can now be estimated reasonably well for many impacts. For others (e.g., maintenance of genetic diversity, community stability, community/national pride) the assigned values are more ephemeral. Sometimes only the measures of the magnitudes of the gains and losses--with no estimates of assigned values--can be provided by the technical analysts to the miraculous decisionmakers who must assign and weigh values quite subjectively.

Summarizing Gains and Losses and Assigned Values (Item 7, Figure 2)

The summary of gains and losses and worths and costs must, by necessity, include incommensurate measures, given the state of the art. Also, some measures must be handled more by narration than by numbers. But that situation will improve over time as the state of the arts advances.

To use an example for reviewing what we have proposed for the impact assessment and valuation framework (Figure 1), assume a simple valuation situation where a proposal is being considered to develop a system of exercise trails where none exist. For even greater simplicity, let us restrict our example to evaluating the health-related benefits of preventing and reducing hypertension. The benefits, then, have been defined as reduced rates of hypertension. Results of physiological studies made on similar populations using similar trails could be used to quantify the magnitude of that reduction/prevention of hypertension. Assigned values could be measured by monetizing those benefits, especially in terms of willingness to pay for use of the trails. Quantification of the assigned values could also involve both nonmonetary economic measures (such as time spent on similar trails by other similar populations) and nonmonetary noneconomic measures (such as the extent and intensity of public support for the trails).

If the reader protests that the proposed analyses are too complex, our response is not "we did not offer you a rose garden." Instead, we suggest that this complexity is the decision reality facing all public decisionmakers. Remember, it was the real world need to make decisions in the face of this complexity and

with limited information that gave rise to the notion of the "magical" black box. It would be ironic if scientists avoid the challenge because of its complexity, while somewhat smugly deriding the decisionmakers' need for those black boxes. We appreciate one reviewer's comment that it seemed we were adding to the dimensions in that black box! We have only tried to describe those dimensions and suggest how better information about them can be obtained by technical analysts. Although defining those dimensions does not make the decision less complex, it opens the black box to more light. Arbitrarily restricting the number of those dimensions serves to redefine the problem to make it amenable to a particular bag of disciplinary tools. This might comfort the analysts skilled in wielding those tools, but the problem still remains with its real world complexity.

IMPLEMENTING THE PROPOSED FRAMEWORK

Before the proposed framework is implemented more widely to guide evaluations of public amenity goods and services, it must be better understood and accepted. Assuming acceptance, the number and complexity of the studies required and the time they will take are a little "mind-boggling," as indicated by Table 2.

In Table 2, we speculate about (1) which of the called for analyses can now be made with reasonable accuracy and validity given the current state of the art, and (2) what would be possible soon (e.g., within 10-15 years) with concerted effort. Our scoring indicates that slightly over one-half (i.e., 6 of 11) of the evaluation tasks are currently being accomplished at 51-75% of potential attainment. Slightly over one-fourth are at 1-25%, and about one-fifth are at 26-50%. We judge that most of the attainment indicated is not on the high end of the ranges suggested. If we are correct, the current analytical abilities indicate need for considerable advancement of the state of the art--which also reflects the current need for miraculous decisionmakers to reach quite deep into huge black boxes. Note especially the degree to which the gains are currently specified, measured, and valued. Considerable progress should be possible soon with concerted effort, for example, to move all but 2 of the 11 (82%) tasks into the 51-75% or higher levels of attainment. The two most difficult tasks will be accurately measuring all relevant gains and estimating their worth in nonmonetary units. They require truly long-term research efforts.

The proposed framework is being partially implemented in resource valuations by public agencies, with some components receiving more attention than others. Perhaps best known is the "system of accounts" recommended by the U.S. Water Resources Council (WRC, 1973, 1979). The WRC system currently guides many impact assessments and valuations of federal land management agencies in the United States. It proposes measures in four accounts labeled (1) national economic development (NED), (2) regional and local economic development, (3) environmental protection, and (4) social impact assessment (SIA). These accounts reflect the need of decisionmakers to consider multiple goals and values. Some of the measures can overlap (e.g., measures of economic efficiency values with some of the environmental protection values), and some acknowledge competition for scarce public resources (economic efficiency

TABLE 2. Estimated Degree to Which the Proposed Evaluation Tasks Are Now Actually Being Accomplished (A) for Publicly Provided Goods and Services and What Might be Possible (P) Within 10-15 Years With Concerted Effort

Task	Estimated degree of task attainment				
	1-25%	26-50%	51-75%	76-95%	100%
Clearly specify the affected goods and services.			A	P	
Identify and measure changes in the amount of affected goods and services that will be produced.			A	P	
Measure probable changes in use of affected goods and services over time.			A,P		
Specify losses.			A	P	
Specify gains.	A		P		
Accurately measure losses.			A	P	
Accurately measure gains.	A	P			
Accurately measure monetary costs of losses.			A	P	
Accurately measure monetary worth of gains (or of the goods and services that produce them).		A	P		
Accurately measure nonmonetary costs of losses.		A	P		
Accurately measure nonmonetary worth of gains.	A	P			

versus local and regional economic development, or this last goal versus environmental protection).

Although current impact-assessment and valuation procedures make some attempt to integrate the different WRC accounts, conventional approaches frequently reflect overly narrow disciplinary perspectives. This restrictive outlook deters making more integrated evaluations and expanding the variables analyzed so that more comprehensive information can be provided to the miraculous decisionmaker.

We build on the WRC system of accounts to show how the proposed framework can be made operational and achieve more integrated and comprehensive valuations. Four areas of improvement are recommended:

1. Improve measures of gains and losses to individuals.
2. Refine existing methods and expand considerably the coverage of SIA's.
3. Refine monetary measures of assigned values.
4. Develop methods for making nonmonetary measures of assigned value.

Improve Measures of Impacts on Individuals

Conventional evaluation practices do not adequately assess gains and losses to individuals. The national economic development account does measure the monetary values assigned by individuals, but the focus is on the aggregate worth of the gains and costs of the losses, not measurement of those gains and losses. The social well-being account considers impacts on groups, not individuals. The regional and local economic development account examines impacts on individuals when measures of income and employment are used, and so do the health-related and other measures made for the environmental protection account. Both accounts need improvement, and other measures of gains and losses to individuals should be better specified and measured.

Decisionmakers, in their needs to weigh many values, desire information on who benefits and who loses from a proposed change. Also, definition and measurement of gains and losses to groups of individuals will help clarify the nature and extent of many of the more ephemeral and "fragile" (Tribe, 1976) values that must be weighed against those more amenable to quantification. Thus, information about how and how much different types of individuals gain or lose from an alternative is useful to public decisionmakers. Certainly, information about likely health-related consequences of excessive cholesterol in the diet, adverse impacts of tobacco use, and relationships between speed limits and human mortality and morbidity has influenced decisionmakers at all levels. More relevant to the allocation of amenity resources, decisionmakers at all levels--consumers to elected officials--would profit by better knowledge of the associated benefits such as increased family solidarity, greater national pride, increased work performance, better mental and physical health, improved self-concept, and better appreciation of basic human dependency on the natural environment. Of course, impacts on every individual cannot be obtained, but patterns can be ascertained.

Not only will information on patterns of individual gains and losses be useful to public decisionmakers; it also will enhance the rationality of the choices of sovereign consumers and voters. For example, if consumers knew more about the positive effects of hiking on health, they might value it more highly, do it more often, and may be more willing to pay more for it through taxes or use fees. Thus, the information on gains and losses to individuals would be useful both to consumers and to public decisionmakers by helping each, in their respective roles, make more informed valuations, and therefore better choices. We realize that many people still smoke and make choices that apparently are not good for them. Nevertheless, we believe that most consumers and voters, as well as allocation decisionmakers, do use available information in their choices, especially over time.

Refine and Broaden Social Impact Assessments

Although the theme of social benefits is pervasive in many of the multiple goals of federal agencies managing amenity resources, the state of the art for assessing these impacts is quite inadequate. Also, current methods of making social impact assessments (SIA's) tend to focus negatively on preventing losses rather than on creating those social conditions or states that enhance overall social welfare (Burch & DeLuca, 1984). Thus, much improvement is needed in how the social impacts are measured, valued, and integrated into public decisions (Finsterbusch & Wolf, 1977).

Particular improvement is needed in deciding which social units (households, communities, societies) are affected by specific allocations. Also needed is a much better understanding of how amenity-related infrastructure at one level facilitates or constrains options at other levels. We know that communities establish conditions that allow lower level family units and individuals to benefit. They do this by allocating amenity resources toward creating and maintaining physical settings that among other things facilitate a sense of place and promote social cohesion. The problem is that little has been done to establish predictive relationships between the improved conditions at the community or macro/collective level and the micro/individual

level. Without such information, the average citizen finds it difficult to recognize and demand facilitating conditions necessary for realizing these types of benefits. They could be "missed" without being known about.

The improved SIA's should be able to identify and measure those social conditions that are desirable for particular types of benefits to be realized by individuals. For example, it has been argued widely that amenity-related environments nurture opportunities for unique types of learning, exploration, skill development, reciprocity, and sharing of information vital for effective functioning; establishing and nurturing social bonds; maintaining a sense of place and continuity; and sustaining a stable life space (Altman & Wohlwill, 1983; Burch, 1986; Cheek & Burch, 1976; Kelly, 1981; West, 1986). Although each of these benefits contributes to the fiber and substance of a society and helps make life worthwhile for its members (Campbell, 1981; Scitovsky, 1978), descriptions of the conditions necessary for these benefits to be realized are largely omitted from currently used methods of impact assessment and valuation (Mishan, 1981). The reason is that we just do not have good predictive ability about these facilitating conditions.

Better means also are needed for assessing the social impacts at different levels within the agency responsible for the evaluations. For example, even though the USDA Forest Service has a national jurisdiction, some of its goals, such as promotion of local and regional development and sustaining community development, reflect subnational concerns. The lower the decision level, the greater the need for information about local impacts and values. Development of national programs (e.g., the Renewable Resources Planning Act 5-year programs and their updates) require little analysis of specific impacts at the local level. In contrast, the plan for the White Mountain National Forest in New England must justify in some detail why tradeoffs are being made between protecting specific scenic areas and harvesting more timber there.

Improve Measures of Economic Efficiency Values

In the introductory section, we established that economic efficiency is a particularly important value to weigh in allocation decisions. At least theoretically, contributions to potential Pareto improvement can be measured independently from many of the other multiple values of concern, and without direct specification and measurement of the gains and losses to individuals and groups of individuals--the need for which has been a central argument of this paper. This possibility is illustrated in Figure 3, which starts with Box 4 of Figure 1 and shows the analyses made "with" and "without" the measurement of gains and losses.

Using the "without" approach to determining economic efficiency (Box 5A and 6A, Figure 3), choices are taken as given and are of interest mainly as a means of estimating the economic value that consumers assign to the goods they choose. No attempt is made to investigate the effect of consumers' choices on their well-being. They are assumed to maximize their utility. The approach can be said to be "utility-based," and consumer sovereignty is assumed to be the basis of value; not only do individual consumers know what is best for their welfare, but they have sufficient knowledge and ability to evaluate the options and choose the one that will maximize their welfare.

In the more integrative "with" approach (Box 5B and 6B, Figure 3), the economic efficiency measures are made using the same methods (e.g., travel costs, contingent valuations, hedonics, auctions) as in the "without" approach for estimating the monetary values of the goods and services, and the integrity of the concept of consumer sovereignty is protected just as well-- and probably better. However, those valuations do not skip from measurement of use to assignment of monetary value as in the "without" approach. Instead, the approach is better integrated with the other evaluations being done, including those of the magnitudes of the gains and losses. In this approach, the economic analysts can be more sensitive to how their efforts can profit by those of the other technical experts.

Better information on the gains and losses associated with the use of particular goods and services would improve benefit-cost analysis. It would enhance the quality of the consumers' choice processes and thereby help target more accurately their willingness to pay or compensations demanded for those goods and services. For example, much of the objective information that helps determine a person's revealed preferences and assigned values comes from sources outside the individual. Examples include knowledge from research about the benefits of avoiding substance abuse (including tobacco), stress management, low cholesterol diets, exercising, proper nutrition, and use of seat belts. Thus, the utility and disutility expected by the consumers--and their willingness to pay--are based largely on known, or expected, gains and losses. Results of systematic research that specifies and measures the gains and losses related to particular amenity goods and services would therefore be useful to the sovereign consumers in their valuation decisions, especially if many of the personal benefits of using those amenity goods and services are not now known, which we suspect is true.

Information on the gains and losses could improve BCAs by helping account for any gaps between willingness to pay and compensation demanded (see chapters in this volume by Gregory & Bishop; Fisher, McClelland, & Schulze; and Brookshire,

Coursey, & Radosevich). One might document, for example, that perceptions of gains and losses differ under these two valuation stances, and that these differences explain the discrepancies (e.g., preference reversals and influences of framing) that have been reported (Kahneman & Tversky, 1979; Tversky, 1972; Tversky & Kahneman, 1981). Also, economic studies of option, existence, and bequest values could be tightened considerably by better understanding the "whys" behind those valuations. For example, what are the benefits of maintaining genetic diversity? Certainly a better understanding of the gains and losses perceived to be associated with these and other demands could help define better the contexts within which particular gains and losses will and will not occur. Defining these contexts will help improve the BCAs; several papers in this volume (Ajzen & Peterson, Brown & Slovic) show that monetary appraisals of value are quite context-dependent. For example, proposals have recently been made that the results of some contingent-valuation studies could be improved if researchers adopted a policy referendum format where the respondents were informed of the likely consequences of alternative actions (Harris, Tinsley, & Donnelly, this volume; Mitchell & Carson, this volume; Randall, 1986, this volume). Specification and measurements of the gains and losses define those consequences.

Better information about the likely gains and losses associated with so-called risk-related allocations (i.e., nuclear energy, toxic wastes, use of pesticides and herbicides) would also improve the monetary analyses made to guide those decisions. The fundamental problems in the risk-related decisions are assignment of probabilities to likely impacts and estimation of the magnitude of those impacts. How likely is it, for example, that a particular nuclear power plant will release different types and level of radiation, and what will be the short-term and long-run consequences to people at different locations? It is almost tautological, and perhaps even trivial, to say that information on these impacts would help reduce these uncertainties. Recent debate about risks associated with the chemicals accumulated in Love Canal in New York is a good case in point; the fundamental problem was that few if any of the residents involved knew what the impacts on their health would be.

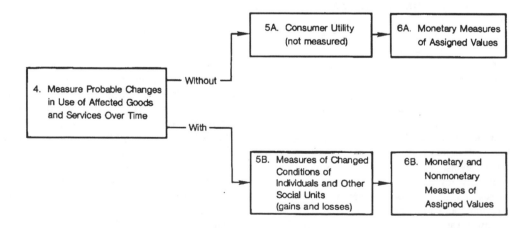

FIGURE 3. Technical valuations with and without direct specification and measurement of gains and losses. (Box 4 is equivalent to Box 4 of Figure 1.)

The proposed approach could also help improve tests of economic efficiency by defining better those user groups who might differ in their willingness to pay for the goods and services with which the differentiated gains and losses are associated. Or gains to a participant (e.g., family solidarity or improved health) might be shown to be dependent on specific attributes (opportunities for family outings or exercise trails) of a particular amenity good or service. Knowledge of these relationships could then improve hedonic studies of the monetary values of those goods and services.

The expanded body of information would also contribute to meeting economic efficiency goals by helping identify which types of amenity goods and services provide similar gains and losses and may thus substitute for each other. Such information is needed in economic valuations to address questions about the resource dependency of particular types of gains. For example, do designated wilderness areas provide unique types of benefits? If not uniquely required, are those areas highly preferred for those benefits, or are no resource dependencies or strong preferences evident?

If one is interested in the dependency of particular types of benefits on certain amenity goods and services or their substitutes, two questions must be answered in sequence (Driver, Nash, & Haas, 1987). First, what types and amounts of gains are realized by users of different goods and services? Second, do these gains differ across goods and services? The second question cannot be answered before the first one. BCAs do not attempt to answer these questions, because they do not define or measure benefits in this way. They can, however, answer an important third question: If the benefits are not uniquely dependent on use of a particular amenity good or service, are there strong preferences (e.g., willingness to pay) that those benefits be realized from that good or service? By taking an integrative cross-disciplinary perspective, answers to all three questions can be obtained, and the BCAs will be more accurate and useful.

Finally, the nonmonetary measures of assigned values can frequently be used to help validate the monetary measures because both attempt to measure relative importance of a good or service. We can envision experimental designs, where willingness to pay measurements are obtained for by test groups who have different amounts of information about the likely gains associated with a particular amenity good or service.

Although most valuations testing economic efficiency are somewhat integrated with the other valuations that are made, those integrations are too weak to realize the above advantages. Only a few economic studies (cf., Johnson & Haspel, 1983; Walsh, Loomis, & Gillman, 1984; Walsh, Miller, & Gilliam, 1983) have included "demand shifters" (e.g., measures of congestion, scenic qualities, relative wildness, bequest concerns about future generations) that directly imply gains to individuals, and those studies did not attempt to define explicitly those possible gains. Our recommendations calls for better integration of economic efficiency valuations with the other valuations made. This can happen without need for any discipline to abandon its theories or methods.

Develop Behavior-Predicting Methods for Making Nonmonetary Measures for Assigned Value

As described previously, the nonmonetary measures of value comprise two classes of metrics: economic and noneconomic. Nonmonetary economic measures include any variables that define the relative willingness of a person to trade a scarce personal resource, other than money, for a particular good or service. Although these resources (e.g., time, personal space, physical property, right to alternative uses) have monetary correspondence, those correlations are not always perfect. A person, for example, who has lexicographically, or through elimination by aspect (Tversky, 1972), decided to preserve leisure time probably would demand a premium wage to forgo such time for work. The nonmonetary economic measures would help tease out these dimensions of economic value.

The nonmonetary noneconomic measures of assigned value are not oriented toward economic exchange, so the variables employed do not quantify directly one's willingness to trade off scarce personal resources to maintain or attain a particular improved condition. These measures usually--if not always--focus on the relative importance of a system of beliefs, which may or may not be related to perceptions of certain rights, as elaborated by McLean and Mills (this volume). How important is it to maintain clean air and clean water above some U.S. Environmental Protection Agency threshold at which adverse impacts on health are likely? Should the elderly be charged discounted user fees because of their contributions to society? Should air visibility be preserved at the Grand Canyon? How important are nearby opportunities to exercise outdoors? The noneconomic measures addressed to these types of assigned value may or may not be related to economic values. When they are, they may correspond to a measure of willingness to pay (or compensation demanded), or the economic value might be expressed as an opportunity cost or as a shadow price.

The held values (i.e., preference states) for which the nonmonetary noneconomic measures of worth and costs are made are quite hard to define; thus, their assigned worths and costs are more difficult to measure. As such, the underlying preferences are commonly expressed by voter sovereignty and by recourse to the courts through the democratic-political and legal processes. As a result, these underlying held values are frequently "protected" by laws that can constrain other preference states from being realized. The gains and losses associated with these types of held values are frequently not specified and often enter the allocation decision process quite subjectively with only intuitive definitions. Intuition, however, can vary greatly from individual to individual. Considerable progress would be made if the gains and losses (to individuals and groups of individuals) associated with these types of held values (e.g., those not well suited for monetary or nonmonetary economic valuations) were measured better. That would reduce considerably the uncertainty in the decisionmaker's black box.

In the past, there has been much confusion between the measures used to quantify the magnitude of a particular gain or loss and a noneconomic measure of the relative importance of those changed conditions. Hopefully, our discussion helped clarify the differences. Measures, for example, of reduced hypertension from aerobic exercises (or of increased family solidarity, more pride in one's country, greater work productivity) are measures of magnitude of the gains to individuals or to groups. In contrast, noneconomic measures of the assigned values say nothing about the magnitude of the gains or losses; they quantify their relative importance, and a gain of small magnitude can have large value (e.g., reduction of a low level but highly toxic hard metal in a water supply).

Many studies have been conducted using both types of non-monetary (i.e., economic and noneconomic) measures of assigned values. Most have reported on introspective appraisals of the relative importance of an attribute or a psychological outcome, such as scenic beauty, social cohesion, or experience preference related to use of amenity goods and services (Altman & Wohwill, 1983; Daniel, Zube, & Driver,, 1979; Driver & Brown, 1986). Some studies have employed a mix of noneconomic and indirect monetary measures, for example, Kellert's (1979) study asked respondents in his national survey of attitudes toward wildlife to trade off preservation of grizzly bears (and other species) with other uses of the resources. Myers (1979) took a different tack and attempted to show, among other things, how loss of species diversity would reduce options for medical advances. Campbell (1981) looked at social variables in his studies of the relative importance of conditions that contribute to life satisfaction or a sense of well-being. In addition, scores of public surveys and opinion polls have incorporated questions abut the relative importance of amenity goods and services, including those of nationally known polling organizations and of federal agencies, such as the National Recreation Household Surveys and the Hunting and Fishing Surveys sponsored by the U.S. Department of the Interior's National Park Service and Fish and Wildlife Service.

These studies have used a variety of techniques for allowing the respondents to self-report their preferences and their valuations. They include use of ratio and other rating scales, transformation curves, and simulation games (Sinden & Worrell, 1979). However, too few of the studies have tested predictability to actual choice behavior. Considerable innovative work is needed in this area to develop better methods and measures. These nonmonetary measures are needed particularly to fill in where monetary measures are weak or absent. It would be helpful to explore also the relation between monetary and nonmonetary measures for different, clearly defined types of values. It might be possible to adjust one to get the other for a specific type of value, which would further reduce the mystery in the black box.

RESEARCH NEEDED

Research needed to implement the framework proposed for valuation consists of (1) differentiation of the amenity goods and services produced, (2) specification of the impacts on individuals and other social units, (3) selection of indicator variables to measure these impacts, (4) measurement of the magnitude of the impacts, (5) determination of the distribution of the impacts, and (6) valuation of the changes. In regard to these needs, we believe that improvement in specification and measurement of gains and losses to individuals and society is central to obtaining

better integrated and more comprehensive valuations. This, in turn, would lead to providing to public decisionmakers more systematically obtained information about the multiple values they must consider.

Clear specification or definition of the goods and services being produced is the first need. Such clarity does not now exist, at least for the amenity goods and services. Product differentiation for those amenity "product lines" comprises a large and separate program of research (Driver, 1985; Driver et al., 1985; Fischhoff, this volume).

Once the goods and services have been defined, the gains and losses must be specified before they can be measured. Studies of what the users of particular goods and services perceive as gains and losses will aid that specification task. Introspective studies will also be needed to help appraise the magnitudes of some types of gains and losses and their assigned values. These documented perceptions will serve as interim, qualitative indexes of those gains and losses until more exact behavior-change measures can be made. Observations of behavioral responses are now possible for other gains and losses. No one method can be proposed because many different approaches from different disciplines will be needed.

Since about 1970, a growing, but still relatively small, amount of research has been done from which inferences can be made about gains to individuals from use of amenity goods and services. Some examples of these likely benefits that need additional systematic study are enhanced child development, greater family solidarity, and improved physiological functioning (including the health-related benefits of exercise), improved abilities to function socially, reduced clinical problems such as drug abuse, improved self-concept and self-reliance, increased work performance, enhanced pride in one's community, and promotion of a wide variety of positive experiences that range from enjoying scenic beauty to spiritual growth to coping temporarily with everyday life stresses (Brown, 1981; Driver & Knopf, 1976; Driver, Nash, & Hass, 1987; Driver, Rosenthal, & Peterson, 1978; Ewert, 1986; Grubb, 1975; Rolston, 1985; Shaw & Zube, 1980; Tinsley, Barrett, & Kass, 1977; Tinsley, 1984; Ulrich, 1981; Young & Crandall, 1984). Work on these and other impacts is needed because only a few studies have focused directly on gains of individuals, as defined in this study (Buccola & Stone, 1975; Ulrich, 1984), and none of these studies can predict patterns of gains and losses for particular changes in amenity goods and services.

Although some useful research has been done on the social impacts of public amenity resource allocations (Burch, 1986; Cheek, 1981; Kelly, 1981; West, 1986), little of that research has clearly documented which particular improved social conditions are created from specific allocations. For example, a growing body of research is addressing the concept of social well-being and life satisfaction and disclosing relationships between overall measures of well-being and particular contributors to such (Campbell, 1981). However, predictive linkages to beneficial changes caused by allocation of public amenity resources have not been established.

The point is that relatively little research has been done on the amenity resource related gains and losses to individuals and other social units. The research conducted has been sporadic rather than part of a concerted effort, and too few longitudinal studies and replications have been made to disclose consistent patterns, in part because the research is extremely complex, and the state of the arts embryonic.[7]

Once a body of knowledge is developed about the gains and losses associated with particular allocations of amenity resources, patterns will emerge just as they have in other cause-effect studies, where similar causes of a change can be studied in replicative research. Once these patterns are identified, it will be unnecessary to conduct separate scientific studies of gains and losses associated with a particular allocation, because the basic information accumulated can be generalized from one allocation to other identical or very similar ones. Except for periodic monitoring, the basic research would provide long-lived utility to resource management.

Even over a long period of time, it is unlikely that all the gains and losses associated with use of amenity resources will ever be specified and measured. By analogy, all causes of mental and physical illnesses are not yet known. But this complexity should not deter research on the gains and losses associated with amenity goods and services any more than it has deterred medical research.

Additional research is needed to develop and refine methods for estimating the worths and costs of the gains and losses both in monetary and nonmonetary units. The types of research needed to improve these valuations have been suggested in previous sections.

A concerted program of research would help implement the proposed approach, which can provide information to enhance the rationality of public amenity resource allocations. However, that research will never answer all of the questions about the complex set of values involved. So, as it does for allocations to the National Institutes of Health, public funding of hospital construction, and development of health-care programs of many sorts, the democratic-political process (public involvement, professional judgment, compromise among elected officials) must continue to guide public amenity resource allocation decisions.

SUMMARY AND CONCLUSIONS

A system of impact assessment and valuation has been proposed that builds on and goes beyond the system proposed by the U.S. Water Resources Council (1973, 1979). The additional information provided would enhance the knowledge of any decisionmaker, whether an individual consumer, resource manager, or elected representative. All of the analysis tasks proposed focus on obtaining information directly from the individuals who are affected and having them assign the values.

The improved knowledge about gains and losses to individuals would be particularly useful to sovereign consumers and voters and, along with changes in social conditions at different levels of social aggregation, would help assure the maintenance of opportunities vital for an effectively functioning society and a sense of well-being. The improved nonmonetary measures of assigned value would both supplement and help validate the monetary measures as well as provide information on values for which the efficiency paradigm does not apply. Improvements made in the monetary measures would facilitate making more

accurate and reliable BCAs. In combination, these improvements would promote meeting the ideal of a republican form of government within which all countervailing values are recognized and articulated clearly in public resource allocation decisions.

The proposed approach could increase the overlap between the different valuations because as each becomes more accurate, it also becomes more comprehensive. While some overlap is inevitable, unwanted double counting can be minimized if the multiple values are analyzed recognizing parallel and supplementary valuation tasks, and attempts are not made to add the different accounts. For example, the approach recommended distinguishes between quantifying the magnitude of the gains and losses associated with a change and measuring the values assigned those impacts. A set of multiple values by itself does not recognize this distinction, nor do enough analysts and users of the results of impact assessments and valuations. This deters more comprehensive evaluations and prompts allegations of double counting, when in actuality different measures for different purposes are being made. For example, even though the proposal was made that nonmonetary, including noneconomic, measures of assigned values be made along with the monetary measures, no proposal was made that these two measures be added. Instead the miraculous decisionmaker will continue to consider each separately and value each input for different reasons. Complex programs of research will be required to implement the proposed approach. Over time the benefits should exceed the costs.

References

Altman, I., & Wohlwill, J. F. (Eds.). (1983). *Behavior and the natural environment (Vol. 6)*. NY: Plenum Press.

Ajzen, I., & Fishbein, M. J. (1980). *Understanding attitudes and predicting social behavior*. Englewood Cliffs, NJ: Prentice-Hall.

Brown, P. J. (1981). Psychological benefits of outdoor recreation. In J. R. Kelly (Ed.), *Social benefits of outdoor recreation* (pp. 13-17). Urbana-Champaign, IL: University of Illinois, Department of Leisure Studies.

Brown, P. J. (1984). Benefits of outdoor recreation and some ideas for valuing recreation opportunities. In G. L. Peterson & A. Randall (Eds.), *Valuation of wildland resource benefits* (pp. 209-220). Boulder, CO: Westview Press.

Brown, T. C. (1984). The concept of value in resource allocation. *Land Economics, 60*, 231-246.

Buccola, V. A., & Stone, W. J. (1975). Effects of jogging and cycling programs on physiological and personality variables in aged men. *Research Quarterly, 46*, 134-139.

Burch, W. R., Jr. (1986). Ties that bind: The social benefits of recreation provision. In *A Literature Review: The President's Commission on Americans Outdoors* (pp. 81-91). Washington, DC: Government Printing Office.

Burch, W. R., Jr., & DeLuca, D. R. (1984). *Measuring the social impact of material resource policies*. Albuquerque, NM: University of New Mexico Press.

Callicott, J. (1985). Intrinsic value, quantum theory, and environmental ethics. *Environmental Ethics, 7* (11), 257-275.

Campbell, A. (1981). *The sense of well-being in America: Recent patterns and trends*. New York: McGraw Hill.

Cheek, N. H., Jr. (1981). Social cohesion and outdoor recreation. In J. R. Kelly (Ed.), *Social benefits of outdoor recreation* (pp. 49-83). Urbana-Champaign, IL: University of Illinois, Department of Leisure Studies.

Cheek, N. H., Jr., & Burch, W. R., Jr. (1976). *The social organization of leisure*. New York: Harper and Row.

Daniel, T. C., Zube, E. H., & Driver, B. L. (1979). *Assessing amenity resource values* (USDA Forest Service General Technical Report RM-68). Fort Collins, CO: Rocky Mountain Forest and Range Experiment Station.

Driver, B. L. (1985). Specifying what is produced by management of wildlife by federal agencies. *Leisure Sciences, 7,* 281-295.

Driver, B. L., & Brown, P. J. (1986). Probable personal benefits of outdoor recreation. In *A Literature Review: The President's Commission on Americans Outdoors* (pp. 63-67, Values). Washington, DC: Government Printing Office.

Driver, B. L., Brown, T. C., & Burch, W. R., Jr. (1987). A call for more comprehensive and integrated evaluations of public amenity goods and services. In F. Kaiser & P. J. Brown (Compilers), *Proceedings of the 18th IUFRO World Congress: Economic Value Analysis of Multiple-Use Forestry* (pp. 204-216). Corvallis, OR: Oregon State University, Department of Resource Recreation Management.

Driver, B. L., & Knopf, R. (1976). Temporary escape: One product of sport fisheries management. *Fisheries, 1,* 21-29.

Driver, B. L., Nash, R., & Haas, G. E. (1987). Wilderness benefits: State of knowledge, in R. C. Lucas (Ed.), *Proceedings of the National Wilderness Research Conference* (General Technical Report INT-220). (pp. 294-319). Ogden, UT: USDA Forest Service Intermountain Forest and Range Experiment Station.

Driver, B. L., Phillips, C., Bergersen, E. P., & Harris, C. C. (1985). Using angler preference data in defining types of sport fisheries to manage. *Transactions of the North American Wildlife and Natural Resources Conference, 49,* 82-90.

Driver, B. L., & Rosenthal, D. H. (1982). *Measuring and improving the effectiveness of public outdoor recreation programs.* Washington, DC: George Washington University.

Driver, B. L., Rosenthal, D. H., & Peterson, G. L. (1978). In Benefits of urban forests and related greenspaces in cities. In *Proceedings of the National Urban Forestry Conference* (Environmental Science and Forestry Publication 80-003) (pp. 91-113) Syracuse, NY: State University of New York, College of Environmental Science and Forestry.

Ewert, A. (1986). Values, benefits and consequences in outdoor adventure recreation. In *A Literature Review: President's Commission on Americans Outdoors* (pp. 71-80, Values). Washington, DC: Government Printing Office.

Finsterbusch, K., & Wolf, C. P. (Eds.). (1977). *Methodology of social impact assessment.* Stroudsburg, PA: Dowden, Hutchinson and Ross, Inc.

Fisher, A. (1986). Comment 1. In D. W. Bromley (Ed.) *Natural resource economics: Policy problems and contemporary analysis* (pp. 201-208). London: Kluwer Nijhoff Publishing.

Freeman, D. M., & Frey, R. S. (1986). A method for assessing the social impacts of natural resource policies. *Journal of Environmental Management, 23,* 229-245.

Grubb, E. A. (1975). Assembly line boredom and individual difference in recreation participation. *Journal of Leisure Research, 7* (4), 256-269.

Johnson, R. F., & Haspel. A. (1983). Economic valuation of potential scenic degradation at Bryce Canyon National Park. In R. D. Rowe & L. G. Chestnut (Eds.), *Managing air quality and scenic resources at national parks and wilderness areas* (pp. 235-245). Boulder, CO: Westview Press.

Kahneman, D., & Tversky. A. (1979). Prospect theory: An analysis of decision under risk. *Econometrica, 47,* 263-291.

Kellert, S. R. (1979). *Public attitudes toward critical wildlife and natural habitat issues: Phase I* (Report to U. S. Department of the Interior, Fish and Wildlife Service). New Haven, CT: Yale University, School of Forestry and Environmental Studies.

Kelly, J. R. (1981). Family benefits from outdoor recreation. In J. R. Kelly (Eds.), *Social benefits of outdoor recreation* (pp. 44-53). Urbana-Champaign, IL: University of Illinois, Department of Leisure Studies.

Mishan, E. J. (1981). *Economic efficiency and social welfare.* London: George Allen and Unwin.

Myers, N. (1979). *The sinking ark: A new look at the problem of disappearing species.* Oxford: Pergamon Press.

Peterson, G. L., Driver, B. L., & Brown, P. J. (in press). The benefits of recreation: Dollars and sense. In R. L. Johnson & G. V. Johnson (Eds.), *Economic valuation of natural resources: Issue, theory and applications.* Boulder, CO: Westview Press.

Randall, A. (1984a). Benefit cost analysis as an information system. In G. L. Peterson & A. Randall (Eds.), *Valuation of wildland resource benefits* (pp. 65-75). Boulder, CO: Westview Press.

Randall, A. (1984b). The conceptual basis of benefit cost analysis. In G. L. Peterson & A. Randall (Eds.), *Valuation of wildland resource benefits* (pp. 53-63). Boulder, CO: Westview Press.

Randall, A. (1986). Valuation in a policy context. In D. W. Bromley (Ed.), *Natural resource economics: Policy problems and contemporary analysis* (pp. 163-200). Boston, MA: Kluwer Nijhoff Publishing Co.

Rolston, H., III. (1981). Values in nature. *Environmental Ethics, 3* 113-128.

Rolston, H., III. (1985). Valuing wildlands. *Environmental Ethics, 7,* 23-48.

Scitovsky, T. (1978). *The joyless economy: An inquiry into human satisfaction and consumer dissatisfaction.* Oxford: Oxford University Press.

Shaw, W. W., & Zube, E. H. (Eds.). (1980). *Wildlife values.* Tucson, AZ: University of Arizona, School of Renewable Natural Resources.

Sinden, J. A., & Worrell, A. C. (1979). *Unpriced values: Decisions without market prices.* New York: John Wiley & Sons.

Tinsley, H. E. A. (1984). The psychological benefits of leisure counseling (i.e., participation). *Society and Leisure, 7,* 125-140.

Tinsley, H. E. A., Barrett, T. C., & Kass, R. A. (1977). Leisure activities and need satisfaction. *Journal of Leisure Research, 9,* 110-120.

Tribe, L. H. (1976). Ways not to think about plastic trees. In L. H. Tribe, C. S. Schelling, & John Voss (Eds.), *When values conflict: Essays on environmental analysis, discourse, and decision* (pp. 61-91). Cambridge, MA: Ballinger Publishing.

Tversky, A. (1972). Elimination by aspect: A theory of choice. *Psychological Review, 79,* 281-299.

Tversky, A., & Kahneman, D. (1981). The framing of decisions and the psychology of choice. *Science, 211,* 453-458.

Ulrich, R. S. (1981). Natural versus urban scenes: Some psychophysiological effects. *Environment and Behavior, 13,* 523-556.

Ulrich, R. S. (1984). View through a window may influence recovery from surgery. *Science, 224,* 420-421.

U. S. Department of Agriculture. (1980). *The RPA Program--1980 Update.* Washington, DC: Forest Service.

U. S. Federal Register. (1982). Regulations for 1975 National Forest Management Act. *Federal Register, 47,* 43038.

U. S. Water Resources Council. (1973). Principles and standards for planning water related land resources. *Federal Register, 38,* 24778-24869.

U. S. Water Resources Council. (1979). Procedures for evaluation of national economic development (NED) benefits and costs in water resource planning. Park K-Recreation. *Federal Register, 44,* 72950-72965.

Walsh, R., Loomis, J., & Gillman, R. (1984). Valuing option, existence and bequest demands for wilderness. *Land Economics, 60,* 14-29.

Walsh, R., Miller, N., & Gilliam, L. (1983). Congestion and willingness to pay for expansion of skiing capacity. *Land Economics, 59,* 195-210.

West, P. C. (1986). Social benefits of outdoor recreation: Sociological perspectives and implications for planning and policy. In *A Literature Review: President's Commission on Americans Outdoors* (pp. 93-102, Values). Washington, DC: Government Printing Office.

Young, R. A., & Crandall, R. (1984). Wilderness use and self-actualization. *Journal of Leisure Research, 16,* 149-160.

Footnotes

[1] The term "benefit-cost analyses" is used generically as a test of economic efficiency and more specifically as a test for potential Pareto improvement (Randall, 1984b, 1986).

[2] For a listing of the multiple goals/values that must be considered by decisionmakers in the USDA Forest Service, see Section 219.1 of the Regulations (U.S. Federal Register, 1982) for the National Forest Management Act of 1976, or the RPA Program-1980 Update (USDA Forest Service, 1980).

[3]Five of the six reviewers of an early draft of this paper commented that we showed disapproval of BCAs. This was not our intention. Instead, we wanted to (1) indicate that while results of BCAs are crucial input to policy and managerial decision processes, other inputs are also needed; (2) describe these other inputs; and (3) show how some of these other types of information can help improve BCAs, and stand on their own in enhancing the rationality of the allocation decision process.

To be explicit this time, our position on BCAs is akin to the one presented by Randall (1986), which in a nutshell says that BCAs provide a needed and useful input to the diffuse policy process, but they should not constitute a solitary decision criterion.

We share some concerns with others, including many economists, about specific aspects of BCAs, but they are directed at refinement, improvement, and qualification--not rejection. Our major concerns relate to the following: status quo income distributions; deciding how to discount the future; the extent to which consumers are adequately informed about the consequences of their choices; how much do many choices in an affluent/ conspicuous and mass consumption society (in which advertising is both pervasive and persuasive) reflect marginal improvements in individual or social welfare; how stable are preferences over time; do decisionmakers emphasize quantitative data over equally important qualitative elaboration under conditions of risk and uncertainty; whether certain moral sentiments might become somewhat anesthetized by attempts to monetize particular environmental services; and the use of technical jargon when attempting to communicate with noneconomists who have different definitions for some key words used (e.g., benefits).

[4]As a way of coping with limited ability to estimate use accurately over time, agencies generally tend to err on the side of planning to provide too much rather than too little of a good or service, so supply and demand are often not in agreement. Also, most functional branches within agencies tend to be optimistic in the projected levels of use of their goods and services. For these reasons, we view Items 3 and 4 (Figure 1) as two separate analytical tasks, both of which can help reduce the gaps between supply and demand.

[5]We do not know why economists use the word "benefit" synonymously with price, or with willingness to pay (or compensation demanded). When all such monetized values are aggregated, they do facilitate tests of a potential Pareto improvement, which is a benefit as that the word is commonly used. Although willingness to pay provides a monetary index of utility or benefit, it actually measures economic worth not benefit. We see no problems--other than semantic inaccuracy--when economists are communicating with other economists. However, their usage of the word benefit does cause confusion, and even unnecessary adverse reaction, when used in their technical input to the multidisciplinary allocation decision process. Technical experts from other disciplines firmly believe they are analyzing benefits and beneficial values. Greater technical accuracy would exist if the modifiers economic efficiency benefits were used. Also, we believe economists' frequent use of the words "the benefits" and "the contributions to social welfare" is quite presumptuous for two reasons: They can now only monetize part of the benefits that are amenable to "pricing," and many benefits are not amenable. Use of the definite article, therefore, incites some noneconomists to be derisive. This depreciates the important information provided on the economic efficiency values. Our point is that the economists are limiting acceptance of their results, and in that way partially undermining their needed contributions.

[6]We argue later that the miraculous decisionmakers can better weigh these expressions of value if they have more complete information on the underlying gains and losses.

[7]A concerted program of research on the gains and losses associated with the use of amenity goods and services will take considerable time and require sizable funding. By analogy, the medical professions faced the same situation a 100 years ago when causes of illnesses were still attributed to the "four humours" and there was much doubt about ever being able to track scientifically health-related causes and effects. Nevertheless, work by Pasteur and Koch in the 19th century stimulated thinking about the germ theory of disease. The state of the art of medical research has advanced greatly since those beginnings. For example, not only are the deleterious health effects of smoking to smokers and nonsmokers being documented, but good estimates are being made of the social costs of those losses. Most of us have benefited from the advances of medical science and are glad there is less guesswork--and the use of fewer leaches. We believe that the proposed research on the gains and losses associated with amenity goods and services, in addition to facilitating better integrated and more comprehensive valuation, would result in considerable social benefit.

Part 2: Approaches to Valuation

Overview

Perry J. Brown
Department of Resource Recreation Management
Oregon State University

A. Allen Dyer
Department of Forest and Wood Sciences
Colorado State University

The papers in this section focus on economic and psychological approaches to valuation. They can be viewed as establishing a baseline from which we can evaluate opportunities and alternatives for enhancing valuation technology.

Considerable work has been done on valuation by scientists in many disciplines. Valuation has been a central concern of natural resource economists, especially those involved in valuing nonmarketed commodities and services. Psychologists, sociologists, and anthropologists also have assessed value and worth of things, concepts, and ideas, although the metrics vary among the disciplines and are quite different from the metrics used by economists. Questions of value are also central to philosophers and are prominent in their literature.

The papers in this section reveal some of the thought and knowledge we have about valuation regarding what it is, its value, and its utility. The authors attempt to review monetary assessment of value, explore the similarities between economic and psychological approaches to human value articulation and choice, and conceptualize contingent valuation in terms of psychological theory.

Important issues include identifying what is being valued, specifying the policy we are trying to evaluate, selecting the best means of determining value, and determining how best to implement that means. The papers in this section deal with all these issues, although each author recognizes that we need to know a lot more before we can be as effective as possible in valuation.

Mendelsohn and Peterson present the economist's definition of monetary value and a specification of the objective of valuation. They argue that, in economic valuation of a good, it is not necessary to be concerned with the use of the good that provides incentive for its purchase, only with the direct value of the good. From this point they discuss fundamental economic theory regarding marketed and nonmarketed goods and relate this theory to natural resource derived goods and services, focusing on recreation as a service that is usually nonmarketed. Among the important observations that Mendelsohn and Peterson make is the assertion that ''... contingent valuation surveys have tended to measure attitudes not monetary values.'' This conclusion is consistent with the observations of Ajzen and Peterson in their review of contingent valuation from the perspective of a social psychologist.

While Mendelsohn and Peterson's paper sets the stage for many of the papers that follow by reviewing the economic theory and arguments involved in monetary valuation, we take exception to their assertion that ''... unless policy depends on why people have values rather than simply what those values are, understanding the motivation or underlying structure behind values may not be important.'' Where valuation itself might not require such information, policy setting always involves why people have values, whether they are the values of policymakers, clients, or other relevant groups. The mere acceptance of monetary values as appropriate or inappropriate in policy making implies particular motives and thus makes policy dependent on why people have certain values.

Kleindorfer and Kunreuther take a quite different approach from Mendelsohn and Peterson by developing a framework for evaluating policies involving pre- and post-accident or disaster actions. In their analysis, several important issues are identified: (1) misperception of probability and consequences by individuals, (2) misprocessing of information, (3) interaction of individ-

uals decision processes with institutions, (4) ex ante concerns regarding ex post consequences, (5) strategic misrepresentation, and (6) uncertainty. Each of these give rise to potential problems in estimates of willingness to pay or willingness to accept in valuation of risk-related policies. The authors also discuss the relevant behavioral considerations in obtaining estimates of value. They conclude that a research need is development of a usable method for multi-attribute valuation. This method should incorporate traditional monetary attributes plus attributes such as dread, familiarity, complexity, regret, and control. They suggest that such a multi-attribute method, which considers recent research from psychology and behavioral economics, could lead to improved policy design and evaluation.

Ajzen and Peterson take a third approach by examining contingent valuation from the perspective of a social psychologist who is an expert in the study of attitudes and behavior. An important outcome of their examination is the discussion of the implications of attitude theory and measurement for the definition and assessment of economic value. One observation they make is that the value of a commodity, whether measured monetarily or as an attitude, must be inferred from responses to the commodity. In this context, willingness to pay (an indicator of value) is an expression of a behavioral intention.

Ajzen and Peterson describe the theory of reasoned action and compare it to utility theory. In the context of valuing public goods, they suggest that the important attitude is that directed at the performance of a particular (and individual) behavior. This is in contrast to attitudes directed toward policies and toward public goods in general. Thus, in assessing attitudes, the context and the object of the attitude are critical elements. By focusing on differences in context and in object, many of the variations in measurement of value using different contingent valuation schemes can be explained. In this regard, the observations of these authors are not unlike the observations of Kleindorfer and Kunreuther.

Ajzen and Peterson also discuss the relationship between monetary and attitudinal estimates of value. They conclude that the two complement each other by examining different aspects of benefits and costs. Whereas the monetary estimate of value yields a rather narrow measure of value and fails to reflect many psychological costs and benefits, attitudinal estimates of value, being rather general, capture a rich variety of costs and benefits, but are useless when monetary estimates are necessary. With both, however, a more complete picture of the costs and benefits is obtained.

In contrast to Ajzen and Peterson's discussion of integrating psychological and economic perspectives into amenity resource valuations, Ulrich explores the analytical arena of integrating nonverbal, physiological manifestations of value for amenity goods and services with the monetary measures. This is a relatively untapped but promising area given that most past physiological measures have centered on the health effects of specific environmental pollutants rather than on the beneficial impacts of public amenities. Ulrich considers the problems of relying solely on verbal response measures and the benefits of identifying more fully the advantageous physiological consequences of alternative amenity resource allocations. Echoing the theme of Driver and Burch's earlier paper in this volume, Ulrich shows that systematic exposure of physiological impacts will help expand the information base on which the sovereign consumer can draw when formulating monetary values in amenity resource studies of willingness to pay or of compensation demanded. He also considers how these additional measures can supplement the monetary measures to provide the public decisionmaker a more comprehensive picture of probable gains and losses.

The papers in this section establish a foundation for understanding economic, psychological, and physiological approaches to valuation, and they begin to address the integration of these three perspectives. No matter what perspective is adopted, one must be clear about the object being valued, the context in which valuation is being made, and the use of the information obtained.

The Definition, Measurement, and Policy Use of Monetary Values

Robert Mendelsohn
Yale School of Forestry and Environmental Studies

George Peterson
USDA Forest Service
Rocky Mountain Forest and Range Experiment Station

In this paper we define the critical concepts surrounding monetary valuation and assess the use of monetary valuation as a tool for public policy. We use the term "monetary value" to refer to numeric values that traditional microeconomic theory and measurement assign to goods and services. Monetary value, as such, is a tightly defined and rigorously defensible concept. It is not, of course, the only possible definition of value. As one reaches out beyond the economics discipline, the concept of value takes on additional meaning and interpretation. Unaware of these additional potential interpretations of the meaning of value, economists have frequently failed to communicate the breadth and limitations of monetary measures.

We also attempt to describe what economists mean by monetary value, and discuss alternative perspectives of value to contrast them with monetary measures. To make this discussion accessible to the multiple disciplines from which it draws, disciplinary terminology is used as little as possible. The paper consequently lacks the formality and precision inherent in disciplinary language. Although perhaps critical to the internal development of concepts inside a discipline, the formality of such language presents a barrier that limits the accessibility of each discipline to others. Thus, at the risk of loss of precision, we seek breadth and a common ground among several relevant social sciences. We simultaneously attempt to explain monetary values to noneconomists and noneconomic perspectives to the economist.

DEFINITION OF MONETARY VALUE

Economists are concerned with the allocation of scarce resources to the production and distribution of goods and services. Resources are considered scarce whenever they are a limiting factor in the production of more desired goods and services. The production of goods and services can be thought of as the solution to two problems. First, given any final production mix of goods and services, limited resources should be marshalled to produce the highest level of goods and services possible. That is, production should occur without waste. Second, the mix of goods and services should be designed to match people's tastes. That is, one should produce the things that people want. In this paper, we focus upon this choice of final consumption, because this choice is at the heart of monetary value.

The Context of Monetary Values

The first step in handling scarcity is to identify all the possible sets of goods and services that can be produced. The second step is to eliminate all sets which result in less of one good without providing more of another. This process results in a best technological set of output choices. For pedagogical purposes, this best set is often illustrated with a guns and butter diagram (Figure 1). The production processes and available resources in society permit the creation of any of the mixes of guns and butter shown in Figure 1. Society, for example, could choose to have just guns

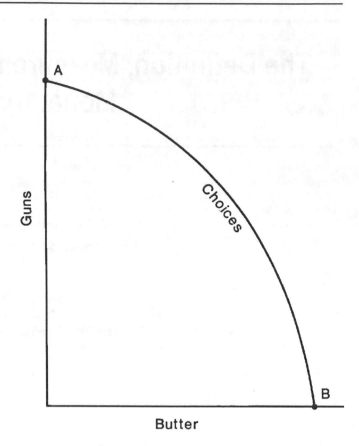

FIGURE 1. Production possibility frontier.

and be at point A, just butter and be at point B, or some mixture of the two goods between A and B. The curve depicted in Figure 1 describes the alternative levels of output that are possible. To choose which mixture is best, we need monetary values.

Economists view monetary values in the context of tradeoffs among different bundles of goods and services. Monetary values reflect the choice of a preferred bundle from a set of possible levels of consumption. Note that the values are defined strictly over different configurations of consumption goods. No Faustian bargains are being conceived in this definition. If one wants more guns, then one must give up butter. The issue is limited to comparing personal consumption bundles. One does not have the choice of selling one's soul for more butter in this framework. Although certainly an interesting subject, it is not what economists mean by values.

Monetary values also are abstracted from how the goods are to be produced. Only final consumption goods and not means of production are assumed to be important motivating factors.

Another point worth reinforcing is the meaning of final goods and services. The final set of goods and services are the objective items acquired by the household (i.e., the items exchanged between the household and suppliers or the environment). For example, a TV set, car, cleaning service, or a doctor's visit are goods and services exchanged between suppliers and households. The outcomes of these purchases, a comfortable convenient ride, a clean house, or good health, are not goods and services in this sense but rather are commodities produced by the household. Although these commodities provide the incentive for the household to purchase the goods and services, it is not necessary to value the commodity to value the good. At least for goods currently being traded, existing trading behavior will lead to valuation of the good directly. Consequently, one can value many goods without understanding the motivation or use of the good.

In the recreation context, this means that one can value a site without valuing the experiences on the site. The value of a day, a memory, or a bagged animal are not prerequisites to site or site attribute valuation. Perhaps more important, the value of commodities are not to be added to the value of the site as an additional benefit. The value of the site is derived from the pleasures or products users find at the site. For example, if a site has many fish, fishermen may value the site highly for the opportunity to catch those fish. This fishing experience may relax users. One cannot, however, argue that relaxation is an additional benefit of the site because it is already counted by the fishermen in their initial bid for the site.

There is one important exception where knowing something about the commodities produced by a household can facilitate the valuation of goods. In some cases, the quality or characteristics of a good are poorly defined. Although one can still talk, in these cases, about the value of a generic type of good, the loss of detail concerning the good itself may be important. The intended use of the good, the expected commodities, can sometimes provide clues to more accurate measures of the good. For example, in recreation, having clues about the activity of households can sometimes help define what characteristics people would be seeking in recreation lands. Similarly, knowing what commodities households produce on certain lands can reveal what attributes of the land they appear to value. In the absence of direct valuation of site characteristics, the inclusion of activities in the analysis of recreation can be helpful.

Even when commodities are included in the valuation of goods, the consumer is still faced with objective measures of choices. Thus, the setting in which economists model values is based on decisions among well-defined bundles of objective consumption goods.

The Source of Monetary Values

Two critical concepts are necessary for understanding the source of monetary values. First, economists believe the values are inherent in the individual. That is, people do not buy goods because suppliers make them. Rather, suppliers make goods because consumers will buy them. The consumer decides what is actually purchased in the marketplace. Goods that suppliers make and consumers do not want sit in supplier inventories. In the recreation context, sites that suppliers make and consumers do not want are underused. Similarly, sites that consumers want but suppliers fail to provide become overcrowded. Second, and perhaps more subtle, the values being measured are the rational motivation behind actual consumer decisions. That is, the values being sought are expected to explain (be consistent with) the observable behavior of the individual.

Economists model the process of ranking and comparing alternatives using indifference curves. An indifference curve

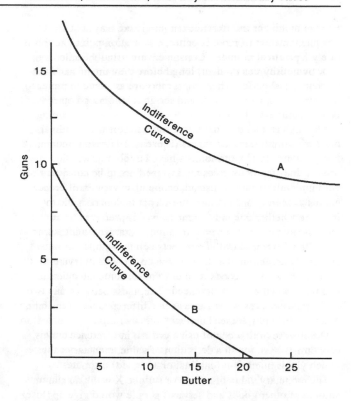

FIGURE 2. Indifference curves: Measures of consumer preferences.

represents all bundles of goods and services that the individual feels are of equal monetary value. That is, the individual would be indifferent to owning any of the bundles of goods and services along a single indifference curve. If any bundle A is preferred to another bundle B, then A is on a higher indifference curve then B. Thus, the indifference curves represent a mapping of preferences over goods and services. For example, Figure 2 presents an indifference curve over guns and butter. Each indifference curve in Figure 2 describes a set of equally satisfying combinations of guns and butter for a specific individual. For example, the individual in Figure 2 feels that having 20 sticks of butter and 10 guns are just as satisfying as having 5 sticks of butter and 15 guns. Because this individual thinks all these bundles are equally satisfying, one could exchange one bundle for another along an indifference curve and the consumer should feel indifferent toward the exchange. In experimental settings, psychologists have had difficulty getting people to reveal their indifference curve. In these settings, people have a tendency to be conservative and hold on to their current bundle. Thus, if given a pen and then offered $5 as a trade, people kept the pen. If given $5 and then offered the pen as a trade, the people kept the $5. Such experiments suggest that the concept of an indifference curve is not part of people's conscious awareness even though their market behavior may be consistent with such a notion.

Figure 2 displays two indifference curves. Indifference curve A is higher or more preferred than indifference curve B. In fact, there is a whole family of these indifference curves. Every bundle lies on one indifference curve. Bundles that contain more and more desirable consumption goods (without giving up others) are on higher indifference curves. There may be a limit to this phenomenon of more is better, a saturation point, but this is rarely a practical problem. Consumers are usually limited by their own resources (budget) long before they tire of having more material goods. Thus, consumers are assumed to prefer to receive more material goods and services holding all other factors constant.

Although researchers have attempted to construct cardinal measures of indifference curves (Stevens, 1959; von Neuman & Morgenstern, 1947), economists have largely rejected this approach. Indifference curves are assumed not to be consistent with intervals or ratios. Instead, economists view indifference curves as merely ordinal measures. That is, it is possible to measure whether one indifference curve is preferred to another but it is not possible to develop an index that would measure either the difference or the ratio between two indifference curves. Thus, economists have given up the idea of trying to measure how many goods it takes to make someone twice as happy, or whether the difference in happiness between any two indifference curves is the same as the difference between some other pair of indifference curves.

Despite the limitations of using ordinal indifference curves, economists have found a definition of value, monetary value, which yields numerical (cardinal or assigned) estimates.

The monetary value of a good or service X is the maximum amount of other goods and services people would give up (lose) to get more (receive less) X. According to economists, the maximum amount is the level of other goods and services that when combined with the new level of X would keep the person on the initial indifference curve. The monetary value of a good is consequently measured using a single indifference curve. The question is how do people trade between other goods and services and X, holding the level of satisfaction constant.

For example, in the recreation context, monetary value is the amount of other goods and services an individual would be willing to give up (receive) in compensation for more (less) recreational goods. In principle, the consumer is being asked to list all the goods he currently consumes that he is willing to forego to get more of the desired recreation object. The individual is being asked to describe the set of bundles (other goods and recreation) that belong on the same indifference curve. No sense of overall loss should be associated with these trades, but rather a sense of indifference.

One possible problem with willingness to pay and willingness to sell questions in contingent valuation experiments is that respondents interpret these questions as dollar amounts that reflect their changed utility. The explanations offered by psychologists for the relatively high response given to compensation demanded questions is that people want a large payment to compensate for a loss. The implication is that respondents interpret these questions as payments for a drop of utility. Thus, one of the potential problems with willingness to pay and willingness to sell questions is that they are imposing cardinal measures on utility rather than making measurements along indifference curves as they are supposed to.

Through experience observing people's choices, two important insights have been gained about people's indifference curves. First, the marginal value of a good declines as one consumes more of the good. Second, the marginal value of goods can often be affected by the availability of other goods. With an observable regularity, consumers tend to value individual items less and less the more they have of them. That is, we observe that as a person has more and more chairs, he will give up less and less of other goods to get more chairs. Consequently, we find that the farmer frequently will willingly stop trading chairs for wheat before he runs out of wheat altogether. To put it another way, we observe that consumers choose broad bundles of goods rather than putting all their resources into any single item.

The second important insight into indifference curves is that a consumer's preference for certain goods is affected by the amount of other goods purchased or available. For example, one's preference for going fishing on any particular day may be different depending upon whether one owned a boat. These two goods are complementary in that the availability of one increases the desire for the other. One example of substitutes is the planning of trips among similar recreation sites. For example, suppose one planned to take a trip to the mountains. The availability of the White Mountains may decrease what one would pay to go to the Catskills. Similarly, the availability of a local beach may decrease what one would pay to visit Cape Cod. Somewhat similar recreation sites often act as substitutes. The more of one, the less a consumer would pay for another. The availability of complementary and especially substitute goods is critical to understanding the value of a marginal item.

Perhaps beginning with Paul Samuelson (1947), an additional concept has slowly become an integral part of this theory. The positive part of microeconomics (see Friedman, 1953) is trying to explain observable economic behavior. The theory has consequently evolved into a preoccupation with values that can be derived from behavior. These values are called revealed preferences (i.e., values revealed through consumer choices). Thus, monetary values are supposed to be consistent with the observed choices of consumers. The source of those values is a black box whose interior structure is intentionally ignored. The model of interest is the model that will explain what consumers actually do.

Monetary values are consequently behavioral values. They are intended to explain how people actually make choices. Because we do not observe values directly but rather we observe behavior, it is perhaps more accurate to say that monetary values are the set of preferences that rationalizes the choices people are observed to actually make.

Linking Monetary Values with Behavior

Given a well-defined map of indifference curves, the consumer's presumed objective is to reach the highest indifference curve possible. Constrained by a set of choices (Figure 1), the consumer determines the bundle of goods and services that will reach the most preferred indifference curve (see Figure 3). Given well-behaved indifference curves and choice sets, this leads consumers to choose the bundle where the indifference curve is just tangent to the set of constraints (see Figure 3). Note that by separating indifference curves (tastes) from choice sets (opportunities), economists have implicitly assumed that indifference curves would not change depending upon the mix of consumption products available. The consumer's actual choice depends upon both taste and opportunities, but taste itself is invariant and stable.

This simple model leads to an important result in a market setting. Within markets, the monetary value of goods and services is their price, the rate of exchange. In a barter economy, monetary value is expressed in physical exchange rates between the goods being traded. Thus, an exchange between a wheat farmer and a carpenter results in an exchange rate between bushels of wheat and a chair. The monetary value of the chair is the number of bushels of wheat needed to buy one chair. If a farmer felt that a chair was worth more than the market exchange rate, he would trade more wheat for more chairs. That is, if the farmer felt the chairs were worth more than the wheat he was giving up, the trade would make him better off. The farmer should continue to make such trades until he either has no more wheat to give or he values the chair at the exchange rate.

At the point where the individual no longer wants to (but can) trade anymore, economists argue that the consumer's value for a unit of a good is equal to the market exchange rates. The individual's personal assessment of the marginal value (the relative worth of one more unit) of wheat versus chairs is the same as the market exchange rate. If the market exchange rate is the same for all people in this market, then everyone will share the same values for a marginal exchange. In market contexts, the market exchange rate is an accurate measure for all consumers of their marginal monetary value.

As economies grew more complex and individuals became more specialized, physical items became an awkward means of exchange. Thus, societies gradually moved towards a common easily transported and stable medium against which all physical items could be traded. This common medium is money. Prices could now be standardized using money as a metric. The monetary value of a traded good became its market price expressed in dollars (or pounds, francs, etc.).

The existence of a common index to compare the exchange rate of all physical goods simplifies our definition of monetary value. Rather than comparing each good X to a long list of other possible goods, we can now compare X to dollars.

The monetary value of a small amount of any traded private good is its market price measured in dollars. The dollars are not intended to be direct measures of satisfaction but rather the small bundle of goods each of us would give up to get more X and remain on our indifference curves. For example, Mr. Jones may give up one trip to the movies ($4.00) and two candy bars ($0.50 each) in exchange for a good novel ($5.00). Mrs. Smith may visit the beauty parlor one fewer times ($17.10) and buy three less packs of chewing gum ($0.30 each) for a lawn chair ($18.00). Because we now have a measure, the market price, by which to compare one small bundle versus another, we can say that Mr. Jones values a good novel at $5.00 and Mrs. Smith thinks lawn chairs are worth $18.00.

The availability of market prices as a measure of the marginal value of traded goods and services has, unfortunately, led to some confusion. Because the price of traded goods is their monetary value, then goods without prices must have no value. Services provided through the public or the environment when not sold would appear to be worthless. This argument, however, is flawed.

Market prices do reflect the marginal monetary value for all goods and services traded in a well-behaved market. If a good traded in such a market has a zero or near zero price, it has a low monetary value. However, many goods are not traded in marketplaces so their monetary value is not reflected in market prices. A good has monetary value whenever people are willing to trade their own wealth for more of the good (or also to prevent having less of the good). Goods can have monetary value but no market value whenever a failure or intrusion in the market prevents exchange. Thus, some goods and services which have perfectly legitimate monetary value are not traded in markets. For example, national defense, public education, health research, clean air and water, and most recreation opportunities in national recreation areas are not bought and sold in the market. Nonetheless, all these goods or services have monetary value as long as people are willing to trade some of their wealth for them. Monetary values do not depend upon whether people actually must pay for the services received. The monetary values can exist whether or not the payment is demanded. Thus, monetary values extend to goods and services that are not traded-- nonmarket goods.

Another source of confusion is the difference between the marginal value of a good and its nonmarginal value. Prices are accurate measures of the marginal value of traded goods. Prices are not accurate measures of the nonmarginal value of a good. For example, in areas such as the Northeast or Pacific Northwest, the marginal value of water is low because water is abundant. However, if less water were available in these regions, the marginal value of water would rise. Thus, applying the marginal value of water when water is abundant to a unit of water when water is scarce would undervalue the scarce water. The value of nonmarginal changes in goods must take account of the fact that the marginal value of goods changes as the amount of the good

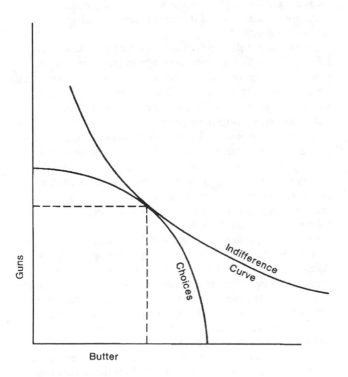

FIGURE 3. Choosing optional bundles.

changcs. Nonmarginal changes of both traded and nontraded goods must be handled differently than marginal changes.

The valuation of nonmarginal changes of goods leads to the concept of consumer surplus. Consumer surplus can be reasonably approximated by the area under a demand curve above current prices (see Figure 4). Note that this area implicitly values each level of good at the price that would pertain if that level were provided in the market. For example, if one were to increase the timber supply from 4 to 6 units, the consumer surplus would be the sum of the 4th unit evaluated at the market price (that occurs when only 4 units are sold), the 5th unit evaluated at the 5-unit market price, and the 6th unit evaluated at the 6-unit market price. The beginning market price, the 4-unit price, would overestimate the per unit value of the change; the last market price, the 6-unit price, would underestimate the per unit value of the change. Consumer surplus, by taking account of the way willingness to pay changes with large changes in the level of goods, is a reasonably accurate measure of the value of nonmarginal changes (Willig, 1976).

The potential confusion between marginal change and nonmarginal change can be seen clearly in discussions of the value of a recreation site to users. The value of a recreation site is a marginal value if taken in the context of a system of such sites. Thus, the value of a site is the market price of a recreation site if such sites were actually bought and sold. In practice, sites themselves are not bought and sold at least with enough regularity to determine market prices. However, trips to sites are bought and sold in the sense that people pay money to transport themselves to sites and thus gain access to them. User fees are also charged at some sites, adding to the cost of access. The travel cost model takes advantage of this market for trips to infer the marginal value of a site. The value of the site is the difference between the current level of trips and no trips. This difference in trips is generally a nonmarginal change. Thus, to value a marginal site, one values the consumer surplus of a nonmarginal change in trips to the site. The consumer surplus of trips to a site as a marginal measure of a site is comparable to the marginal price of a small timber sale. If one were to eliminate a nonmarginal number of sites or a nonmarginal number of timber sales, then this marginal value of a site or a timber sale would no longer be appropriate. However, the consumer surplus of trips, the marginal recreation value of a single site, is directly comparable with the marginal value (the market stumpage value) of timber sales from that site.

Cumulating Individual Values

The basic building block of monetary values is the individual's preference. In the case of traded goods consumed by individuals, the individual and social values are assumed identical. That is, if Mr. Smith is observed to value his last purchased can of peas at the market price, then the social value of this can of peas is the value that Mr. Smith places upon it. Because peas are traded in the marketplace, if someone else valued the peas more highly than Mr. Smith, the other individual would presumably have paid more for the peas and bought them himself. The process of trading in the marketplace, barring market imperfections, results in market goods going to the highest bidder. Thus, the value the individual places upon an individually consumed good is a reasonable measure of the highest possible use in society of that unit of goods.

Income cannot affect prices and therefore values. As the income of an individual increases, opportunity constraint expands permitting the individual to spend more for all the things the individual wants. Thus, a rich person can afford to spend more than a poor person for the same thing. If the income distribution suddenly changed, monetary values for income sensitive goods could also change. The change would depend upon how the income was actually redistributed. As people become more wealthy, they purchase more income-elastic goods. Thus, a society with most of its income devoted to a few individuals may purchase more luxury goods than a society with more equal incomes. Aggregate demand curves therefore depend on the existing income distribution.

Some goods, called "public goods," are not consumed by a single individual (Samuelson, 1954). For example, national defense, clean air, outdoor recreation areas, or fisheries are all resources shared by more than one user. In contrast, stumpage, grazing land, and mining are primarily private goods, consumed totally by the party given the rights to use the land at each moment in time. The value of jointly consumed (nonrival) resources is not captured entirely by what any one single person will pay for them. The value of public goods, because they are jointly consumed, is the sum of what all the users would individually pay for the good. Thus, the aggregate monetary value of Yellowstone National Park is the sum of what all the people

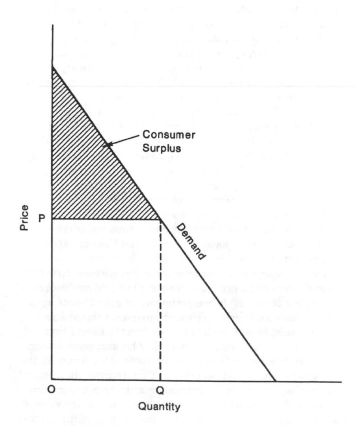

FIGURE 4. Consumer's surplus.

who enjoy the park would individually pay rather than do without the park.

Note that private markets have trouble providing public goods. The nonrival quality of public goods suggests that whoever enjoys the public good more, should pay more for it. This poses a problem to the owners of public goods because it is difficult to distinguish between people who would be willing to pay a lot and people who would be willing to pay a little. Private owners are consequently forced to charge a single price for use and so are unable to collect the total revenue associated with a marginal unit of the public good. Further, the price they charge will be a monopoly price, which maximizes the revenue from the good. Private ownership of public goods consequently leads to undersupply.

Because governments do not have to pay for the provision of public goods through user fees, they are potentially better able to provide public goods to society. It is this ability to separate valuation from fees that makes the government a potentially better supplier of private goods than the marketplace. That is not to say that all public goods should be free, but merely to point out that collection of revenue for many public goods is difficult and are not necessarily a limiting factor in their production.

Just because governments can potentially produce public goods more efficiently than the private sector, of course, does not guarantee that they will do so. For example, if a government mimicked the private sector and managed public resources to collect as much revenue as costs, the government, just like the private sector, would undersupply public goods. The ideal management of a public good is to equate the monetary value of a unit of the public good with its cost. Whether or not to collect any revenue from the public good depends on how difficult it is to fund the costs of the resource through user fees versus other sources of tax revenue, equity, and administrative costs.

Another problem with market prices of goods as a measure of social value is the presence of externalities, the production of by-products that cause damage that the creator does not have to pay for. Of greatest concern is the production of disamenities, such as pollution that imposes costs on other consumers, which the polluter (who could be either a producer or a consumer himself) does not take into account. To the extent that society regulates pollution, noise, and other such disamenities, the magnitude of this problem is reduced and is potentially eliminated. However, with imperfect regulation, several consumption and production activities continue to produce side effects that they do not have to pay for. In such cases, market prices overestimate the value of these goods and services. The true monetary value of marginal goods and services that produce disamenities is the market price minus the value of the marginal disamenity. For example, if a homeowner buys a particularly noisy lawnmower at the market price of $129 but his neighbors are willing to pay $30 for a quieter neighborhood, the lawnmower is really only worth $99.

Monetary Values and Policy Decisions

In this section, we discuss the use of monetary values to assist in making public policy decisions. In particular, we are interested in circumstances where the government is attempting to decide how to allocate resources to produce competing goods and services. For example, how should resources be allocated within the U.S. Forest Service to produce forage, timber, mining, wildlife, and recreation? Given the available land and an aggregate budget, one could construct a set of scenarios that represents different possible combinations of each of these goods and services, similar to the guns and butter diagram of Figure 1. The consumer could then be asked to trade between timber, mining, forage, recreation, and wildlife to choose a final bundle.

We note six possible reasons why monetary values may not be adopted to make public policy, and discuss the validity of each reason. The six reasons we focus on are:

1. Political power is distributed differently from the distribution of wealth.
2. People do not fully understand the consequences of their decisions.
3. People's conscious values are inconsistent with their own behavior.
4. People cannot consciously cope with the necessary choices.
5. The monetary values are measured inappropriately.
6. Monetary values are misunderstood and would be acceptable if understood.

In contrast to choices among typical consumer goods, most consumers do not buy the timber, use the grazing rights, mine the minerals and energy, enjoy the wildlife, and recreate in any single national forest (or even across the whole system). That is, they have no personal experience trading between the goods that society must consider when managing the resources. Thus, the ability of consumers to trade private goods does not infer that they have the same experience, capacity, or fluidity with the outcomes of social decisions. To paraphrase the insights of Tversky and Kahneman (1981), individuals often have labile or poorly formed public policy values (especially environmental values). People are not familiar with trading among public options.

To use monetary values in this social decision context, economists observe how people or firms trade between each of these services and all other goods (dollars), and from these trades infer how people would trade between the social options. Thus, for example, the recreationist pays for travel to the site. This is a tradeoff between the recreation service of the site and the goods and services (including traveling somewhere else) the person would have purchased if the site was unavailable. The timber or pulp company pays for stumpage. The amount of money each company is willing to pay for stumpage depends upon the price of stumpage from other sources and the tradeoff consumers are making between boards, plastics, steel, paper, electronic equipment, etc. By comparing the recreationist's trade of dollars against recreation with the timber company's trade of dollars for stumpage, the economists infer the relative value of recreation against stumpage.

The use of monetary values in this context implicitly assumes that the tradeoffs people make between each service and all other goods provide an appropriate index by which to compare each of the services directly. Thus, the market price of timber can be compared against the market price of mining or grazing lands and the nonmarket value of recreation and wildlife not

AUGUSTANA UNIVERSITY COLLEGE
LIBRARY

because people are trading personally between all these goods but rather because users are trading each of these goods against a common index of all other goods (dollars). Thus, economist's use of monetary values incorporates a complex set of trades and production functions which extend far beyond the forest.

Keeping the above case in mind, let us now examine each of the six reasons why monetary values may be rejected. With each reason, we will attempt to discuss the strengths and weaknesses of each argument.

Distribution of Wealth and Political Power

Monetary values are predicated on the existing income distribution. One reason why some people have a strong demand for a good is because they have more wealth. The monetary price for Rolls Royce automobiles, for example, is dominated by the tastes of the very wealthy. If the wealth of a society were redistributed in a different way across the population, a different set of market prices (marginal monetary values) may well result. If political power is distributed across society in a way that is different from the distribution of wealth, the values aggregated through political power may well conflict with the aggregated monetary values. Thus, to the extent that the distribution of wealth and political power differs, the political system may have an independent measure of value because it aggregates individual tastes differently.

Three issues should be considered when comparing economic versus political allocation of resources. First, if the distribution of rights is different, which distribution is more just? The second issue concerns which mechanism is better at allocation given the initial rights distribution. Finally, is the distribution of power that different between the two systems to warrant dramatically different outcomes?

Determination of the most just allocation of rights is a weighty philosophical discussion. On the one hand, the ancient Greek philosophers such as Aristotle argued that government should be ruled by the few (a wise and educated few). On the other hand, social egalitarians argue that equality is just. Egalitarianism itself has spawned the competing viewpoints in modern America's debate. On the one hand, some argue for equality of opportunity--the same rules for all. On the other hand, others argue for equality of outcome--the same income or resources for all. The current income distribution in the United States is a reasonable approximation of equality of opportunity. The current voting laws in the United States are closer to equality of outcome--one man, one vote. To take sides on this issue is beyond the scope of this paper; we merely wish to point out the source of controversy.

The second critical issue concerns the ability of the political versus the economic system to aggregate viewpoints given the initial distribution of rights. For example, when political power is concentrated in the hands of relatively few individuals, what has been the historical record? As elegantly stated by Lord Dalton, "Power tends to corrupt; absolute power corrupts absolutely." There are few examples where absolute political power

has resulted in enlightened leadership, especially in the last century.

Even with more democratic or pluralistic forms of government, there is a debate about the ability of the political system to make allocative decisions. For example, even in a one-man, one-vote system, there is always the danger that the majority will use political power to terrorize the minority (the tyrannical majority discussed by Buchanan and Tullock [1974]). That is, minority values will be given zero weight no matter how strong. These problems are mitigated by having constitutional rights, but such rights have only occasional impact on allocative decisions.

In a pluralistic democracy, minorities themselves can do quite well. Concentrated interest groups have a disproportionate incentive to organize and lobby because few people have much to gain. The few can gain control of large resources as long as the costs of the program, which the few fight for, are spread out among many others (Stigler 1975). Finally, pork barreling, where representatives are responsible only to local interests, is a serious problem. In an attempt to "bring home the pork," they often leave the public pantry bare. There are serious problems with the way that democratic political processes allocate resources. Even if one agreed that the equity provided through the political system was important, the allocation of resources through public means causes such inefficiency, it is not obvious that a real improvement in outcome is evident.

Finally, it is clear that the distribution of wealth is not equal in the United States or most other places in the world. In contrast, at least in democratic nations, each man is allegedly given the same right to vote. In more autocratic governments, political power is more concentrated than economic power. At this level, it would appear that economic and political power distributions can be quite different. It is also true that for some goods, the amount of income one possesses would dramatically change one's demand for a good. Thus, for example, the number of exotic cars demanded by a nation would change as power became concentrated. However, for many other goods, the demand for the good does not change greatly with income. In these cases, even if the income distribution was shifted, aggregate demand would hardly be affected. That is, because both wealthy and poor want the good, as power shifts between them, the demand for the good does not change greatly. A great deal of recreation demand is not sensitive to income. Consequently, the aggregate demand for recreation would not be greatly affected as income was shifted from one party to another.

Of course, certain special services such as fishing in an isolated northern Canadian lake or running the rapids of the Grand Canyon may attract more rich people than poor people. For these resources, a person's wealth would affect his willingness to pay and thus a different income distribution might change the monetary value of the resource. However, for the average use, poor people appear to be willing to pay just as much as rich people to gain access to sites. The difference in the distribution of rights between economic and political systems should not severely impact the demand for and therefore the allocation of recreation opportunities. Thus, the income distribution may have little impact on the monetary values of recreation and so should not be used as a reason to avoid using monetary values.

Understanding the Consequences of Public Policy

Lack of information is often given as a reason why the public fails to comprehend the value of some specific resources. Monetary values reflect decisions consumers actually make given their understanding of the consequences of their private decisions. If people have never experienced a good, however, it is possible that they would like it more than they think. That is, people may not be aware of how much they would value a good and so their current behavior would lead to an underestimate of the value of the good. Current users of goods often believe that nonusers would enjoy the good if they only tried it. This argument has been raised by numerous voices in the environmental area. Naturalists are frequently arguing that if people could only experience the awe of floating down the Grand Canyon or the beauty of untouched wilderness or the power of a whale as it leaps from the water, then they would place a greater weight on preservation. In the absence of such experiences, consumers fail to purchase access to these natural wonders and so "undervalue" them.

In support of such arguments, it is clear that many people took up hiking ardently only after having been convinced by some avid hiker friend or eloquent natural writer of the hidden pleasures. The economic rationale for the need for advertising is that it is making consumers aware of their true preferences and options. Information is valuable in a complex world and it is indeed evident that with more information, people will change their observed market behavior and thus monetary prices.

The idea that one should inform people about the benefits they will receive from using public goods is laudable. If in fact the information is new and valuable to people, they will change their behavior. New monetary values will then be reflected in this changed behavior. The argument that consumers are unaware of their private gains from using public resources is consequently not a reason to abandon the use of monetary values but rather simply a reason to engage in advertising.

Abandoning monetary values because of lack of information is dangerous because it is no longer clear who has "informed values." Users may argue that they are informed because they have experience with the good. But how much experience is necessary to determine whether one really would enjoy an activity? Must you try an activity many times before a deep understanding is reached? If initial use is expensive, how are we to be sure that users have not self-selected themselves out of the general population and thus represent a minority set of informed values rather than the informed value of the general population? This problem of separating who is informed versus who really enjoys using a resource limits the practicality of using informed values.

In our opinion, the chance that people will fail to understand their private choices is not nearly as likely as that they will fail to understand their public choices. With public choices, people have much less incentive to become informed. In this case, the individual's lack of information works in favor of monetary values over uninformed public attitudes. Whenever a tradeoff is sufficiently complex or unfamiliar, people's perception of the relative value of the goods being traded in public policy likely will be different from the monetary value. If the voters fail to grasp the full extent of the consequences of public actions, they will tend to hold values with respect to actions that may conflict with their true self-interest.

For example, in the case cited above where the public must choose between the various uses of the national forest, people will tend to favor those services with which they are most familiar. Thus, the timber and pulp companies will favor stumpage, the mineral and energy companies will favor mining, the livestock companies will favor grazing, hunters will favor wildlife, and hikers will favor recreation. None of these groups may understand the importance of the resource for other uses. Their political attitudes about which use is most important is based on their understanding. Monetary values, in contrast, would reflect much of the complexity of a modern economic system, which the typical individual is unlikely to comprehend. For example, the price of stumpage would reflect the availability of stumpage from other sources, current production methods in the timber and pulp industries, and the desired consumption of many final products such as houses, furniture, newspapers, and books. Similarly, in situ mineral prices reflect current mining and milling techniques, other sources of minerals and energy, and the demand for another long list of final products such as guns, plastics, cars, and gasoline. Recreation demand for hiking and camping or wildlife reflects the cost of access to these sites as well as the pleasure many citizens derive from activities in undeveloped settings.

If the reason people's attitudes conflict with monetary values is that they do not understand the consequences of political choices, it would appear that monetary values are preferable. Monetary values, in this case, capture the complexity of our economic system with a richness that ordinary citizens should not be expected to grasp. Correctly measured, monetary values provide guidance for our statesmen to lead the public to good social decisions.

Conscious Attitudes May Conflict with Behavior

Even with full information about the consequences of a public decision, people's conscious values may conflict with behavior. This discrepancy between attitudes and behavior has long been a subject of inquiry to social psychologists. At the extreme, this internal conflict between conscious values and behavior borders upon insanity as people perform actions over which they have no control. However, in a more subtle way, the conflict between behavior and attitudes is part of all our lives. To completely match behavior to conscious values is to thoroughly know and control oneself.

To illustrate the complexity of a common decision, let us take the simple choice of ice cream flavor. Monetary measures reflect what ice cream flavor you actually choose. If you think you like chocolate-flavored ice cream more than vanilla and you are observed to buy chocolate even when vanilla is on sale, then your behavior and attitudes are consistent. However, suppose you asserted that you liked chocolate better but that you were observed to buy vanilla just as often as chocolate. When confronted with this discrepancy, you might reply that chocolate is more fattening, bad for your health, or that you are afraid the chocolate would stain your white blouse, and therefore you often buy vanilla. But except for these factors, you do prefer chocolate to vanilla. One's reply to attitudinal surveys may reveal opinions that underlie monetary values. A person's feelings about health, weight, and appearance all play a role in one's desire for flavors. For these opinions to be properly reflected in behavior, however, a respondent must weigh the importance of each opinion and predict the net effect. In practice, the respondent may find it difficult to sort these factors out and give consistent responses.

As deep as some people's understanding of themselves goes, complete mastery remains elusive. Although we may all be able to explain away our erratic or whimsical behavior, the real issue is not whether we can find an excuse for past behavior but rather can we predict future behavior. The limits of our knowledge of ourselves is consequently one of the bounds separating attitudinal from behavioral values. Our conscious attitudes can be no more accurate than our perceptions of ourselves.

The discrepancy between behavior and held values can be perceived in an entirely different fashion, however. People's held values may describe what citizens should do in contrast to what they actually do. Let us define the desired set of values that people would like to have as aspired values. For example, dieters frequently argue that they should not have dessert but cannot resist. Their actions describe their behavioral values but their comments describe their aspired values. When making public decisions, people may want society to live up to aspired, not behavioral, values. That is, they may truly wish that society acts in a way that is better than the way each individual acts. It is perfectly reasonable (even if perhaps inconsistent) to argue that aspired values, not behavioral values, should be the motivating force behind social decisions.

Although, in principle, aspired values are a laudable approach, they are besieged by three serious problems. First, they are hard to measure. Second, honest men and women disagree about appropriate aspired values. Third, aspired values are often framed in absolute terms and so are difficult to aggregate or compare. Because aspired values are not necessarily linked with observed behavior, one is forced to measure aspired values through attitudinal surveys which remain subject to methodological problems. Further, many authors who argue for aspired values fail to recognize that there may be no single aspired value. Instead, these authors substitute their individual values for aspired values and argue that different values come solely from ignorance. Aspired values do not appear to be absolute truths but rather products of people's experiences. This approach must deal with the fact that different people have different aspired values.

One reason why aspired values are different from behavioral values is that behavior reflects the compromises we often make with our ideals. In this sense, behavioral values would appear to be inferior to aspired values because aspired values reflect untainted ideals. This aspect of aspired values, however, exacerbates the general problem of heterogeneous viewpoints. Aspired values, because they do not have to reflect the real tradeoffs in life, are often presented in absolute terms. For example, some people feel strongly that women should choose for themselves whether or not to have an abortion. Other people feel strongly that abortions are wrong. These are absolute principles, which deny any sense of a tradeoff. Consequently, no compromise position addresses these conflicting views. A similar conflict

exists with respect to animal rights (endangered species) and wilderness. Aspired values as absolute statements almost explicitly reject any notion of relativity (the comparison of one person's views against another's). As a practical matter, in a heterogeneous society, it is not at all clear how one could use absolute aspired values to make public choices.

Failure to Cope with Choices

Another plausible criticism of the usefulness of the monetary value approach is that society may be unwilling to face the reality of certain tradeoffs. Moral dilemmas, where people are forced to choose among competing immoral outcomes, can lead to a conscious attempt to avoid the tradeoff concept altogether. Policies become symbols of the right thing to do rather than acceptable compromises. For example, the Endangered Species Act is supposed to protect all species from extinction. The law is absolute in tone and symbolizes the high regard we have for other species. Even though in practice the law is limited by administrative priorities, enforcement budgets, and Congressional override, the conscious tradeoff has been avoided. Another such avoidance occurs throughout our public health regulatory framework. Pollutants, insecticides, herbicides, and food additives are all supposedly regulated to protect our health. No tradeoffs are explicitly mentioned in the law. Yet, upon careful review, we find that no chemicals are perfectly safe either. We have the illusion of having risked no safety and yet in reality we choose a point between all other things and more public health. Monetary values are omitted from these policy decisions because the monetary values highlight the fact that we are still making tradeoffs.

Perhaps a more subtle version of this distortion is that people may believe there is only a narrow band of choice. Having only a limited possible choice set, the alternative with the most of some desired characteristic is preferred. For example, people may feel there are only a few alternatives with regards to wildlife and that the most possible wildlife is the preferred choice. A careful measure of wildlife value is not necessary. It may as well be infinite because of the choices available, one always wants more. In the above circumstances, the precision of monetary values may be unnecessary and even undesirable.

Poor Methodology

An important reason to use monetary values for social decisions is that they are well defined and relatively easy to measure. Even the monetary value of nonmarket goods can frequently be captured with advanced revealed preference techniques. For example, there are several revealed preference approaches to measure nonmarket goods (Mendelsohn & Brown, 1983; Mendelsohn & Markstrom, this volume). Of course, with every measurement technique, one must make standing hypotheses to connect reality with theory. It is also true that measurement in field applications can fail to have sufficient quality control.

Finally, it is evident that at least for nonmarket goods, many dimensions of quality or experience have not yet been captured by the empirical literature. Thus, one must be sanguine about the universal use of monetary values for all things.

Recent authors have recommended the use of attitudinal surveys as a measure of monetary value. If successful, this tool could dramatically expand the list of nonmarket goods that could be valued. Although at times successful, the contingent valuation literature has tended not to recognize the discrepancy between behavior and attitudes. Further, questions are often asked that are unambiguous only to the professional economist (who would probably not answer them correctly on purpose). The complexity and subtlety of the concepts of monetary value appear to be difficult to transmit. Thus, contingent valuation surveys have tended to measure attitudes not monetary values. The results are consequently subject to multiple interpretations.

For example, there is a long-standing controversy about the difference between willingness to pay and willingness to accept in the contingent valuation literature. Willingness to pay reflects the money that people would be willing to exchange for more of the recreation good and still be just as happy as they are now. Willingness to accept reflects the money they would have to be given to be just as happy as with less of the resource. In both cases, the intention is that the person remains on the same indifference curve both before and after the change. With both concepts, a single indifference curve is the point of reference to judge the recreational good. The difference between the two measures is that they use different indifference curves as points of reference.

The indifference curve associated with the willingness to pay (WTP) concept assumes the individual must pay for any improvement in the resource, the willingness to accept (WTA) concept assumes the individual already owns the right to the improved resource. In both cases, the issue is making tradeoffs between changes in the level of service and income along a single indifference curve.

Generally, we would expect that the WTA payment is larger than the WTP concept. The WTA indifference curve is higher than the WTP indifference curve because one "owns" the improvement in the resource to start with and therefore has more income. If people with more income would generally buy more of the good, then this higher indifference curve also implies a higher value on the improvement. WTA should therefore exceed WTP because of this income effect.

However, the economics profession has widely concluded that the two measures ought to be close in most applications (Willing, 1976). The context of most recreation goods offers no exception. First, recreation forms a small part of overall wealth and thus whether or not you own the resource is not very important. Owning an improvement in the resource will not greatly increase your wealth. Second, measuring an increase in the value of recreation with higher income has been difficult. In the recreation case, income does not appear to affect the value people place on resources. Either of these points would be sufficient to suggest that WTP and WTA are similar. However, given both of them, it is difficult to argue that WTP and WTA should be sizably different in the recreation example.

Nonetheless, the contingent valuation literature has consistently reported that WTA is five to six times larger than WTP (e.g., Knetsch & Sinden, 1984). Contingent valuation methods clearly are not measuring either monetary or behavioral values in this case. As discussed earlier, these questions probably are being interpreted by individuals as the value of changes in utility rather than the amount of goods needed to remain at the same utility. In any case, as long as examples such as these are common in the literature, contingent valuation estimates or at least certain estimates of monetary values clearly must be viewed cautiously.

The general problems with the contingent valuation approach, however, also illustrate another important point. Attitudinal values are hard to measure. The way questions are posed, the sample chosen for interview, and the method of interview can all influence the response. People's own conscious knowledge of themselves is limited. Further, at least contingent valuation research has not developed as comprehensive or as uniform analytical methodologies as have been developed for revealed preference techniques. Other attitudinal methods developed in psychology have not demonstrated their immediate applicability to social decision making. Especially when comparing attitudinal responses to market prices, there is little question that monetary values are more precisely measured. Thus, although there are limitations to the measurement of monetary values for all goods, the monetary value estimates are generally more reliable than any alternatives.

Misunderstanding Monetary Value

Clearly one of the most important reasons that monetary values have as little weight in public policy decisions as they currently have is that they are not understood. Many actors in the policy process look upon monetary values as merely a measure of the commercial or development potential of a natural resource. As popularly conceived, monetary values are seen as failing to capture important health, spiritual, and aesthetic values. As an extreme example, some suggest that the monetary value of our national parks is equal to the money people spend on the visit buying souvenirs, meals, and lodging. This conception of monetary values, however, is incorrect. The monetary value of the park is not the expenditures visitors make on all these ancillary items. The expenditures on food, lodging, and souvenirs reflects the monetary value of the souvenirs, food, and lodging. The monetary value of the park is the amount of income people would forego rather than losing the park altogether.

Monetary values incorporate many valid opinions such as the desire for health, outdoor experience, aesthetics, and naturalism. Although these specific opinions are not measured, their input into behavior is captured in monetary values. Thus, for example, as people have become more aware of the value of exercise for health, they have increased their monetary value for outdoor recreation. Economists have explicitly chosen not to model why people have the values they have. That is not to say, however, that the motives that cause people to have their observed values is not reflected in those behavioral values.

Why people have adopted certain values is an interesting question. However, unless policy depends on why people have values rather than simply what those values are, understanding the motivation or structure behind values may not be important.

Only in special cases will policy decisions depend upon how values are formed. For example, the establishment of a national welfare system gave being on welfare a credible status in society. The number of people willing to be on welfare turned out to be much larger than was anticipated. Similarly, establishing wilderness areas has increased the demand for these roadless areas over undesignated but otherwise similar areas. Policies can affect monetary values by changing people's tastes for goods and services. In such circumstances, understanding why people form the values they have is important. One must go to the hidden structures underlying monetary values in these cases.

CONCLUSION

In this paper, we have attempted to describe what monetary value is and what it is not. In the process, we have carefully explored the concepts underlying the economist's notion of monetary value. We have noted that this measure is explicitly a behavioral approach in that it predicts or matches choices individual consumers actually make. Monetary values are not as successful in predicting public policy choices. We also discussed six major reasons why monetary values have not been more deeply embraced by policymakers.

Placing monetary values in perspective, we then attempted to assess the relative merits of each of these reasons. For example, lack of understanding about the meaning of monetary values, lack of information about the consequences of public decisions, and concern over the distribution of income are positive explanations of why monetary values fail to be accepted, but they do not provide deep normative support for continuing this practice. In contrast, holding informed attitudes that conflict with behavior and inadequate methodology may be legitimate reasons why society should continue to hold monetary values with at least a modicum of suspicion. Finally, there is the issue of moral dilemmas. It is not clear whether society should be permitted to ignore monetary values with a pretense that real choices are avoidable. It is an open question whether a rational approach to policy built upon an explicit distortion of evidence is preferable to explicitly choosing between unpleasant alternatives.

References

Buchanan, J., & Tullock, G. (1974). *The calculus of consent.* Ann Arbor, MI: University of Michigan Press.

Friedman, M. (1953). *Essays in positive economics.* Chicago, IL: University of Chicago Press.

Knetsch, J., & Sinden, J. (1984). Willingness to pay and compensation demanded: Experimental evidence of an unexpected disparity in measures of value. *Quarterly Journal of Economics, 100,* 507-521.

Mendelsohn, R., & Brown, G. (1983). Revealed preference approaches to valuing outdoor recreation. *Natural Resource Journal, 23,* 607-618.

Samuelson, P. (1947). *Foundations of economic analysis.* Cambridge, MA: Harvard University Press.

Samuelson, P. (1954). The pure theory of public expenditures. *Review of Economics and Statistics, 36,* 386-389.

Stevens, S. S. (1959). *Measurement, psychophysics, and utility.* In W. Churchman & P. Ratoosh (Eds.), *Measurement: Definitions and theories.* New York: John Wiley & Sons.

Stigler, G. (1975). *The citizen and the state: Essays on regulation.* Chicago, IL: University Press.

Tversky, A., & Kahneman, D. (1981). The framing of decisions and the psychology of choice. *Science, 211,* 453-458.

von Neuman, J., & Morgenstern, O. (1947). *Theory of games and economic behavior.* Princeton, NJ: Princeton University Press.

Willig, R. (1976). Consumer's surplus without apology. *The American Economic Review, 66,* 589-597.

Contingent Value Measurement: The Price of Everything and the Value of Nothing?

Icek Ajzen
Department of Psychology
University of Massachusetts

George L. Peterson
USDA Forest Service
Rocky Mountain Forest and Range Experiment Station

During recent years, economists have become increasingly interested in placing dollar values on goods and services not exchanged in the marketplace. The impetus for the development of appropriate methods arose from the need for benefit-cost assessments related to public goods (Cummings, Brookshire, & Schulze, 1984). If values of public goods can be estimated in a manner that makes them directly comparable to market prices, then it becomes possible for policymakers to determine the economically efficient mix of market and nonmarket goods. For example, with appropriate information about the value of air quality, it would be possible to compare the marginal cost of pollution control in the service of improved air with its marginal benefit. The contingent valuation method (CVM) has become a commonly used tool for valuing natural amenities and other public goods that are not traded in the marketplace (Cummings et al., 1984; Davis, 1963; Randall, 1984). The main purpose of this paper is to evaluate the CVM in light of economic and psychological views of value. In the process, we examine psychological value in terms of attitude theory and measurement, compare it with economic approaches, and discuss the implications of attitude theory and measurement for the definition and assessment of economic value.

INFERRING VALUE

The value of any commodity, whether traded in the marketplace or not, cannot be directly observed. It is a latent, hypothetical attribute that only can be inferred from observable cues. The kinds of cues that can properly be used to infer a commodity's value depend on our definition of the construct and on the objectives of value assessment; that is, on who wants to know and why.

Value in an Economic Context: Price

Most economists define value in a strict and narrow sense. The economic value of a commodity is no more, and no less, than the amount of money a person is willing to give up to get the commodity, or the amount of money the person requires as compensation for loss of the commodity. This value is inferred from actual behavioral choices in the exchange of goods and money.

The neoclassical theory of consumer demand asserts that consumers behave as if they were maximizing a utility function subject to a budget constraint. The consumer's preference ordering for different bundles of goods is assumed to be representable by a utility function, U. For example, if Bundle A is preferred to Bundle B, then $U(A) > U(B)$. The magnitude of the utilities is irrelevant to the theory; all that matters is that the function correctly orders alternative bundles of goods.

A key concept in the economic definition of value is compensation. *Compensating variation* is the maximum amount of money the consumer is willing to pay for a change in the quantity of a given commodity. If the change is adverse, then the compensating variation is negative and represents the minimum amount of money the consumer is willing to accept as compensation for the change. The key point about compensating variation is that the consumer is indifferent between the status quo and making the payment or accepting the compensation.

Of course, the amount of money a person is willing to pay for a commodity (i.e., the commodity's economic value) will change with the context. For goods exchanged in the marketplace, the context is that of a real market, but even a "real" market varies, depending on the degree of distortion or imperfection present in the market, and on the nature of the goods in question and their alternatives. When a real market context is not available, as in the case for nonmarketed goods, precise specification of the context becomes especially important.

Contingent Valuation

Randall (1984) identified two broad classes of techniques for quantifying the economic value (compensating variation) of a nonmarket good: the expenditure function approach and the contingent valuation approach. If the utility function is assumed to have certain mathematical properties, then it is sometimes possible to estimate compensating variation for a nonmarket good by estimating the demand for a related market good. The key relationship between the market good and the associated nonmarket good is weak complementarity (i.e., when the nonmarket good is no longer available, demand for the related market good must fall to zero).

With the contingent valuation approach, no special properties about the form of the utility function are assumed. To determine compensating variation, consumers are directly questioned regarding their willingness to pay or accept compensation for a specified change. The key assumption of the contingent valuation method is that consumers are able and willing to answer such questions truthfully.

As noted in the introduction, the CVM was developed in an attempt to permit cost-benefit analyses of public goods. Implicit in its use is the view that market price is an appropriate measure of a commodity's social benefits, and contingent value is to serve as a substitute for the unavailable market value of a public good. We shall consider these issues in a later section. First, however, we compare this economic view of value with a psychological perspective.

Value in a Psychological Contest: Attitudes

As defined by psychologists, the value of a commodity is broadly conceived, and can be inferred from a variety of different responses involving the commodity. The concept most commonly used by social psychologists to refer to the value of any object is the concept of *attitude*. An attitude is a disposition to respond favorably or unfavorably to a commodity, person, institution, or event. Although formal definitions of attitude vary, most contemporary social psychologists seem to agree that the characteristic attribute of attitude is its evaluative (pro-con, pleasant-unpleasant) nature (e.g., Bem, 1970; Edwards, 1957;

Fishbein & Ajzen, 1975; Hill, 1981; Osgood, Suci, & Tannenbaum, 1957; Oskamp, 1977). This view is strengthened by the fact that, as we shall see below, standard attitude scaling techniques result in a single score that locates an individual on an evaluative dimension viz-a-vis the attitude object (cf. Fishbein & Ajzen, 1975; Green, 1954).[1]

Like value, attitude is a hypothetical construct that, being inaccessible to direct observation, can only be inferred from measurable responses. Given the nature of the construct, these responses must reflect positive or negative evaluations of the attitude object. Beyond this requirement, however, there is virtually no limitation on the kinds of responses that can be considered. To simplify matters, it is possible to categorize attitude-relevant responses into various subgroups. The most popular classification system goes back at least to Plato and distinguishes between three categories of responses: cognition, affect, and conation (see Allport [1954], Hilgard [1980], and McGuire [1969] for general discussions). Within these categories, it is useful to separate verbal from nonverbal responses.

Cognitive Responses

In the first category are responses that reflect perceptions of, and information about, the attitude object. To illustrate, consider some responses we might use to infer attitudes toward national parks. Cognitive responses of a verbal nature are expressions of *beliefs* that link national parks with certain characteristics or attributes. Beliefs to the effect that national parks provide opportunities for recreation, that they preserve wildlife, etc., might be taken as evidence of a positive attitude. By way of contrast, an unfavorable attitude would be implied by expressions of beliefs suggesting that national parks are wasteful of taxpayers' money, that they are overcrowded, and the like. Cognitive responses of a nonverbal nature are more difficult to assess, and the information they provide about attitudes is usually more indirect. For example, we might argue that people with favorable attitudes toward national parks have relatively low thresholds for the perception of attitude-relevant positive stimuli, while people with unfavorable attitudes have relatively low thresholds for negative stimuli. To infer attitude toward national parks, therefore, we might measure how long it takes a person to appreciate the significance of cartoons depicting national park scenes in either a favorable or an unfavorable light.

Affective Responses

The second category of responses from which attitudes can be inferred has to do with evaluations of, and feelings toward, the attitude object. Here again, we can distinguish between affective responses of a verbal and of a nonverbal kind. Verbal responses of affect toward national parks, for example, can be expressions of pleasure or disgust, appreciation or disdain. Thus, a person who claims to enjoy national parks, or to "feel good" about their availability, would seem to hold a favorable attitude, but a person who indicates that the mere thought of national parks is maddening would seem to hold a negative attitude.

Various physiological and other bodily reactions are often assumed to reflect affect in a nonverbal fashion. Among the reactions considered are the galvanic skin response (electrical conductance of the skin), constriction and dilation of the pupil, heart rate, the reactions of facial muscles, etc. One of the difficulties inherent in methods that rely on responses of this kind is the problem of distinguishing between reactions that imply favorable attitudes and reactions that imply unfavorable attitudes, although recent research has reported some progress in this regard (Cacioppo et al., 1986).

Conative Responses

Responses of a conative nature are behavioral inclinations, intentions, commitments, and actions with respect to the attitude object. Starting again with the verbal side, we can consider what people say they do, plan to do, or would do under appropriate circumstances. Thus, people with negative attitudes toward national parks might indicate that they would refuse to spend more than a few hours in a national park, would oppose a campaign to clean up a national park, or discourage their children from camping in national parks. Those with positive attitudes, on the other hand, might express intentions to donate money to a fund for a national park, plan to encourage their children to visit national parks, or indicate a readiness to read about national parks. As we shall see below, willingness to pay and to accept compensation for a public good, the responses used in contingent valuation, are best considered conative responses of a verbal nature.

Nonverbal conative responses indicating favorable or unfavorable attitudes toward national parks are also easily imagined. Thus, people who actually read books or articles about national parks, who take their children to national parks, and who participate in a clean-up drive of a national park would be classified as having positive attitudes, whereas people who refuse to take part in a clean-up drive or who write letters to newspapers complaining about the waste of using taxpayers' money for the construction and maintenance of national parks would be said to have negative attitudes.

In sum, an individual's favorable or unfavorable attitude toward a public good, or toward any other object, institution, or event, can be inferred from verbal or nonverbal responses toward the public good in question. These responses can be of a cognitive nature, reflecting perceptions of the commodity, or beliefs concerning its likely characteristics; they can be of an affective nature, reflecting the person's evaluations and feelings; and they can be of a conative nature, indicating how a person does or would act with respect to the commodity.

A Hierarchical Model of Attitude

For many theorists, the distinction between cognition, affect, and conation is more than just a system for classifying responses from which attitudes can be inferred. These theorists assume that each response category reflects a different theoretical *component* of attitude (e.g., Katz & Stotland, 1959; Smith, 1947). In this view, attitude is a multidimensional construct consisting of cognition, affect, and conation. Although each of these components varies along an evaluative continuum, it is assumed that the evaluations expressed in them can differ greatly (Breckler,

1984; Ostrom, 1969). Thus, a person might feel secure in a national park (positive affect) but, at the same time, believe that national parks are poorly maintained (negative cognitive component) and refuse to spend a weekend camping in a national park (unfavorable conative component).

In recent years, a controversy has developed around this issue: Should attitude be conceptualized as a unitary or as a multidimensional construct? A number of attempts have been made to confirm the discriminant validity of measures designed to tap the different components (e.g., Bagozzi, 1978; Breckler, 1984; Kothandapani, 1971; Ostrom, 1969). Depending on the method used and the assumptions made, the research findings have variously been interpreted either as supporting a tripartite model or as supporting a single-factor model (see the exchange between Dillon and Kumar [1985] and Bagozzi and Burnkrant [1985]). The major issue seems to revolve around whether differences between measures of the cognitive, affective, and conative components are a result of differences in method (i.e., as theoretically uninteresting method variance) or .true differences between conceptually independent constructs.

Closer inspection reveals, however, that it is not necessary to choose between the multi- and unidimensional views of attitude. The tripartite model of attitude offered by Rosenberg and Hovland (1960), which serves as the starting point of most analyses, is actually a *hierarchical* model that includes cognition, affect, and conation as first-order factors and attitude as a single second-order factor. Thus, the three components can be defined independently and yet comprise, at a higher level of abstraction, the single construct of attitude. To extend this line of reasoning, recall that each component is made up of verbal and nonverbal response classes, and that each of these is further comprised of a large number of specific response tendencies. Thus, attitudes are always inferred from specific responses to the attitude object. We can classify these responses into broader categories and assign different labels to those categories, but we are still dealing with the same attitude. The findings of empirical research are quite consistent with this view in that a single factor is found to account for much of the variance in attitudinal responses, and the correlations among measures of the three components, although leaving room for some unique variance, are typically of moderate to high magnitude (e.g., Breckler, 1984; Kothandapani, 1971).

Assessment Procedures

Our discussion of attitude measurement is not intended to provide a thorough treatment of the subject. Many methods are available, some quite sophisticated in terms of the stimulus situations they create, the ways they assess responses, and the statistical procedures they employ (Edwards, 1957; Fishbein & Ajzen, 1975; Green, 1954). The purpose of the present treatment is merely to introduce the reader to some of the basic principles involved, especially those principles that have some bearing on our later discussions of contingent valuation. Most methods used to infer attitudes rely on verbal responses to questionnaire items. Therefore, our discussion of attitude measurement will focus on verbal responses, but it should be kept in mind that the same procedures can be applied equally well to observation of nonverbal responses.

Direct Assessment

The simplest procedure in many ways is to ask respondents to report directly on their own attitudes. Many studies in social psychology have employed direct probes of this kind. In the context of valuing public goods, consider the following example:

What is your attitude toward setting aside more public land as natural preserves?

Very much   Very much
in favor :___:___:___:___:___:___:___:___:___:___:opposed

In many cases, single items of this kind have proved quite adequate for the assessment of particular attitudes. However, this method has potential drawbacks, in particular the question of *reliability*, or the extent to which repeated assessment of the same attitude produces equivalent results. Single responses tend to be quite unreliable, leading to low correlations between repeated observations. For this reason, and for other reasons discussed below, it is usually preferable to use multi-item measures.

Perhaps the best-known multi-item measure used to obtain a relatively direct indication of attitude is the *semantic differential*, developed by Osgood et al. (1957). Designed originally to measure the meaning of a concept, it is now used in a variety of contexts. As a measure of attitude, the semantic differential consists of a set of bipolar evaluative adjective pairs, such as *good-bad*, *harmful-beneficial*, *pleasant-unpleasant*, *desirable-undesirable*, and *awful-nice*. Each adjective pair is placed on opposite ends of a 7-point scale, and respondents are asked to mark each scale as it best reflects their evaluation of the attitude object. Thus, the following evaluative semantic differential could be used to assess attitudes toward national parks:

National Parks are:

pleasant : ___:___:___:___:___:___:___:	unpleasant
harmful : ___:___:___:___:___:___:___:	beneficial
good : ___:___:___:___:___:___:___:	bad
awful : ___:___:___:___:___:___:___:	nice

Responses are scored from -3 on the negative side of each scale to +3 on the positive side, and the sum over the four scales is a measure of the respondent's attitude toward national parks.

Indirect Assessment

The contingent value method is, of course, a direct assessment procedure. Direct measures of the multi-item kind have proved useful in attitude research. They are easily developed and, for this reason, are popular, especially in the context of laboratory studies. For some purposes, however, they are somewhat limited because they may elicit relatively superficial responses. Indirect measures of attitudes, on the other hand, provide opportunities for respondents to review different aspects of a given domain. The responses they give to a set of specific questions are then used to infer the disposition under investigation.

We previously discussed the different kinds of verbal responses that can be used to infer attitudes. Usually, the items that appear on a questionnaire are statements of beliefs, behavioral intentions, or actual behavior, and respondents are asked to indicate their agreement or disagreement with each statement. Different methods are available to select items from a large initial pool, ensuring that the set of items comprising the attitude scale is representative of the total domain. To review these methods in detail is beyond the scope of this paper; we will briefly describe only the two most popular scaling procedures: Thurstone and Likert scaling. (This description is based on the discussion of attitude measurement in Ajzen and Fishbein [1980, pp. 14-16].)

For example, consider the following statements designed to assess attitudes toward locating an airport near a wildlife preserve:

1. An airport at location X will frighten animals in the preserve.
2. I would visit the preserve if there were an airport at location X.
3. Locating an airport at X will make visits to the preserve less enjoyable.
4. An airport at location X will cause considerable air pollution.

Thurstone (1931) assumed that different opinion statements of this kind express varying degrees of favorableness or unfavorableness toward the attitude object, and he developed several methods that permit assigning scale values to opinion statements, scale values that define the statements' locations on the evaluative dimension. In the most widely used Thurstone procedure, the "equal-appearing interval scale," the initial, large pool of items is given to a sample of judges representative of the research population, and these judges are asked to rate the favorableness of each item on an 11-point scale. The median or mean rating provided by the judges is the item's scale value. Two criteria are used to select items for the final attitude scale. The criterion of ambiguity first eliminates items with large disagreements among judges (i.e., items that have a large variance around the mean scale value). The resulting item pool is administered to a sample of respondents asked to check all items with which they agree. The criterion of irrelevance is then used to eliminate items that fail to discriminate among respondents with different attitudes. The final scale is comprised of items with scale values spaced more or less equally along the evaluative continuum that have met both selection criteria. When administered, respondents are asked to check all items with which they agree, and attitude scores are obtained by computing the median or mean scale value of the endorsed items.

Likert (1932) proposed a somewhat simpler procedure by dispensing with the need for judges. His method of summed ratings also begins with the construction of a large pool of opinion statements. Instead of using judges to determine each item's scale value, the investigator decides whether agreement with an item implies a favorable or an unfavorable attitude. Items that appear neutral or ambiguous are eliminated. The remaining items are administered to a sample of respondents who, typically, are asked to indicate their agreement or disagreement with each statement on a 5-point scale: agree strongly, agree, undecided, disagree, disagree strongly. Responses are assigned values from 5 (strong agreement) to 1 (strong disagreement) for positive items, and in reverse order for negative items. A preliminary attitude score is computed for each individual by summing over all response values for that individual. Item selection is accomplished by means of the criterion of internal consistency: The items that exhibit the highest correlations with the preliminary total attitude score are retained on the final scale.

Each statement on an attitude scale links the attitude object (e.g., locating an airport near a wildlife preserve) with a certain attribute or consequence (e.g., frightens animals, induces me to visit the preserve, etc.). It can be seen that attitude scaling methods require two kinds of information with respect to each item: (1) whether the person agrees or disagrees with the item (or the extent of his agreement/disagreement), and (2) whether agreement implies a positive or a negative attitude (or the degree of evaluation implied by agreement). The first type of information refers to the strength of the respondent's *belief* that the attitude object has a certain attribute, while the second type of information is concerned with his *evaluation* of the attribute. Likert and Thurstone scaling methods determine attribute evaluations normatively, for the population at large, while belief strength is assessed for each individual respondent. It is also possible to obtain both types of information directly from the individual respondents.

Examination of the Thurstone and Likert scaling methods reveals that an estimate of attitude (A) is obtained by multiplying belief strength (b) and outcome evaluation (e), and summing the resulting products across all responses:

$$A \propto \Sum b_i e_i. \tag{1}$$

A SOCIAL PSYCHOLOGICAL VIEW OF CONTINGENT VALUATION: THE THEORY OF REASONED ACTION

Willingness to pay or to accept compensation is an expression of a behavioral intention or, perhaps, a behavioral commitment. In any case, it represents a willingness to perform a behavior. Ajzen and Fishbein (1977, 1980; Fishbein & Ajzen, 1975) have made it clear that the determinants of a behavior often differ greatly from the determinants of attitudes (i.e., value judgments) in relation to some object, institution, or event. This issue will be discussed within the framework of the "theory of reasoned action" (Ajzen & Fishbein, 1980; Fishbein & Ajzen, 1975). Considerable evidence in support of the theory has accumulated in a variety of experimental and naturalistic settings (e.g., Ajzen, 1971; Ajzen & Fishbein, 1980; Ajzen, Timko, & White, 1982; Manstead, Proffitt, & Smart, 1983; Smetana & Adler, 1980). The behaviors involved have ranged from simple strategy choices in laboratory games to actions of appreciable personal or social significance, such as having an abortion, smoking marijuana, and choosing among candidates in an election. The constructs employed by the theory of reasoned action are fundamentally motivational in nature. According to the theory, the immediate antecedent of any behavior is the *intention* to perform the behavior in question. The stronger a person's intention, the more the person is expected to try, and hence the greater the likelihood that the behavior will actually be performed. The theory of reasoned action specifies two conceptually independent determinants of intention. One is a personal factor termed *attitude toward the behavior* and refers to the degree to which a person has a favorable or unfavorable evaluation of the behavior in question. The second predictor of intention is *subjective norm*, a social factor referring to the perceived social pressure to perform or not to perform the behavior. Attitude and subjective norm, each weighted for its relative importance, are assumed jointly to determine behavioral intention. The discussion of the theory up to this point is summarized symbolically:

$$B \sim I \propto [w_1 A_B + w_2 SN], \qquad [2]$$

where B is the behavior of interest, I is the person's intention to perform behavior B, A_B is the person's attitude toward performing behavior B, SN is the person's subjective norm concerning performance of behavior B, and w_1 and w_2 are empirically determined weighting parameters that reflect the relative importance of attitudes and subjective norms.

The theory of reasoned action also deals with the antecedents of attitudes and subjective norms; antecedents, that in the final analysis determine intentions and actions. At the most basic level of explanation, the theory postulates that behavior is a function of salient information, or beliefs, relevant to the behavior. Two kinds of beliefs are distinguished: *behavioral beliefs*, which are assumed to influence attitudes toward the behavior, and *normative beliefs*, which constitute the underlying determinants of subjective norms. Each behavioral belief links the behavior to a certain outcome, or to some other attribute such as the cost incurred by performing the behavior. The outcome's subjective value then contributes to the attitude toward the behavior in direct proportion to the strength of the belief (i.e., the subjective probability that performing the behavior will lead to the outcome under consideration). To obtain an estimate of attitude (A), belief strength (b) is multiplied by outcome evaluation (e), and the resulting products are summed across all salient behavioral beliefs, as shown in Equation 1 above. This model of attitude toward a behavior is similar to other expectancy-value models of attitude (e.g., Feather, 1959; Rosenberg, 1956).

Normative beliefs are concerned with the likelihood that important referent individuals or groups would approve or disapprove of performing the behavior. The strength of each normative belief is multiplied by the person's motivation to comply with the referent in question, and an estimate of subjective norm is obtained by summing the resulting products across all salient referents.

In contrast to the theory of reasoned action, traditional utility theory assumes that each person acts as an individual utility maximizer; the demand for goods and services is not, explicitly, a function of what others expect of the individual. The theory of reasoned action, and the research it has generated, suggest otherwise. If the contingent value method is to accurately reflect the amount of money a person would actually be willing to pay or to accept as compensation, the hypothetical situation described to the person must reflect the social pressure that may exist in the real-life setting. If it does not, then contingent valuation may systematically overestimate or underestimate the monetary value of a public good.

In the context of valuing public goods, the most important implications of the theory of reasoned action are related to the attitude toward a behavior construct. Note that this attitude is directed at the performance of a particular behavior (e.g., paying for cleaner air, driving to a national park, etc.) and not at an object, institution, or event (e.g., attitudes toward a clean lake or toward some other environmental amenity), the targets of traditional attitude measures. Perhaps a bit more difficult to see, attitude toward a behavior also differs from attitudes toward policies, such as attitudes toward cleaning up our air, building a national park, etc. These latter attitudes, although they deal with behavior, do not address the individual's *own* behavior. Thus, an individual can have a positive attitude toward reserving public land for a national park, yet place no particular value on visiting the park (and have no intention to do so) nor value or intend to pay for the project.

To understand the reasons for these differences, we must, according to the theory of reasoned action, examine the underlying determinants of the three kinds of attitudes: attitudes toward public goods, attitudes toward policies dealing with public goods, and attitudes toward paying for a public good (or performing some other behavior with respect to it, such as using the public good or accepting compensation for loss of its use). In each case, the underlying determinants are assumed to be a set of salient beliefs that can be elicited in a free-response format. However, the kinds of beliefs elicited from respondents will tend to differ. In the case of attitudes toward public goods, these beliefs associate the good in question with various attributes. Thus, if asked about their beliefs concerning a proposed national park, respondents may list its recreational value, the natural beauty of the landscape, the variety of wildlife available, etc. Some of the same beliefs may be emitted when respondents consider the advantages and disadvantages of establishing the national park in question, but other considerations may enter as well. For example, we may discover that such a policy is considered wasteful of taxpayers' money or that it is valued because of the employment it would create for area residents. Finally, still other beliefs may emerge in relation to paying for establishment of the national park, in relation to paying for the right to enter it, or in relation to accepting compensation for loss of the privilege to use the park. People may believe that the establishment and maintenance of a national park is the responsibility of government and that they should therefore not have to pay for it or that by paying an entrance fee they gain the right to hunt or fish, activities that may be highly valued. The question of compensation may, by implication, produce beliefs that enhance the subjective value of a public good. For example, if asked how much he or she would have to be paid to sell a hunting license, a person may infer that hunting licenses are hard to get and that therefore should be paid more than its original cost. The formation of inferential beliefs of this kind could explain the frequently observed difference between monetary estimates of value obtained by means of contingent valuations based on willingness to pay and willingness to accept compensation.

In short, by shifting the focus from attitudes toward a public good to questions of policy or personal action, different kinds of considerations may enter the picture. An example of how even relatively minor shifts of this kind can change the relevant beliefs is available in the context of consumer behavior (Ajzen & Fishbein, 1980). Beliefs about Chevrolets (in general) and about buying a Chevrolet in the next 3 years were listed by a sample of undergraduate students. The most frequently emitted beliefs were examined and two sets of beliefs were found to differ greatly from each other. Beliefs about Chevrolets were concerned with product attributes such as moderate price and dependability, easy service, and the fact that the car is made in America, while beliefs about buying a Chevrolet dealt with the consequences of this behavior, including payment of costly insurance premiums and high upkeep costs. As might be expected, these differences in beliefs produced very different attitudes toward Chevrolets and toward buying a Chevrolet in the next 3 years. Measures of these two attitudes were obtained by means of semantic differential scales, and the correlation between them was only .30.

To return to the valuation of public goods, our discussion suggests that the value placed on the good itself may differ greatly from the value of a policy designed to provide for the public good, and this latter value may in turn have little to do with willingness to pay for the good in question or to accept compensation for its loss. Contingent valuation is usually viewed as a method for establishing the (economic) value of a public good. In point of fact, however, by focusing on personal action (i.e., willingness to pay or to accept compensation for a specified change), it is best viewed as placing a value on a behavior with respect to the good in question. Of course, nothing is wrong with such an approach as long as we realize what the method does and does not provide. Later in this paper we compare this approach to one which shifts the focus of valuation from personal action to the question of policy.

A Psychological Assessment of Contingent Valuation

Intentions and Behavior

The contingent valuation method is sometimes questioned on the grounds that social psychological research has revealed poor relations between verbal attitudes and overt actions. Thus, it is argued, the amount of money a person says he would be willing to pay may have little to do with the amount of money he actually would pay. This particular concern seems to be largely misplaced, however. Although measures of general attitudes toward an object are frequently unrelated to specific actions with respect to the object (Ajzen & Fishbein, 1977), the contingent value method is not concerned with such global attitudes. Instead, as we saw, it elicits indications of specific behavioral intentions. Under appropriate conditions, behavioral intentions are reasonably good predictors of later behavior (Ajzen, 1985).

Volitional Control

The first requirement for a strong association between intentions and actions is that the behavior under consideration be under volitional control (Fishbein & Ajzen, 1975). A behavior may be said to be *completely* under a person's volitional control if the person can decide at will to perform it or not to perform it. Conversely, the more that performance of the behavior is contingent on the presence of appropriate opportunities or on possession of adequate resources (e.g., time, money, skills, cooperation of other people, etc.), the less the behavior is under purely volitional control. Because people can usually spend the amount of money they are willing to spend, this may not be a particularly serious problem in the context of contingent valuation. Nevertheless, several issues related to behavioral control are worth noting.

One resource that will obviously affect ability to pay is the person's wealth and income. Although economic definitions of value explicitly incorporate this constraint, the contingent value method tends to leave the matter implicit. When indicating how much they would be willing to pay for a public amenity, respondents presumably take into consideration the amount of money available to them, alternative uses they might have for their money, etc. However, this is not necessarily the case, and it might be preferable to instruct respondents explicitly to take these matters into account.

Other factors that may reduce the intention-behavior relation in the context of public amenity use have to do with opportunities. A person may indicate willingness to pay a certain amount of money for a hunting license, for example, but actually may never find the time to go on a hunting trip. Thus, even though a hunting license may be offered sometime following contingent value assessment, expressed willingness to pay may find no expression in actual behavior.

Change of Mind

A second requirement for a strong intention-behavior relation is that the intention must not have changed in the interval between the time it was assessed and the time the behavior is observed. The longer the time interval, the more likely is the occurrence of unforeseen events that may change the intention. It follows that accuracy of prediction will usually vary inversely with the time interval between measurement of intention and observation of behavior.

Note, however, that the concern of economists is usually focused at the aggregate level, rather than at the level of the individual. Because changes in the intentions of different individuals are often likely to balance out, aggregate intentions are apt to be relatively stable over time. This implies that intention-behavior correspondence at the aggregate level may be quite high even when, at the individual level, changes in intentions produce low predictive validity. Evidence in support of this hypothesis is provided by research on family planning. In a study by Bumpass and Westoff (1969), women with two children were asked how many children they intended to have in their completed families. Six to 10 years later (near the end of their reproductive periods), they were reinterviewed to obtain information about the number of children they actually had. Only 41% of the women had exactly the number of children they planned; the remainder had more or fewer children than intended. On the average, however, the women's actual family size corresponded precisely to the intended family size (3.3 children on average).

Correspondence

Perhaps most important for strong intention-behavior correlations in the context of contingent valuation is the requirement that the measure of intention corresponds in its level of generality to the behavioral criterion (cf., Ajzen, 1982; Ajzen & Fishbein, 1977). Any intention and any behavior can be defined in terms of four elements: the action involved, the target at which the action is directed, the context in which it occurs, and the time of its occurrence. Measures of intention and behavior correspond to each other to the extent that their action, target, context, and time elements are assessed at identical levels of generality or specificity. The generality or specificity of each element depends on the measurement procedures employed. A single observation of an action is a highly specific behavioral indicator involving a given response directed at a particular target and performed in a given context at a given point in time. An example might be "driving (the action) 25 miles (the context) to a national park (the target) on a given Sunday morning (time)." By aggregating across one or more elements, measures of intention and behavior can be made arbitrarily general. Thus, the general behavioral tendency with respect to a national park could be assessed by getting information about various relevant actions in different contexts and at different points in time: driving to the park on various occasions, using its facilities, taking friends to the park, etc. According to the principle of correspondence formulated by Ajzen and Fishbein (1977), consistency between intention and behavior is a function of the degree to which indicators of these two variables are formulated at the same level of generality or specificity. The more similar the action, target, context, and time elements of the intention to the elements of the behavior, the stronger should be the statistical relation between them (Foa, 1958; Guttman, 1957; Olweus, 1980).

The question of correspondence is closely related to the problem known as *hypothetical bias* in the contingent valuation literature. Expression of willingness to pay for a specified change will obviously be affected by information about the change given to the respondent. Hypothetical bias refers to the possibility that the description of the hypothetical situation may differ in systematic ways from the actual situation in which an exchange of money could be observed. Schulze, d'Arge, and Brookshire (1981) compared the following two questions that might be posed to respondents: "How much are you willing to pay for less air pollution?" versus "How much are you willing to pay for an annual average reduction in oxidant concentrations of .10 parts per million in the seven block radius around Hollywood Boulevard and Vine Street?" (p. 158). The first question is too general, the second too specific and technical. To ensure proper correspondence between measures of intention and behavior, and at the same time enable respondents to provide meaningful answers, it is necessary to avoid technical jargon, to define the proposed change at a reasonable level of specificity, and to assess both intention and behavior at that same level.

Even when carefully worded, however, any single description of a hypothetical situation will remain to some extent ambiguous. Consider, for example, the question of how much a person would be willing to pay for entrance to a proposed national park. We could describe the location and size of the park and some of the available facilities. Still, many details will have to be left out. Is the visit to occur when the park is crowded or relatively empty?; on a weekend or during vacation?; in the winter or summer?; will the visit include an overnight stay or not? Clearly, we cannot consider all these possibilities in a single question. This is one of the reasons why social psychologists prefer to assess attitudes in an indirect, multi-item format. Each item or question can explore a somewhat different aspect of the domain.

Although it would require a more thorough survey, this approach is also feasible in the case of contingent valuation. Respondents could be asked to indicate how much money they would be willing to pay, given contextual variations, if the park had camping facilities, if a fishing license were included in the entrance fee, if the visit were to occur during peak season, and so forth. The average across the different estimates could then be taken as a measure of willingness to pay. Actual behavior would, of course, also have to be observed in an equally varied set of circumstances. By aggregating across contexts with respect to intentions as well as behaviors, we maintain close correspondence and thus ensure a strong intention-behavior correlation.

PRICE VERSUS PSYCHOLOGICAL VALUE

Amount of money paid for a good--whether established in exchange or by means of contingent valuation--is assumed to reflect the good's benefits to the consumer. The cost of the good is, of course, usually given in monetary terms. When benefits are also assessed in monetary terms, it becomes possible to compare a good's benefits to its costs in benefit-cost analyses. As an economic tool, therefore, contingent valuation--with all its potential measurement problems--can be of great use. One must take care, however, not to equate willingness to pay for a good with its psychological value, especially when dealing with public goods. As Cummings et al. (1984) noted in their assessment of the contingent valuation method, "... market prices serve, at best, as weak approximations for relevant measures of social value" (p. 12).

From a psychological point of view, the value of a commodity broadly reflects people's perceptions of the commodity's favorable and unfavorable attributes (i.e., people's attitudes toward the commodity in question). No single reaction with respect to the commodity is sufficiently representative of the evaluative disposition to serve as a measure of attitude. As we discussed, attitudes are inferred from a variety of responses aggregated to obtain a broad dispositional index. It follows that expressions of willingness to pay or to accept compensation are too narrow and specific to serve as measures of psychological value.

There are other reasons to be weary of equating willingness to pay with psychological value. Thus, the relations between demand, supply, and price on one hand, and psychological value on the other, are complicated and not well understood. An increase in price will tend to reduce demand for a commodity but may, paradoxically, increase its psychological value. Conversely, an increased supply will tend to reduce price and increase demand, but it may also reduce the commodity's psychological value.

Perhaps the most important difference between economic and psychological measures of value is that, in contrast to willingness to pay, which is extremely sensitive to situational factors, attitudes are relatively stable dispositions that reflect a commodity's value across time and context. It is for this reason that people can talk about a good being overpriced or a bargain: The subjective value of a good can be smaller or greater than the price demanded. In other words, considerations underlying willingness to pay or accept compensation may differ greatly from considerations that enter into establishing the good's psychological value. Willingness to pay for cleaning up a nearby lake polluted by industry can serve as an example. Although the psychological value of a clean lake may be considerable, the act of paying for this project may imply acceptance of responsibility. If industry is blamed, people may think that the industry in question should pay for the cleanup. As a consequence, the value of a clean lake may be high, but willingness to pay will be low.

The Psychological Value of Public Goods

Monetary estimates of value can be used not only to compare a public good's benefits to its costs but also to compare its benefits to the benefits derived from alternative goods that may or may not be traded in the marketplace. Thus, we may want to compare the value of cleaning up a polluted lake with the value of developing the lumber industry in the same geographical location. The monetary value of developing a lumber industry can be computed by conventional means and compared to the monetary value of cleaning up the lake as estimated by the contingent valuation method. The above discussion suggests, however, that this approach tells us little about the *psychological* value of a public good, nor was it designed to do so.

The attitude approach, based on Ajzen and Fishbein's (1980) description of the attitude formation process, is designed to capture the psychological benefits and costs of public (as well as private) goods. The basic idea is that changes in the availability of nonmarket as well as market goods can be valued by assessing attitudes toward those changes. To understand the logic and procedures involved, it is necessary to consider attitudes and their underlying determinants in greater detail.

The Informational Basis of Attitudes

As we noted earlier, attitudes toward instituting a given policy are determined largely by beliefs about the advantages and disadvantages of that policy. Generally speaking, we form beliefs about a policy (or any other object) by learning to associate it with certain advantages and disadvantages (perceived benefits and costs). Automatically and simultaneously, we acquire attitudes toward the policy; that is, we learn to value positively policies we believe have positive characteristics, and we acquire unfavorable attitudes toward policies we associate with negative characteristics (Fishbein, 1967).

In the course of a person's life, his experiences lead to the formation of many different beliefs about various objects, ac-

tions, and policies. These beliefs may be the result of direct observation, they may be acquired indirectly by accepting information from outside sources, or they may be self-generated through inference processes (Fishbein & Ajzen, 1975). Some beliefs persist over time, others are forgotten, and new beliefs are formed. Although a person may hold a large number of beliefs about any given policy, it appears that only a relatively small number, maybe 5 to 10 beliefs, are *salient* at any given moment. According to the theory of reasoned action, these salient beliefs are the immediate determinants of the person's attitude.

To understand why a person holds a certain attitude toward a policy, it is necessary to assess his salient beliefs about that policy. Perhaps the simplest and most direct procedure involves asking the person to list the advantages and disadvantages of the policy using a free-response format. For example, to elicit the beliefs underlying a person's attitude toward cleaning up a lake, we could ask the following questions:

1. What do you believe are the advantages of cleaning up Lake X?
2. What do you believe are the disadvantages of cleaning up Lake X?
3. What else do you associate with cleaning up Lake X?

The respondent is asked to briefly list the beliefs that come to mind. The first few beliefs emitted can be taken as the person's salient beliefs concerning the policy of cleaning up Lake X.

The procedure described thus far permits exploration of the unique set of beliefs that underlie a given person's attitude toward a policy. For many purposes, however, we are more interested in the beliefs commonly held within a target population than in the beliefs of any particular individual. These *modal salient beliefs* can be ascertained by eliciting beliefs from a representative sample of the population in question; the beliefs most frequently listed by this sample constitute the modal set for the population.

Relating Beliefs to Attitudes

The expectancy-value model of attitude described earlier shows how salient beliefs can influence a person's attitude. Generally speaking, the more favorable the consequences associated with a given policy, and the stronger these associations, the more favorable the attitude should be (see Equation 1). For example, assume that one of the beliefs (salient in the research population) about cleaning up Lake X is the belief that doing so will make it possible to swim in the lake. The evaluation of this consequence is simply the attitude toward it; that is, the extent to which swimming in the lake is valued positively or negatively. This evaluation is usually assessed by means of one or more bipolar evaluative scales:

Making it possible to swim in Lake X is:

valuable ____ ____ ____ ____ ____ ____ ____ worthless

To measure the strength of a person's belief, we obtain a subjective probability estimate that indicates the perceived likelihood that the proposed policy will result in a given outcome. For example,

Cleaning up Lake X will make it possible to swim in the lake.

likely ____ ____ ____ ____ ____ ____ ____ unlikely

Each evaluation and each belief strength is scored from -3 (worthless, unlikely) to +3 (valuable, likely), and the product of the two scores is computed. As shown in Equation 1, the sum of these products over all salient beliefs provides an estimate of the attitude toward the policy. Further, it is possible to sum separately the products of positive and negative beliefs. The former sum can serve as a measure of the policy's perceived benefits, the latter of its perceived costs.

Thus far, we have considered only the problem of assessing attitudes toward one policy at a time. We can, however, use the same methods to compare attitudes associated with different policies, irrespective of whether they involve market or nonmarket goods. For example, we could elicit modal salient beliefs about cleaning up Lake X and about building a highway in the same general area. We could then construct appropriate questionnaires to assess belief strength and outcome evaluations with respect to the two sets of beliefs and compute estimates of attitudes toward the two policies. Comparison of these attitudes might show a clear preference for one policy over the other.

We could, of course, also assess the two attitudes directly (by means of two short semantic differentials) or simply ask for preference ratings between the two policies. However, the indirect method has several advantages. As noted earlier, the indirect method is preferable because it permits a better exploration of the attitudinal domain. Moreover, by eliciting beliefs salient in the population, we obtain a description of the considerations that, according to theory, *determine* the attitudes in question. Finally, and perhaps most importantly, by assessing specific beliefs, we can separate perceived benefits of a policy from its perceived costs, thus enabling a cost-benefit analysis.

Outlines of a Procedure

A useful valuation procedure must permit direct comparison of the utilities and disutilities people associate with different policies. Even with the belief-based measure of attitudes, it is sometimes difficult to make this comparison because the modal beliefs elicited with respect to one policy are apt to be quite different from those elicited with respect to another policy.

The solution to this problem lies in the development of a modal set of salient beliefs that is general enough to be applicable to all kinds of policies, or at least to those policies that are to be compared. A possible approach at the most general level is suggested by Rokeach's (1970, 1973) work on human values. Through content analyses of responses provided by the participants in his extensive research program, Rokeach has constructed the following list of 18 "terminal values":

A comfortable life	An exciting life
A sense of accomplishment	A world at peace
A world of beauty	Equality
Family security	Freedom
Happiness	Inner harmony
Mature love	National security
Pleasure	Salvation
Self-respect	Social recognition
True friendship	Wisdom

These 18 values could be considered a set of salient outcomes for any policy. Thus, respondents could be asked to evaluate "a comfortable life," "a world of beauty," "a sense of accomplishment," etc., and to indicate the likelihood that various policies (e.g., building a dam, reserving land for a park, cleaning up a lake, etc.) would help or hinder attainment of these outcomes. If a policy helps attainment of some terminal value, it is counted as a benefit; when it hinders attainment of a value, it is counted as a cost. For some purposes, however, Rokeach's terminal values may represent too general a set of beliefs; they may miss many of the important considerations that enter into comparisons of particular policy alternatives. In those instances, it would be necessary to construct a general set of salient beliefs appropriate for the comparisons that are to be made. For example, if the different policies all involve alternative uses of the same public land, we could, in a pilot study, elicit beliefs about each proposed use. The final set of modal salient beliefs would include all frequently mentioned outcomes, and especially those common to the alternative policies. In either case, the summed belief by evaluation products for each policy is taken as a measure of the policy's psychological value. In this manner, it becomes possible to compare the costs and benefits of a given policy as well as the relative values of different policies within a given population. It is also possible to compare various subpopulations in terms of the values they place on different policies.

SUMMARY AND CONCLUSIONS

In this paper, we discussed some of the problems associated with the contingent value method. Among other things, we argued against the equation of willingness to pay, no matter how ascertained, with psychological or social benefits. Willingness to pay is a relatively narrow, economic measure of value that does not do justice to the broad costs and benefits that may be associated with a public good. Based on a theory of attitudes and behavior, we showed that the psychological value of any good, whether traded in the marketplace or not, is influenced by considerations that may differ greatly from the kinds of beliefs associated with willingness to pay or to accept compensation. Further, due to differences in underlying beliefs, it is important to distinguish between attitudes toward a good itself, attitudes toward performing some behavior in relation to the good (such as paying money for it or accepting compensation for loss of the good), and toward a policy designed to produce a change with respect to the good in question.

Based on considerations related to attitude theory and measurement, we outlined a possible approach to the assessment of psychological value. This procedure relies on an expectancy-value model and estimates attitudes toward a policy or a public good by means of a set of beliefs salient in the population of interest. The overall attitude is considered a measure of the good's value, while subsets of beliefs concerning the good's perceived advantages and disadvantages can be used to obtain estimates of benefits and cost, respectively.

Comparison of goods in terms of attitudes or subjective evaluations, while advantageous in some respects, is not without its problems. Like contingent valuation, attitude measurement is subject to various response biases. Although an indirect procedure that infers attitudes from perceived advantages and disadvantages is perhaps less subject to such biases than the more direct contingent valuation method, the possibility of hypothetical, strategic, and social desirability biases cannot be ruled out and must be taken into consideration.

The critical drawback of the attitude-based valuation method, however, is the mirror image of the problem associated with the contingent valuation method. While the latter is problematic as a measure of a good's psychological or social benefits, the former cannot easily be used to assess the good's costs in monetary terms. It is difficult if not impossible to assess attitudes toward various amounts of money (costs), attitudes that could then be compared with attitudes (values) associated with public goods. Attitudes toward money or toward spending money in the abstract are rather meaningless. They can be assessed only in a specific context (e.g., spending $30 for a hunting license). However, such a measure would be similar to an indication of willingness to pay, which is the basis for the contingent valuation method. Little is to be gained by assessing attitudes toward paying for a good instead of intentions to do so.

In sum, attitudinal estimates of a public good's value are relatively general in nature, capturing the rich variety of costs and benefits associated with the good. They are useless, however, when monetary estimates of costs and benefits are essential. On the other hand, the contingent valuation method, or any other method designed to estimate a public good's monetary value, tends to yield a rather narrow measure of value that fails to reflect many important psychological costs and benefits. In fact, when misused, it may give us, in Oscar Wilde's words: "the price of everything and the value of nothing." When properly applied, however, the contingent value method and attitudinal assessments of value complement each other by examining different aspects of a public good's costs and benefits.

References

Ajzen, I. (1971). Attitudinal vs. normative messages: An investigation of the differential effects of persuasive communications on behavior. *Sociometry, 34,* 263-280.

Ajzen, I. (1982). On behaving in accordance with one's attitudes. In M. P. Zanna, E. T. Higgins, & C. P. Herman (Eds.), *Consistency in social behavior: The Ontario Symposium* (Vol. 2) (pp. 3-15). Hillsdale, NJ: Erlbaum.

Ajzen, I. (1985). From intentions to actions: A theory of planned behavior. In J. Kuhl & J. Beckman (Eds.), *Action-control: From cognition to behavior* (pp. 11-39). Heidelberg: Springer-Verlag.

Ajzen, I., & Fishbein, M. (1977). Attitude-behavior relations: A theoretical analysis and review of empirical research. *Psychological Bulletin, 84,* 888-918.

Ajzen, I., & Fishbein, M. (1980). *Understanding attitudes and predicting social behavior.* Englewood-Cliffs, NJ: Prentice-Hall.

Ajzen, I., Timko, C., & White, J. B. (1982). Self-monitoring and the attitude-behavior relation. *Journal of Personality and Social Psychology, 42,* 426-435.

Allport, G. W. (1954). The historical background of modern social psychology. In G. Lindzey (Ed.), *Handbook of social psychology* (Vol. 1) (pp. 3-56). Cambridge, MA: Addison-Wesley.

Bagozzi, R. P. (1978). The construct validity of the affective, behavioral, and cognitive components of attitude by analysis of covariance structures. *Multivariate Behavioral Research, 13,* 9-31.

Bagozzi, R. P., & Burnkrant, R. E. (1985). Attitude organization and the attitude-behavior relation: A reply to Dillon and Kumar. *Journal of Personality and Social Psychology, 49,* 47-57.

Bem, D. J. (1970). *Beliefs, attitudes and human affairs.* Belmont, CA: Brooks/Cole.

Breckler, S. J. (1984). Empirical validation of affect, behavior, and cognition as distinct components of attitude. *Journal of Personality and Social Psychology, 47,* 1191-1205.

Bumpass, L., & Westoff, C. (1969). *The later years of child bearing.* Princeton, NJ: Princeton University Press.

Cacioppo, J. T., Petty, R. E., Losch, M. E., & Kim, H. S. (1986). Electromyographic activity over facial muscle regions can differentiate the valence and intensity of affective reactions. *Journal of Personality and Social Psychology, 50,* 260-268.

Cummings, R. G., Brookshire, D. S., & Schulze, W. D. (1984). *Valuing public goods: An assessment of the contingent valuation method* (EPA Contract #CR-81107-01-0). Unpublished Manuscript, U. S. Environmental Protection Agency, Washington, DC.

Davis, R. (1963). Recreation planning as an economic problem. *National Resources Journal, 3,* 239-249.

Dillon, W. R., & Kumar, A. (1985). Attitude organization and the attitude-behavior relation: A critique of Bagozzi and Burnkrant's re-analysis of Fishbein and Ajzen. *Journal of Personality and Social Psychology, 49,* 33-46.

Edwards, A. L. (1957). *Techniques of attitude scale construction.* New York: Appleton-Century-Crofts.

Feather, N. T. (1959). Subjective probability and decision under uncertainty. *Psychological Review, 66,* 150-164.

Fishbein, M. (1967). A consideration of beliefs and their role in attitude measurement. In M. Fishbein (Ed.), *Readings in attitude theory and measurement* (pp. 257-266). New York: John Wiley & Sons.

Fishbein, M., & Ajzen, I. (1975). *Belief, attitude, intention, and behavior: An introduction to theory and research.* Reading, MA: Addison-Wesley.

Foa, U. G. (1958). The contiguity principle in the structure of interpersonal relations. *Human Relations, 11,* 229-238.

Green, B. F. (1954). Attitude measurement. In G. Lindzey (Ed.), *Handbook of social psychology* (Vol. 1) (pp. 335-369). Reading, MA: Addison-Wesley.

Guttman, L. (1957). Introduction to facet design and analysis. In *Proceedings of the Fifteenth International Congress of Psychology, Brussels* (pp. 130-132). Amsterdam: North-Holland Publishing Co.

Hilgard, E. R. (1980). The trilogy of mind: Cognition, affection, and conation. *Journal of the History of the Behavioral Sciences, 16,* 107-117.

Hill, R. J. (1981). Attitudes and behavior. In M. Rosenberg & R. H. Turner (Eds.), *Social psychology: Sociological perspectives* (pp. 347-377). New York: Basic Books.

Katz, D., & Stotland, E. (1959). A preliminary statement of a theory of attitude structure and change. In S. Koch (Ed.), *Psychology: A study of a science* (Vol. 3) (pp. 423-475). New York: McGraw-Hill.

Kothandapani, V. (1971). Validation of feeling, belief, and intention to act as three components of attitude and their contribution to prediction of contraceptive behavior. *Journal of Personality and Social Psychology, 19,* 321-333.

Likert, R. A. (1932). A technique for the measurement of attitudes. *Archives of Psychology, No. 140.*

Manstead, A. S. R., Proffitt, C., & Smart, J. L. (1983). Predicting and understanding mothers' infant-feeding intentions and behavior: Testing the theory of reasoned action. *Journal of Personality and Social Psychology, 44,* 657-671.

McGuire, W. J. (1969). The nature of attitudes and attitude change. In G. Lindzey & E. Aronson (Eds.), *The handbook of social psychology (Vol. 3) (2nd ed.) (pp. 136-314). Reading, MA: Addison-Wesley.*

Olweus, D. (1980). The consistency issue in personality psychology revisited--with special reference to aggression. *British Journal of Social and Clinical Psychology, 19,* 377-390.

Osgood, C. E., Suci, G. J., & Tannenbaum, P. H. (1957). *The measurement of meaning.* Urbana, IL: University of Illinois Press.

Oskamp, S. (1977). *Attitudes and opinions.* Englewood-Cliffs, NJ: Prentice-Hall.

Ostrom, T. M. (1969). The relationship between the affective, behavioral, and cognitive components of attitude. *Journal of Experimental Social Psychology, 5,* 12-30.

Randall, A. (1984). Theoretical bases of non-market benefit estimation. In G. L. Peterson & A. Randall (Eds.), *Valuation of wildlife resource benefits* (pp. 77-88). Boulder, CO: Westview Press.

Rokeach, M. (1970). *Beliefs, attitudes, and values.* San Francisco, CA: Jossey-Bass.

Rokeach, M. (1973). *The nature of human values.* New York: Free Press.

Rosenberg, M. J. (1956). Cognitive structure and attitudinal affect. *Journal of Abnormal and Social Psychology, 53,* 367-372.

Rosenberg, M. J., & Hovland, C. I. (1960). Cognitive, affective, and behavioral components of attitudes. In C. I. Hovland & M. J. Rosenberg (Eds.), *Attitude organization and change* (pp. 1-14). New Haven, CT: Yale University Press.

Schulze, W. D., d'Arge, R., & Brookshire, D. S. (1981). Valuing environmental commodities: Some recent experiments. *Land Economics, 57,* 151-172.

Smetana, J. G., & Adler, N. E. (1980). Fishbein's value x expectancy model: An examination of some assumptions. *Personality and Social Psychology Bulletin, 6,* 89-96.

Smith, M. B. (1947). The personal setting of public opinions: A study of attitudes toward Russia. *Public Opinion Quarterly, 11,* 507-523.

Thurstone, L. L. (1931). The measurement of attitudes. *Journal of Abnormal and Social Psychology, 26,* 249-269.

Footnote

[1]Factor analysis and multidimensional scaling techniques make it possible to separate the total attitude space into subdomains, and to assign a different score to each domain. The overall attitude, however, is measured by the total score.

Ex Ante and Ex Post Valuation Problems: Economic and Psychological Considerations

Paul R. Kleindorfer
Center for Risk and Decision Processes
University of Pennsylvania

Howard Kunreuther
Center for Risk and Decision Processes
University of Pennsylvania

Consider two problems that reflect risks to both individuals and society: (1) failure of individuals to voluntarily buckle seat belts, and (2) opposition by communities to siting a hazardous waste disposal facility in their jurisdiction. These problems have some similarities. They both entail a relatively low probability of an accident that may cause fatalities or serious health effects. Both technologies also produce benefits to society. The automobile enables one to achieve mobility; hazardous waste is a by-product of productive activities by industry.

These two problems are also different. Automobile safety is generally viewed as a private good, with limited external costs and benefits to others. The hazardous waste problem has significant externalities and public bad characteristics. For example, a community that hosts an incinerator or landfill absorbs the risks and costs while providing benefits to the region via the industrial output that creates the waste. The automobile is a well-known technology and accidents are a part of life. Hence, little dread or fear of the unknown is associated with car accidents. Furthermore, few people are affected by accidents when they occur. In contrast, a hazardous waste facility is associated with potential negative consequences that instill dread and fear in the minds of residents in the host community. Hazardous waste accidents can also cause severe disruption to a community as illustrated by Love Canal in New York and Times Beach, Missouri.

In this paper we develop a framework for evaluating policies for dealing with both these types of low probability events. In particular, we are interested in integrating actions taken prior to an accident or disaster (i.e., ex ante policies) and those implemented after one occurs (i.e., ex post policies). In evaluating the costs and benefits of these policies, the following issues seem particularly important to address:

1. Many individuals misperceive the probability and consequences of the event. If people feel that the chances of an auto accident are small (''It can't happen to me because I am a far better driver than the average driver'') (Svenson, 1981), then they may not be interested in incurring the small cost and potential inconvenience of safety measures such as wearing a seat belt. Similarly, community residents are often alarmed at the potential consequences of a noxious facility even though the scientific evidence may suggest that the dangers are minimal.

2. Individuals misprocess information. If individuals use simple heuristics to make choices due to the complexity of the decisions facing them, then they will not behave in ways predicted by normative theories such as maximization of expected use. Without an understanding of the decision process associated with choice, policymakers may recommend programs that will not work in practice. For example, suppose individuals use a threshold model of choice so that if the perceived probability of an accident is below a given level, they ignore potential consequences in determining whether to voluntarily adopt protective activities. In this case, subsidizing air bags may have little impact on the adoption decision, assuming that the perceived accident probability is below a critical level; thus, the protective activity is not worth considering (Pauly, Kunreuther, & Vaupel, 1984).

3. Individual decision processes interact with institutions. The type of institutional arrangements (real and perceived) surrounding a potential hazard will affect the way individuals deal with valuation issues. For example, if a regional authority announces that one of five communities will be chosen by random lottery as a host site for a noxious facility, then a community's willingness to pay (WTP) for having the site elsewhere and it's willingness to accept (WTA) the site in its backyard will be quite different from those that would result if another institutional arrangement were used (e.g., lowest WTA is chosen as the site and all other site candidates pay their WTA).

4. Individuals are concerned about ex ante decisions as they relate to ex post consequences. For example, residents in a community proposed as a hazardous waste site may not see ex ante compensation as a meaningful solution if they feel that appropriate ex post monitoring and control measures will not be enforced once the site is in place. Attributes such as dread and fear of the unknown may be important aspects of their decision because once the facility is in place, the community has to live with the site and deal with the consequences of an accident. Similarly, drivers considering adopting a protective activity may consider who will pay for the costs of an accident. If they feel they will receive subsidized medical care for hospital expenses, then this may impact their ex ante decision.

5. Individuals may misrepresent their true valuation or behave strategically. In responding to valuation assessment surveys or other policy evaluation measures, individuals may have incentives to behave strategically, not indicating their true valuation of alternative options but rather the maximally self-serving irrefutable valuation. For example, residents of a community may have an incentive to overstate the required compensation to accept a waste facility if they know they can receive almost anything they demand (e.g., because no other sites currently are being considered).

6. Technical and scientific uncertainty make it difficult for individuals and policymakers to establish accurate estimates for many parameters of interest. For example, individuals may have no reasonable basis for estimating health effects from a hazardous waste disposal facility, and experts may disagree on such effects or may simply be unable to assess the complex processes leading from the waste facility to health effects. These uncertainties cloud not only the policy evaluation and choice process but also significantly affect the legitimization of policies. Thus, individuals may exploit the existence of uncertainties to hinder the implementation of the policy or they may require high compensation to still their claimed woes.

Each of these factors play important roles in people's ex ante decisions on what action to take. In this paper we discuss the traditional economic framework for understanding the valuation of benefits of public policy options related to risks, and consider how recent findings from psychology and behavioral economics might affect the valuation of benefits for individuals. We also examine the impact of institutional arrangements on valuation issues, concentrating on the above factors, and present some hypotheses about the level of governmental regulation of risks that is likely to be acceptable. We conclude the paper with suggested research issues connecting valuation and policy analysis.

RISK VALUATION PROBLEMS

We briefly consider the traditional economic framework for dealing with some of the issues raised above (for more details on this framework, see Kleindorfer and Kunreuther [1981]). Consider a benevolent, selfless policymaker who is trying to determine in what ways, if any, the government should intervene in some risk-related activity. The problem confronting the policymaker is to select an action that reflects the values of the society. The traditional theory assumes that each economic agent involved is the best judge of his or her own utility. Therefore, the choice of a socially optimal policy is based on a measure of welfare, which depends only on the utility functions of the actors involved. If we label these actors 1, 2,..., N, a simple measure of welfare would be the aggregate amount of money or willingness to pay (WTP) of these individuals to see a specified public policy alternative enacted, rather than staying with the status quo specifically:

$$B(z) = \sum_i B_i(z),\qquad\qquad [1]$$

where $B_i(z)$ is the WTP of actor i. The standard approach to benefits $B_i(z)$ is the contingent valuation method (CVM) (See Cummings, Brookshire, and Schulze [1985] for a current summary of the theoretical foundations and applications of the CVM approach to the evaluation of public policy involving risk.) This approach elicits $B_i(z)$ through survey methods (Smith, Desvousges, & Freeman, 1985) or through controlled experiments (Brookshire, Coursey, & Schulze, 1985). Individual $B_i(z)$ values are then aggregated and compared to implementation and governance costs to determine a ranking of alternative policies z. The simplest model in which to illustrate the CVM approach assumes that preferences depend on policy options only through their impact on ex post wealth. An example involving the evaluation of two alternative seatbelt policies illustrates this simple case.

The policies of interest are voluntary seatbelt usage (z_0) versus a law requiring mandatory use of seatbelts with fines for noncompliance (z_1). Figure 1 depicts a simple decision tree for this problem for an individual with wealth W where losses are measured in dollar values. If the individual buckles up (x=1) then his loss should there be an accident (L(1)) is less than if he does not wear a seatbelt (x=0) and has an accident (L(0)). He incurs a cost C(1) for buckling up. However, he stands a chance of a fine F if he does not wear a seatbelt and is stopped by a policeman (with probability q) while driving. For each policy (z_0 or z_1) the rational individual would choose the optimal x (1 or 0) by comparing the expected utility of the respective branches in this decision tree.

The resulting optimal expected utility is denoted by $E[U(z_i)]$ for each policy zi. By the nature of these policies, it is clear that $E[U(z_0)] > E[U(z_1)]$ for rational individuals because they can freely choose whether to buckle up or not under policy z_0 but

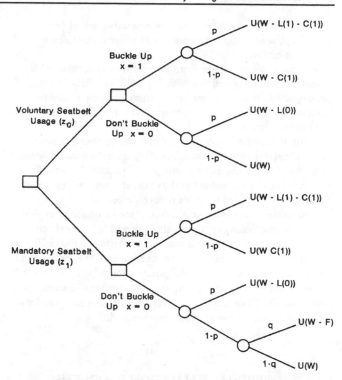

FIGURE 1. Decision tree for consumer's decision to wear seat belt based on two alternative policies.

they are coerced (by fine) to do so under policy z_1. Let $B_i(z_0,z_1)$ represent the difference in expected use between implementing policy z_0 instead of z_1. $B_i(z_0,z_1) > 0$ and is precisely the WTP that individual i would pay to reinstall the policy z_0 if the policy z_1 were established. Alternatively, the same rational individual would be willing to see z_1 implemented if he were given a payment $B_i(z_0,z_1)$, his WTA, or if he felt that he would receive some special benefit (i.e., no threat of a fine) if forced to buckle up. Finally, by summing across individuals, one obtains the total social benefits of sticking with the status quo, as in Equation 1 above.

One can argue with the above type of analysis on several counts. First, the additive form of welfare analysis (simply summing WTA or WTP values) is only valid under restrictive conditions (see Crew & Kleindorfer, 1986). More importantly for our purposes here, this analysis assumes that individuals are well-informed and rational. In particular, they know all relevant probabilities and losses. However, as we indicated in the introduction, growing evidence indicates that many individuals and firms are neither well-informed nor rational. Therefore, it seems important to inquire how departures from these assumptions might influence the analysis and conclusions of this theory and what the implications of these findings are for regulatory policies. Several implications are immediate in this regard.

First, consumer and industry behavioral responses to particular policies will change if their decision processes or perceptions change. Because benefits, B, are evaluated on the basis of expected behavior, we see that such process changes have implications for the outcome of policy analysis. For example, if many individuals underestimate the chances of certain low probability events, they may not take voluntary protective action (e.g., buckle up) where objective data would suggest this to be an attractive option.

Second, if consumers or firms are misinformed, reasonable objections can be raised to evaluating policies solely in terms of the expected utility as expressed by these consumers and firms. That is, some form of regulation may be called for to counteract misinformation.

Third, if actors misperceive probabilities or consequences of uncertain states (usually optimistically), then the general public may object to the socially optimal policy ex ante. However, victims may object (and collect) ex post if a nonoptimal policy leads to unanticipated negative consequences.

With these considerations in mind, it seems useful to explore several recent findings from psychology and behavioral economics relating to possible biases and heuristics, which individuals may use in processing information and choosing individual actions in response to public policy alternatives. Our special interest here is in understanding the consequences of such biases and heuristics from responses to valuation/elicitation questions associated with contingent valuation methods.

INDIVIDUAL VALUATION PROBLEMS

When individuals either misperceive risks or use decision rules that differ from expected utility maximization, then ex ante behavior by individuals may not conform to the predictions by policymakers. We first present an example of how misperception of probability affects standard welfare analysis and then examine alternative strategies for dealing with alternative choice rules.

Misperception of Probability and Outcomes

Considerable evidence from controlled laboratory experiments indicates that individuals use a wide variety of heuristics and exhibit systematic biases in estimating probabilities (Kahneman, Slovic, & Tversky, 1982). To illustrate the effect of ex ante misperceptions of risk on public policy strategies, consider the problem discussed by Kleindorfer and Kunreuther (1981) of evaluating whether a passive restraint feature such as an air bag should be required as standard equipment for all new automobiles.

Suppose that the welfare measure of interest is the expected number of fatalities per year (Table 1). For each of the two alternatives (mandatory versus optional installation of air bags), we tabulated the welfare consequences of different informational patterns (evaluating welfare by using the behavior of the average consumer). For ease of exposition, we neglected the automobile industry in this analysis and assumed that all consumers shared the same (mis)information.

When consumers evaluate the probability of a dangerous accident as $p = 0.001$, they will behave (i.e., they will drive and use active safety restraints) in such a way that estimated fatali-

TABLE 1   Illustration of Welfare Analysis When Actions Are Misinformed

	Consumer's information or beliefs (W_E)		Actual information (W_F)	
	$p^a = 0.001$	$p^a = 0.002$	$p^a = 0.001$	$p^a = 0.002$
Air bags mandatory				
Actual $p = 0.001$	9	9	9	20
Actual $p = 0.002$	15	15	8	15
Air bags optional				
Actual $p = 0.001$	15	15	15	33
Actual $p = 0.002$	25	25	12	25

$^a p$ = consumer's estimated probability of a dangerous accident (per auto/per year).

ties per year (in thousands) will be $W_E = 9$ (Table 1). Suppose, however, that consumers estimate the probability of a dangerous accident to be $p = 0.001$ when in reality $p = 0.002$. In this case consumers' estimates of fatalities remain at $W_E = 9$ while the actual figure has now increased to $W_F = 20$.

We may ask what action a policymaker should take here. To make matters simple, we assume that the policymaker knows that $p = 0.002$ and that actual $p = .001$. Then from Table 1 the following welfare measures are relevant for policy choice: (1) if air bags are mandatory, $W_E = 9$ and $W_F = 20$; and (2) if air bags are optional, $W_E = 15$ and $W_F = 33$.

The consumers estimated that 6,000 lives will be saved per year if air bags are mandatory whereas, in fact, 13,000 will be saved. At an add-on price of, say $100, citizens might be willing to make air bags mandatory, if they knew and believed the actual fatality figures, but they might be opposed to such action in its current, misinformed state. In this instance, the policymaker would have to determine how much weight to give to consumers' perceptions and how much to give to their knowledge in deciding whether to push for mandatory installation of air bags or not. If the policymaker is also uncertain about fatality figures (or if these are disputed by various experts), then legitimization of a policy contrary to consumers' (possibly misperceived) optimal policy would clearly be difficult.

Alternative Choice Models

Suppose that individuals do not take protective action (e.g., do not wear a seat belt) because they use a threshold model of choice and hence tune out the potential consequences. In this case, the alternatives facing the policymaker are either to increase the perceived probability of a severe accident so that it is above the threshold or to rely on incentive or regulatory mechanisms for forcing the person to pay attention to the potential consequences for imposing the protective mechanism on the individual (e.g., requiring air bags in all automobiles). Similarly, suppose individuals are concerned with other attributes aside from the impact of risk on wealth levels when making their choices. Then, either the analyst/policymaker has to address the multi-attribute nature of risk directly by providing better information or modify strategies through incentive systems so that the problem is framed in a way that monetary outcomes are of central importance.

Providing Better Information

Recent survey techniques used by Smith et al. (1985) for hazardous waste risks have introduced the concept of a risk ladder to alleviate the information processing problem. Using this concept, individuals are asked to make comparative risk judgments with events such as risk of dying from cigarette smoking or an airplane crash. The implicit assumption is that "dying" is characterized by a single attribute and that individuals can more easily specify WTP by dealing with more familiar hazards than without using this type of reference point.

We know from the psychometric studies of risk perception (Slovic, Fischhoff, & Lichtenstein, 1979) that many dimensions are associated with specific hazards so that comparisons of the chances of dying from two different events may mask the underlying factors (e.g., fear and unknown risks) that influence attitude toward a potential hazard. Considerably more research needs to be undertaken to link WTP to the different dimensions of risk that psychometric studies have uncovered. Hence, there may be problems in interpreting WTP.

The time frame in which probabilities are presented may also influence an individual's WTP. The expected utility model assumes that individuals will behave the same whether information is presented on the probability of a disaster on a per year or per auto trip basis or over some longer time dimension. Consider automobile accidents for an individual driver. The chance of being killed on any trip is 0.000003; suffering a disabling injury is 0.00001. However, if one calculated the probability of being killed in 50 years of driving, the figure increases to 0.01 and the probability of experiencing at least one disabling injury increases to 0.33. Slovic, Fischhoff, and Lichtenstein (1978) used these figures in controlled laboratory experiments to determine whether or not behavior would be influenced by a change in the time perspective. They found that individuals given lifetime probabilities responded more favorably to the use of seat belts and air bags than people exposed to trip by trip statistics. This behavior would be consistent with a threshold model of choice if the critical probability level above which individuals paid attention was independent of time.

Incentive Systems

Dread or other aspects of cognitive stress may cause people to avoid thinking about risks (Loewenstein, 1986). This may have no effect (other than reducing their anxiety level) if they need not take an action to reduce the probability or consequences of the risk. This would be the situation confronting a resident after the siting of a waste facility in the community, to the extent that the community had competent monitoring and control procedures (e.g., for water quality). If, however, individuals do not think carefully about risks and safety options ex ante, they will likely undertake suboptimal levels of protective activity. In these cases, contingent valuation methods will be dealing with individuals who do not wish to think about the risk in question. Here, it may be useful to develop incentive systems to motivate individuals to reframe the problem so that they perceive the potential benefits of certain actions. A few examples of such incentive systems for protective activities follows:

1. A reward system could be used. For example, suppose that all individuals observed to wear seat belts when coming to work are given an opportunity to enter a lottery with a prize of a given probability r and gain G. Those individuals who treat the chances of an accident as if it were zero would base their decision on whether to adopt protection by comparing use of the seatbelt:

$$rU(W+G-C) + (1-r)U(W-C), \qquad [2]$$

and nonuse of seatbelt:

$$U(W), \qquad [3]$$

where C is the cost of buckling up and W is wealth. Recent experience with reward systems suggest that they may help increase the use of seatbelts (Geller, 1984). Similar rewards have been helpful in stimulating the adoption of preventive health measures. For example, employees at the Speedcall Corporation received an extra $7 per week if they did not smoke on the job. Within a month of the program's initiation, the percentage of employees smoking fell from 67% to 43%. At the last assessment, the percentage smoking had been reduced to 20% (Warner & Murt, 1984).

2. One possible way of encouraging individuals to purchase automobiles with automatic seatbelts or airbags is to provide a reduction in (or partial refund of) their insurance premiums due to a reduced expected cost of medical care from car accidents. Nationwide Insurance Co. has estimated that the reduction in insurance premiums for the use of automatic seatbelts would be $19 per year or $130 in present value terms (over the life of the car). Because the average cost of an automatic seatbelt has been estimated to be $106, the aggregate savings would be $24 (Nordhaus, 1984).

3. If information campaigns and positive incentive systems are not successful, then some type of fine or penalty could be instituted, as in many states today for the mandatory seatbelt case. In the past, these programs have been resisted in the United States, but have met with considerable success in other countries. Robertson (1978) reported that between 50% and 80% of passengers and driver buckled up as a result of this legislation. One exception was Puerto Rico, which introduced a $10 to $25 fine in 1974. The seatbelt usage rate there was approximately the same as it was before the law, possibly due to limited enforcement and the relatively low fines.

Multi-Attribute Valuation Problems

If individuals are worried about specific types of risks due to factors such as dread and fear of the unknown, then some attention should be paid to addressing these concerns. Initially, it is important to determine what factors are important to different stakeholders with respect to a given hazard. This can be done either through a psychometric analysis (Slovic et al., 1979) and/or a value tree analysis (von Winterfeldt, 1987) whereby individuals indicate what their principal concerns are with respect to a given hazard.

Once the factors important to individuals are clearly understood, strategies can be designed to deal with these attributes. For example, if residents of a community are concerned with the safety of a disposal facility, once it is in operation, then specific regulations and monitoring procedures may have to be implemented as part of the siting process. If individuals dread the consequences of automobile accidents so that they prefer not to watch ads that graphically paint the consequences of not wearing a seat belt, then this information strategy may not achieve its desired effects (Robertson, 1978). This latter example illustrates the complexity in dealing with appropriate policies and the relevant multi-attribute use functions of consumers. People may tune out certain messages that raise a set of concerns that they prefer not to think about for reasons of cognitive dissonance (Akerlof & Dickens, 1982).

VALUATION ISSUES: INSTITUTIONAL PERSPECTIVES

Decision processes of boundedly rational individuals can lead to misperceptions of risk and simplified decision rules. These, coupled with such attributes as dread and regret, lead to difficult and complex valuation problems at the individual level. Additional problems in benefits valuation are caused by institutional arrangements.

Institutional arrangements are organizations, information channels, and dispute resolution mechanisms used for planning, implementing, and controlling transactions related to a particular risk. It should be evident that these arrangements will influence how people think about risks and, therefore, how they respond to valuation questions. For example, if people believe they will receive government relief in the event of a flood, they may locate their house in a flood plain (Kunreuther et al., 1978). Similarly, if mandatory seatbelt laws are strictly enforced and fines are levied for violators, one would expect significantly higher seatbelt usage than if some other institutional arrangements were in place.

More generally, when considering their choices of protective activity in the face of risks, individuals and firms consider both the ex ante cost to them of such choices as well as the ex post consequences in terms of the risk itself. These consequences are themselves conditioned by the institutional arrangements in place or which the individual or firm believes will be in place. Thus, actual and perceived institutional arrangements will affect the perceived ex post consequences, which individuals use as

TABLE 2 Stakeholder/Strategy Matrix for Siting a Hazardous Waste Facility

Stakeholder	Stage 1: Locating the site — Monetary or in-kind compensation	Stage 2: Living with the site — Compensation for property value decreases	Stage 2: Living with the site — Environmental regulation	Stage 3: Accident — Insurance and ex post compensation
Host community	x	x	x	x
Other communities	x			
Developer	x	x		
Waste generator	x			x
State siting authority	x		x	
Federal government agencies (e.g., EPA)			x	x
Insurance industry				x

one element in their evaluation of policy and choice options. To make these points more specifically, consider the hazardous waste siting problem.

We can imagine three stages in the life of a hazardous waste facility. In Stage 1, the facility is planned and built. In Stage 2, the residents of a community must live with the facility. In Stage 3, a possible accident might occur. We show these three stages and likely institutional arrangements (marked with an X in Table 2) for compensating the host community for the disamenities it suffers from hosting the facility.

In Stage 1, a bidding mechanism or other benefits assessment mechanisms (Kunreuther, Kleindorfer, Knez, & Yaksick, in press) are used to determine ex ante compensation required to assist the community in its planning processes and to begin to compensate the community for increased direct and indirect costs associated with hosting the community (e.g., for increased fire, policy, and emergency response measures). In Stage 2, gross receipts taxes collected on a per ton basis would provide continuing compensation to maintain the required infrastructure to partially compensate for increased dread and anxiety, which the facility might cause community residents, and to provide compensation for resulting property value decreases. In Stage 3, insurance and other relief (e.g., medical surveillance) might be provided in the event of an accident at the facility.

Table 2 just considers the policy instruments related to compensation. An entirely analogous table could be drawn up for policy instruments related to monitoring and control of safety of the facility. Another table could also illustrate access to information on the operations and safety of the facility by community residents. Each of these tables would provide a detailed picture of some attribute of potential interest and value to community residents. Table 2, of course, relates to the wealth dimension. Other value dimensions might include "sense of control," "dread risk," and "unknown risk." These complex value dimensions, taken together, might provide a reasonable picture of the overall value assessment of a resident to the prospect of having such a facility in the community.

Now imagine residents being asked (as is presently being done in New Jersey, Massachusetts, and Ontario) how much compensation they would require as a host community to have the facility in their backyard. Neglecting misrepresentation issues for the moment, the community's response clearly will depend on their perception and valuation of the consequences for the quality of their lives in each of the stages listed above. Moreover, these consequences clearly depend on the institutions in place to assure compensation and safety of the facility over the course of its life.

One implication of this claimed institutional relativism of valuation assessments is that one must understand what respondents to valuation studies are assuming will be institutions in place to effect the consequences of their choices. Suppose, for example, residents of a potential host community consider the above complex three-stage scenario when asked what their willingness to accept (WTA) payment would be for a facility. Suppose further that residents only consider avoided infrastructure (or other ex ante) costs when asked what their willingness to pay (WTP) would be to have the facility located elsewhere. Under these circumstances, it would be little wonder if WTP were significantly less that WTA. The reason would not be the typically advanced rationale (see Smith et al., 1985) of shifting reference points or other utility-shaped arguments, but rather simply the result of alternative considerations by individuals in responding to the WTA and WTP questions.

If perceived institutions are important, as claimed above, it might be useful to consider a strategy of attempting to have everyone accurately anticipate the actual institutions that will be in place for dealing with a risk. For example, following Kydland and Prescott (1977), one would like potential homeowners to believe that the government will not pay disaster relief to them if they locate their homes in the flood plain. However, when a flood or disaster does occur, the government has in fact provided such relief in the past. Thus, individuals might realistically anticipate such relief, whatever the government may claim to the contrary ex ante.

The key questions in the risk area are who decides on the level and location of the risky activity, who pays in the event of specific problems, and on the basis of whose information are these first two issues carried out? If society decides ex ante (i.e., public policymakers do the deciding), then a kind of free-riding takes over with respect to who has the responsibility for the risk should anything go wrong. The key would seem to be to decide simultaneously ex ante and ex post compensation and control methods, and as Kydland and Prescott (1977) argue, to have ex ante decisions adhered to ex post. However, this forced linking of ex ante and ex post valuations and obligations does not always work in practice. The reasons are reminiscent of those in the transactions cost literature on the infeasibility of neoclassical contracting (Williamson, 1985).

A perfect contract between society and its individual citizens for regulating a risk would describe exactly all of the above issues and the contingent responsibilities of each party for all conceivable events. This is clearly an impossibility. Most risks are just too complicated to understand, plan for, and arrange contingent responsibilities. As a result, individuals tune out specific risks and leave these up to regulators to control. Rather than a risk-specific contract being written, we rely on general adjudication processes, both ex ante and ex post, to deal with a wide range of contingent responsibilities. That is, we operate much more in the sense of an administered contract framework (Goldberg, 1976) whereby regulators and the judiciary deal with a few specific issues at a time ex post rather than with a risk-specific neoclassical contract spelled out ex ante. This administered contract approach probably encourages rent seeking ex post, and it also likely does not encourage informed consent or action ex ante. In some areas, however, it may be the best we can do to provide reasonable governance modes for a wide variety of diverse risks, while leaving citizens with a sense of "perceived institutional reality," which has a chance of dealing with the complexities of our risky society.

Nonetheless, this discussion raises the question as to whether some areas of risk are sufficiently important so that some (perhaps imperfect) contract linking ex ante and ex post behavior is advisable to motivate individuals and firms to inform themselves and to take efficient steps ex ante in anticipation of ex post consequences.

IMPLICATIONS FOR RISK REGULATION AND VALUATION

The preceding discussion raises three issues of importance for the valuation and regulation of risk: imperfectly informed consumers, institutional relativism, and social versus private risk bearing.

If individuals are imperfectly uninformed, their valuations and actions will reflect these properties. The resulting imbalance between what individuals believe is best and what an informed policymaker considers best (in their name) presents a fundamental valuation dilemma. This dilemma arises directly from the juxtaposition of consumer sovereignty and the inherent complexity of health and safety risks. Under consumer sovereignty, societal welfare valuations are based on underlying preferences and beliefs of citizens. However, complexity and uncertainty lead to incompletely informed citizens or to citizens' preferences and beliefs that are extremely complex and difficult to assess, interpret, or aggregate for evaluating and legitimating alternative policy options. Policymakers, however, can be informed about the risks associated with particular hazards but may not be knowledgeable about what factors influence individual and firm decisions. The policymaker needs to know these factors and also needs to determine how different policies are likely to affect consumer and firm behavior. The type of regulatory programs that evolve should reflect this understanding.

To illustrate, consider the case of siting a landfill or incinerator in a community. If the policymaker is convinced that the key problem is related to an expected increase in loss of lives from the facility, then some type of compensation proposal might be negotiated so that, for example, the affected community received new health-related facilities that promised to save more lives than would be affected by the disposal facility. If, however, the principal concern by residents was in the unknown risks from the potentially noxious facility, then the compensation package would likely be rejected unless the residents were convinced that they would be able to shut down the facility if it was either poorly operated or creating unanticipated risks.

When asked for value judgments related to risk, citizens make assumptions about the institutions that will determine how various options related to this risk will affect them. Such institutional assumptions form an essential background or reference point for responses to valuation issues. Citizens' perceptions of the legitimacy and ease of implementing various options will likely affect their responses to valuation procedures. Therefore, the institutional background of CVM surveys for risk evaluation must be credible and understandable.

A central question concerning institutional legitimacy is the extent to which governmental intervention is desirable and credible. If such intervention/regulation is not prima facia credible, then the evaluation of alternative regulatory options will not be taken seriously.

The essential point raised here is whether citizens believe that the risk in question is a private or a public "good." The more public the actual risk, the stronger the case for governmental regulation and, arguably, the weaker will be the incentives for citizens to make careful ex ante (private) valuations and choices of protective activity to ameliorate ex post consequences. Given this, it is interesting to consider the level of governmental regulation of risk that might be acceptable as a function of how "public" the risk in question is perceived to be. To analyze this, consider first the following standard hierarchy for increasing "paternalism" or regulatory control in response to social risks:

1. No governmental intervention: individuals are entirely responsible for their own evaluation processes and choices.
2. Information intervention: the government collects and disseminates information to consumers and firms, which is believed to be well informed of the nature of the risk or on ameliorating consequences.
3. Positive incentives: payouts by the government to induce certain behavior (e.g., subsidized flood insurance premiums).
4. Negative incentives: fines or special taxes levied to discourage certain behavior.
5. Formal directives or regulations: laws requiring specific behavior by consumers or firms, frequently coupled with some government ownership of risk management resources.

The issue posed above is the appropriate level of government intervention (i.e., how far down the above ladder to proceed for a given risk). The traditional justification of regulation is to patch up some imperfection in a market economy. The main thrust of our analysis has been on the "demand side" (i.e., misprocessing and nonprocessing of information by individuals and firms). On pure welfare grounds, one would expect that regulation would have an important role to play in correcting such informational imperfections as these. However, the valu-

ation dilemma indicated above is also a regulatory dilemma in that individuals will be reluctant to see strong governmental intervention if they underestimate the risk, and they will be unwilling to accept a risk (however strongly backed by policymakers) if they overestimate the risk.

The following attributes are probably important in determining an acceptable governmental intervention for a given risk:

1. The "dread risk" of individuals affected by the risk (Slovic et al., (1979).
2. The "unknown risk" of individuals affected by the risk (Slovic et al., 1979).
3. Negative externalities involved--the degree to which the results of misprocessing or nonprocessing of information are borne by decisionmakers as opposed to noninvolved others.
4. The intensity of belief of individuals in the correctness of their own actions.
5. The scientific and technical uncertainty associated with the risk.

The general thrust of our (perceived) public goods argument is that the greater the level of the first three factors, the higher the (perceived) benefits of governmental intervention in mitigating the risk and associated externalities. Yet the higher the last two factors are, the more difficult it will be for policymakers to legitimate their actions, to the extent that these run counter to those believed to be correct by the citizenry. To be slightly provocative, but without much more than casual empirical evidence to rely on, we state these points in the form of a few hypotheses:

1. The larger the catastrophic potential and the less perceived control individuals have for a given hazard (both of which increase the hazard's dread risk), the more likely individuals will want to have control ex ante and government relief ex post.

An example of this hypothesis is the area of hazardous waste disposal facilities. As Elliot (1983) pointed out, communities do not simply wish to be compensated for hosting a waste facility, they wish to exercise control and have access to information about the on-going operations of the facility. Arguably, such monitoring and control reduces dread risk to an "acceptable level" where compensation can then be effective. Concerning ex post relief, many examples (e.g., product safety, disaster relief, and environmental regulation) strongly support the notion that individuals believe they have a right to ex post relief if a catastrophe occurs. This, after all, is the purest function of the state in social risk bearing.

2. The more complex a hazard is and the less familiar it is (both of which increase the hazard's unknown risk), the less likely individuals will be to undertake purposeful protective activity ex ante and the more receptive they will be to stronger governmental intervention.

A prime example of this hypothesis is prescription drugs. Because neither consumers nor doctors are in a position to evaluate new products, strong Federal Drug Administration (FDA) regulations are widely viewed as desirable.

3. The higher the impact of misperception by affected individuals on noninvolved third parties (i.e., the higher the negative externalities), the more ready society will be to accept stronger governmental intervention.

Thus, society is willing to have government play only an informational role with respect to cigarette smoking, yet a much stronger role in dealing with heroin or drunk-driving. These latter problems have strong negative externalities as reflected in drug-related crime and accident victims.

4. The larger the technical and scientific uncertainty associated with a risk (i.e., the higher the "unknown risk"), the weaker will be governmental intervention because of policy legitimization problems.

The above hypotheses are admittedly only conjectural. Our primary reason for stating them is to highlight the complex relationships between the problems of valuation, regulatory institutions, and public acceptability of risks and risk regulating institutions. From the point of view of policy valuation via methods like CVM, implications of this analysis include reference points, acceptable risks, and compensable risks.

A clear institutional and understandable personal reference point like the status quo must be established for respondents. This reference point should embody credible institutions and understandable consequences for the respondent as a function of policy options. An example of such a reference point is a specific and understandable standard for water quality established by the U.S. Environmental Protection Agency (EPA) based on risk assessments on carcinogenicity.

The characteristics of regulatory intervention, policy options, and (perceived) residual risks that are conceivably acceptable to a group of affected citizens must first be determined. Only in this range of conceivable acceptability can valuation questions be meaningfully answered.

Within the range of acceptable risk and risk management institutions, compensation and valuation can play an important role in selecting efficient risk management options, communicating and legitimating these to the public, and gaining their implementation.

In any such acceptability and valuation analysis, valuation of risks must be much broader-based than the traditional contingent valuation approach that relies on monetary equivalents of expected use. The growing body of evidence cited in this paper suggests that risks are multi-attribute in nature. A more detailed evaluation of these multiple "risk" attributes than has been traditionally undertaken by economists is desirable for several reasons.

For policy evaluation, it is important to know what level of dread and unknown risk is associated with a hazard. This is not just to determine individuals' reactions to hazards. It is also crucial in designing policies to deal with such risks. Compensation may not be the appropriate policy instrument to deal with either dread or unknown risk. Increased monitoring and control may be the least costly and most effective manner for dealing with these factors.

For motivating individuals to undertake more efficient actions themselves in dealing more effectively with hazards from a societal welfare vantage point, policymakers must understand a good deal more about the decision processes of individuals than is embodied in the standard use theory valuation approach.

Differences in ex ante and ex post valuations of individuals in various population segments will provide key insights to the policymaker on which policies are likely to be implementable prior to a disaster and legitimated after the fact by these groups. Opposition to particular policies may not be an inexorable given. More complete valuation studies of the sort suggested here may lead to finding the right mix of policy instruments based on an understanding of how different segments of the population see the problem.

Similarly, better valuation of risks will allow better communication of policy alternatives (and their intended purpose in serving the public's real interest) to the public. What may be thought of as an intransigent, uninformed public, using a simple monetary valuation approach, may look like a qualitatively different public using a broader valuation approach.

All of this suggests that one of the key research needs in the area of valuing risks and strategies is the development of a usable approach to multi-attribute valuation, which will allow for the traditional monetary attributes, but which also considers such factors as dread, familiarity, complexity, regret, and control. This will not be an easy task, and is also likely to be context dependent because each of the mentioned attributes is itself likely to be a compound attribute of several other properties and factors inherent in a particular risk or hazard. Nonetheless, recent research from psychology and behavioral economics indicates that the development of multi-attribute valuation is a worthwhile challenge, which may provide the basis for improved policy evaluation and design for risks involving health and safety of individuals.

References

Akerlof, G. (1970). The market for lemons: Quality uncertainty and the market mechanism. *Quarterly Journal of Economics, 84,* 488-500.

Akerlof, G., & Dickens, W. T. (1982). The economic consequences of cognitive dissonance. *American Economic Review, 72,* 307-319.

Brookshire, D., Coursey, D., & Schulze, W. (in press). Experiments in the solicitation of private and public values: An overview. In L. Green & J. Kagel (Eds.), *Advances in behavioral economics.*

Crew, M., A., & Kleindorfer, P. R. (1986). *The economics of public utility regulation.* London: MacMillan.

Cummings, R. D., Brookshire, D. S., & Schulze, W. D. (1985). *Valuing public goods.* Totowa, NJ: Rowman & Allanheld.

Elliot, M. (1983). *Coping with conflicting perceptions of risk in hazardous waste facility siting disputes.* Unpublished doctoral dissertation, Massachusetts Institute of Technology, Cambridge, MA.

Geller, E. S. (1984). Motivating safety belt use with incentives: A critical review of the past and a look to the future. *In Advances in belt restraint systems: Design performance and usage* (Report No. 141). Society of Automotive Engineers.

Goldberg, V. P. (1976). Regulation and administered contracts. *Bell Journal of Economics, 7,* 426-448.

Kahneman, D., Slovic, P., & Tversky, A. (1982). *Judgement under uncertainty: Heuristics and biases.* Cambridge: Cambridge University Press.

Kleindorfer, P., & Kunreuther, H. (1981). Descriptive and prescriptive aspects of health and safety regulation. In A. Ferguson & R. Leveen (Eds.), *The benefits of health and safety regulations* (pp. 25-42). Cambridge: Ballinger.

Kleindorfer, P., & Kunreuther, H. (1987). *Insuring and managing hazardous risks: From Seveso to Bhopal and beyond.* Berlin: Springer-Verlag.

Kunreuther, H., Ginsberg, R., Miller, L., Sagi, P, Slovic, P., Borker, B., & Katz, W. (1978). *Disaster insurance protection*. New York: John Wiley & Sons.

Kunreuther, H., Kleindorfer, P. R., Knez, P. J., & Yaksick, R. (in press). The role of compensation for siting noxious facilities: Theory and experimental design. *Journal of Environmental Economics and Management*.

Kydland, F., & Prescott, E. C. (1977). Rules rather than discretion: the inconsistence of optimal plans. *Journal of Political Economy 85*, 473-492.

Loewenstein, G. (1986). *Expectations and risk of intertemporal outcomes*. Unpublished manuscript, Center for Decision Research, University of Chicago, Chicago, IL.

Nordhaus, W. (1984). *Supplementing notice of proposed rule-making on federal motor vehicle safety standards* (Docket No. 74-14, Notice 35, June 13, Reference 10). Occupant Crash Protection. Washington, D.C.

Pauly, M., Kunreuther, H., & Vaupel, J. (1984). Public protection against misperceived risks: Insights from positive political economy. *Public Choice, 43*, 45-64.

Robertson, L. (1978). Automobile seat belt use in selected countries, states and provinces with and without laws requiring seat belt use. *Accident Analysis and Prevention, 10*, 5-10.

Slovic, P., Fischhoff, B., & Lichtenstein, S. (1978). Accident probabilities in seatbelt usage: A psychological perspective. *Accident Analysis and Prevention, 10*, 281-285.

Slovic, P., Fischhoff, B., & Lichtenstein, S. (1979). Rating the risks. *Environment, 21*, 14-20, 36-39.

Smith, K., Desvousges, W. H., & Freeman, A. M., III. (1985). *Valuing changes in hazardous waste risks: A contingent valuation analysis* (Draft Interim Report, 2 vols.). Washington, DC: Environmental Protection Agency.

Svenson, O. (1981). Are we all less risky and more skillful when our fellow drivers are? *Acta Psychologica, 47*, 143-148.

von Winterfeldt, D. (1987). Value tree analysis: An introduction and an application to offshore drilling. In P. Kleindorfer & H. Kunreuther (Eds.), *Insuring and managing hazardous risks: From Seveso to Bhopal and beyond* (pp. 349-376). Berlin: Springer-Verlag.

Warner, K., & Murt, H. (1984). Economic incentives for health. *Annual Review of Public Health, 5*, 107-133.

Williamson, O. E. (1985). Assessing contract. *Journal of Law, Economics and Organization, 1*, 177-208.

Toward Integrated Valuations of Amenity Resources Using Nonverbal Measures

Roger S. Ulrich

Department of Geography

University of Delaware, Newark

The growing interest among economists in placing dollar values on amenity resources is understandable in view of mounting needs and pressures to use benefit-cost assessments with respect to goods not traded in markets. If dollar estimates similar to market prices can be derived for natural amenities and other public goods, these values would have considerable usefulness for justifying programs or budgets, developing and analyzing policies, and efficiently allocating limited investment resources (Kaiser, Brown, & Davis, this volume).

Although the practical advantages of value estimates for public goods are widely recognized, many authors have expressed concern that dollar estimates obtained by methods such as contingent valuation (CV) are often narrow expressions of value, and accordingly may widely miss the mark of representing social benefits (Ajzen & Peterson, this volume; Boulding & Lundstedt, this volume). Also, evidence suggests that if CV methods are applied to hypothetical or unfamiliar situations, where individuals lack experience relevant to assigning meaningful dollar values, then the CV estimates may be biased or lack validity. To alleviate these and other CV problems, several papers in this volume have emphasized the need to employ verbally-based psychological approaches, such as attitudinal questionnaires and preference ratings, in combination with contingent valuation procedures (Ajzen & Peterson; Chestnut; Harris, Tinsley & Donnelly; Schroeder & Dwyer). In this regard, Ajzen and Peterson describe various verbally-based methods for obtaining comparatively broad assessments of the psychological or social value of public goods.

As is evident in this volume, the views of economists and noneconomists tend to differ with respect to the conceptualization of value and methods advocated for measuring value. Despite these differences, a common denominator to both groups is heavy reliance on verbal responses as the basis for value estimates. For instance, in the great majority of CV studies, respondents are asked to indicate verbally their willingness to pay, or their compensation demanded, for a public good or service. (Exceptions to the reliance on verbal data by economists include, for instance, travel cost methods that incorporate trip behavior, and approaches that use simulated markets to evaluate actual payments.) As noted, noneconomists as well as many economists have argued in favor of integrating CV methods with other types of verbally-based procedures (e.g., attitudinal questionnaires) to assess gains and losses more precisely and comprehensively.

In this context, the present paper represents a different direction in its focus on nonverbal procedures for identifying and measuring value. Because of the great variety of nonverbal measurement procedures, many technically complex, a comprehensive survey of methods relevant to amenity resource valuation is beyond the scope of this paper. The discussion will not address the few types of nonverbal indicators already familiar to economists (e.g., certain overt behaviors such as actual payments). Instead, a major objective is to illustrate the usefulness of selected types of nonverbal procedures (behavioral and physiological) by describing examples of research concentrating on natural amenities. Another purpose is to discuss advantages associated with integrating these types of nonverbal methods with verbally-based procedures for assessing both nonmonetary and monetary values. As the research examples will show, nonverbal methods can identify important beneficial conse-

quences that may not be revealed by verbal inquiry and would otherwise remain hidden to researchers and consumers. The position of this paper is that unless consumers or CV respondents are informed concerning these benefits, economic estimates may substantially under-represent social value. Also, as will become evident in the discussion, nonverbal approaches offer possibilities for identifying and measuring beneficial consequences of public goods in terms of data that have scientific credibility and which tend to carry weight in judicial proceedings concerned with social values. In a limited number of instances, certain nonverbal indicators (e.g., relating to health and performance) can be linked to real market prices, thereby avoiding problems potentially associated with CV, and at the same time creating opportunities for evaluating the validity of estimates obtained from CV and other economic valuation methods.

In addition to addressing the valuation of nonmonetary and monetary benefits of public goods, this paper discusses the usefulness of nonverbal methods for assessing *detrimental* consequences associated with perceived environmental risks and stressors. As will be shown, there are strong scientific grounds for concluding that the use of nonverbal procedures in combination with verbal methods is necessary if valid estimates of value are to be obtained for many environmental stressor situations. The need for nonverbal methods arises because individuals exposed to a long-term environmental problem or stressor typically engage in cognitive coping, which often denies or sharply diminishes the problem in their verbally-expressed conscious awareness. Although coping may lower stress and other detrimental consequences expressed in verbal responses (e.g., willingness to pay), higher levels of detrimental impacts can be clearly indicated by nonverbal measures.

The next section advances the position that consumers require information concerning salient benefits or detriments of goods as a basis for assigning meaningful economic values. However, a fundamental obstacle to consumer awareness stems from the fact that researchers have not yet identified beneficial and detrimental consequences of most public goods. Against the background of this very conspicuous research need, the next section overviews a wide range of nonverbal measures that potentially can be used to increase our understanding of the nonmonetary and monetary values of public goods. Two subsequent sections then discuss examples of investigations that use nonverbal methods to identify and measure various benefits of natural amenities. The discussion then shifts to environmental risks and stressors, and the need to integrate nonverbal procedures with verbal methods in order to enhance the validity of nonmonetary and monetary estimates of detrimental consequences. This is followed by a brief overview of limitations of nonverbal procedures. A final section summarizes the main conclusions of the paper.

INFORMATION, CONSUMER AWARENESS, AND MEANINGFUL VALUE ESTIMATES

The amount and types of information available to consumers concerning a particular nonmarket good are major factors affecting whether economic value estimates are meaningful. At one extreme are valuation situations where a contingent valuation respondent has considerable relevant experience and is personally informed concerning salient benefits and other features of the good. If the respondent also has experience in real markets with goods having roughly similar characteristics--and especially, has previous exposure to the same good in a market context--then CV estimates should be similar to market prices. Not surprisingly, evidence indicates that for familiar goods (e.g., pints of strawberries), CV estimates based on hypothetical markets correspond closely to payments actually made in simulated markets.

But validity problems certainly will arise when respondents lack familiarity with a vaguely defined good, and are not provided information by the investigator concerning salient benefits and other characteristics. Estimates may also be biased, for instance, when the commodity is familiar but respondents lack experience with it in a real market. An example of an extreme informational problem would be if respondents knew nothing about a good, thus, lacking a basis for making well-founded value judgements. Yet even with very little information, people can still report meaningless values to investigators, usually on the basis of unconscious judgmental rules or heuristics (Kahneman, Slovic, & Tversky, 1982; Mitchell & Carson, in press). Economists have been justifiably concerned about the risk of obtaining hypothetical value data by asking hypothetical questions about unfamiliar goods (Fisher, McClelland, & Schulze, this volume).

Between the informational extremes of familiar goods and goods unknown to respondents are the great majority of public amenities for which meaningful values are needed for policy decisions--for instance, mountain scenery, a desert panorama, or a river for trout fishing. Certain consumers have considerable first-hand experience with such amenities, whereas most individuals have some familiarity but are not well-informed. For situations where respondents lack awareness, validity considerations strongly imply that the investigator should judiciously provide information to make possible more well-founded value judgements. The provision of information relevant to important characteristics should help respondents/consumers better understand the commodity in their utility functions, and thereby make better decisions regarding willingness to pay. In emphasizing that consumer awareness is a requirement for achieving sound estimates, there is no suggestion here that the investigator should supply a detailed array of information, which could overload the respondent. Considerable research has shown that large amounts of information tend to work against reasoned judgements, perhaps especially in short-term contexts such as CV interviews (Fischhoff, this volume). Also, risks of bias are associated with providing information; for instance, different ways of labeling or presenting material can have significantly different influences on judgements (e.g., "wilderness area" vs. "commercial timber stand", Brown & Slovic, this volume). However, these potential disadvantages appear secondary compared to the major validity problem inherent in a lack of awareness on the part of respondents.

In situations where research has shed light on benefits/detriments of a public good, what subset of this information should be conveyed to uninformed CV respondents? When the good is a tangible setting or environmental aspect that can be experienced

by respondents or other consumers, information priorities should include, among others, effects on physiological well-being, ability to function or work effectively, and health. As later sections of this paper will show, nonverbal procedures are exceptionally suited to investigating these types of consequences. In the case, for instance, of direct physiological or health effects (e.g., blood pressure), information may often influence respondents' "salient beliefs" with respect to a good, and accordingly have important influences on attitudes and values (Ajzen & Peterson, this volume). Health information appears pertinent to a number of the "terminal values," which Rokeach (1973) has advanced as a set of salient, general beliefs. Inclusion of health information seems crucial when effects are potentially pronounced yet are not perceivable by most individuals experiencing the environment. Consider the example of a water feature that appears pristine to an uninformed observer or recreationist, but actually is contaminated by toxic chemicals. Unless this knowledge is conveyed to respondents, CV estimates might markedly overvalue the benefits for users (or not reflect social costs of the pollution). Further, if CV respondents were not informed of the contamination, the value estimates would be vulnerable to challenge in judicial and other decision-making contexts where health effects usually are assigned considerable importance.

Apart from health material, what other types of information should be provided when the investigator is informed about a good but respondents or consumers are not? One approach is to have the public decide through the vehicle of a preliminary survey that precedes the CV phase. An initial survey could be conducted using attitudinal or preference measures to assess psychological values for benefit/detriments identified by previous research. By indicating the relative salience or importance of characteristics of the good, the preliminary survey would enable the investigator to select more objectively a subset of information for presentation in the subsequent CV phase. Characteristics of greatest psychological value would presumably be relevant to making judgements about dollar values. As already noted, the amount of information selected for the CV survey should be limited in quantity to facilitate meaningful comprehension by respondents. The information should be moderately specific but avoid technical jargon (Ajzen & Peterson, this volume; Harris et al., this volume). A full account of the initial survey findings, along with material too technical for inclusion in the CV survey, should be conveyed to decisionmakers with the CV estimates to provide more complete information.

The foregone comments presuppose that investigators themselves have access to knowledge about the beneficial and detrimental characteristics of public goods. Despite progress in some research areas, such as identifying psychological benefits of wilderness recreation activities (Driver & Brown, 1986), the reality is that the benefits of most natural amenities are by no means well understood. Doubtless, numerous important beneficial consequences have not yet been identified, much less measured with precision. In this regard, important positive consequences (e.g., effects on health, capacity to function or work effectively) likely remain outside the conscious awareness of even frequent users of natural amenities. Without greater knowledge available both to investigators and consumers, the informational foundation for assigning values will remain incomplete for most public goods--and in some cases, will be largely nonexistent. A general conclusion that emerges is that advances in achieving sound value estimates will be heavily contingent on progress in research that defines more clearly amenity goods. Among other advantages, this progress would likely lead to increasingly effective applications of CV methods to many public goods, which at present we know little about and are often of greatest concern to decisionmakers. Otherwise, CV may be relegated the reputation of a limited approach that yields meaningful values for already familiar, well-defined goods, which frequently have little importance for policy.

A point basic to this paper is that research approaches that combine nonverbal and verbal methods have excellent potential for defining and measuring consequences of public goods. The next section overviews numerous nonverbal measures applicable to amenity valuation. This is followed by descriptions of research examples that illustrate in greater detail the use of selected nonverbal procedures.

NONVERBAL MEASURES

Categories

In general terms, nonverbal measures fall into two broad categories: *behavioral* and *physiological*. The behavioral category encompasses an extremely wide range of observable or overt actions, which can indicate beneficial or detrimental consequences for individuals or groups of attributes of environments. Examples of behavioral measures include choices made by wilderness users in terms of specific recreational activities or locations, recidivism or rehabilitation rates for delinquent youths as a function of whether they have had a wilderness challenge experience, littering, sleep patterns, alcohol use, frequency and duration of social contacts, attendance rates at workplaces or schools, and incidents of family violence. Most behavioral measures relate to psychological or other nonmonetary gains or losses; however, many behaviors also have monetary relevance (e.g., employee absenteeism), and certain behavioral indicators can be linked rather directly to real prices (e.g., physician office visits). One important subcategory of behavioral measures is termed by psychologists as *performance* indicators. Whereas economists tend to associate "performance" with such behavioral measures as employee productivity, psychologists use the term in reference to levels of functioning (e.g., accuracy, speed, persistence) on a wide variety of tasks requiring attention and cognitive processing (e.g., embedded figures tasks, proofreading). Some performance measures are reliable and sensitive indicators of environmental influences on individuals or groups, especially stressor effects (Glass & Singer, 1972; Hockey, 1983).

The second broad category of nonverbal measures--physiological--is used most frequently by behavioral scientists to record responses or activity levels in four general bodily systems: (1) the electrocortical, (2) autonomic, (3) skeleto-muscular, and (4) neuroendocrine. Measurements of activity in the first three systems are usually made from skin surfaces using electrodes. Prominent measures of electrocortical activity include evoked brain potentials and brain waves (e.g., alpha waves, beta waves). Autonomic system indicators include many useful physiological measures (e.g., blood pressure, heart rate, respiration, electrical conductance/resistance of the skin, pulse wave transit time). Skeleto-muscular system indicators typically involve measurements of muscle tension, which are made by recording the electrical activity of specific muscles. In contrast to electrocortical, autonomic, and skeleto-muscular indicators, the neuroendocrine system involves biochemical measurements of various hormones in blood or urine samples. Although procedures such as obtaining urine samples from subjects may seem to some readers to be invasive methods, these useful indicators are arguably no more invasive than, say, a lengthy contingent valuation interview; further, some physiological measures certainly are less invasive than CV interview methods. (For surveys of physiological measures potentially applicable to outdoor environments see Andreassi [1980], Baum, Fleming, & Singer [1985], and Ulrich [1979a].)

Concerning the applicability of physiological measures to amenity contexts, it should be emphasized that most perceivable changes in an individual's physical surroundings will be expressed in activity levels in one or more physiological systems (Greenfield & Sternbach, 1972). For instance, exposures to different types of landscape scenes have different influences on brain electrical activity, which in turn can be interpreted as comparatively positive or negative consequences (Ulrich, 1981). Physiological measures are exceptionally suited to the study of stressful influences of environments, and to measuring restorative or therapeutic effects of amenity environments on stressed individuals. With respect to stress situations, as well as a wide range of other contexts, data concerning such responses as blood pressure and muscle tension are widely regarded as objective and credible indicators of physiological well-being. Physiological measures also have excellent potential for shedding light, for instance, on the attention-holding properties of different natural amenities, and for distinguishing emotional influences in terms of the arousal or activation dimension (Ulrich, 1979b). Recent advances have greatly expanded the usefulness of physiological methods for assessing positive and negative emotional responses (Dimberg, 1986, 1987; Ohman, in press).

If changes in certain *behaviors* (e.g., cigarette usage) are observed for long periods in individuals or groups, it may prove justified to link the findings to beneficial or detrimental health outcomes. The eventual determination of possible health benefits of natural amenities will require longitudinal studies that monitor physiological and behavioral changes over several months or years. However, direct health impacts of natural amenities can also be investigated using certain short-term research designs, especially if the study groups are comprised of hospital patients or other health care recipients. A later section will describe a research example wherein beneficial health consequences of a natural amenity are identified and measured for a group of hospital patients.

In the case of both general categories of nonverbal measures (behavioral, physiological), it is often advantageous to use the methods in integrated research approaches that include verbal measures. Compared to research designs that use only one type of measure, integrated approaches that obtain data from different response modes yield a wider range of inferences or conclusions, and usually are considerably stronger from the standpoint of validity concerns. Regarding the latter, one important indication of the validity of findings is the extent of convergence or consistency among findings obtained from different types of measures. For instance, an outcome of general convergence among verbal data (e.g., willingness to pay, attitudes) and nonverbal indicators (e.g., behaviors) would imply validity and suggest that the findings warranted confidence. On the other hand, a pronounced lack of consistency across data from different response modes would suggest that the conclusions were suspect and accordingly should be taken with a grain of salt.

Specifying Beneficial Consequences Using Nonverbal Methods

Research Example Illustrating Behavioral Measures of Beneficial Health Influences of a Natural View

This research example illustrates the use of multiple behavioral indicators to identify and measure short-term health consequences of a natural view for hospitalized individuals. Numerous studies have found that when verbally-expressed preferences are compared for urban and unspectacular natural scenes, adult groups in Western societies rather consistently prefer nature. For individuals experiencing stress or anxiety, many natural views--in contrast to urban scenes lacking nature--appear to have therapeutic effects because they apparently elicit positive feelings, reduce fear, hold interest, and might block or reduce stressful thoughts (Ulrich, 1983). Empirical support for this nature restoration effect initially consisted of verbal data from self-report questionnaires (Ulrich, 1979b). To extend this line of research and possibly identify other beneficial consequences of visual exposures to nature, surgical patients in a suburban Pennsylvania hospital were studied to determine whether a bedside window view of nature might be positively related to various nonverbal indicators of recovery and health (Ulrich, 1984). Such patients usually experience considerable stress or anxiety, and their hospital confinement restricts their access to outdoor environments almost entirely to window views. Recovery data were obtained for pairs of patients with the same surgery (cholecystectomy, a common gall bladder operation), who were closely matched for factors such as sex, age, weight, tobacco use, and general medical history. The patients were assigned to rooms that were nearly identical except for the view through the window. One member of each matched pair had a view of a small stand of deciduous trees, whereas the other overlooked a brown brick building wall. A variety of nonverbal (behavioral) health-related information was taken from patient records, including number of days of hospitalization after surgery, number and strength of drug doses taken for pain and anxiety, minor postsurgical complications (e.g., persistent headache and nausea requiring medication), and all nurses' notes about observed psychological indicators and behaviors relevant to a patient's condition.

Comparison of the tree-view and wall-view groups showed that those patients overlooking the natural scene spent significantly less time in the hospital (7.96 days compared with 8.70

TABLE 1 Comparison of Drug Doses Taken for Pain per Patient for Wall-view and Tree-view Groups

| Analgesic strength | Number of Doses Per Patient | | | |
| | Days 0-1[a] | | Days 2-5 | |
	Wall group	Tree group	Wall group	Tree group
Strong	2.56	2.40	2.48	0.96
Moderate	4.00	5.00	3.65	1.74
Weak	0.23	0.30	2.57	5.39

[a]Day 0 was day of surgery; Day 1 was first recovery day. Drug intake figures for days 0-1 were not significantly different between groups, probably because patients were too drugged or too absorbed by intense pain to attend to their windows. For days 2-5, the variation between groups was significant (p < .01). (data from Ulrich, 1984).

days per wall-view patient). Also, the tree-view patients tended to have lower weighted scores for minor postsurgical complications, and had far fewer negative evaluative comments in nurses' notes (e.g., "upset and crying" or "needs much encouragement"). Further, the wall-view patients required many more doses of pain drugs classed as moderate or strong, which included such potent narcotic analgesics as morphine and Dilaudid (Table 1). By contrast, individuals with the view of nature more frequently were given weak analgesics (e.g., Tylenol, aspirin). This combination of nonverbal findings constitutes strong evidence that the view of trees had comparatively therapeutic influences on patients. The pattern of convergence across different behavioral measures with respect to beneficial consequences of the trees conveys greater scientific credibility than could be achieved with the great majority of single measure research designs. The use of multiple measures partly accounts for the apparent widespread acceptance of the findings within the medical profession (Baron, 1986).

Implications for Value Assessment of Research Example Using Behavioral Measures

By and large, positivist scientific investigations attempt to shed in-depth light on a narrow slice of an issue or context; presumably, many research steps over time, coupled with advances in theory development, eventually yield a broad yet accurate picture of understanding. Reflecting this posture, the objective of the hospital study was to evaluate in a scientific manner whether an urban forest amenity was the source of specific beneficial consequences for a narrowly defined population. The study placed higher priority, for instance, on employing a multiple measures design than on achieving a broader assessment of social benefits for the public. At first glance, this research example might seem to have only peripheral relevance for many economists, especially those seeking to provide economic value estimates based on a single measure such as willingness to pay. Closer examination, however, suggests that the methods and findings of the window-view study have several implications for economic value assessment.

From the standpoint of CV applications, the study identifies specific benefits that otherwise would remain unknown to investigators as well as respondents/patients. Some patients have a vague intuitive awareness of responding positively to a "room with a view." Questionnaire-based research has clearly shown that most patients consider an attractive natural window view as very important (Verderber, 1983). However, in the absence of research using nonverbal measures to identify health outcomes, patients could hardly have a well-founded understanding of potential benefits for their health. An attitudinal survey that incorporated information from research using health related nonverbal measures would likely reveal that patients assign high levels of importance to at least some of the potential beneficial health consequences of a natural view. Following the position taken earlier, information about these valued features of the amenity would warrant inclusion in a subsequent CV survey to help form the basis for more informed consumer judgements. Although CV studies would often encounter complications in health care contexts stemming from insurance payments, many respondents/consumers would probably indicate a willingness to pay extra (as they do, for instance, for private versus semiprivate rooms) for such advantages as (1) the possibility of a somewhat shorter hospital stay, (2) less need for potent narcotic painkillers that have several negative side-effects, and (3) the strong likelihood of a less negatively-toned emotional state during recovery. More generally, research using behavioral measures holds considerable promise for enabling CV investigators to take into account, and write specific questions about, a wide range of potentially important beneficial consequences of natural amenities that have not yet been identified or which we know little about.

Apart from implications for CV, the hospital study suggests opportunities for an approach to economic valuation wherein certain health-related behavioral measures could be linked to real prices. Goods and services provided by the health sector typically have prices (e.g., dollar cost figures for occupying different types of hospital rooms, for taking medications, for physician services, etc.). Consumption of priced goods and services can in certain contexts serve as a set of comparatively objective indicators concerning the influences on well-being of amenity resources. For instance, the hospital study found that patients overlooking trees took fewer moderate and strong analgesic injections, but received more tablets of weak pain drugs such as acetaminophen (Table 1). Although charge schedules can vary considerably between hospitals, injections of strong analgesics usually are more expensive than oral doses of weak analgesics. The tree-view group required far fewer of the more costly doses, suggesting a cost-savings benefit for the urban forest amenity.

The prices of the pain drugs are market prices, although they may be distorted by health insurance or government influences. Estimates based on these and other market-like health prices would probably tend to have more credibility in many policy situations that CV generated estimates, but they may not reflect portions of consumer surplus. This approach to economic valuation would not make it possible to link a real price to every benefit comprising the bundle of consequences typically associated with a public good. However, by establishing tenable connections between certain important components of the bundle and real prices, comparatively solid foundation points would be constructed under portions of a broader assessment, tending to reduce the magnitude of overall error. For example, if eight beneficial attributes were identified for a public good, and four could be tied to real prices, leaving four which could be assessed meaningfully by CV or other economic methods, the error variance for the entire bundle might be reduced in most cases. (This example notwithstanding, it is almost certainly the case that many of the real gains in welfare produced by public goods can only be assessed with validity using nonmonetary methods.)

In addition to producing credible monetary value estimates in certain contexts, health-related behavioral measures approaches could prove useful from the standpoint of evaluating other economic valuation methods. By relating specific benefits to real prices, many opportunities could be created for evaluating the validity of estimates generated by CV and other procedures.

As a rough indication of the broader economic implications of the hospital study--offered cautiously by this noneconomist author--it can be noted that in 1987, spending for short-term general hospital care in the United States will exceed $130 *billion* (American Hospital Association, 1986). This huge figure does not include costs for long-term institutions and federal facilities. Expenditures for hospital care are so large, and continue to escalate so rapidly, that even a slight reduction in inpatient days (e.g., a 1-2% reduction) could produce annual savings of several hundred million dollars. The tree-view patients in the study, compared to the wall-view group, spent 8.5% fewer postsurgical days in the hospital. If the findings are shown by other studies to hold for many categories of patients known to experience anxiety, it would appear that large savings in health costs might be achieved if hospitals were designed and sited to provide patients with attractive, therapeutic views of nature. The extremely high dollar costs of medical care also have important implications for an alternative perspective on economic valuation. The approach of linking health measures to market prices could prove useful in estimating credible *lower bound* economic values that could be high for some natural amenities. These tenable lower bound estimates should then be reported to decisionmakers along with findings concerning nonmonetary gains to provide a more comprehensive informational basis for allocation decisions.

Research Example Illustrating Physiological Measures of Stress-Reducing Influences of Natural Amenities

In addition to behavioral indicators, there is a clear need for research on beneficial consequences of public goods that utilizes integrated combinations of verbal and *physiological* measures (e.g., blood pressure, brain electrical activity, muscle tension, neuroendocrine indicators). Physiological measures have been neglected by investigators, and little is known about the beneficial physiological effects of experiences with outdoor settings. As noted earlier, research approaches that combine verbal and physiological (or other nonverbal) measures make possible a wider range of inferences and are usually strong from the standpoint of convergent or cross validation considerations.

The efficacy of the physiological category of nonverbal measures in specifying benefits is evident in the findings from a study that investigated the extent to which exposure to different outdoor settings facilitate or hamper an individual's recovery from uncomfortable stress (Ulrich & Simons, 1986). A stress reaction is the process whereby a person responds psychologically, *physiologically*, and usually with behaviors, to a situation that threatens well-being (Baum, Singer, & Baum, 1982). The physiological component consists of numerous responses in different systems, such as the cardiovascular (autonomic), skeleto-muscular, and neuroendocrine, which mobilize the individual for coping with the situation. In the study, 120 individuals first viewed a stressful film, and then were exposed to color/sound videotapes of different outdoor environments. Recovery from stress during the environmental presentations was assessed by, among other physiological methods, recording muscle tension, electrical conductance of the skin, and pulse transit time, a nonevasive measure that correlates highly with systolic blood pressure. In general terms, stress recovery is associated with decreased muscle tension, reduced skin conductance, and increased pulse transit time (decreased blood pressure). Verbal measures were also integrated into the study. Subjects were asked to provide ratings of their feelings before and after the stressor film, and after the recovery videotape, using a standard questionnaire.

Each subject was exposed to one of six different, simulated outdoor settings as the recovery condition following the stressor film. Previous research has suggested that the use of realistic color/sound videotapes is a valid procedure for stimulating real environments (Zube, Vining, Law, & Bechtel, 1985). The six environments displayed for stress recovery included four unblighted urban settings where the presence of autos and pedestrians varied systematically, and two unspectacular natural settings (forest and stream). To simplify discussion of the findings, the stress recovery data have been collapsed across the six settings into three broader environmental categories (nature, pedestrian mall, traffic).

Analysis of the recovery phase revealed significant environment x recovery period interactions for all physiological measures, indicating that recovery trajectories over time differed as a function of type of environment. More specifically, the findings clearly showed that individuals recovered faster and more completely from stress when they were exposed to nature as opposed to any of the urban settings (Figure 1). Adding considerable weight to this conclusion is the uniform consistency across physiological indicators with respect to the greater stress reducing effects of nature. Because the various measures assessed activity in different, weakly interrelated bodily systems, even short-term exposures to nature may have therapeutic consequences that tend to be generalized in physiological systems.

Additional important insights concerning the beneficial effects of the nature presentations emerged from the verbal (questionnaire) data regarding the individuals' emotional states. In general, verbal findings were consistent with physiological results. For instance, subjects exposed to nature evidenced lower physiological stress, and reported feeling better after the presentations. The integration of physiological and verbal methods made possible a broader spectrum of findings and suggested a higher level of validity for the main conclusion of reduced stress following a period of exposure to nature.

Implications for Value Assessment of Physiological Research Example

The preceding findings strongly suggest that the natural settings, compared to the urban, had more positive emotional and physiological effects. Regarding the value implications of the nonverbal data, there is little question that physiological well-being is an important psychological value for most people. Hence, these types of physiological findings regarding a public good would warrant consideration in a broad assessment of social value. Apart from consumers, considerable importance is often accorded physiological consequences by decisionmakers, courts, and some legislative contexts. One indication of the credibility of physiological measures, and of the recognition of physiological well-being as an important social value, is that many physiological effects (e.g., blood pressure) traditionally are considered permissible data by courts. A related point is that physiological findings often carry weight in environmental impact statements. If physiological evidence is obtained regarding specific beneficial or detrimental consequences, courts are more likely to decide that these characteristics must be considered, often irrespective of whether economic values can be assigned.

Compared to the hospital findings described earlier that were based on behavioral measures, results obtained from physiological methods are less directly useful for economists. Unlike certain behaviors (e.g., drug intake by patients), data on blood pressure, stress hormone levels, brain waves, etc., usually cannot be linked to real prices. Also, unlike some long-term physiological changes, the health consequences of short-term beneficial physiological (and psychological) influences have not been determined. The present state of knowledge concerning relationships between positive effects of short-term environmental experiences and health is too limited to permit conclusions with respect to such major health end points as hypertension. In this regard, the determination of possible health benefits of stress-reducing effects of natural amenities will eventually require longitudinal investigations spanning several months or years. Likewise, with regard to wilderness recreation, long-term studies will be needed to investigate many possible beneficial consequences (e.g., social adjustment, family stability). However, within the limits of a shorter-term research perspective, there are numerous possibilities for relating therapeutic influences of natural settings in many stress contexts to improvements in performance criteria (e.g., problem-solving accuracy), to positive behavioral indicators such as helpfulness, and perhaps to certain behaviors of economic relevance such as absenteeism.

The stress recovery research using physiological indicators, like the hospital study based on behavioral measures, identified certain beneficial consequences of natural amenities that are probably outside the conscious awareness of consumers. Consistent with the position endorsed earlier, CV respondents should be given information about physiological consequences that likely have psychological value. The information provided should be limited to physiological effects that can be understood by most laypersons. Some physiological effects can be conveyed using terms that are meaningful to perhaps most people (e.g., "lower blood pressure"). However, many findings from physiological studies are technical and require considerable scientific language to communicate. This aspect of physiological measurements, coupled with the lack of direct links to dollar values,

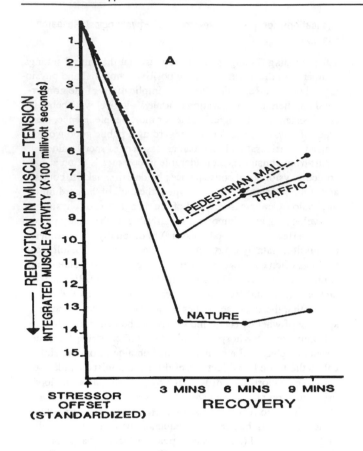

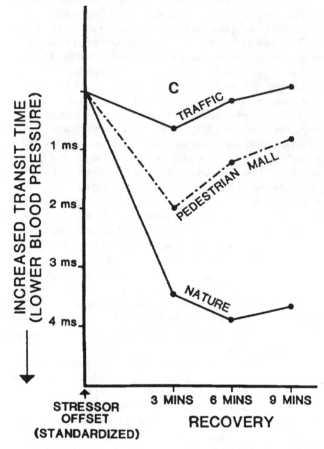

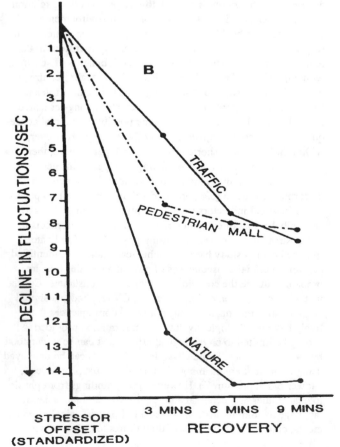

FIGURE 1. Measures of (A) muscle tension (EMG), (B) skin conductance, and (C) pulse transit time during recovery from stress in subjects exposed to three categories of outdoor settings (data from Ulrich & Simons, 1986).

underlines the clear need for a comprehensive approach to value accounting for many amenity contexts, as described by Driver and Burch (this volume). Such an approach would explicitly take into account nonmonetary information, including physiological evidence, in addition to information about economic values. Both nonmonetary and monetary categories of gains and losses would be considered by decisionmakers, in keeping with the view that benefit-cost analysis, in concept, should be based on a broad consideration of possible valued consequences, including those that are not amenable to economic efficiency analysis (Driver & Burch, this volume; Peterson & Brown, 1985). If scientific research has yielded credible evidence of beneficial or detrimental physiological consequences, an ostensibly objective valuation process that ignores such findings will be vulnerable to challenge and loss of credibility. Alternatively, in cases where physiological or other credible data about real gains or losses in welfare are not amenable to sound economic analysis, it would be untenable on scientific grounds to force the findings through an economic valuation procedure for the sake of adhering exclusively to an economic accounting system. Any precision and validity characterizing the physiological conclusions would be compromised if the findings were transformed to monetary estimates by methods that introduced substantial error. In this example, only some form of comprehensive accounting approach could simultaneously allow explicit consideration of the physiological evidence, and preserve the scientific character and credibility of the data.

INSIGHTS FROM PHYSIOLOGICAL MEASURES CONCERNING POSSIBLE LIMITS TO THE SUBSTITUTABILITY OF ENVIRONMENTS

If a natural amenity has a beneficial consequence that is important and unusual (i.e., not produced by the vast majority of other types of settings) this distinctiveness may contribute a significant dimension of value. In some cases, a public good may have unique characteristics; for instance, the uniqueness of the scenery of Yosemite Valley is widely regarded as an important component of the value of the environment. With respect to a more common or unspectacular natural amenity, it may be relevant for value assessment to evaluate whether or not substitutes are available for the benefits of the setting. If substitutes are not readily available to consumers in the geographical locale, the amenity might be assigned higher value.

Integrated research approaches using various physiological measures may be uniquely well-suited to yield insights concerning the availability of substitutes for producing positive influences on well-being. For example, it will be recalled that natural settings promoted stress recovery much faster and more completely than urban environments (Figure 1). In terms of the general magnitude of physiological stress recovery, there are certainly substitutes available for the natural settings. For instance, depending on dosage, oral tranquilizers can produce greater physiological relaxation, although the onset is not as rapid as for exposures to the common natural amenities (about 3 minutes or less for the natural exposures). Also, injections of various tranquilizers and barbiturates can have much stronger relaxation influences; onset times can be even faster than for natural scenery if the drugs are administered intravenously. However, in addition to their economic costs, these substitutes involve a wide range of substantial detrimental consequences not associated with exposures to nature. Alternatively, some individuals can be successfully trained in self-relaxation techniques, and within 20 minutes or less are able to achieve physiological stress reductions similar to or greater than those produced by the unspectacular natural settings in the study.

The range of substitutes may be far more limited if consideration is restricted to the influences of physical environments. In the stress recovery research, undistinguished natural settings produced much faster and more complete recovery than a sample of unblighted, comparatively attractive urban environments lacking nature. Other physiological research using recordings of brain electrical activity suggests that passive exposures to everyday natural settings have significantly different--and more positive--physiological effects than exposures to the great majority of unblighted urban settings lacking nature (Ulrich,

1981). In my judgement, it may prove quite difficult to locate urban settings lacking nature that have physiological relaxation consequences matching those of the unspectacular natural amenities in the study. Although physiological evidence to date is limited, the speculation seems justified that urban settings lacking nature may not prove to be substitutes for even undistinguished natural amenities from the standpoint of beneficial physiological consequences on stressed individuals. Perhaps future studies will find that exposures to natural versus urban settings have broadly different patterns of physiological influences across varied contexts--including, for instance, contexts where individuals are bored or chronically under-stimulated.

The possible nonsubstitutability of urban areas for natural settings in terms of various beneficial physiological consequences might prove important for decisionmaking. This stems from the reality that in decision contexts, urbanization is so frequently the alternative to a natural setting. Accordingly, integrated research approaches using physiological measures may contribute to a deeper understanding, and to a credible documentation, of beneficial consequences or values that could be lost with the elimination of nature. In addition to identifying tangible differences in the consequences of experiences with different general categories of environments (e.g., natural vs. man-made), physiological measures are probably sensitive enough to reveal differences in the influences of a common natural setting versus a more distinctive, spectacular natural environment.

Valuation of Detrimental Consequences of Environmental Risks and Stressors

The monetary and nonmonetary valuation of detrimental consequences associated with long-term exposures to environmental risks and stressors presents potentially major measurement and validity problems, which may not arise for beneficial consequences. These problems are related to the fact that risks and stressors confront individuals with psychological challenges in terms of perceived threats to well-being. The appraisal of threat generates duress, which must be dealt with, adjusted to, or somehow resolved. A large literature in clinical psychology indicates that over time the process of coping and responding often profoundly alters the individual's cognitive evaluation, attitudes, and emotions with respect to a stressor (Lazarus, 1966). Because these changes are reflected in verbally expressed feelings and attitudes, it can be assumed they also correlate with judgements about economic values such as willingness to pay. In short, verbally based economic estimates with respect to an environmental problem will often be strongly influenced by psychological coping processes. These influences may be a serious threat to the validity of verbal measures, including willingness to pay, as indicators of detrimental influences. A link with previous sections is provided by the solution proposed for the measurement problem. By integrating nonverbal measurements with verbal methods, more well-founded, valid inferences will be obtained concerning social losses from environmental risks or stressors.

Ambient Environmental Stressors

The concern here is with obtaining valid findings for a broad class of environmental problems that Campbell (1983) has termed "ambient stressors." These are long-term conditions that affect wide areas or large groups of people. Examples include air pollution, water pollution, community noise, crowding, and some instances of visibility reduction. Campbell draws a conceptual distinction between ambient stressors and more acute, disruptive, temporally discrete stressors (Lazarus & Cohen, 1977) that place urgent demands on coping resources (e.g., bereavement, job loss, tornado damage). Although ambient stressors are nonurgent, their long-term character may require coping and adaptation responses over extended time periods (Campbell, 1983). Convincing evidence from many studies covering a wide range of contexts indicates that ambient environmental stressors can elicit substantial stress in large groups of people (e.g., Cohen, Evans, Stokols, & Krantz, 1986; Evans, 1982). The involuntary character of many ambient stressor situations probably is an important factor heightening their detrimental consequences. If an individual initially judges that exposure to a risk is voluntary or partially under his/her personal control, the threat usually will be appraised as less serious, sometimes to the point of being grossly underestimated. Examples of risks having a voluntary component are illness from cigarette smoking and injury from downhill skiing. By contrast, an individual's *initial* appraisal of an ambient environmental stressor may be heightened when exposure seems largely outside personal control.

Coping Responses to Prolonged Environmental Problems

A critical factor for value assessment is the nature of *long-term* coping responses to these types of environmental problems. Individual differences in responses occur as a function of several variables (e.g., personality, economic resources). Evans and Tafalla (in press) concluded that people living in areas impacted by ambient environmental stressors have essentially three coping/ adjustment options: passive resignation, migration, or various actions to influence the situation (instrumental coping). The latter encompass actions such as involvement in political activities or installing additional window panes to attenuate noise. Research suggests that relatively few individuals engage in actions or active coping; also, most cannot migrate (Evans & Jacobs, 1981). Hence, the great majority of individuals appear to respond with apathy and passive resignation as the environmental problem becomes prolonged (Evans & Tafalla, in press; Rankin, 1969). Passive resignation is accompanied by progressive denial, rationalization, or other coping that diminishes the appraised severity of the risk. Many individuals may evaluate the stressor in light of their quite limited coping options, resulting in "reappraisal" of the negative circumstances as benign, thereby reducing their psychological stress (Lazarus, 1968). This latter coping has similarities with the predictions of Festinger's (1957) dissonance theory: individuals will alter their conscious

appraisal of the risk (i.e., increasingly believe that the risk poses little or no problem), because to believe otherwise would create a stress-producing lack of congruence between their course of action (living in the impacted area) and their cognitions concerning themselves as sensible or rational persons. With long-term exposure to the problem, these various coping responses are more psychologically adaptive than maintaining the initial, comparatively high risk appraisal, and experiencing ongoing negative emotions. Thus, most people affected initially by an ambient stressor, and who cope passively, will evidence attenuation over time in their risk appraisals and psychological stress. After several weeks or months of exposure, verbal reports from these individuals may suggest that the stressor is neutralized or no longer has detrimental consequences. A CV survey conducted at this point would likely obtain comparatively low values for willingness to pay to reduce consequences of the environmental problem. The CV investigator, or researcher using attitudinal scales or other verbal measures, might well conclude that habituation or adjustment has occurred, and that social costs of the stressor are now relatively low. In fact, the validity of these findings would be exceedingly problematic. This becomes clear when stress is understood as a "whole body phenomenon" (Baum et al., 1985) associated with a range of important negative influences in response systems not tapped by verbal methods. In the case of ambient environmental stressors, psychological coping can lower verbal indicators, but chronic, higher levels of stress may still be clearly expressed in nonverbal indicators, including physiological measures and behaviors.

Long-Term Detrimental Consequences: Valid Findings Require Multiple Measures

Although there are different definitions and models of stress, there is wide agreement that responses to stressors and risks have salient nonverbal as well as psychological and verbal components. The mobilization required for coping with a threat typically is associated with changes in physiological functioning in numerous systems. Additionally, contemporary models emphasize a third category of stress markers--behavioral (Baum et al., 1985; Cohen et al., 1986). The increasing use of behavioral measures stems partly from the finding that exposures to stressors reliably produce declines in cognitive performance on a wide variety of tasks. Also, after cessation of an environmental stressor, researchers have consistently reported persistent, detrimental behavioral *after effects* such as declines in frustration tolerance and proofreading (Glass & Singer, 1972). Validity concerns constitute very strong grounds for advocating the use of a multimeasures research approach that assesses detrimental consequences using psychological and nonverbal indicators. Convergence among measures from different response modes would justify greater confidence in findings, including results obtained from verbal measures such as willingness to pay.

However, detrimental effects characterized by lack of convergence among data from different response modes can occur after prolonged exposure to an ambient environmental stressor. As suggested earlier, lack of convergence (and possibly, divergence) may be recorded when rationalization, denial, or other coping has reduced conscious awareness of risk, but prolonged passive resignation and helplessness are expressed in chronic physiological and behavioral symptoms. In this regard, research on long-term responses to the nuclear reactor accident at Three Mile Island (TMI) provides a rather dramatic illustration of the shortcomings of stress assessment strategies that rely exclusively on verbal measures. As Baum, Fleming, and Singer noted (1985), at least one TMI study using questionnaires found that stress for area residents had disappeared 3-4 months following the accident. Findings from several self-report studies suggested that stress levels had diminished considerably within 6-9 months after the accident. It is reasonable to assume that verbally expressed willingness to pay--although a comparatively narrow and less sensitive indicator of stress than those employed--would correlate with these verbally-based stress findings. However, 17 months after the accident, Baum and his colleagues found clear evidence of chronic stress using a combination of verbal, physiological, and behavioral measures (Baum, Gatchel, & Schaeffer, 1983). TMI area residents, compared to various control groups, exhibited higher levels of epinephrine and norepinephrine, stress-related hormones. Also, behavioral measures (performance on a proofreading task and an embedded figures task) revealed cognitive performance deficits for TMI residents comparable to those associated with responses to acute laboratory stressors--a most impressive and disturbing finding in view of the nearly 1.5-year interval since the accident. Findings obtained from verbal measures were mixed; responses to some questions suggested stress, whereas other questions indicated no differences between TMI area residents and control groups. Sole reliance on the verbal data would have led to ambiguity or possibly the false conclusion that TMI area residents were not experiencing stress (Baum et al., 1985). Likewise, it seems possible that if willingness to pay data had been obtained in the study, values would have substantially under-represented the real losses in welfare to area residents. By integrating verbal and nonverbal measures, this TMI study achieved a broad and scientifically credible picture regarding detrimental consequences of the environmental stressor.

At this point it might be argued that lower risk appraisals resulting from psychological coping represent real welfare gains in situations such as TMI; hence, comparatively low CV estimates obtained after months of coping with an ambient stressor might be accurate or valid indicators of detrimental consequences. This point of view, however, would conflict with validity criteria that are widely accepted in the scientific community--which emphasize convergence among findings from different modes as a condition justifying confidence in the data obtained from any given measure. Moreover, one possible extension of the coping/gain argument is that if research identifies detrimental consequences that are outside the conscious awareness of many impacted individuals (e.g., chronically elevated blood pressure), the information should not be communicated to the public because it would create coping difficulties, heighten risk appraisals, and accordingly produce losses in welfare. In other words, "what consumers don't know, or are not informed about, won't hurt them." Also, in the face of findings from multiple nonverbal measures (e.g., cardiovascular, biochemical) that converge in indicating chronic stress, any argument that low (i.e., nonconvergent) willingness to pay values are appropriate indicators of detrimental consequences would invite a derisive

reply from, among other quarters, the medical community. Finally, questions concerning social equity are raised by the view that real gains may result when psychological coping sharply lowers verbal indicators of stress, but does not attenuate nonverbal manifestations. Individuals in higher income categories have several coping alternatives when confronted with long-term environmental risks, including active adjustments such as migration, which probably eventually produce "whole body" stress recovery. Lower income groups, however, often have no option except to remain permanently in the affected area and adapt passive coping strategies such as resignation and denial.

IMPLICATIONS FOR CV ASSESSMENT OF LONG-TERM ENVIRONMENTAL PROBLEMS

Clearly, the identification and measurement of nonmonetary and monetary losses from prolonged environmental problems require assessment of responses in different modes. Research strategies should integrate verbal measures, including reported willingness to pay, with physiological and/or behavioral indicators. An outcome of general synchrony between verbal data and those from a nonverbal mode would imply validity, and would increase the credibility of value estimates based on reported willingness to pay. However, lack of general convergence would suggest that CV estimates did not warrant confidence.

The latter outcome, however, would not necessarily imply that the objective of obtaining meaningful CV estimates should be abandoned for the particular risk situation. One possibility would be to perform a second CV study wherein respondents were provided information regarding specific detrimental consequences. They might be informed, for instance, that many residents of the area were suffering from chronically elevated blood pressure (a documented influence of some ambient environmental stressors). Because of the apparent chronic character of cardiovascular and endocrine responses to many long-term environmental stressors, attention might be justifiably called to the possibility of increased risk for hypertension (Gatchel & Baum, 1983). It seems likely that providing such information to CV respondents would increase willingness to pay judgements. A potential drawback would be that the reactivity of the respondents might be increased to the point of introducing error. Also, it appears certain that the CV interview itself would be a stressor. In some contexts, it might prove necessary to accept these drawbacks in view of the importance of obtaining more meaningful willingness to pay estimates.

If the investigator is faced with nonconvergence of verbal data and those from a nonverbal mode, an alternative approach to economic valuation would involve collecting additional physiological or health-related behavioral data concerning the environmental problem. In view of the long duration in these contexts of negative physiological influences, and of possible chronic behavioral symptoms (e.g., drug and alcohol consumption), it may often be warranted to consult health experts to obtain estimates regarding increased morbidity and consumption of health care (the latter might also be measured directly). These estimates could then be linked to prices, and lower bound estimates could be obtained concerning detrimental consequences of the environmental problem. The economic estimates should then be provided to decisionmakers along with findings concerning nonmonetary consequences, which are not reflected in the monetary estimates, to provide a broader informational base for more comprehensive valuations.

LIMITATIONS OF NONVERBAL MEASURES

As with all measures, nonverbal measures (behavioral, physiological) have limitations, and are not applicable to some situations. Single physiological or behavioral indicators should not be used alone, a caution that usually also applies to verbal indicators. When physiological findings are obtained for unstressed individuals, these data can sometimes prove ambiguous when used as the only basis for inferring well-being. However, when physiological methods are used in combination with other types of measures, including verbal or behavioral, results often are more easily and confidently interpreted. Compared to verbal methods, nonverbal procedures, especially physiological methods, tend to be time-consuming and more costly. In the case of most physiological research, each subject must be assessed individually, usually for a considerable amount of time, making it difficult to study large groups. Further, many physiological measurements require expensive, bulky, and sensitive equipment that is awkward in field conditions. Certain physiological indicators vary as a function of variables such as temperature and humidity; several are influenced by active movements of the subject, and some are so sensitive to movements (e.g., brain electrical activity) that subjects must be monitored while seated motionless in a chair having armrests. Because of these considerations, many physiological measurements are better suited to laboratory research than to field studies. This does not, however, preclude their effective and sound application to questions relating to outdoor environments. Numerous studies have supported the ecological or external validity of using various realistic media in laboratories to simulate salient properties of real outdoor settings (e.g., visual and auditory characteristics). Also, laboratory-based physiological strategies offer some very important advantages compared to measures of other response modes, such as temporally continuous measurement (Figure 1). The single most important problem limiting physiological measures is the fact that few researchers working in the broad area of environmental valuation are trained in their use.

Certain physiological measurements can be used conveniently in field conditions, and have great potential for contributing to research on, among other issues, restorative effects of wilderness experiences. Some physiological stress indicators based on hormone measurements (catecholamine levels) are suited to field studies, especially when chronic effects or stress changes over many hours are concerns (e.g., Singer, Lundberg, & Frankenhaeuser, 1978). Other catecholamine indicators obtained from blood samples present major difficulties for field use, such as short half-life durations or unacceptable invasiveness or risk due to a requirement for vein puncture. On the other hand, advances in electronics miniaturization are making the recording of some important physiological responses increasingly practical for field or wilderness settings. Compact, self-contained, unobtru-

sive units worn by subjects can record or transmit data such as heart rate.

Health-related behavioral measures, such as consumption of medications or length of hospitalization, have certain advantages as credible indicators of beneficial or detrimental consequences--and they can sometimes be linked to real prices. But the number of contexts where they can be applied is limited. The most conspicuous opportunities are various types of health settings located proximate to natural amenities--hospitals, homes for the ages, blood banks, etc. Also, there are many possibilities for using health-related behavioral measures in residential situations. Health-related measures will be especially effective when applied to important targets of opportunity found mostly in urban or fringe areas. The possibilities for wilderness applications are more restricted. These will usually involve the identification of a wilderness setting having particular environmental characteristics dictated by control and other considerations in a multiple-measures design. As was previously emphasized, there is a great number of useful behavioral indicators in addition to health-related measures; thus, an appropriate combination of behavioral and verbal measures could potentially be identified for the vast majority of contexts, regardless of whether a laboratory or field approach is used, or a wilderness or urban fringe setting is investigated.

SUMMARY AND CONCLUSIONS

The beneficial consequences of most amenity resources are by no means well understood; there is a clear need for research that uses integrated, multiple-measures strategies to specify the benefits of natural amenities. The current lack of knowledge means that neither researchers nor consumers/respondents are informed about many public goods of concern to decisionmakers. When consumers are not informed about goods, there is simply no scientifically credible basis for contending that their economic value judgements should be well-founded or necessarily meaningful. This represents a major validity problem for contingent valuation in many amenity contexts. Further, economic estimates obtained by other methods will also be susceptible to very substantial error when goods are not identified or well defined and real gains in welfare are overlooked. Accordingly, advances in achieving sound value estimates for many amenity resources will be contingent on progress in research that defines more clearly the characteristics of the goods. As findings become available, CV respondents should be informed about important consequences so that they can better understand the commodity and thereby make better decisions regarding willingness to pay. General guidelines and strategies are suggested for selecting information for presentation in interviews.

Verbal measures alone may be sufficient for investigating *benefits* in many contexts. In this regard, the use of attitudinal scales in combination with reported willingness to pay will yield more comprehensive and precise assessments of psychological value. Whenever possible, investigators should also incorporate nonverbal measures in their research strategies. Integrated designs using these measures make possible a wider range of conclusions and are stronger with respect to validity concerns.

This paper distinguishes two broad categories of nonverbal indicators (behavioral and physiological), overviews numerous measures in each category, and discusses why these methods have major advantages in many amenity valuation contexts. For example, behavioral measures related to health are credible and sometimes can be linked directly to real prices. Because health costs can be very high, validation approaches that incorporate certain behavioral measures could yield economic estimates--including lower bound figures--that may be exceptionally high for some natural amenities. A drawback of health-related behavioral measures is that the possibilities for wilderness applications are limited. Compared to many behavioral indicators, the physiological category of nonverbal measures is less directly useful for economists because the findings can rarely be linked to real prices.

Nonetheless, findings from physiological procedures (e.g., blood pressure effects) have scientific credibility, carry weight in environmental impact statements, and typically are considered permissible data by courts. Hence, most physiological findings are not amenable to economic efficiency analysis, yet neither can they be ignored in decision making without inviting serious challenge. This point, coupled with the fact that many other credible data regarding nonmonetary beneficial consequences cannot be transformed to credible monetary estimates, indicates the clear need for a *comprehensive* approach to value accounting for amenity contexts. Such an approach should explicitly consider information about nonmonetary consequences, in addition to taking into account meaningful information about monetary values.

Research examples discussed in this paper illustrate that both general categories of nonverbal measures--behavioral and physiological--can identify and measure real increases in welfare that may be outside the conscious awareness of consumers, and probably are not reflected in verbal measures, including willingness to pay. Physiological methods are perhaps unique in their potential to shed light on the possible nonsubstitutability of different environments with respect to positive influences on well-being. For decades, research based on physiological/health measures has been of central importance in identifying detrimental consequences of toxic substances in the environment; by comparison, we have only recently made a small beginning in using this powerful category of methods to uncover what may eventually prove to be numerous important beneficial consequences.

Verbal measures should never be used alone to assess *detrimental* consequences associated with prolonged exposure to environmental risks or stressors. Contemporary theory and findings in environmental and health psychology indicate that for long-term environmental problems, the validity of verbally-based indicators such as willingness to pay is exceedingly problematic. Validity considerations dictate the use of integrated research strategies that measure responses using verbal, physiological, and often behavioral indicators. An outcome of general convergence between verbal data and those from a nonverbal mode would support the credibility of value estimates based on willingness to pay. On the other hand, lack of convergence would indicate that CV estimates did not justify confidence, and that alternative approaches for estimating economic value were in order. In sum, nonverbal measurements have several important advantages; they also can work in a complementary manner

with verbal measures, and they have great promise for contributing to the identification and sound measurement of nonmonetary and monetary consequences of public goods.

Acknowledgment

As a noneconomist attempting to blend a variety of ideas and behavioral science material with valuation issues, I benefitted considerably from interaction with economist colleagues, especially George Parsons and Lee G. Anderson.

References

American Hospital Association. (1986). *Hospital statistics.* Chicago, IL: American Hospital Association.

Andreassi, J. L. (1980). *Psychophysiology: Human behavior and physiological response.* New York: Oxford University Press.

Baron, R. J. (1986). Finding new models in medicine. Editorial. *Journal of the American Medical Association, 255,* 3404-3405.

Baum, A., Fleming, R., & Singer, J. E. (1985). Understanding environmental stress: Strategies for conceptual and methodological integration. In A. Baum & J. E. Singer (Eds.), *Advances in environmental psychology, Vol. 5: Methods and environmental psychology* (pp. 185-205). Hillsdale, NJ: Lawrence Erlbaum.

Baum, A., Gatchel, R. J., & Schaeffer, M. A. (1983). Emotional, behavioral and physiological effects of chronic stress at Three Mile Island. *Journal of Consulting and Clinical Psychology, 51,* 565-572.

Baum, A., Singer, J. E., & Baum, C. S. (1982). *Stress and the environment.* In G. W. Evans (Ed.), Environmental stress (pp. 15-44). New York: Cambridge University Press.

Campbell, J. M. (1983). Ambient stressors. *Environment and Behavior, 15,* 355-380.

Cohen, S., Evans, G. W., Stokols, D. & Krantz, D. S. (1986). *Behavior, health, and environmental stress.* New York: Plenum.

Dimberg, U. (1986). Facial reactions to fear-relevant and fear-irrelevant stimuli. *Biological Psychology, 23,* 153-161.

Dimberg, U. (1987). Facial reactions, autonomic activity and experienced emotion: A three component model of emotional conditioning. *Biological Psychology, 24,* 1-18.

Driver, B. L., & Brown, P. J. (1986). *Probable personal benefits of outdoor recreation.* Report prepared for the President's Commission on Americans Outdoors. Rocky Mountain Forest and Range Experiment Station, USDA Forest Service, Fort Collins, CO.

Evans, G. W. (Ed.). (1982). *Environmental stress.* New York: Cambridge University Press.

Evans, G. W., & Jacobs, S. V. (1981). Air pollution and human behavior. *Journal of Social Issues, 37,* 95-125.

Evans, G. W., & Tafalla, R. (in press). Measurement of environmental annoyance. In H. S. Koelga & E. P. Koster (Eds.), *Environmental annoyance.* Amsterdam: Elsevier.

Festinger, L. (1957). *A theory of cognitive dissonance.* Evanston, IL: Tow, Peterson.

Gatchel, R. J., & Baum, A. (1983). *An introduction to health psychology.* Reading, MA: Addison-Wesley.

Glass, D. C., & Singer, J. E. (1972). *Urban stress: Experiments on noise and social stressors.* New York: Academic Press.

Greenfield, N. A., & Sternbach, R. A. (Eds.). (1972). *Handbook of psychophysiology.* New York: Holt, Rinehart, and Winston.

Hockey, G. R. L. (Ed.). (1983). *Stress and fatigue in human performance.* New York: John Wiley & Sons.

Kahneman, D., Slovic, P., & Tversky, A. (1982). *Judgement under uncertainty: Heuristics and biases.* Cambridge: Cambridge University Press.

Lazarus, R. S. (1966). *Psychological stress and the coping process.* New York: McGraw-Hill.

Lazarus, R. S. (1968). Emotions and adaptation: Conceptual and empirical relations. In W. J. Arnold (Ed.), *Nebraska Symposium on Motivation.* Lincoln: University of Nebraska Press.

Lazarus, R. S., & Cohen, J. (1977). Environmental stress. In I. Altman & J. Wohlwill (Eds.), *Human behavior and environment: Advances in theory and research,* (Vol. # 1), (pp. 89-125). New York: Plenum.

Mitchell, R. C., & Carson, R. T. (in press). *Using surveys to value public goods: The contingent valuation method.* Washington, DC: Resources for the Future.

Ohman, A. (in press). The psychophysiology of emotion: An evolutionary-cognitive perspective. In P. Ackles, J. Jennings, & M. Coles (Eds.), *Advances in psychophysiology* (Vol. 2). Greenwich, CT: JAI Press.

Peterson, G. L., & Brown, T. C. (1985). The economic benefits of recreation: Common disagreements and informed replies. In A. E. Watson (Ed.), *Proceedings: Southeastern Recreation Research Conference* (pp. 17-33). Statesboro, GA: Department of Recreation and Leisure Services, Georgia Southern College.

Rankin, R. E. (1969). Air pollution control and public apathy. *Journal of the Air Pollution Control Association, 19,* 565-569.

Rokeach, M. (1973). The nature of human values. New York: Free Press.

Singer, J. E., Lundberg, U., & Frankenhaeuser, M. (1978). Stress on the train: A study of urban commuting. In A. Baum, J. Singer, & S. Valins (Eds.), *Advances in environmental psychology* (pp. 41-56). Hillsdale, NJ: Lawrence Erlbaum.

Ulrich, R. S. (1979a). Psychophysiological approaches to visibility. In *Proceedings of the Workshop on Visibility Values* (pp.93-99). In D. Fox, R. J. Loomis & T. Greene (Eds.), USDA Forest Service Report WO-18. Fort Collins, CO: Rocky Mountain Forest and Range Experiment Station.

Ulrich, R. S. (1979b). Visual landscapes and psychological well-being. *Landscape Research, 4,* 17-23.

Ulrich, R. S. (1981). Natural versus urban scenes: Some psychophysiological effects. *Environment and Behavior, 13,* 523-556.

Ulrich, R. S. (1983). Aesthetic and affective response to natural environment. In I. Altman & J. Wohlwill (Eds.), *Human behavior and environment, Vol. 6: Behavior and the natural environment* (pp. 85-125). New York: Plenum.

Ulrich, R. S. (1984). View through a window may influence recovery from surgery. *Science, 224,* 420-421.

Ulrich, R. S., & Simons, R. F. (1986). Recovery from stress during exposure to everyday outdoor environments. In J. Wineman, R. Barnes, & C. Zimring (Eds.), *The costs of not knowing: Proceedings of the Seventeenth Annual Conference of the Environmental Design Research Association* (pp. 115-122). Washington, DC: Environmental Design Research Association.

Verderber, S. F. (1983). Designing for the therapeutic functions of windows in hospital rehabilitation environment. In P. Bart & G. Francescato (Eds.), *Knowledge for design: Proceedings of the 1982 Conference of the Environmental Design Research Association* (pp. 476-492). College Park, MD: University of Maryland Press.

Zube, E. H., Vining, J., Law, C. S., & Bechtel, R. B. (1985). Perceived urban residential quality: A cross-cultural bimodal study. *Environment and Behavior, 17,* 327-350.

Part 3: Concerns About Economic Measures

Overview: Gains, Losses, and Contingent Valuation

Herbert W. Schroeder
USDA Forest Service
North Central Forest Experiment Station

John F. Dwyer
USDA Forest Service
North Central Forest Experiment Station

The contingent valuation method (CVM) for estimating resource values has increased in popularity among economists and policymakers over the past decade. Several studies have employed the method, and, where comparisons have been made, the results are generally comparable with market transactions and with estimates from travel cost and hedonic methods. Questions remain concerning the validity of CVM, but continued development and use of travel cost and hedonic approaches have shown that they too have problems and limitations. Also, interest in quantitative estimates of option, existence, bequest, and other nonuser benefits has increased; direct estimates of these values can be obtained in dollar terms only with a contingent valuation approach. Consequently, contingent valuation methods have gained a firm foothold among techniques for estimating the economic value of nonmarket resources. The method has, however, encountered a significant obstacle concerning the valuation of gains versus losses.

A Problem for Economists and Policymakers

Economic theory states that willingness to pay (WTP) for a nonmarket resource should approximately equal compensation demanded (CD) for loss of the resource. Scientists and policymakers using the contingent valuation method, however, have observed a wide divergence between estimates of WTP and CD. The percentage difference between the two measures is generally the greatest with evaluation of the most emotionally-laden issues, such as changes in environmental quality, which is where contingent valuation is often used and the valuation of losses is important.

When these large differences arise, a decisionmaker interested in the benefit-cost criterion has several options. First, the CD estimates derived from the contingent valuation experiment can be used in the analysis, in the belief that they are valid estimates of the compensation demanded to cover losses. Second, estimates of CD can be developed from the WTP estimates using mathematical formulae. These results are generally only slightly higher than the willingness-to-pay estimates. Third, the direct estimate of willingness to pay can be used with the assumption that it is a lower bound on compensation demanded.

The choice of which of these three options to follow can have significant implications for policy. If direct estimates of willingness to accept compensation from a contingent valuation model are used in benefit-cost analysis, the result is likely to strongly favor the avoidance of losses--particularly losses of rights and privileges to which individuals have strong emotional attachment, such as wilderness, wildlife, clean air and water, and free flowing streams. The two other choices will give less relative weight to such losses.

A fourth option, of course, would be to forego the use of CVM to estimate dollar values entirely, in the belief that the WTP-CD divergence casts doubt on the validity of CVM and perhaps on economic measures of gains and losses in general. Without a good explanation of why WTP and CD diverge, it is impossible to say which of these courses of action is best.

The purpose of this paper is to outline possible explanations for the difference between WTP and CD from the viewpoints of economists and psychologists, reconcile those viewpoints, and suggest areas of future research on valuation of environmental gains and losses. This discussion is based on the papers that appear in this section of the book, the ideas expressed during group discussions of those papers (which we chaired), and our own viewpoints.

Loss Aversion

One possible explanation for differences between WTP and CD is strategic behavior, in which individuals deliberately bias their responses to produce a desired outcome. This is, however, an issue with both WTP and CD, and would not contribute to the difference between the two measures unless it was far more serious with one than the other. Perhaps a more likely explanation is that human beings are loss averse (i.e., they generally tend to avoid losses).

Examples of loss aversion are not hard to find in everyday life. For example, a child asks for and after some debate with its parents receives a teddy bear at the circus; but then some time later the child is asked to give up the teddy bear. In most instances it would be far more difficult--and require far more compensation--to get the child to give up the teddy bear after possessing it, as opposed to asking the child to forego having one before it was acquired. Similarly, individuals may become attached to rights and privileges that they currently hold, and may demand significant compensation to give them up, or refuse to give them up at all. However, in the absence of these rights and privileges individuals may not be willing to pay such large amounts to obtain them in the first place.

Perhaps a right or privilege changes (increases) in value after an individual has acquired it because the individual gains greater knowledge or experience in using it and greater emotional attachment to it. Psychologically, people often seem to define their identities in terms of their rights, privileges, and possessions, so that the prospect of surrendering something after it has been possessed for a time is like losing a piece of the self, and provokes a strong defensive reaction.

The force of loss aversion tendencies in CVM survey may be strengthened by the unfamiliar nature of the tasks presented to respondents, particularly where they must make statements of compensation demanded to give up a resource. Individuals are sometimes asked to "sell" rights or privileges that they have never contemplated selling, and in some instances did not previously consider to be theirs. In addition, in CVM experiments there is a question of who will or should compensate them for their loss or whether they will actually be compensated at all. Consequently, individuals' response to the scenarios presented to them are likely to be conditioned by their uncertainty concerning rights, responsibilities, and liabilities as well as uncertainty about the value that they attach to the right or privilege in question.

Faced with uncertainty about how to assign dollar values to goods that they have no experience in trading, loss averse individuals may state a low willingness to pay value or a high compensation demanded value to insure that they will be no worse off after the exchange than before. The elicitation process may also provoke zero bids, refusals to bid, or infinite bids in instances where individuals do not relate to or agree with the context or process (rights, payment vehicles, liabilities, etc.) of the questions.

Viewpoints of Economists and Psychologists

Faced with the dilemma of large differences between estimates of WTP and CD, when economic theory suggests the estimates should be quite similar, economists look for a solution in terms of improved techniques for removing bias in CVM. Economists, as a group, are somewhat uncomfortable with survey techniques because their models are traditionally based on observed behavior and not the results of surveys and experiments. Therefore, they turn to psychologists and other social scientists for possible solutions. Psychologists, with their stronger orientation to experiments, survey techniques, and questionnaires, have much to offer in terms of technique.

Psychologists, however, do not seem so inclined to view the divergence between WTP and CD as a problem. To them it is a valid and interesting finding in its own right. Rather than attributing the divergence to measurement bias and looking for ways to eliminate it, they are more likely to take it at face value, as showing that people genuinely do value gains differently from losses. This is an intuitively reasonable interpretation. After all, gaining and losing are different experiences, evoking emotional and behavioral responses that differ in both quality and intensity. To see this, one need only compare the behavior of a dog being offered a bone with the response of the same dog when someone tries to take the bone away. Loss is a threat, and we are programmed by evolution to respond to threats quickly, decisively, and forcefully. For any organism, responding to immediate threats is the first behavioral priority. The emotional response of a CVM respondent faced with the prospect of losing access to a favorite recreation site, like that of a dog defending its favorite bone, or the child seeking to retain its toy, may be deeply rooted in our evolutionary past. CVM surveys may in fact be measuring the intensity of these emotional responses, and it is not at all surprising that the results for gains and losses are different. To require that WTP and CD be equal may be to ignore or distort a basic characteristic of human behavior that has important consequences for environmental decision making.

Therefore, the basic reaction of many psychologists to the work of economists in valuation is that alternative approaches to the valuation question are needed, not "fine tuning" of the CVM techniques. These approaches would use different criteria and techniques that psychologists see as more effective in assessing public responses to changes in the availability of environmental amenities, and do not necessarily involve dollar values. Economists who have traditionally been asked to estimate dollar values for resources, are reluctant to forego dollar measures--which are in increasing demand by some managers and policymakers--for alternative approaches that do not develop dollar estimates. Most economists are quick to point out that dollars are certainly not the only measure of public values and that noneconomic factors are also considered in public decision making. Few economists and even fewer policymakers

argue for strict reliance on the benefit/cost criterion for public decision making. However, some psychologists fear that, while saying this, economists are working vigorously to apply dollar values as guides to public decision making in contexts where they have dubious validity, and that once dollar values are established, decisionmakers will rely on them to the exclusion of other less quantitative information. Also, in the traditional CVM, the respondent is usually put in a position where his or her decisions regarding public goods are based entirely on dollar values--a most unnatural position for the individual. Even though the individual's responses and those of others in the experiment would be weighed in conjunction with other criteria in a final management or policy decision, at the time of the experiment this does not ease the burden on the respondent.

Part of the difficulty in public decision making is that we do not have an empirical criterion against which to validate our decisions. Presumably, the social value of an agency's decision is somehow related to public acceptance and satisfaction with the state of the world created by the decision. Unfortunately, unidimensional (e.g., dollar) measures of net social value can never be empirically validated, because they cannot avoid making assumptions about equity to aggregate the values of individual gainers and losers.

A Possible Synthesis of Viewpoints

Perhaps the differing viewpoints of economics and psychology will be easier to resolve if we clearly recognize the normative character of economic theory. That is, rather than viewing economics as a description of how people actually make decisions and assign values, we should view it as one possible set of rules for how individuals and society ought to make decisions. The question then becomes: Are the normative assumptions of the economic model legitimate in the arena of amenity resource decision making?

The validity of a descriptive theory is established empirically using the scientific method, but the legitimacy of a normative theory can only be established politically and philosophically. The WTP/CD difference, "wild" bids, and nonresponses in CVM experiments may indicate that people frequently do not conform to the standards of economic reasoning; but the standards may still be legitimate as guides for "good" decision making.

The economic concept of value is meaningful and useful as long as individuals accept the normative legitimacy of economic reasoning, and can provide value statements consistent with the requirements of such reasoning. If a person accepts the validity of economic reasoning for amenity resource decisions, then it seems reasonable to require the person to make value statements consistent with the assumptions of economic theory. If the person's responses turn out to be inconsistent with these requirements (as is the case in many empirical studies of decision making), then it would be reasonable to point out the inconsistency to the individual and ask that his or her responses be rethought and revised.

It seems pointless, however, to elicit economic value statements from people who do not accept economic reasoning as legitimate in a particular context. Protest responses and statements of zero or infinite value in CVM surveys suggest strongly that some people in fact do not accept the legitimacy of economic reasoning in amenity decision making. Therefore, a necessary step prior to conducting a CVM survey should be to determine whether the affected publics perceive economic reasoning as legitimate within the decision context. If there are contexts in which economic reasoning is not perceived by the public as a legitimate approach to decision making, then we should turn to other approaches for valuing amenity resources in those contexts.

An alternative to unidimensional measures of value would be a decision-making approach that preserves the multidimensional character of the decision problem, instead of collapsing the decision onto a single scale of dollars, utility, or whatever. Realistic multi-attribute descriptions of future states of the world could be presented to the public and to decisionmakers in a way that would help them evaluate the desirability of proposed alternatives. Psychologists and decision theory researchers have already made some progress towards developing such methods.

Suggested Research

These considerations suggest a number of areas where research efforts would be highly productive in applying psychological research to the area of nonmarket resource values:

1. The inability of economic theory to explain the large differences between WTP and CD provides psychologists and others with ample room for deriving explanations for a phenomenon with significant implications for research and public decision making. Research should examine the role of loss aversion in natural resource decision making, and its implications for attempts to place values on amenity resources. Studies might focus on the differing emotions and behaviors evoked by prospects of gaining or losing environmental amenities, and how these reactions are expressed in actual decision-making situations.
2. In-depth interviews and "process tracing" should be conducted with individuals before, during, and after CVM experiments, to learn about their thought processes and decision strategies during the experiment. The experiments should involve a range of goods and services, including some that are "ordinary," as well as unique, environmental resources, and should address both WTP and CD. In-depth

interviews could focus on individual responses to (1) the idea of selling the goods or services in question; (2) the assignment of rights implied by the sale; (3) the manner of selling goods, services, or rights; and (4) the way that prices are varied in the experiment, etc. Particular attention should also be given to individuals who refuse to participate in all or any part of the experiment, give zero or inordinately large bids, or who give much different responses to questions concerning WTP and CD. Several in-depth studies of this type would better explain what is happening in CVM experiments, than would continued replication of comparative studies of WTP and CD.

3. Psychologists and economists should cooperate to develop empirical methods to assess individual's perceptions of the legitimacy of economic valuation and other approaches to amenity resource decision making. These methods should then be applied to a variety of decision-making contexts involving both gains and losses of amenity resources. Public perception of the legitimacy of economic approaches may well vary with the context being considered. Such studies may point out instances where economic evaluations of amenity resources are not readily acceptable to particular individuals.
4. Methods for contingent valuation studies should be developed that include tests of whether individuals' value responses are consistent with assumptions of economic theory. These methods should also resolve inconsistencies through continued interaction with the individuals, in effect training them to apply economic reasoning to their own values and preferences, assuming that the individual has accepted the legitimacy of economic reasoning for the problem at hand.
5. Methods for presenting realistic multi-attribute representations of future states of the world, and for assessing public preference for alternative states of the world should be investigated. Such an approach would not seek to reduce gains and losses to dollar measures, nor to aggregate gainers' and losers' values into a single net benefit figure.

Conclusion

In summary, future research on amenity resource valuation should develop improved methods for obtaining both dollar and nondollar measures of benefits. Perhaps an even more important task is to identify the conditions and limits under which each approach will produce valid, meaningful, and useful results.

Specifying Value Measurements

Baruch Fischhoff
Eugene Research Institute
Eugene, Oregon

Values are involved in all human actions. As a result, they are a part of all social sciences. Methods for measuring values include attitude surveys, observation of market behavior, creation of hypothetical markets, and intensive interactions with decision analysts. Variants on all these methods have been tried in determining people's values for environmental resources. The other papers in this volume present the theoretical and empirical legacy of these different efforts. Whatever method is used, certain fundamental issues must be faced. These include defining the resources that are to be valued, ensuring that people have understood the evaluation question, and assessing the validity of their responses. The present paper offers a general framework for considering these basic methodological issues.

A measurement technique should be sensitive to meaningful differences among measured objects and insensitive to meaningless ones (see Campbell & Fiske, 1959). For example, a police radar detector should give different readings when directed at cars traveling at different speeds, but not when held by different troopers or in different arm positions by a single trooper. The response patterns elicited by a lie detector should vary with respondents' belief in the truth of their answers, but not with their trust in the procedure, their confidence in the examiner, or their level of ambient arousal. A test of academic aptitude should give higher scores to students who are good guessers on multiple-choice questions and who subscribe to majority-culture norms if those skills facilitate academic success, but not if they do not. A survey of unemployed workers should find a higher percentage who report being "actively looking for work" when the prospects for finding work improve or when those who admit to giving up can keep their unemployment benefits.

Validating such measurements requires additional measurements, the availability of which varies from case to case. For calibrating radar detectors, independent measures of vehicle speed are readily available on car speedometers (although it might take some doing to collect them): It is harder to determine precisely how a detector was employed in a particular application. For lie detectors, corroborative evidence can help infer what respondents really believe about the truth of their statements; it is more difficult to ascertain what beliefs and emotions the setting itself elicits. For aptitude tests, the same psychometric procedures used to produce the tests can be used to measure potential influences such as "testwiseness" and cultural "smarts." The same survey techniques that ask unemployed workers if they are still in the market for a job can ask how they view current economic opportunities and whether they expect to be penalized for candor. Once these auxiliary measurements are in place, one should be able to establish whether the focal measurement is properly sensitive or insensitive.

THE STANDARDIZATION STRATEGY

Unfortunately, most auxiliary measurements face analogous validation problems, and require auxiliary measurements of their own. To reduce the number of features of a measurement situation that might, in principle, have to be studied, measurers usually rely heavily on standardization. For example, troopers are trained to operate radar detectors in a precisely specified

way. Lie detector operators try to make their sessions similar to one another and to the sessions conducted by other operators. Aptitude testing creates a standardized "reality," which is then applied identically to every subject tested. Survey researchers attempt to standardize their questions, as well as the social interaction between interviewers and interviewees.

Crucial to standardization is knowing what to standardize. Factors that make no difference need not be controlled. Factors that make little difference may be allowed some modest variability. If factors that affect measurements cannot be controlled, then some theory is needed to disentangle their effects.

THE EMPIRICAL BASIS OF STANDARDIZATION

Ideally, the effect of every possible factor would be established prior to taking (or interpreting) any measurement. Without such knowledge, measurements are inherently ambiguous. That ambiguity is sometimes clearest when it produces controversy. For example, court cases have hinged on the effects, if any, of variations in radar and lie detector procedures. The commercial success of aptitude tests is threatened by charges that they are affected by such "irrelevant" factors as coaching and previous testing experience. Considerable research has attempted to dispel or substantiate such charges. Ambiguity is least likely to be recognized and explored when there is a deeply-rooted convention regarding how data are to be collected; thus, the effects of possible procedural variations are never tested.

Practically speaking, few of the potentially confounding factors can be explored thoroughly. The number that have been examined signals the maturity of a field. There are perhaps thousands of studies on aptitude testing procedures, hundreds on lie detection, dozens on radar detection, and relatively few on surveying the unemployed.

In the absence of directly relevant empirical studies, one turns to indirectly relevant ones. For example, the "mere" tens of studies on what affects reported employment status (Bailar & Rothwell, 1984) can be supplemented by the thousands examining which factors influence interviews focused on other topics. Indeed, some scholars have attempted to aggregate such studies into theories of interviewing capable of explicating the overall impact of experimental procedures on responses (Mitchell & Carson, in press; National Research Council, 1982; Payne, 1952; Turner & Martin, 1984).

Where both data and theories are lacking, only lore is left to guide interpretation. Because human behavior is so complex, a myriad of factors could, conceivably, affect any response, especially if interpretation is approached with radical skepticism. As a result, effects of most factors are left to the informed speculation of those who design the measurements and use their results. The most extensive, and least visible, use of such judgment in measurement design is in determining what factors not to standardize. The importance of some of these factors may be explicitly discounted. However, the vast majority are just neglected because they are incapable of making a difference and do not merit serious consideration. For example, it is often convenient to ignore time of day when conducting surveys, to increase the chances of finding respondents at home. If survey researchers make this decision explicitly, they might defend it by arguing that circadian rhythms have too little effect on responses (to these particular questions) to bear standardization; or the question might not even occur to them, any more than they might worry about factors such as weather, street noise, or interviewers' eye, hair, or clothes color and biorhythm. Within any discipline, there is often strong informal agreement about such nuisance factors, based on undocumented experience and intuition. The unwritten character of these norms of indifference make it hard for outsiders to design studies that members of a discipline will find acceptable.

Even when uncontroversial, such norms have an ad hoc character, as unintegrated scraps of collected wisdom. They are usually more satisfying when tied to a unifying theory, which allows these interpretative principles to support one another, so that subsequent evidence must overturn them all if it is to overturn any one. For example, physical theory provides a basis for ignoring many aspects of the circumstances in which radar detectors are operated (e.g., latitude, pavement color). This account of which factors affect measurements seems much more trustworthy than the comparable account of the contextual factors that could not possibly affect behavior on lie detector tests.

Behavioral scientists are frequently surprised by neglected boundary conditions that prove to have powerful effects on behavior. Indeed, the history of behavioral science often seems driven by such surprises, which open new areas of investigation (McGuire, 1969). For example, reading from a prepared text keeps survey interviewers from expressing their own views verbally, but not from providing subtle cues by how they carry themselves, inflect their voices, and record responses. Although a source of heartache for survey researchers, these cues are a gold mine for students of nonverbal communication. Other scientists have made careers out of others' heartaches, such as how dress influences person perception, how question order affects reported attitudes, how response mode affects responses, and how stress affects the accuracy of reading and transcribing quantitative responses. Just one example of how complex these human interactions can be is the finding that matching the apparent race of interviewer and interviewee produces more extreme responses to race-related attitude questions, without having much other effect (e.g., not even on the race of the individuals who are nominated as favorite entertainers) (Turner & Martin, 1984).

DEALING WITH REACTIVE TESTING

Knowing which factors can influence responses shows what to standardize, but not how to standardize. In some cases, normative guidelines specify the measurement procedure. With radar detectors, contextual factors should be set in whatever way encourages police radar speed to match driver speedometer speed. With aptitude tests, the conventional wisdom is to avoid creating conditions that reward test wiseness or membership in the dominant culture. With lie detection, any factor (e.g., tester's demeanor) that induces stress should be eliminated. When a factor cannot be entirely eliminated (e.g., the tester must have some demeanor), then the common prescription is to

hold that factor constant. For example, lie detection may induce some stress no matter how the test is staged and the subject prepared. If, however, those conditions can be controlled, then operators can try to learn something from differences in the stress level associated with different questions. Concentrating on differences is, of course, not helpful for measuring absolute arousal levels. It could mislead if the change in arousal caused by lying depended on the arousal caused by other factors (i.e., was sensitive to the somewhat arbitrary method of standardization).

The meaning of changes would also be problematic if respondents were uncertain about the truth of their answers (e.g., if they did not remember exactly where they were on the evening of a crime or did not know whether they would steal from an employer if given the chance) and this uncertainty produces an unstable level of arousal. In that case, the measurement technique would not yield an interpretable signal. Its signal would be misleading if respondents reduced their uncertainty by attempting to "read" from the situation what the tester believes the right answer to be or expects them to say. That reading might make them first to feel like liars or like trusted employees, and then to respond with the corresponding arousal levels. To forestall this possibility, testers strive for an impassive demeanor. Yet, for a cue-hungry respondent, that, too, might be interpreted as meaningful (e.g., as hostility or suspicion). The resulting measurement would be partly true, insofar as it captures one way that respondents are capable of viewing themselves. However, it would be only part of the truth, insofar as respondents could also see themselves otherwise. To reduce this threat, all aspects of the testing situation that catch subjects' attention must convey the proper, neutral impression. Such total control would reveal subjects' lack of clarity.

When subjects are uncertain about the truth of their answers, the only way to get a clearer measure of the truth that they are meant to reveal (e.g., what they saw, what they would do) is to sharpen respondents' perceptions by reactive testing. The usual (and negative) image of reactive testing is of a strongly suggestive setting (e.g., one communicating mistrust), which changes the respondent in a direction desired by the measurer (Rosenthal & Rosnow, 1969). A more constructive approach is somehow to help respondents remember what they saw (Wells & Loftus, 1984) or envision their own future behavior. Such interventions are anathema to many social scientists, who are loathe to change respondents in any way. However, a direct attempt to sharpen perceptions may have more interpretable (and salutary) effects than an attempt at impassivity that exerts unintended and unanalyzed influences. Of course, a commitment to complete experimental control carries no guarantee of its attainment. It may be no more possible to resolve a respondent's uncertain feelings than it is possible to create an impression of impartiality or to ensure that lying causes a measurable change in arousal.

USING ILL-DEFINED QUESTIONS

Even when their beliefs are well articulated, lie-detector subjects can only provide sharp answers if they are asked sharp questions. With questions concerning facts, achieving clarity should be relatively straightforward if "good English" queries about what subjects did, or observed, are used. The art of doing so is not unlike the art of formulating good questions for achievement tests or demographic surveys. One common threat in the practice of these arts is ambiguous terms; another threat is terms that are clear, but mean different things to different people. With standardized questions, careful pretesting can clarify how terms are interpreted by individuals in the target population(s). With unique questions, such as those posed in lie detector sessions, good clinical skills are the main safeguard for detecting and correcting residual confusion. Those skills must be considerable with a confusing setting that invites second guessing.

To be made clear to respondents, questions must first be clear to the questioners. The operators of lie detectors rely on their clients (e.g., employers, the police) for their questions. Thus, those clients must know exactly what they mean, for example, by "find out if these prospective employees are going to steal from us (or reveal proprietary information, or be sympathetic to union activity)." If they do not, then responsible operators must either decline the job or create their own questions (representing what the clients might have asked had their thinking been clearer). Survey researchers face similar difficulties with clients who want to know how well the public likes them, their product, their industry, their candidate, or their advertising message. There are typically many ways of defining both "like" and the potential objects of that affection.

Unless researchers are willing and able to coax more precise specifications out of their clients, they are likely to end up with such ill-defined questions as, "Do you like nuclear power?" A thoughtful respondent might, even should, ask whether "like" means "am enthusiastic about," "am willing to tolerate," or "would choose it among competing energy technologies." However the verb is interpreted, the thoughtful respondent would also ask what aspects of the technology are to be evaluated. For example, "Can I consider its effect on the distribution of wealth and centralization of political power in this country? Or, is this just a question of economic benefits versus environmental risks, or just a question about relative production costs?" If "like" means "prefer relative to competing energy technologies," then the set of possible alternatives needs to be defined. For example, does it include an aggressive program of energy conservation? Should those comparison technologies be considered in their current state, or in the state they might attain with a massive research and development investment (e.g., for solar power)? Depending on the purpose of the questioning, any of these might be the right definition (Fischhoff, 1983).

DEVELOPING PRECISE QUESTIONS

Formulating such an attitude question is, in many ways, no less complicated than formulating the mandate for a policy analyst paid to evaluate nuclear power as an energy option. Deciding what "like" means is akin to deciding what policy analytic procedure (e.g., cost-benefit analysis, multi-attribute utility analysis) to use in measuring the attractiveness of nuclear power. Specifying the relevant (and irrelevant) features of the technology and its alternatives is akin to operationalizing that

procedure. Doing so requires many seemingly technical decisions that can markedly affect the results of the analysis. Indeed, unless one alternative dominates all competitors (in the sense of being superior in all respects), the choice of definition will, in principle, determine the alternative chosen (Fischhoff & Cox, 1985; Fischhoff, Lichtenstein, Slovic, Derby, & Keeney, 1981; Stokey & Zeckhauser, 1978; von Winterfeldt & Edwards, 1986).

If these features are not specified explicitly by those who ask questions, then they must be inferred by those who answer them. To apply their craft, policy analysts must provide whatever details are omitted by the policymakers hiring them. Doing so puts the analysts in the position of setting social policy--by determining what matters. Conscientious analysts will press their clients for details. Their success will depend on how well articulated the policymakers' philosophy is and how candidly they can discuss it in public (e.g., can they admit to assigning a value to human life or to ignoring distributional effects?). The comparable challenge for attitude researchers is discerning exactly why their clients want to know about people's opinions. That is, what political or marketing or theoretical questions hinge on the answers? To ask precise survey questions, researchers need precise client questions. If researchers just guess at what their clients wanted to ask, then they may develop sharp survey questions, the answers to which do not serve their clients' needs (a fact which may or may not be recognized). If researchers leave their own questions vague, then respondents must impute the missing details to provide complete, thoughtful answers. Where there is good societal consensus on what the issues are (e.g., regarding nuclear power), respondents might guess correctly what precise question was intended--just as people usually know the kind of answer sought by "How are you?" Whether respondents make the correct inference will depend on whether they share clients' cultural and linguistic norms. Whether incorrect inferences are discovered will depend on what methodological precautions are taken.

If clients cannot supply the details necessary for formulating precise questions, then it may mean that the issues are not well articulated in their own minds. In such cases, it might seem strange to expect precise answers from respondents. They, too, might be insensitive to the nuances of question formulation, resulting, for example, in quite similar responses to questions that are actually quite different.

For example, over the past 15 years, there have been substantial changes in the publicly accepted "facts" regarding nuclear power and in the focal topics in the debate over its future. Events like the Three Mile Island accident have focused attention on and magnified nuclear power's apparent risks. Events like the Washington Public Power Supply System default have focused attention on and raised concerns about its economic benefits. Nonetheless, there has been relatively little change in both the questions asked by public opinion surveys and the responses to them (Rankin, Nealey, & Melber, 1984). Despite the changing facts and foci in the public debate, the questions have remained quite general and the responses have remained quite stable (divided very roughly into 40% in favor, 40% opposed, and 20% undecided). To treat these responses as thoughtful opinions, one would have to argue, first, that respondents have interpreted the general question to fit the issues of their day (i.e., in some sense it is not the same question, despite having the same wording) and, second, that the changing issues and information had no aggregate effect on opinions about nuclear power. An alternative interpretation is that instead of elaborating the details of a value question, respondents simply give a ''gut level'' response. As long as the issue is relatively remote from respondents' central concerns, their responses should be relatively unmoved by public events. It would be a mistake, however, to take such responses as indicative of deeply held beliefs or predictive of actual behavior (Ajzen & Fishbein, 1977; Schuman & Johnson, 1976). On the slightly more specific and significantly more central question of whether respondents would want a nuclear power plant in their neighborhood, there have been dramatic changes in attitudes (Farhar-Pilgrim & Freudenburg, 1984).

SEEING QUESTIONS IN CONTEXT

Insensitivity to the nuances of question wording need not imply insensitivity to the nuances of the social settings within which they are asked. Socialized individuals have elaborate and general schemas for interpreting interpersonal interactions. As a result, even settings intended to be neutral and unrevealing may be mined for hints as to what the interviewers are thinking. For example, ''What do they want me to say? How intense are my feelings expected to be? What is the range of opinions expected? How hard am I expected to think? Is there anything to be gained by misrepresenting my views (e.g., avoiding stigma, influencing public policy)?'' The resulting responses may say more about how respondents view the social setting than about how they view the topic of the question (DeMaio, 1984; Rosenthal & Rosnow, 1969).

The pressure that an interview setting exerts on survey responses is akin to the pressure that social forces exert on responses to goods in the marketplace (e.g., the price paid for a new consumer product or an added feature of an existing product). A good's apparent cost of production and scarcity should set some rough limits on what can be charged for it. However, consumers may also be sensitive to, or even hungry for, cues regarding questions such as, ''What are others willing to pay? What is this like that I've purchased (or rejected) in the past? Will people view me differently if I own this? (and, Do I care if they do?)'' It is merchandisers' job to shape, first, how consumers complete those missing details of the questions posed by the market and, second, how they provide answers. The decisions that emerge from this process may be interpreted as ''revealing consumers' preferences.'' However, those are not necessarily the same preferences that would have been revealed had the question been posed (and interpreted) in different ways.

Whether particular preferences are revealed consistently should depend on whether the market consistently evokes the same (incomplete) perspective. Consistency is enhanced when customers not only buy a product, but also identify themselves as the kind of person who buys it. Brand and party loyalty can be signs of such commitment, in which an initial ''purchase'' evokes a subset of a person's values which, in time, assumes precedence and permanence.

THE VALIDITY OF PREFERENCES

Whether revealed preferences are also ''true'' preferences is, in part, a definitional question. All but the most basic, biological preferences arise from the interaction between people and their environment (including the objects, people, and symbols in it). Either by analysis or by experience, people must determine what they prefer in the myriad of decisions that the world throws (or might throw) at them. The number of possible evaluation questions or formulations of those questions is so large the people cannot know what they prefer in most specific decisions until those questions have been put to them.

For the marketer, the ''true'' question is the one put forth by the marketplace; the preferences that it elicits are the ones that matter, those that find expression in action. The possibility that a different presentation might evoke a different ''true preference'' is, of course, a matter of great practical concern. However, the possibility that these actions may not represent the actors' best interests is not meaningful. By contrast, investigators attempting to measure people's values are troubled by the thought that their questions reveal only a portion of what respondents believe. One exception might be those political pollsters whose stock in trade is finding just that one question that will elicit the greatest expression of support for their client candidate or issue.

THE FULL SPECIFICATION STRATEGY

The ability to manipulate expressed preferences (deliberately or inadvertently), like the ability to shape market preferences, reflects people's sensitivity to what is presented (including its social context), combined with their relative insensitivity to what is left out. A theoretically appealing response to this differential sensitivity is to spell out all pertinent details, thereby ensuring that nothing important is missed (i.e., presenting those details in an explicit and comprehensible form, while making certain that none of the interview's auxiliary details belie its explicit message). For the measurer, this strategy requires extensive normative and descriptive knowledge. The former is needed to determine the right question and specify its details. The latter is needed to anticipate how respondents will perceive what is presented to them.

For respondents, this strategy requires such a thorough understanding of the substantive issues that they can address whatever formulation they receive. That may be asking a lot, especially when the investigators (or their clients) have generated (what is for them) the right question only after extended deliberations. One threat to comprehension of the question is overloading the respondent with all the details that need to be considered in addressing the full question. A second threat is finding either the very idea of a fully specified question or the particular formulation chosen to be a foreign way of thinking. If respondents feel confused, then they could give ''Don't know'' or protest responses. On the other hand, doing so may seem like an admission of failure, which also disenfranchises them regarding that issue. It may seem preferable to make some guess at what one's opinion would be, given full comprehension. With the relatively simple questions usually used in survey research, no-response rates are typically quite low, however obscure or involved the underlying topic (Smith, 1984).

Among those respondents willing to answer complex questions, a likely result of overload is insensitivity to some of the details. If it is too hard to take it all in, then respondents may just leave part of it out. One sign of such measurement failure is giving similar responses to stimuli (e.g., market goods, attitude questions) that differ considerably, but in ways that attract little attention. An example might be people's ignorance regarding many details of the insurance policies that they themselves have bought (Kunreuther et al., 1978). The details are all spelled out, and strongly affect the value of the policy. However, there are too many of them to be taken in and integrated into an overall assessment of what policies are worth. It takes some combination of regulatory action, market pressures, and agents eager for repeat business to make the premiums that purchasers pay approximate what policies are worth. The widely disparate rates that consumers pay per unit of protection (e.g., life coverage obtained through straight term, whole life, and travel coverage) may reflect, in part, the difficulty of even trying to absorb all the details.

THE ROLE OF RESPONDENT EXPECTATIONS

The gap between what respondents say and what they would have said had they attended to all the details should be greatest when time is limited, when motivation is weak, and when respondents' "default assumptions" (what they would expect unspecified details to be) are wrong. For example, potential purchasers of a life insurance policy might expect premiums to be quoted in annual amounts, reimbursement to be the same for all types of deaths, and coverage to remain constant over the life of a policy. If their expectations are sufficiently strong, respondents may not even examine those aspects of policies, instead focusing their limited attention on details that seem less predictable. If they do notice being offered, say, a declining term policy with double indemnity for accidents and a biannual premium, they may have difficulty knowing how to evaluate these usually standard features.

Social norms and industry standards ensure that many goods and questions are presented in fairly familiar formulations. However, that need not be the case. Marketing objectives may foster formulations designed to frustrate comparison with competing goods (e.g., bundling life insurance with complex investment opportunities; using different size boxes, nutritional additives, and premiums with breakfast cereals). Political maneuvering may produce proposals designed to appeal to such complex constituencies that it is hard to evaluate them or those who vote for them. Researchers' theoretical interests may lead them to pose questions with unusual limiting conditions (e.g., "Do you expect to have a[nother] child in the next 4 years, assuming that you stay married and we don't have a major recession?"). One response to unfamiliar formulations is, again, refusing to participate, with the attendant risks of being ignored or disrespected. A second is trying to assume the measurer's novel perspective on the spot. A third is answering as though a more familiar ques-

tion had been asked. None of these strategies is likely to provide satisfactory responses to the former elicitor.

ADAPTING RESPONDENTS TO QUESTIONS

One plausible treatment for overload or unfamiliarity is helping respondents answer the question that has been put to them. Possible mechanisms include giving respondents extended time to think about the question, allowing them to discuss its implications, and providing alternative perspectives for their consideration. Unfortunately, these methods are neither easy, proven, nor compatible with customary measurement philosophy. To varying degrees, they require spending more time with respondents, making that time quality time (e.g., by providing more accomplished interviewers), generating or developing normative analyses of how the issue might be judged, and taking seriously respondents' complaints and discomforts. Such methods might help respondents discern and express their values (yet create an illusion of greater thoroughness). They might also have no effect, confuse respondents (by overwhelming them with unfamiliar possibilities), or induce some systematic bias (by providing some pervasive alternative perspective or inadvertently suggesting that one perspective is more appropriate). Fear of this last possibility drives most measurement procedures to adopt the stance of being neutral instruments that project stimuli against subjects and faithfully record the ensuing responses. An aptitude test with multiple-choice questions whose answers are coded directly onto sheets designed for computer processing might exemplify this philosophy. It could also be seen in impassive lie detector operators and survey interviewers who refuse to give any overt hint regarding the meaning of their procedures.

Such impassivity attempts to ensure uniform application of a procedure designed to minimize the risk of influencing responses by anything that the measurer does deliberately. The preferred risk is influencing responses inadvertently--by confusing respondents, eliciting an unrepresentative subset of their potentially relevant perspectives, or just evoking a shallow response. Given these risk preferences, most methodological work focuses on developing questions that stand alone, needing no interactive clarification.

Where this is not a plausible aspiration, the methodological cupboard is relatively bare. Perhaps the most relevant skills are resident in clinical psychologists, counselors, decision analysts, and the like. Through intensive interaction, they attempt to help clients understand their own values. Although the exploration of possible responses may be more or less directive, the problem itself is meant to be the client's. However successful these techniques may be, helping people solve their own problems is still somewhat different than helping them understand an interviewer's question and what they think about it. With respondents' own problems, there is always some reservoir of relevant thoughts to stabilize and direct thinking.

None of these difficulties would exist if people knew exactly what they thought and wanted regarding all possible formulations of all possible issues. Such comprehensiveness is, perhaps, not only an unreasonable expectation but also an insidious aspiration. People who feel that they could (and should) have some opinion about everything risk ending up with thoughtful opinions about nothing (Ellul, 1966).

The demands of adapting to novel questions and formulations arise not only with questions about the world, but with many questions about oneself. For example, one possible definition of being "unemployed" is "having worked less than 1 hour in the preceding week" and "still looking for work." The first of these two conditions is a question of fact that could, in principle, be resolved objectively (i.e., by consulting all possible employers). It is examined by asking questions on labor force surveys as a matter of convenience (Bailar & Rothwell, 1984).

The second condition is a quasi-fact, ultimately requiring a subjective assessment by the respondent. That might be an easy chore for someone fresh out of work or school who is actively pounding the pavement and sending out vitae. Whether they are "still looking for work" might be less clear for individuals who are discouraged about finding new jobs, enjoying their new-found leisure, or thinking about returning to school for some retraining. State employment services use this concept by specifying, for example, the weekly number of potential employer contacts needed to qualify as "looking for work." That specification may serve bureaucratic needs and express the social philosophy underlying the state's unemployment compensation policy, without capturing how the unemployed think about their predicament. The unemployed may view their job contacts as a ritual having little to do with their personal definition of "looking for work." Or they may take the contacts seriously, but be uncertain about whether their past failures leave any reason to go on looking. In such situations, they do not know whether they are unemployed, in the terms of the official definition.

THE SOURCE OF QUESTIONS

Most measurement is strongly measurer-centered. In one sense, this is natural and unavoidable: People ask questions about things that interest them. In another sense, however, it is still quite natural, but possible and even desirable to avoid: People would like to receive the answers to their questions in a readily usable form. With physical measurements, this desire is often satisfied without sacrificing any measurement validity. For example, modern electronics make it possible to convert the physical evidence received by a radar detector into a digital readout. The wide acceptance of detectors suggests that the desire for convenience has not overly compromised accuracy.

With social measurements, satisfying the measurer's convenience is more likely to carry a price. For example, to meet the perceived needs of educational administrators, the developers of aptitude tests reduce complex human properties to numerical summaries. Critics argue that what those numbers capture is at best an unrepresentative subset of true human aptitudes. Although they may accept some of this criticism, defenders of the tests would argue that richer accounts of ability provide too little additional information to justify the additional expense of creating and processing them, given current measurement techniques.

Test developers are less ready to accept a second charge associated with measurer-centeredness, namely that their tests reflect a perspective (or culture or world outlook or linguistic commu-

nity) that is foreign to many subjects. Such a test would be unduly sensitive to a supposedly irrelevant factor, subscription to the developers' perspective, and unduly insensitive to concomitant factors, such as subjects' confusion, misunderstanding, and need to translate what they know into the tester's terms. The edifice of psychometric techniques allows some of these possibilities to be examined empirically, while others engender the same appeals to faith that defend the use of numerical summaries. A third charge against measurer-centered procedures is that they are reactive, changing respondents through the questioning process. Possible mechanisms for such change include providing new information, suggesting new perspectives, inhibiting the expression of certain views, and forcing consideration of previously neglected issues.

ADAPTING QUESTIONS TO RESPONDENTS

Faced with similar threats, anthropologists set as a goal "de-provincializing rationality," understanding respondents' world outlook sufficiently well to see how they conceptualize an issue. Achieving this goal is a daunting task for even a single issue, much less the diversity of issue-respondent combinations faced by measurers. Within resource constraints, it is hard to manage much more than focus groups, intensive discussion with individuals like those who will eventually be questioned.

Even when complete empathy is achieved, a gap still may exist between what respondents have to offer and what measurers (or their clients) need for their theoretical or practical purposes. That is, they may understand the measurers' issues, but not what they think about it, beyond being able to identify some relevant values that might, in time, be coalesced into an opinion on the specific issue. If the gap cannot be filled (reactively) by helping respondents extend themselves to the new issue, the measurers may be best off asking the most relevant question that respondents can conveniently answer. Then, the measurers, rather than the respondent, can close the gap between what needs to be asked and what can be answered. Using whatever theory and insight are available, the measurer would then attempt to deduce what respondents would think about the issue were they to address it in depth. Treating such extrapolated responses as actual answers may discomfort some measurers. Among other things, it means that the measurer assumes responsibility for filling the gap, rather than leaving it implicitly to the respondent. The hope is that the measurer can do a better job, benefiting from the opportunities for reflection, analysis, and peer review that come with an open process--compared with the struggle of individual respondents to project themselves into a new question. In addition, the openness of the adjustment procedure may itself serve as a constant useful reminder that respondents do not really know what they think on the question.

An alternative strategy is to ask clients to reformulate their issues into ways that are more compatible with respondents' natural way of thinking. In addition to serving the technical purpose of encouraging more comprehensible questions, doing so would also serve the social purpose of putting respondents' concerns at the center of policymaking, marketing, theorizing, or whatever other purpose motivated the measurement effort.

CONCLUSION

Valid measurements of people's values are sensitive to all relevant features of the objects (e.g., goods, policies, candidates) being evaluated and insensitive to all irrelevant features. Relevance is, in part, a normative question, resolved by the measurers' determination of which features of the object are legitimate factors in its evaluation. For marketing purposes, for example, that set of features may emphasize those aspects of objects that can be manipulated to enhance an object's attractiveness. In most cases, the set includes descriptions of the quantity or magnitude of the object being evaluated. Typically, the set of features excludes any aspects of the measurement setting that might be construed as communicating what respondents' values should or be misconstrued as belonging to the evaluated object. Within these normative constraints, relevance is a descriptive question, resolved by respondents' choice of which features in the permitted set to value.

A normative failure of measurement means that the measurer (or client) has identified the measured object incorrectly or imprecisely. A descriptive failure means that respondents are unable to identify or express their relevant values. Either failure is more likely for complex and novel evaluations, where there has been insufficient opportunity to articulate the relevance of basic values for the specific evaluation. In such cases, measurers may not know what they want to ask about and respondents may not know what they want, vis-a-vis the question presented to them. Uncertain measurers may not ask the right question for their purposes, perhaps unwittingly changing their question from application to application. Where respondents' values are equally inarticulate, they may not notice the changes either. Where they are more attuned to the nuances of formulation, the variability in their responses may be misinterpreted as instability rather than sensitivity. Uncertain respondents may produce confused and inappropriate responses whose deficiencies may or may not be recognized (by respondent or measurer). Perhaps the worst situation arises when measurer and respondent have incomplete and incompatible perspectives, rendering effective communication largely impossible, while the measurement procedure prevents the sort of unstructured confrontation that can reveal (and perhaps resolve) misunderstandings.

Attaining normative clarity requires substantive understanding of the object being evaluated. The following section briefly describes an attempt to clarify these issues in one specific context, obtaining judgmental evaluations of changes in visibility.

Perception of Visibility

The regulation of technologies, in the United States, is increasingly dominated by a belief in the possibility of comprehensive quantitative analysis. Various forms of risk and benefit assessment are employed to estimate the effects of potentially hazardous actions. Once estimated, those effects are subjected to techniques like cost-benefit analysis, decision analysis, and multi-attribute utility analyses in the hopes of reducing them to a common numeraire (Bentkover, Covello, & Mumpower, 1985; Fischhoff et al., 1981; von Winterfeldt & Edwards, 1986). Fol-

lowing that reduction, the logic of each technique provides summary guidance on the advisability of the evaluated actions.

Where the belief in quantification exists, effects that cannot be readily and credibly measured tend to be neglected. Recognizing this, scientists concerned with hard-to-measure effects have been straining to improve their measurement methodology. Deterioration in visibility is one such environmental threat whose importance in regulatory decisions may be diminished or disturbed by quantification difficulties. Lest visibility be ignored, researchers have embarked on ambitious programs designed to assess how visibility is affected by various environmental interventions and how much those effects are worth to people.

Both pursuits are complicated by the inevitable role of psychological processes in integrating the physical consequences of those interventions (Malm, Kelley, Molenar, & Daniel, 1981; Middleton, Stewart, & Leary, 1985). Although the visual system has been studied carefully over the last century, a subjective element remains in how changes in the air are interpreted, which cannot be predicted entirely from physical data. As a result, it is not enough to get the (difficult) atmospheric chemistry right to predict how environmental interventions will be seen.

Once they have been seen, changes in visibility must be evaluated. A natural place to look for evidence of "revealed" preferences is in marketplace behavior (Griliches, 1971; Ridker & Henning, 1967). Unfortunately, changes in visibility are rarely, if ever, bought and sold directly. An alternative strategy is to look at how differences in visibility affect the prices of goods thought to be sensitive to visibility. Although some valiant attempts have been made to pursue this strategy (Brookshire, Thayer, Schulze, & d'Arge, 1982), they are fraught with methodological difficulties, including how to measure ambient visibility, how to determine what consumers perceive visibility to be, and how to establish that consumers have assigned visibility a clear role in their overall decisions.

As a supplement to these market-based studies, a pioneering group of economists has experimented with interview-based studies, in which consumers are asked to bid for environmental changes within the context of hypothetical markets (Cummings, Brookshire, & Schulze, 1986; Engelbrecht-Wiggans, 1980; Randall, Ives, & Eastman, 1974; Tolley et al., 1986). These investigators have persevered despite the skepticism of a profession that has traditionally had little faith in mere "expressed preferences." Those doubts have been eroded by a number of factors, including the lack of a credible "revealed preference" method (for discerning values from marketplace behavior), the ever-increasing number of scientists performing such bidding studies, and the failure to observe in those studies any clear evidence of "strategic behavior" (wherein respondents misrepresent their actual values to distort the study's overall results).

Threats to Measurement

Although these techniques break important new ground for economics and social research, they also raise difficult theoretical questions (Cummings et al., 1986; Rowe & Chestnut, 1982). Perhaps the foremost of these is whether respondents possess sufficiently well-articulated values for the particular good offered in the experiment to answer the interviewers' highly specific bidding questions. If not, then their responses may not represent what they would have said after prolonged, thoughtful deliberations. Thus, despite the focus on visibility, responses in these interviews may be no more definitive expressions of true value than consumers' responses to the visibility component of market questions.

In either the interview or the market setting, one possible result of respondent confusion is neglecting visibility, relative to more easily considered consequences (e.g., dollar costs). A second possible result is a search by respondents for hints (from interviewers or marketers) as to what a reasonable response might be. Those hints might be sought in the wording of questions, the nonverbal communication of interviewers, the nuances of packaging, or the social staging of the interview. If these unintentional hints vary across interviews or studies, then the value assigned to visibility may vary as well, suggesting that people do not care that much about it (if they did, then they should be able to provide consistent evaluations). Whatever inference is made about the worth of visibility, the lack of a robust evaluation methodology may effectively diminish its role in regulatory decisions.

The existence of such apparently unstable or "labile" values regarding significant issues has become a topic of growing interest in survey research, experimental psychology, and behavioral economics (Fischhoff, Slovic, & Lichtenstein, 1980; Hogarth, 1982; Kahneman & Tversky, 1979). Within the bidding game (or "contingent valuation") literature, it has emerged as inexplicable inconsistencies between responses to games that have differed in seemingly irrelevant procedural details, such as the "starting point" (i.e., the first potential bid offered for respondents' approval or rejection) or the "payment vehicle" (i.e., the means by which the payment would be collected). As part of a project sponsored by the Electric Power Research Institute, we are exploring these general issues in the context of visibility (Fischhoff & Furby, 1987a, b).

A Secondary Analysis

Our initial effort has been to examine the consistency of visibility evaluations reported in some two dozen studies from the published and unpublished literature. We began with a theoretical analysis of how visibility could be defined as a good, in terms of both what respondents are asked to evaluate and why they might choose to value it. Subsequently, we characterized the collected studies in terms of this framework.

At this point, our analysis indicates great diversity in what investigators have chosen as the appropriate definition of "visibility," as well as in what features of the good they have felt it necessary to specify explicitly to make the evaluation question meaningful to respondents. On a methodological level, this variability in definitions complicates comparing studies. Ordinarily, convergence in the results from different studies is encouraging, suggesting robust evaluations. However, when the good in question varies across studies, it is unclear whether those variations do not matter or simply are not noticed. In the latter case, there may be too much convergence of responses in studies that are actually asking quite different questions.

The goal of our secondary analysis is to assess the extent to which the values observed in different studies have been sensitive to meaningful differences in procedure and insensitive to meaningless ones, and to provide a summary of what is known empirically about the value of visibility. That review is meant to facilitate exploiting the large body of existing data for regulatory purposes. The variability in these definitions raises the question of whether the risk management community can provide a clear, consensus specification of visibility as a good. The experts may have as hard a time as lay people in articulating their perception of what is important. Insofar as the choice of definition makes a statement about what visibility should mean, its resolution is a normative question. As part of our analysis, we will describe the options available in defining visibility, discussing the policy implications of each (Fischhoff & Cox, 1985).

Once a definition has been chosen, the problem remains of how to get reliable quantitative responses to it from people who may care a lot about visibility yet not know exactly how much they care. Eliciting such responses requires a descriptive understanding of how people interpret different representations of a good and how they express their values. We hope to begin some empirical work on these questions in the not-too-distant future. Our current thinking is that a viable methodology for value measurement must be quite respondent-centered. In a sense, people are now being asked to answer the questions that economics is not eager to touch. An alternative strategy is to find out where people do have stable values and fit the economics around them. It may emerge that there is a core of essential issues related to the value of visibility that are not credibly reduced to quantitative terms. We will consider these issues in the context of visibility, with an eye toward their implications for the general aspiration for comprehensive, quantitative analysis of environmental issues.

References

Ajzen, I., & Fishbein, M. (1977). Attitude-behavior relations: A theoretical analysis and review of empirical research. *Psychological Bulletin, 84,* 888-918.

Bailar, B. A., & Rothwell, N. D. (1984). Measuring employment and unemployment. In C. F. Turner & E. Martin (Eds.), *Surveying subjective phenomena* (Vol. 2) (pp. 129-142). New York: Russell Sage.

Bentkover, J. D., Covello, V., & Mumpower, G. (Eds.). (1985). *Benefits assessment: The state of the art.* Dordrecht, The Netherlands: Reidel.

Brookshire, D. S., Thayer, M. A., Schulze, W. D., & d'Arge, R. C. (1982). Valuing public goods: A comparison of survey and hedonic approaches. *American Economic Review, 72,* 165-177.

Campbell, D. T., & Fiske, R. W. (1959). Convergent and discriminant validity by the multitrait-multimethod matrix. *Psychological Bulletin, 56,* 81-105.

Cummings, R. G., Brookshire, D. S., & Schulze, W. D. (1986). *Valuing public goods: The contingent valuation method.* Totowa, NJ: Rowman & Allenheld.

DeMaio, T. J. (1984). Social desirability and survey measurement: A review. In C. F. Turner & E. Martin (Eds.), *Surveying subjective phenomena* (Vol. 2) New York: Russell Sage.

Ellul, J. (1966). *Propaganda.* New York: Knopf.

Engelbrecht-Wiggans, R. (1980). Auctions and bidding models: A survey. *Management Science, 26,* 119-142.

Farhar-Pilgrim, B., & Freudenburg, W. R. (1984). *Nuclear energy in perspective: A comparative assessment of the public view.* In W. R. Freudenburg & E. A. Rosa (Eds.), *Public reaction to nuclear power: Are there critical masses?* Boulder, CO: Westview.

Fischhoff, B. (1983). "Acceptable risk": The case of nuclear power. *Journal of Policy Analysis and Management, 2,* 559-575.

Fischhoff, B. (1984). Setting standards: A systematic approach to managing public health and safety risks. *Management Science, 30,* 823-843.

Fischhoff, B., & Cox, L. A., Jr. (1985). Conceptual framework for regulatory benefits assessment. In J. D. Bentkover, V. T. Covello, & J. Mumpower (Eds.), *Benefits assessment: The state of the art* (pp. 51-84). Dordrecht, The Netherlands: Reidel.

Fischhoff, B., & Furby, L. (1987a). *Measuring values: A conceptual framework for interpreting transactions with special reference to contingent valuation of visibility.* Eugene, OR: Eugene Research Institute.

Fischhoff, B., & Furby, L. (1987b). A review and critique of Tulley, Randall et al., *"Establishing and valuing the effects of improved visibility in the eastern United States."* Eugene, OR: Eugene Research Institute.

Fischhoff, B., Lichtenstein, S., Slovic, P., Derby, S., & Keeney, R. (1981). *Acceptable risk.* New York: Cambridge University Press.

Fischhoff, B., Slovic, P., & Lichtenstein, S. (1980). Knowing what we want: Measuring labile values. In T. Wallsten (Ed.), *Cognitive processes in choice and decision behavior.* Hillsdale, NJ: Erlbaum.

Freudenberg, W. R., & Rosa, E. A. (Eds.). (1985). *Public reaction to nuclear power: Are there critical masses?* (pp. 117-141). Boulder, CO: Westview.

Griliches, Z. (Ed.). (1971). *Price indexes and quality change.* Cambridge, MA: Harvard University Press.

Hogarth, R. M. (Ed.). (1982). *New directions for methodology of social and behavioral science: The framing of questions and the consistency of response.* San Francisco, CA: Jossey-Bass.

Kahneman, D., & Tversky, A. (1979). Prospect theory. *Econometrica, 47,* 263-292.

Kunreuther, H. R., Ginsberg, L., Miller, P., Sagi, P., Slovic, P., Borkin, B., & Katz, N. (1978). *Disaster insurance protection: Public policy lessons.* New York: John Wiley & Sons.

Malm, W., Kelley, K., Molenar, J., & Daniel, T. C. (1981). Human perception of visual air quality (uniform haze). *Atmospheric Environment, 15,* 1875-1890.

McGuire, W. J. (1969). Suspiciousness of experimenter's intent. In R. Rosenthal & R. L. Rosnow (Eds.), *Artifact in behavioral research.* New York: Academic Press.

Middleton, P., Stewart, T. R., & Leary, J. (1985). On the use of human judgment and physical/chemical measurements in visual air quality management. *Journal of the Air Pollution Control Association, 35,* 11-18.

Mitchell, R. C., & Carson, R. T. (in press). *Using surveys to value public goods: The contingent valuation method.* Washington, DC: Resources for the Future.

National Research Council. (1982). *Survey measure of subjective phenomena.* Washington, DC.

Payne, S. I. (1952). *The art of asking questions.* Princeton, NJ: Princeton University Press.

Randall, A., Ives, B., & Eastman, C. (1974). Bidding games for valuation of aesthetic environmental improvements. *Journal of Environmental Economics and Management, 1,* 132-149.

Rankin, W. L., Nealey, S. M., & Melber, B. D. (1984). Overview of national attitudes towards nuclear energy. In W. R. Freudenberg & E. A. Rosa (Eds.), *Public reaction to nuclear power: Are there critical masses?* (pp. 41-68). Boulder, CO: Westview.

Ridker, R. G., & Henning, J. A. (1967). The determination of residential property values with special reference to air pollution (St. Louis, Missouri). *Review of Economic Statistics, 49,* 246-257.

Rosenthal, R., & Rosnow, R. L. (1969). *Artifact in behavioral research.* New York: Academic Press.

Rowe, R. D., & Chestnut, L.G. (1982). *The value of visibility: Theory and applications.* Cambridge, MA: Abt Books.

Schuman, H., & Johnson, M. (1976). Attitudes and behavior. *Annual Review of Sociology, 2,* 161-207.

Slovic, P., Fischhoff, B., & Lichtenstein, S. (1982). Response mode, framing, and information processing effects in risk assessment. In R. M. Hogarth (Ed.), *New directions for methodology of social and behavioral science: The framing of questions and the consistency of response* (pp. 21-36). San Francisco, CA: Jossey-Bass.

Smith, T. W. (1984). Nonattitudes: A review and evaluation. In C. F. Turner & E. Martin (Eds.), *Surveying subjective phenomenon, (Vol. 2).* New York: Russell Sage.

Stokey, E., & Zeckhauser, R. (1978). *A primer of policy analysis.* New York: Norton.

Tolley, G., Randall, A., Blomquist, G., Brien, M., Fabian, R., Fishelson, G., Frankel, A., Grenchik, M., Hoehn, J., Kelly, A., Krumm, R., Mensah, E., & Smith, T. (1986). *Establishing and valuing the effects of improved visibility in eastern United States.* Washington, DC: U.S. Environmental Protection Agency.

Turner, C. F., & Martin, E. (Eds.). (1984). *Surveying subjective phenomenon (Vol. 2).* New York: Russell Sage.

Von Winterfeldt, D., & Edwards, W. (1986). *Decision analysis and behavioral research.* New York: Cambridge University Press.

Wells, G. L., & Loftus, E. F. (Eds.). (1984). *Eyewitness testimony: Psychological perspectives.* Cambridge, England: Cambridge University Press.

Norms and Behavior in Philosophy and Social Science

Douglas MacLean
Center for Philosophy and Public Policy
University of Maryland.

Claudia Mills
Center for Philosophy and Public Policy
University of Maryland.

Half a century ago, the logical positivists tried to separate sharply the normative from the empirical. Underlying positivism was a view about science that maintained a fundamental distinction between facts and values and that generated a correspondingly naive view about the value-free methods of science.

Most philosophers of science today would reject the idea that facts and values can be clearly distinguished. Values seep into science at many junctures, for example, determining what to count as evidence, how to report findings, and the bases for accepting and rejecting theories. Those who theorize about science are now more comfortable discussing the value of various scientific enterprises.

The relationship between facts and values and between normative and empirical claims, even in the physical sciences, is more complicated than the positivists believed. As in philosophy, these relationships raise crucial problems in the social sciences, especially where normative theories play an important role.

Philosophers who construct normative theories may have a tendency to ignore relevant facts. They often make hand-waving appeals to their intuitions or to what "we believe," without explaining why these appeals should lend credence to the conclusions that follow. If we examine our normative convictions critically --perhaps even empirically--we can find many reasons not to be sanguine. It may be a regrettable fact that normative philosophy does not have better empirical grounding, but it is not surprising. Philosophers, after all, are not trained to work from empirical data. Often, they think that theirs is an *a priori* discipline, like mathematics.

It is more remarkable, however, to notice similar tendencies in the work of social scientists. They too can be blinded by their normative convictions and led to make *a priori* claims about how people actually behave or about how they would behave under certain circumstances.

Our interest in this subject has been stimulated by some recent work in what is now called behavioral decision theory. This is empirical work, much of which is designed explicitly to clarify the distinction between normative and empirical claims in economics, decision theory, and policy analysis. This work has general philosophical interest as well.

FACTS, NORMS, AND INTUITIONS

Normative philosophy and normative social science (i.e., all those disciplines or subdisciplines where moral, social, or political theory, or where conceptions of rational thought and action, play central roles) begin with intuitions. "Ethical theories have to start from somewhere" Williams (1985) wrote (p. 93). After finding various other possible foundations for moral philosophy unsatisfactory, he concluded that "the only starting point left is ethical experience itself" (p. 93). We will argue to a similar conclusion.

By claiming that intuitions are the foundations of normative inquiry, however, we do not suggest that these disciplines rely on some mysterious cognitive faculty that puts us directly in touch with true and objective values, as some earlier "intuitionist" moral theories may have suggested. We agree with Wil-

liams that intuitions are our "spontaneous convictions, moderately reflective but not yet theorized" (p. 94). Calling them spontaneous convictions suggests, correctly, that intuitions are usually invoked without being supported by appeals to evidence. Williams characterized intuitive responses as "assured and unprompted" (p. 97).

However, our intuitions sometimes rely on empirical assumptions about our psychological makeup, circumstances of our world, the range of politically feasible options, or our culture's shared moral experiences. They are to this extent vulnerable to empirical testing, and vulnerable in other ways as well. Intuitions may be the foundations of normative inquiry, but they are corrigible foundations.

One obvious problem with intuitions is that our firmest convictions may not be as widely shared as we think; almost certainly they will not be as widespread as we think they ought to be. Intuitions are culture-bound and shaped by our particular psychologies and historical circumstances. One philosopher's intuitions may be his convictions alone, or they may turn out to be shared by few people beyond the circle of his like-minded colleagues or those committed to the same theory.

The only way to know whether normative convictions are in fact universally shared, or would be under certain ideal conditions, is to gather evidence. This is something philosophers are not prone to do, nor is it always easy to know where to look for evidence, even for those who are better trained in empirical methods. How could we know, for example, whether people are happier if they are free? How can we determine actual consumer behavior under ideal circumstances where there is perfect information and no transaction costs? Although our normative convictions about these matters clearly have empirical content, it is not at all clear what that content is.

Another problem is that norms can conflict. An investigation may be required to determine whether a conclusion supported by one set of intuitions might not be undermined by other equally plausible intuitions. But this will be an investigation into moral reasoning and justification, not an empirical survey. Kagan (1986), one philosophical critic of reliance on intuitions, argued that "rival theories can be played off against intuitions about particular cases; and such intuitions can never be decisive."

A third problem is that even our widely shared intuitions may have suspicious pedigrees. Singer (1974) maintained that our firmest moral convictions derive "from discarded religious systems, from warped views of sex and bodily functions, or from customs necessary for the survival of the group in social and economic circumstances that now lie in the distant past" (p. 516). Relying on intuitions can make normative inquiry conservative and reactionary. According to Singer, we use our convictions to create theories to "pat ourselves on the back" for having the convictions we do.

Arguments that rest ultimately on intuitions might thus be circular or question-begging. Parfit (1984) pointed out that if some theory "has been taught for more than two millennia, we must expect to find some echo in our intuitions....[It] cannot be justified simply by an appeal to the intuitions that its teaching may have produced" (p. 130). Normative theories must be critical; they must allow us to abandon intuitions in the light of reason and to be prepared to accept counter-intuitive conclusions. As several decision theorists have pointed out, if our normative theory of choice was also an adequate descriptive account of our decision-making behavior, it would serve no useful purpose (e.g., Raiffa, 1968).

Given these problems and tendencies, we might be tempted to agree with the conclusion of Brandt (1979) that "it is puzzling why an intuition--a normative conviction--should be a test of anything" (p. 21). Intuitions are clearly problematic and no doubt complicate the relationship between empirical and normative claims, but we cannot simply reject them because we have no place else to begin in moral reasoning.

Parfit (1984) described two ways of doing ethics or arguing about morality: One is the Low Road, that merely appeals to our intuitions. The other is the High Road, Meta-Ethics. If we can give the best account of the nature of moral reasoning, we can hope that this will imply particular claims about morality. We can hope that our Meta-Ethics will imply conclusions in Ethics. (p. 447)

Anti-intuitionist moral theorists, as Parfit suggests, turn to the high road of meta-ethics in the hope of developing a theory of moral reasoning to allow them to rise above moral intuitions.

We are not aware of any developed view about moral reasoning that inspires confidence that the appeal to rationality alone will yield any substantive moral conclusions. The history of moral philosophy, dating back at least to Kant, suggests that substantive moral claims cannot be derived from a theory of rationality or practical reasoning alone.

Accounts of moral reasoning, moreover, also appeal to intuitions--if not relatively concrete moral intuitions, then more abstract and consequently less well-grounded normative convictions about what is reasonable. In formal models of rational choice (e.g., expected utility theory), we are asked to accept as intuitive some rather abstract axioms about which most people have no firm convictions. Whatever normative appeal attaches to these axioms is derived as much from the elegance and structure of the system of which they are a part as from our independent judgments about the normative force of the substitution axiom or the sure thing principle. Granted, we are not likely to be illicitly importing intuitions that are vestiges from our premoral (or pre-rational) pasts into our acceptance of an axiomatic normative theory. But we are being invited, at least implicitly, to think that mathematics provides the model for the structure of rational thought, and that rational decisions must involve maximizing something. If this is not an artifact of a discarded religion, it does at least show a cultural bias.

We do not suggest that these theories must provide an incorrect model of moral reasoning, but only that they also appeal in the end to intuitions. There is no reason why we should place more confidence in abstract intuitions than in our more concrete, moral convictions. The latter will be more solid, even though they may also be tainted.

Finally, concrete moral norms also determine our understanding of rationality and our ideas about proper forms of moral reasoning. For example, whether reactive attitudes like regret and reproach are rational, or just how morality makes room for acting on purely personal rather than impersonal reasons, cannot be settled by considerations of moral reasoning alone. Our understanding about these important questions appeals inevitably to our moral intuitions.

Thus, we should look instead to ethical theories that do not try to avoid intuitions but attempt instead to incorporate them into

deliberations in ways that respect their fallibility. Rawls (1971) defended a theory of this kind. He described moral reasoning as a process of trying to arrive at a "reflective equilibrium" between theory and intuition, which aims to save as many of our intuitions as possible while producing a rational structure of principles that makes clear which intuitions have to be rejected or modified. On this conception of morality, intuitions are corrigible, but they are also the basis upon which our principles and theories are constructed: "There is a definite if limited class of facts against which conjectured principles can be checked, namely our considered judgments in reflective equilibrium" (Rawls, 1971, p. 51).

In the process of developing a theory and arguing for principles that will save our intuitions and resolve conflicts, we must also bring in general facts about human psychology and political feasibility (Rawls, 1971). Thus, empirical claims are explicitly incorporated into moral reasoning and normative principles are tied to empirical facts.

We see no conflict between accepting intuitions as the starting point for normative philosophy and social science and accepting the criticisms we described earlier of a reliance on them. This means only that our method of reasoning must include procedures for criticizing and justifying intuitions that help us avoid the pitfalls described by the critics.

We must recognize, first, that intuitions are empirically vulnerable. This is partly because of the way facts and norms are intermingled in reasoning about morality and rationality, but also because of the ways, as a matter of empirical fact, we care to have the normative convictions we do.

We must ensure that our intuitions are generally plausible. The best way to do this is to rely on intuitions that are both widely believed and well supported by critical reflection. If either of these conditions fails, then we are justified in suspending belief or in demanding further justification.

Finally, to avoid question-begging and circular reasoning, we must critically evaluate the uses of intuitions in normative inquiry. Norms supply us with reasons, but these are reasons in the sense of justification, not necessarily reasons in the sense of causes. Justification is a normative issue, about which we might have reasonable convictions; causes are empirical issues, not to be settled *a priori.*

The force of these prescriptions is best appreciated by examining some of the errors and confusions that occur when normative and empirical claims are not properly distinguished or are thoughtlessly combined in normative theories. Our main example will focus on an issue in economics and policy analysis, which is directly related to some interesting work in behavioral decision theory.

COASE AND HIS CRITICS

"The Problem of Social Cost" is a well-known article by Coase (1960) that has altered the way many people think about law and economics. Coase was responding to the work of Pigou (1920), which led economic and policy theorists to become concerned with the "externalized" costs of economic activities. These costs, like pollution, are borne by society at large and lead to underpricing of commodities because they tend not to be counted as costs of production. Pigou regarded the social cost of production as the "actual" cost, which he intended to include these externalities. He maintained that social costs should be internalized, or that prices should reflect actual costs, and proposed that this could be accomplished only by legally imposed fines and bounties on externalities.

Pigou's suggestion for implementation was regarded as unfeasible, but legal reformers at the time did argue for internalizing at least those social costs that resulted in harm by replacing the traditional negligence standards in tort law with strict liability standards. Pigou and his followers thus maintained that producers should be held responsible for the full cost of production. This was an intuition or a normative conviction, which they attempted to justify on economic grounds.

Coase attacked this justification and Pigou's conception of social cost. He argued instead that the problem of social cost is a reciprocal one, which requires both a perpetrator and a victim:

> The question is commonly thought of as one in which A inflicts harm on B and what has to be decided is: how should we restrain A? But this is wrong....The real question that has to be decided is: should A be allowed to harm B or should B be allowed to harm A?

This is clearly a normative question, and Coase addressed it by arguing for two conclusions. The first, which has come to be known as Coase's theorem, is that in an ideal situation--defined as a situation where there are no transaction costs--parties will bargain to the same result no matter how entitlements or liabilities are assigned. Coase stated that where "the damaging business is not liable for any of the damage which it causes, the allocation of resources will be the same ... as it was when the damaging business was liable for damage caused" (p. 6).

Thus, Coase denied that the existence of externalities leads to underpricing. If A inflicts harm on B, then the harm will remain so long as the cost of the harm is less than the cost of removing it; if A is liable, then A will compensate B; and if A is not liable, B will accept the harm. If the cost of the harm exceeds the cost of removing it, then if A is liable, A will remove the harm, and if A is not liable, B will pay to remove it. Income will be distributed differently, according to how the entitlements and liabilities are assigned, but no economic inefficiencies are involved. The prices of commodities will remain the same. Thus, Coase concluded: "The ultimate result (which maximizes the value of production) is independent of the legal position if the pricing system is assumed to work without cost" (p. 8).

This is an empirical, predictive claim. Coase's justification for it, however, consisted not of economic data establishing that this is in fact how consumers or firms behave in ideal situations, but rather of a few simple hypothetical examples suggesting that this is how reasonable people ought to behave. His appeal, therefore, was to intuitions about reasonable economic behavior, intuitions clearly driven by a normative theory about rational choice and behavior. Coase did not acknowledge or attempt to defend this theory, perhaps (judging from his use of the indicative rather than the subjunctive mood) because he believed that actual behavior coincides with normative behavior (i.e., that the behavior of actual people under ideal market circumstances coincides with the behavior of ideal people under these same circumstances).

If this was Coase's reasoning, then it is formally acceptable. It relies reasonably on an intuition, granted certain assumptions. The coincidence of actual behavior or beliefs and relatively obvious norms, we have suggested, provides as firm a foundation for a normative argument as we can imagine. Coase believed the norm is obvious and the corresponding behavior and beliefs actual.

Coase's reliance on hypothetical examples rather than empirical data is not necessarily a weakness in his argument, for, as his second argument makes clear, his theorem has no practical application. Transaction costs are virtually always present in the world in which we actually live. According to Coase, for the pricing system to work smoothly, the market must be regulated at least to the extent that rights and liabilities are clearly assigned. Often they are not, and it is always costly to make these corrections through regulation. His second argument was that we cannot simply assume that the social cost of regulating to correct these defects will be less than the cost of not regulating: "What has to be decided is whether the gain from preventing harm is greater than the loss which would be suffered elsewhere as a result of stopping the action which produces the harm."

Although this appears to be a straightforward normative conclusion, it is qualified by another of his remarks. Coase acknowledged that moral reasons may exist for assigning entitlements one way rather than another and that these may be worth some degree of inefficiency. Thus, he concluded that "welfare economics must ultimately dissolve into a study of aesthetics and morals" (p. 43). Moral considerations and the economic inefficiencies that result from acting on them are treated by Coase as separate, extraneous matters, not central to his principal argument that rights and entitlements can be treated economically as factors of production whose distribution will not affect economic efficiency. Then, together with the assumption that the problem of social cost is reciprocal and, thus, no more the responsibility of the perpetrator than of the victim, economic activity should be regulated primarily to correct economic inefficiencies. Regulations should not be undertaken unless their expected benefits exceed their expected costs.

Our interest in Coase's argument lies in showing how his empirical assumption about how people will behave under ideal circumstances is crucial to his normative convictions about the reciprocity of social costs and the justification of regulation. One of Coase's examples involved a cattle-raiser's herd damaging a farmer's crop. Coase maintained that whether the farmer is entitled to damages or not has no effect on the size of the herd the cattle-raiser will actually keep: "This will be the same as it would be if the cattle-raiser had to pay for damage caused by his cattle, since a receipt forgone of a given amount is the equivalent of a payment of the same amount" (p. 7).

The claim that opportunity costs (receipts forgone) are equivalent to out-of-pocket costs (payments) is a cornerstone of the theory of rational choice to which Coase subscribed. This belief led him to an assertion about how people do behave or how they will behave. However, the empirical claim is false, and because it is false, Coase cannot appeal to it to justify the intuition that helps support his normative views. The falsity of this claim has been established by behavioral experiments but prior to this it was known (although perhaps not when Coase wrote his article) that opportunity costs are not empirically equivalent to out-of-pocket costs in the sense that people are not willing to sell a commodity or an entitlement for the same price as they would be willing to buy it. The equivalence is merely normative, and because it is, according to our suggestions for establishing the normative status and relevance of intuitions, it cannot simply be appealed to as an intuition but must have an independent justification.

Numerous empirical studies have demonstrated that buying and selling prices are not equivalent (e.g., Knetsch & Sinden, 1984). In some attempts to measure indirectly the economic value of different kinds of environmental protection to hunters and other users of wilderness and wetlands, expressed selling prices are typically 4-16 times higher than expressed willingness to pay (Knetsch & Sinden, 1984). This effect has also been noticed more directly in other contexts. For example, wage rate differentials for hazardous and nonhazardous occupations, which are otherwise similar, increased dramatically after 1970 when the Occupational Safety and Health Act was passed (Brown, 1980). Presumably workers then regarded a safe workplace as their right and increased its value, as a selling price, over what they were willing earlier to pay for it.

Some legal theorists have been quick to embrace these findings and use them to argue against Coase. They have suggested rationalizations of the difference in buying and selling behavior that fit their moral intuitions. Kennedy (1981) stated that "people generally have greater concern for and attachment to things as they are than to things as they could be," and that "people are disinclined to disrupt an equilibrium state" (pp. 401-402). He cited, as "a matter of empirically demonstrable fact" (p. 402), our moral intuition about the difference in strength between duties not to harm and duties to aid. It is not entirely clear in Kennedy's article how this intuition, even if it is widely held and reflected in behavior, explains the effect. Perhaps it can, but nowhere in the article or its many references is it indicated that this demonstrable fact has, in fact, been demonstrated. By assuming *a priori* that his intuition is reflected in consumer behavior, Kennedy committed the same mistake as Coase. Both are led by their normative convictions to make *a priori* claims about consumer behavior. With the benefit of hindsight, Kennedy correctly predicted the behavior, but that is no reason to think his intuitive account explains it correctly.

Kelman (1979), another legal theorist, similarly argued against Coase that legal entitlements will create and reinforce a sense of moral right, which will explain the relevant finding:

If the consumer...values pure water more highly because he is entitled to it,...[h]e will not give up his right to pure water for the $100 cost of abatement because he values the right too highly. But pure water, a good like any other on the market that he can buy or not, may not be worth $100 to him. Perhaps society learns what to value in part through the legal system's description of our protected spheres. (p. 695)

Kelman made two related claims here. The general claim was that a society's legal policies will have a causal impact on its citizens' evaluative sensibilities. The second assertion, an application of the more general claim, was that gaining an entitlement to a good will increase its perceived value.

The interesting general claim seems intuitively plausible. Of course we should look for confirming evidence, but it would be surprising if a social institution as important as a legal system did not have a powerful effect in shaping the moral conscious-

ness of its citizens. Surely the image of blacks in the United States has changed as a result of civil rights legislation. But the truth of the application cited by Kelman is not so obvious that it can be taken *a priori*.

Kelman suggested that the consumer values the entitlement to pure water, which he is not willing to abandon lightly. But deciding to exchange pure water for $100 is to exercise an entitlement, not to abandon it. Why should the right increase the value of the water? Moreover, if the argument is a general one, it should be symmetrical: It should also be true that we value $100 more if we have it (and the entitlement to it) than if we do not have it or are trying to get it. Perhaps we do, but it is not so obvious that we value the money we have more than the money we want. Or perhaps something about unspoiled rivers, wilderness, or other environmental goods can explain why their perceived value is affected by whether or not we believe we have entitlements to them. We suggest later why this might be the case, but if true, this is the fact that needs to be explained.

These critics are mirror images of Coase. They commit the same mistakes. Normative convictions lead them both to make *a priori* claims about empirical matters (i.e., the prediction or explanation of consumer behavior). Coase made incorrect predictions, and we also suggest that Kennedy and Kelman's explanations of Coase's false predictions were incorrect as well.

THE EXPLANATION OF SOME EMPIRICAL FINDINGS

The field of behavioral decision theory has been shaped by the work of two psychologists, Daniel Kahneman and Amos Tversky. Their behavioral theory, which they call prospect theory, attempts to demonstrate and explain some of the widespread violations of the axioms and assumptions of expected utility theory. Much of their work consists of showing how these violations are systematic.

Two features of prospect theory help to explain the behavioral effects involved in the difference between buying and selling. The first is the framing phenomenon. Kahneman and Tversky (1979) maintained that people do not attempt to maximize any kind of objectively defined utility function. Rather, our preferences tend to be determined by what we see as gains and losses, defined in relation to some neutral reference point. This reference point may or may not be determined by something objective, like a person's current asset position. It may also be determined by other factors, such as the individual's expectations or by how a problem is presented or described.

Gains and losses, as measured from the reference point, are treated differently. The utility function for losses is steeper for most people than it is for gains. This feature of prospect theory is called loss aversion. People also tend to be risk seeking in the domain of losses (i.e., people prefer a gamble to a sure loss with a similar "expected value") and risk averse in the domain of gains (people prefer a sure gain to a gamble). Together, these features can explain certain behavior that fundamentally violates expected utility theory. If framing determines whether prospects are viewed as gains or losses, and if gains and losses are valued differently, then preferences can change with different decision frames. Tversky and Kahneman's (1981, 1986) well-known Asian Disease example illustrates this effect.

Asian Disease

Imagine that the U.S. is preparing for the outbreak of an unusual Asian disease, which is expected to kill 600 people. Two alternative programs to combat the disease have been proposed. Assume that the exact scientific estimates of the consequences of the programs are as follows:

Survival Frame

If Program A is adopted, 200 people will be saved.   [72%]

If Program B is adopted, there is a 1/3 probability that 600 people will be saved, and 2/3 probability that no people will be saved.   [28%]

Mortality Frame

If Program C is adopted 400 people will die.   [22%]

If Program D is adopted, there is 1/3 probability that nobody will die, and 2/3 probability that 600 people will die.   [78%]

When the prospects are framed in terms of survival, the majority of respondents prefer A to B, but describing the same prospects in terms of mortality induces the majority of people to take up a different reference point, from which the different treatment of gains and losses leads to a reversal of preferences.

The fact that people can be manipulated into making inconsistent responses by clever descriptions of a decision problem is not in itself exciting or important. We should be concerned, however, with the explanation of the cognitive processes that lead to these reversals. This is the crucial empirical issue.

There are two intuitively plausible explanations for this inconsistency in responses. The first, suggested by some philosophers, appeals to the moral intuitions mentioned by Kennedy (1981). Most people, we assume, think the obligation to avoid killing is stronger than any obligation to save lives. We must not kill innocent people, even for great social gain; yet we are not required to accept great sacrifices to save lives that would otherwise be lost, were we to do nothing. Not everybody accepts these intuitions, but most people do. Thus, when the Asian Disease example is presented in the survival frame, people are inclined to think of 200 lives that would be saved if Program A is chosen but that would be put at significant risk by choosing Program B. If these 200 lives are lost, they are lost as a result of our decision to choose B over A, and the moral prohibition against causing 200 deaths is more stringent than the obligation to try to prevent the deaths of the additional 400. In the choice between C and D, however, people are inclined to focus on the 600 deaths that will be caused in the absence of any combative program. Because we have, it is assumed, only a relatively weak obligation to prevent deaths caused through no fault of our own, it is less important to ensure that 200 are saved and more attrac-

tive to take the gamble of saving the full 600. After all, whatever action we take here is to our moral credit.

Having suggested this explanation of these different preferences by appealing to moral intuitions, few philosophers, we think, would go on to defend this particular reversal. After all, when the two frames are presented simultaneously, the alternatives can be seen to involve identical choices under different descriptions. Moral intuitions are appealed to, therefore, to give a causal or behavioral explanation of the common responses. The intuitions may be normatively justifiable; the behavior they give rise to, in this instance, is not.

Moral intuitions doubtless play a significant role in determining preferences and choices. The stronger the normative appeal of the intuition, one might think, the stronger this causal role will be. This is precisely where it is important to distinguish normative from empirical issues. The causal role of moral intuitions is an empirical issue; as such, it needs to be tested. The tests made by Tversky and Kahneman (1981, 1986), and other experimenters following their lead, suggest that this is not the best explanation of the preference reversal in the Asian Disease example.

A different explanation of loss aversion comes from decision theorists attempting to reconcile the normative theory with empirical results. Several of these revisionists have suggested that the concept of utility has to be broadened to include not just the utility of the outcomes of choice (e.g., the utility of money or of lives saved) but also of the "cognitive" factors that attach to the act of choosing (e.g., Bell, 1982). Specifically, these theorists have suggested that people are strongly influenced by the potential for regretting their choices when risks "turn out badly." People will give up some expected value of outcomes to avoid potential regret.

Regret avoidance may be a strong human motivation. It may even be rational to avoid regret or blame, whether or not the regret or blame itself has a rational foundation. But it is seldom made explicit in these reconciliation attempts whether regret avoidance is part of a normative theory of rational choice or part of an empirical theory that explains behavior. Regret avoidance is an intuitively plausible way to explain some important empirical findings, such as the well-known "Allais paradox" (Allais, 1953). However, regret avoidance and the moral argument are both ad hoc explanations. Because both have independent normative appeal, it is easy to assume that people act according to them and thus that they apply causally as well. Tversky and Kahneman's (1981, 1986) example of "Conditional Gambles" further illustrates the problem.

Conditional Gambles

a sure gain of $100, or   [72%]

a 50% chance to gain $200 and a 50% chance to gain nothing.   [28%]

Assume yourself richer by $500 than you are today. You are forced to choose between:

a sure loss of $100, or   [36%]

a 50% chance to lose nothing and a 50%
chance to lose $200.   [64%]

The moral explanation is rendered implausible by the Conditional Gambles example. The same kind of reversal that occurs in the Asian Disease example also occurs when the stakes are money rather than lives and when the consequences affect the welfare of the actor alone. Nor can potential regret explain this set of preferences. Regret theories cannot distinguish the two problems in Conditional Gambles, because they assume the prospects are evaluated in relation to each other, rather than to some common reference point. In Conditional Gambles, the difference between the consequence of one's choice and the consequence of having chosen differently is identical in both problems. Prospect theory gives a more basic and general explanation of the empirical findings than the moral explanation or the appeal to potential regret.

Further evidence from a number of other, simple experiments seems to reinforce this conclusion. In one experiment, for example, Knetsch and Sinden (1984) gave half their subjects tickets to a lottery and the other half $3.00. When the first group was given an opportunity to sell their tickets for $3.00, 82% kept them, but when the second group was allowed to buy lottery tickets for their $3.00, only 38% wanted the tickets. Simple experiments like this one undermine the relatively sophisticated or morally appealing explanations of preference reversals or buying and selling differentials in more complicated contexts. Appeals to the value of entitlements, rights, or potential regret have an intuitive plausibility in the richer contexts, but little plausibility here. What sensitivity to the value of the entitlements in question could conceivably explain why people tend to keep whichever of the lottery ticket or the money they are initially given? Loss aversion is a more convincing explanation for these simple cases, and it is sufficient to explain the more interesting and important cases as well. It is the simplest and best explanation of some general behavior.

We do not suggest that other factors cannot also influence our decisions, but parsimony and other theoretical considerations should lead us to the more basic explanation, which can apply to a wider range of phenomena. The evidence suggests that the best empirical account of the difference in buying and selling behavior is cognitively simple--a combination of framing effects and loss aversion. If moral principles, the value of legal entitlements, or potential regret also influence our behavior in these cases, as perhaps we think they should, then different and further empirical evidence will be needed to establish this fact.

NORMATIVE CONSIDERATIONS

We have been concerned so far to make two basic points. The first is the importance of distinguishing normative from empirical claims. We noted some errors and fallacies that occur when these are conflated. In particular, it is a mistake to think that because some claim has considerable normative appeal, it must be part of the explanation of human behavior. A normative justification is a reason for thinking that some principle ought to

help determine a person's preferences and decisions, but it is not a reason for thinking that it actually does. Normative claims are justified by moral reasoning, which appeals to intuitions. Causal claims are empirical claims, and they need to be tested and justified by appeal to evidence and data. People do not always behave according to their own normative convictions; otherwise, phenomena like weakness of the will could not occur. The confusions that result when normative and behavioral claims are not properly distinguished can also have important implications for policies, as they have in discussions of the problem of social cost.

Our second point was that prospect theory gives the best explanation of a set of important behavioral violations of normative theories. Framing effects, combined with loss aversion, are sufficient to explain some of the complicated and important cases, and this explanation is confirmed by some simple experiments in which more subtle hypotheses--appealing to moral intuitions, income effects, the consciousness-raising effects of entitlements, and so forth--plainly fail to apply. Generality is a virtue of an explanation. If a single hypothesis can explain behavior as complicated as the difference in wage rates for hazardous work before and after the passage of the Occupational Safety and Health Act, as well as effects as simple as the fact that if you give someone a $2.00 pen, he or she probably will not sell it for its market value, but if you give someone $2.00, the person probably will not buy the pen, this generality then tends to confirm the hypothesis.

This leaves us with an important question: What should we say normatively about loss aversion? Recall that in our discussion of the problem of social cost, some morally plausible intuitions would have led to the same behavior predicted by loss aversion. Our argument concerned the best empirical explanation of the difference between buying and selling prices. But we might appeal to our normative convictions to justify that behavior. Thus, loss aversion might in some cases be morally defensible or even praiseworthy, and if behavior is morally defensible, then it is also rational if by rational we simply mean reasonable and not something more technical or narrow like the strict pursuit of self-interest or maximizing expected utility according to the axioms of a normative theory of choice.

At the same time, loss aversion is a far too widespread and general phenomenon simply to embrace as a moral or rational norm. We respond with the majority in the Asian Disease example, but we confess that this preference shift cannot be justified. It shows only how most people can be manipulated by the framing of a decision problem. We would hope to be able to overcome this kind of manipulation. A clever experimenter could probably lead us to keep a lottery ticket, or to refuse to buy one, in the same way that most people can be so manipulated, but we find no normative justification for the loss aversion demonstrated in these cases. So framing and loss aversion are to be neither simply defended nor attacked on normative grounds. Loss aversion appears to be a basic psychophysical reaction that may be reasonable in some contexts but unreasonable in others. The moral issues will not be settled by this behavior. They must be treated independently, and we must appeal to other normative convictions in doing so.

Where should this moral inquiry begin? Our discussion suggests that it might well start with the closely related issues involved in framing and entitlements. Empirical work in behavioral decision theory has shown that entitlements will affect preferences and are thus necessary to determine what will be taken to be efficient outcomes. The conditions of efficiency depend on the assumptions of entitlements that go into the framing of the problem.

Some will no doubt think that, as a normative matter, this should not make any difference. Buying and selling prices should be equivalent. We should, as Coase (1960) recommended, be able to take an "opportunity cost approach" to policy questions and "compare the total product yielded by alternative social arrangements" (p. 43), and we should be able to determine opportunity costs independently from entitlements. Generally speaking, according to this way of thinking, the different ways of framing outcomes, probabilities, or acts ought normatively to be equivalent. We disagree. "A finger twitch that initiates a sequence of events resulting in a human death" and "a murder" are not morally equivalent descriptions of an event, even though in some sense both descriptions may be true of the same event. In morality and in the law, murder and causing a death are quite different. The resolution of issues about responsibility and punishment often depends on which of competing descriptions, equivalent in some sense, is appropriate. Context, intentions, and other moral factors, therefore, can determine how a problem ought to be framed. Independent normative considerations will determine which framings or descriptions are morally or rationally equivalent.

Entitlements will be essential factors in these considerations. As a dramatic example, consider the morally unproblematic right not to be raped. The importance and value of this right cannot possibly be reduced or made equivalent to what we might determine that citizens in some given social circumstances ought rationally to pay for protection against rape. It would be morally outrageous to suggest that the latter measure can be used to determine full compensation for rape victims or that the incidence of rape should be the same in societies, regardless of whether citizens paid to protect victims from rape or whether rapists were allowed to rape as long as they were willing to compensate their victims. A society that allocated moral and legal entitlements in this latter way would be acting according to a moral code that we would find incomprehensible.

This example suggests how we might understand the consciousness-raising feature of entitlements. We found it puzzling why a legal entitlement to pure water should increase the value we place on the water, as Kelman (1979) suggested. We could not understand why the value of something to a person ought to be affected by him or her owning it. It would be normatively unreasonable and empirically bizarre to think that owning something is necessary to appreciate its value fully--that we perhaps undervalue whatever we do not own. When Cecil Rhodes (quoted in Arendt, 1958) wrote, "Expansion is everything....I would annex the planets if I could" (p. 124), we understand this to be not a sensitive desire to appreciate other cultures and people more highly, but simply the ranting of a mad imperialist. The suggestion is also counterintuitive. It is the grass we do not own that is commonly supposed always to be greener.

The consciousness-raising effect of entitlements comes when we stop thinking of all legal entitlements and moral rights on the model of property rights, which we fully and properly exercise when we buy and sell. The right not to be raped is not merely the right a person has to her own body as her property. This is

why violations of that right cannot be regarded as a legal issue of takings, which is justified if compensation is offered. The right not to be raped, like many other rights, derives not from ownership but from the dignity of the person. It does not arise from a legal convention, as the right to drive on the right-hand side of the street does. Rather, the laws of any civilized society must protect that right because of its independent moral importance. The question of how much we ought to spend as a society to offer what degree of protection against rape is a separate and difficult policy question, which will be informed by the moral severity of rape, but the amount we determine is appropriate cannot be regarded as full market value for the unconsented use of another person's body.

Likewise, coming to think that we are entitled to live in a land with areas of wilderness protected for posterity, or to a workplace safe from certain health risks, might have similar consciousness-raising effects. We might come to see these as moral rights that cannot strictly be regarded on the model of property rights. We might see ourselves as having special duties to conserve our environmental legacy for future generations; we might rethink the respect we are owed as members of the nation's work force, and so on. This will lead to an appreciation of rights that might well and reasonably affect our willingness to exchange these things for other benefits. If so, then it will be highly misleading simply to attach some financial increment to a good as an expression of the value we place on our entitlement to it. Reducing all rights to property rights will not allow us to conduct the proper kind of normative investigations into these important areas of social policy.

A defensible theory of moral rights, which does not reduce all rights to property rights, would have to demonstrate how the protection of rights does not call for too great a sacrifice of welfare. It would also probably have to explain how rights have compelling but not absolute force, and when they can be overridden because of other considerations. In this paper, we have not tried to present such a full-blown conception of moral rights. However, we have tried to show, in a general way, how moral issues must be treated independently of patterns of economic behavior and how certain moral rights and entitlements might influence our other preferences and decisions.

References

Allais, M. (1953). Le comportement de l'homre rationnel devant le risque: Critique des postulats et axiones de l'ecole Americaine. *Econometrica, 21,* 503-546.

Arendt, H. (1958). *The origins of totalitarianism.* New York: Meridian.

Bell, D. (1982). Regret in decisionmaking under uncertainty. *Operations Research, 30,* 961-981.

Brandt, R. (1979). *A theory of the good and the right.* Oxford: Clarendon Press.

Brown, C. (1980). Equalizing differences in the labor market. *Quarterly Journal of Economics, 94,* 113-134.

Coase, R. (1960). The problem of social cost. *Journal of Law and Economics, 3,* 1-44.

Kagan, S. (1986). The present-aim theory. *Ethics, 96,* 746-759.

Kahneman, D., & Tversky, A. (1979). Prospect theory: An analysis of decision under risk. *Econometrica, 47,* 263-291.

Kelman, M. (1979). Consumption theory, production theory, and ideology in the Coase theorem. *Southern California Law Review, 52,* 669-698.

Kennedy, D. (1981). Cost-benefit analysis and entitlement problems: A critique. *Stanford Law Review, 33*, 387-445.

Knetsch, J., & Sinden, J. A. (1984). Willingness to pay and compensation demanded: Experimental evidence of an unexpected disparity in measures of value. *Quarterly Journal of Economics, 98*, 507-521.

Parfit, D. (1984). *Reasons and persons*. Oxford: Clarendon Press.

Pigou, A. C. (1920). *The economics of welfare*. London: Macmillan.

Raiffa, H. (1968). *Decision analysis*. Reading, MA: Addison Wesley.

Rawls, J. (1971). *A theory of justice*. Cambridge, MA: Harvard University Press.

Singer, P. (1974). Sidgwick and reflective equilibrium. *Monist, 58*, 490-517.

Tversky, A., & Kahneman, D. (1981). The framing of decisions and the psychology of choice. *Science, 211*, 453-458.

Tversky, A., & Kahneman, D. (1986). Rational choice and the framing of decisions. *Journal of Business, 59*, 251-278.

Williams, B. (1985). *Ethics and the limits of philosophy*. Cambridge, MA: Harvard University Press.

Measures of Willingness to Pay Versus Willingness to Accept: Evidence, Explanations, and Potential Reconciliation

Ann Fisher
Office of Policy Analysis
U. S. Environmental Protection Agency

Gary H. McClelland
Department of Psychology
University of Colorado

William D. Schulze
Department of Economics
University of Colorado

For some public amenity resources, values cannot be obtained by traditional benefit estimating approaches such as the travel cost method or the hedonic property value method. Examples include experiencing the peace and magnificence of the Grand Canyon without the noise of helicopters and small airplanes echoing from its walls, knowing that a wilderness area is being preserved in its natural state, or knowing that an endangered species is being given an opportunity to re-establish itself.

The travel cost method will be inadequate when nonusers have substantial values for such public amenity resources, or when experiencing the amenity is not part of the trip's purpose (e.g., viewing the Potomac River on the way to work each day). The hedonic property value method will be inadequate when few or no residences are near the resource for which value estimates are needed or when people who do not live nearby also have values for the resource. An alternative to these market-based methods is the contingent valuation method (CVM), in which people are asked directly to reveal their values of public amenity resources contingent upon the circumstances hypothesized in the scenario presented to them.

This paper reviews some major issues concerning use of the CVM, and discusses the observed disparity between values when people are asked how much they are willing to pay (WTP) for a benefit versus how much they are willing to accept (WTA) to give up that same benefit. This disparity appears to contradict traditional economic theory, so we examine the evidence on this disparity and offer some conjectures as to its source. In the last section, we suggest what this implies for using either WTP or WTA methods in a CVM study for policy analysis.

PROBLEMS WITH CVM

Economists have been skeptical about the reliability of the CVM. The primary concern has been that hypothetical questions produce hypothetical answers. Secondary concerns have been raised about at least five other issues. Is the question framed in such a way that respondents understand the information and are not biased by the way it is presented? For example, is it reasonable to expect respondents to understand precisely what an improvement in the visual air quality of the Grand Canyon would mean? Does the payment vehicle cause a bias because its nature suggests a reference range for the value or because respondents could view the payment vehicle as inappropriate? For example, asking respondents how much they would be willing to have their water bill increased to pay for a particular benefit may constrain responses to the range of "reasonable" water bills. Does the starting point in a bidding game CVM application bias responses? Asking respondents "Would you be willing to pay $X?" may suggest the range near $X as reasonable responses. Do respondents react differently to various interviewers and are there important differences between in-person, telephone, and mail surveys? Finally, do respondents respond strategically, hoping to influence the policy to be based on the survey results but not expecting to bear the full consequences of their own bids? Schulze, d'Arge, and Brookshire (1981) and Mitchell and Carson (1985) discuss these and other biases that can occur when using CVM.

Many of these problems can be minimized by careful questionnaire design and conduct of the survey itself. For example, pretesting with intensive questioning of respondents about their reactions to each question can lead to an improved format. Cummings, Brookshire, and Schulze (1986) concluded that accurate responses are more likely if respondents are familiar with the commodity, have experience with it in a market context, and if there is little uncertainty about the hypothetical outcomes being valued. Unfortunately, these "reference operating conditions" will fail to be met, in varying degrees, by many of the public amenity resources for which policy decisions must be made. Ongoing research may shed light on how much accuracy suffers when these reference operating conditions are relaxed.

For potential biases caused by the payment vehicle, its careful choice can avoid having respondents feel that it is inappropriate for the specific valuation task. Keeping it general (e.g., "higher prices for all goods and services") and using a direct question rather than a bidding game can reduce the reference range problem. Of course, this must be balanced against the evidence that people have more difficulty responding to a direct question ("How much would you be willing to pay?") than a bidding game question ("Would you be willing to pay $10?").

If a bidding game is chosen, alternative starting points can be tested (e.g., as in Desvousges, Smith, & McGivney, 1983). Testing for interviewer bias generally shows minimal effects when trained interviewers are used, and this problem can be eliminated completely by using a mail survey. Tests for strategic bias generally show that it is not a problem, and psychologists find that people responding to a survey usually try to answer honestly and accurately (Kahneman, 1986).

A major criticism of using estimates from past CVM studies has been that samples often were small and not representative of the population to which the value estimates were applied. This reflects the fact that economists began investigating this approach without the full benefit of what psychologists had learned about how people process information in a survey setting, and what market researchers had learned about how people react to questions about hypothetical new products. Thus, early CVM studies were oriented more toward whether the method might work--especially for public amenity resources--than toward producing value estimates that could be used in policy decisions. Recent studies have paid more attention to designing samples representative of the populations of interest, so that the value estimates potentially can be used for policy decisions.

With respect to the hypothetical question/hypothetical answer issue, there is evidence that people do not give statistically different answers when responding to hypothetical willingness to pay questions compared with actually purchasing an ordinary private good (Dickie, Fisher, & Gerking, 1987). In related work, Heberlein and Bishop (1985) compared contingent valuation results with actual prices for permits to hunt geese and deer. In the willingness to accept portion, CVM estimates were 60 percent higher than prices hunters actually accepted to sell their goose permits. For deer permits, the mean CVM value was lower than the mean actual selling price, but large variances kept these from being statistically different. Heberlein and Bishop (1985) found CVM results of willingness to pay were larger but not statistically different from the prices hunters in the experiment actually paid to acquire permits. In summary, the results from Dickie et al. (1987) and the WTP, but not the WTA, findings by Heberlein and Bishop (1985) show that responses to hypothetical survey questions can match actual behavior.

The problems discussed above do not appear to overwhelm the potential usefulness of CVM. Rather, these problems represent a list of design issues that need to be considered carefully when planning a CVM study. We need to know more about the seriousness of these problems and about how far the three reference operating conditions for CVM suggested by Cummings et al. (1986) can be relaxed. On the whole, however, there seems to be grounds for at least cautious optimism.

WTP VERSUS WTA

In a contingent valuation study, the respondent's willingness to pay (WTP) measures the maximum value of other goods and services that he or she is willing to give up to achieve an improvement, say, in a public amenity resource, or to prevent a deterioration in that resource. Correspondingly, a respondent's willingness to accept (WTA--often called compensation demanded, CD) is the minimum that he or she must be paid to forgo the resource improvement or to accept its deterioration.

When expressed in terms of price changes, the theoretical difference between WTP and WTA is negligible so long as income and wealth effects are small (Willig, 1976). (Some natural resource amenities may represent large wealth effects at least for some people. In such cases, the theoretical difference between WTP and WTA could not be presumed to be negligible and it would be critical to use the conceptually correct perspective whether it be WTP or WTA.) Consumers will experience changes in most public amenity resources in terms of quantities rather than prices, because these resources generally are not traded in markets. For changes in terms of quantities, Randall and Stoll (1980) and Takayama (1982) have provided theoretical results similar to those Willig presented for price changes. Thus, theory implies that questionnaires asking people how much they will pay to acquire a good should usually yield responses similar to questionnaires asking how much they would have to be paid to forgo that good.

However, a number of economic studies have found unexpectedly large differences between WTP and WTA responses (Table 1). WTA generally exceeds WTP by substantial amounts, and in no instance does WTP exceed WTA (Table 1). For the commodities examined, large income and wealth effects are unlikely. Hence, these data represent a strong rejection of the theoretical argument that WTP amounts ought to equal WTA amounts. Gordon and Knetsch (1979) may have been the first to suggest that these disparities may deserve serious attention. The evidence is made stronger by Gregory's (1986) experiments in which WTA was significantly greater than WTP in 16 of 21 comparisons involving 1,700 participants. Also lending support are several psychological tests of utility models conducted in the 1960's. For example, Coombs, Bezembinder, and Goode (1967) and Slovic and Lichtenstein (1968) both asked subjects to state "minimum selling prices" (= WTA) and "maximum buying prices" (= WTP) for lottery tickets. As in the economic studies, WTA always exceeded WTP.

TABLE 1. Measures of WTP and WTA

Study		WTP[a]	WTA	WTA/WTP
Hammack and Brown (1974)	[1][b]	$247.00	$1044.00	4.2
Banford, Knetsch, and Mauser (1979/1980)	[2]	43.00	120.00	2.8
		22.00	93.00	4.2
Sinclair (1976)		35.00	100.00	2.8
Bishop and Heberlein (1979)		21.00	101.00	4.8
Brookshire, Randall, and Stoll (1980)	[1]	43.64	68.52	1.6
	[2]	54.07	142.60	2.6
	[3]	32.00	207.07	6.5
Rowe, d'Arge, and Brookshire (1980)	[1]	4.75	24.47	5.2
	[2]	6.54	71.44	10.9
	[3]	3.53	46.63	13.2
	[4]	6.85	114.68	16.6
Coursey, Hovis, and Schulze (1987)	[1]	2.50	10.50	3.8
	[2]	2.75	4.50	1.6
Knetsch and Sinden (1984)	[1]	1.28	5.18	4.0
Heberlein and Bishop (1985)		31.00	513.00	16.5

[a]All amounts are in year-of-study dollars.

[b]The bracketed numbers refer to either the number of valuations received or the number of experimental trials conducted per person.

IS WTP BETTER THAN WTA?

The disparity between WTP and WTA results generates the question of which, if either, is an accurate measure of a respondent's true values? One possible explanation for the disparity is that WTP is constrained by the consumer's budget, while WTA has no similar constraint. Believing that the budget constraint represents the more realistic situation, Cummings et al. (1986) recommended a fourth reference operating condition for using CVM: that WTP measures be used rather than WTA measures.

However, WTP might not always be the correct perspective. For example, Coombs et al. (1967) and Slovic and Lichtenstein (1968) used a third condition in which subjects stated a "fair price" not knowing until later whether they were to be the buyer or the seller in the transaction. The values obtained in this condition were intermediate between the values obtained in the WTP and WTA conditions, but somewhat closer to the WTA values. This suggests that at least for some situations WTA may be more appropriate than WTP and that maybe neither is quite correct.

Further complicating the choice of WTP over WTA are studies by Kahneman and Tversky (1984); McNeil, Pauker, Sox, and Tversky (1982); Slovic, Fischhoff, and Lichtenstein (1982); Thaler (1980); Tversky and Kahneman (1981); and others. These studies have demonstrated that the same outcome is valued differently depending on whether that outcome is framed as a gain or as a loss. For example, McNeil et al. (1982) found that preferences of physicians and patients between hypothetical therapies for lung cancer depended on whether the probabilistic outcomes were described in terms of mortality (lives lost) or survival (lives gained). Surgical therapy was less preferred relative to radiation therapy when treatment outcomes were described in terms of mortality rather than in terms of survival. As a nonprobabilistic example, Thaler (1980) noted that the credit card industry lobbied vigorously to have differences between cash and credit prices for consumer purchases labeled as a "cash discount" rather than a "credit card surcharge." Supposedly, this would make the credit price appear to be the normal price against which consumers would assess gains and losses.

Tversky and Kahneman (1981; see also Kahneman & Tversky, 1984) use their Prospect Theory (Kahneman & Tversky, 1979) as an explanation for the differential effects of framing outcomes as either gains or losses (Gordon & Knetsch, 1979). According to Prospect Theory, outcomes are evaluated against a neutral reference outcome, the status quo. Deviations from the neutral reference outcome have diminishing marginal value, but the response to losses is more extreme than the response to gains. This yields an S-shaped value function with a kink at the neutral reference position (Figure 1). If WTA implies the evaluation of a loss (i.e., how much must someone be paid to accept a loss relative to the current situation) and if WTP implies the evaluation of a gain (i.e., how much is someone willing to pay to get a gain relative to the current situation), then the gain/loss function from Prospect Theory predicts WTA > WTP, which is clearly the result from both economic and psychological studies.

If Prospect Theory is correct, then to choose either WTP or WTA as the appropriate perspective requires an assessment of the consumer's initial position and whether the contemplated policy change would be considered as a gain or a loss. Beliefs about one's property rights may be an important factor in defining the initial position. Property rights may be explicit or implicit, and an individual's beliefs about his or her property rights may differ from the policymaker's (or researcher's) assessment. Even worse, certain ways of asking the question may imply to the respondent whether he or she does have property rights. For the moment, assume that individuals, researchers, and policymakers agree about the distribution of property rights, regardless of whether they are explicit or implicit.

If the proposed amenity change will lead to an improvement from the status quo and individuals' rights are vested in the status quo, then the appropriate perspective is willingness to pay to achieve that improvement. On the other hand, if individuals believe that a deterioration already has occurred and the proposed change would restore (or at least move them toward) their prior position (to which they have property rights), then the appropriate perspective is WTA: What would they have to be paid to give up their right to the improvement?

Alternatively, if the proposed change would decrease the amount or quality of the available amenity and respondents

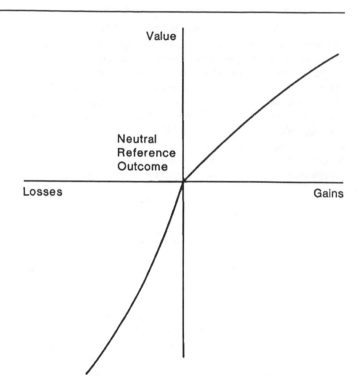

FIGURE 1. A value function for Prospect Theory.

believe that they have property rights to the present situation, then the WTA measure reflects what they would have to be paid to accept the lower level of the amenity. However, if the property rights are vested in industry or in another community, then WTP measures what they would be willing to pay to get property rights to the present level of amenity, rather than suffer its deterioration.

In practice, many decisions will involve situations where people believe that they have property rights to the improved amenity. Thus, if the observed disparities between WTP and WTA reflect a shortcoming of expected utility theory rather than an artifact of how the CVM has so far been applied, attempts to adhere to the fourth reference operating condition could seriously underestimate the value of proposed amenity changes when the WTA perspective is more appropriate than WTP.

Attempts to Resolve This Disparity

One important aspect of the studies described above that have compared WTP and WTA is that they involve commodities not ordinarily traded in markets. In addition, each person is given only one experience in the hypothetical market for these commodities, and his or her response is based on that single experience. Each of us can think of examples of our first experience in the market for a particular good. Sometimes we made mistakes in our purchase decisions, especially when not much information was available about the characteristics of that good and what its typical market price might be.

As a way to test the importance of market experience in explaining the disparity between WTP and WTA, Coursey, Hovis, and Schulze (1987) conducted laboratory experiments with an unfamiliar commodity. They compared the usual one-shot hypothetical response with a "semihypothetical" response where participants had some familiarity with the commodity, and with an auction where half of the respondents actually "consumed" the commodity.

The commodity used for the experiment is a "bad" rather than a "good:" sucrose octa-acetate (SOA), the only known laboratory substance that is bitter yet nontoxic. In WTP experiments, participants offer to pay to avoid "consuming" SOA. Consuming SOA means tasting it by holding 1 ounce of concentrated SOA solution in the mouth for 20 seconds. In WTA experiments, participants are offered money to taste SOA.

In Part I of the experiment, SOA was described carefully, as is typical of descriptions in many CVM scenarios. Then, participants submitted their WTP or WTA bids. In Part II, individuals tasted a few sample drops of SOA before giving their WTP to avoid tasting or their WTA to taste the full ounce. The monitor then attempted to raise (lower) the WTP (WTA) bids in 25-cent increments.

In Part III of the experiment, eight individuals per group participated in a Vickrey auction designed to induce individuals to reveal their values for SOA. In each trial in a WTP group, the fifth highest bid was reported as the reigning price. The four individuals with higher bids then voted whether to pay the reigning price (rather than their own bid) to avoid tasting SOA. A trial was final (after four initial practice trials) only if all four agreed. The losers then had to taste SOA, but paid nothing. The WTA auctions mirrored the WTP ones. The results are summarized in Figure 2.

Several findings of the experiment were interesting. For the WTP experiments, the purely hypothetical results in Part I, the semihypothetical results in Part II, and the auction results in Part III were not statistically different. Similarly, for the WTA experiments, the Parts I and II results and the initial Part III results were not statistically different. However, these WTA results were statistically different from the corresponding WTP results, except for the ending trial (compare w and w' in Figure 2). By the ending trial, WTA converged strongly toward WTP under the market-like pressures of the auction.

These results seemed to indicate that when people gain experience with an ordinary type commodity, their WTA values actually were much like their WTP values. Because the WTP values were not statistically different from the ("experienced") auction results, this suggests that WTP can be elicited with some accuracy in a CVM study, at least for ordinary goods.

On the other hand, Gregory and Furby (1986) wondered why participants needed learning experience only for the WTA responses, rather than for both WTP and WTA. Among other possibilities, they were concerned that the results may be influenced by differences in instructions to WTP and WTA groups and in the endowment given to the two groups.

Regardless of possible caveats to the Coursey et al. (1987) study, the real issue is whether estimated disparities between WTP and WTA are "real" for public goods. Coursey, Brookshire, Gerking, Anderson, and Schulze (1984) conducted a study for SOA as a public good that paralleled the private good study. The major difference was that everyone in the group either had to consume SOA or else the whole group was able to avoid it, depending on the group's aggregate WTP or WTA amounts.

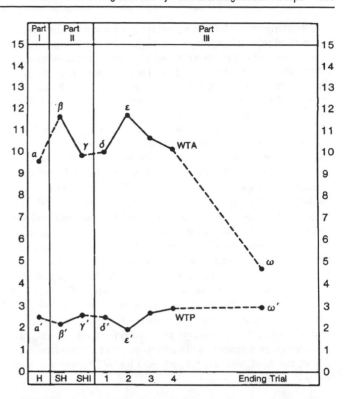

FIGURE 2. Overall average experimental responses. Each point represents overall average of the 32 individuals who participated in each of the WTA and WTP experiments.

The results have some similarities to the SOA private good study, and some important differences. One difference is that the hypothetical WTP measures are statistically larger than the WTP auction values. As was the case for SOA as a private good, the hypothetical WTA measures are statistically greater than their corresponding WTP measures for SOA as a public good. As in the private good study, WTA values converge toward WTP, but for the public good the auction WTA still significantly exceeds the auction WTP. Furthermore, the auction WTP results are statistically similar for SOA as a private good and as a public good. This seems to indicate that although WTP can be elicited accurately for private goods using the CVM and that this estimate may suffice even when WTA is the appropriate perspective for the decision, this appears not to hold when the commodity is a public good. For public goods, it may be necessary to calibrate the results (e.g., adjust them downward by a known fraction) or to use a more elaborate auction procedure to get WTP or WTA; even the auction method may yield WTA > WTP.

One possible reason for observing a value function like that in Figure 1 may have to do with the sorts of decisions respondents typically make. With the exception of their own labor (which usually is exchanged according to a reasonably long-term implicit contract), most people simply are not used to selling things that they own. Occasional sales of their old car or house hardly give experience comparable to the frequent purchases of food, clothing, gasoline, etc. The fact that the WTA framework may be less familiar to people may cause their initial WTA responses to diverge more from the "true" WTA, compared with the divergences between initial and "true" WTP. Also, for those few times when people have selling experiences, it may be in their best interest to behave strategically by not revealing their reservation price at the outset. Strategic behavior is less common for the typical purchase, however, where the buyer must either take or leave the item's posted price. Thus, relatively less experience with strategic behavior when making purchases (compared with selling activities) also may tend to make initial WTA bids higher than initial WTP bids.

In another experiment, Brookshire and Coursey (in press) used CVM, a single iteration field auction, and a laboratory auction for trees to be planted in a new neighborhood park. Their median value function results were similar to the value function of Prospect Theory (Figure 1). Of their three valuation methods, the results for CVM showed the largest disparity between WTP and WTA. The differences between the CVM and the single iteration field auction were not significant, suggesting that a single iteration auction may not be adequate. However, the laboratory auction process produced more reasonable results. In particular, the value function was smooth instead of kinked at a neutral reference point as suggested by Prospect Theory. If we accept the market-like auction results as those representing real values, then the Brookshire and Coursey (in press) results suggest that when WTA measures are needed for public goods, an iterative auction process will yield more accurate measures than CVM, but that CVM may be sufficient for WTP measures of the value of public goods.

NEW RESULTS ON GAINS AND LOSSES

In a CVM study of residents living near a hazardous waste site, Schulze, McClelland, Hurd, and Smith (1985) carefully worded the WTP and WTA versions so that losses and gains should cancel one another according to Prospect Theory. For example, in the WTP version, the payment "loss" is balanced against a commodity structured as a loss; people are given a choice between reopening the now closed landfill or paying to prevent its reopening. In the WTA version, the respondent is faced with a gain-gain situation. The respondent is "given" property rights to the situation before the landfill was closed, and asked to state the least amount of money he or she would accept in lieu of closing the landfill. Although these questions seem less "natural" than the ones typically used in CVM studies, it was thought that they might eliminate biases (identified by Kahneman & Tversky, 1979) if people cannot cope with trading gains for losses. A similar set of questions was asked about the presence of the landfill or an identical neighborhood without the landfill.

Because of some extremely high responses to the questions, the median bids are much lower than the mean bids (Table 2). It is not unusual for statisticians to trim 5 percent from each tail of a distribution to remove unreasonable outliers. Doing so moves the means closer to the medians, as shown in the second column of Table 2. Some of the high bids seem unrealistic because people probably would be better off financially by abandoning their homes instead of paying their stated WTP. Protest zero bids also are common in CVM studies, so trimming on the lower end also seems sensible.

Even the trimming leaves a clear pattern of WTA > WTP. The reason for this is not obvious. It may be that the careful wording

TABLE 2. Contingent Valuation of the OII Landfill

Type	Mean bids at level of outlier treatment			Median bid
	0%	10%	15%	
Valuing the closure of the OII Landfill				
WTP	$88.02	$38.36	$25.73	$10.00
(N)	(250)	(226)	(212)	
WTA	835.20	649.07	558.85	300.00
(N)	(179)	(161)	(153)	
Valuing the presence of the OII Landfill				
WTP	221.73	189.79	165.56	25.00
(N)	(272)	(246)	(232)	
WTA	751.38	618.88	598.39	500.00
(N)	(218)	(196)	(186)	

of questions (so that a respondent was faced either with a gain-gain situation or with a loss-loss situation) simply failed because respondents had strong preconceptions about their own initial reference position with respect to the hazardous waste site. In other words, respondents really did not place themselves at the neutral reference outcome (or origin) specified in the scenarios. Unfortunately, no questions were asked that would allow the determination of how respondents conceived their property rights relative to the ones specified in the scenarios.

CAN DISPARITY BE RESOLVED?

Expected utility theory has attractive features, but evidence about the disparity between WTP and WTA continues to accumulate. Perhaps economists and psychologists can work together to explain these disparities, using such tools as state-dependent utility functions, Prospect Theory, and the concepts of cognitive dissonance. So far, the result simply is not clear and more theoretical and empirical work is required to resolve the disparity.

Based on the above review of the empirical evidence, we can make some theoretical suggestions about the disparity. This disparity may be represented as the sum of two separate factors: strategic bias (SB) and loss aversion (LA). That is,

$$WTA - WTP = SB + LA.$$

SB includes such things as sellers' attempts to get more from the buyer by stating values much higher than their true reservation price. As suggested above, these strategic biases are more likely to be a problem for WTA than WTP because of most respondents' lack of selling experience relative to buying experience. Thus, SB is likely to make WTA > WTP.

LA refers to the differential valuation of gains and losses as suggested by Prospect Theory and in particular to the fact that losses are more aversive than a gain of the same magnitude is pleasurable. LA probably increases with stronger psychological commitment or personal involvement in the commodity. Such investment tends to make the commodity a "personal possession" with a history of memories and expectations. For example, a ribbon won as a reward in an amateur athletic contest will have far greater value to its owner than to anyone considering buying the ribbon. That is, the owner's WTA would be much higher than any buyer's WTP due to the differential emotional investment in the commodity. Strong beliefs about property rights would likely create the same effect. Personal possessions with strong commitments will not be parted with cheaply. LA will tend to make WTA > WTP and the disparity will be larger the greater the commitment and involvement in the commodity.

The concepts of SB and LA help explain the range of the disparity. In Table 1, WTA/WTP ranges from about 2 to over 10. In the Schulze et al. (1985) study of the hazardous waste site, ratios as large as 30 to 1 were obtained (Table 2). It appears that the ratio is smallest for those situations in which LA is presumably low. For example, it is reasonable to presume that the subjects in the SOA experiments had no experience and little or no investment in the outcome. In that situation, the WTA/WTP ratio was relatively small and could be eliminated with market-like pressures. In such circumstances, the disparity may be a function primarily of SB, which can be reduced with experience. On the other hand, in the hazardous waste site study, the possible loss involved one's health for which there is undoubtedly a high emotional investment. In that case, LA is large and when combined with SB produces a large disparity.

More research clearly needs to be done to understand which situations produce the largest disparity and for which situations WTP or WTA is more appropriate. In the meantime, policy decisions must be made about our natural resource amenities. The prudent decisionmaker will need to be aware of the conceptually appropriate reference point for valuing the amenity change, and how any available value estimates are related to that reference point. In many instances, estimation errors may be tolerable in the sense that a known underestimate still exceeds the cost of the policy, or a known overestimate still falls short of the cost of the policy. In other cases, the decisionmaker will have to do what he or she is paid to do--exercise judgment.

References

Banford, N. D., Knetsch, J. L., & Mauser, G.A. (1979/1980). Feasibility judgements and alternative measures of benefits and costs. *Journal of Business Administration, 11*, 25-35.

Bishop, R. C., & Heberlein, T. A. (1979). Measuring values of extra market goods: Are indirect methods biased? *American Journal of Agricultural Economics, 27*, 926-930.

Brookshire, D., & Coursey, D. L. (in press). Measuring the value of a public good: An empirical comparison of elicitation procedures. *American Economic Review*.

Brookshire, D. S., Randall, A., & Stoll, J. R. (1980). Valuing increments and decrements in natural resource service flows. *American Journal of Agricultural Economics, 62*, 478-488.

Coombs, C. H., Bezembinder, T. G., & Goode, F. M. (1967). Testing expectation theories of decisionmaking without measuring utility or subjective probability. *Journal of Mathematical Psychology, 4*, 72-103.

Coursey, D. L., Brookshire, D. S., Gerking, S., Anderson, D., & Schulze, D. (1984). *Laboratory experimental economics as a tool for measuring public policy values* (Draft Report). Washington, DC: U.S. Environmental Protection Agency.

Coursey, D. L., Hovis, J. J., & Schulze, W. (1987). The disparity between willingness to accept and willingness to pay measures of value. *Quarterly Journal of Economics, 8*:679-690.

Cummings, R. G., Brookshire, D. S., & Schulze, W. D. (1986). *Valuing environmental goods: Assessment of the contingent valuation method.* Totowa, NJ: Rowman & Allanheld.

Desvousges, W. H., Smith V. K., & McGivney, M. P. (1983). *A comparison of alternative approaches for estimating recreation and related benefits of water quality improvements* (Report No. EPA-230-05-83-001). Washington, DC: U.S. Environmental Protection Agency.

Dickie, M., Fisher, A., & Gerking, S. (1987). Market transactions and hypothetical demand data: A comparative study. *Journal of the American Statistical Association, 82*, 69-75.

Gordon, I. M., & Knetsch, J. L. (1979). Consumer's surplus measures and the evaluation of resources. *Land Economics, 55*, 1-10.

Gregory, R. (1986). Interpreting measures of economic loss: Evidence from contingent valuation and experimental studies. *Journal of Environmental Economics and Management, 13*, 325-337.

Gregory, R., & Furby, L. (1986). *Auctions, experiments and contingent valuation.* Unpublished manuscript, Decision Research, Eugene, OR.

Hammack, J., & Brown, G. M., Jr. (1974). *Waterfowl and wetlands: Toward bioeconomic analysis.* Baltimore, MD: Johns Hopkins University Press.

Heberlein, T. A., & Bishop, R. C. (1985). *Assessing the validity of contingent valuation: Three field experiments.* Unpublished manuscript, University of Wisconsin, Madison.

Kahneman, D. (1986). Comments by Professor Daniel Kahneman. In R. G. Cummings, D. S. Brookshire, & W. D. Schulze, *Valuing environmental goods: Assessment of the contingent valuation method* (pp. 185-194). Totowa, NJ: Rowman & Allanheld, 185-194.

Kahneman, D., & Tversky, A. (1979). Prospect theory: An analysis of decision under risk. *Econometrika, 47*, 263-291.

Kahneman, D., & Tversky, A. (1984). Choices, values, and frames. *American Psychologist, 39*, 341-350.

Knetsch, J. L., & Sinden, J. A. (1984). Willingness to pay and compensation demanded: Experimental evidence of an unexpected disparity in measures of value. *Quarterly Journal of Economics, 99*, 507-521.

McNeil, B., Pauker, S., Sox, H., Jr., & Tversky, A. (1982). On the elicitation of preferences for alternative therapies. *New England Journal of Medicine, 306*, 1259-1262.

Mitchell, R. C., & Carson, R. T. (1985). *Typology of threats to validity in contingent valuation studies.* Unpublished manuscript, Resources for the Future, Washington, DC.

Randall, A., & Stoll, J. R. (1980). Consumer's surplus in commodity space. *American Economic Review, 70*, 449-454.

Rowe, R. D., d'Arge, R. C., & Brookshire, D. S. (1980). An experiment on the economic value of visibility. *Journal of Environmental Economics and Management, 7*, 1-19.

Schulze, W. D., d'Arge, R. C., & Brookshire, D. S. (1981). Valuing environmental commodities: Some recent experiments. *Land Economics, 57*, 151-172.

Schulze, W. D., McClelland, G., Hurd, B., & Smith, J. (1985). *Estimating benefits for toxic waste management: An application of the property value method* (Draft Report). Washington, DC: U.S. Environmental Protection Agency.

Sinclair, W. S. (1976). *The economic and social impact of the Kemano II Hydroelectric Project on British Columbia's fisheries resources.* Vancouver, British Columbia, Canada: Fisheries and Marine Services, Department of the Environment.

Slovic, P., Fischhoff, B., & Lichtenstein, S. (1982). Response mode, framing, and information-processing effects in risk assessment. In R. Hogarth (Ed.), *New directions for methodology of social and behavioral science: Question framing and response consistency* (pp. 21-36). San Francisco, CA: Jossey-Bass.

Slovic, P., & Lichtenstein, S. (1968). Relative importance of probabilities and payoffs in risk taking. *Journal of Experimental Psychology Monograph, 78*, 1-18.

Takayama, A. (1982). On consumer's surplus. *Economic Letters*, 35-42.

Thaler, R. (1980). Toward a positive theory of consumer choice. *Journal of Economic Behavior and Organization, 1*, 39-60.

Tversky, A., & Kahneman, D. (1981). The framing of decisions and the psychology of choice. *Science, 211*, 453-458.

Willing, R. D. (1976). Consumers' surplus without apology. *American Economic Review, 66*, 589-597.

Willingness to Pay or Compensation Demanded: Issues in Applied Resource Valuation

Robin Gregory
Decision Research
Eugene, Oregon

Richard C. Bishop
Department of Agricultural Economics
University of Wisconsin, Madison

Discussions of economic value frequently begin with a statement that the value of something is equal to individuals' maximum willingness to pay for it. While this is a convenient shorthand, it tells only part of the story; economic theory reminds us that a second welfare measure, reflecting the minimum compensation individuals demand, is equally valid. Theory further asserts that, in practice, individuals' willingness to pay and compensation demanded in most cases should be reasonably similar.

Both willingness to pay (WTP) and compensation demanded (CD) measures are familiar to economists because the potential compensation test forms the theoretical foundation for cost-benefit analysis. This decision rule states that a proposed policy or project is deemed economically justified on efficiency grounds only if the gainers (those who would be made better off) could compensate the losers (those who would be harmed) and still be better off. Whether compensation is actually required is normally considered a distributional issue, one that may be important but that is essentially noneconomic in character.

When considering the values of environmental assets such as clean water, visibility, and recreational fishing (resources that are not directly traded in markets), application of the compensation test is often desirable but may be more difficult than in cases involving market commodities. Assessing whether gainers would be able to compensate losers still requires at least a rough measure of the amount of compensation that the losers might demand, but the accuracy of environmental value estimates is difficult to assess. Furthermore, because the legal rights in many environmental and natural resource situations are not well defined, weighing the claims of potential gainers and losers frequently involves difficult value judgments. Simply identifying who is a winner and who is a loser may not be straightforward.

In this paper we attempt to sort through some of these issues. Criteria to help choose between WTP and CD value measures are reviewed, and some limits of their application in the context of the potential compensation test are examined. Next, we discuss whether the choice between payment- and compensation-based measures of potential losses is likely to be important. Finally, we examine the accuracy of WTP or CD value estimates and their ability to provide useful and defensible information to resource managers and project analysts. Throughout this paper, we assume that information on economic values is needed by decisionmakers and is relevant to understanding the problems that they face. Furthermore, our emphasis on the economic dimension should not be interpreted as diminishing the importance of noneconomic aspects of resource management or public policy decisions.

The Potential Compensation Test as a Guide for Evaluation

Welfare economics recognizes that any public policy initiative creates effects on individuals that may be important, both to those people and to other members of the society in which they live. A basic rule for assessing these effects, first proposed by Pareto late in the 19th century, is that a policy can be said to represent an unambiguous improvement in social welfare only if it makes no one worse off and at least one person is made better off. Operationally, this criterion is of little use, because means are not established for determining net social gains in the usual case where the proposed action imposes costs on some participants in the course of providing benefits to others. Unless an explicit mechanism for benefit-sharing is established, those bearing the costs of an initiative could be left worse off and the Pareto criterion would not be fulfilled.

Recognition of this limitation stimulated Kaldor (1939) and Hicks (1943) to develop a second criterion based on the concept of compensation, with a policy said to create an increase in social welfare if those who gain could fully compensate those who lose and still consider their final position (i.e., after the payments were made) to represent a welfare improvement. The compensation need not actually be paid; therefore, the Hicks-Kaldor criterion is one of potential rather than actual Pareto improvement. This criterion implies a policy objective of maximizing the net value of social output: Some will win and some will lose, but society overall will benefit from changes that pass the compensation test (i.e., the sum of the individual value changes will be positive).

Several economists (e.g., Little, 1960) have argued that a more explicit link should be made to the distributional implications of this rule; others (e.g., Haveman & Weisbrod, 1975) have emphasized the potential significance of transactions costs (e.g., associated with administrative or informational requirements). However, economists generally have accepted the potential compensation test as a basis for welfare assessments, agreeing that distributional effects should be analyzed and reported to the decisionmaker but that distributional recommendations involve value judgments that are beyond economics.

The idea that those who gain should be able to compensate those who do not has both a clear intuitive appeal and a strong theoretical justification. However, application of this basic concept in the context of valuing environmental and natural resource situations is likely to encounter several unresolved issues related to the identification of winners and losers and the estimation of their respective gains and losses.

Consider the following two examples of resource valuation disputes. In the first example, a logging company wants to obtain improved access to land that it owns by building a road across private property, and seeks permission from the owner. As long as the owner's CD is less than the benefits anticipated by the company, the existence of unambiguous property rights suggests that a solution is likely to be found quite easily because the relevant mode is that of benefit-sharing; negotiations may be sticky (e.g., because the landowner engages in strategic behavior), but a mutually satisfactory outcome clearly is possible.

With public resources the definitions of gainers and losers can be much more ambiguous. Consider an area of national forest that either can be cut for timber or preserved as wilderness. At first glance, it seems natural to evaluate a timber company's request to clearcut the area by designating loggers as the gainers and environmentalists as the losers. According to this view, the compensation test would entail asking whether the loggers can compensate the environmentalists. The timber company might argue, however, that it is a long-established enterprise on the public lands and that the area in question is simply the next step in a long-standing pattern of economic activity. In welfare economic terms, it is arguing that establishing a wilderness is the proposed change and that proper application of the compensation test would entail asking whether the environmentalists could compensate the loggers. Once substantial differences in WTP and CD are considered possible, the outcome of the compensation test may rest on which group is assigned status quo ante property rights in such situations. Economics does not provide normative guidance about such assignments of rights.

Several additional limitations of the compensation test as a guide to valuing the gains and losses of individuals require explicit recognition:

1. People may not be clear about their own preferences (i.e., they may not know their utility functions). Even in the simple cases described above, individuals may find it difficult to know what they want, or to think about the long-term costs and benefits of alternative plans, especially when both options (e.g., logging and wilderness) involve some uncertainty (e.g., how carefully will the logging be done? How much will it cost to maintain the area as a wilderness?). People also may find that there is just too much to think about at one time, so that cognitive limitations associated with information recognition and processing lead to confused (e.g., intransitive) or unstable preference orderings.

2. A second limitation reflects a distinction between situations where there are winners and losers and others where there are only losers. The potential compensation criterion assumes conscious action on the part of an agency, and does not address the question of what to do when losses are not intentional (e.g., associated with acts of weather or fate rather than government). For example, homeowners in residential areas that suffer losses due to flooding are not automatically compensated, pending judgment regarding their observance of zoning restrictions and other measures that serve to incorporate socially-sanctioned expectations regarding the probability that flood-related losses will occur. Property losses may be compensable out of government contingency funds, but in such cases the decision often is political or humanitarian rather than economic in nature and compensation rarely covers more subjective welfare claims (e.g., relating to emotional damages).

3. A single party may experience both benefits and costs; thus, transfers from winners to losers would need to be assessed within the same community, group, or individual. In the examples noted above, development of the forest company lands may mean that area residents would enjoy more jobs or higher average wages, but they also could suffer marked declines in recreational opportunities or in water quality. In such cases, people may find it difficult to trade off or carefully weigh the various types of benefits and costs related to a proposed resource development project. A further complication would arise if individuals simply accept the benefits as being in the natural course of events (i.e., coincident with a perspective that employment opportunities are part of every citizen's endowment or that life will improve year-by-year) but view the losses as costs for which compensation is expected.

4. Applications of the potential compensation test must normally involve aggregate measures such as personal income (money) gains and losses, changes in areas under market demand functions, and savings in monetary costs. If the assessment instead is made directly by individuals (who represent the theoretically correct judge of impacts), a quite different picture could emerge. For example, some people may consider themselves to be losers (in a welfare sense) despite an income gain, perhaps because of increased congestion in their community. Others may code the welfare change in terms that are inherently noncommensurate, for example in terms of particular lifestyle components. Other people may oppose any change, because of misgivings regarding sponsorship (e.g., by the state or federal government) or simply because change itself is viewed as a cost (even if the result is an "improvement" in conditions, e.g., an increase in the trout population of a favorite fishing stream).

How well aggregate measures are able to capture these more subjective effects is an open question. One diagnostic, which suggests there are problems associated with application of the compensation criterion, concerns the number and status of outlying responses and of nonparticipants. For example, in studies conducted by economists in the context of proposed declines in air quality (Rowe, d'Arge, & Brookshire, 1980) or hunting opportunities (Brookshire, Randall, & Stoll, 1980), as many as one-half the participants refused to answer the compensation question asked of them. One explanation for the extreme values or nonparticipation relates to the symbolic value of many environmental goods and the strong feelings that people may have regarding basic amenities such as clear air, clean water, and quiet. Because symbols tend to be subjectively defined, sensitive to context, and highly changeable over time, defining the winners and losers in a given natural resource situation may depend on the extent to which symbolic dimensions of a dispute are recognized by participants or emphasized by others with a stake in the final decision. A related explanation is that some events may be viewed as inherently noncompensable, such as the extinction of an animal species or a decline in life expectancy. Benefit-sharing is therefore no longer the relevant evaluation mode because exchange of the asset is itself considered invalid.

5. Another problem in applying the compensation test, which relates back to the two examples given earlier, stems from the frequent ambiguity of both institutional and individual entitlements to nonmarket environmental goods. Much has been written about the difficulty of assessing benefits and costs in the context of proposed changes in resource endowments due to the absence of well-defined property rights. One approach taken by researchers in the field is to argue for a clearer delineation of such rights (Fisher & Raucher, 1984); another route develops the case for recognition of implicit rights, which generally refer to a class of basic entitlements (e.g., clean air, protection from noise) held by people without previous explicit legal sanction (Kennedy, 1981).

Exactly how such rights are to be defined generally is not specified. For example, liability rules would protect an entitlement but allow for its transfer on the basis of a state-determined judgment rather than one made by individuals, whereas inalienable entitlements would forbid the sale of a right except under specified circumstances (Calabresi & Melamed, 1972). In the context of amenity resources, however, it is often unclear who (or which collective body) should be given the opportunity to decide on the initial entitlement. Moreover, it is not obvious that the Pareto criterion refers to ownership or rights (whether explicit or implicit). Instead, the criterion would seem to imply protection of the welfare level experienced by each individual and as perceived by that person (Knetsch, 1983). If someone believes he or she is worse off because of an action, then this person has suffered a welfare loss that is potentially deserving of compensation and this loss does not necessarily need to be related to any question of property-based (or, more generally, thing-based) rights. Obviously, the identification of winners or losers as well as the outcome of a potential compensation test could be quite different depending on the extent to which other than property-based or legally-sanctioned entitlements are recognized.

6. A final limitation of the potential compensation test is based in several specification problems that must be addressed in conducting economic analyses of resource-use options (Fischhoff & Cox, 1986). One example concerns how the selected unit of analysis is defined. People's roles as part of both social groups (e.g., households) and institutional structures (e.g., firms) contribute to the formation and expression of their values. Furthermore, people are not completely stable in their preferences; variations may occur over the course of a day, week, or year. The specification of units in the analysis therefore will affect the final estimates of value that are obtained, as well as establish an implicit lower bound as to what is of interest to analysts. For example, if the household is selected as the preferred unit, then the distribution of costs and benefits within the household will be ignored.

At a practical level, decisions can be made on each of these points so that the analysis is allowed to proceed; however, these decisions will likely be controversial. Because these decisions require judgments in addition to the guidance provided by the compensation test, they represent limitations of that test and, by implication, limitations of the economic analysis of resource policy options. This argument suggests that (a) careful attention should be given to how these choices have been made when comparing the results of resource evaluations, and (b) inputs from other disciplines may be needed to help with this set of important decisions that analysts are called upon to make.

Measures of Payment and Compensation

A person could pay to obtain a valued good or to avoid something undesirable; alternatively, a person could accept compensation either to relinquish a valued good or to forego a desirable opportunity. Conventional economic theory argues that, in similar contexts, a person's maximum willingness to pay to avoid an undesirable good or event should be about the same as the minimum compensation the person demands to accept it. This argument was first made by Hicks (1943), Henderson

(1941), and other originators of the new welfare economics, and has been reviewed carefully in a number of articles (e.g., Currie, Murphy, & Schmitz, 1971) and texts (e.g., Freeman, 1979; Just, Hueth, & Schmitz, 1982).

More recently, the expectation of approximate equivalence between WTP and CD estimates of value was argued quite forcefully in general terms by Willig (1976) and in terms of environmental tradeoffs by Randall and Stoll (1980). Willig's major contribution was the calculation, based on empirically estimable parameters, of strict upper and lower bounds on the ability of a WTP measure to estimate CD values (and vice versa). His calculations show that, under normal conditions, the choice of value measure will be unimportant because both willingness to pay and compensation demanded approaches should yield results that closely approximate the area under the ordinary demand curve. Randall and Stoll expanded this argument in terms more relevant to unpriced environmental goods.

The economic arguments for equivalence in WTP and CD measures of value distinguish between those cases where the environmental good or service in question is relatively important to people and those where it is not. Willig (1979), for example, makes this point explicitly, arguing that the observed and theoretical relationship between consumer's surplus measures may not be similar if the project under study has a large income effect, if the ratio of ordinary consumer's surplus to income is large, or if all price changes are not in the same direction. However, when income effects are quite small (i.e., the change in welfare associated with a change in the amount of some asset is considered relatively unimportant), then differences in WTP and CD estimates of economic value are expected to be negligible.

Contingent valuation techniques have been used to assess the value of recreational hunting and fishing opportunities, participation in a lottery, a local postal service, proposed changes in risk, a television program, alternative parking space assignments, and various changes in air and water quality. In all these cases, substantial differences in WTP and CD values of the same good have been observed. The magnitude of the disparity ranges from about 2.5:1 for proposed changes in fishing sites (Banford, Knetsch, & Mauser, 1980; Sinclair, 1976) to as much as 16:1 for a proposed change in visibility (Rowe et al., 1980). These results are reviewed in some detail in the existing literature and will not be discussed further here except to note that (a) the average difference in WTP and CD measures of environmental values derived in contingent valuation studies appears to be approximately 3:1 or 4:1, and (b) income effects alone cannot adequately explain such disparities (Gordon & Knetsch, 1979).

Differences in WTP and CD evaluations have also been observed when controlled experiments and market-like data were employed. Among the better-known experiments comparing CD and WTP values are those conducted by Bishop and Heberlein (1979) and their associates (Bishop, Heberlein, & Kealy, 1983; Bishop, Heberlein, Welsh, & Baumgartner, 1984) on the value of goose- and deer-hunting permits in Wisconsin. Tests by Bishop and Heberlein that employed real money demonstrated substantial differences in WTP and CD approaches to valuing the same good; other cash experiments by Knetsch and Sinden (1984) and Gregory (1986) yielded similar results. Thus, the divergence between WTP and CD is not just the result of some problem with contingent valuation as a value estimation procedure.

Another group of researchers has employed auction mechanisms (and, more generally, the controlled laboratory techniques of experimental economics) in an attempt to elicit WTP or CD responses under conditions considered more akin to those of a competitive market (Coursey, Hovis, & Schulze, in press). Experiments have been conducted with a variety of different goods (e.g., strawberries, and a bitter-tasting substance called sucrose octa-acetate or SOA) in settings intended to simulate consumer behavior toward both private and public goods (Coursey & Schulze, in press). In the public good experiments, a significant difference was reported in WTP and CD responses both before and after the auction was implemented. A statistically insignificant difference was reported between the post-auction WTP and CD responses in the private good experiments using SOA (Coursey, Brookshire, Gerking, Anderson, & Schulze, 1985). However, a re-examination of these results using slightly different statistical procedures shows that the difference in post-auction WTP and CD responses remains significant (Gregory & Furby, in press).

This body of empirical results raises serious doubts concerning the ability of any WTP measure to closely estimate CD responses. Numerous explanations have been offered for the observed differences in payment- and compensation-based values. Probably the most common explanation cites measurement errors, arising from problems of bias or other sources of "...weakness in the survey instrument..." (Dwyer & Bowes, 1978, p. 1008). The unfamiliar nature of the survey process (which in most cases effectively prohibits consultation with peers, references to external information sources, or repeated transactions with the amenity good), creates a situation that may be "quite artificial" for many participants and therefore may elicit invalid responses because equilibrium conditions have not been established (Bishop et al., 1983). Other explanations of the disparity explicitly refer to the hypothetical nature of contingent valuation questions and their consequent lack of comparability with market exchanges (Coursey et al., 1985), or emphasize that the predictions of consumer's surplus (or any other normative) theory cannot be refuted by the results of any specific empirical tests (Rowe et al., 1980).

Therefore, one response to the disparity in predicted and observed values is to ignore empirical tests of compensation demanded and rely instead on theoretical arguments to support the use of CD estimates derived from WTP measures. This approach has been followed, for example, in estimating the net benefits of proposed changes in air quality (Brookshire, Ives, & Schulze, 1976) and recreational hunting opportunities (Brookshire et al., 1980). In the latter case, the authors found differences of "...up to an order of magnitude..." between participants' observed and derived compensation demanded, but concluded the observed values were unreliable and "... in any particular situation, the proper measure of value can be identified on the basis of theoretical considerations" (Brookshire et al., 1980, p. 487). A related response is to conclude that the theoretically-supported equivalence of payment- and compensation-based measures implies that correct (i.e., unbiased) estimates of compensation would be similar to individuals' responses to decremental WTP questions (that ask people's willingness to pay to avoid a proposed decline in economic circumstances). This approach is explicitly suggested in the Water Resource Council's (1983) *Principles and Guidelines*, for example, and is implicit

in the numerous studies of environmental losses that only ask payment-based evaluation questions.

An alternative response--and this is the view of the present authors--is to look at people's expressed values of required compensation as subject to some error but also as indicative of meaningful differences in how people typically view WTP and CD measures of value. The implication of this response is not that observed disparities in WTP and CD measures provide precise evidence of differences in resource values, but rather that results of the research conducted to date are sufficiently consistent so as to indicate that considerably more attention should be given to improving methods for eliciting compensation responses.

Evaluating the Accuracy of WTP and CD Measures

Thus far in this paper we have argued that differences in payment- and compensation-based measures of economic losses may be both real and significant, and we have pointed out a number of limitations of the potential compensation criteria as a guide to estimating compensation values. One important remaining question concerns the accuracy of WTP and CD measures of environmental value. Two principal positions are discussed in the literature: (a) contingent WTP measures are fairly accurate (i.e., +/- 50%) but CD measures are not (e.g., Cummings, Brookshire, & Schulze, 1984), and (b) contingent WTP measures represent a lower bound on true values whereas CD measures represent an upper bound (e.g., Bishop et al., 1983).

So long as both the payment setting and the asset under consideration are familiar and well-defined, we conclude that contingent WTP measures used in the context of potential environmental gains probably will yield fairly accurate estimates of resource values. When used to estimate potential environmental losses, the available empirical evidence suggests that WTP measures will likely underestimate individual's compensation demanded, perhaps significantly. Nevertheless, a measure of individuals' willingness to pay to avoid a loss could serve as a lower bound on the "true" compensation demanded by losers. In both cases, WTP measures of resource value can provide useful information for improved resource management decisions.

Compensation demanded measures of a potential resource loss also should be most valid when the evaluation context and payment setting are familiar and the environmental asset is clearly defined. However, the existence of a number of special problems suggest that accurate compensation demanded measures of economic value may be especially difficult, or even impossible, to obtain. These include the following possibilities:

1. People may not recognize that compensation is due (e.g., for the loss of an environmental asset that never was considered to be their own).
2. People may be inclined to bid strategically because of the absence of a clear budget constraint, although it may be possible to link compensation estimates with payment consequences (as has been attempted by Kunreuther, Kleindorfer, Knez, & Yaksick, in press, in the context of noxious facility sitings).

3. People may refuse to consider any exchange once their implicit entitlement seemingly is recognized by the compensation-based form of a valuation question.

Despite these problems, it often will be reasonable to interpret information from contingent CD measures of well-defined and familiar environmental assets as representing an upper bound on people's true economic value. This suggestion would seem to be supported on the basis of both field and laboratory results obtained to date (Bishop et al., 1983, 1984; Welsh, 1986). Whether economic (dollar) values are necessarily relevant to the allocation decision at hand, and whether they are fully able to capture people's values for the asset under consideration or instead reflect only one piece of a larger value structure (as implied by Brown, 1984, and others), are important questions that deserve careful investigation.

In cases where the environmental asset is unfamiliar or difficult to define specifically, the accuracy of contingent WTP and CD value estimates is much more difficult to assess. Consider, for example, some of the questions that might arise when interpreting the results of contingent surveys that ask participants to value national improvements in air or water quality (e.g., Mitchell & Carson, 1984; Tolley, Randall, Blomquiest, & Hoehn, 1984). Can respondents clearly perceive the full implications for themselves if air or water resources across the U.S. were to be improved or degraded? What assumptions do people make about tradeoffs between levels (e.g., the fate of fishing opportunities if swimmable levels of water quality were achieved)? What do terms such as visual range or swimmable levels imply in respondent's minds about related parameters such as air color or water clarity? Similar questions about participants' perceptual and conceptual capabilities also could be raised in other contexts, for example that of contingent surveys of wildlife existence values (Boyle & Bishop, in press).

Contingent valuation exercises in such cases must necessarily compromise technical and descriptive detail to provide a brief, easily understood survey. Obviously, where empirical verification of the validity of contingent valuation is lacking, a healthy degree of skepticism is warranted. Nevertheless, and particularly for WTP, results from competently done studies still may be helpful for policy formulation. Results from field and laboratory experiments involving relatively familiar, well-defined products indicate that people do try to give accurate values and no evidence indicates that they stop doing so when they encounter more difficult problems. Accuracy may be affected, but there is no reason to assume that the results are mere "noise."

Overall, these views suggest a mood of cautious optimism for the researcher engaged in a contingent valuation study or the policymaker called upon to interpret the results. If winners and losers can be clearly identified, if the asset in question is familiar, and if the willingness to pay of those who gain from a decision is close to the compensation demanded of those who lose, then the recommendation for a project can be made with some confidence. If the winner's willingness to pay exceeds the loser's compensation demanded, and the number of nonrespondents is low, then there is a strong case for arguing that the compensation test is met and that a proposed action would be a good investment.

When the contingent willingness to pay of those who gain is less than the willingness to pay of those who lose, then the

compensation test can be said to have failed because losers' contingent compensation demanded will likely be still higher. When the loser's contingent compensation demanded substantially exceeds the winner's contingent willingness to pay, or when the number of nonrespondents and/or outliers is unacceptably high, then the limitations of the potential compensation test and the uncertainties surrounding WTP and CD response accuracy create serious problems for the analyst or policymaker. In such a case, two obvious recommendations are to (a) do the best job possible, in terms of identifying winners and losers, debiasing responses, and creating realistic evaluation settings; and (b) carry out at least limited sensitivity tests by using alternative elicitation and data analysis procedures. Beyond that, not a great deal can be said at the present time.

Conclusion

The available empirical evidence from contingent valuation studies, actual cash transactions, and controlled laboratory experiments indicates that theoretical predictions of close correspondence between WTP and CD measures of environmental values are unlikely to be confirmed in practice. People typically seem to think about, and assign values to, amenity environmental goods quite differently depending on which side of an exchange they are on. Being asked to give up an environmental good or an outdoor recreational activity seems to demand something quite different of people than being asked to pay to avoid the loss.

The endowment effect, implicit in prospect theory (Kahneman & Tversky, 1979) and discussed by Thaler (1980) and other economists, suggests that a general reluctance to exchange that which is considered to be one's own may play a role in creating the disparity, but it provides no guidance as to how improved measures of compensation demanded could be elicited or how their validity could be assessed as part of a benefit-cost decision framework.

Some empirical evidence indicates that contingent valuation procedures overestimate individuals' compensation demanded while giving relatively more accurate measures of their willingness to pay (Heberlein & Bishop, 1985). If shown to be robust, contingent expressions of compensation demanded could be used as an upper bound on true compensation demanded. If a proposed project or policy showed the willingness to pay of gainers as expressed using contingent valuation mechanisms to exceed the compensation demanded of losers (also in terms of contingent values), then there would be a case for arguing that the compensation test is met. However, if the winners' contingent willingness to pay was less than the losers' willingness to pay, then the compensation test would fail. And if winners' willingness to pay was less than the losers' compensation demanded, then it would be unclear whether the compensation test was met or not.

Additional work on measuring people's compensation demanded should be viewed as an integral part of economists' efforts to develop policy relevant values for environmental goods. The issue is not merely an interesting academic puzzle. The correct analysis of potential compensation payments--when they are due, to whom, in what amounts and in what form--lies at the heart of defensible policies regarding many of the most pressing environmental and natural resource problems.

References

Banford, N., Knetsch, J., & Mauser, G. (1980). Compensating and equivalent variation measures of consumer's surplus: Further survey results. *Journal of Business Administration, II*, 25-35.

Bishop, R., & Heberlein, R. (1979). Measuring values of extramarket goods: Are indirect measures biased? *American Journal of Agricultural Economics, 61*, 926-930.

Bishop, R., Heberlein, T., & Kealy, M. (1983). Contingent valuation of environmental assets: Comparisons with a simulated market. *Natural Resource Journal, 23*, 619-633.

Bishop, R., Heberlein, T., Welsh, M., & Baumgartner, R. (1984). *Does contingent valuation work? Results of the Sandhill Experiment*. Paper presented at the Association of Environmental and Resource Economists Conference, Ithaca, NY.

Boyle, K., & Bishop, R. (in press). The total value of wildlife: A case study involving endangered species. *Water Resources Research*.

Brookshire, D., Ives, B., & Schulze, W. (1976). The valuation of aesthetic preferences. *Journal of Environmental Economics and Management, 3*, 325-346.

Brookshire, D., Randall, A., & Stoll, J. (1980). Valuing increments and decrements in natural resource service flows. *American Journal of Agricultural Economics, 62*, 478-488.

Brown, T. (1984). The concept of value in resource allocation. *Land Economics, 60*, 231-246.

Calabresi, G., & Melamed, A. (1972). Property rules, liability rules and inalienability: One view of the cathedral. *Harvard Law Review, 85*, 1089-1128.

Coursey, D., Hovis, J., & Schulze, W. (in press). On the supposed disparity between willingness to accept and willingness to pay measures of value. *Quarterly Journal of Economics*.

Coursey, D., & Schulze, W. (in press). The application of laboratory experimental economics to the contingent valuation of public goods. *Public Choice*.

Coursey, D., Brookshire, D., Gerking, S., Anderson, D., & Schulze, W. (1985). *Experimental methods for assessing environmental benefits: Volume II* (Draft Report). Washington, DC: U.S. Environmental Protection Agency.

Cummings, R., Brookshire, D., & Schulze, W. (1984). *Valuing environmental goods: A state of the arts assessment of the contingent valuation method* (Draft Report). Washington, DC: U.S. Environmental Protection Agency.

Currie, J., Murphy, J., & Schmitz, A. (1971). The concept of economic surplus and its use in economic analysis. *Economic Journal, 81*, 741-791.

Dwyer, J., & Bowes, M. (1978). Concepts of value for marine recreational fishing. *American Journal of Agricultural Economics, 60*, 1008-1012.

Fischhoff, B., & Cox, A. (1986). Conceptual framework for benefits assessment. In J. Bentkover, V. Covello, & J. Mumpower (Eds.), *Benefits assessment: The state of the art* (pp. 51-84). Dordrecht, The Netherlands: D. Reidel.

Fisher, A., & Raucher, R. (1984). Intrinsic benefits of improved water quality: Conceptual and empirical perspectives. *Advances in Applied Micro-Economics, 3*, 37-66.

Freeman, A. M. (1979). *The benefits of environmental improvement*. Baltimore, MD: Johns Hopkins University Press.

Gordon, I., & Knetsch, J. (1979). Consumer's surplus measures and the evaluation of resources. *Land Economics, 55*, 1-10.

Gregory, R. (1986). Interpreting measures of economic loss: Evidence from contingent valuation and experimental studies. *Journal of Environmental Economics and Management, 13*, 325-337.

Gregory, R., & Furby, L. (in press). Auctions, experiments and contingent valuation. *Public Choice*.

Haveman, R., & Wiesbrod, B. (1975). The concept of benefits in cost-benefit analysis: with emphasis on water pollution control activities. In H. Peskin & E. Seskin (Eds.), *Cost-benefit analysis and water pollution policy* (pp. 37-66). Washington, DC: The Urban Institute.

Heberlein, R., & Bishop, R. (1985). *Assessing the validity of contingent valuation: Three field experiments*. Paper presented at the Conference on Man's Goals in Changing the Global Environment, Venice, Italy.

Henderson, A. M. (1941). Consumer's surplus and the compensating variation. *Review of Economic Studies, 8*, 117-121.

Hicks, J. (1943). The four consumer's surpluses. *Review of Economic Studies, 11*, 31-41.

Just, R., Hueth, D., & Schmitz, A. (1982). *Applied welfare economics and public policy*. Englewood Cliffs, NJ: Prentice Hall.

Kahneman, D., & Tversky, A. (1979). Prospect theory: An analysis of decision under risk. *Econometrica, 47*, 263-291.

Kaldor, N. (1939). Welfare propensities in economics and interpersonal comparisons of utility. *Economic Journal, 49*, 549-552.

Kennedy, D. (1981). Cost-benefit analysis of entitlement problems: A critique. *Stanford Law Review, 33*, 387-445.

Knetsch, J. (1983). *Property rights and compensation*. Toronto, Ontario, Canada: Butterworth & Co.

Knetsch, J., & Sinden, J. (1984). Willingness to pay and compensation demanded: Experimental evidence of an unexpected disparity in measures of value. *Quarterly Journal of Economics, 99*, 507-521.

Kunreuther, H., Kleindorfer, P., Knez, P., & Yaksick, R. (in press). A compensation mechanism for siting noxious facilities: Theory and experimental design. *Journal of Environmental Economics and Management*.

Little, I. M. D. (1960). *A critique of welfare economics* (2nd ed.). Oxford: Clarendon Press.

Mitchell, R., & Carson, R. (1984). *Willingness to pay for national freshwater quality improvements* (Report). Washington, DC: U.S. Environmental Protection Agency.

Randall, A., & Stoll, J. (1980). Consumer's surplus in commodity space. *American Economic Review, 70*, 132-149.

Rowe, R., d'Arge, R., & Brookshire, D. (1980). An experiment on the economic value of visibility. *Journal of Environmental Economics and Management, 7*, 1-19.

Sinclair, W. (1976). *The economic and social impact of the Kemano II Hydroelectric Project on British Columbia's fisheries resources*. Vancouver, British Columbia, Canada: Fisheries and Marine Service, Department of the Environment.

Thaler, R. (1980). Toward a positive theory of consumer choice. *Journal of Economic Behavior and Organization, 1*, 39-60.

Tolley, G., Randall, A., Blomquist, G., & Hoehn, J. (1984). *Establishing and valuing the effects of improved visibility in the eastern U.S.* (Draft Report) Washington, DC: U.S. Environmental Protection Agency.

Water Resource Council. (1983). *Economic and environmental principles and guidelines for water and related land resources implementation studies*. Washington, DC: U.S. Government Printing Office.

Welsh, M. (1986). *Exploring the accuracy of the contingent valuation method: Comparisons with simulated markets*. Unpublished doctoral thesis, University of Wisconsin, Madison.

Willig, R. (1976). Consumer's surplus without apology. *American Economic Review, 66*, 589-597.

Willig, R. (1979). Consumer's surplus without apology: Reply. *American Economic Review, 69*, 469-474.

Part 4: Methods of Monetary Valuation

Overview

Thomas C. Brown
Rocky Mountain Forest and Range Experiment Station
Fort Collins, Colorado

Richard G. Walsh
Department of Agriculture and Natural Resource Economics
Colorado State University
Fort Collins, Colorado

The three papers in Part 4 discuss alternative approaches to estimating the economic value of nonmarket (e.g., amenity) products. They summarize the relevant theoretical framework and discuss problems in empirical application. The authors are cautiously optimistic about the ability of the methods to obtain reasonably accurate measures of monetary value. A common theme among the papers is that meaningful monetary valuation of amenity goods and services is possible and is moving ahead on both conceptual and empirical levels.

The papers assume that people provide relevant value information via their actual or contingent purchase, or sale behavior. Thus, they assume that individuals are the best judges of the value of their actions and that they can evaluate tradeoffs in light of real constraints and approximate optimal decisions relative to their own preference structures.

The authors discuss three types of markets used for obtaining monetary value information. Mendelsohn and Markstrom use data on observed expenditures in actual markets to estimate the value of related goods not directly sold in markets. The unpriced good might be a characteristic of the priced good (as proximity to parks is to houses) or a separate good that can only be obtained if the priced good is purchased (as use of a free campground is to the purchase of travel to reach the campground). Hoehn and Swanson discuss the use of hypothetical markets, wherein people's responses about what they would do in hypothetical purchase, sale, or referendum situations, to indicate monetary value. Brookshire, Coursey, and Radosevich present results from use of experimental markets. Like the first approach, this involves actual exchange rather than predictions about hypothetical situations, and like the second approach, directly values the good in question rather than inferring value from purchases of related goods.

Mendelsohn and Markstrom briefly describe the approaches and underlying assumptions of five methods that infer the value of unpriced goods from actual market behavior for related goods. Four of these methods use travel and/or time expenditures to infer the value of recreation sites or the characteristics of such sites: the simple, multiple site, generalized, and hedonic travel cost methods. The fifth method, the hedonic price method, uses expenditures on property, or wages accepted in different locations, to infer the value of environmental characteristics associated with such property or locations.

Mendelsohn and Markstrom's paper is written for those who are not familiar with the travel cost and hedonic methods. Noneconomists will find the sections on the simple travel cost and hedonic methods particularly useful; they quite clearly describe how the values of recreation sites and environmental characteristics, respectively, are inferred from the value of the marketed commodities via statistical demand analysis. Some observers have mistakenly concluded that the travel cost method assumes the value of a recreation site is proportional to the cost of traveling to the site. The authors dispel this idea with a clear description of value as consumer surplus (i.e., net willingness to pay above what users pay in travel costs).

Hoehn and Swanson's paper is concerned with the adequacy of value measures obtained in hypothetical markets for use in benefit-cost analysis. The first section of the paper reviews potential sources of error in contingent valuation surveys. The second section summarizes a model of contingent behavior that considers the components of an individual's contingent valuation decision process and the theoretical implications of those components for the individual's response. The final section lists the conclusions to be drawn from the model for use of contingent valuation.

The section of Hoehn and Swanson's paper on the model of contingent behavior describes three sources of error in contingent valuation responses and shows how these sources of error could affect responses. The three sources of error are (1) the communication process whereby the good to be valued and other aspects of the valuation situation are communicated to respondents, (2) the constrained search and value decision process that respondents face, and (3) the possible incentives for respondents to adjust their valuations to influence policy decisions that might result from the contingent survey. Hoehn and Swanson use their model to show how each of these sources of error would cause respondents to deviate from the responses that would mirror the values obtained if the goods were exchanged in an ideal market.

Hoehn and Swanson present many interesting points about their model of contingent behavior in a rather terse fashion; thus, some points may not be perfectly clear to the uninitiated. For this reason, we review some of those points here. Consider first their analysis of the effect of "communication error" on respondents' valuations. For simplicity, we focus on Hicksian compensating measures (e.g., on willingness to pay for a positive change from the current reference point). Hoehn and Swanson's analysis proceeds as follows:

1. If there is error in the way respondents process the information presented to them about the good to be valued, this may lead to uncertainty on the respondents' part about the nature of the change.
2. Ignoring other possible problems with communicating and comprehending the prospective change, and assuming people are risk averse, this uncertainty will always lead to a lower willingness to pay than would result in the absence of uncertainty.
3. Whether a respondent perceives the change to be better or worse than the true perception of the change, this undervaluation will be present in risk averse individuals.
4. Assuming across respondents a random (and therefore symmetrical) deviation from the correct perception of the change, the mean willingness to pay will be less than or equal to the ideal (no communication error) value.

The implication of this conclusion for benefit-cost analysis, is that willingness to pay measures obtained from a proper survey design will not exceed the ideal measure. However, it is important to remember its underlying assumptions, including that (1) there is a true or correct perception of the good to be valued, (2) the process of communicating and comprehending this perception leads to uncertainty on the part of respondents, (3) respondents are risk averse (in Hoehn and Swanson's language, that a typical respondent has a "concave utility function"), and (4) the communication error does not cause a skewed distribution in perception of the good among respondents that could result in an overestimate of willingness to pay. Thus, for example, risk positive responses and biased perceptions of the good (perhaps because of significant prior inclinations or a desire to please the interviewer) are assumed away.

Another point of clarification concerns the second potential source of error, the constrained search and value process that respondents face during value formulation. Again, assuming a Hicksian compensating payment measure of a positive change, the respondent seeks to determine the maximum amount that he or she is willing to pay to obtain the prospective change. Hoehn and Swanson assume that (1) respondents, regardless of communication error or their attitude toward risk, approach that maximum from below, inching up to the maximum willingness to pay; and (2) because of the time and resource constraints of the contingent valuation method context, respondents may therefore fail to complete the process and may state something less than their maximum willingness to pay. This conclusion again suggests that the contingent willingness to pay measure will not overestimate the true value, providing a conservative estimate for benefit-cost analysis. The important behavioral assumption here is that more time and cognitive effort will move the response only in one direction, toward the maximum. Thus, the possibility of a respondent making a guess at the maximum, and then moving in whatever direction arises as more time and effort go into the valuation, is precluded.

Hoehn and Swanson have presented an ambitious framework for analyzing contingent valuation responses. They have begun a process of dissecting the value formulation and value statement process. Perhaps their proposals about contingent valuation behavior are best considered as hypotheses, which will hopefully be empirically tested.

Brookshire, Coursey, and Radosevich use experimental markets with student subjects to examine the now well-documented asymmetry between willingness to pay to obtain a good and compensation demanded to give up the good. Because this dichotomy is counter to the expectations of standard consumer theory, it has aroused considerable interest among economists. Brookshire et al.'s results provide yet another example of this dichotomy. However, and most important, they show that, in the course of repeated iterations of a Vickrey auction carried out before the actual transaction, compensation demanded tended to fall while willingness to pay tended to remain stable or rise. In terms of the median responses of subject groups, the two measures converged. In terms of mean responses, which were subject to the effect of extreme responses that appear to reflect strategic behavior, the two measures crossed; mean willingness to pay was greater than compensation demanded by the end of the auction iterations.

Because of the outlier problem, Brookshire et al. prefer the results based on group median responses. In this view, compensation demanded gradually fell with bidding iterations to approach willingness to pay, which remained rather constant. As the authors state, the drop in compensation demanded could be explained in terms of reduction in loss aversion. Loss aversion would elevate compensation demanded to give up a good, but would have little or no affect on willingness to pay because we are all quite familiar with giving up (i.e., spending) money. Loss aversion would be expected to diminish as individuals become more familiar with trading the good, as they did during the iterations of the Vickrey auction.

Regardless of the explanation for the original dichotomy, the gradual convergence lends support for the economist's expectation that willingness to pay and compensation demanded do not differ in a market context.

To the extent that the iterations of Brookshire et al.'s experiments represent additional time and effort spent on value formulation, the experiments are one test of Hoehn and Swanson's hypotheses. Hoehn and Swanson's model suggests that the willingness to pay responses in the experiment, being Hicksian compensating measures, will not decrease with iterations. Brookshire et al.'s results are in accord with this expectation. The Hoehn and Swanson model is ambiguous with respect to the experiment's compensation demanded responses, which are Hicksian equivalent measures.

Benefit-cost analysis is one approach to organizing information and evaluating proposed changes in resource allocation. While certainly not the only available approach, it is widely used and has considerable appeal in our democratic and capitalistic system of government. The papers in Part 4 take the need for benefit-cost analysis as given, and consider important issues concerning incorporation of nonmarket goods into the benefit-cost framework. Thus, they help move us toward an improved understanding of the monetary value of nonmarket goods.

Toward a Satisfactory Model of Contingent Valuation Behavior in a Policy Valuation Context

John P. Hoehn
Department of Agricultural Economics
Michigan State University

Cindy Sorg Swanson
USDA Forest Service
Rocky Mountain Forest and Range Experiment Station

An individual's ability to make economic choices is limited by many factors. Some of these factors are elements of the choice context--the structure of information, penalties, and rewards. Other factors are cognitive. We incorporate these contextual and cognitive constraints into the standard economic choice model in order to better understand contingent valuation behavior.

In our model, contingent valuation presents an individual with a contingent policy choice. In response, an individual invests time and effort to formulate a valuation. The valuation process is subject to both contextual and cognitive constraints. These constraints result in value responses that tend to diverge from the ideal Hicksian value measures. In a Hicksian compensating framework, individuals tend to understate willingness to pay and overstate willingness to accept compensation.

The implications of our model help to organize existing empirical evidence and to clarify the policy relevance of contingent valuation. Most importantly, though contingent valuation may not be ideal, it does appear to be satisfactory as a practical method for measuring benefits and costs. Given a policy domain that includes both beneficial and detrimental alternatives, contingent valuation identifies at least a subset of policies that are truly beneficial.

In this paper we provide a brief overview of contingent valuation's strengths and identify the dominant sources of error that may affect the contingent choice context. We then discuss a behavioral model that encompasses the major constraints on contingent choice and develop the model's implications for the design contingent valuation formats.

AN OVERVIEW OF THE CONTINGENT VALUATION METHOD

A standard economic valuation of natural resource change seeks to answer an apparently straightforward question: Given an initial natural resource policy, s^0, and a prospective policy, s^1, are the affected individuals made better off or worse off by a change from s^0 to s^1? In answering this question, an economic analysis evolves through several initial stages. First, to the extent possible, the linkages between policy action and its impacts on human well-being are identified. Second, measures of value are selected and adapted to a policy context that may include substantial uncertainty and a variety of indirect gains and losses. Finally, appropriate valuation techniques are matched with the identified gains and losses.

In valuing the unpriced or nonmarket impacts of a policy change, contingent valuation (CV) typically exhibits three important advantages. First, the impacts subject to valuation parallel the predicted impacts of policy. Thus, for a subset of natural resource services, a CV format may pose an individual choice context that parallels the policy choice under consideration: "If a policy were to change natural resource services from s^0 to s^1 at a cost to you of \$b, would you accept or reject the change?" Second, CV formats are adaptable to the implicit property rights setting of policy and may be elicited in either a Hicksian compensating or equivalent form. Finally, consistent with the aggregate policy choice context, CV is forward looking or prospective (Brookshire & Crocker, 1981) and option price is a natural valuation construct.[1]

Several types of evidence tend to validate the policy relevance and reliability of CV data. In terms of indirect evidence, a large body of social-psychological research examines the correspondence between self-reported behavioral intentions and actual behavior (Ajzen & Fishbein, 1977; Ajzen & Peterson, this volume). This research indicates that given a close correspondence between the described and the actual action, the target of the action, the behavioral context, and the timing, one can expect a high correlation between an intended behavior and the realized behavior. Thus, from this literature, one would expect a high degree of correspondence between contingent and actual payment behavior when close correspondence between contingent and actual policy choice context exists.

More directly, empirical application of CV has generated four types of corroborating evidence (Hoehn & Randall, in press). First, CV results are systematically related to respondents' socioeconomic characteristics as well as the availability of substitute resource services. Second, CV data tend to reflect actual choice behavior. Third, CV data are comparable to the value results obtained in applications of other relevant techniques, such as the hedonic and travel cost methods. Finally, where rigorous hypothesis tests are possible, outcomes are consistent with the economic validity of CV data.

With the accumulation of favorable evidence, CV research is beginning to formally investigate alternative models of CV behavior. The dominant alternative (taken by economists) is the textbook economic model of individual behavior: Faced with the contingent policy proposal, the economic agent instantaneously assimilates the policy description, optimizes across all possible alternatives, and selects the optimal value response.

Although the textbook model predicts the general quality of CV data, it does not seem to account for at least three puzzling aspects of CV behavior. First, individual value responses and rankings appear to be unstable over short time intervals (Randall, Blomquist, Hoehn, & Stoll, 1985; Sorg, 1982). Second, with willingness to accept formats, elicited valuations are sometimes unexpectedly large (Brookshire, Randall, & Stoll, 1980; Randall, Ives, & Eastman, 1974). Finally, willingness to accept and willingness to pay responses typically diverge to a greater degree than suggested by theory (Bishop & Heberlein, 1979; Brookshire, et al., 1980; Gordon & Knetsch, 1979).

The general objective of this paper is to build on recent efforts to develop a systematic model of CV behavior. Rather than reject the economic model per se, this research adapts the economic model to the constraints of the CV context. Three aspects of CV are of particular interest: (1) the problem of conveying complex policy information to respondents, (2) the respondent's process of value formulation, and (3) strategic incentives that may arise from the payment rule or aggregate policy implementation rule.

POTENTIAL SOURCES OF ERROR IN CONTINGENT VALUATION OUTCOMES

At various stages in the development of the CV research program, different researchers have proposed various taxonomies for categorizing the potential sources of error in CV formats and outcomes. As a result, important influences on CV behavior have become somewhat obscured (Cummings, Brookshire, Schulze, & Coursey, 1984). Among the existing taxonomies, one can identify four nonexclusive sets of errors (Cummings et al., 1984): (1) the hypothetical context of CV, (2) the information conveyed by the CV format, (3) the strategic behavior of individuals as they try to affect policy outcomes, and (4) the large differences between values obtained with a willingness to pay (WTP) format and values obtained with a willingness to accept (WTA) format. By reviewing the empirical evidence regarding these errors, the apparent underlying influences can be extracted.

Errors in the Hypothetical Context

Hypothetical effects are said to arise as individuals evaluate the gains and losses posed by a prospective policy (Brookshire & Crocker, 1981). Some evidence for hypothetical bias can be drawn from the results of Bishop and Heberlein (1980) and from the psychological literature. In a comparison of contingent and simulated markets, Bishop and Heberlein found that contingent valuation results tend to understate a simulated market measure of willingness to pay and overstate the likely measure of willingness to accept. Research by Slovic (1969) also indicated a difference between hypothetical and actual choice behavior. In a broad review of the psychological literature, Cummings, Brookshire, and Schulze (1986) found mixed evidence of outcome differences for "actual and hypothetical payment" (p. 14) situations. Three factors appear to contribute to the errors that may arise from the hypothetical context. First, as information is conveyed from the format to the individual, errors in perception and comprehension are likely to occur. Policy impacts are often complex and unfamiliar. The time constraints of an interview restrict the amount of time for repetition and review. This problem of communication may result in a "lack of consonance between the commodity 'offered' in the [contingent market] and the individual perceptions of that commodity" (Cummings et al., 1986, p. 15). These errors in perception and comprehension may lead to subsequent errors in the stated valuations.

Second, the decision processes of an individual require time and effort. Once the physical impacts of policy are understood, an individual must begin to rearrange activities and market goods purchases: "If water quality improves in a distant recreation area, am I likely to visit? Will fishing improve? Are there likely to be larger crowds? What current purchases might I give up to pay for the change?" Research substantiates the intuition that such decisions take time. Cognitive research clearly indicates that an individual's ability to process the required information is, at any point in time, limited (Calder, Insko, & Yandell, 1974; Rummelhart, 1977). Pommerehne, Schneider, and Zweifel (1982) showed that individuals tend to shift toward more profitable gambles as they are allowed more time to iterate through a choice process. The results of Hovis, Coursey, and Schulze (1985) and Smith (1979) tend to underscore the correlation between time and improved decisions. Given the correlation between time and reliable decisions, it seems possible that the

time constraints of the typical CV context may cut short an individual's decision processes and induce errors into CV outcomes.

Third, Cummings et al. (1984) suggested that framing effects (Kahneman & Tversky, 1979) may be more pronounced in a CV context than where choices are actually accomplished. However, no existing empirical evidence strongly supports this conjecture (see Cummings et al., 1986).

Information Bias

Information bias arises as individuals formulate an expectation of policy impacts subject to the information conveyed by a CV format (Rowe, d'Arge, & Brookshire, 1980). Such an expectation is conditioned, in part, upon the description of policy impacts as well as other elements of the CV format such as the payment mechanism and bid elicitation procedure. If the information conveyed to respondents does not correspond to the actual policy under evaluation, the information may be biased and may in turn induce a bias in valuation.

Information bias is sometimes erroneously identified as a change in valuation induced by a change in policy description or format design. For instance, an empirical--but flawed--test of information bias might elicit respondents' valuations subject to two different sets of policy information. If the two sets of valuations were shown to be different, information bias might be identified as the cause of the discrepancy. This conclusion, however, is unwarranted. The test simply illustrates that respondents are sensitive to changes in policy relevant information. To demonstrate information bias, one must demonstrate that (1) elements of the policy description and actual policy fail to correspond, and (2) these elements have a significant and systematic impact on elicited valuations.

Two format design elements are sometimes identified with information bias: (1) the starting points in an iterative bidding routine and (2) the choice of payment vehicle (Rowe et al., 1980). Starting points refer to the initial dollar amounts posed by certain forms of iterative bidding routines. These procedures begin with a question of the form: "Would you accept or reject the policy...if it cost $b?" Across a sample of respondents, several different starting points are usually used. If, in ex post analysis, starting points are statistically correlated with final bids, starting point bias exists.

Empirical evidence for starting point bias is mixed. Bishop, Heberlein, Welsh, and Baumgartner (1984) and Rowe et al. (1980) found evidence of starting point bias in their respective CV results. Brookshire and Randall (1979), Brookshire, Thayer, Schulze, and d'Arge (1982), and Thayer (1981) found no evidence of starting point bias in their applications of the iterative bid procedure. Overall, starting point effects appear to stem from (1) acquiescence on the part of the respondent or (2) respondent fatigue due to a lengthy sequence of iterative bidding (Rowe et al., 1980). Therefore, to reduce the prospect of starting point bias, it is important to (1) stress the prospect of actual payment of the stated valuation and (2) iterate to the point of indifference as quickly as possible. In addition, if starting point effects are detected in ex post analysis, the sensitivity of the final results to starting point effects should be examined. Finally, under auxiliary assumptions, it is possible to measure the quantitative impact of starting point effects and to estimate an unbiased measure (Thayer, 1981).

In most cases it is possible to eliminate starting points altogether. Recent studies implement a two-stage iterative procedure without starting points (Randall, Hoehn, & Tolley, 1981; Tolley et al., 1984). In the first stage, a respondent is asked to state the maximum cost that he/she would be willing to sustain to obtain a proposed policy change. Using the first-stage stated valuation as a starting point, the second stage implements a conventional iterative bidding routine. In this two-stage procedure, the starting point is endogenous to an individual's own valuation process.

A third possible source of information bias is the CV payment vehicle. Studies by Daubert and Young (1981), Greenly, Walsh, and Young (1981), and Rowe et al. (1980) found significant differences in final valuations associated with different payment vehicles. Brookshire and Randall (1979) and Brookshire et al. (1980, 1982) found no evidence of payment vehicle effects. In interpreting these results, two points are important. First, as suggested in the discussion of format design, specific payment vehicles are a substantive feature of the general policy description. An individual may view a policy financed by a lump sum charge as different from a policy financed by an increase in an ad valorem tax. Thus, with a substantive change in payment vehicles, valuations may also change. Second, specific payment vehicles are not necessary for realism or credibility in CV formats. Adequate CV performance can be obtained by use of a generalized lump sum cost (Randall et al., 1981; Tolley et al., 1984). As suggested in the discussion of format design, if the objective is to value the general environmental impacts of policy, there is no need to stress a specific payment vehicle.

Strategic Effects

Strategic effects stem from an individual's attempt "to influence the outcome or results of the [evaluation] by not revealing a true valuation" (Rowe et al., 1980, p. 6). In a general public decision setting, the prospect of strategic behavior has been recognized at least since the 18th century (Hume, 1888). In the 19th century, Wicksell (1969) argued that individuals asked to contribute to the provision of a nonrival, nonexclusive good would view their own contribution as affecting only the price and not the availability of prospective services. Wicksell concluded that individuals would contribute nothing toward provision. More recently, Samuelson (1954) concluded that an efficient pricing of nonrival, nonexclusive goods is impossible because it is in "the self interest of each person to give false signals..." (p. 388).

During the last 2 decades a large amount of literature has developed that challenges the generality of incentives leading to "false signals." Clarke (1971), Groves (1973), and Groves and Ledyard (1977) have demonstrated the possibility of designing incentives compatible with truthful revelation. Substantial empirical work also exists (Bohm, 1972; Ferejohn, Forsythe, & Noll, 1979; Marwell & Ames, 1979; Schneider & Pommerehne, 1981; Smith, 1979; Sweeny, 1973). From a review of empirical

studies, Smith (1980) concluded that "incentive compatible public good mechanisms are possible and...operational..."

Even without explicit incentives for truth-telling, strategic effects appear weak. In an experimental context, Bohm (1972), Scherr and Babb (1975), and Schneider and Pommerehne (1981) found little evidence of pronounced strategic behavior. Smith (1979, 1980) tested the strength of strategic incentives against a set of institutions designed to encourage a truthful statement of values. Smith's results suggested that even weak incentives for truth-telling may be enough to counter the prospect of strategic behavior. Evidence from CV research is consistent with the broader literature. Brookshire, Ives, and Schulze (1976), Mitchell and Carson (1981), and Rowe et al. (1980) found no evidence of strong strategic behavior in a CVM setting.

Differences in WTP and WTA

A final potential source of error is an unexpectedly large divergence in empirical measures of WTA and WTP. The theoretical analyses of Randall and Stoll (1980) and Willig (1976) suggest that the quantitative differences between WTA and WTP are, *a priori*, likely to be small. Empirical results consistently violate this *a priori* expectation. Studies by Gordon and Knetsch (1979), Hammack and Brown (1974), Knetsch and Sinden (1985), and Rowe et al. (1980) reported differences between WTA and WTP that were much greater than would be predicted on *a priori* grounds. Nevertheless, the cause of such a divergence remains unclear.

Some evidence regarding the source of divergence was found in the laboratory experiments of Hovis et al. (1985). In their study, WTA and WTP value responses were monitored through a sequence of bidding iterations. At the outset of bidding, WTA and WTP diverged to the extent usually observed in empirical studies. As bidding continued, WTP rose moderately and WTA declined sharply. After a number of iterations, WTA and WTP converged to a point much more consistent with the theoretical results. The divergence of the initial and final WTA valuations was much greater than the divergence of the initial and final WTP valuations. The results indicated that incomplete decision processes lie at the heart of the WTA-WTP divergence.

Conclusions Regarding the Potential for Error

The preceding review identifies two underlying effects that may generate a potential for error in CV outcomes. First, there is the problem of communicating complex information subject to the time constraints of the CV format and the assimilative capacities of the respondent. Given time constraints on review and repetition, errors in perception and comprehension may lead to errors in valuation. Second, the search process implicit in a value formulation process may be constrained and incomplete in a CV context. The valuation problem is often complex and requires an individual to search through routine activities and rearrange market goods purchases. Time for value formulation is, however, limited. Incomplete decision processes appear to lead to such empirical effects as the divergence of WTA and WTP.

Other sources of error are less problematic. Starting point effects are detectable and controlled by an appropriate format design. Payment vehicle effects reflect a substantive change in the general description of policy. The use of specific payment vehicles appears to be unnecessary, except to reflect the content of an actual policy proposal.

Lastly, strategic effects do not appear to dominate CV outcomes. However, the absence of strong strategic effects may be more problematic than their presence. The lack of strategic response may indicate that the respondent views the entire CV experiment as rather academic and remote from actual policy processes (Brookshire et al., 1976). Confidence in CV outcomes would be stronger if the operative incentives were more clear.

In summary, given attention to CV design, the potential for error can be reduced to three underlying possibilities: (1) errors in communication, (2) time constrained search processes, and (3) the likely incentives that determine the extent of truthful or strategic behavior.

CONTINGENT BEHAVIOR AND IMPROVED FORMAT DESIGN

Improved control and understanding of CV format design and outcomes requires systematic explanation of CV behavior. A successful model of contingent behavior would serve several purposes. First, it would encompass the three sources of error previously outlined and thereby generalize the empirical results of past case studies. Second, it would predict the quality of CV data as the valuation context changes. Third, it would result in testable, refutable consequences. Lastly, the relationships identified by the model could be used to (1) assess the adequacy of CV data in economic evaluation and (2) guide the design of improved CV formats.

Recent research by Hoehn and Randall (Hoehn, 1983; Hoehn & Randall, 1983, in press) suggested the possibility of a systematic explanation of CVM behavior. Their basic approach was to adapt the standard economic choice model to the constraints of the CV context. Their analysis encompassed the primary potential sources of error we previously identified: (1) errors in communication, (2) time constrained decision processes, and (3) the likely incentives of the CV context. Implications for policy analysis and CV format design can be extracted from the model used by Hoehn and Randall.

Contingent Behavior and Value Outcomes

A typical CV format confronts an individual with two problems: a value formulation problem and a value statement problem. The value formulation problem arises from the difficulties of valuing an unfamiliar policy change. Value formulation encompasses two potential sources of error: (1) errors in comprehension that may arise as an individual attempts to assimilate new information and (2) the time constrained decision or search process. The value statement problem encompasses strategic behavior.

To identify the impact of value formulation and value statement on CV outcomes, a point of reference or value datum is needed. Because the objective is to elicit an economically relevant valuation, an appropriate datum would be the Hicksian value measure formulated under ideal conditions. Under these ideal conditions:

1. Information about a policy change is communicated without error.
2. Respondents instantly search and optimize across the opportunities presented by a policy change.
3. Incentives are entirely compatible with a full statement of the formulated valuation.

In the ideal case, for a policy that would change resource services from s^0 to s^1, the respondent's ideal Hicksian compensating (HC) measure is:

$$HC = m^0 - e(p, s^1, u^0), \qquad (1)$$

where m^0 is the respondent's initial income, p is the vector of market prices, u^0 is the respondent's well-being or utility level under the initial policy s^0, and $e(p, s^1, u^0)$ is an expenditure function. In the present case, the expenditure function states the minimum level of income that would just maintain the respondent's initial well-being under the post-policy level of natural resource services, s^1. With a change in s that increases well-being, the expenditure function decreases and HC is greater than zero. For policy changes that improve well-being, HC is identical to the compensating measure of willingness to pay. For policy changes that diminish well-being, the expenditure function increases and HC measures an individual's compensating willingness to accept.

The respondent's ideal Hicksian equivalent (HE) measure is:

$$HE = m^0 - e(p, s^0, u^1), \qquad (2)$$

where u^1 represents the individual's uncompensated post-policy level of well-being. In the case of the equivalent measure, the expenditure function states the minimum level of income that would just maintain the uncompensated post-policy level of well-being under the initial set of environmental conditions, s^0. The expenditure function increases (decreases) with increases (decreases) in u^1. Thus, with the equivalent measure, HE measures a respondent's willingness to pay to avoid a detrimental policy change and HE measures a respondent's willingness to accept compensation to forego a beneficial policy change.

Value Formulation

In an actual CV context, value formulation takes place under conditions less than ideal. From the preceding discussion, two sources of error are particularly relevant to the actual CV context: (1) errors in communication and (2) the constrained search and value decision process.

Communication error may arise as policy information is communicated over what are likely to be noisy and error-prone sensory communication channels. The CV format may attempt to communicate s^1 but the actual message communicated is likely to be $\hat{s}^1$ where $\hat{s}^1$ is a random transformation of s^1. In terms of an individual respondent, such communication error may induce greater uncertainty about the intended effects of policy. However, if the format information itself is unbiased, one might expect the error to average out. Thus, the expected value of the communication error for an individual respondent might well be zero, so that $s = E[\hat{s}]$.

Interestingly, a communication error with zero expected value may have a nonzero impact on elicited CV valuations. Under fairly general conditions, an individual's expenditure function is convex in s and the utility function is concave in s. Using Jensen's inequality (Mood, Graybill, & Boes, 1974) and the definition of the expenditure function, it is straightforward to show that the expenditure function subject to uncertainty, $e(p,\hat{s}^1,\hat{u}^0)$, is not less than the expenditure function formulated under ideal conditions, $\hat{e}(p,s^1,u^0)$. Therefore, the Hicksian compensating measure formulated subject to communication error, fHC, does not exceed the ideal Hicksian compensating measure, HC:

$$fHC = m^0 - \hat{e}(p,\hat{s}^1,u^0) \leq HC. \qquad (3)$$

Given its different logical structure, the relation between the formulated equivalent measure and ideal equivalent measure is just the inverse of the relation between the formulated and ideal compensating measures. The equivalent measure formulated subject to communication error, fHE, is not less than the ideal equivalent measure:

$$fHE = m^0 - e(p,s^0,u^1) \geq HE \qquad (4)$$

because $\hat{u}^1 \leq u^1$ where $\hat{u}^1$ is an individual's anticipated post-policy level formulated subject to communicated error (for discussion, see Hoehn [1983] and Hoehn and Randall [in press]). Overall, communication error would result in a formulated compensating valuation, fHC, that does not exceed the ideal compensating measure, HC, and a formulated equivalent measure, fHE, that is not less than ideal equivalent measure, HE.

To this point it is implicit that individual decision processes are instantaneous. In fact, the decision processes of value formulation take time and demand significant cognitive resources. Having assimilated the policy relevant information, a respondent begins the process of assessing the policy's impacts on his/her activities and deciding on a valuation. Each of the two Hicksian value measures imposes a different set of demands on the value formulation process.

If the format is designed to elicit a Hicksian compensating measure, an individual seeks to determine the maximum amount of income that he/she is willing to pay (or accept) to get the prospective policy change. As shown in Equation 3, this maximum willingness to pay (accept) is the difference between the respondent's initial income and the minimum level of expenditure that would leave the individual at his/her initial level of utility at the post-policy level of resource services. Hoehn and Randall's model suggests that due to the time and resource constraints of the CV context, a respondent fails to complete the time consuming and cognitively demanding minimization process. Instead, subject to the constraint on utility or well-being, the respondent identifies a level of expenditure, $\bar{e}(p,\hat{s}^1,u^0)$. Because $\bar{e}(p,\hat{s}^1,u^0)$ maintains initial utility and $\hat{e}(p,\hat{s}^1,u^0)$ is the minimum

expenditure that maintains initial utility when subject only to communication error, $\bar{e}(p,\hat{s}^1,u^0)$ must not be less than $\hat{e}(p,\hat{s}^1,u^0)$. Using Equation 3, the time and resource constrained formulated valuation, fHC_t, is:

$$fHC_t = m^0 - \bar{e}(p,s^1,u^0) \leq fHC \leq HC. \qquad (5)$$

Thus, the Hicksian compensating measure, fHC_t, formulated subject to both communication error and the resource constraints of the CV context does not exceed the ideal Hicksian compensating valuation, HC.

In addition, as indicated by the subscript t, the formulated compensating measure is a function of the time and effort spent in decision making. As the amount of time and effort allocated to the formulation process increase, fHC_t also tends to increase.[2] On average, one would not expect an increase in the amount of time and decision resources allocated to value formulation to increase the divergence between fHC_t and HC.

A format designed to elicit a Hicksian equivalent measure confronts the individual with a somewhat different search and decision problem: An individual must determine the maximum amount of income that he/she is willing to pay (accept) to avoid (forego) the prospective policy. To formulate the Hicksian equivalent measure as described by Equation 4, an individual must (1) forecast his/her well-being under the prospective policy, u^1, and (2) determine the minimum level of expenditure that would maintain that prospective level of well-being under the initial level of resource services, $\hat{s}^0$.

The two-step decision problem imposes two oppositional forces on the formulated equivalent measure, fHE_t. The forecasting problem tends to push fHE_t upward while the payment formulation problem tends to push fHE_t downward. The outcome of these two countervailing forces is not clear. Therefore,

$$fHE_t >|< HE. \qquad (6)$$

The equivalent measure, fHE_t, subject to both communication error and the constraints of the CV context may be greater than, less than, or equal to the ideal equivalent measure, HE.

The impact of additional time and effort on the equivalent measure is also unclear. Whether fHE_t increases or decreases depends on the amount of time and effort allocated to forecasting the prospective level of well-being versus the amount of time allocated to payment formulation.

Value Statement

Once a valuation is formulated, the respondent faces a problem of value statement--of whether to accurately report the formulated valuation, fHC_t or fHE_t. For instance, in some cases, an individual may believe that it is in his/her best long-term interest to respond truthfully to the valuation question. In these cases, the individual states fHC_t or fHE_t, whichever is relevant. However, an individual may also perceive more immediate incentives to distort fHC_t or fHE_t. In this case, an individual may decide to distort fHC_t or fHE_t, and report some other sHC_t or sHE_t, respectively.

The most immediate value statement incentives stem from the relation between the CV choice, the likelihood of policy implementation, and the distribution of policy costs. Hoehn and Randall's model identifies two, often implicit, elements of the CV context that determine the structure of incentives: (1) an (implicit) implementation rule and (2) the (implicit) payment rule. The implementation rule defines the relationship between an individual's response and the likelihood that the project is actually implemented. The payment rule describes an individual's payment in the event that a prospective policy is actually implemented.

Three of the Hoehn and Randall incentive structures are particularly relevant to the CV context.

Case 1. An individual supposes that (1) the prospective policy will be implemented if benefits exceed costs, and (2) in the event of implementation his/her payment will be proportional to his/her stated bid.

If an individual views the value statement problem in terms of Case 1, the probable personal benefits of implementation are weighed against the probable personal costs. The stated valuation may therefore be a compromise between a statement of the full fHC_t or fHE_t, and state nothing. If forced by the incentives of the CV format into a compromise, an individual states something not greater than the full formulated valuation. Therefore, with perceived incentives given by Case 1, sHC_t does not exceed fHC_t, and sHE_t does not exceed fHE_t.

Case 2. An individual supposes that (1) the prospective policy will be implemented if benefits exceed costs and (2) his/her payment is the per capita or average cost of project implementation.

With perceived incentives described by Case 2, an individual who suspects that his/her fHC_t or fHE_t deviates from the true sample mean valuation would report valuations sHC_t or sHE_t to exaggerate that deviation. The intention would be to shift the measured sample mean valuation toward his/her own formulated valuation. Such behavior tends to increase the variance of the stated valuations. Under fairly general conditions, the sample of stated valuations can still be used to estimate a valuation with a statistical expectation that understates fHC_t or fHE_t. Thus, in terms of expected values, the analyst can obtain estimate of sHC_t that does not exceed fHC_t, and an estimate of sHE_t that does not exceed fHE_t.

Case 3. The respondent assumes that (1) the prospective policy will be implemented if a plurality of individuals responds favorably to an impact-payment pair, and (2) his/her payment will be equal to the described per person costs of implementation.

Case 3 is essentially a voting or referendum rule. With this rule, an individual can do no better than respond "accept" to a payment that is less than fHC_t or fHE_t, and respond "reject" to a payment that is greater than fHC_t or fHE_t. Faced with an iterated schedule of prospective costs, an individual would accept all policy-payment pairs until the prospective payment exceeds fHC_t or fHE_t. In this manner, the individual identifies a stated valuation sHC_t that is equal to fHC_t, and a sHE_t that is equal to fHE_t.

Overall, the likely incentives of the CV context reveal little possibility for strategic overstatement of the formulated valuations. Each of the likely incentive structures indicates that, at

worst, the estimated average stated valuation understates the average formulated valuation. Importantly, if individuals view the CV context as a referendum or poll, stated valuations are likely to be identical to formulated valuations.

Summary

Applications of the CV confront respondents with two basic problems: value formulation and value statement.[3] In terms of a Hicksian compensating format, the net effect of value formulation and value statement lead to a systematic effect on the elicited valuations. Under the range of conditions discussed in this section, CV elicits a compensating measure that does not overstate the ideal compensating measure:

$$sHC_t \leq fHC_t \leq HC. \qquad (7)$$

With a Hicksian compensating format, benefit measures elicited in terms of the stated willingness to pay, $sWTP^c$, do not overstate the ideal WTP^c. Measuring costs in terms of stated willingness to accept, $sWTA^c$ ($= -sHC_t$) does not understate the ideal cost measure, WTA^c.

The net effect of value formulation and value statement on the stated Hicksian equivalent measures is less clear. Although the likely incentives suggest an understatement of fHE_t, the value formulation process itself leads to an ambiguous relation between fHE and HE.

HYPOTHESES AND IMPLICATIONS OF THE CONSTRAINED CHOICE MODEL

The model outlined above can be used to develop a number of testable empirical implications or hypotheses. Existing empirical evidence does not appear to be inconsistent with these implications. The model also assists in understanding apparent empirical anomalies. In addition, the model predicts certain outcomes that have been confirmed by recent empirical research. Below, we briefly consider the more pertinent empirical implications and the corresponding empirical evidence.

Learning

The model suggests that (1) the formulated compensating measure of willingness to pay does not decrease, and (2) the formulated compensating measure of willingness to accept does not increase as additional time and decision resources are allocated to the value formulation process. This result is consistent with the recent experimental results of Bergstrom and Stoll (1985).

Initial Divergence between $sWTP^c$ and $sWTA^c$

The model suggests that $sWTP^c \leq WTP^c$, and $WTA^c \leq sWTA^c$. Thus, the $sWTP^c$ and $sWTA^c$ are likely to diverge to a greater extent than suggested by standard theory. As discussed earlier, this divergence is consistent with the empirical evidence.

Non-Divergence of sWTP^c and sWTA^c over Time

The model implies that sWTP^c does not decrease and sWTA^c does not increase as more time and effort are allocated to the value formulation process. This implies that sWTP^c and sWTA^c do not diverge as more time and effort are allocated to the CV decision problem. This implication is consistent with the recent results of Hovis et al. (1985).

HC Does Not Overstate HC

In other words, the stated compensating measure of willingness to pay does not overstate the ideal compensating measure of willingness to pay, and the stated compensating measure of willingness to accept does not understate the ideal compensating measure of willingness to accept. Although this is difficult to test due to the need for a proxy for the ideal measure, this implication of the model appears consistent with the empirical results of Bishop and Heberlein (1980), Brookshire et al. (1982), and Hoehn (in press).

Iterative Bids Dominate the Values Obtained with a WTP Format

Suppose respondents view an iterated accept-reject format as a voting or referendum format and a "How much are you willing to pay" format is interpreted as incentive Case 1 or Case 2. The valuations obtained with an iterative bid format are certain to dominate those obtained with a WTP format due to (1) the amount of time allocated to the value formulation process and (2) the implicit structure of incentives. This result is consistent with the recent empirical results of Sorg (1982).

Overall, the initial model suggests five sets of immediate empirical implications. Notably, these implications appear to be consistent with both existing empirical evidence, including both the regularities and the perceived anomalies.

OPTIMAL AND SATISFACTORY BENEFIT-COST MEASURES

A routine objective of benefit-cost analysis is to determine whether a given policy prospect is a potential Pareto improvement. A policy prospect is a potential Pareto improvement (PPI) if those who gain from policy change could fully compensate those who lose from policy change. In terms of the Hicksian compensating measures, a policy change is a PPI if:

$$0 \leq HC. \tag{8}$$

In applied benefit-cost analysis, empirical measures of gain or loss are used as indicators of a PPI. However, different empirical approaches may yield benefit-cost indicators with different properties relative to the PPI criterion. It is therefore useful to define a set of benefit indicator performance criteria in relation to the PPI test.

An optimal benefit-cost indicator is "one that identifies all proposals that offer PPI as having positive net value and all non-PPI proposals as having negative net value" (Hoehn & Randall, in press, p. 26). Hoehn and Randall noted that while an optimal benefit-cost indicator is ideal, the inevitable compromises of empirical evaluation may admit the usefulness of a benefit indicator that is systematic but not optimal. In a policy environment where many policy proposals are presented as desirable, a benefit-cost indicator that correctly and systematically identifies some portion of the true PPI may be quite useful. In terms of this objective, a satisfactory benefit-cost indicator (SBI) is "one that identifies at least a portion of the true PPI proposals as having positive net value and all non-PPI alternatives as having negative net value" (Hoehn & Randall, in press, p. 27). An SBI is satisfactory if:

$$SBI \leq HC \tag{9}$$

for all prospective policies. Finally, an unreliable benefit-cost indicator is one that is simply not systematically related to the PPI criterion or, in other words, to HC.

By combining these benefit-cost indicator criteria with the qualitative results regarding CV outcomes, Hoehn and Randall (in press) showed that--given an appropriate choice of format design--the Hicksian compensating measures obtained through contingent valuation are satisfactory benefit cost indicators because:

$$sHC_t \leq HC. \tag{10}$$

As more time and effort are devoted to value formulation, the sHC_t tend to become more satisfactory--that is, the formulated valuations more closely approximate the optimal. Given (1) sufficient time and effort and (2) a format with a referendum structure, the sHC_t would approximate an optimal benefit-cost indicator.

IMPROVING THE DESIGN OF CONTINGENT VALUATION FORMATS

Our review of CV emphasizes that the method encompasses a broad class of valuation designs. CV formats may vary widely and may generate, in turn, wide variation in CV outcomes. The analysis indicates that the variation in contingent value data can be controlled by appropriate format choices. The analytical findings suggest at least five guidelines for the design of satisfactory CV formats:

1. With adequate attention to format design and under a wide range of circumstances, valuations obtained in a Hicksian compensating framework result in satisfactory benefit-cost indicators. Thus, where the initial level of well-being is the appropriate reference level, the Hicksian compensating measure should be used and can be expected to yield satisfactory benefit-cost estimates. There appears to be no reason to avoid the use of WTA[c].

2. The elements of CV design should be reviewed with respect to four features: (1) the description of policy conveyed to a respondent, (2) the implicit implementation rule, (3) the implicit payment rule, and (4) the amount of time allocated to value formulation. To the extent that a format design alters one of these four features, a shift in stated valuations can be expected.

3. The implicit implementation rule and the implicit payment rule determine the incentives for value statement. Because the fixed policy cost form of the bid elicitation procedure is suggestive of the referendum model, use of the fixed cost form yields more satisfactory benefit-cost estimates. The accept-reject structure of the fixed cost form reduces the possibility of falsely rejecting a true PPI alternative.

4. An iterative bidding framework is likely to increase the amount of time devoted to valuation and, thereby, increase the satisfactoriness of value outcomes.

Finally, CV outcomes may be further enhanced by format structures that reduce the complexity of the value formulation problem. Tables and graphs that ease the assimilation of information are likely to increase the satisfactoriness of CV outcomes. Computerized formats may be effective in aiding review and repetition or in assisting with simple calculations that an individual may find useful in rearranging prospective market purchases.

CONCLUSION

Our goal was to review and extend recent efforts to develop a systematic model of CV behavior. The literature on the CV was reviewed to identify the major structural elements of the CV choice context. Three major influences were identified: (1) the problem of conveying complex policy information to respondents, (2) the respondent's time and resource constrained process of preference search and valuation, and (3) strategic incentives that may arise from the implicit aggregate policy implementation and payment rule.

We also reviewed recent efforts to develop a theory of CV behavior. By adapting the standard economic model of behavior to the CV context, we showed that the three major influences identified above may indeed have a significant impact on CV outcomes. For the contexts analyzed, CV does not overstate the ideal Hicksian compensating value measures. In a Hicksian compensating setting, willingness to pay is not overstated and willingness to accept is not understated. A referendum format is likely to yield to most satisfactory measures of willingness to pay and willingness to accept. Unfortunately, the Hicksian equivalent measures are less predictable. In a Hicksian equiva-

lent setting, the elicited willingness to pay and willingness to accept measures may either understate or overstate the ideal measures of willingness to pay and willingness to accept.

Overall, predictive models of contingent behavior are in an early stage of development. Nevertheless, initial results appear to be consistent with existing data. It does appear possible to identify the key features of the contingent choice context and, through format design, to control the quality of contingent value outcomes.

References

Ajzen, I., & Fishbein, M. (1977). Attitude-behavior relations: A theoretical analysis and review of empirical research. *Psychological Bulletin, 84,* 888-918.

Bergstrom, J. C., & Stoll, J. R. (1985). *Cognitive decision processes, information, and contingent valuation.* Paper presented at the annual meeting of the American Agricultural Economics Association, Ames, IA.

Bishop, R. C., & Heberlein, T. A. (1980). *Simulated markets, hypothetical markets, and travel cost analysis: Alternative methods of estimating outdoor recreation demand.* Staff Paper Number 187, Department of Agricultural Economics, University of Wisconsin, Madison.

Bishop, R. C., & Heberlein, T. A. (1979). Measuring values of extramarket goods: Are indirect measures biased? *American Journal Agricultural Economics, 64,* 927-930.

Bishop, R. C., Heberlein, T. A., Welsh, M. P., & Baumgartner, R. M. (1984). *Does contingent valuation work? Results of the Sandhill Experiment.* Paper presented at the annual meeting of the American Agricultural Economics Association, Cornell University, Ithaca, NY.

Bohm, P. (1972). Estimating demand for public goods: An experiment. *European Economic Review, 3,* 111-130.

Brookshire, D. S., & Crocker, T. D. (1981). The advantages of contingent valuation methods for benefit cost analysis. *Public Choice, 36,* 235-252.

Brookshire, D. S., Ives, B., & Schulze, W. D. (1976). The valuation of aesthetic preferences. *Journal of Environmental Economics and Management, 3,* 325-346.

Brookshire, D. S., & Randall, A. (1979). *Experiments in valuing wildlife services.* Phase I Interim Report to the U.S. Fish and Wildlife Service, University of Wyoming, Laramie.

Brookshire, D. S., Randall, A., & Stoll, J. R. (1980). Valuing increments and decrements in natural resource service flows. *American Journal of Agricultural Economics, 62,* 478-488.

Brookshire, D. S., Thayer, M. A., Schulze, W. D., & d'Arge, R. C. (1982). Valuing public goods: A comparison of survey and hedonic approaches. *American Economic Review, 72,* 165-177.

Calder, B., Insko, C., & Yandell, B. (1974). The relation of cognitive and memorial processes to persuasion in a simulated jury trial. *Journal of Applied Social Psychology, 4,* 62-92.

Clarke, E. H. (1971). Multipart pricing of public goods. *Public Choice, 11,* 17-33.

Cummings, R. G., Brookshire, D. S., & Schulze, W. D. (Eds.). (1986). *Valuing environmental goods: Assessment of the contingent valuation method.* Totowa, NJ: Rowman and Allanheld.

Cummings, R. G., Brookshire, D. S., Schulze, W. D., & Coursey, D. L. (1984). *Valuing environmental goods: A state of the arts assessment of the contingent valuation method.* Unpublished manuscript, Department of Economics, University of New Mexico, Albuquerque.

Daubert, J. T., & Young, R. A. (1981). Recreational demands for maintaining instream flows: A contingent valuation approach. *American Journal of Agricultural Economics, 63,* 666-676.

Ferejohn, J., Forsythe, R., & Noll, R. (1979). An experimental analysis of decision making procedures for discrete public goods: A case study of a problem in institutional design. In V. L. Smith (Ed.), *Research in experimental economics,* Greenwich, CT: JAI Press.

Gordon, I. M., & Knetsch, J. L. (1979). Consumers' surplus measures and the evaluation of resources. *Land Economics, 55,* 1-10.

Graham, D. A. (1981). Cost-benefit analysis under uncertainty. *American Economic Review, 71*, 715-725.

Greenly, D. A., Walsh, R. C., & Young, R. A. (1981). Option value: Empirical evidence from a case study of recreation and water quality. *Quarterly Journal of Economics, 95*, 657-673.

Groves, T. (1973). Incentives in teams. *Econometrica, 41*, 617-663.

Groves, T., & Ledyard, J. (1977). Optimal allocation of public goods: A solution to the 'free-rider' problem. *Econometrica, 45*, 783-809.

Hammack, J., & Brown, G. M. (1974). *Waterfowl and wetlands: Toward bioeconomic analysis.* Baltimore, MD: Johns Hopkins Press.

Hoehn, J. P. (in press). Contingent valuation and the prospect of a satisfactory benefit cost indicator. In R. C. Johnson & G. V. Johnson, (Eds.) *Economic valuation and natural resources: Issues, theory, and applications.* Boulder, CO: Westview Press.

Hoehn, J. P. (1983). The benefit cost evaluation of multi-part public policy: A theoretical framework and critique of estimation methods. Unpublished doctoral dissertation, University of Kentucky, Lexington.

Hoehn, J. P., & Randall, A. (1987). A satisfactory benefit cost indicator from contingent valuation. *Journal of Environmental Economics and Management, 14*, 226-247.

Hoehn, J. P., & Randall, A. (1983). *Incentives and performance in contingent policy evaluation.* Paper presented at the summer meeting of the American Agricultural Economics Association, West Lafayette, IN.

Hovis, J., Coursey, D. C., & Schulze, W. D. (1985). *A comparison of alternative valuation methods for nonmarket commodities.* Unpublished manuscript, Department of Economics, University of Wyoming, Laramie.

Hume, D. A. (1888). *Treatise on human nature.* Oxford: Oxford Press

Kahneman, O., & Tversky, A. (1979). Prospect theory. *Econometrica, 47*, 263-291.

Knetsch, J., & Sinden, J. A. (1985). Willingness to pay and compensation demanded: Experimental evidence from an unexpected disparity in measures of value. *Quarterly Journal of Economics, 100*, 507-521.

Marwell, G., & Ames, R. E. (1979). Experiments on the provision of public goods. *American Journal of Sociology, 84*, 1335-1360.

Mitchell, R. C. & Carson, R. T. (1981). *An experiment in determining willingness to pay for national water quality improvements.* Draft report, Washington, DC: Resources for the Future.

Mood, A. M., Graybill, F. A., & Boes, D. C. (1974). *Introduction to the theory of statistics.* New York: McGraw-Hill.

Pommerehne, W., Schneider, S., & Zweifel, P. (1982). Economic theory of choice and the preference reversal phenomena: A reexamination. *American Economic Review, 72*, 569-574.

Randall, A., Blomquist, G. C., Hoehn, J. P., & Stoll, J. R. (1985). *National aggregate benefits of air and water pollution control* (Draft Final Report). Washington, DC: Environmental Protection Agency.

Randall, A., Hoehn, J. P., & Tolley, G. S. (1981). *The structure of contingent markets.* Paper presented at the annual meeting of the American Economic Association, Washington, DC.

Randall, A., Ives, B., & Eastman, C. (1974). Bidding games for valuation of aesthetic environmental improvements. *Journal of Environmental Economics and Management, 1*, 132-149.

Randall, A., & Stoll, J. R. (1980). Consumer's surplus in commodity space. *American Economic Review, 70*, 449-454.

Rowe, R. D., d'Arge, R. C., & Brookshire, D. S. (1980). An experiment on the economic value of visibility. *Journal of Environmental Economics and Management, 7*, 1-19.

Rummelhart, D. (1977). *Introduction to human information processing.* New York: John Wiley & Sons.

Samuelson, P. A. (1954). The pure theory of public expenditures. *Review of Economics and Statistics, 36*, 387-389.

Scherr, B. A., & Babb, E. M. (1975). Pricing public goods: An experiment with two proposed pricing systems. *Public Choice, 23*, 35-53.

Schneider, F., & Pommerehne, W. W. (1981). Free riding and collecting action: An experiment in public microeconomics. *Quarterly Journal of Economics, 95*, 689-704.

Slovic, P. (1969). Differential effects of real versus hypothetical payoffs on choices among gambles. *Journal of Experimental Psychology, 80*, 434-437.

Smith, V. L. (1979). Incentive compatible experimental processes for the provision of public goods. In V. L. Smith (Eds.), *Research in experimental economics.* Greenwich, CT: JAI Press.

Smith, V. L. (1980). Experiments with a decentralized mechanism for public goods decisions. *American Economic Review, 70*, 584-599.

Sorg, C. (1982). *Valuing increments and decrements of wildlife resources: Further evidence.* Unpublished master's thesis, Department of Economics, University of Wyoming, Laramie.

Sweeny, J. W. (1973). An experimental investigation of the free-rider problem. *Social Science Research, 2*, 277-292.

Thayer, M. A. (1981). Contingent valuation techniques for assessing environment impacts: Further evidence. *Journal of Environmental Economics and Management, 8*, 27-44.

Tolley, G. A., Randall, A., Blomquist, G. C., Fabian, R., Fishelson, G., Frankel, A., Hoehn, J. P., Krum, R., & Mensah, E. (1984). *Establishing and valuing the effects of improved visibility in the eastern United States.* Report prepared under United States Environmental Protection Agency cooperative agreement CR80776-01-1, University of Chicago, Chicago, IL.

Wicksell, K. (1969). A new principle of just taxation. In R. A. Musgrave & A. T. Peacock (Eds.), J. M. Buchanan (Trans.), *Classics in the theory of public finance.* New York: St. Martin's Press. (Original work published 1896).

Willig, R. D. (1976). Consumers' surplus without apology. *American Economic Review, 66*, 589-597.

Footnotes

[1]Brookshire and Crocker (1981) discuss this and other advantages of CV in some depth. See Graham (1981) for a discussion of the use of option price in policy evaluation.

[2]Formally, Hoehn and Randall (in press) showed that fHC_t does not decrease but may increase with the allocation of additional time and decision resources.

[3]The analysis of the value search process, communication error, and value statement are subject to rather different assumptions regarding the utility function. The findings regarding the value search process hinge on concept of minimization on a set $X = \{x \mid u(x,s^1) \geq u^0\}$, where x is a commodity bundle and $u(\ )$ is a utility function. Under weak assumptions of continuity, the set X is closed and bounded below. Therefore, a minimum expenditure bundle exists. The individual either finds this minimum expenditure bundle or does not. If the individual does not find the minimum level of expenditure, he/she settles for a higher level of expenditure that still yields u^0. The communication error and value statement processes are analyzed assuming that the utility function is concave. It is not clear whether substantially different conclusions would result if the concavity assumption were relaxed.

The Use of Travel Cost and Hedonic Methods in Assessing Environmental Benefits

Robert Mendelsohn
Yale School of Forestry and Environmental Studies

Donald Markstrom
USDA Forest Service
Rocky Mountain Forest and Range Experiment Station

One of the pressing issues of our time is the preservation and management of valuable natural resources that are not traded in markets. Although we have a number of laws that recognize the social value of natural areas, good measures of the monetary value of the environment are rare. Consequently, as the development value of natural areas rises, there is ever increasing pressure to amend protectionist laws and regulations to allow more development and more pollution. To balance these development pressures, it is important to develop comparable measures of the monetary value of nonmarket goods, such as a clean environment, wilderness areas, and wildlife. In this paper, we discuss two promising revealed preference methods to measure the monetary value of natural resources that are not traded in markets: generic travel cost and hedonic methods.

It might seem strange to focus solely on the elements of the environment for which no markets have been established. After all, why ignore the vast natural resources traded in the market place, such as oil, minerals, land, crops, livestock, and trees? However, as discussed in Mendelsohn and Peterson (this volume), these traded goods have well-defined and measurable monetary values, their market prices. In this paper, we focus on nonmarket resources that are not so easily valued, specifically recreation on public lands.

A crude measure of the value of recreation lands has been used for several decades: the annual count of visitors. The number of visitor days reflects the general interest in a site. Thus, a site with 200 visitors is presumed to be of greater value than a site with 100 visitors. This basic concept was extended to take account of the length of stay by counting recreation visitor days (RVD). The longer a visitor stayed, the more RVD's accumulated. Although sufficient to distinguish national sites from local parks, the count of RVD's is an awkward measure to compare against alternative land uses such as timber or mining. How many visitor days does it take to be comparable with 1,000 barrels of crude oil or 500 tons of coal?

To find a unit of comparison against other traded goods, RVD's had to be converted to dollars. The first estimates of the value of an RVD came from simple travel cost models (e.g., Clawson & Knetsch, 1966) with subsequent estimates also being made by contingent valuation techniques (e.g., Sorg & Loomis, 1984). The value of an RVD, recreation visitor day, is defined as the average consumer surplus (in dollars per day) for a visitor to a site. Thus, the RVD concept has been developed to help managers measure the aggregate recreation value of a site (average RVD value times the number of RVD's).

The RVD concept, however, gives a land manager little guidance to the benefits of managing existing land because it is entirely divorced from land qualities. That is, the concept does not value improvements to the land. One attempt to introduce land qualities in this framework is to distinguish RVD's by activity (Driver & Tocher, 1970). Thus, a separate estimate of RVD values by hiking, hunting, fishing, swimming, and boating provides at least some guidance to the land manager as to whether or not to focus on trails, wildlife, fish, beaches, or boat launches. RVD's were further differentiated by the inclusion of Recreation Opportunity Spectrum (ROS) zones as a measure of the development level of the setting in which the activity takes place (Driver & Brown, 1978). The ROS classifications includes six distinct settings ranging from primitive to urban. Even more recently, several techniques have been developed to value the individual characteristics of land. These include property hedonic (Freeman, 1979; Wilman 1981), multiple site travel cost (Burt & Brewer, 1971; Cichetti, Fisher, & Smith 1976), generalized travel cost (Desvousges, Smith, & McGivney, 1983; Freeman, 1979; Vaughn & Russell, 1983) and hedonic travel cost models (Brown & Mendelsohn, 1984; Englin & Mendelsohn, 1985; Mendelsohn, 1984).

Beginning with the simple travel cost model and continuing through the more sophisticated methods, the purpose of the valuation methods was to find a monetary value for an RVD, an RVD activity day, an RVD activity day by ROS class, and finally for the characteristics of land. By confining the research to monetary values, the economic work focused upon objective or behavioral values. A subsequent branch of research has investigated the motivations behind these behavioral values by attempting to look at the package of experiences people are seeking in outdoor recreation (Driver & Brown, 1978; Driver & Tocher, 1970) such as family solidarity, mental health, physical health, and increased work productivity. This research, however, is more difficult than the monetary valuation because it involves subjective views of entities that have no direct behavioral counterpart. Although this subjective research is interesting, we confine our discussion in this paper to behavioral values.

One unfortunate limitation of recreation analysis of public lands is the expression of values in terms of an RVD. Empirical evidence suggests that RVD's are not additive. For example, a 2-day trip by two people is not necessarily worth a 1-day trip by four persons or a 4-day trip by one person. This inherent flaw in the RVD concept has mistakenly led some administrators to believe there is a flaw in the underlying valuation procedure. However, it should be recognized that valuation techniques such as the travel cost model need not express recreation values in terms of RVD's. In fact, the best use of travel cost models is to estimate the entire net recreation value of a site.

In the next few sections, we review the underlying methodology of the property and wage hedonic models and the simple, multiple site, generalized, and hedonic travel cost models. We try to identify, in each case, the special assumptions of each technique, the appropriate setting for the method, and the kinds of applications attempted to date.

PROPOSED METHODOLOGIES

As mentioned in the introduction, the five methodologies we explore in this paper have been used to measure different things. The simple travel cost model, for example, is designed to value an entire site by estimating the demand for trips to the site. The hedonic property (wage) method determines the value of environmental factors surrounding private property (employment) by exploring the variation in sale values (wages) within a private market. The multiple site travel cost model is intended to value types of sites and to explore interactions among systems of sites. The generalized travel cost model attempts to value site characteristics by examining subtle shifts in the demand for trips to various sites. Finally, the hedonic travel cost method estimates the value of site characteristics by examining how users choose which site to visit.

Simple Travel Cost

The simple travel cost model has been used for almost 3 decades to value recreation sites. The approach was first suggested by Harold Hotelling in a letter to the Park Service and has since been developed by Marion Clawson, Jack Knetsch, and many others. The simple travel cost method values a single site by observing how much people are willing to pay to come visit the site. The model presumes that people will make repeated trips to a site until the marginal value of the last trip is just worth what they have to pay to get there. Choosing to take a trip is just like choosing to buy a dress in a store except that the price of the trip is the travel cost expended rather than money given to a merchant.

Typically, we observe that as one buys more and more of any consumption item, the value of the last unit purchased falls. The same pattern applies to recreation trips. The more trips a person takes, the less one values one more trip. Inframarginal trips, the first few trips, may be worth a lot more to an individual than the last trip. People keep purchasing more and more of a good until their marginal valuation exactly equals the price of the good. The last trip must therefore be worth the travel cost.

If all trips were worth just the travel cost, then the site itself would have no value. If one took the site away, the people would no longer have the trips but they would have all the money they spent on the trips. Thus, if each trip was just worth the money spent on it, the site itself would be worthless. The value of sites thus lies in the excess value of the trips over and above the travel costs. If the earlier trips are worth more than the last trip, they are also worth more than the travel cost. The value of the site per person is the excess value of the inframarginal trips over the travel costs.

To measure the value of inframarginal trips, the travel cost model assumes that people who happen to be further away are the same as people who live closer except that they face higher travel costs. Suppose the nearby people had travel costs of $5.00 per trip and went 10 times whereas the next most distant set of people had travel costs of $5.50 and went 9 times. If all these people are alike, everyone would value the 9th trip at $5.50 and the 10th trip at $5.00. The more distant people consequently do not take the 10th trip (because it costs more than $5.00 for them). The closer individuals value the 9th trip more than they have to pay for it. In fact, the added value of the 9th trip is $0.50. If the site were taken away, the more closer individuals would lose this extra $0.50. Of course, they would also lose more than this because they would lose the other inframarginal trips (the 8th, 7th, 6th trip, etc.) as well.

This simple logic is captured in a formal model relating visitation rates to travel costs. By measuring how often people come to the site from different distances, one can infer the value of each trip. Thus, one can actually measure the travel costs of people who come to the site an average of one time, two times, three times, etc. One testable hypothesis of this model is that people faced with higher travel costs tend to come to a site less often. This hypothesis has been tested on numerous data sets and is broadly supported.

The formal travel cost model thus relates visitation rates to travel costs. For example, one might postulate the following model:

$$V = a + b\,T + c\,W, \tag{1}$$

where V is visitation rates, T is travel costs, and W is a measure or vector of socioeconomic variables. Researchers have found that the coefficient on travel costs, b, is almost always negative as expected (e.g., Clawson & Knetsch, 1966; Dwyer, Kelly, & Bowes, 1977). The first step in the travel cost model is to estimate an equation such as the one above from data about visitors and where they come from. The socioeconomic variables are used to correct for observable differences between people. Corrected for observable differences, the assumption that people from different distances are really alike seems more reasonable.

Once a model such as Equation 1 has been estimated, it is possible to calculate the value of a site. As mentioned earlier, the value of the site is captured by the difference between the marginal value of each trip and its marginal cost. The marginal cost of the trip is just the actual travel cost of the person. The marginal value of a trip is the travel cost of the more distant person who has made this trip their last. Thus, the area underneath the visitation trip curve (Equation 1) minus the costs of actual travel measures the individual's valuation of the site. In economic language, the site visitation function is a demand curve for trips. The value of the site is the consumer surplus for trips.

Because many people can value a recreation site jointly, the value of the site is the sum of what all the people would be willing to pay to maintain it. Thus, one would measure the consumer surplus of people from every distance away from the site and take the sum of the resulting values. Assuming that visitation rates are being measured in terms of annual attendance, this process would yield an annual value for the entire site. The present value of this annual flow could then be calculated using an appropriate discount rate.

To calculate the simple travel cost model, one needs, at a minimum, data concerning the origin of users to a specific site. Coupling this data with information about travel costs (perhaps from maps) and population (from the U.S. Census), one can calculate a travel cost curve. Because people from different origins are not always alike, it is helpful to supplement this data with socioeconomic information about each origin. For example, income, education, and number of small children may tend to affect desired visitation rates. By controlling for such factors, it is more likely that the only true difference between towns is the travel costs.

It has never been clear exactly what unit of observation is most appropriate for the simple travel cost model. Some studies use individual visitors as the unit of observation. Unfortunately, when people travel as groups, the travel cost of each individual is just his/her share of the travel costs of the entire party. This presents difficult problems of how to divide party travel cost. An alternative approach is to use the party or a car as the unit of observation and to include a measure of party size as an independent variable. The advantage of this latter approach is that the travel costs of the party are well defined. The extent that party size influences valuation can be revealed in the analysis.

Another issue with respect to the simple travel cost model (and in fact all the behavioral models) is how to measure travel costs. Once origin is known, measuring the distance each person must travel to get to the site is relatively straightforward. However, the appropriate cost per mile is a more troublesome figure.

On the one hand, we have estimates from the American Automobile Association (AAA) about the average total costs of driving a car. These figures include oil and gas as well as maintenance, insurance, taxes, and the annualized purchase price of the car. It is not clear that people take all these costs into account when making trip decisions. After all, the purchase price of the car and that year's insurance has already been paid for whether the person takes one more trip or not. On the other hand, all the time spent traveling to the site is not included in the AAA figures. For example, is this time as valuable as work time (the wages of the individual) or is the travel time a pleasure in and of itself? Exactly what cost per mile should be used in travel cost models is not at all clear.

Another problem with travel cost models is that some people visit more than one destination on a trip. If a person has other reasons for taking a trip, how much of the travel cost should be ascribed just to the site? For example, if a person from Philadelphia has a business trip to Boston and then visits the White Mountains, how much of the total trip should be assigned to the White Mountains? Generally, this is not obvious. However, it has been observed that people from further away are more likely to visit multiple sites. Consequently, it seems reasonable to limit the distance in travel cost models to approximately 300 miles from the site. All people coming from further than 300 miles are not included in the estimation of the travel cost model (although they are included in the consumer surplus calculations).

Hedonic Price Method

The hedonic method is based on the simple notion that people choose specific goods because of their objective characteristics. Originally designed to control for the quality difference among goods (Griliches, 1971), the hedonic price method gradually became a tool to measure the value of good's attributes. In this paper, we focus on valuing environmental attributes associated with the purchase of goods. The specific goods, in this case, are houses and jobs. The model suggests that because people select the good for its characteristics, then the value of the characteristics are reflected in the price of the good. Thus, an otherwise similar house located in a nicer environment should sell for a higher price. The differential in that price reflects the value of the environment. Similarly, if there were two identical jobs but one was located in a lovely city and the other was not, employers should be able to hire people for less money for the job in the nicer location. The amount of money people would give up to live in a nicer environment is equal to the value of the environment to them.

Because many attributes tend to be different from one hour to another and one job from another, to estimate the value of any one characteristic, one must control for all others. One approach to this statistical problem is to find identical pairs of houses except that one house has the environmental good and the other does not. The difference in sale value between the houses would then reflect the value of the environmental good. Unfortunately, it is difficult to find pairs of houses so closely matched that the major remaining difference between the houses is the attribute being valued. A second approach is to control for the differences

between houses with an explicit statistical model. Although there are problems with this technique as well, this latter approach has been used in the literature (e.g., Anderson & Crocker, 1971; Ridker & Henning, 1967; Wilman, 1981).

The hedonic method begins with a statistical model of how characteristics affect the price of the good. In this model, all attributes expected to affect the market price of the house or job are measured and included in some mathematical form. For example, the hedonic model could be linear where the value of the good is a linear combination of all the characteristics:

$$V = a + bZ_1 + cZ_2 + dZ_3 + ... + u, \qquad (2)$$

where Z reflects the vector of characteristics, V is the market price of the good, and a, b, c, etc., is a set of characteristic prices. This model would then be estimated using a multiple regression technique. The data would include a number of market transactions from a single market. As long as there is sufficient independent variation across the sample for each attribute and that attribute is valued, the hedonic technique should be able to measure the independent contribution of the attribute.

One of the serious questions about the hedonic method is whether or not the characteristics can be controlled through the statistical model. For example, the appropriate functional form for the hedonic equation is not known *a priori*. Halvorsen and Pollakowski (1979) consequently recommended that a formal Box-Cox transformation be attempted to explore for the correct flexible functional form. Unfortunately, this approach focuses too strenuously on explaining the total variation in sales price rather than the contribution of the environment. The Box-Cox test may not always be appropriate (Cassell & Mendelsohn, 1985).

A second control problem concerns the list of included variables. Even the most painstaking data collection process is bound to leave out some attributes that affect good purchase decisions. The issue then becomes what is the effect of left-out variables. If there is any sample correlation between the left-out variables and the environment, the price coefficient on the environment will be biased. Because including all variables in a hedonic model is impossible, the art of hedonics suggests that researchers focus on attributes that may be correlated with the environment. Specifically, because the environment tends to have strong spatial patterns, the researcher must try to locate all other important variables with similar spatial patterns.

With nonlinear hedonic market equations such as the following popular semilog form:

$$\log (V) = a + bZ_1 + cZ_2 + ... + u, \qquad (3)$$

the price of a characteristic is no longer the coefficient of that characteristic but rather the marginal contribution of the attribute to market price. For example the price of attribute Z_1 in Equation 3 is:

$$P(Z_1) = d\log (V)/d Z_1 = b\log (V). \qquad (4)$$

Note that as this attribute increases, the marginal price of Z_1 increases. The price gradient is upwards sloping with this functional form.

Early practitioners of the hedonic price method (Anderson & Crocker, 1971; Ridker & Henning, 1967) were misled by the slope of these price gradients to think that they had estimated demand or supply curves for the attribute. This is not precisely the case. The hedonic price gradient is merely a collection of prices occurring at one moment in time within a single market. Multiple prices for the attribute can occur at different levels of the attribute because the attributes themselves cannot be untied from the bundles in which they are located. Thus, for example, the price of a second bathroom is the difference in market value between one- and two-bathroom houses. There is no need for the price of a third bathroom to equal the price of the second because the third bathroom price is determined by the difference in prices between two- and three-bathroom houses. As long as people cannot take the third bathroom out of a three-bathroom house and sell it to houses with one bathroom, the price of bathrooms could well vary depending upon the number of bathrooms.

The hedonic model presumes that people have enough choices in the market so that they can adjust their package of attributes to buy just the right amount of each. That is, people will buy more and more of each characteristic until they value the characteristic relative to all other goods at the market price. The estimated hedonic price consequently reflects the marginal value of the characteristic for all people who purchase that level of characteristic. Anyone who has bothered to buy a house knows that it is almost impossible to find the house with just the right amount of every desired characteristic. However, it is also apparent that in choosing among houses, one consciously jockeys the attributes of each house against all others. Thus, the model may serve as a reasonable approximation of the true choice behavior even if it is not exact.

To understand how people react to nonmarginal changes in a characteristic, one must know more than just the market price. The estimated hedonic price is an underestimate (overestimate) of a nonmarginal reduction (increase) in any attribute. To estimate the precise value of nonmarginal changes, one must understand how consumers react to changes in prices. That is, one must estimate a demand curve for each characteristic.

Hedonic property and wage studies, however, have been severely hampered in their attempt to estimate hedonic structural equations. Most studies of properties and jobs really only have data from a single market. As shown in a series of papers (Brown & Rosen, 1982; Diamond & Smith, 1985; Mendelsohn, 1985) single markets cannot support structural equation estimation without making ridiculous assumptions. The only approach which looks promising is to use multiple markets (Cassell & Mendelsohn, 1982; Palmquist, 1984; Witte, Sumka, & Erickson, 1979). Even with the multiple market approach, however, systematic differences between markets can obfuscate results. Further, the data requirements are expensive. Thus, the primary use of the hedonic method will continue to be to measure prices or marginal benefits.

A final issue that needs to be addressed with respect to the hedonic model is that it captures only those variables that are apparent to home buyers. Thus, if a tremendous amount of soot or visible smog is in an area, one can reasonably expect market prices to be sensitive to the effect. However, if the environmental good is a tasteless, odorless gas, an underground toxic leak, or an invisible water pollutant, it is no longer apparent that the hedonic method will capture the monetary value of the good. The hedonic method will only measure what people are aware of. If a pollutant is not evident to the senses, its true value to people will be evident in hedonic prices only if there is extensive advertising.

Multiple Site Travel Cost

One complication of the simple travel cost model that has been suggested in the literature is to account for the proximity of alternative sites (e.g., Burt & Brewer, 1971). It is well known that the visitation rate to a specific site is heavily influenced by the availability of substitute sites. This can be accommodated within the simple travel cost framework by including the travel costs to the relevant alternative sites as additional independent variables. For example, one could amend Equation 1 with the following:

$$V = a + bT + cW + dP, \qquad (5)$$

where P is a vector of the travel costs to alternative sites.

The multiple site approach could also be adapted to examine the value of a system of sites. Thus, instead of valuing one particular site, one would value an entire configuration of sites. The specific value of changing a site from one type to another or of adding a site to an existing system could then be examined with a single set of estimates. Equation 5 would be replaced by a system of equations, one for each type of site. The model assumes that people would always go to the closest site of each type. Thus, the model would include the travel costs to the nearest of each type of site and there would be a separate regression for each type of site:

$$V1 = a_1 + b_1 T_1 + c_1 W + d_1 P_1, \qquad (6)$$

$$V_2 = a_2 + b_2 T_2 + c_2 W + d_2 P_2,$$

$$\cdots \qquad \qquad \cdots$$

$$Vn = an + bnTn + cnW + dnPn.$$

The advantage of estimating the demand for a system of sites is that one could evaluate adding or subtracting any existing type of site to the system with the single demand estimation. To make a similar comparison with single site travel cost (Equation 5), one would have to make a separate analysis for each type of site. If one relied on simple travel cost (Equation 1), one would have to make a separate analysis of each site even within a type of site to arrive at similar estimates.

One disadvantage of the multiple site approach is that one needs more information to make the estimation work. In addition to knowing the origin of visitors from any one site, one also needs to know the location of alternative sites they visit. Instead of measuring a single distance from each origin, a multiplicity of distances need to be measured. In the case of the White Mountains, one could easily include the many alternatives available within the National Forest. However, to be complete, one would also want to include more distant alternatives such as the Green Mountains, the Catskills, Cape Cod, and the Maine coast.

Because the demand equation (Equation 6) series represent a system, it is important that the system be internally consistent. For example, suppose one converted a low quality site to a high quality site. This would be equivalent to subtracting a low site and adding a high site. If one used the low quality site equation to value the removal of the low site first, then the high quality site would not be in place yet. When the high quality site was being evaluated second, the low quality site would now be gone. Suppose we measured the addition of the high quality site first and then measured the low quality site removal value. It is important that either way we measure the change, we get the same answer from the system. By requiring that certain cross travel cost coefficients inside the system be consistent with each other, this symmetry can be achieved.

Generalized Travel Cost

Generalized travel cost is a method of measuring the value of site characteristics using the simple travel cost model. If two groups of people face identical travel costs to sites except that one group enjoys a slightly better site than the other, then the extra quality of the one site will be evident in the visitation rates. That is, the slightly better site will have slightly more visitation, controlling for distances, than the inferior site. The extra value of the difference in characteristics would be reflected in the additional consumer surplus of the better site.

To implement this model, one needs measures of the objective characteristics of each site, Z. For example, Z could be improvements made by the trustee or just natural qualities. The travel cost model would be amended to include these features, e.g.:

$$V = a + bT + cW + eZ. \qquad (7)$$

If the attribute is a desired characteristic, the coefficient on e would be positive. Controlling for all other factors, the more of the characteristic, the more visits people would make. Of course, the effect of a characteristic need not be this simple. It could be that people would take more visits at specific distances if there were more of a particular feature. For example, as a gorge gets deeper and wider, people may be willing to visit from further away but the closer people may not want to visit much more often. To capture this more general response, one could use the following more complicated model:

$$V = a + bT + cW + eZ + fTZ. \qquad (8)$$

The above model allows the demand for the site to become more inelastic as it gets more of a valued characteristic without necessarily increasing visitation greatly. That is, the relationship between visitation and distance could become steeper with a more valued site. This is important because it infers that inframarginal trips are ever more valuable than the last trip. The site

value may increase dramatically without greatly affecting visitation rates. In fact, this type of argument may reveal that the White Mountains are a special site in New England and thus of greater value both in terms of the number of visitors and the average value per visit.

As with all the methods that value characteristics, this approach requires measurements of the attributes of each site. Further, to value attributes, it is necessary to compare several sites with varying levels of attributes. Depending upon the number of attributes one wished to measure, one would need many sites.

Specific to the generalized travel cost model, is an assumption that the distances to alternative sites are the same. Thus, the model usually does not include the distance to alternative sites. This is a troublesome assumption in most applications of the generalized travel cost model. Usually, the researcher has obtained site variation by comparing very different sites. The distances to alternative sites may therefore vary from one person to the next. In fact the alternative sites have often been located in entirely different regions. For the researcher to take account of these substitute sites, the researcher would have to judge what sites were similar across users. The models have consequently ignored substitute sites and are therefore subject to bias and large random errors. It is not evident whether the omission of substitutes tends to overwhelm the more subtle measurement of site characteristics or not.

This problem may possibly be overcome by relying on intertemporal data instead of cross sections. By studying a single site over time, it may often be reasonable to assume that substitutes have remained unchanged. By identifying particular sites that have changed in interesting ways, one could be able to value the changed characteristic. For example, if a forested area was clear cut near a site, one could see what impact this had on site valuation. Similarly, as the clear cut site becomes reforested, one could observe how recreation is affected. Alternatively, one could observe the impacts of other management decisions such as renovating sites, improving highways, maintaining trails, or enlarging parking lots.

Hedonic Travel Cost

The hedonic travel cost model, like the generalized travel cost model, focuses on measuring the value of the characteristics of sites. Unlike the traditional travel cost model, however, the hedonic travel cost model focuses on the choice of site given an origin rather than the set of origins observed given a site. Thus, in spirit, the hedonic travel cost model is closer to the multiple site than the generalized travel cost model.

The underlying assumption of all the characteristic models is that people choose to visit a site because of its observable characteristics. At the heart of the hedonic travel cost model is the notion that people are revealing their preferences through their choice of sites. By driving an extra mile or more for a specific characteristic, people reveal that a characteristic is important to them. Their willingness to pay for that attribute is reflected in the additional travel cost they are willing to bear to obtain more of the attribute.

To handle multiple attributes, the method assumes that a site can be represented as a package of attributes. People then select among all the available packages depending upon their personal values and the additional costs of each package. The marginal contribution of each attribute can then be untangled by observing choices made over sufficiently dense sets of packages. By regressing the travel costs of whole bundles upon the characteristics of those bundles, one can reveal the marginal travel costs associated with each attribute. For all the people who choose that level of attribute, the marginal value of the attribute will be equal to the marginal travel cost associated with that last level of the attribute. Thus, the coefficients of the hedonic regression of travel costs on characteristics will reveal the marginal value of attributes.

For example, suppose that the hedonic regression of travel costs T on characteristics Z was of the following form:

$$T = a + bZ_1 + cZ_2 + dZ_3. \tag{9}$$

The coefficients of each attribute would reflect the marginal value of that attribute for all people who visited that site from the origin being measured. For example, suppose that Z_1 measured age of the trees in this site. The coefficient b would measure what people would pay for an extra year of age on the trees they visit. Suppose further that Z_2 was a dummy variable for a developed campsite. The coefficient c would measure how much more people would pay for developed over alternative campsites.

For the hedonic method to work, people must have choices of sites to visit. Thus, one could not use the hedonic method to value a single site on an island. There must be sites that have, and others that do not have, the desired characteristics. Further, the more characteristics one wishes to measure, the more sites one must have to choose from. For example, suppose there are but two types of sites, some set in valleys and some in high mountains, and all the sites of each type are alike. Although many features may be unique to the high mountain sites such as elevation gain, view, alpine meadows, wildflowers, and wildlife, this data set would only be able to value the entire set of features. Unless some of the high elevation sites had each feature whereas others did not, the individual contribution of each characteristic could not be discerned with this data.

Because the cost of travel to a set of sites is dependent on the location of origin, there could be very different hedonic regressions to spatially separated origins. Thus, the hedonic regressions must be estimated separately for each origin. This is an attractive feature of the hedonic method because it provides independent verification of the value of attributes. Each origin provides a separate test that a specific characteristic may be of positive value.

A second advantage of using multiple regressions is that one can learn from the fact that individuals face different opportunities. For example, the price of an attribute may be high in one place but low in another. By observing how people react when facing different attribute prices, one can learn about their tastes for large changes in attributes. For example, some attributes may have elastic demands. People may like the attributes but they are not willing to pay very much for them. Other attributes have inelastic demands suggesting that users would pay a great deal rather than do without the attribute altogether. Some especially unique characteristics such as old growth timber, bald eagles, and temperate rain forests tend to have inelastic demands. People may not be willing to pay a great deal to have a lot more of these characteristics around (nearby the existing ones) but they would pay a great deal not to lose the existing levels.

To estimate how people would respond to changes in the amount of each attribute offered, one could regress the hedonic prices estimated in the hedonic regressions upon the level of characteristics observed. For example, one could use the following equation:

$$P_1 = a + bZ_1 + cW, \tag{10}$$

where P_1 was the estimated price from the price regressions for characteristic Z_1. The regression could be expanded to include the quantities of other characteristics that may substitute or complement Z_1. A set of socioeconomic variables W could also be included in the regression to explain the variation in tastes among individuals.

Unlike the hedonic price regressions, which were computed separately for each origin, the demand regression (Equation 10) is computed across all origins in the sample. By observing how much of each characteristic people buy when faced with different prices, one can learn how much people would value substantial changes in the levels of site attributes.

To estimate the hedonic price model, one needs to know which of many sites people visit. By collecting such observations from a host of origins, one can estimate both the marginal value of a characteristic as well as the demand for that characteristic.

CONCLUSION

In this paper, two generic methods to value nontraded environmental goods were examined: travel cost and hedonics. Both methods attempt to reveal values by observing actual market behavior. They consequently fall under the general heading of revealed preference techniques. The values they attempt to estimate are monetary values that are totally consistent with market prices for traded goods.

In both cases, we attempt to value the environment by examining purchases of related market goods. In the case of travel cost, the related market good is a trip. By observing the demand for trips to a site, one can infer the value of the site. With the hedonic approach, the related good is a house or a job. By observing how the market price for houses or jobs is affected by environmental goods, one can estimate how much people would pay for more of the environmental good near their job or house. As with any measurement technique, some aspects of the measurement process are not perfect. Thus, both the hedonic and travel cost methods are subject to error. There is no reason to believe, however, that either technique is biased *a priori*. Further, additional research could narrow the existing band of uncertainty around these estimates. In particular, a careful study of the value (disamenity) of traveling would have an important impact on the travel cost model and careful sampling of observations within a market could provide added support for the hedonic price models.

References

Anderson, R., & Crocker, T. (1971). Pollution and residential property values. *Urban Studies, 8,* 171-180.

Brown, G., & Mendelsohn, R. (1984). The hedonic travel cost method. *Review of Economics and Statistics, 66,* 427-433.

Brown, J., & Rosen, H. (1982). On the estimation of structural hedonic price models. *Econometrica, 50,* 765-768.

Burt, O., & Brewer, D. (1971). Estimation of net social benefits from outdoor recreation. *Econometrica, 39,* 813-828.

Cassell, E., & Mendelsohn, R. (1985). The choice of functional forms for hedonic equations: Comment. *Journal of Urban Economics, 18,* 135-142.

Cassell, E., & Mendelsohn, R. (1982). *Estimating the demand for the characteristics of housing.* Paper presented at the American Economics Association Meeting, New York.

Cichetti, C., Fisher, A., & Smith, V. K. (1976). An econometric evaluation of a generalized consumer surplus measure: The Mineral King controversy. *Econometrica, 44,* 1259-1276.

Clawson, M., & Knetsch, J. (1966). *Economics of outdoor recreation.* Baltimore, MD: Johns Hopkins University Press.

Desvousges, W., Smith, V. K., & McGivney, G. (1983). *A comparison of alternative approaches for estimating recreation related benefits for water quality improvements* (Report No. EPA-230-05-83-001). Washington, DC: U. S. Environmental Protection Agency.

Diamond, D., & Smith, B. (1985). Simultaneity in the market for housing characteristics. *Journal of Urban Economics, 17,* 280-292.

Driver, B., & Brown, P. (1978). The opportunity spectrum concept and behavioral information in outdoor recreation supply inventories: A rationale. In H. Gyde Lund and others (tech. coords.), *Integrated Renewable Resource Inventories Workshop* (pp. 24-31) Gen. Tech Report RM-55, Fort Collins, CO: USDA Forest Service, Rocky Mountain Forest and Range Experiment Station.

Driver, B., & Tocher, S. (1970). Toward behavioral interpretation of recreational engagements, with implications for planning. In B. Driver (Ed.), *Elements of outdoor recreation planning.* Ann Arbor, MI: University of Michigan Press.

Dwyer, J., Kelly, J., & Bowes, M. (1977). *Improved procedures for valuation of the contribution of recreation to national economics development.* Water Resources Center, University of Illinois, Urbana-Champaign.

Englin, J., & Mendelsohn, R. (1985). *Measuring the value of managing forest for outdoor recreation.* Unpublished manuscript, Washington, DC. U. S. Forest Service.

Freeman, M., III. (1979). *The benefits of environmental improvements.* Baltimore, MD: Johns Hopkins Press.

Griliches, Z. (1971). *Price indices and quality control.* Cambridge, MA: Harvard University Press.

Halvorsen, R. & Pollakowski, H. (1979). Choices of functional form for hedonic price equations. *Journal of Urban Economics, 10,* 39-49.

Mendelsohn, R. (1985). Identifying structural equations with single market data. *Review of Economics and Statistics, 67,* 525-529.

Mendelsohn, R. (1984). An application of the hedonic travel cost framework for recreation modeling to the valuation of deer. In V. K. Smith & A. Witte (Eds.), *Advances in applied microeconomics* (3rd ed.) (pp. 89-101). JAI Press, Greenich, CT.

Palmquist, R. (1984). Estimating the demand for housing characteristics. *Review of Economics and Statistics, 66,* 394-404.

Ridker, R., & Henning, J. (1967). The determinants of residential property values with special reference to air pollution. *Review of Economics and Statistics, 49,* 246-257.

Sorg, C., & Loomis, J. (1984). *Empirical estimates of amenity forest values: A comparative review* (General Technical Report RM-107). Fort Collins, CO: Rocky Mountain Forest and Range Experiment Station, U. S. Department of Agriculture, Forest Service.

Vaughn, W., & Russell, C. (1983). *The national benefits of water pollution control: Fresh water recreational fishing.* Baltimore, MD: Johns Hopkins Press.

Wilman, E. (1981). Hedonic prices and beach recreation values. In V. K. Smith (Ed.), *Advances in applied microeconomics* (pp. 77-104). Greenwich, CT: JAI Press.

Witte, A., Sumka, H., & Erickson, H. (1979). An estimate of a structural hedonic price model of the housing market: An application of Rosen's theory of implicit markets. *Econometrica, 47,* 1151-1173.

Market Methods and the Assessment of Benefits: Some Further Results

David S. Brookshire
Department of Economics
University of Wyoming

Don L. Coursey
School of Business
Washington University

Karen M. Radosevich
Department of Economics
University of Wyoming

In a recent paper, Coursey, Hovis, and Schulze (1987) reported the results of a series of experiments designed to examine the robustness of willingness to pay (WTP) and willingness to accept (WTA) value measures for a commodity. The authors measured values that individuals placed on the consumption of a bitter, unpleasant taste. Measurements of value were collected over six regimes. Hypothetical values were elicited before and after the individuals had an opportunity to experience the commodity, and values were obtained in a competitive market environment. These three elicitation methods were used in conjunction with a WTA and in a WTP framework to yield six value measures (three questions crossed within the two frameworks).

The investigation yielded three principle results. First, hypothetical value measures obtained in the WTA framework were biased upwards from values obtained in the market. Second, hypothetical value measures obtained using the WTP framework corresponded more closely to final market values than hypothetical WTA values. Apparently, psychological factors did not influence hypothetical WTP values to the degree observed for the WTA values. Third, the demand revealing properties of the market mechanism used to elicit values caused the WTP and the WTA value measures to eventually converge. The results were based on individual consumption of a commodity that provided dissatisfaction.

We extended the comparison of WTP and WTA measurements to the case of a commodity that provides positive satisfaction to the individual. The six value measures used by Coursey et al. (1986) were collected for a positive good.

The most significant result obtained in this extension was that WTP and WTA value measures again converged in the marketplace. However, the dynamics of the convergence process were not consistent with psychological explanations of value. Psychological models of preference formation predict that WTP and WTA value measures will converge for both negative and positive good experiences. This result was strongly supported by the results of Coursey, Hovis, and Schulze (1987) and the study reported herein. However, as we explain, the exact pattern of the convergence can also be predicted by the psychologist's model. This pattern dictates that WTP measures for a negative good should remain constant over the form of elicitation technique used. The WTA value measure and the WTP value should converge over the course of market transactions, as shown in Coursey et al.'s study. However, we also obtained the same pattern of convergence for a positive good, contradicting the theoretical predictions of psychological theory, which implies that WTA value measures should be constant while WTP measures will converge from below to the WTA values.

Theoretical Background

A central problem in measuring the value of a commodity is the unexpectedly large empirical difference obtained in WTP versus WTA compensation studies. Theoretically, elicitation procedures designed to ask an individual for payment to acquire larger levels of a good's provision should provide similar measurements in absolute value as those designed to ask the same individual how much compensation is required to give up the same provision of a good. Thus, value measurements ought to be symmetrical when the quantity of a good is either increased or decreased, especially when quantities in question are relatively small (except for an [usually small] income effect [Randall & Stoll, 1980; Takayama, 1982; Willig, 1976]). However, when this theory was tested in the field, WTP measures were consistently and significantly smaller than corresponding WTA measures. Additionally, the differences in the two measures were much larger than could be accounted for by income effects (Brookshire, Coursey, & Schulze, in press; Coursey & Schulze, 1986; Cummings, Brookshire, & Schulze, 1986).

Economic speculation about this asymmetry has centered on the strategic biases associated with different elicitation procedures. Conventional wisdom emphasizes nonoptimal provision of public goods when individual values are solicited outside of a market or "market-like" context. Consequently, if respondents treat an evaluation procedure as a nonmarket process, their logical strategy is to exaggerate actual values. In a WTP environment, they tend to respond with value measures that understate their actual demand for the good. Likewise, in a WTA environment, they tend to overstate the compensation required to reduce the level of a good's provision. Without the addition of a market-like elicitation procedure that induces truthful revelation of value, the gap and associated asymmetry between WTP and WTA measures should not be expected to disappear.

Psychologists attribute the asymmetry in value measurements to a more fundamental problem. Their central argument hinges upon the conjecture that an individual may not exhibit a coherent set of preferences for a good. Specifically, the prospect theory of behavior includes an analysis of value that compares different levels of a good's provision to a neutral frame of reference point. This reference point is usually a current level of provision of the good. The most important implication of this model is that decreases in the quantity of the public good away from this reference point are valued at a marginally higher rate than corresponding increases in the quantity of the good above the reference point. This phenomena of losses looming larger than gains is usually referred to as loss aversion. The main implication of loss aversion is that when equal increases and decreases in the quantity of a good are valued, one should not expect symmetry between WTP and WTA measures.

Although explanations of preference asymmetry differ between economics and psychology, two common features prevail. Both argue that it is impossible to separate the measured value of a good from the elicitation procedure through which that value is obtained. The economist argues that any biases in measured value over different elicitation techniques directly reflect the strategic incentives associated with these techniques. The psychologist argues that any biases are more likely to arise from variations in the frame by which values are elicited.

The second common element relates to the joint professional belief that the value asymmetry can and will disappear in a market-like environment. A market-like environment will accomplish the dual role of providing incentive compatibility and learning experience to the individual. The most important attribute of the market-like environment to the economist is the incentive property. Specifically, the economist is concerned with designing allocation processes that provide the greatest possible incentive for truthful revelation of value. Once truthful values are obtained, any sources of bias that lead to the asymmetry should disappear. Psychologists argue that the market-like environment is important because recurrent and reversible transactions can take place in the market. The importance of these transactions lies in the fact that attitudes towards losses may change as the individual becomes familiar with the experience of obtaining a good and then giving it up. After a period of time, what is given up will eventually be perceived as an opportunity cost rather than a loss. Loss aversion phenomena can then be expected to become a less predominant factor in the valuation measurement process (see Kahneman's comments in Cummings et al. [1986] for background regarding this argument).

Fortunately, mechanisms that place individuals in a market-like situation, where they strongly reveal demand for a good, have been developed by public choice theorists and refined by experimental economists. These mechanisms provide the social scientist with a set of demonstrated guidelines with which to develop more accurate elicitation procedures.

Recently, economists and psychologists have considered the implications of the loss aversion phenomena for the biases inherent in value measurement. Brookshire, Coursey, and Schulze (1986) have examined the four possible types of questions that can be asked about a good. The two most natural forms of questions that might be asked are: "How much would you be willing to pay to obtain a good that would provide you with increased satisfaction?" and "How much would you have to be compensated to accept a good that would provide you with a decrease in satisfaction?" There are, however, two additional ways in which the questions could be asked: "How much would you be willing to accept to give up a good that would provide you with an increase in satisfaction?" and "How much would you be willing to pay to avoid accepting a good that would provide you with a decrease in satisfaction?"

Brookshire et al. (1986) showed that the latter two ways of asking the questions yielded theoretical answers that were unbiased with respect to the individual's true value for the good, because individuals do not simultaneously compare losses and gains when forming their answers to the questions. Kahneman (1986) has recently and independently proven a similar result, which he referred to as the quadratic structure of choice.

Thus, WTP measures for the negative good will have less of a tendency for bias. Additionally, if a market mechanism can drive the two measures of value together, then WTA value should do all of the converging. That is, the pattern of convergence should be asymmetric, with WTA values doing all of the moving. As noted in the introduction, this pattern was observed for the negative good experiments.

The above theory also applies to a positive good. In this case, WTA values should have less of a tendency for bias. If the market mechanism causes the measures to converge, then WTP should do all of the work and converge from below to the WTA value. We examined this extension of the theory into the domain of a positive good in a series of experiments.

Experimental Design

The commodity chosen for use in the earlier negative good experiments was a bitter, unpleasant taste experience--sucrose octa-acetate. Sucrose octa-acetate is safe, breaking down into sugar and vinegar in the body, but tastes unpleasant (Green, 1941; Linegar, 1943). In the WTA experiments, subjects were offered payment to taste sucrose octa-acetate. In the WTP experiments, subjects offered to pay to avoid tasting sucrose octa-acetate. Tasting involved holding a 1-ounce cup of a concentrated sucrose octa-acetate solution in the mouth for 20 seconds.

Sucrose octa-acetate had the important property in the previous experiments of unfamiliarity to the subjects. In extending the experimental design to a positive good, we wanted to retain this property of unfamiliarity. Thus, we chose another liquid with pleasant taste properties in the new set of experiments. This liquid was raspberry juice, a commercially available mixture of raspberry and apple juice. In the WTA experiments, subjects were offered payment to avoid tasting the juice. In the WTP experiments, subjects offered to pay to consume the juice. Tasting involved drinking an 8-ounce cup of raspberry juice. (A copy of the instructions for the WTP experiments is included in Appendix A; a copy of the WTA instructions is included in Appendix B.)

Three groups of eight students recruited from undergraduate classes at the University of Wyoming participated in the WTP experiments and three similar groups of eight students participated in the WTA experiments. No subject participated in more than one experiment. The conduct of the positive good experiment mirrored the negative good experiment.

Part I of each experiment consisted of asking each of eight subjects either how much they would pay to hypothetically drink the juice (WTP experiments) or hypothetically how much they would have to be compensated to avoid drinking the juice (WTA experiments). The bids produced in the first part of the experiment were termed purely hypothetical (H) bids, because individuals had not yet sampled the juice.

Part II of the experiment involved three steps. In the first step individuals tasted a few sample drops of juice. In the second step individuals were again asked for their WTP or WTA bids to drink a full 8-ounce cup of juice. We referred to these values as semihypothetical (SH) bids. In the third step, the experimental monitor attempted to raise (lower) the WTP (WTA) bids in 25-cent increments. The process was initiated from the level of the individual's stated semihypothetical bid. As soon as an individual refused to further raise (lower) their bid, the monitor recorded the final bid as the individual's semihypothetical iterated (SHI) bid. All subjects were addressed on a one-to-one basis. This procedure was designed to give individuals some limited experience with the commodity and to determine how closely hypothetical values might correspond to final auction values. The procedure for obtaining hypothetical values closely followed the field survey mechanism proposed by Randall, Ives, and Eastman (1974).

In Part III of the experiment, eight individuals in a group participated in a Vickrey auction designed to elicit individual competitive bids. Four 8-ounce cups of the juice were auctioned to the group of eight individuals. For brevity, only the structure of the WTP auction is described below. The WTA auction was conducted in a mirror-like manner, except where noted.

Each individual in the WTP auction was given a 10-dollar credit to use in the auction (no credit was given in the WTA auction). During each trial, each individual first submitted his or her bid to drink one cup of the juice. Bids were then collected by the monitor and rank ordered from highest to lowest. The fifth highest bid was then reported back to the eight subjects as the reigning price.

The four individuals with bids higher than the reigning price were told that they have "won" the auction implying that they could pay the reigning price (not their own bid) to drink the juice. The losers paid nothing but would not be able to drink the juice if the trial was final.

To determine if the trial was final, unanimity was required among the winners. If no winner objected, the trial was considered final. Further, the first four trials were nonbinding in that even if no winner objected, another trial was conducted. The fifth trial and on could produce a potentially binding outcome. The experiment ended either with no objections among winners, in which case four individuals paid to drink the juice and four individuals did not get to drink the juice, or, in the case where an objection remained after 10 trials, all parties did not get to drink the juice.

Both the unanimity requirement and the nonbinding practice trials have been shown to be helpful in promoting learning and, as a result, in revealing true values in induced value experiments (Coursey & Smith, 1984; Miller & Plott, 1985; Smith, 1982; Smith, Williams, Bratton, & Vannoni, 1982). In particular, the unanimity requirement allowed a "winner" who had made a mistake to reject the outcome and force another auction trial.

Results and Discussion

Individual data collected during the three WTP and the three WTA experiments included hypothetical bids from Part I, semihypothetical and iterated semihypothetical bids from Part II, and the first and last trial bids from Part III of the experiments (Table 1 and 2). We concentrated on the last trial of the auctions because this version of the auction allowed different experiments to end on different trials. Included are summary statistics for each of the experiments.

Two of the three WTP experiments showed a marked tendency for mean bids to increase over the course of the experiment, while all of the WTA experiments exhibited declining bid values as the elicitation environment became more competitive (Figure 1).

The data were strongly influenced by outliers (Table 1 and 2). Graphical effects of these outliers were underweighted in the median presentation of bidding behavior (Figure 2). Again, two of the three WTP experiments showed at least some degree of bid increases in the market portion of the experiment, while all of the WTA experiments exhibited more or less monotonic decreases in median bidding behavior as the degree of competition increased in the experiment.

For pooled groups of experiments, mean values in the WTP and the WTA experiments tended to converge by the fifth trial of the auction (Figure 3). However, the strategic overbidding of a single individual in the last trial of the experiments caused this convergence to degenerate on the last trial. This strategic bidding, although not expected in the Vickrey auction, appeared to dominate the last period results. For this reason, we focused on the median values for the pooled groups of experiments illus-

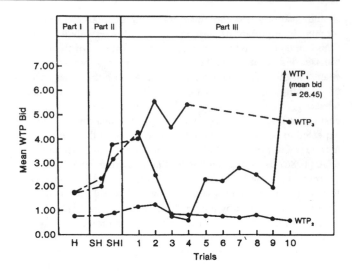

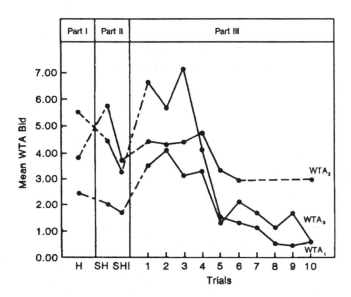

FIGURE 1. Mean willingness to pay (WTP) or willingness to accept (WTA) (in dollars) for a private good (juice) by individual groups.

trated in the right hand panel (Figure 3). These median values indicated a bias of WTA values above WTP values in both Part I and Part II of the experiments. This bias decayed in the market auction part of the experiment; thus, by the end of the experiments, median WTP and WTA values were equal.

These results strongly supported the conclusion that WTP and WTA measures of value will converge in a repetitive market environment, similar to earlier results obtained for the negative good experiment. Apparently, the learning experiences that occur in the marketplace, although not well understood by either the economics or psychological profession, facilitate this convergence.

However, as an examination of the results of this study indicates, the dynamic convergence pattern does not conform to the predictions of any loss aversion based model. WTA values of measure again do almost all of the converging work. WTA values begin above WTP measures of value; however, instead of

TABLE 1. Individual Willingness to Pay (in Dollars) for a Private Good (Juice)

Subject	Hypothetical bid	Semi-hypothetical bid	Semihypothetical iterated bid	First auction trial bid	Ending auction trial bid
Experiment 1:					
1	0.75	0.50	0.55	0.50	0.15
2	5.00	15.00	20.00	20.00	6.50
3	0.35	0.35	0.35	0.50	50.00
4	0.25	0.75	1.50	7.00	3.00
5	0.30	0.10	0.10	1.00	50.00
6	5.25	0.25	0.25	0.25	100.00
7	1.00	1.50	2.00	5.00	1.50
8	0.75	0.45	0.45	0.45	0.45
Mean	1.71	2.36	3.15	4.34	26.45
Median	0.75	0.48	0.40	0.75	4.75
SD[a]	2.13	5.12	6.84	6.82	36.76
Experiment 2:					
1	0.50	0.50	0.50	0.45	0.45
2	1.25	0.50	0.50	0.80	0.60
3	1.00	1.00	1.50	3.00	1.50
4	1.00	2.00	2.25	1.00	0.85
5	0.75	0.75	0.75	0.40	0.40
6	1.00	0.50	0.50	0.50	0.50
7	0.25	0.40	0.45	0.80	0.40
8	1.00	1.00	1.00	2.00	0.75
Mean	0.84	0.83	0.93	1.12	0.68
Median	1.00	0.62	0.62	0.80	0.55
SD	0.33	0.53	0.64	0.92	0.37
Experiment 3:					
1	1.00	1.00	1.25	3.00	3.00
2	2.00	3.00	15.00	15.00	8.50
3	1.50	2.50	3.00	4.00	5.00
4	2.50	1.00	1.00	3.25	6.60
5	1.50	2.00	2.25	0.50	3.50
6	2.00	3.00	4.00	4.00	6.00
7	2.00	3.00	3.75	2.00	5.00
8	1.00	0.50	0.50	0.40	1.20
Mean	1.69	2.00	3.84	4.02	4.85
Median	1.75	2.25	2.62	3.12	5.00
SD	0.53	1.04	4.69	4.66	2.28
Total:					
Mean	1.41	1.73	2.64	3.16	10.66
Median	1.00	0.88	0.88	1.00	1.50
Standard	1.29	2.98	4.76	4.82	23.36

[a]SD = Standard deviation.

TABLE 2. Individual Willingness to Accept Payment (in Dollars) for Not Receiving a Private Good (Juice)

Subject	Hypothetical bid	Semi-hypothetical bid	Semihypothetical iterated bid	First auction trial bid	Ending auction trial bid
Experiment 1:					
1	5.00	3.00	2.00	5.00	2.00
2	2.00	2.00	1.25	4.00	2.00
3	20.00	10.00	9.00	9.00	0.01
4	1.00	1.50	1.00	1.00	1.00
5	2.00	1.00	0.75	1.00	0.01
6	5.00	10.00	5.00	15.00	0.10
7	5.00	5.00	4.50	5.00	0.01
8	5.00	4.00	2.00	15.00	0.10
Mean	5.62	4.56	3.19	6.88	0.65
Median	5.00	3.50	2.00	5.00	0.10
SD[a]	6.05	3.60	2.83	5.62	0.90
Experiment 2:					
1	3.50	1.75	1.00	1.75	2.00
2	6.25	6.25	6.25	6.25	6.25
3	0.50	8.50	4.00	8.50	4.10
4	1.00	1.00	1.00	2.00	4.00
5	10.00	10.00	10.00	10.00	2.00
6	5.00	10.00	0.00	1.00	1.00
7	2.00	5.00	4.00	2.00	3.00
8	3.00	4.00	3.75	4.00	2.00
Mean	3.91	5.81	3.75	4.44	3.04
Median	3.25	6.12	3.88	3.00	2.50
SD	3.13	3.51	3.26	3.42	1.68
Experiment 3:					
1	1.00	0.75	0.10	3.00	0.05
2	5.00	3.00	2.50	4.00	0.10
3	1.00	2.00	1.75	2.00	1.00
4	5.00	5.00	5.00	5.00	1.25
5	0.50	0.40	0.00	3.00	0.25
6	0.25	0.00	0.00	0.00	0.00
7	5.00	3.00	2.50	10.00	0.25
8	2.25	2.25	2.25	2.25	2.25
Mean	2.50	2.05	1.76	3.66	0.64
Median	1.62	2.12	2.00	3.00	0.25
SD	2.15	1.66	1.72	2.96	0.80
Total:					
Mean	4.01	4.14	2.90	4.99	1.45
Median	3.25	4.00	2.12	4.00	1.00
S	4.15	3.33	2.70	4.22	1.62

[a]SD = Standard deviation.

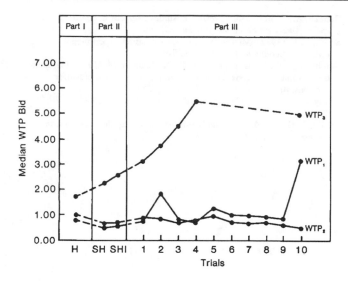

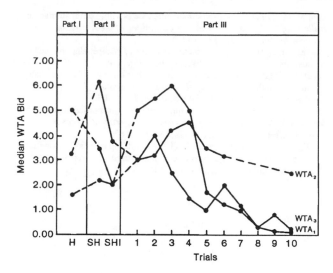

FIGURE 2. Median willingness to pay (WTP) or willingness to accept (WTA) (in dollars) for a private good (juice) by individual groups.

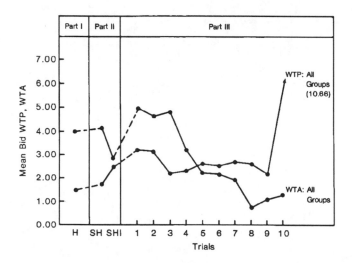

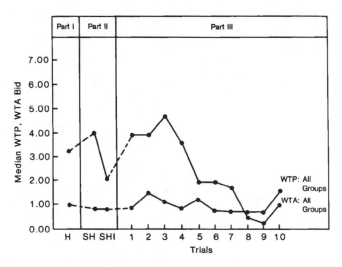

FIGURE 3. Mean and median willingness to pay (WTP) or willingness to accept (WTA) (in dollars) for a private good (juice), all groups.

the WTP values increasing in the convergence process, these values decay downward. Thus, additional dynamic asymmetries appear to be associated with "goods" versus "bads," which have not been captured by the theory.

Finally, regarding the stability of the data across the positive and negative good experiments, there appears to be a much larger element of relative "noise" in the positive good experiments compared to the negative good experiments. This noise is manifested in the variance of the values reported in the experiments, as evident in a comparison of the data sets for the two experiments. Additionally, a larger element of skewness is present in the positive good experiments. This skewness is evident in the differences observed for mean and median values. The cause of these distributional differences and their effects upon the conduct of public policy remain an important area for further research.

References

Brookshire, D. S., Coursey, D. L., & Schulze, W. D. (in press). *Experiments in the solicitation of private and public values: An overview*. In L. Green & J. Kagel (Eds.), Advances in behavioral economics. Ablex.

Brookshire, D. S., Coursey, D. L., & Schulze, W. D. (1986). *Valuing public goods*. Unpublished manuscript, University of Wyoming, Laramie.

Coursey, D. L., Hovis, J. J., & Schulze, W. D. (1987). On the supposed disparity between willingness to accept and willingness to pay measures of value. *The Quarterly Journal of Economics, 8,* 679-690.

Coursey, D. L., & Schulze, W. D. (1986). The application of laboratory experimental economics to the contingent valuation of public goods. *Public Choice, 49,* 47-68.

Coursey, D. L., & Smith, V. L. (1984). Experimental tests of an allocation mechanism for private, public, or externality goods. *Scandinavian Journal of Economics, 86,* 468-484.

Cummings, R. G., Brookshire, D. S., & Schulze, W. D. (1986). *Valuing environmental goods: An assessment of the contingent valuation method*. Totowa, NJ: Towman & Allanheld.

Green, M. W. (1941). Sucrose octa-acetate as a possible bitter stomachic. *Bulletin of the National Formulary Committee of the American Pharmaceutical Association, 10,* 131-133.

Kahneman, D. (1986). *The quadratic structure of choice.* Unpublished manuscript, University of California, Berkeley, CA.

Linegar, C. R. (1943). Acute and chronic studies on sucrose octa-acetate by the oral method. *Bulletin of the National Formulary Committee of the American Pharmaceutical Association, 11,* 59-63.

Miller, G., & Plott, C. (1985). Revenue generating properties of sealed-bid auctions. In V. L. Smith (Ed.), *Research in experimental economics* (Vol. 3), Greenwich, CT: JAI Press, Inc. 159-182.

Randall, A., Ives, B., & Eastman, C. (1974). Bidding games for valuation of aesthetic environmental improvements. *Journal of Environmental Economics and Management, 1,* 132-149.

Randall, A., & Stoll, J. R. (1980). Consumer's surplus in commodity space. *American Economic Review, 70,* 449-454.

Smith, V. L. (1982). Microeconomic systems as an experimental science. *American Economic Review, 72,* 923-955.

Smith, V. L., Williams, A., Bratton, K., & Vannoni, M. (1982). Competitive market institutions: Double auctions versus sealed bid-offer auctions. *American Economic Review, 72,* 58-77.

Takayama, A. (1982). On consumer's surplus. *Economic Letters, 10,* 35-42.

Willig, R. D. (1976). Consumer's surplus without apology. *American Economic Review, 66,* 589-597.

Appendix A

PART I

You have volunteered to participate with seven other individuals in an experiment dealing with economic and psychological decisionmaking. Your responses to each question will be kept completely confidential.

This experiment consists of three parts. In this first part, Part I, you will be required to make totally hypothetical, monetary responses to different decisionmaking situations that will affect you and the group.

When you have finished reading all of the instructions for Part I indicate to the experiment monitor that you are ready to proceed. Please do not talk with any other member of the group now or at any other time during the experiment. Please turn the page and continue reading the instructions.

Description of Part I: Bidding Games

In this first part of the experiment you will be asked to make a totally hypothetical monetary response to a predicament that will affect you. You will be asked how much money you hypothetically would be willing to pay to taste a pleasant liquid.

Tasting the liquid means you would drink an 8-ounce volume of the liquid. The hypothetical monetary response that you will make is the *largest* amount of money that you would be willing to pay to taste the pleasant liquid.

After all participants have read these instructions, the monitor will review these conditions once more. If afterwards you do not understand the content of these instructions and would like to again review this material or ask a question, feel free to do so. Please wait for the monitor's instructions before proceeding.

PART II

This is the second of the three parts of the experiment. As before, your responses to each question will be kept completely confidential.

In this second experiment you will again be required to make hypothetical monetary responses to a decisionmaking situation. When you have finished reading *all* of the instructions for Part II indicate to the experiment monitor that you are ready to proceed. As before, please do not talk with any other member of your group.

In this part of the experiment, you and the other members of the group will actually sample the liquid. Sampling the solution will involve flowing a few drops of the solution over your tongue. You will then be asked to make a new hypothetical

monetary response representing the amount of money you would be willing to pay to allow yourself to taste the liquid. Again, you will be asked for the *maximum* amount of money you hypothetically would pay to allow yourself to taste the pleasant solution.

After all participants have read these instructions, the monitor will explain the conditions once more. If afterwards you do not understand the content of this part of the instructions and would like to again review this material or ask a question, feel free to do so. Please wait for the monitor's instructions before proceeding.

PART III

Instructions

This is the third and final part of the experiment. You, as before, are participating in a group exercise with seven other individuals. Together you form a group of eight individuals who must make a series of collective decisions. You and your fellow group members will engage in an auction that will be carried out by means of a sealed-bid process. However, you will not be permitted to speak with the other members of the group. The decisionmaking process involved must be carried out in silence.

Specifically, this part of the experiment consists of three phases. The first phase involves a group bid-making process. This is the *Auction Phase*. The second phase, the *Voting Phase,* involves the members of the group voting on whether or not to accept the outcome of the *Auction Phase*. The third phase involves making final the allocations of monetary rewards to the group members. This is called the *Allocation Phase*.

You, as well as each of the group members, will be given a credit of _____, which is yours to keep as long as you consent to remain active in this experiment.

Like any auction in which buyers come together to bid for a desired commodity, your task, as well as the task of the other group members, is to make a bid to "buy" the opportunity of subjection of yourself to a pleasant taste experience. In other words, you will submit a "dollars and cents" offer that you feel best represents the amount of money you would pay to taste one 8-ounce cup of the pleasant liquid. Because you have already sampled the liquid you should have a good idea of its "flavor."

In this experiment, four cups of the pleasant liquid will be allocated. The most that you or any other participant possibly will taste is one cup. Thus, depending on the bidding process, four of the individuals will end up tasting one cup each and the other four individuals will taste nothing. During the auction phase of the experiment you must determine your bid and then submit that bid to the monitor. This bid indicates the monetary value of your WTP to taste the liquid. You will write your bid with your name, subject number, and trial number on the Bidding Form provided and hand it to the monitor.

Once all bids have been collected, the monitor will rank the eight bids from highest to lowest and determine a "Reigning Bid." This Reigning Bid is important to remember. The Reigning Bid is determined in the following way. Suppose the ranking of the eight bids representing the group members' WTP to taste the liquid turns out to be (from highest to lowest):

$$\$10, \$9, \$8, \$7, \$6, \$5, \$4, \$3.$$

The Reigning Bid is the *fifth highest* bid, and in this example is $6. All bids greater than the Reigning Bid will be tentatively *accepted* as winning bids. That is, each group member who bid *above* the Reigning Bid (those four who bid $10, $9, $8, $7) will tentatively have to pay for tasting the liquid and, therefore, will be required to taste the liquid.

However, each member of the group whose bid is accepted will only have to pay a price to taste the liquid equal to the Reigning Bid. Thus, in the example above, the individuals who bid $10, $9, $8, $7 will tentatively pay only the Reigning Bid, or $6, to taste the liquid. These "winners" are winners because they are allowed to taste the liquid by paying from their _____ the "Reigning Bid" price and because they don't actually have to pay what they were originally willing to pay to taste the liquid.

Now, on the other hand, all those group members whose bids are equal to the Reigning Bid or less than the Reigning Bid will be tentatively *rejected*. That is, each member who bid (as in our example above) $6, $5, $4, $3, will tentatively not have to pay to taste, but will not taste one cup of the fluid. These people keep the _____ they have been given plus the $3.00 for participating.

With the end of the Auction Phase (that is, the determination of the Reigning Bid and those group members whose bids were accepted), the group enters the second phase of the experiment.

This second phase is the "Voting Phase." The experiment has been designed to allow for up to 10 trials during which the group would be involved in decisionmaking. In other words, a trial consists of the Auction Phase *and* the Voting Phase. During each trial those members of the group whose bids were tentatively "accepted" (that is, above the Reigning Bid), and only those members, will then vote on whether to accept results of that trial. The result, here, is the price that each of the "winners" pay to taste the liquid. For this result to be finalized, the vote (of accepting to pay the amount of the Reigning Bid to taste the liquid) must be a unanimous "Yes." If any one or more of the members voting, votes "No" then a new bidding phase or Auction Phase and Voting Phase will start.

Notice on the Record Sheet given to you that the ten possible trials have been divided into two categories. The first four trials are denoted as the "Opening Trials" and the latter trials, Trial 5 through 10 are denoted as the "Closing Trials." In the opening trials, Trials 1 through 4, the voting process will not be binding. Those group members whose bid was above the Reigning Bid will vote on the outcome, and the voting results will be announced but will not be final. Only in the Closing Trials will the voting process be binding. Thus, if in the fifth trial, for example, the vote is unanimously "Yes" to accept the outcome, the Voting Phase stops (that is the trial ends) and the third phase, the "Allocation Phase," begins. Agreement can occur in any of the Trials 5 through 10. But, if the group fails to reach agreement by the end of the tenth trial then all eight members of the group will keep their _____ and no one will be required to taste one cup of the fluid.

After all participants have read these instructions, the monitor will explain the conditions once more. If afterwards you do not understand the content of this part of the instructions and would like to again review this material or ask a question, feel free to do so. Please wait for the monitor's instructions before proceeding.

Appendix B

PART I

You have volunteered to participate with seven other individuals in an experiment dealing with economic and psychological decisionmaking. Your responses to each question will be kept completely confidential.

This experiment consists of three parts. In this first part, Part I, you will be required to make totally hypothetical, monetary responses to different decisionmaking situations that will affect you and the group.

When you have finished reading all of the instructions for Part I indicate to the experiment monitor that you are ready to proceed. Please do not talk with any other member of the group now or at any other time during the experiment. Please turn the page and continue reading the instructions.

Description of Part I: Bidding Games

In this first part of the experiment, you will be asked to make a totally hypothetical monetary response to a predicament that will affect you and every member of the group. You will be asked how much money we would have to pay you as compensation from a group fund as well as every other individual in the group for not tasting a pleasant liquid. But, in this fund, there is only a limited amount of money. As long as the total amount of money that the group demands for compensation (the sum of all the group members' requests) is less than or equal to the amount of money in the fund then everyone will be paid the amount they request for not tasting the pleasant liquid.

Tasting the liquid means you would drink an 8-ounce volume of the liquid. Thus, the hypothetical monetary response that you will make is the *smallest* amount of money you would require from the group fund as compensation for you and the other members of the group to voluntarily not taste the pleasant liquid.

After all participants have read these instructions, the monitor will review these conditions once more. If afterwards you do not understand the content of these instructions and would like to again review this material or ask a question, feel free to do so. Please wait for the monitor's instructions before proceeding.

PART II

This is the second of the three parts of the experiment. As before your responses to each question will be kept completely confidential.

In this second experiment you will again be required to make hypothetical monetary responses to a decisionmaking situation. When you have finished reading *all* of the instructions for Part II indicate to the experiment monitor that you are ready to proceed. As before, please do not talk with any other member of your group. Please turn the page and continue reading the instructions.

In this part of the experiment you and the other members of the group will be required to actually sample the liquid. Sampling the solution will involve flowing a few drops of the solution over your tongue. You will then make a new hypothetical monetary response representing your WTA as compensation from a general fund for not tasting the liquid. You will be asked, hypothetically, the *minimum* amount of money we would have to pay you as well as each member of your group as compensation from the fund to voluntarily not taste the pleasant solution.

The money offer that you make after having sampled the liquid is the *smallest* amount of money you would require as a group member from the group fund as compensation for not being subjected to the pleasant stimulus.

After all participants have read these instructions, the monitor will explain the conditions once more. If afterwards you do not understand the content of this part of the instructions and would like to again review this material or ask a question, feel free to do so. Please wait for the monitor's instructions before proceeding.

PART III

Instructions

This is the third and final part of the experiment. You, as before, are participating in a group exercise with seven other individuals. Together you form a group of eight individuals who must make a series of collective decisions. You and your fellow group members will engage in an auction that will be carried out by means of a sealed-bid process. However, you will not be permitted to speak with the other members of the group. The decision-making process involved must be carried out in silence.

Specifically, this part of the experiment consists of three phases. The first phase involves a group bid-making process. This is the *Auction Phase.* The second phase, the *Voting Phase,* involves the members of the group voting on whether or not to accept the outcome of the *Auction Phase.* The third phase involves making final the allocations of monetary rewards to the group members. This is called the *Allocation Phase.*

Your task, as well as the task of the other group members is to determine an amount of money (or compensation) to be paid to you for not subjecting the group to the pleasant taste experience. In other words, you will submit a "dollars and cents" bid that you feel best represents the amount of compensation you must be paid from the group fund for not drinking 8 ounces of the pleasant liquid.

If the combined bids of the group are equal to or less than the amount of money in the general fund, then *all eight of you will actually be paid the amount you requested to not taste the liquid.* The amount of money actually in the general fund will not be announced to you by the experimental monitor.

During the first phase of the auction you must determine your bid and then submit that bid to the monitor. You will write your bid with your name, your subject number, and the trial number on the Bidding Form provided to you and then hand it to the monitor. Once all the Bidding Forms have been collected, the monitor will compare the amount that the group has requested, as a whole, to the amount of money in the general fund.

There are three possible outcomes in the *Auction Phase.* First, the sum of the group bids is greater than the amount of money in the general fund. If this is the case, no payments can be made but the group will be allowed to try bidding again in a new trial. That is, each member will resubmit a new bid on a new Bidding Form. The group's total bids will be re-added to determine whether or not the sum of the bids can be covered by the general fund. The auction provides for a maximum of 10 trials where each trial involves this process of calculating the group's total request for payment. If at the end of 10 trials the group fails to request payment supportable by the general fund, then each member will be paid *nothing* and *will* have to taste the liquid.

The second possible outcome is that the sum of bids just equals the amount of money in the general fund. In this situation each member of the group votes on whether or not to accept this outcome as final. If the voting is a unanimous "Yes," then each member will be paid the amount that he or she bid on the Bidding Form for that trial. However, a unanimous vote must occur before any payments are made. That means each member must vote "Yes" on his or her Voting Form in order for the group to actually be paid to not taste the liquid.

The third and final possibility is that the sum of bids made by the group is less than the general fund. In this case each group member will receive a "bonus" that is proportional to the amount of money under-requested. Assume for the moment that there were just four people in your group. Assume also that the sum of bids from the group equals $10.00 and the general fund has $20.00. Also assume that your bid was $3.00 and the other members' bids were $1.00, $2.00, and $4.00. The group under requested by $10.00, which will be divided up proportionally to the group members' original bid and distributed as a bonus to the group members. If your bid was $3.00 your bonus would be (3/10) of $10.00 or $3.00, making a total payment to you of $6.00.

The bonus to the other members would be (1/10) of $10.00 or $1.00, (2/10) of $10.00 or $2.00 and (4/10) of $10.00 or $4.00 making total payments to the other group members of $2.00, $4.00, and $8.00, respectively.

After the bonus, the group is in the same situation as when the sum of the bids by the group just equals the general fund. The group must then vote, based upon the adjusted bid value to determine whether it will accept the outcome. Remember, voting must be a unanimous "Yes" for the results to be finalized. If one individual votes no, then the group enters a new trial in which new bidding and voting occurs.

Notice on the Record Sheet provided to you that the 10 possible trials have been divided into two categories. The first four trials are denoted as the "Opening Trials" and the latter trials, Trial 5 through Trial 10, are denoted as the "Closing Trials." In the opening trials the voting process will not be binding. The voting results will be announced but *will not be final*. Only in the Closing Trials can the voting process be binding. For example, if in the fifth trial the vote is unanimously "Yes" to accept the outcome, the Voting Phase ends. Agreement can occur in any of the Trials 5 through 10. But, if the group fails to reach agreement by the end of the tenth trial then all eight members of the group will earn no money, and everyone will be required to taste the fluid.

Summary

I. Auction Phase

1. Each group member enters his or her name, trial number, and bid on one of the Bidding Forms and hands it to a monitor. The monitor will then determine whether or not the group's bid sum is less than, equal to, or greater than the general fund used to pay the group to not taste the liquid.

2. The monitor then announces to the group the outcome of the bidding phase and hands back the Bidding Forms to each individual. The group members will know the actual amount that has been requested as well as his or her own (possibly adjusted) bid, but not the bid of each of the other group members.

3. If the sum of bids is greater than the general fund, the group will enter the next trial. If the sum of requests equals or is less than the general fund then the second or voting phase begins. (Bids may be adjusted for bonuses.)

II. Voting Phase

1. The voting phase only occurs when the sum of bids from the group equals or is less than the general fund used to pay the group to not taste the liquid. If this is the case, then individuals in the group will write their name and trial number on a Voting Form and vote "Yes" or "No" on whether to accept the outcome of being paid their original bid or their adjusted bid. All voting forms will be collected by the monitor and tabulated. A unanimous vote must occur for the outcome to be accepted by the group.

2. Recall, that the first four trials of the Auction are the Opening Trials. If a unanimous vote occurs at this time, then a new trial begins automatically. If a unanimous vote occurs in the "Closing Trials," Trials 5-10, then the outcome is binding and all individuals would be paid their original or their adjusted bid. If a vote occurs in the Closing Trials that is less than unanimous, then a new trial automatically begins.

III. Allocation Phase

1. The end of each Voting Phase signals the end of each trial. If the trial number is less than or equal to four, a new trial automatically begins regardless of the result in the Voting Phase.

2. When the group is in the Closing Trials of the experiment and the vote is unanimous, each group member will be paid the amount indicated on the Bidding Form for that trial.

If you do not understand the content of these instructions and would like to review the written instructions or ask a question, please do so. If you understand the above material please indicate now to the monitor that you are ready to proceed with Part III of the experiment.

Part 5: Methodological Issues in Economic Valuation

Overview

Terry C. Daniel
Department of Psychology
University of Arizona

Cindy Sorg Swanson
USDA Forest Service
Rocky Mountain Forest and Range Experiment Station

The two papers in Part 5 cover a range of issues that are of fundamental importance to the valuation of environmental amenities. Harris, Tinsley, and Donnelly raise questions regarding the sensitivity, reliability, and validity of contingent (and other economic) value measurement (CVM) methods. At a more basic level these authors present a critical analysis of the appropriateness of the "free capitalist market" as a model for valuing public amenity resources. Mitchell and Carson focus more upon the methodological sufficiency of contingent valuation studies from the perspective of survey research criteria. They offer a detailed analysis of unintended biases that may be introduced into contingent value assessments.

Both papers are critical of current contingent value applications. However, neither paper advocates abandoning the approach altogether, and both offer constructive questions and suggestions for improvement. Harris et al. suggest the development of a "Modified Direct Survey" approach, which calls for a shift from hypothetical market methods toward a policy referendum format and for more interaction between the contingent value surveyor and the respondents to help articulate environmental amenity values. Mitchell and Carson admonish contingent value researchers to pay more attention to methodological features of their studies to avoid introducing unintended biases in CVM assessments. They specifically address the need for adequate respondent samples, careful choice of administration format, and proper presentation of the hypothetical valuation scenario, including the description and sequencing of the amenities to be evaluated.

In the following pages we briefly review and discuss some of the important issues that are raised in these two papers. It is not our intention to repeat their arguments--the authors have done a commendable job of presenting a great deal of complex material clearly and concisely. Rather, we single out a few issues that we feel are particularly important and that provide a forum for presenting some of our own perspectives on the valuation of amenity resources.

HARRIS, TINSLEY, AND DONNELLY

Harris et al. (this volume) trace the motivation for economic valuations of environmental amenity resources to the benefit-cost analysis (BCA):

> ...which relies upon the use of monetary measures as a test for potential Pareto-improvement.

The basis for BCA, in turn, is attributed to the "neo-classical/ rational planning" paradigm. The need for commensurate values in BCA has generally been met by using monetary values, most often represented as *prices* (or shadow prices) derived from some market (or hypothetical market) context. For example, prices, or the amounts that people would be "willing to pay," are determined for environmental amenities such as access to wilderness or some level of atmospheric visibility or landscape scenic beauty. These amenity prices might then be compared to prices paid for associated, and often competing, commodity resources such as timber, minerals, water, or grazing to determine the most efficient environmental management policies.

If all of this were to work according to theory, some of the knottiest problems of public policy could be reduced to simple arithmetic. Harris et al. and other authors in this volume, however, find a number of reasons to question the validity of economic valuations. A representative concern is that the willingness to pay that people report in contingent value surveys may not accurately reflect the value of the amenity resource being assessed. Many reasons are offered for this concern; some are very particular and focused on specific details of survey procedure and some are based on more fundamental concerns about the theoretical and philosophical assumptions underlying the methods. The problems and the changes recommended to solve them can be fit into four broad categories: change the methods, change the people, change the world, and change the theoretical model.

Change the Methods

It is argued that the accuracy and usefulness of economic valuations can be improved by more careful attention to the details of the assessment methods. Harris et al. and Mitchell and Carson both emphasize the need for methodological improvements. Some of the proposed changes in CVM methods are intended to improve the internal *reliability* of value estimates, i.e., the extent to which separate applications of the same CVM instrument produce the same estimates. In particular Harris et al. cite the need for "stability," consistently in measures over time, and "equivalence," consistency over changes in irrelevant contextual factors (e.g., interviewers).

Controlling random error in surveys is important, but there is a danger in placing too much emphasis on internal reliability. Indeed, high reliability in amenity resource valuations could be achieved by a carefully controlled survey on a subject for which respondent's have little or no understanding. To the extent that respondents have no opinion of their own, the survey instrument itself will determine responses. Thus, the resulting value estimates may be very precise and quite reliably predict values that will be obtained on another administration of the survey. However, the results may have little or nothing to say about values held by people outside of the particular survey situation; that is, high reliability may be achieved at the expense of external *validity*.

In this context, Harris et al. are concerned about the representation of the hypothetical market scenario--is the CVM scenario appropriate to the "real world" value being assessed? They note the lack of correspondence between the decision-making context established by the CVM survey and that more typically encountered by humans in real decision situations:

> People typically make evaluative decisions in the marketplace where an array of goods and their attributes, including price, are available for consideration.

In contrast, they characterize the CVM survey as more similar to the door-to-door sales situation where people are confronted with: a hypothetical decision problem that typically involves a limited number of consumer choices during an abbreviated period of time.

A more appropriate scenario, they suggest, is the "amenity resource supermarket" where a variety of amenity and commodity goods are available, with prices already attached, and the consumer must make choices in the face of a limited budget.

Aside from the obvious difficulties of actually, or even hypothetically creating a supermarket such as that proposed, it is unlikely that it would provide much help in valuing environmental amenities. As the authors note in other parts of their paper, there may well be fundamental inconsistencies between markets, whether door-to-door or supermarket, and people's conceptualizations of environmental amenities and the values thereof. If this were so, methodological improvements of CVM, or other market-based economic valuation procedures, while possibly increasing the precision and reliability of assessments, would do little to increase the validity or appropriateness of these measures for making policy decisions about public environmental amenity resources.

Change the People

Harris et al. also raise the possibility that CVM assessments fail because the people surveyed are not very clear about their values. Respondents are often unable (or unwilling) to make the effort required to consider their values in depth and to report them with the precision required by monetary measures. They cite iterative auctions and group consensus approaches as useful efforts to correct this situation, but conclude that neither goes far enough. Harris, et al. offer an "Interactive Computerized Knowledge-Based Value Counseling" approach as a way to help respondents learn about and report their amenity resource values.

There would, of course, be some technical difficulties in implementing such an approach. Some of the problems could be solved by use of micro-computer "expert systems" programs that would handle the interaction with respondents in a flexible, but controlled and standardized, fashion. More problematic, however, is determining what material is appropriate to present to respondents, and how to interpret the value changes that are induced through this counciling/learning process. By design, the respondent that enters this value counciling process is not the same as the respondent who finishes it. To what population (public), then, should the values obtained be generalized?

The generalization problem is encountered by any public involvement procedure (such as "transactive planning") that requires intensive interaction between representatives of the public and professional analysts or planners. Often the result of these procedures is that the public participants come to view the environmental problem in the more analytic, "rational" manner adopted by professionals. This may be good or bad, but it always makes suspect any generalization of the judgements/values of the participants to the more general public from which they were originally sampled. Carefully selected (sometimes elected) representatives of concerned citizen's groups may spend many hours in intensive interactions with planners to arrive at a consensus regarding some important controversial environmental issue. When the agreed upon solution is reported to their constituency, however, the solution, and even the representatives,

may be rejected as not reflecting the values (and feelings) of the group.

A danger in Harris et al.'s. value counciling approach is that the resulting values may only represent people who have had the "benefit" of the counciling. The vast majority of the public will continue to hold less educated, but non-the-less intensely felt values. In most situations, it will be the reactions of that latter public that determine the success or failure of an environmental policy.

Change the World

One reason that people find it difficult to assign consistent and meaningful dollar values to amenity resources is that they do not have adequate relevant experience. For the most part, people have not had the opportunity to purchase directly scenic vistas, clear air, or other environmental amenities. Thus, when faced with a hypothetical amenity purchase in a hypothetical market, they are justifiably uncertain of what they would be willing to pay.

One approach to dealing with this problem, one which may get to the heart of the economic efficiency of natural resource allocation, is privatization of public amenity resources. That is, instead of providing the public with wilderness recreation, wildlife, and scenery at no (or nominal) cost, actual prices could be established if access to these amenities were traded in an open competitive market.

Harris et al. cite several difficulties with implementing this approach, including proper assignment of property rights, the change in role for public land agencies and accounting of transaction costs. Beyond these problems, privatization raises a number of other issues: Should access to amenity natural resources be restricted to those willing and able to pay for them (unlike education or highways, for example); will access fees to public lands be covered by welfare (wilderness experience stamps, AMENITY-CARE?); will amenity resource markets be pure capitalist, competitive markets (if so, they may well be the only resources extracted from public lands that are traded in such a market)? Privatization, or quasi-privatization, might provide a means for establishing prices for amenity natural resources, but it would leave many questions regarding the *value* of these resources unanswered.

Change the Model

Harris et al. point out that economic valuation methods that are being developed and tested for application to amenity resource assessment are based on a private market model. In such a market, the value of an amenity is determined by the price it brings in competition with other goods and by competition between individual buyers. This model, the authors argue, places amenity resources in a context that emphasizes use rather than intrinsic value, short-term individual preferences rather than long-term social consequences, and treats natural rights as property rights:

These contexts are especially problematic for decision making about unique public resources that are viewed as part of each individual's endowment and subject to irreversible change. In particular, amenities that have been traditionally viewed as priceless or beyond market transactions because of intergenerational, spiritual, and other factors may be bound by traditions of public subsidy and government intervention that distort people's conception of their willingness to pay.

Reliance on the private market model is what rationalizes efforts to compare CVM-based measures of willingness to pay to the prices people pay in some actual or contrived market. The goal of "nonmarket" economic valuation methods is to estimate how much people would be willing to pay for various environmental amenities "if there were a competitive market."

Harris et al. propose that a model based on "public finance theory" would be more appropriate:

In contrast, the theory of public goods allocation asserts that public goods are more appropriately allocated on the basis of political referenda than a private market....

The authors go on to recommend the "Modified Direct Survey" approach based on the policy referendum model and employing the interactive, value counciling format discussed above. Still, Harris et al. continue to cling to the monetary index of value, though the outcome of their method:

...would be a monetary index of preference, as opposed to any true indicator of willingness to pay.

What is unclear is how this monetary index of value should be interpreted. Do the authors intend that this index be treated only as a relative (interval) scale measure of value? If so, one of the key advantages claimed by monetary indices would be lost-- amenity resource values could not be compared, in commensurate terms, with values for competing commodity resources. The calculus of public policy making would not be greatly simplified. Further, the situational transitivity sought by economic valuation methods (a dollar is a dollar is a dollar) would be discarded. This is not to imply that any of the nonmarket valuation methods that seek to emulate a market currently offer such benefits. The question is whether the effort to achieve market-like (absolute) dollar values for amenity resources should be abandoned in name as well as in practice.

MITCHELL AND CARSON

Mitchell and Carson focus attention on issues relating to the Contingent Valuation Method. They suggest that contemporary CVM research has placed too much emphasis on demonstrating CVM validity, such as lack of strategic behavior, starting point and other biases. As a result, the quality of individual studies with regard to survey design, sample size, and sampling procedures has not received adequate attention. There is a pressing need, Mitchell and Carson argue, to turn from validating CVM as a whole to addressing individual methodological issues.

In an effort to move away from validity issues to individual study issues Mitchell and Carson suggest a "Methodological Evaluation Approach." In this approach there are several issues requiring scrutiny, including (1) wording of the CVM scenario, (2) administration of the instrument, (3) adequate sample size,

and (4) sequencing of amenities to be valued. Each level is briefly discussed below.

Word of the Scenario

The wording of the CVM scenario is critical to insure a fit between the subject matter, theoretical requirements, and policy requirements. The trade-off between generality and specifics of the policy must be kept in mind because minor changes in the policy description can greatly affect willingness to pay bids. Therefore, the closer the fit between the survey and the policy the greater the confidence in the reported results.

Also critical to the wording is the need for respondents to understand the scenario as the researcher intended. Respondents must be motivated to give valued responses by believing the scenario and by finding the choice situation plausible. Contrary to previous suggestions, the payment vehicle will and should affect willingness to pay bids as the vehicle is a real and important aspect of the policy.

These and related "information biases" are discussed in detail by Mitchell and Carson. Indeed, the CVM literature seems at times to be fixated with excessive concern about various "biases" that are suspected of influencing assessment results; a "bias bias" may be in effect. Implicit in many of these concerns is the premise that there exists a "true value," and that by eliminating all biases from surveys that value would be found. Alternatively, eliminating biases from value surveys may be more like peeling an onion; after the biases are peeled away there may be nothing left to measure. *Values* may be inherently situational or context bound; for example, there may be no determinable value of wilderness experience *per se*, even though a particular wilderness experience may have very great value for a specific person (or set of persons) in some specific context.

Mitchell and Carson acknowledge that amenity resource values are context dependent. It should be expected that value indices will differ from one assessment to another, depending upon the population represented by the respondent sample, the setting in which the survey is conducted, and on aspects of the social policies implied and the perceived personal consequences for the respondent. Value indices that result from CVM surveys, then, must be qualified by these and other contextual factors as, indeed, the "true values" must. Concern about bias in economic valuation should not be focused on finding some context-free true value; rather, care should be taken in the survey design and implementation so that the surveyor and users of the survey results are not misled as to what is being measured. Further, the reporting of CVM results should include a clear account of the relevant contextual factors, with appropriate constraints on conclusions and generalizations based on those results.

Survey Administration

Administration of the survey involves tradeoffs, which may dictate whether an in-person, mail, or telephone survey is more appropriate. Three characteristics must be considered when choosing the survey method: (1) complexity of the policy; (2) motivation necessary to work through the survey; and (3) ability to extrapolate assessments to untested populations, which requires specific sampling strategies.

In-person methods most easily capture all characteristics but they are also the most costly and time consuming. Telephone surveys preclude the use of visual aids and also tend to be more impersonal resulting in the inability to motivate respondents. Mail surveys allow the use of visual aids and avoid interviewer bias; however, they do require an ability to read and understand, they preclude involved sequencing patterns, and they are most susceptible to nonresponse bias. Whichever method is used, standardization of implementation is critical to allow comparisons across respondents. This will require pretesting and training of interviewers.

Sequencing

Recent evidence indicates that sequencing of items to be valued in a survey can greatly effect the results obtained. In general, independently measured benefits can not be aggregated because of the tie between sequencing and the estimates obtained. Each good is treated incrementally in a survey, therefore a marginal value is given for each added good. Previous goods are treated as potential substitutes for each additional good. As a result, the sequencing in a survey must follow policy sequencing and results can not be disaggregated into component parts.

Respondent Sampling

Sampling design and implementation requires deciding how many people to survey, whom to survey, and how to select specific individuals. The population to which the assessment results are to be generalized must be defined, including identification of any significant subgroups. Once the population is defined, a method of sampling respondents from that population must be determined. This may be a stratified sample of households in a neighborhood, randomly generated telephone numbers, or a specific clientele mailing list. Finally, individuals must be approached and sampled such that valid willingness to pay bids are obtained. Some criterion must be used to deal with nonresponse bias, outliers, and item nonresponse. Some level of nonresponse is to be expected because the survey often involves complex issues.

Certainly sample size and representativeness are essential factors for any survey research. However, given the other conceptual and methodological issues that remain unresolved for the CVM, excessive concern about respondent sampling may be premature. For example, if the CVM context (hypothetical market model) is inappropriate for public amenity resources (as Harris et al. suggest), the value indices produced will not be valid regardless of how thoroughly the respondent population is defined and sampled. Larger, more carefully selected samples

can only increase the reliability of the indices; i.e., the error of measurement (at any prescribed confidence level) can be reduced by increasing the sample size, but this will not provide any additional assurance that the value index obtained, however precise, is valid for making environmental policy.

A related issue has to do with the (implied) precision of the point estimates of value that are typically reported in CVM surveys. Many nonmarket values are reported as a single point estimate without any reference to the error of estimate or the confidence interval associated with the index. Such a practice seems particularly inadvisable when estimates frequently have measurement errors of 50% and greater. Further, the use of the dollar metric implies an absolute (ratio) scale of measurement. Yet, Mitchell and Carson (and many others) suggest that comparisons of values obtained between CVM studies, much less efforts to generalize values to some "real world" situation should be approached with considerable caution. While there may be substantial press for such absolute point values from the political arena, to simplify and "objectify" public policy decisions, there seems little scientific justification for such values at the current stage of amenity resource valuation methodology. Perhaps research effort would be better spent on studies to ascertain functional relationships (in interval or even ordinal terms) between specific amenity resource values and changes in relevant environmental characteristics (or management policies).

CONCLUSIONS

Harris et al. question the theoretical and philosophical basis of applying nonmarket economic valuation methods to the assessment of environmental amenities. They argue that the "free capitalist market" analogy is inherently inappropriate to public amenity resources, and advocate assessment methods based on a policy referendum model. Further, they call for methods that create an assessment context more consistent with actual human decision-making processes. A "Modified Direct Survey" approach that features increased interaction with respondents in a Social Judgement Theory context is offered as an alternative to current hypothetical market methods.

Mitchell and Carson also suggest that the referendum model has merit, but focus most of their paper on more specific methodological issues. They conclude that willingness to pay bids are closely tied to features of the survey design. It is critical, therefore, that the complete survey, the population, sample size, sample design, treatment of outliers, and any other information that has direct bearing on the reported values be reported along with the resulting monetary indices. Given the potential influence of all of these factors, CVM surveyors are advised that the CVM context should conform as closely as possible to the "real world" context to which the value assessment is to be applied.

In combination, these papers give economic valuation researchers much to think about. Even if the challenges Harris et al. raise for the basic market model are somehow met, Mitchell and Carson make it clear that there are still substantial methodological problems to be resolved. Both papers call for a more intensive and careful research and development effort to improve the reliability and validity of economic valuation methods. Both agree that for now the results of CVM and other nonmarket assessments must be interpreted and applied with considerable caution. What is less clear is how decisions about public amenity resources are to be made in the mean time.

As some wise person once said, "If you do not know where you are going, any road will do." It may be useful to reconsider the question that CVM and the other nonmarket economic evaluation methods seek to answer. Harris et al. begin by pointing to benefit-cost analysis as an important impetus for development and application of economic valuation methods to public amenity resources. In the BCA context it is essential to have dollar values (prices) for the benefits and costs at issue. Certainly public policy decisions and management of the public lands has spawned a great many BCA computations in recent years, but one could justifiably be skeptical about the influence these computations have actually had on decisions. Not infrequently, BCA serves more for *post hoc* rationalization of decisions, even where "hard" commodity resources are concerned.

At best, public policy decisions are only complexly related to economic values, whether for market commodities or for non-market amenity resources. Thus, the need or even the usefulness of finding the correct *price* (if there were a market...) for public amenity resources might well be questioned. At another level there is certainly a need to know the *value* of public amenity resources, and how different environmental policies affect those values. Policies will be made and implemented and the conflicts between and among commodity and amenity resources will continue to require some resolution.

Given the state-of-the-art of nonmarket valuation methods, there seems little justification for rushing into standardizing and institutionalizing techniques, much less for trying to achieve consensus on the "correct" price/value for specific environmental amenities. Rather, a continuation of a multi-method approach, drawing upon the expertise of economists, psychologists, political scientists, and others, would seem to be indicated. In that context, forums such as that provided by this volume and the associated Estes Park Conference are essential for fostering interdisciplinary communication and cooperation. The common goal of all of these approaches is to better understand amenity resource values, and to insure that these values are more effectively considered in the making of environmental policy.

Evaluating the Validity of Contingent Valuation Studies

Robert C. Mitchell
Clark University
Worcester, MA

Richard T. Carson
Department of Economics
University of California
San Diego, CA

The contingent valuation (CV) method was developed by resource economists to measure the benefits of difficult-to-value environmental amenities. In contrast to the established methods of travel cost and hedonic price, which use consumer choices in related markets to (indirectly) value nonmarketed goods, CV uses surveys to create hypothetical markets in the good so that respondents can directly express their willingness to pay for changes in the supply of nonmarketed goods under specified contingencies. The CV approach offers two notable advantages over the indirect methods: It directly measures the willingness to pay measure prescribed by welfare theory and it is capable of valuing a much broader range of amenities than the behavior-based methods, including those not yet provided. Providing the results are valid, these advantages make it a potentially attractive methodology for valuing recreation benefits, especially for facilities that are contemplated but not yet provided.

The question of validity--or the degree to which CV estimates are accurate representations of the respondents' true willingness to pay (WTP)--is of vital importance in any assessment of CV as a methodology. This question has been raised in two quite distinct ways. The first is to ask: "Is the method valid?" This is the question asked by many economists who feel much more comfortable with benefit measurement approaches based on what people do than with a survey-based method such as CV that relies on what people say they would do. From these economists' perspective, the latter approach is unlikely to measure people's real preferences because self-interested respondents will be motivated to either give responses shaped by strategic considerations or responses based on a less than optimal effort to search their preferences and arrive at a value for the amenity. The second approach is to ask a more specific question, "To what extent are the findings of a given CV study valid?" This tends to be the approach taken by survey researchers and cognitive psychologists (among others). These researchers are not inclined to dismiss the ability of surveys to measure behavioral intentions out-of-hand, but they know from experience that survey findings, particularly those that involve difficult-to-answer questions, are vulnerable to response effects that occur when the interview process or the wording of the questionnaire influences the respondents' answers.

In this paper, we suggest that the preoccupation of CV researchers in previous years with demonstrating that the method is valid has led to a relative neglect of the important issue of the quality of individual studies. We discuss the consequences of this situation and offer an approach to the assessment of individual CV studies.

THE EFFORT TO VALIDATE THE METHOD

During the past decade, a major concern of CV researchers has been to convince economist skeptics that the hypothetical character of CV surveys is not sufficient grounds for dismissing the method out-of-hand. The result has been that most applications of the CV method, until recently, have had the avowed purpose of assessing its validity. Matters of survey design, sample size, and sampling procedures have taken second place to the implementation of experimental designs using split samples to test for such things as strategic behavior and the effect on the mean WTP amounts of varying such design features as the payment vehicle or the starting point. The results of these experiments have been interpreted as generally favorable to the method.[1]

The most prominent validation strategy, however, has been to show that CV studies do as good a job of measuring benefits as their more favored indirect counterparts. For example, WTP estimates from a CV study have been compared with estimates of an amenity, measured in a series of travel cost and hedonic price studies (Bishop, Heberlein, Welsh, & Baumgartner, 1984; Heberlein & Bishop, 1986) to what people would pay in real dollars for hunting permits in a simulated market. Although suggestive, these comparisons have their limitations. In the first place, it is well recognized that estimates based on the indirect methods, such as a hedonic price estimate of air pollution reduction benefits, are themselves prone to error, owing to that fact that their indirect relationship with the good being valued necessarily requires the use of largely arbitrary assumptions to arrive at a WTP amount (Cummings et al., 1986). Because indirect estimates cannot be regarded as measures of the true WTP amount, they cannot serve as absolute criteria for the validity of a CV measure. Instead, they are parallel measures of the same unmeasured construct. In the language of psychometrics, the greater the correlation between the measures, the greater the evidence for construct (not criterion) validity. This means that the validity of both measures is supported by such a finding, not just the CV measure. A second limitation of the CV-indirect comparisons is that they are restricted to a subset of amenities for which the indirect methods can be used. This includes recreational sites, hunting opportunities, and air visibility in Los Angeles, but excludes national water quality and other public goods for which the CV method is most needed.

These limitations notwithstanding, the credibility ascribed to the indirect measures by resource economists has meant that results of CV-indirect comparisons have assumed the status of a crucial validity test for the CV method. The most extensive assessment of these results was made by Cummings et al. (1986) in their review of 15 hypothetical-indirect comparisons from eight studies. Cummings et al. first developed a "reference accuracy level" based on the accuracy of other benefit measurement methods, which they set at +/- 50%. All of the hypothetical-indirect comparisons they examined either met the reference accuracy level or were no higher than 60% of each other. This degree of overall correspondence led Cummings et al. to conclude that the CV method is reasonably accurate, at least when used to value amenities also accessible by indirect methods. In their words:

Assuming that, within the range of +50%, value estimates derived from indirect market methods include "true" valuations by individuals, these results suggest that CVM (contingent valuation method) values may yield "accurate" estimates of value in cases where individuals have had some opportunity to make actual previous choices over that commodity in a market framework. (Cummings et al., 1986, p. 102).

Positive research findings such as these have helped to address the concerns of the skeptics and have played a crucial role in establishing the CV method's credibility, as had other research that established the method's theoretical foundation (Freeman, 1979; Randall, Ives, & Eastman, 1974; Randall &

Stoll, 1980). As a result, several government agencies now certify that contingent valuation is an acceptable procedure for measuring water quality benefits (Water Resources Council, 1979), water project benefits (Moser & Dunning, 1986), and damages under Superfund legislation (U. S. Department of the Interior, 1986). Economists (including journal editors) and policymakers are increasingly inclined to take the findings of CV surveys seriously.[2] In addition, an ever increasing number of researchers are using the CV method to value nonmarketed goods. We know of more than 100 studies that have used the method between 1965 and 1986 (Mitchell & Carson, in press).

As with any method, studies using the contingent valuation approach vary greatly in quality. In the CV case, this variability is compounded by the newness of the method, the many lacunae in our knowledge of respondent behavior in surveys, the inherent difficulty in obtaining dollar amounts for hypothetical provisions of public goods, the frequent lack of sufficient resources to conduct methodologically adequate CV surveys, and the fact that many people responsible for conducting and reviewing CV studies have had no previous experience or training in conducting sample surveys.

While the early CV researchers' emphasis on research that would help legitimate the CV method was no doubt essential for the method's survival, this emphasis on the success or failure of the method *as a whole* has been at the expense of attention to the methodological quality of individual studies. As noted, the experimental character of the early CV studies and their focus on hypothetical-indirect comparisons did not include attention to such matters as pretesting, sample design and sample size, interviewing procedures, and adjustments for nonresponses. While researchers conducting these early studies often used their data to draw conclusions about aggregate benefits, these estimates were usually treated as suggestive or illustrative rather than definitive.

THE VALIDITY OF INDIVIDUAL CV STUDIES

Now that the CV method has achieved a measure of credibility, there has been a marked shift in the last few years from experimental applications designed to validate the method, to policy applications where the goal is to obtain benefit estimates that can be used in making decisions about the provision of public goods. Policy analysts at the federal and state level are increasingly asking whether the findings of particular CV studies are suitable for use in the regulatory analysis of proposed regulations. Some of these decisions are beginning to be contested in court settings where attorneys and expert witnesses argue the relevance and merits of the CV survey on which the decision is based. As a result, the question "To what extent are the findings of *this* study valid?" is being asked with increasing frequency.

This is an important question with no simple answers. In this paper, we develop an approach for evaluating individual CV studies on theoretical, policy, and methodological grounds with emphasis on the latter. Before doing so, however, we examine an alternative approach to the assessment of individual studies, which was recently proposed by Cummings et al. (1986).

THE FORMAL CRITERIA APPROACH

Although Cummings et al. (1986) primarily focused on the validity of the CV method, they also recognized the need to assess the quality of individual studies. This led them to propose what might be called the formal criteria approach to this problem. On the supposition that the CV studies used in the CV-indirect method comparisons that met the 50% reference level were acceptably accurate, they advanced the idea that the characteristics these studies share with the "institution underlying indirect market methods" (Cummings et al., 1986, p. 102) may serve as criteria to evaluate the accuracy of other CV studies. They called these criteria "reference operating conditions" (ROCs). They reasoned that if a new CV study meets the full set of ROCs, its findings would be valid in the sense that they could be presumed to be within 50% of the true value.

The ROCs originally proposed by Cummings et al. (1986)[3] were:

1. Subjects must understand, be familiar with, the commodity to be valued.
2. Subjects must have had (or be allowed to obtain) prior valuation and choice experience with respect to consumption levels of the commodity.
3. There must be little uncertainty.
4. Willingness to pay, not willingness to accept, measures are elicited.

These four ROCs were thought to capture the characteristics of market situations, such as buying a new refrigerator or deciding to visit a particular park, which made them amenable to accurate consumer valuation. For example, because consumers normally buy consumer goods rather than sell them, they would be most comfortable with a CV format that asks how much they would pay (ROC 4). ROC 3 is based on research in psychology and experimental economics that shows that when people are uncertain their valuation decisions may be prone to distortions introduced by extraneous aspects of the valuation situation.[4] To the extent that one or more of the ROCs is not satisfied, Cummings et al. (1986) believed the range of accuracy will expand beyond the 50% reference level, reflecting the errors associated with the excluded ROC.

CV researchers and others have debated the validity of the original set of ROCs proposed in Cummings et al.'s (1986) draft report. The ROCs were based on the assumption that a consumer market model is the appropriate model for CV studies. We have argued that in many cases, particularly for public goods, a political market model is preferable because people value public programs and amenities in referenda (Carson, Hanemann, & Mitchell, 1986; Mitchell & Carson, 1986a, in press). Acceptance of a referendum model would imply quite different ROCs; for example, voters often make binding choices about amenities with which they have relatively slight familiarity.

Even if a "correct" set of ROCs were identified, the formal criteria approach to validating individual CV studies would still suffer from fundamental problems. One problem is the usefulness of the 50% accuracy level. On the one hand, this implies a higher level of precision than is warranted. If a genuine criterion was available to compare to a CV estimate, it might be appropriate to accept accuracy levels. However, convergent validity involves comparing two estimates, neither of which can be assumed to represent the unmeasured variable. Although it is reassuring when the two measures of the same concept are close to one another, the possibility exists that both are inaccurate (the confidence economists have in indirect measures notwithstanding). It therefore seems inappropriate to speak confidently about percent levels of accuracy. On the other hand, if one accepts the premise that an accuracy criterion is feasible and desirable, an accuracy range of 50% is probably too large. Applying such an error range to benefit estimates would, in many cases, fail to provide useful guidance to policymakers. Accepting this criteria as the best one can do--the implication of Cummings et al.'s (1986) analysis--is equivalent to feeling satisfied "if one's bullet hits the target anywhere no matter how far it lands from the bulls eye." While at times this may be all that is possible, acceptance of a +/- 50% criterion removes the motivation to obtain more accuracy.

The other, and fundamental, problem is that the ROCs dwell solely on formal criteria and omit consideration of various theoretical and methodological factors, which must be taken into account in evaluating the accuracy of individual CV studies. Taken literally, the formal criterion approach seems to imply that as long as the amenity being valued in a CV survey meets the ROCs, any conscientious application of the method will yield acceptable (+/- 50% of the true value) estimates. In fact, a study could meet Cummings et al.'s (1986) original ROCs or any or all of their 11 alternative ROCs and still be inaccurate. To cite an extreme case, estimates based on a haphazard sample of 50 people using a questionnaire that has not been adequately pretested for respondent comprehension, which does not describe the amenity changes properly and is vulnerable to one or more of the many biases to which CV surveys are subject, will not yield useful WTP estimates no matter how familiar the respondents are with the amenity being valued.

THE METHODOLOGICAL EVALUATION APPROACH

The aim of a CV survey is to obtain a population estimate for people's WTP for a given amenity. To evaluate a particular study, researchers must scrutinize various factors of the study:

1. The wording of the CV scenario is critical because it provides the stimulus to which the respondents respond. The researcher who designs a CV study creates a hypothetical scenario for the respondent, of which some features, such as the quantity of the good, are intended to be taken into account by the respondent when he or she assesses the value of the amenity. Other features, which may include the government agency that would provide the good or the sequence of the questions, are intended to provide a plausible background for the valuation situation without themselves influencing the valuation outcome.
2. The administration of the instrument is important because the method of administration may introduce errors independent of the scenario's wording.

3. The adequacy of the sample design and its implementation will have an independent effect on the accuracy of the population estimates.
4. The sequence in which substitute or complement amenities are valued will influence the size of the WTP amounts. In the following sections, we discuss each factor.

The Scenario

One of the difficulties in designing a CV instrument is that it must meet the dual criteria of satisfying the requirements imposed by economic theory and the need of respondents for a meaningful and understandable set of questions. Someone who wishes to evaluate a study must have access to the complete text of the survey, as administered. In addition, it is useful to have information about why the researchers designed it to include what they learned from their pretests. Table 1 shows a set of design criteria that must be met by any CV scenario, and the consequences of not meeting them. Each of the five criteria is a necessary but not sufficient condition for a valid scenario; together they may be regarded as necessary and sufficient.

The first two criteria concern the fit between the subject matter of the scenario and the requirements of theory and policy. If, for example, the scenario describes the wrong property right or

TABLE 1. Scenario Design Criteria and Contingent Valuation Measurement Outcomes

Is the Scenario...	If not, respondent will...	Measurement consequence
Theoretically accurate?	Value wrong thing (theoretical misspecification).	Measure wrong thing.
Policy relevant?	Value wrong thing (policy misspecification).	Measure wrong thing.
Understandable by respondent as intended?	Value wrong thing (conceptual misspecification).	Measure wrong thing.
Plausible to the respondent?	Substitute another condition, or Not take seriously.	Measure wrong thing. Unreliable, bias-susceptible don't know, or protest zero.
Meaningful to the respondent?	Not take seriously.	Unreliable, bias-susceptible don't know, or protest zero.

budget constraint, the data are incompatible with economic theory. From a policy perspective, perhaps the most crucial thing is that the scenario adequately describes the amenity change that the policymaker wishes to value. If the findings of a CV study of risk benefits was intended to apply to low level risk reductions, such as from 2 in 1 million to 1 in 1 million, a scenario that describes risks of 1 in 1,000 or even 1 in 100,000 would be misspecified. Similarly, the description of a new recreational area should include all its salient features if the WTP amounts are to properly represent its true value. It is important, in this context, to be aware of the tradeoff between generality and specificity in the descriptions of amenities in CV surveys. The researcher often wishes to apply his or her results to a variety of settings that require findings insensitive to the details of a particular scenario, for example, the location of a recreational area in Ohio rather than Indiana or the use of a utility bill payment vehicle instead of a "higher prices and taxes" vehicle. However, we know that sometimes what seem to be minor changes in the description of an amenity can have large effects on the elicited WTP amounts. Therefore, the closer the fit between the amenity valued in a CV survey and the amenity that a policy analyst wishes to value, the greater the confidence the analyst can have that the CV findings are relevant to the policy decision.

Presuming that the scenario is properly specified from the standpoints of theory and policy, it is necessary to communicate the scenario accurately to the respondents. Conceptual misspecification occurs when respondents understand the scenario in a different way than the researcher intended. This problem tends to be underestimated by researchers untrained in survey research techniques. As Sudman and Bradburn (1982) observed:

> The fact that seemingly small changes in wording can cause large differences in responses has been well known to survey practitioners since the early days of surveys. Yet, typically, the formulation of the questionnaire is thought to be the easiest part of the design of surveys--so that, all too often, little effort is expended on it. (p. 1).

For example, some respondents think of "environmental problems" as including trash on city streets and local crime, a broader range of concerns than someone using the term in a survey instrument is likely to want it to mean. Comprehension problems can seriously distort WTP estimates. If some respondents think they are being asked about drinking water in a study that is attempting to ask them about surface water quality in lakes, rivers, and streams, or if they think they are being asked to say what a "fair" price would be for an amenity instead of the highest amount they would pay for it before doing without it, or if they think a risk reduction they are asked to value will reduce the risk to zero when in fact there will still be some risk from a contaminant, the researcher will end up measuring the wrong thing. This places an unusually heavy burden on the designer of a CV survey to undertake a careful and, if necessary, extensive program to try the instrument out under various conditions (pretesting) (Converse & Presser, 1986).

Just because a respondent understands or could understand the scenario does not mean that he or she would necessarily be motivated to make the effort necessary to take the hypothetical situation into account and determine the value of the amenity to him or her. Two factors are particularly important in motivating valid responses to CV scenarios. The first is the plausibility of the scenario. This involves a variety of factors, all of which enhance the perceived realism of the hypothetical market. Is the hypothetical market sufficiently believable to the respondent that he or she will take it seriously? If a good is currently provided for a relatively nominal cost, such as a license to hunt or the use of a state park, respondents may find it difficult to believe that it can have a value significantly higher than these reference amounts even if this is in fact the case. Is it conceivable to the respondent that the outcomes described in the scenario could occur? Some respondents, who do not believe nuclear power can be made "safe," will be incredulous if a scenario asked them how much they would pay for programs to reduce the risk from a given nuclear power plant to nearly zero. Is the choice situation one that makes sense to the respondent? An electric utility bill will be a more plausible payment vehicle than a sales tax for an air visibility scenario because the former has a more understandable connection to the cause of the visibility changes than does the latter. A hypothetical referendum often makes more sense to respondents than a hypothetical private goods market for nonmarketed goods. In all these ways, plausibility reduces the uncertainty in the respondent's mind about the choice situation.

Two undesirable outcomes may occur if the respondent perceives the scenario as implausible. One outcome is that respondents may substitute what they believe to be a more plausible condition for the one described in the scenario. Asked to value a recreational area via a scenario that has the users pay for it, respondents may (consciously or unconsciously) assume that the government would pay for it out of taxes and under value it in their WTP amounts. The result would be a WTP amount for the appropriate good under conditions other than intended by the researcher. The second outcome is that the respondent would not be motivated to take the valuation exercise seriously. To the extent that this occurs, a variety of measurement consequences, none of them desirable and some subversive of accurate benefit estimates, may occur. The respondent might take a "wild guess" at an amount, which would affect the reliability of the WTP estimate, or the respondent might be motivated to minimize the effort involved in answering the valuation question by saying "don't know," by giving a protest zero (i.e., a $0 willingness to pay amount offered to appease the interviewer and which does not represent a true $0 valuation), or by giving a biased WTP amount. A classic example of bias is when respondents' WTP amounts vary systematically according to whether a $1 or $10 amount is used as a starting point for a bidding game elicitation framework.

Bias, in the sense we are using it here, refers to systematic errors. Unlike random error, which is amenable to assessment by sampling and replicating the survey, there is no applicable body of theory by which validity can be assessed (Bradburn, 1982; Carmines & Zeller, 1979) because we lack an explanatory model of the cognitive processes that underlie respondents' verbal self-reports (Bishop, 1981). In these circumstances, the prevention of systematic error necessarily has an *ad hoc* character about it, although survey researchers have developed rules-of-thumb, based on experience and a growing body of survey experiments, which serve to minimize bias.[5]

The question of bias is complicated in CV surveys by the general absence of a measurable true WTP value for public goods, which can be used to assess the validity of a given study. Thus, bias must be inferred from our partial understanding of respondent behavior--if you ask the question this way, people will likely distort their answers--or from evidence in the survey showing that changing the wording of the scenario in ways that are not expected to affect the WTP amounts, in fact does so. The possibility of starting point bias was indicated by theory, suggesting that under conditions of uncertainty, respondents might take initial amounts as information about the "correct" value for the good. The effect was demonstrated in several CV experiments. "Not expected" is a key phrase here, because some differences may in fact be legitimate contingent effects.

This observation requires some explanation, for until recently there was some confusion in the CV literature on this point. It was earlier assumed that only the nature and amount of the amenity being valued should influence the WTP amounts; all other scenario components, such as the payment vehicle and method of provision, should be neutral in effect (Rowe, d'Arge, & Brookshire, 1980). Therefore, according to this view, an experimental finding that the WTP amounts for a given study differ according to whether a utility bill or a sales tax payment vehicle is used was evidence of "information bias." More recently, Arrow (1986), Kahneman (1986), and Randall (1986) have argued against this view, holding that important conditions of a scenario, such as the payment vehicle, *should* be expected to affect the WTP amounts. According to their view, which we accept, respondents in a CV study are not valuing levels of provision of an amenity in the abstract, they are valuing a *policy* that includes the conditions under which it will be provided and the way the public is likely to be asked to pay for it. This notion that a public good does not have a value independent of its method of financing goes back to at least Wicksell (1967) and is fully consistent with economic theory.

The uncertainty induced by scenario implausibility promotes susceptibility to bias because respondents in this condition are susceptible to treating supposedly neutral elements of the scenario, such as the starting points, as clues to what the value of the amenity should be. Table 2 summarizes seven types of bias that result from respondents being influenced by the interview situation or treating elements of the contingent market as providing information about the "correct" value for the good. In each case, the respondent's WTP amount is distorted by the scenario feature in a directional fashion. For example, the under-motivated respondent may assume the amenity is important by the fact that an interviewer has gone to the trouble of asking him or her about it and give a higher amount than he or she would give if properly motivated to express the value it really has to the respondent (importance bias).

Finally, the relevance of the amenity to the respondent also can play a role in motivating thoughtful responses. If the CV study interviews Colorado residents about an expansion in skiing opportunities, it probably will be more difficult to motivate those residents who do not ski to take the study seriously. If so, the same array of measurement consequences described above for implausible scenarios are likely to occur and, because even in Colorado the number of nonskiers is likely to be large, the results could seriously distort the benefit estimates. Interviewer bias, for example, might induce many of these people to say they would be willing to pay a nominal amount to avoid appearing "cheap" in the eyes of the interviewer. Aggregated

TABLE 2. Biases From Compliance and Implied Value Cues (from Mitchell & Carson, in press)

Bias	Description
Compliance bias	
Sponsor bias	A respondent gives a WTP amount that differs from his or her true WTP amount in an attempt to comply with the presumed expectations of the sponsor (or assumed sponsor).
Interviewer bias	A respondent gives a WTP amount that differs from his or her true WTP amount in an attempt to either please or to gain status in the eyes of a particular interviewer.
Implied value cues	
Starting point bias	The elicitation method or payment vehicle directly or indirectly introduces a potential WTP amount that influences the WTP amount given by a respondent. This bias may be accentuated by a tendency to "yea" saying.
Range bias	The elicitation method presents a range of potential WTP amounts that influences a respondent's WTP amount.
Relational bias	The description of the good presents information about its relationship to other public or private commodities that influence a respondent's WTP amount.
Importance bias	The act of being interviewed suggests to the respondent that one or more levels of the amenity has value.
Position bias	The position/order in which valuation questions for different levels of a good (or different goods) suggests to respondents how those levels should be valued.

over a large number of nonskiers, annual WTP amounts of 1 or 2 dollars offered by people who really, if they considered the matter, would value the amenity at $0, could substantially bias the estimate upwards.

ADMINISTRATION OF THE INSTRUMENT[6]

Survey instruments may be read to the respondent in person or over the telephone, or they may be sent in the mail with a request to fill out and return. In recent years, the high costs of in-person surveys and methodological developments in telephone survey technology have led the major academic survey research centers to experiment successfully with telephone interviews, a methodology that commercial polling houses had used for many years (Groves & Kahn, 1979). The sampling problems presented by unlisted telephone numbers have been overcome by the use of computer-based random digit dialing techniques.[7] An even less expensive survey method is the mail survey, which, unlike telephone interviews, permits the use of visual aids. Here, too, methodological advances have improved the technique. It used to be thought that low response rates (e.g., 20-30%) were inevitable in mail surveys, but techniques now available can result in higher (i.e., 50-70%) response rates for mail surveys under some circumstances.[8] However, these techniques require considerably more effort and expense.

Which characteristics of CV questions should influence the choice of method? At least three come to mind. First, CV questions often involve complex scenarios that require careful explanation and that benefit from the use of visual aids and close control over the pace and sequence of the interview. Second, the need to obtain dollar values requires a method that can motivate respondents to make a greater-than-usual amount of effort. Third, the need to extrapolate from the sample to make benefit estimates for populations necessitates the use of survey methods that support techniques to compensate for missing data, a topic we discuss in the next section.

Based on these criteria, the in-person survey, where the interviewer conducts the interview in the respondent's dwelling, is the method of choice for most CV situations. The physical presence of the interviewer offers the greatest opportunity to motivate the respondent to cooperate fully with a complex or extended interview and the interviewers can be expected to probe unclear responses and provide observational data (Schuman & Kalton, 1985). In-person interviews also lend themselves to the use of various types of visual aids, or "display cards," to help convey information or complex ideas, and they support techniques to replace missing responses with responses estimated by using missing data techniques.

The large potential cost savings in using telephone and mail surveys has not gone unnoticed by CV researchers. Several have used mail surveys (Bishop & Boyle, 1985; Bishop & Heberlein, 1979; Bishop et al., 1984; Schulze et al., 1983; Walsh, Loomis, & Gillman, 1984), and others have conducted CV surveys by telephone (Carson, Hanemann, & Mitchell, 1986; Mitchell & Carson, 1986b; Oster, 1977; Roberts, Thompson, & Pawlyk, 1985; Sorg & Nelson, 1986; Sorg et al., 1985). Randall, Blomquist, Hoehn, and Stoll (1985) compared all three methods in their study of the national aggregate benefits of air and water pollution control.[9] Not considering cost, what are the tradeoffs between these methods and the more expensive in-person technique?

The greater impersonality of telephone surveys compared with in-person interviews reduces the ability of the interviewer to motivate the respondent. The absence of visual cues during the telephone interview also makes it harder for the interviewer to adjust the interview to the respondent's circumstances, nor can the interviewer use visual aids to help communicate the scenario.[10] The result is that respondent attention spans for descriptive material are much lower in telephone surveys than in surveys where the interviewer is present and the description can be reinforced by visual aids. This makes it difficult, if not impossible, to maintain respondent interest and attention while communicating even moderately lengthy CV scenarios.

Although mail surveys have an advantage over telephone interviews--the ability to use visual aids--and an advantage over both in-person and telephone interviews in avoiding the possibility of interviewer bias, they suffer from several important shortcomings from the CV point of view. Mail surveys require the respondent to read and understand the description given in the scenario. Unfortunately, the reading level of a surprising number of Americans is quite low. According to the National Assessment of Educational Progress, which conducted a study of literacy among a national sample of 3,600 young adults between the ages of 21 and 25, 6% were unable to read a short sports story in a newspaper, 20% could not read as well as the average eighth grader, 37% could not present the main argument in a newspaper column, and only 43% could use a street map (Kirsch & Jungeblut, 1986). These data understate reading comprehension problems because the young adult sample has a higher level of education than comparable cohorts of older people. It would appear that unless the scenario in a mail questionnaire is short and simple, or the respondent is reasonably well-educated and also highly motivated, there is an unacceptably large chance that the respondent may miss important details or misinterpret one or more aspects of the scenario. Another set of problems results from the self-administered character of mail surveys. This makes it difficult to use skip patterns, where the choice of follow-up question depends on the respondent's answer to previous question, or to tailor the interview to the individual respondent's needs. A well-trained interviewer can pace the interview according to the circumstances of the interview, repeat questions when the respondent indicates puzzlement or uncertainty, and answer respondent questions (within the limits imposed by the interview protocol).[11]

The self-administered mail survey also does not prevent the respondents from browsing through the questionnaire before they start to fill it out. This precludes the use of multiple scenarios where respondents answer each question in a fixed sequence and without knowledge of the following scenarios. Mail surveys also can distort the sample because those who fail to fill out and return the questionnaire are typically those who have the least degree of interest in the amenity being valued.

While in-person interviews are clearly the technique of choice for CV surveys, experience with telephone and mail CV surveys suggest that, except for the sample nonresponse bias problem (which we discuss below), their shortcomings may be largely overcome provided the respondents are familiar with the amenity[12] or the scenario is relatively simple.[13] For example, when Bishop and Heberlein (1979) sent a mail questionnaire to goose hunters, those receiving the questionnaire were well acquainted with the hunting opportunity they were asked about and their nonresponse rate was extremely low for a mail survey. The offshore recreational divers interviewed by Roberts et al. (1985) over the telephone were also familiar with the type of diving amenity they were valuing.

However, as the material becomes more complex and less familiar to the respondents, the results are less satisfactory. We used a relatively simple referendum format in a telephone survey of people's values for reduced risks of contracting giardiasis from San Francisco's water supply (Mitchell & Carson, 1986b). In this case, our use of the telephone method involved a clear tradeoff between cost and precision. Despite considerable instrument development by an academic survey research organization experienced in conducting difficult telephone interviews, we found it necessary to omit a number of important aspects of the hypothetical situation from the scenario presentation, which could have been easily incorporated into a personal interview situation.

Irrespective of how a survey is administered, a major requirement is to ensure that the data it obtains are comparable--that is, the information is gathered in a standardized fashion so that one person's answers can be compared with those given by another person. To this end, survey organizations devote considerable care and resources to pretesting questionnaires and training interviewers. Pretesting is the survey equivalent of the test flight. Just as no plane manufacturer would go into production without rigorously testing its latest design, no survey writer would assume that a questionnaire on a new topic, especially if the questionnaire is complex, could be sent directly to the field without careful tryouts under field-like conditions. Even experienced survey practitioners are often surprised when certain questions work better than they had anticipated and others, which they thought were winners, turn out to be fatally ambiguous. Pretests normally consist of an extended period of trial and error experimentation with draft versions of the questionnaire to see which alternative question wordings and orderings work best. If the topic is novel, the pretest process may include preliminary in-depth research, perhaps using focus groups to learn how people conceptualize and talk about the topic (Desvousges, Smith, Brown, & Pate, 1984; Mitchell & Carson, 1986b; Randall et al., 1985).

Comparability also imposes demands on how interviewers conduct themselves in surveys. As Riesman (1958) observed, the basic task of the interviewer is to "adapt the standardized

TABLE 3. Potential Sampling Biases in CV Surveys (from Mitchell & Carson, in press)

Bias	Description
Population choice bias	The population chosen does not adequately correspond to the population to whom the benefits and/or costs of the provision of the public good will accrue.
Sampling frame bias	The sampling frame used does not give every member of the population chosen a known and positive probability of being included in the sample.
Sample nonresponse bias	The sample statistics calculated using those elements from which a valid WTP response was obtained differ significantly from the population parameters on any observed characteristic related to willingness to pay. This may be due to unit or item nonresponse.
Sample selection bias	The probability of obtaining a valid WTP response among sample elements with a particular set of observed characteristics is related to their value for the good.

questionnaire to the unstandardized respondents" (p. 267). Except for mail surveys, questioning is a social process. Each interaction between an interviewer and a respondent is unique because of the particular circumstances in which the interview occurs and the personal characteristics of the two participants. To "adapt the questionnaire," without distorting or changing it, the interviewer has to motivate the respondent to enter into a "special" kind of relationship. Sudman and Bradburn (1982) described how interviews differ from ordinary conversations:

> The survey interview...is a transaction between two people who are bound by special norms; the interviewer offers no judgement of the respondents' replies and must keep them in strict confidence; respondents have an equivalent obligation to answer each question truthfully and thoughtfully. In ordinary conversation we can ignore inconvenient questions, or give noncommittal or irrelevant answers, or respond by asking our own question. In the survey interview, however, such evasions are more difficult. The well-trained interviewer will repeat the question or probe the ambiguous or irrelevant response to obtain a proper answer to the question as worded. (p. 5)

It is precisely at the point of probing and handling respondent queries that comparability can be lost unless the interviewer rigorously follows instructions not to offer any information or explanations other than those described in the handbook for the study.[14]

Sample Design and Implementation

Probability sampling procedures provide surveys with a straightforward way to generalize from the responses of a relatively small number of respondents to much larger populations. These procedures are based on the principle that *each* economic agency (such as an individual or a household) in the population of interest has a known probability of being selected. Sampling issues had not received much attention in the CV literature until recently, (see Bishop & Boyle, 1985; Desvousges, Smith, & McGivney, 1983; Mills, 1986; Mitchell & Carson, 1984; Moser & Dunning, 1986) despite the fact that they represent a substantial threat to the accuracy of aggregate WTP estimates.

Deciding who to interview for a CV study and how to locate and interview these people involves a series of decisions. First, the researcher must decide how to define the population of economic agents likely to be influenced by the change in the level of the public good. Do they include the residents of a particular town or other geographic area? Are they those who use the amenity? Another choice to be made is whether the agents are to be individuals or households. Next, the researcher must decide how to actually identify or list this population. This list or method of generating such a list is known as a sampling frame. The actual sample is drawn from this list. The third step is to attempt to obtain valid WTP responses from each of the economic agents chosen to be in the sample. Unfortunately, a sizable number of respondents will fail, for some reason, to give valid WTP amounts. These nonresponses can lead to nonresponse and/or sample selection biases unless corrective steps are undertaken. The eventual benefit estimates can become biased as a result of the sampling decisions and procedures at any or all of these stages. Four types of potential sampling design and execution bias have been identified (Table 3).

Population choice bias occurs when the researcher misidentifies the population whose values the study is intended to obtain. Populations may be defined in terms of the element (e.g., individual recreator), sampling unit[15] (e.g., cars entering recreation areas), extent (e.g., in two counties in northern California), and time (e.g., during July 1988). Choosing the correct population is simplest when the population who will pay for the good (or who would be presumed to pay according to a given payment vehicle, such as a local tax) coincides with the population who will benefit. It becomes more problematic the greater those who pay and those who benefit diverge, for example, in the case of the huge Four Corners Power Plant at Fruitland, New Mexico (Randall et al., 1984). Residents of the area and visitors who come to enjoy the scenery use the public good of air visibility without paying the cost of maintaining it. This payment obligation is (would be) borne by those in Los Angeles (and elsewhere) who purchase their electricity from the utility that owns the plant. Nevertheless, area residents and visitors may be a crucial population for a WTP study of the aesthetic benefits of local air visibility, because they directly experience the benefits.

After the population of interest has been identified, the sampling frame must be defined. The frame may be an existing list of the sample units of interest or, more commonly, a method of generating a list. If the population and the sampling frame diverge, *sampling frame bias* can occur. This type of bias makes it difficult, if not impossible, to accurately generalize the results of the study to the population initially defined by the researcher, even if there are no other problems in carrying out the survey.

The procedures for defining the sampling frame vary according to the type of survey method use--personal, phone, or mail.[16] The sampling frame for in-person surveys of people who live in a given area are normally based on a physical enumeration of geographically-defined, occupied dwelling units. Where the area is large, various types of area stratification and clustering techniques have been developed to reduce the enumeration costs (Cochran, 1977). Nongeographically based populations often pose more difficult problems for in-person surveys. Suppose those who use a beach or visit a park comprise the population of interest. A valid sampling frame should make it possible for the sample to represent the visitors according to the time of day they visit, the day of the week, the season of the year, and, possibly, by how they use the facility. The sampling frame for telephone surveys can either be chosen from the numbers listed in phone books, with the problem of unlisted numbers (both voluntary and involuntary),[17] or, more preferably, the random digit dialing method. This latter method, which selects numbers at random from the universe of usable numbers for the population of interest (see Frey, 1983), ensures that unlisted as well as listed numbers are included in the sample. Mail survey sample frames are based on lists of potential sampling units. They face the problem of obtaining lists of up-to-date addresses for every economic agency in the population of interest. This is often a difficult task for surveys of the general public because of the frequency with which people in our society change their residences. There are likely to be fewer problems of this type when the appropriate sampling frame consists of a current list of addresses held by a government agency, such as the holders of fishing or hunting licenses.

The remaining types of bias-- *sample nonresponse bias* and *sample selection bias*--occur because of nonresponse. No matter what sampling plan and survey method is used in a CV survey, some level of nonresponse to the WTP questions is virtually inevitable, with the consequence that the number of those who give valid WTP amounts will be smaller than the number of originally chosen sample elements. There are two distinct ways in which a member of the sample can fail to respond to a WTP question. In the first, unit nonresponse (Kalton, 1983), the person (or household) fails to answer the entire questionnaire. This occurs when people cannot be found at home by phone or in-person interviewers, when they refuse to be interviewed when asked to participate by the interviewer, or when those sampled in a mail survey fail to return the questionnaire.

The second way, item nonresponse, occurs when a respondent answers some or most of the questionnaire but fails to answer a particular question of interest, such as the WTP question.[18] With the exception of questions that ask for the respondent's income, item nonresponse rates exceeding 5-7% are relatively rare in ordinary surveys (Craig & McCann, 1978). In CV surveys, however, nonresponse rates of 20-30% for the WTP elicitation questions are not uncommon when (1) the sample is random and therefore includes people of all education and age levels; (2) the scenario is complex; and (3) the object of valuation is an amenity, such as air visibility, which people are not accustomed to valuing in dollars. Up to a certain point, these higher levels of nonresponse to the WTP questions are acceptable or even desirable. It is unrealistic to expect that 95% of a sample will be able and willing to expend the effort necessary to arrive at a well-considered WTP amount for certain types of amenities. Given the choice between having respondents offer unconsidered guesses at an amount or having them say they do not know how much it is worth to them, the latter behavior is preferable, provided appropriate procedures to compensate for the resulting item nonresponse are used.

Unit and item nonresponse results in the loss of valid WTP amounts from those originally chosen for the sample, and both can contribute to sample nonresponse and sample selection bias. If 1,000 households were drawn by probability-based methods for a CV sample and valid WTP amounts were obtained for only 800 of these households, the researcher would have to determine what effect the missing 200 households have on the WTP estimate (i.e., if the values for the 800 people in the realized sample--those for whom valid WTP amounts are available-- accurately represent the values for the amenity held by the population from which the original 1,000 household sample was selected). If nonresponse in a CV survey was not associated with the WTP values held by the original sample, the failure to interview some respondents from the original sample would not cause bias (provided the sample size were reasonably large),[19] although it would affect the reliability of the estimates. A lack of association cannot be assumed, however. In the first place, researchers have found that respondent refusal is often associated with lack of interest in the topic of the survey (Stephens & Hall, 1983), and it would seem reasonable that those who are less interested in the amenity stand a good chance of holding different values for it than their more interested counterparts. Second, response rates typically vary across population subgroups, such as lower income people, and there is ample evidence that WTP amounts are often associated with the characteristics of these subgroups as are other types of survey variables (Kalton, 1983).

To determine whether observed nonresponse results in bias for a given study, two questions need to be asked. One is whether response rates differ across identifiable categories or groups of households (e.g., users vs. nonusers, different educational levels) and the other is whether systematic differences exist between those within a particular group who responded and those who did not. Bias will occur to the extent that these between and within-group differential response rates exist and are related to the value for the good. A given CV study may suffer from a between-group sample nonresponse bias, a within-group sample selection bias, or both.[20] *Sample nonresponse bias* would occur if, for example, the sample under-represented the proportion of low income households in the population and low income households held different WTP amounts for the amenity than households of other income levels. Even if the proportion of low income households in a study's sample was representative, the study could still suffer from *a sample selection bias*--either by differential selection or by a higher rate of item nonresponse--if the low income people who gave usable WTP amounts differed in their preferences for the good from those low income people who did not express their values for the good.[21]

The in-person, telephone, and mail survey methods have different vulnerabilities to the sample nonresponse and selection biases. In comparison to the other two methods, mail surveys are particularly prone to errors from these sources, especially the latter. This occurs because not only are the unit response rates for mail surveys lower than those for phone or in-person surveys, but also the potential for sample selection bias is higher because of their self-administered character and the concomitant lack of control the researcher has over the process of getting the respondent's cooperation and eliciting his or her answers.

With telephone and in-person surveys, it is normally possible to assume that the nonresponses are not related to the subject matter of the survey. In the first place, the failure to interview people who are not found at home or who are incompetent in the interview has nothing to do with their personal reaction to the survey's topic. Second, those who refuse to be interviewed in these types of surveys, usually do so before they know the specific topic of the survey.[22] Third, studies of people who refuse personal or telephone interviews (Smith, 1983; Stinchcombe, Jones, & Sheatsley, 1981) suggest that refusals occur because of general rather than survey-specific reasons.

These assumptions cannot be made for those who receive a mail survey and fail to return it. Unless the recipient throws the package out without opening it, his or her decision whether to respond or not (including the decision to lay it aside for a while) is likely influenced by examination of the cover letter and the questionnaire. Research has shown that the less salient a mail questionnaire is to a potential respondent, the less the likelihood that the respondent will take the time to fill it out and sent it back (Heberlein & Baumgartner, 1978; Tull & Hawkins, 1984).[23] In the case of public goods, interest in the subject matter is likely to be correlated with the value the good has to the respondent, thus, nonrespondents to mail surveys may hold lower or even $0 values for the good compared with respondent value of equivalent demographic categories. Thus, mail surveys have a strong potential for sample selection bias--information from those who happen to give valid WTP answers cannot be

used to infer or to impute WTP values for the nonrespondents.[24] This is one reason why market research texts (e.g., Tull & Hawkins, 1984) do not recommend their use for general populations.

Some CV researchers have argued that nonresponse bias is not likely to be significant on the basis of the findings of a study conducted by Wellman, Hawk, Roggenbuck, and Buhyoff (1980). This study compared early and late respondents to a non-CV mail survey about outdoor recreation, which achieved a 70% response rate. The authors argued, on the basis of apparent similarities between these groups on a number of characteristics, that "time, effort, and dollars spent in intensive followups to increase recreation survey response rates might better be expended on other phases of the research process" (p. 171). This finding is an insufficient basis to assume random nonresponse because Wellman et al. did not study the 30% of their sample who failed to respond to the survey. There are no grounds for believing that late respondents to mail surveys such as theirs are a valid surrogate for the nonrespondents and *a priori* (see above) and empirical (Anderson, Basilevsky, & Hum, 1983) evidence to the contrary.

The Measurement Sequence

CV researchers often want to combine separately measured components of a benefit. These components may be different benefits for separate geographical locations (e.g., the Grand Canyon, the Rocky Mountain Region, and the eastern United States), or benefits for different parts of a larger program (e.g., the air and water quality components of the national environmental program). In a series of important papers, Hoehn, Randall, and Tolley (Hoehn, 1983; Hoehn & Randall, 1982; Randall, Hoehn, & Tolley, 1981; Randall et al., 1985) showed why, under many conditions, independently measured (by contingent valuation) subcomponent benefits cannot be aggregated without overcounting. They also showed that when subcomponent benefits are measured sequentially in the same study, the order in which the subcategories are presented to respondents influences the values ascribed to each, with the goods valued first receiving higher values than later mentioned goods, assuming no other changes in the scenario. The combined entities might be the benefits for a given amenity for different geographical areas, such as air quality in the Grand Canyon, the Rocky Mountain Region, and the eastern United States (*geographical sequence aggregation bias*), or benefits for different components of an overall program, such as the air and water pollution control components of the National Environmental Pollution Control Program (*multiple public good sequence* aggregation bias). They attribute this behavior to the fact that respondents value each good sequentially as if it were a marginal increment to the existing set of environmental amenities that they enjoy instead of valuing it as an initial possible increment.[25]

The essential problem is that a particular policy change is not well specified with regard to another policy change unless the sequence of the two changes is known by respondents. Respondents in an area that has several polluted lakes will value cleaning up the first lake in their area more than the second lake for several reasons. First, the presence of the cleaned-up, first lake is available as a substitute for a second, cleaned-up lake.[26] Second, the individual's allocation of money for the first lake reduces the money he or she has available for cleaning up the second lake. If separate CV studies value the lakes individually, however, respondents will treat the lake they are asked to value as if it were the first lake. An overvaluation of the benefits of a combined cleanup will occur if the separate values are added together. If the lakes are valued in sequence in a single study by a sample of respondents, the benefit estimates for the individual lakes (but not the entire set of lakes) will be biased unless the valuation sequence replicates the actual sequence in which the cleanup will occur.[27] It should be clear that any good being valued has a place in a sequence relative to some other goods-- either the other good was provided before, at the same time, or later than the good being valued.

Randall et al. (1985) considered the problem of how to disaggregate WTP estimates for all national environmental programs into specific program components such as air and water pollution control. They showed that unless the sequence in which the components will be implemented is known or unless some strong separability conditions on the utility function are met, there is no unique disaggregation of the component values. The essential problem is that the substitution and income elasticities are unknown.[28] Researchers are advised to design CV studies that value a specific good, and to avoid applying values offered in one study to other situations that have significantly different contexts.

CONCLUSION

Contingent valuation surveys are a particularly demanding use of the survey research method because respondents often have difficulty answering the questions. Respondents are likely to be uncertain about the value (in dollars) that they hold for an amenity. The formidable methodological challenge of this undertaking, the lack of expertise most economist practitioners have in survey research techniques, the newness of the method, and the varying degree of resources available to the researcher make it highly likely that the quality of CV-based benefit estimates will vary considerably. The tendency in the CV literature, however, has been to ignore the issue of methodological quality and to treat one CV study as good as another. We argued that this is a legacy of CV researchers' great emphasis on showing that the method is valid. Now that the method has gained acceptance, and policymakers are beginning to take CV-based benefit estimates into account in making policy decisions, it is vital to pay attention to the validity of individual studies.

Validity refers to the degree to which the benefit estimates from a given CV survey may be regarded as representative of the "true" willingness to pay held by the population to which the estimates are generalized. Owing to the absence of prices for these goods in real or adequate markets, which is why the CV method is needed, validity cannot be established by comparing the survey result against a criterion, nor is it generally possible to establish its convergent validity by comparing the CV estimate with an estimate of the value of the same amenity obtained by an indirect market method, such as hedonic pricing or travel cost. What can and must be done is to assess the study's methodology with the aim of determining the degree to which its results are free of bias from factors identified in advance as potential sources of error. We offered a framework for undertaking such an assessment, which was organized around four aspects of the research process. To the extent that a study is found to be adequate on these dimensions, the research consumer will have greater confidence in the study's findings.

We began with a discussion of the scenario used to obtain the WTP amounts and outlined five broad criteria (see Table 1) that a CV scenario must meet if it is to accomplish the researcher's policy and theoretical intentions. Next, we turned to the process of conducting the survey including the implications of using the in-person, telephone, or mail techniques. We then considered the adequacy of the sample design and its implementation. The fourth aspect was the potential problem posed by the sequence in which amenities are valued when they are substitutes or complements.

Each aspect offers opportunities, often numerous, for error. It is incumbent on researchers to address these issues in the design of the study and in the presentation of its findings. To adequately evaluate a study, the research analyst must have access to the complete questionnaire and reasonably complete information about the sample, for example, the pretesting, the administration of the instrument, the response rate, the techniques used to handle outliers, and the findings of any experimental manipulations incorporated into the study design. Where a particular source of bias is regarded as an especially plausible threat, the researcher is well advised to devise a formal test for its presence. Provided the sample size is adequate, the survey method lends itself to experiments where equivalent subsamples receive different treatments to determine their effect on the WTP amount. CV research has an impressive tradition of conducting such experiments.

The type of assessment we have described will enable the analyst to rule out a large number of possible sources of bias. If validity problems are identified, the study's estimates can be qualified accordingly. It will, of course, be impossible to rule out error from other unexamined factors, but CV studies are not unique in this regard. Travel cost and hedonic price studies also require careful evaluation and, in the end, an act of trust that their findings are valid. The framework we have presented is based on current knowledge; the more we understand about respondent behavior in CV surveys, the better we will be able to know where the problems in a given study are likely to lie, if indeed, there are problems.

References

Anderson, A. B., Basilevsky, A., & Hum, D. P. M. (1983). Missing data. In P. H. Rossi, J. D. Wright, & A. B. Anderson (Eds.), *Handbook of survey research*. New York: Academic Press.

Arrow, K. J. (1986). Comments. In R. G. Cummings, D. S. Brookshire, W. D. Schulze (Eds.), *Valuing environmental goods*. Totowa, NJ. Rowman and Allanheld.

Bishop, G. F. (1981). Survey research. In D. D. Nimmo & K. R. Sanders (Eds.), *Handbook of political communication*. Beverly Hills, CA: Sage.

Bishop, R. C., & Boyle, K. J. (1985). *The economic value of Illinois Beach State Nature Preserve*. Unpublished Report, Heberlein, Baumgartner Research Service, Madison, WI.

Bishop, R. C., & Heberlein, T. A. (1979). Measuring values of extra-market goods: Are indirect measures biased? *American Journal of Agricultural Economics, 61*, 926-930.

Bishop, R. C., Heberlein, T. A., Welsh, M. P., & Baumgartner, R. A. (1984). *Does contingent valuation work?: A report on the Sand Hill Study*. Paper presented at the Joint Meeting of the Association of Environmental and Resource Economists and the American Economics Association, Cornell University, Ithaca, NY.

Bradburn, N. M. (1982). Question-wording effects in surveys. In R. M. Hogarth (Ed.), *Question framing and response consistency*. San Francisco, CA: Jossey-Bass.

Brookshire, D. S., & Crocker, T. D. (1981). The advantages of contingent valuation methods for benefit-cost analysis. *Public Choice, 36*, 235-252.

Brookshire, D. S., Thayer, M. A., Schulze, W. P., & d'Arge, R. C. (1982). Valuing public goods: A comparison of survey and hedonic approaches. *American Economic Review, 72:*165-176.

Carmines, E. G., & Zeller, R. A. (1979). *Reliability and validity assessment*. Beverly Hills, CA: Sage.

Carson, R. T., Hanemann, W. M., & Mitchell, R. C. (1986). *Determining the demand for public goods by simulating referendums at different tax prices*. Unpublished manuscript, University of California, San Diego.

Cochran, W. G. (1977). *Sampling techniques* (3rd ed.). New York: John Wiley & Sons.

Converse, J. M., & Presser, S. (1986). *Survey questions: Handcrafting the standardized questionnaire*. Beverly Hills, CA: Sage.

Craig, C. S., & McCann, J. M. (1978). Item nonresponse in mail surveys: Extent and correlates. *Journal of Marketing Research, 15*, 285-289.

Cummings, R. G., Brookshire, D. S., & Schulze, W. D. (Eds.). (1986). *Valuing environmental goods: A state of the arts assessment of the contingent method*. Totowa, NJ: Rowman and Allanheld.

Desvousges, W. H., Smith, V. K., Brown, D. H., & Pate, D. K. (1984). *The role of focus groups in designing a contingent valuation survey to measure the benefits of hazardous waste management regulations* (Draft Report to the U.S. Environmental Protection Agency). Research Triangle Park, NC: Research Triangle Institute.

Desvousges, W. H., Smith, V. K., & McGivney, M. P. (1983). *A comparison of alternative approaches for estimating recreation and related benefits of water quality improvements* (Report No. EPA-230-05-83-001). Washington, DC: U. S. Environmental Protection Agency, Office of Policy Analysis.

Dillman, D. A. (1978). *Mail and telephone surveys--the total design method*. New York: John Wiley & Sons.

Dillman, D. A. (1983). Mail and other self-administered questionnaires. In P. H. Rossi, J. D. Wright, & A. B. Anderson (Eds.), *Handbook of survey research*. New York: Academic Press.

Freeman, A. M., III. (1979). The benefits of environmental improvement: Theory and practice. Resources for the Future, Washington, DC. 272 p.

Frey, J. H. (1983). *Survey research by telephone*. Beverly Hills, CA: Sage.

Greenley, D. A., Walsh, R. G., & Young, R. A. (1981). Option value: Empirical evidence from a case study of recreation and water quality. *Quarterly Journal of Economics, 96*, 657-672.

Groves, R. M., & Kahn, R. (1979). *Comparing telephone and personal interview surveys*. New York: Academic Press.

Heberlein, T. A., & Baumgartner, R. (1978). Factors affecting response rates to mailed questionnaires: A quantitative analysis of the published literature. *American Sociological Review, 43*, 447-462.

Heberlein, T. A., & Bishop, R. C. (1986). Assessing the validity of contingent valuation: Three field experiments. *Science of the Total Environment, 56*, 99-107.

Hoehn, J. P. (1983). *The benefits-costs evaluation of multi-part public policy: A theoretical framework and critique of estimation methods*. Unpublished doctoral dissertation, University of Kentucky, Lexington.

Hoehn, J. P., & Randall, A. (1982). *Aggregation and disaggregation of program benefits in a complex policy environment: A theoretical framework and critique of estimation methods*. Paper presented at the American Agricultural Economics Association summer meeting, Utah State University, Logan.

Kahneman, D. (1986). Comments. In R. G. Cummings, D. S. Brookshire, & W. D. Schultze (Eds.), *Valuing environmental goods*. Totowa, NJ: Rowman and Allanheld.

Kalton, G. (1983). *Compensating for missing survey data*. Ann Arbor: Survey Research Center, University of Michigan.

Kirsch, I. S., & Jungeblut, A. (1986). *Literacy: profiles of America's young adults* (National Assessment of Education Progress Report No. 16-PL-02). Princeton, NJ: Educational Testing Service.

Mills, A. S. (1986). *Survey sampling issues in empirical research*. Paper presented at the Conference on Research Issues in Resource Decisions Involving Marketed and Nonmarketed Goods, U. S. Department of Agriculture, San Diego, CA.

Mitchell, R. C., & Carson, R. T. (1984). *A contingent valuation estimate of national freshwater benefits: Technical report to the U.S. Environmental Protection Agency*. Washington, DC: Resources for the Future.

Mitchell, R. C., & Carson, R. T. (1986a). Some comments on the state of the arts report. In R. G. Cummings, D. S. Brookshire, & W. D. Schulze (Eds.), *Valuing environmental goods*. Totowa, NJ: Rowman and Allanheld.

Mitchell, R. C., & Carson, R. T. (1986b). Property rights, protest, and the siting of hazardous waste facilities. *American Economic Review, 76*, 285-290.

Mitchell, R. C., & Carson, R. T. (in press). *Using surveys to value public goods: The contingent valuation method*. Washington, DC: Resources for the Future.

Moser, D. A., & Dunning. M. (1986). *A guide for using the contingent value methodology in recreation studies*. Fort Belvoir, VA: Institute for Water Resources.

Oster, S. (1977). Survey results on the benefits of water pollution abatement in the Merrimack River Basin. *Water Resources Research, 13*, 882-884.

Randall, A. (1986). The possibility of satisfactory benefit estimation with contingent markets. In R. G. Cummings, D. S. Brookshire, & W. D. Schulze (Eds.), *Valuing environmental goods*. Totowa, NJ: Rowman and Allanheld.

Randall, A., Blomquist, G. C., Hoehn, J. P., & Stoll, J. R. (1985). *National aggregate benefits of air and water pollution control* (Interim Report). Washington, DC: U.S. Environmental Protection Agency.

Randall, A., Hoehn, J. P., & Tolley, G. S. (1981). The structure of contingent markets: Some experimental results. Paper presented at the Annual Meeting of the American Economic Association, Washington, DC.

Randall, A., Ives, B. C., & Eastman, C. (1974). Bidding games for valuation of aesthetic environmental improvements. *Journal of Environmental Economics and Management, 1*, 132-149.

Randall, A., & Stoll, J. R. (1980). Consumer's surplus in commodity space. *American Economic Review, 70*, 449-455.

Plackett, K. M., & Plackett, R. L. (1981). Experimental design for categorized data. *International Statistical Review, 49*, 111-126.

Research Triangle Institute. (1979). *Field interviewer's general manual*. Research Triangle Park, NC: Research Triangle Institute.

Rich, C. L. (1977). Is random digit dialing really necessary? *Journal of Marketing Research*. August.

Riesman, D. (1958). Some observations on the interviewing in the teacher apprehension study. In P. Lazarsfeld & W. Thielens, Jr. (Eds.), *The Academic mind: Social scientists in a time of crisis* (pp. 266-370). Glencoe, IL: Free Press.

Roberts, K. J., Thompson, M. E., & Pawlyk, P. W. (1985). Contingent valuation of recreational diving at Petroleum Rigs, Gulf of Mexico. *Transactions of the American Fisheries Society, 114*, 214-219.

Rowe, R. D., & Chestnut, L. G. (1983). Valuing environmental commodities revisited. *Land Economics, 59*, 404-410.

Rowe, R. D., d'Arge, R. C., & Brookshire, D. S. (1980). An experiment on the economic value of visibility. *Journal of Environmental Economics Management, 7*, 1-19.

Schulze, W. D., Cummings, R. G., Brookshire, D. S., Thayer, M. A., Whitworth, R., & Rahmatian, M. (1983). *Methods development in measuring benefits of environmental improvements: Experimental approaches for valuing environmental commodities* (Vol. II). Draft Manuscript, U. S. Environmental Protection Agency, Office of Policy Analysis and Resource Management, Washington, DC.

Schulze, W. D., d'Arge, R. C., & Brookshire, D. S. (1981). Valuing environmental commodities: Some recent experiments. *Land Economics, 57*, 151-169.

Schuman, H., & Kalton, G. (1985). Survey methods. In G. Lindzey & E. Aronson (Eds.), *Handbook of social psychology* (pp. 635-698). New York: Random House.

Smith, C. K., & Desvousges, W. H. (1987). An empirical analysis of the economic value of risk changes. *Journal of Political Economy, 95,* 89-114.

Smith, T. (1983). The hidden 25 percent: An analysis of nonresponse on the 1980 general social survey. *Public Opinion Quarterly, 47,* 386-404.

Sorg, C. F., Loomis, J. B., Donnelly, D. M., Peterson, G. L., & Nelson, L. J. (1985). *Net economic value of cold and warm water fishing in Idaho* (Resource Bulletin RM-11) Fort Collins, CO: Rocky Mountain Forest and Range Experiment Station.

Sorg, C. F., & Nelson, L. J. (1986). *Net economic value of elk hunting in Idaho.* (Resource Bulletin RM-12). Fort Collins, CO: USDA Forest Service, Rocky Mountain Forest and Range Experiment Station.

Stephens, S. A., & Hall, J. W. (1983). *Measuring local policy options: Question order and question wording effects.* Paper presented at the annual conference of the American Association for Public Opinion Research, Buck Hill Falls, PA.

Stinchcombe, A., Jones, C., & Sheatsley, P. (1981). Nonresponse bias for attitude questions. *Public Opinion Quarterly, 45,* 359-375.

Sudman, S. (1976). *Applied sampling.* New York: Academic Press.

Sudman, S. (1983). *Applied sampling.* In P. H. Rossi, J. D. Wright, & A. B. Anderson (Eds.), Handbook of survey research (pp. 145-194). New York: Academic Press.

Sudman, S., & Bradburn, N. M. (1982). *Asking questions: A practical guide to questionnaire design.* San Francisco, CA: Jossey-Bass.

Tull, D. S., & Hawkins, D. I. (1984). *Marketing research: Measurement and Method* (3rd ed.). New York: Macmillan.

U. S. Department of the Interior. (1986). Final rule for natural resource damage assessments under the Comprehensive Environmental Response Compensation, and Liability Act of 1980 (CERCLA). *Federal Register, 51*(148), 27674-27753.

Walsh, R. G., Loomis, J. B., & Gillman, R. A. (1984). Valuing option, existence, and bequest demands for wilderness. *Land Economics, 60,* 14-29.

Walsh, R. C., Sanders, L. D., & Loomis, J. B. (1985). *Wild and scenic river economics: Recreation use and preservation values.* Report to the American Wilderness Alliance, Department of Agriculture and Natural Resource Economics, Colorado State University, Fort Collins, CO.

Water Resources Council. (1979). Procedures for evaluation of national economic development (NED): Benefits and costs in water resources planning, Level C, Final Rule. *Federal Register 44*(242):72892-72976.

Wellman, J. D., Hawk, E. G., Roggenbuck, J. W., & Buhyoff, G. J. (1980). Mailed questionnaire surveys and the reluctant respondent: An empirical examination of differences between early and late respondents. *Journal of Leisure Research, 12,* 164-172.

Wicksell, K. (1967). A new principle of just taxation. In R. A. Musgrave & A. T. Peacock (Eds.), *Classics in the theory of public finance* (pp. 29-41). New York: St. Martins.

Footnotes

[1]See Brookshire and Crocker (1981) and Schulze, d'Arge, and Brookshire (1981). For another view see Rowe and Chestnut (1983). Cummings, Brookshire, and Schulze (1986) and Mitchell and Carson (in press) offer a more recent assessment of these experiments.

[2]As shown, for example, by the publication of CV studies in the *Quarterly Journal of Economics* (Greenley, Walsh, & Young, 1981), the *American Economic Review* (Brookshire, Thayer, Schulze, & d'Arge, 1982), the *Journal of Political Economy* (Smith & Desvousges, 1987), and the more specialized natural resource economic journals.

[3]The Cummings et al. (1986) volume has an unusual structure. It consists of a lengthy draft report written by the editors in which they review the evidence for the method's validity, a series of papers and comments presented by other CV researchers and outside scholars at an all day conference convened to consider their report, and a final "Summary and Conclusions" chapter where Cummings et al. present their final views on the matters covered in the "draft report." What may be termed the "original" ROCs are those set forth in the draft report.

[4]To assess the relationship between the ROCs and the accuracy of hypothetical CV markets, Cummings et al. (1986) examined the degree to which each of the seven CV studies involved in the hypothetical-indirect comparisons met the ROCs. The amenities valued by the three CV studies that showed the highest correlation with their indirect counterparts (within 50% or less) satisfied all the ROCs. These amenities involved common and visible things (e.g., air pollution in Los Angeles) and municipal facilities (e.g., schools and community services) in a western boomtown.

[5]See Mitchell and Carson (in press) for a further discussion of this issue and a preliminary framework for understanding respondent behavior in CV surveys.

[6]This section is based on material in Mitchell and Carson (in press).

[7]See Frey (1983) for a discussion of random digit dialing and other aspects of telephone survey methodology.

[8]See Dillman (1978, 1983) and Tull and Hawkins (1984) for useful and somewhat different perspectives on mail and telephone survey practice.

[9]On the basis of their study, which obtained relatively similar findings for mail and in-person interviews, Randall et al. (1985) concluded that the in-person interviews were not superior to their mail questionnaires. Unfortunately, the response rates they achieved for each methodology were too low (44% for in-person and 36% for mail) to make a definitive judgement on this issue. They also did not address the important sample nonresponse problems which mail surveys are particularly vulnerable to.

[10]It may sometimes be possible to mail materials to households before conducting the telephone interviews. See Sorg et al. (1985) for an example.

[11]It must be emphasized that standard survey practice forbids interviewers from providing *ad hoc* explanations when respondents look puzzled, or improvising answers to respondent questions. They are instructed to read *only* the material provided to them, which may, however, include set answers, previously prepared by the researchers, to questions that the pretesting showed might pose difficulties for some respondents. This additional material is only used if the respondent specifically raises the issue.

[12]This is why mail and telephone interview techniques are likely to work best for recreational users.

[13]Discrete choice formats (where a respondent is offered a single price on a take-it-or-leave-it basis) are usually required under these circumstances with some loss of information and additional complexity in statistical analysis over the continuous choice format.

[14]The Research Triangle Institute's (1979) *Field Interviewers General Manual* offers an informative overview of the interviewer's role and training.

[15]We often use "unit" when "element" is technically the correct term in what follows because of our frequent defining of households as the relevant definition of an economic agent. In this and many other (but not all) instances, the population unit and the population element are equivalent.

[16]For nontechnical descriptions of sampling frame development procedures see Sudman (1976, 1983) and Tull and Hawkins (1984).

[17]Approximately 95% to 96% of American households have telephones. Rich (1977) reported that the rate of unlisted numbers in urban areas increased 70% between 1964 and 1977. Groves and Kahn (1979) reported an unlisted rate of 27% for their latest national sample. According to Frey (1983), "when you add new, but unpublished, listings to this figure, it is possible that at any one time, nearly 40 percent of all telephone subscribers could be omitted from the telephone directory" (p. 62).

[18]Item nonresponses on WTP questions fall into four general categories: (1) don't knows, (2) refusals, (3) protest zeros, and (4) responses that fail to meet an edit for minimal consistency.

[19]Many CV surveys in the literature use relatively small sample sizes (less than 500, often much less). The loss in statistical power may severely limit the ability of such surveys to conduct methodological experiments or to estimate population statistics within a meaningfully narrow confidence interval. These matters were discussed in detail by Mitchell and Carson (in press).

[20]The term "nonresponse bias" as used in the survey research literature often refers to both the between- and within-group biases.

[21]It should also be clear that the failure to observe a characteristic related to WTP (e.g., income) can change a sample nonresponse bias into a sample selection bias and that obtaining a previously unobserved characteristic can change a sample selection bias into a nonresponse bias. To be more explicit, let:

$$WTP = f(X,b) + U, \quad (1)$$

where $f(X,b)$ is a regression function based on X, a matrix of predictor variables, and U is a vector of error terms. Sample nonresponse bias occurs when the sample distribution of X's differs significantly from the joint population distribution of X's, and sample selection bias occurs when the sample distribution of U differs significantly from the population distribution of U.

[22]This presumes, as is the case with many surveys, that the interview topic is described in general terms at the point when the respondents' coopera-tion is first requested, to avoid this type of bias. For example, the interviewer would say "we are conducting a study of people's views about certain kinds of environmental issues" instead of the more specific "how much people are willing to pay to reduce the risk of cancer from trihalomethane contamination in their drinking water."

[23]Undoubtedly some of those who neglect to respond to mail surveys do so for reasons unrelated to the topic. The nature of mail surveys is such, however, that no interviewer is present to record that a potential respondent is sick or has traveled abroad for a month and these nonresponses cannot be distinguished from those who refuse to answer the surveys.

[24]For a discussion of the techniques available to compensate for bias due to nonresponse, see Mitchell and Carson (in press).

[25]This type of behavior should not be unexpected, because economic theory clearly predicts that one should observe respondents giving decreasing marginal valuations of close substitutes.

[26]Where the income effect is small, the second good in the sequence may be valued more than if it had been the first, if the two goods are complements.

[27]Walsh, Sanders, and Loomis (1985) conducted a CV study of the benefits of preserving up to 15 wild and scenic rivers in Colorado. They clearly demonstrated the decreasing benefits of preserving additional rivers.

[28]Some techniques discussed in Randall et al. (1985) may be used to obtain an upper or lower bound on the WTP amounts independent of sequence if the researcher is prepared to make some fairly weak assumptions about the curvature of the marginal benefit curves.

Research Methods for Public Amenity Resource Valuation: Issues and Recommendations

Charles C. Harris
Department of Wildland Recreation Management
University of Idaho

Howard E. A. Tinsley
Department of Psychology
Southern Illinois University

Dennis M. Donnelly
USDA Forest Service
Rocky Mountain Forest and Range Experiment Station

Randall (1985) concisely described the purpose of benefit-cost analysis (BCA), which relies upon the use of monetary measures as a test for potential Pareto-improvement:

> In 1908, E. Barone...suggested that proposals for change be evaluated by a compensation test....If the gainers from some proposed change could compensate those who would otherwise lose to the full extent of their threatened losses, and still enjoy a net gain, that change could be judged acceptable even if compensation did not actually occur. The compensation test is clearly utilitarian in nature,...and resolves the difficulties inherent in interpersonal comparisons of cardinal utility by reformulating the test to require interpersonal aggregation of money-valued gains and losses.
>
> Since consensual changes--those that leave some net beneficiaries and no net losses, and therefore could be implemented without objection--had come to be called Pareto-improvements, it is unsurprising that proposals that passed the test of potential compensation were designated Potential Pareto-improvements (PPIs)....
>
> BCA is a test for PPIs. The pragmatic task in BCA is to employ appropriate empirical methods within an economic-theoretic framework consistent with the PPI concept, to determine ex ante whether it is likely that a proposed change would, if implemented, generate a PPI (or, less often, to determine ex post whether a previously implemented change had produced a PPI) (pp. 168-169).

We recognize the validity of Randall's view of BCA as one particular, useful kind of information among many to be considered in a diffuse, participatory policy decision process. We also recognize the appropriateness and efficacy of BCA as a tool for achieving efficiency, which we view as a laudable goal. However, we question the efficacy of particular approaches that have been developed to measure monetary values--ones to which people fundamentally relate within a market context.

Alternative, noneconomic approaches have also been developed that assess welfare changes with nonmonetary scales or other measures of well-being. These approaches are the product of diverse behavioral sciences such as psychology, sociology, and political science. These social sciences have developed different paradigms for valuing specific impacts of public resource allocation decisions (Driver & Burch, this volume).

The following discussion includes an analysis of the conceptual and theoretical underpinnings of economic approaches currently being developed to estimate values for nonmarket goods, an assessment of existing evidence about the validity and reliability of specific valuation techniques, a description of additional research needed to further test the validity and reliability of these methods, and a consideration of alternative conceptual and measurement approaches that might ensure more reliable and valid monetary measures of value.

ECONOMIC VALUATION METHODS: BASIC CONCEPTUAL ISSUES

Ultimately, the validity of a measurement device can be judged only in the context of the theoretical foundations upon which that measure is based. Thus, knowledge of economic theory and its assumptions is prerequisite to an informed evaluation of economic methods of value measurement. The paradigm implicit in BCA and its foundations is one that Randall (1985) has termed "the neoclassical/rational planning" paradigm: It presumes that a market structure is a useful and appropriate vehicle for analyzing changes in welfare.

Significant advantages are realized by the use of dollar values. Monetary values provide a common metric upon which different potential uses of natural resources can be compared. In addition, monetary values are easily understood. Lay persons can more readily grasp the significance of dollar values than metric systems based on other values such as service, human development, or artistic expression. However, disadvantages also are apparent in using dollar values as a basis for comparison.

From an economics perspective, the value of a good is equated with its price in a market context or its shadow price in a nonmarket context. Some question the extent to which these economic indices of value reflect the full value of an environmental good (e.g., Andrews & Waits, 1978; Brown, 1984; Driver & Harris, 1981; Rolston, 1985). Their inadequacy is suggested by a variety of factors, many of which are related to the contexts in which monetary valuation occurs. Monetary indices necessarily focus on human-use value (whether consumptive or nonconsumptive) rather than intrinsic value (Rolston, 1985), on the short-term atomistic preferences of individuals rather than long-term social consequences (Kahn, 1966), and on natural rights as property rights that can be purchased or appropriated (Randall, 1985).

These contexts are especially problematic for decision making about unique public resources that are viewed as a part of each individual's endowment and subject to irreversible change. In particular, amenities that have been traditionally viewed as priceless or beyond market transactions because of intergenerational, spiritual, and other factors may be bound by traditions of public subsidy and government intervention that distort people's conception of their willingness to pay.

Economists have long recognized that free-enterprise economic systems are best represented as mixed rather than pure capitalist systems. Given the existence of market failures and their impacts on social welfare, government intervention and nonefficiency-based measures of welfare have long played a major role in the actual workings of these economies. Resource economists recognize the existence of numerous and inconsistent schools of economic thought about the theory of public-private interactions in these economies (Randall, 1985). Nevertheless, the methods currently being refined for valuation of nonmarket goods presuppose that theory based on private market interactions should be readily applicable to the conceptualization of the problem posed by nonmarket economic valuations.

Because a measure's validity is partly dependent on the correctness of the theory underlying it, this presupposition and the issues it raises (Schulze & Howe, 1985) relate directly to this paper's central theme of the need to establish the validity and reliability of existing methods for valuing nonmarket goods. A major theoretical issue for these methods is that those goods are public ones traditionally allocated by nonmarket mechanisms. Outputs of the national forest system, for instance, are subsidized by government and allocated as public goods in ways that differ from market-based allocation processes. Implicitly, government has chosen to base its management and production decisions about all forest outputs (not just amenity resources) on their existence as public, merit goods. Yet, although the USDA Forest Service is subsidizing the timber industry in the name of maximizing net social welfare (Beuter, 1986), the saw and pulp logs it produces continue to be viewed as market commodities, thereby perpetuating the conception that these and other outputs need to be valued on a monetary basis for economic analysis.[1]

MEASUREMENT ISSUES FOR ECONOMIC METHODS OF VALUING PUBLIC AMENITY RESOURCES

Attention to basic measurement theory and issues in the social sciences is critical for properly assessing the validity and reliability of scientific methods and measures applied by those disciplines. In this section, we focus on measurement issues raised by the three primary economic methods for valuing nonmarket goods: travel cost methods (TCMs), hedonic pricing methods (HPMs), and contingent valuation methods (CVMs).

The Validity of Nonmarket Economic Valuation Methods

The validity of a behavioral measure is the extent to which differences in measurements obtained with it reflect true differences among individuals on the behavior or trait being measured. More simply, the validity of a measure refers to the extent to which it actually measures the theoretical construct it is purported to measure. Three classes of evidence have been cited as necessary to establish the validity of psychometric measures (Novick, 1985): content (or face) validity, criterion validity, and construct validity.

1. Content validity tests the extent to which a measure adequately reflects the domain of a construct (Nunally, 1978). As in the case of economic methods for valuing nonmarket goods, the measurement instrument:

   ...must stand by itself as an adequate measure of what it is supposed to measure. Validity cannot be determined by correlating the...(measure) with a criterion, because the...(measure) is the criterion of performance...Rather than test the validity of measures after they are constructed, one should ensure validity by the plan and procedures of construction. (Nunally, 1978, pp. 91-92)

For methods of nonmarket economic valuation, the construct of concern has, in the past, been the value for a nonmarket amenity good derived from market-like structures; the domains of concern here, then, are the market structure that is created with the valuation method, the procedures used to present that market and elicit values, and the specification of the good to be valued (i.e., clearly defining its attributes and qualities).

Public finance theory questions the propriety of a market-based model as a basis for allocating public goods, given its premises that individuals pursue their own self-interest in competitive interactions. In contrast, the theory of public goods allocation asserts that public goods are more appropriately allocated on the basis of political referenda than a private market (e.g., Musgrave & Musgrave, 1976). The work of some researchers developing methods for nonmarket economic valuation supports that assertion (see Mitchell & Carson, 1986). The concluding sections of this paper explore some implications of this policy referendum approach and the potential benefits of integrating this approach with social judgment theory.

2. Criterion validity assesses the extent to which a measure of a construct is related to other measures recognized as meaningful criteria. An obvious criterion measure for EVMs would be actual market prices.[2]

3. Construct validity is of particular concern for establishing validity because it focuses on the extent to which a measurement strategy or instrument actually is measuring an abstract construct, such as the value placed on a public amenity good, that cannot be identified with a single, specific, and observable behavior; and all theories in science involve statements about constructs rather than concrete variables (Nunally, 1978). Psychometric theory, in explaining the concept of construct validity, states that:

Because constructs concern domains of observables, logically a better measure of any construct would be obtained by combining the results from a number of measures of such observables than by taking any one of them individually....any particular measure can be thought of as having a degree of construct validity depending on the extent to which results obtained from using the measure would be much the same if some other measure, or hypothetically all the measures, in the domain had been employed in the experiment.... There are three major aspects of construct validation: (1) specifying the domain of observables related to the construct; (2) from empirical research and statistical analyses, determining the extent to which the observables tend to measure the same thing, several different things, or many different things; and (3) subsequently performing studies of individual differences and/or controlled experiments to determine the extent to which supposed measures of the construct produce results which are predictable from highly accepted theoretical hypotheses concerning the construct....(Nunally, 1978, p. 98)

Accordingly, the theory underlying the construct needs to be stated in detail. For a measure to be judged, a valid representation of a construct, variations on that measure should have a predictable relationship to variations on other, theoretically-related variables (Cronbach & Meehl, 1955).

A lack of construct validity may reflect a number of factors:

1. Problems with the model developed to operationalize that theory and the instrument(s) developed on the basis of that model. One of the critical factors determining the construct validity of the various economic methods for nonmarket valuation is the theoretical and methodological validity of each; thus, one approach to establishing the validity of these methods is to assess the validity of the assumptions of each, formulate propositions about the relationships of a monetary indicator of value with other variables on the basis of a theory, and then test these propositions.

2. Construct validity stresses the variety of types of evidence that can be used to indicate validity. The correlation coefficient is one such measure, but other methods can be used to validate a test, including comparisons of group differences, analyses of changes in performance across time, assessments of internal consistency, and studies of the measurement process itself.

3. While no one validity study does more than increment to a small degree the confidence we can have in a particular measure, a single, well-established negative result limits the generalizations we can make from a study of a construct. A major contribution of construct validity is to emphasize the inconclusive nature of validity. Because human behavior--including responses to measurement instruments--is complexly determined, no instrument can be conclusively judged to be valid; rather, validity is a matter of degree.

In the following sections, the content, criterion, and construct validity of nonmarket economic valuation methods are discussed and the reliability of the methods is assessed. Then, suggestions are made about further research needed to test the validity of the assumptions and thus of the techniques.

The Content Validity of Economic Methods for Valuing Nonmarket Goods: Research Design

The design of a study is a particularly important determinant of the validity of measurements obtained with it. As previously noted, the plan and procedures for obtaining value estimates can affect significantly the validity of those estimates. Research design often represents some compromise between use of research methods that are most appropriate for a study's purpose, on the one hand, and economy of time, resources, and effort, on the other. The elements of research design, including the development of data collection methods, sampling design, sample selection, and data analysis and interpretation, have received varying degrees of attention and care across the studies published to date concerning methods of collecting people's values for nonmarket goods (see Mitchell & Carson, this volume). Perhaps the major conclusion from a review of studies of these methods is that they generally represent exploratory research (i.e., their emphasis is on discovery of insights and development of methods) as opposed to research that is either descriptive (i.e., accurately portraying the characteristics of a population and determining relationships among events and characteristics) or explanatory (i.e., establishing causal relationships).

The exploratory nature of many of these studies is reflected in the research methods used. The methods applied in the CVM studies have been examined in depth; Mitchell and Carson (this volume, 1986) explored the range of design-related shortcomings of past CVM survey efforts, while others, like Harris, Driver, and McLaughlin (1987) and Edwards and Anderson (1987), call for the application of standard survey research methods such as proper sampling, testing for nonresponse bias, and the use of the total design method in CVM research. The need for experimental design and statistical tests when comparing values and developing and testing hypotheses has also been recognized (Cummings, Brookshire, & Schulze, 1986). Some studies fail to fully acknowledge the implications of the lack of

fit between the data collected and the model estimated on the basis of that data for the HPM, TCM, and hedonic travel cost method (HTCM) (Brookshire, Schulze, Thayer, & d'Arge, 1982; Brown & Mendelsohn, 1984; Vaughn & Russell, 1983).

Assumptions underlying statistical estimation in the TCM also must be validated if the content validity of this method is to be confirmed. One is that variation in travel costs is sufficient for statistically identifying the demand function, and that all factors influencing demand (e.g., travel costs, experience with a type of recreation, availability of substitute sites, attractiveness of the site) are properly represented in the TCM model (Rosenthal et al., 1980). Further testing of the validity of these assumptions and the extent to which TCM results are sensitive to them is needed. From a household production perspective, the experience obtained from that site may represent different commodities for different types of trips. For example, persons taking day trips, weekend trips, or vacations (extended trips) to a site are likely to experience it differently than local residents. Local residents are more likely to have prior experience with the type of recreation at the site, take its attractiveness more for granted, and have a greater number of substitutes for it than vacationers. In this context, dropping multipurpose, multidestination trips from a TCM modeling effort may introduce systematic bias into benefit estimation, given the likelihood that many more vacationers are taking multipurpose trips to a site than are locals.

A variety of economic statistical and numerical issues are raised by even the simple TCM (Stynes, 1985a). Efforts to meet the statistical requirements of the TCM and minimize any specification bias by developing more appropriate specifications of the demand curve that account for time costs (Cesario & Knetsch, 1970), substitutes (Caulkins, Bishop, & Bowes, 1985), and quality and congestion influences (McConnell, 1980) further complicate this approach. After decades of research, confusion and disagreement persist on the specification issues raised by the TCM. Allen, Stevens, and Barrett (1981) summarized the current situation, asserting that "the nature and extent of bias due to model specification is likely to vary from situation to situation...the selection of an appropriate specification is indeed a difficult task" (p. 179). In addition, considerable variation in value estimates has been found depending upon how data is aggregated (Sutherland, 1982) and the functional form used to estimate the demand function. Although some issues such as the inclusion of the opportunity costs of travel time in demand modeling have been reasonably resolved (Cesario & Knetsch, 1970; Smith, Desvousges, & McGivney, 1983), very little is known about other issues such as the role of alternative sites as substitutes or complements.

In addition to these concerns, the work of some researchers (e.g., Rosenthal, 1985; Stynes, 1985) also raises questions about the effectiveness of more complex specifications and elaborate measures for improving the TCM. Stynes, for example, expressed the concern that "the subtleties of estimating a per capita demand function call for extensive sensitivity analysis and technical judgment" (p. 6, 1985), a concern supported by the findings and conclusions of Smith and Desvousges (1985) and Smith, Desvousges, and Fischer (1985).

A hopeful sign is that research on methods of nonmarket economic valuation has become increasingly more sophisticated in research methods and design. Some recent efforts (e.g., Desvousges, Smith, & McGivney, 1983; Mitchell & Carson,

1986) have used the services of professional survey researchers, and increasing attention is being given to the use of defensible research methods. This improvement is critical; the validity of the values obtained with these economic methods is as dependent on the adequacy of the research design for the measurement effort as it is on the construct validity and reliability of the measures applied and the correctness of the model on which those measures are based.

Given the exploratory nature of research to date and the resultant inability to generalize from most of these studies, attempts to generalize from the results of specific studies must be done with caution. This concern has been clearly articulated by Smith and Desvousges (1985), who caution that:

> Our progressive refinement in the generalized travel cost model illustrates how sensitive the benefit estimates can be to the modeling and estimation judgements made in deriving them. This finding, in turn, implies that the transfer of recreation benefit estimates that have been derived for a specific site under one set of conditions to a new site under a different set of conditions must be done cautiously. Judgment can play an exceptionally important role in the definition and use of economic models. Our re-evaluation of the generalized travel cost model indicates how important one class of decisions associated with estimation can be. (p. 380)

The hedonic TCM (HTCM) also raises issues that some research suggests cannot be resolved on any theoretical basis. These include the definition of a residential zone, establishment of criteria for acceptable estimates of implicit prices, and the definition of the level of consumption of site characteristics used in demand modeling (Smith & Kaoru, 1985). The decisions made to resolve these issues can have a large effect on demand and benefit estimation for site characteristics. Smith and Kaoru (1985) estimated an array of alternative models, also emphasizing the role of practical judgment in making decisions about the implementation of the HTCM. Their findings indicate an inability to develop reasonably plausible and robust estimates of the elements of the model. In a comment directly related to the validity of the HTCM, they concluded that "the model cannot be routinely applied to value changes in site characteristics until the theoretical implications of these implementation decisions are fully understood" (p. 26).

The Criterion Validity of Nonmarket Economic Valuation Methods

The criterion validity of a nonmarket economic valuation measure is established by determining that it is highly correlated with a criterion variable such as actual market price. Mitchell and Carson (1986) have described studies by Bishop and Heberlein (1979, 1986), Bishop, Heberlein, and Kealy (1983), Bohm (1972) and Dickie, Fisher, and Gerking (1985), which they interpret as providing evidence for the criterion-related validity of CVMs. In these studies, CV estimates based on hypothetical markets were compared with amounts that respondents actually paid in simulated markets; those amounts provided a criterion for evaluating the validity of the CV measures. Mitchell and Carson concluded that these studies provide support for the criterion-related validity of the CVMs used. The close approximation of the CV values under consideration to the actual market prices should not be surprising, however, given the fact that the goods being valued (e.g., hunting permits, pints of strawberries) were familiar, well-defined goods with which respondents likely would have had prior market experience that would influence their decision-making processes.

The Construct Validity of Nonmarket Economic Valuations: Theoretical and Methodological Issues

The theoretical models underlying the methods economists have developed for valuing nonmarket goods and the assumptions of those models raise a variety of issues that bear directly on establishing the construct validity of these valuation methods. We summarize some of those issues for the TCM, HPM, and CVM.

The TCM

The construct validity of the TCM rests on acceptance of assumptions necessary for the use of travel costs as a proxy for price. The validity of some of these assumptions needs to be established, as does the robustness of the TCM.[3] Basic tenets or characteristics of the early, simple TCMs were that:

1. The value of the site is estimated in terms of value per trip rather the value of those joint outputs actually represented by recreation experiences.
2. Recreationists' travel expenditures are made solely to obtain a good (use of a recreation site), and people do not travel just for the experience of traveling.[4]
3. Although trips may be taken to realize a variety of benefits (only some of which may be purely recreational and still fewer of which may be derived from particular characteristics of the site), a partitioning of the value assigned to a site on the basis of these varied benefits is infeasible.
4. Information about the specific characteristics of the site and their contribution to the total site value is unavailable and unconsidered.
5. The only purpose of a given trip is to visit one particular site and thus only the marginal travel costs associated with that site should be included in estimating site demand.
6. The site is unique and has no substitutes.

To overcome some of the shortcomings of early, simple TCMs, more advanced approaches to the TCM have been proposed that seek to incorporate the influence of site characteristics (Caulkins et al., 1985; Vaughn & Russell, 1983), substitutes (Burt & Brewer, 1971; Cicchetti, Fisher, & Smith, 1976; Rosenthal, 1985), and multiple destinations (Haspell & Johnson, 1982) in demand modelling.

These approaches assume that shortcomings of the simple TCM can be adequately resolved through more sophisticated model development. Recent research (e.g., Rosenthal, 1985) provides grounds for questioning this assumption and illustrates the need for further research to determine the most effective approach to incorporating the influence of alternative sites as substitutes in the TCM.

In addition, the complementary effects of recreation sites on recreation demand and values as estimated with the TCM have yet to be addressed. The role of recreation areas as complements for one another is likely to be an especially important feature of sites located at major tourism destinations. In these instances, the clustering of attractions is important for attracting the volume of tourism and recreation activity sufficient for supporting private tourism enterprises (Gunn, 1979).

The HPM

The HPM, based on the work of Lancaster (1966), Rosen (1974), and others, was developed on the idea that choice of a private goods bundle (e.g., a purchase of a private good representing a bundle of valued attributes) can be an indicator of the value of a related public good. The assumptions underlying this approach raise issues about its construct validity on both psychological and economic grounds. Those issues include (1) the need to correctly specify the hedonic price function (Desvousges et al., 1983; Freeman, 1979), (2) the separation of demand and supply curves necessary for estimating demand and supply curves (Bartik, 1987; Epple, 1987), (3) the reality that amenity resources (e.g., a national park) are rarely bundled in market goods, and (4) assumptions about the nature of human decision making (e.g., the purchase of one or more private goods or services represents the choice of a specific level of public good to be provided; each individual/household recognizes and considers the implications of each of the attributes associated with the purchase of a private good or service).

The HTCM attempts to account for the influence of uniqueness of a site on its value by directly considering the choice of site characteristics. Information about individuals' decisions to travel to recreation sites is used to estimate implicit prices for the site's characteristics, but the private good upon which the required demand functions are based is travel, as is the case with the TCM. This approach thus builds on concepts underlying both the TCM and the HPM.

A range of concerns has been expressed about the assumptions and procedures of the HTCM. Although demands for the characteristics of a public good like a recreation site can be estimated without the single market identification problem discussed by Brown and Rosen (1982), the other untested assumptions associated with the HPMs and TCMs apply to this approach. Further, because the HPM and HTCM are the approaches most recently developed for application to resource valuation, they have been examined the least thoroughly of any economic methods for valuing nonmarket goods. Analyses of the construct validity of the HPM and HTCM are needed, given the issues raised by their assumptions and procedures (see Ladd & Zober, 1977, 1979; Ratchford, 1979). Because these models attempt more subtle measurements, their validity is more problematic in the event of specification error than the simple TCM.[5] Smith and Kaoru (1985) have concluded that important conceptual issues must be resolved before the construct validity of the HTCM can be established.

The CVM

Implicit assumptions of the CVM about people's decision-making and information-processing capabilities raise fundamental questions about CVM's construct validity. A basic issue here is the extent to which attributes of people's information processing and decision-making processes limit the accuracy with which contingent values can be measured. Researchers working on the development of the CVM are showing an increased interest in identifying and remedying distortions in the results of their valuation methods (see Berger, 1984; Bishop & Heberlein, 1986; Cummings et al., 1986); nonetheless, the CVM assumes that people have the capability to readily assign market-like values to nonmarket commodities in valid and useful ways.

Harris et al. (1987) question this assumption and its corollary that, through valuation judgments, "...willingness-to-pay measurements transform more global and unarticulated preferences into specific, precise monetary values that accurately index the preferences that would be carefully researched and ordered if the good or service were traded in a competitive market" (p. 3). Researchers in a number of behavioral disciplines are attempting to answer questions about the abilities and methods used by people to make everyday decisions. These questions are especially pertinent to the decisions required by the CVM, which typically has presented people with a sometimes novel and usually complex problem-solving task that assumes market-like behavior in the context of a hypothetical, nonmarket situation.[6] The findings from psychological research on human decision-making provides a number of bases upon which to question the assumptions of CVMs.

Human information processing and decision-making abilities.--First, the literature questions the validity of the assumption that the typical respondent has the capability to respond to contingent valuation surveys with well-reasoned and carefully calculated value judgments. Accurate assessments using these methods require vigilant information processing and the use of optimizing strategies. Yet considerable research in cognitive and social psychology suggests that, in fact, people use faulty thought processes and take cognitive shortcuts involving simplistic decision-making processes (e.g., Bettman, 1979; Bradburn, Ripps, & Shevell, 1987; Fischhoff, 1977; Nisbett & Ross, 1980; Radner, 1975; Slovic, 1972), which result in different value responses than would be obtained if the vigilant and complex processes called for by the CVM were used.

Simon (1957) asserts that human beings have only limited rationality with which to solve complex decision-making problems. These limitations frequently result in simplistic decision-making processes that do not reflect utility maximization (Simon, 1986). Among the simplified procedures that people typically use are suboptimizing (i.e., choosing an alternative that maximizes some properties of the decision at the expense of others) and satisficing (choosing an alternative that meets a minimum set of requirements). Empirical research examining these processes (e.g., Shoemaker, 1982; Thaler, 1980) suggests that the utility maximization process is less likely to be used in decision making than is implied by most CVMs.

Psychological research has revealed a variety of factors that can influence decision-making processes. Faulty recall and inference (Bradburn et al., 1987; Nisbett & Ross, 1980), cognitive defenses (Janis & Terwilliger, 1962), reliance on reference group (Argyle, 1969; Huston, 1974), obedience to authority (Milgram, 1974), and attitude change processes (Cacioppo, Petty, & Stoltenberg, 1985; McGuire, 1969) are some of the factors that may impact the quality of human decision making.

In the context of the CVM, the present administration of CVM instruments, in striving to achieve scientific rigor and objectivity, present a social setting and human interactions that are necessarily formal and impersonal. People who find themselves in these kinds of situations may feel that they are being socially coerced into participating in problem-solving situations that likely raise concerns, doubts, and questions in their minds. In particular, people may respond with concerns about the interviewer's expectations of them and the proper way of dealing with the situation--a way that is minimally stressful but adequately conscientious.

In failing to account for these and other psychological factors, past research has generated seemingly random CV values in some cases, with demographic variables failing to explain systematic differences in people's bids. Tests of the randomness of CV bids (e.g., Berger, 1984; Desvousges et al., 1983; Schulze et al., 1983) provide insufficient support for Randall, Hoehn, and Brookshire's (1983) assertion that CV measures are likely to predict actual behavior; this lack of support raises questions about the degree of construct validity of CV measures.

Elicitation effects in the face of respondent ignorance or uncertainty.--A second issue stimulated by the psychological literature concerns the extent to which people's responses are influenced in unknown or undesirable ways by the value elicitation methods used and the context within the questions are asked. The CVM typically assumes that people have well-defined ideas about the worth or desirability of possible events and that, although these ideas often may not be articulated in people's minds, proper questioning can elicit judgments accurately representing people's estimates of monetary values for unpriced goods. They seemingly have overlooked the more subtle and profound danger that, under conditions of respondent ignorance or uncertainty, the survey method may significantly influence the formulation and expression of values.

People typically make evaluative decisions in the marketplace where an array of goods and their attributes, including price, are available for consideration. Consequently, they may not even know how to begin thinking about decision problems posed by CVMs. Imagine a scenario that logically extends the assumptions of the CVM, wherein people could actually purchase desired quantities of environmental goods from an "amenity resource supermarket" that actually sells a variety of public amenities (ranging from endangered wildlife species and air quality to wilderness and wild-and-scenic rivers) along with the tangible goods people typically consume on a daily basis. From this perspective, the information processing and decision-making processes that consumers use assume a different light than that cast by existing methods for obtaining contingent values. This scenario confronts the consumer with a reasonably fixed amount of discretionary income and a vast number of amenity goods from which to choose. In addition, prices have been set for each good, based on the machinations of the marketplace in combination with whatever government interventions have adjusted those prices; the worth of these goods is thus reflected in their price, assuming that people are price setters (rather than takers) and that any price supports or ceilings imposed adequately represent their social benefits. This scenario also assumes that people will willingly spend a portion of the discretionary funds to purchase some minimum amount of those amenity goods they desire most, and it places their purchase

decisions in the larger context of past purchases and future choices. In contrast, the scenario implicit in existing CVMs is that people must resolve a hypothetical decision problem that typically involves a limited number of consumer choices during an abbreviated period of time.

Differences in the above two scenarios raise research questions that the current focus on accuracy of scientific measurement in CVMs does not treat. Most basic is whether the decision processes of people acting in a market context are the same as those used in a field setting where a survey instrument is introduced. People likely make purchase decisions in a market context that poses a variety of conditions that receive only limited consideration, if any at all, in CVMs. The relevance of market decision processes for their applications to the CV process should be investigated; in particular, clarification of the ways in which CV decisions are formulated and a comparison of these formulations with those used for purchases of market goods are needed.

People typically initiate and control the search and decision processes involved in their market purchase decisions. In contrast, administration of the CVM is better represented by the Fuller Brush representative who has only a limited variety of brushes to sell. In completing the CVM, people are compelled to make purchase/expenditure decisions in a comparatively short period of time, in the context of one or a few isolated goods, about a product for which they had not initiated the choice process, and in the presence of a total stranger. These purchase conditions seldom occur in the real world, the exception being the case of door-to-door salespersons, and folk wisdom about people's responses to these kinds of intrusions does little to recommend similar methods in CVM research as a basis for allocating important public amenity resource.

In one study, for example, the researcher (Berger, 1984) concluded that CVM bids received were "good will" bids that were inflated because of the pressure respondents perceived to give a socially acceptable, higher bid. The contingent market presented to people was deemed "so artificial and foreign...that they are unwilling or unable to follow the normal processes of preference research" (Berger, 1984, p. 173).

This conclusion is consistent with our concern about the extent to which CVM techniques enable people to use the methods they typically use for making evaluative judgments. If people usually compare the range of available products, their attributes and their prices in making decisions in the marketplace, how do people make evaluative judgments in a nonmarket context where these decision criteria are unavailable? We suggest that people can most readily articulate their preferences where the judgment task involves simple and familiar experiences, the range of reasonable values is given, and the trade-offs among the attributes of the thing being valued are explicit and comparable. The CVM often presents people with complex, unfamiliar decision problems, which people likely do not know how to begin thinking about, much less solve. Research is especially needed to test the validity of estimates that may be influenced by the methods used as much or more than people's actual preferences.

Stress and human decision making.--A final question derived from psychological research on information processing and decision making is whether people can participate usefully in a decision-making effort when that effort is minimally or overly stressful. This question represents the concern common to all survey researchers that the problem-solving tasks posed by their survey questions may either burden respondents (e.g., Cocheba & Langford, 1981; Desvousges et al., 1983; Seller, Stoll, & Chabas, 1985; Walsh, Gillman, & Loomis, 1982); or, alternatively, not be taken seriously (e.g., Berger, 1984). Investigations have shown that many respondents fail to respond to CV questions or refuse to respond in relatively large numbers when given the opportunity. Mitchell and Carson (1986) noted that, "whereas an item nonresponse (sic) rate of eight to ten percent would be regarded as high in an ordinary opinion survey, rates of 20 to 30 percent or even higher are not uncommon in CV surveys.... certain subgroups, such as people who are older and those with low levels of education, contribute disproportionately to these high non-response rates" (pp. 11.4-11.5). Given these concerns, the effects of stress levels on both the validity and reliability of estimates derived with the CVM need to be tested.

Validity of the CVM as the lack of systematic bias.--Economists' efforts to establish the construct validity of CV estimates has typically focused on examining possible sources of systematic bias in these values and on psychological factors affecting the valuation process (Berger, 1984; Carson & Mitchell, 1985; Cummings et al., 1986; Desvousges et al., 1983; Mitchell & Carson, 1986). As we have suggested, the conclusion that a technique is providing measurements in which no systematic bias can be found is one indication of the technique's validity; however, that conclusion is only a necessary and not a sufficient condition for establishing a measure's validity.

The significance of the various sources of bias introduced by the CVM that have been examined with research is clouded by the differing interpretations and conclusions drawn in reviews of that research. Studies of these kinds of bias, which include strategic bias (Bohm, 1972; Brookshire, Ives, & Schulze, 1976; Rowe & Chestnut, 1983; Rowe, d'Arge, & Brookshire, 1980), starting point bias (Boyle & Bishop, 1984; Brookshire, d'Arge, Schulze, & Thayer, 1981; Brookshire, Randall, & Stoll, 1980; Desvousges et al., 1983; Mitchell & Carson, 1981; Randall et al., 1978; Rowe et al., 1980; Thayer, 1981; Thayer & Schulze, 1977); and payment-vehicle bias (Brookshire et al., 1977, 1980, 1981; Daubert & Young, 1981; Greenley, Walsh, & Young, 1981; Rowe & Chestnut, 1983; Rowe et al., 1980) have provided mixed evidence about their influence on CV values.

Our view is that these types of bias could be interpreted as specific examples of a more general information bias (i.e., the influence of the amount, kind, and form of information provided in the CVM instrument on the values provided by respondents). One would expect that the information provided as well as the way it is framed through problem formulation, instrument design, and question wording would influence the responses to a survey instrument (Kahneman & Tversky, 1984; Tversky & Kahneman, 1981).

Of perhaps greater concern is the hypothetical nature of the decision problem and the potential for hypothetical bias posed by the CVM (Bishop & Heberlein, 1979; Cummings et al., 1986; Feenburg & Mills, 1980; Harris & McGown, 1986; Mitchell & Carson, 1986; Rowe & Chestnut, 1983). The basic issue here is that the very nature of contingent valuation poses a hypothetical, and thus potentially inconsequential, decision problem. Consequently, stated responses may differ from deci-

sions made in an actual choice situation. Given the extensive body of literature exploring the discrepancies between responses to hypothetical questions and actual behavior (see Harris et al., 1987), we conclude that this type of bias may make a major contribution to the lack of validity of CVM values. Although some (Carson & Mitchell, 1985; Mitchell & Carson, 1986) disagree, other researchers who have empirically examined CVMs conclude that hypothetical bias does exist and represents a significant problem (e.g., Berger, 1984; Bishop & Heberlein, 1979; Coursey, Schulze, & Hovis, 1983).

The Construct Validity of Nonmarket Economic Valuation Methods: Convergent Validity

Over the last 2 decades, a variety of studies of the convergent validity of the value estimates obtained with two or more economic methods for valuing nonmarket goods have been reported. Convergent validity refers to evidence that different measures of a construct (e.g., the TCM, HPM, and CVM for measuring the value of a nonmarket good) yield similar results (Campbell & Fiske, 1959). Thus it provides one basis for determining the construct validity of the measures whose results are being compared.

Comparative analyses to assess the convergent validity of the various methods have predominantly compared the CVM with either the TCM or the HPM, producing mixed results. An early study was conducted by Knetsch and Davis (1966), who compared a TCM estimate of the benefits of recreation (an approximation they recognized as being crude) with a CVM estimate for the same good. After a casual, largely subjective inspection of the data, they declared those estimates to be "close." In contrast, Bishop and Heberlein (1979) reported an equally qualitative comparison of the TCM and CVM. They concluded that the mean estimated value of goose-hunting permits obtained with the two EVMs was not close. Desvousges et al. (1983) were among the first to apply statistical tests to a series of comparisons of benefits attributable to water quality improvements obtained using the TCM and CVM. Their findings have been summarized as ambiguous (Cummings et al., 1986), and the authors themselves noted that their implementation of the TCM failed to consider the influence of substitute sites on benefit estimation.

A similar limitation was acknowledged but then largely ignored by Smith et al. (1985), who compared benefit estimates derived from a simple TCM, a generalized TCM, and a CVM. They found that the results obtained from the two TCM estimates were different and that the results obtained with the simple TCM were comparable to those obtained using the CVM. Their findings and those of others (Smith et al., 1985; Smith & Kaoru, 1985) suggest that value estimates derived from TCMs and HPMs are highly sensitive to the subjective judgments of researchers. Additional studies comparing the monetary values placed on recreation opportunities, as measured with the CVM and TCM, have been reported by Seller et al. (1985), Fisher and Raucher (1984), Sorg and Loomis (1984), and Thayer (1981). In general, they provide mixed evidence for the consistency of the value measurements obtained with these approaches.

At present, only weak and inconsistent evidence is available to support the convergent validity of economic methods of valuing nonmarket goods. Consequently, the extent and quality of the evidence could not be interpreted as meeting the standards for measurement validation established by the American Psychological Association (Novick, 1985). Moreover, the limits of convergent validity must be acknowledged. These investigations represent one of many methods of obtaining construct validity, but they do not fully address the issue of validity. Good convergent validity would be obtained, for example, if two individuals measured a football field using a 13-inch ruler and a 39-inch yardstick. The results of these measurements would correlate, but the measures would not be valid.

Comparisons of values obtained with the CVM and HPM also raise the problem of inadequate tests of convergent validity. Favorable comparisons of value estimates obtained with the CVM and HPM were reported by Brookshire et al. (1982, 1984). However, because a goodness-of-fit coefficient was not reported for either the hedonic wage or hedonic property equations, any comparison of estimates obtained with those equations is suspect. Cummings et al. (1983) highlighted this concern, noting that:

> ...these results do not 'prove' the accuracy of survey measures for public good values;...survey and hedonic values may be biased vis-a-vis 'true' social values for public goods...if successful, however, repeated experiments of the type reported above may go far in redefining some of the economists' reservations concerning the use of survey methods for valuing public goods. (p. 12)

"Repeated experiments" lose any significance, however, if the methods being used are producing invalid results. Tests of goodness-of-fit would provide one basis for establishing the content validity of these hedonic values.

Analysis of a multitrait-multimethod matrix (Campbell & Fiske, 1959) is one methodology developed in psychology to more rigorously assess the construct validity of survey measures. Rosenthal, Waldman, and Driver (1984) used this approach in a study of recreation preferences, and Tinsley and Kass (1980) and Tinsley, Driver, and Kass (1981) used it in validating the Paragraphs About Leisure (PAL) and the Recreation Experience Preference (REP) scales (two instruments used to assess the psychological benefits of leisure), respectively. The multitrait-multimethod matrix has yet to be used in valuation studies.

This analysis requires that the values of two or more nonmarket goods be derived using measures based on two or more economic methods of measurement. High correlations among the measurements of a given nonmarket good obtained with the different methods indicates the convergent validity of the procedures. The lack of a correlation among value measurements obtained using the same method for different goods is required to provide evidence of discriminant validity (i.e., not only do different measures provide correlated values for the same good, but they provide uncorrelated values for different goods). Both convergent and discriminant validity evidence are required to establish the construct validity of a procedure.

Because generalizability of the results of particular studies is limited, the usefulness of efforts to assess convergent validity by comparing value estimates from different studies representing an array of conditions is also limited. The work of some researchers has clarified the problematic nature of these comparisons and the need for more uniform applications of methods under more uniform conditions to increase the meaningfulness of these comparisons (e.g., Sorg & Loomis, 1984).

The Reliability of Economic Methods for Valuing Nonmarket Goods

The reliability of a measure is concerned with random measurement error (due to transient aspects of the respondent, situation, or procedures that may vary from one measurement to another). The greater the degree to which random error confounds the accuracy of the measurements obtained with a survey instrument, the less reliable that instrument is deemed to be; a high degree of reliability has long been considered a primary requirement that must be met before an instrument can be used for research (Novick, 1985).

Although economics has traditionally analyzed and interpreted data at an aggregate level (mean value estimates are calculated and the reliability of those estimates is assumed to be ensured with a large sample size), the assumption that individual biases nullify each other at the aggregate level of analysis used in the economic methods under consideration here has been questioned by some researchers (e.g., Kleindorfer & Kunreuther, 1983; Pratt, Wise, & Zeckhauser, 1979; Schelling, 1978; Schoemaker, 1982). In addition, the requirement that respondents be randomly sampled has been sometimes overlooked in economic research.[7] Findings generally suggest that samples are self-selecting; respondents to CVM studies, for instance, tend to be more affluent and educated. The reliance on nonprobability samples weakens the argument that random errors are nullified by large samples. Furthermore, some of the research on the CVM is characterized by small samples, and the number of useable values is further reduced by anomalies in the data such as nonresponses, protest bids, and outlier bids (see Mitchell & Carson, this volume).

The reliability of measurements obtained using the CVM is of particular concern because this direct survey approach uses a method of data collection that is particularly susceptible to transitory influences on individual respondents. Consequently, the CVM raises a number of issues examined by survey researchers. An operational definition of reliability is the consistency of two or more measurements in which only one aspect of the measurement process differs. Among the aspects allowed to differ are the time of administration (in this context, consistency results in "stability") and the person administering the instrument (in this context, consistency results in "equivalence"; Kidder, 1980). Factors that might influence the stability of an individual's measured values include personal factors that change over time, such as fatigue, mental set, and health. The administration of a CV instrument may be influenced by differences between interviewers or by a lack of consistency within a single interviewer across time. Neither the stability nor equivalence of CVM measures has been formally tested in CVM research, but a few studies provide some circumstantial evidence of the stability of CV values (Bishop & Heberlein, 1979; Mitchell & Carson, 1985; Rowe et al., 1980).

The reliability of the TCM, HPM, and HTCM also merits consideration. Measurement error is not likely to pose a problem for these methods if the necessary data on private goods characteristics and the market values of those goods are available and accurate, and if pains are taken to carefully compile the required information. Unfortunately, some researchers have used these methods without evaluating the reliability of their data. In the case of the HTCM and TCM, the reliability of measurement may be a particularly important issue in that the more complex a model and its assumptions, the greater its sensitivity to random error. Mendelsohn and Brown (1983), in particular, have suggested that the complex modeling involved in the HTCM renders it more sensitive to measurement error than the simple TCM.

Research is needed on the issue of reliability. Also, more information is needed about how the degree of reliability influences the usefulness of economic approaches to nonmarket valuation. In one of the few studies examining this issue, Brown, Sorhus, Yang, and Richards (1983) described the effects of error in travel cost measurement. Noting that errors in reported trip costs can result in substantial misestimates of consumer surplus, they concluded that "further research is obviously needed to test for accuracy of consumer surplus estimates using various approaches" (p. 157).

FURTHER ASSESSMENT OF THE PSYCHOMETRIC PROPERTIES OF EVMS

Concerns exist, even among economists, about the efficacy of nonmarket economic valuation theories and the specific techniques developed to implement them; these concerns are apparent in the comments of authors of other papers in this volume. Because few formal tests to rigorously examine the reliability and validity of measures currently in use have been conducted, systematic research is needed to assess their psychometric properties if the use of these methods is to be pursued.

Care should be taken to assess the reliability of measures, and, where necessary, revisions to ensure their reliability should be undertaken. Careful and extensive pretesting to determine and correct problems with any instrument has long been a basic approach in survey research to increase instrument reliability. Past attempts to improve survey instruments have used focus groups, observed or tape-recorded interviews, systematic debriefing of respondents, and analysis of preliminary surveys involving only a few respondents (Mitchell & Carson, 1986).

In addition, the use of large sample sizes, robust statistical techniques, and experimental designs that affirm the stability and equivalence of measurements will be of value in minimizing the random error in EVMs. In the case of the CVM, for example, the typically large variance in responses requires a large sample size to derive sufficiently precise sample statistics for useful analysis. The use of robust statistical techniques (e.g., the alpha trimmed mean recommended by Mitchell and Carson (1986), is another way of increasing the reliability of CV measures by systematically detecting and dealing with the effects of outliers. However, the presence of outliers may indicate problems with the validity of a measure. Further research on the significance of outliers is needed before they can be discounted as sources of random error.

Formal research is also needed that uses experimental designs to systematically test the stability of measurements over time and their equivalence across interviewers and other variations of survey administration. Other sources of error may affect the accuracy of nonmarket economic valuation measures in ways that are difficult to detect. In the case of CVMs, for example, Kahneman (1986) postulated the possible influence of symbolic demand, whereby people may respond to a good being valued in general terms rather than in terms of specifics describing that good. For example, when surveyed about their willingness to pay additional taxes to maintain fishing in one particular region in Canada, respondents gave the same amount as that proffered to maintain fishing in Canada as a whole. Kahneman recommended that CV research should routinely manipulate potential anchors, suggestive numbers, or other factors to test for these effects. This should be done in testing the reliability of CVMs, particularly during pretesting.

More extensive research is also needed on the validity of nonmarket economic valuation methods. As suggested earlier, the task of rigorously testing the efficacy of the assumptions underlying these methods has only begun. In addition, continued examination of the implications of the procedures used and researcher judgements involved in operationalizing those models is needed.

In particular, formal research to assess the construct validity of nonmarket economic valuation measures should be conducted. Rigorous experiments using formalized procedures such as multitrait-multimethod analysis have yet to be used. In addition, economists and psychologists should collaborate to learn more about amenity resource valuation as a decision-making process. The potential of focus groups and process or protocol analysis (Buggie, 1983; Calder, 1977; Payne, 1976) has yet to be tapped, and value decision processes need to be better understood and the factors influencing them better defined, as several economists have recently emphasized (e.g., Hanneman, 1985; Simon, 1986; Smith, 1985, 1986). Development of a research thrust based on exploring the methods and ramifications of applying social judgment theory to the policy referendum model (discussed later in this paper) would help meet this need.

Research on the content validity of these evaluation methods is also needed. For example, if the good being valued is inadequately represented in a CVM survey instrument, the potential of bias is introduced. This potential is of particular concern when the good is unfamiliar, seems implausible, or lacks meaning. Even when the good is well presented with a written scenario and accompanying graphics, one cannot presume that people will respond to a real good that they have actually experienced in the same way they imagine they would when confronted with a hypothetical situation.

As a precondition for any type of valuation process, the nature and attributes of the amenity resource good for which value estimates are being obtained need to be better defined and specified. For example, camping opportunities in a national forest could be defined more exactly as management products by differentiating them in terms of the type of camping and setting desired (see Driver & Harris, 1981). Researchers have suggested that a psychological approach may be helpful in specifying some of these products, where that specification is based on users' preferences for, and evaluation of, product attributes that include activity, setting, and experience attributes (Driver, 1985;

Driver, Phillips, Bergersen, & Harris, 1985). These products need to be adequately defined and measurable units of quantity assigned to them before meaningful values can be estimated for them. The importance of people understanding and being familiar with a good for the valuation process is recognized (Cummings et al., 1986; Mitchell & Carson, 1986), but research has far to go in resolving the difficult issues posed by product specification and the transferability of a market-based approach to nonmarket goods like public amenity resources (see Driver & Burch, this volume).

In addition, other issues raised for the content validity of the TCM, HPM, and HTCM modelling and estimation procedures required for these methods need to be addressed. Sensitivity analysis of the methods is particularly needed to determine the extent to which value estimates are sensitive to various specifications of the demand curve, data aggregations, functional forms, and numerous other procedural influences on modelling outcomes, as Stynes (1985) has begun to do.

DEVELOPING A MODIFIED DIRECT SURVEY APPROACH

Although all economic methods for valuing nonmarket goods have advantages and disadvantages, we believe the direct survey approach (now best represented by the CVM) holds the greatest promise for the development of valid, reliable measures of the monetary value of public amenity resources. However, we also believe that this approach must be modified substantially.

One change reflects differences in our conceptualization of the psychology of the basic decision-making process required for valuation from that of other researchers (e.g., Berger, 1984; Bishop & Heberlein, 1986; Cummings et al., 1986) who discuss CVM-based judgments in the context of attitude theory and the theory of reasoned action (Ajzen & Fishbein, 1980; Fishbein & Ajzen, 1975). Our fundamental divergence from this perspective concerns the ideas that (1) the intention to perform a given behavior, which is antecedent to that behavior, is in the case of the CVM a person's willingness to pay, and (2) a person's attitude is thus directed toward the behavior of paying. Our conceptualization is that the hypothetical nature of the CVM willingness-to-pay measure means that the responses obtained to it are not, in reality, an expression of a behavioral intention. We propose a perspective based on consumer behavior theory, whereby the closest approximation of that intentional expression is found in real market behaviors: People intend to make a purchase or allocate scarce financial resources based on considerations of price (i.e., willingness to pay) that is only one of a potentially wide variety of constraining and facilitating factors (costs and benefits) about which people formulate and consider beliefs and attitudes. The model of an attitude toward a behavior is like other expectancy-value models of the subjective expected utility class (Fischoff, Goitein, & Shapira, 1982). Like other models of this class, it involves the product of subjective probability that an outcome will occur times the evaluation of that outcome; however, the link between this evaluation process and the preference research that consumers are thought to practice in their purchase or allocation decision making has yet to be clarified.

Our contention is that, if the CVM approach as it is now conceived is to be pursued, the relevant behavior upon which researchers should focus is not the decision to pay some amount for a good. The relevant behavior is the actual commitment of scarce dollars to obtain or maintain that good, while considerations of the amount of discretionary dollars available, the benefits realized and, most significant, the amount of dollars one is willing to pay or allocate are central to the decision-making process but are antecedent to the purchase/allocation decision and its behavioral outcome. We argue that the refinement of the CVM on the basis of this conceptualization would improve the method's construct validity. Going one step further, we also contend that, if a structure for evaluating trade-offs in a meaningful way and providing valid monetary values for public amenity resources is to be developed, a direct survey valuation method (DSVM) based on this initial framework provides a beginning, but it must be modified in major ways.

The Policy Referendum Model

The first change we propose is one of conceptualization. The DSVM should provide respondents with more than the opportunity to try to assess and then reveal their preferences in a monetary metric. It should be designed to provide a more familiar approach (developed on the basis of relevant theories of consumer and voting behavior) that helps people learn their preferences and how they might express the values they place on nonmarket goods with the more precise, monetary index that dollar values represent. Theory and research on the CVM has begun moving in this direction with the development of a policy referendum model for resource valuation. Mitchell and Carson (1986) described this model, which we believe is a more appropriate one for valuing public resources, but one that is problematic in its own right:

> The results from actual referenda on environmental improvements or other public goods offer one approach to measuring benefits which, though limited in application, has some very desirable properties. In a referendum, voters indicate whether or not they are willing to provide a specific level of a public good according to a specified payment scheme. The decision on how to vote is based on the voter's assessment of whether the marginal utility of the public good is greater than the marginal utility of the amount she would have to pay. The public goods market is in essence created by the election setting and the wording of the referendum. Unlike...(CVM) methods, which use hypothetical markets, the amount and method of payment is specified and enforced in this case. (p. 2-14)

While Mitchell and Carson (1986) noted the rarity of referenda for environmental goods, they suggested that the policy referendum model offers an attractive institutional framework for valuation efforts:

> Critics sometimes seem to suggest that the CV method requires people to do something which is totally novel. In fact, as our discussion of referenda shows, governments do periodically attempt to ascertain people's willingness to pay for specified levels of amenities. It is for this reason that we will

propose that referenda are a more appropriate model for CV studies than ordinary market behavior...referenda (also) offer an attractive institutional framework for CV studies themselves. Although they did not attempt to simulate a referendum as such, Bishop and Heberlein (1979...) have successfully used CV instruments to ask respondents to say whether they are willing or not to pay a given price for the provision of a good. By asking people how they would vote in a hypothetical referendum if the cost to their household of a given amenity level was a specified price, and by offering a sufficient range of prices to a large enough sample in this manner, demand curves for the good can be determined. Large samples are expensive, but the simplicity of this elicitation technique makes the use of less expensive mail or phone survey techniques possible. Alternately, the WTP amount may be elicited within a referendum framework by asking respondents whether they would vote for or against a referendum for providing the amenity. For those who would vote yes, a followup question would ascertain the highest amount they would be willing to pay if the referendum passed. This is the approach we used in our drinking water study. (p. 2-17)

This referendum model implies an alternative set of guidelines to the "reference operating conditions" for the market-based model for CV proposed by Cummings et al. (1986); those alternative guidelines are that:

1. Respondents must understand the commodity to be valued, how it will be provided, and how it will be paid for.
2. They should be given as simple a choice as possible.
3. There must be little uncertainty about the provision of the good.
4. WTP, not WTA, measures are elicited.
5. Outliers should not be permitted unduly to influence the results.
6. Respondents should be permitted to abstain from the valuation process.

As other papers in this volume establish, the primary problem for the referendum model is reflected by Guideline 4 above; this model, like the market-based CVMs, implicitly requires a measure of willingness-to-pay rather than willingness-to-accept, even though the latter is often the requisite value measure for the loss of public goods that people do (or logically should) consider as part of their endowment. We recommend a different approach, which we detail in the rest of this section.

Interactive Computerized Knowledge-Based Value Counseling

A second change for the DSVM is necessitated by the fact that the term value as we apply it here refers not simply to market or shadow price. More generally, it refers to assigned value as described by Brown (1984), where the context within which the valuation occurs is considered and, in addition, the full range of benefits and costs is reflected (Driver & Harris, 1981). Tapping this kind of value would require educating people and clarifying for them the attributes of the good, the potential impacts of a proposed change in the existing quantity of that good, the con-

stituency that should be considered, and a host of other details. Ultimately, what would be derived via this learning and value formulation process would be a monetary index of preference, as opposed to any true indicator of willingness to pay.

The process being proposed here is similar to that provided in psychological counseling, in that it provides a useful, structured situation through which people are enabled to more clearly and precisely determine and articulate their values within the context of a well-specified judgment task. This clarification process would likely result in both a learning process and attitude change for respondents, whereby their attitudes toward a proposed change in the quality or quantity of a given amenity resource would be altered, resulting in a change in the value they hold for that resource.

The use of interactive, knowledge-based (expert-system) computer programs (e.g., Rolandi, 1986) for value clarification and elicitation could be developed as the most effective way of creating a process for eliciting reliable value estimates. This use of preprogrammed computer information bases could help minimize interviewer bias and thereby maximize the measure's reliability.

Development of this value-counseling process in the context of a referendum (i.e., voting) approach would avert criticisms of nonmarket economic valuation methods, which currently introduce inequity with a market system that determines social values on the basis of an existing income distribution. Although economists generally skirt the equity issue (as not germane to their analysis) and focus their attention on efficiency criteria, this issue is particularly pertinent to the valuation and allocation of public, social goods such as amenity resources. The problem of developing a viable, commonly accepted means for determining a social welfare function remains unresolved (Arrow, 1949). The CVM as it is now conducted does nothing to remedy its disproportionately higher weighting of the values of people who, because they have greater discretionary incomes, are able and therefore willing to pay more for a good.

We believe the nature and importance of public amenity resources requires that their valuation be premised and structured on a basis different from the private market approach implicit in all existing nonmarket economic valuation methods. Given their emphasis on self-interest over altruism (see Sen, 1977), competition over cooperation, and the status quo at the expense of future developments, those methods may, in many cases, offer inequitable, possibly unethical, and at least illogical paradigms on which to build a process for valuing public goods. Further, allocation decisions about social, nonmarket goods often involve the possibility of irreversible impacts on unique resources, about which people hold emotionally-charged opinions. These kinds of decisions merit more careful and reasoned judgments than those made for personal good consumption. The unavoidable reliance of existing methods for valuing nonmarket goods on the various subjective judgments required for their implementation is sufficient justification for shifting the burden of judgment from the technical analysts making those judgments to the public actually attempting to value a nonmarket good.[8]

The focus of current experimental approaches on developing auction mechanisms--such as sealed-bid auctions (Vickrey, 1961) and group consensus mechanisms (Groves & Ledyard, 1977)--is a step in the right direction for improving the validity and reliability of CVM valuation. Recent laboratory experiments to develop auction mechanisms for resource valuation (Brook-shire, Coursey, & Schulze, 1985; Coursey et al., 1983; Coursey, Schulze, & Hovis, 1984; Hovis, Coursey, & Schulze, 1983) seek to overcome several problems, including a person's lack of familiarity with a good and the opportunity to learn about it and one's value for it in the CVM, the hypothetical nature of the CVM, and the disparity between willingness to pay and willingness to accept measurements.

However, we concur with Gregory and Furby's (in press) concerns that the work of Coursey et al. (1984) raises a range of conceptual, research design, statistical, and interpretive issues that challenge the usefulness of this approach for providing meaningful information about amenity resource values. Contrary to researchers' claims, auctions may be lacking as a mechanism for increasing people's familiarity with a nonmarket good, for their learning more about their personal preferences and values, or for producing values of greater validity; while the approach admittedly reduces the hypothetical bias of which the CVM has been accused, the artificiality of auction-based markets also reduces their generalizability for obtaining market-like values for nonmarket commodities (Coursey et al., 1984).

Consequently, a third and fundamental change that we propose is the development of a new valuation approach that applies social judgment theory (SJT) (Hammond, Stewart, Brehmer, & Steinmann, 1974; Hammond, Mumpower, & Smith, 1977) via interactive, knowledge-based computer technology to the policy referendum model. Details of the development of SJT, its basis on the Brunswikian theory of the "lens model," and its operationalization are beyond the scope of this paper. The important aspect of SJT for the problem of monetary, non-market valuation is its emphasis on providing respondents with cognitive aids for improving human judgment at the same time that it seeks a better understanding of human judgment. The results of SJT research analyzing persons' cognitive systems indicate that an effective cognitive aid for persons making policy judgments (as is required in policy referendum noting behavior) is needed that pictorially displays the weights, function form, and uncertainties in persons' judgment policies as well as in judgment tasks. By using interactive computer graphics, people involved in the process of interpersonal learning that SJT provides can have pictorial representations of their judgment policies; those representations provide people with complete, accurate feedback about their judgment policies--which otherwise would be unavailable and with which they can reconsider the policy judgment task and their final judgment.

SJT analyzes an individual's cognitive judgement system in four steps, outlined here with an example that places resource valuation within the context of a policy referendum model:

1. The identification of the judgment problem step includes defining the judgment to be made--say, the amount of acreage of roadless forest in Idaho to be allocated to timber production versus wilderness preservation. First, the information (cues) on which judgment should be based needs to be identified, including decision criteria such as perceived gains and losses (e.g., meeting timber production targets, maintenance of resource-dependent communities, availability of recreation/tourism opportunities); behavioral variables and other invariant conditions (e.g., the percent of forest now in a roadless condition, projected timber yield); and

outcome variables (e.g., percent of quality wilderness acreage preserved). Finally, formal properties (e.g., distributions, ranges, and intercorrelations) of the set of cue variables would be determined. Research to correctly identify this information is critical for the rest of the process.

2. The exercise of judgment task, consisting of a number of cases representing the judgment problem, is completed, where each case represents a different combination of values on several cues. For example, trade-offs among cues such as loss of logging jobs, increase in tourism activity, and preservation of gene pools could be made explicit and quantifiable through a budget allocation devise; each profile represents a different allocation (in percentage terms) of a budget to different cues, and each individual indicates his judgments by rating several profiles on a numerical scale.

3. The analysis of judgment step is performed through statistical analyses where the values of the cues are independent variables and the individual's judgments constitute the dependent variable. Again, while the details of ways to implement this step (e.g., use of linear versus nonlinear judgment models) are beyond the scope of this discussion, the crucial point is that this analysis develops a model useful as a cognitive aid for helping an individual learn his/her value trade-off structure.

4. Display of results is the final step of the judgment analysis process. The weights and functional form derived from the previous step are presented immediately to the individual by means of computer graphics displays. Comparisons of the output of various judgment systems that reflect different assumptions about the context of the valuation problem could be made. With the development of the option for subject-controlled revision of weights and function forms and/or request for more detailed information, each respondent could directly change the weights and function forms in his/her judgment policy based on prior judgment outcomes or new information. He/she could then view the new outcomes and make successive revisions in his/her judgment policy. The result would be measurements with a monetary valuation method that incorporates sensitivity analysis as part of the valuation judgment process. Further, given that valuation decision making may involve highly complex, hierarchical judgment problems, multilevel and multistage judgment modelling and analysis could also be accommodated by computer graphic and knowledge-based systems.

The above analysis could be readily developed and applied with the flexibility and power of the knowledge-based systems now available for users of personal computers (PCs). Given the widespread availability of portable PCs, a DSNM based on SJT and its application to describing cognitive systems could be feasibly and economically administered to a small but representative sample of the population of concern. Further, if structured with a clear, easily understood presentation of information, this DSVM could assume a game-like quality that respondents would both enjoy (ensuring high compliance rates) and become absorbed in (ensuring vigilant decision making about values). Work by Weiss (1982) and his associates has chronicled the advantages of computerized interactive testing in the ability area of psychology. Tailored testing procedures, as these are called, achieve greater precision of measurement and economy of test time than conventional tests. Computerized administration of the test can result in greater precision of measurement, increased utility of the test, and reduced cost of its administration.

Perhaps most critically, this DSVM would avoid many of the concerns expressed in other papers in this volume and elsewhere (e.g., Boulding, 1977; Smith, 1986) about existing economic methods for valuing nonmarket goods. Reliability of measurement could be ensured with repeated trials performed by a given respondent, and the measure's validity would be enhanced both by the DSVM's focus on describing and analyzing the respondent's valuation process and by its role as an aid in the decision making basic to that process.

NEEDED RESEARCH

Three major directions for future research are suggested by existing theory and technique in psychology. We have already discussed the first--the need for systematic research to assess the psychometric properties of existing nonmarket evaluation methods. Second, attention should be given to the tasks of developing some consensus about an acceptable theoretical framework for valuing public amenity resources, and then developing a set of standardized, easily-applied economic valuation procedures. Third, the extension of existing methods and the development of new approaches for the valid valuation of public amenity resources deserves attention.

Consensus on Theory and Simplification of Application

A broad perspective on the efficacy of existing nonmarket valuation methods suggests that, if and when their validity and reliability is established, the ultimate test of these methods will rest on their widespread acceptance and use. A direction for future research, then, will be for social scientists to initiate efforts to establish a broad-based consensus among legislators, agency policy/decisionmakers, and concerned social scientists about acceptable evaluative analysis, a viable conceptualization of the valuation process, and defensible methods for measuring values and incorporating them into the political process.

Of particular importance, the pragmatic concerns of some lawmakers and agency decisionmakers with the efficacy of nonmarket economic valuation methods remain an unresolved issue. They will remain so until attempts at building agreement about resource valuation theory and methods are successful. In part, this concensus will require the development of methods perceived to make "good common sense" as well as being theoretically and methodologically sound.

In addition, the full implementation of these methods may require a simplification and standardization of procedures that may be at cross-purposes with complex decision problems or the need for site-specific or resource-specific valuation models and methods. The sometimes extensive data-collection efforts and technical expertise required for existing methods currently

results in most managers using unit day values rather than TCMs or CVMs, and an assessment is needed of how much additional accuracy in value estimates from the TCM and CVM is achieved with the additional costs incurred with their use. If a theoretical consensus and readily applied set of implementation procedures for these methods cannot be developed, their ultimate usefulness for BCA will remain in question.

Extending Existing Approaches and Developing New Ones

A final direction that future research could pursue is that of expanding upon and modifying existing nonmarket economic valuation methods or developing new approaches that have potential for more valid valuation of public amenity resources.

For example, one more dramatic approach that might be taken to achieve economic efficiency would be to create a structure for leasing public resources such as national forests to entities in the private sector, whose activities could then be regulated through the stipulations and specifications of leasing contracts.[9] If the ultimate objective of existing methods is to help achieve an efficient allocation of scarce resources through a market structure, quasi-privatization offers the most direct means of creating a structure that would actually yield market prices. Although implementation of this approach would require certain (perhaps infeasible) conditions, such as the clear definition and assignment of property rights, a shifting of the role of land management agencies from a managerial to a regulatory one, an accounting of transaction costs, and other perhaps unachievable changes, it might be a more cost-effective means of achieving the ends implicit in existing EVMs.

Further study of people's abilities to perform valuation tasks in the context of human decision-making processes is needed. Past applications of the CVM, for example, have been premised on the assumption that consumer decision processes used in the marketplace can be readily transferred to tasks of valuing nonmarket goods. Questions needing further attention include: To what extent does the normative model of economic person underlying the CVM and the decision making it relies upon conform to people's actual economic behaviors? Can people's valuation processes be modelled to help validate the soundness of the values obtained with the CVM? Can new methods developed on the basis of other nonmarket institutions (e.g., political referenda) and a clarification of people's decision structures and processes through applications of SJT provide more appropriate and effective for obtaining values than existing EVMs?

Advantage should be taken of the propensities of survey respondents to be accommodating by developing and using the more interactive approach to value clarification and specification discussed in this paper. This approach parallels the call from some resource planners for replacing the traditional, comprehensive rational planning approach with a transactive planning methodology. Instead of management experts formulating alternatives, evaluating them, choosing the one they deem to be optimum, and then presenting their choice to minimally involved but often highly concerned publics, those publics should serve as planning partners who are integrally involved throughout the transactive planning process (McLaughlin & Force, 1985). In large part, this transactive alternative to the rational-planning mode of many resource management agencies reflects the underlying perception that planning should ultimately be as much a subjective, interactive, and political process as an objective, rational, and quantifiable one.

An interactive planning approach would be advanced by structured value-counseling sessions that enable participants to become familiar with both the good to be valued and the valuation task. Sessions using computerized knowledge-based systems could provide clarification of the context of the problem at hand and ultimately help the participants learn about their values. This approach could help ensure that people's value responses are well-reasoned ones that are not invalidated by the cognitive complexity and stress that may accompany the relatively brief and unfamiliar decision-making process that typifies CVMs.

Although the results of this interactive counseling and policy judgment approach may also fall short of the ideal of objective, reliable, and valid instrumentation sought in survey research, the literature reviewed here and elsewhere suggests that this ideal may remain unrealizable for nonmarket economic valuation methods in their current forms. Given the richness, complexity, and novelty of the value specification task and the grossness of values presently obtained with these methods, interactive elicitation procedures could provide equally defensible and perhaps more valid measures. From a behavioral perspective, a trade-off may be necessary here--one of less reliability (due to the possible influence of researchers on values in the process of the value clarification and learning process) for greater validity (resulting from the greater understanding of the decision problem, familiarity with the good being valued, and the more carefully researched preferences that value counseling sessions might provide). This tradeoff should be an acceptable one--especially if meaningful measurement is the researcher's highest priority, as it must be for the whole exercise to have any true value.

References

Ajzen, I., & Fishbein, M. (1980). Attitudes-behaviors relations: A theoretical analysis and review of empirical research. *Psychology Bulletin, 84,* 888-918.

Allen, P. G., Stevens, T. H., & Barrett, S. A. (1981). The effects of variable omission in the travel cost technique. *Land Economics, 57,* 173-180.

Andrews, R. N. L., & Waits, M. J. (1978). *Environmental values in public decisions: A research agenda.* Unpublished manuscript, School of Natural Resources, University of Michigan, Ann Arbor.

Argyle, M. (1969). *Social interactions.* New York: Atherton Press.

Arrow, K. J. (1976). *Social choice and individual values* (2nd ed.). New York: John Wiley & Sons.

Bartik, T. J. (1987). The estimation of demand parameters in hedonic price functions. *Journal of Political Economics, 95,* 81-88.

Becker, G. S. (1976). *The economic approach to human behavior.* Chicago, IL: University of Chicago Press.

Bettman, J. R. (1979). *An information processing theory of consumer choice.* Reading, MA: Addison-Wesley Publishing Co.

Berger, G. J. (1984). *Applications and assessment of the contingent valuation method for hazardous waste policy in the Washington, DC area.* Unpublished doctoral dissertation, University of New Mexico, Albuquerque.

Beuter, J. (1986). *The economics of below-cost timber sales.* Paper presented to the College of Forestry, Wildlife and Range Sciences, University of Idaho, Moscow.

Bishop, R. C., & Heberlein, T. A. (1979). Measuring values of extra-market goods: Are indirect measures biased? *American Journal Agricultural Economics, 61,* 926-930.

Bishop, R. C., & Heberlein, T. A. (1986). Does contingent valuation work? In R. G. Cummings, D. S. Brookshire, & W. D. Schulze (eds.), *Valuing public goods: An assessment of the contingent valuation method* (pp. 123-147). Totowa, NJ: Rowman and Allanheld Publishers.

Bishop, R. C., Heberlein, T. A. & Kealy, M. J. (1983). Contingent valuation of environmental assets: Comparison with a simulated market. *Natural Resource Journal, 23,* 619-634.

Bohm, P. (1972). Estimating demand for public goods. *Kyklos, 23,* 775-791.

Boulding, K. E. (1977). Prices and other institutions. *Journal of Economic Issues, 11,* 809-821.

Boyle, K. J., & Bishop, R. C. (1984). *Lower Wisconsin River recreation: Economic impacts and scenic values.* Staff Paper No. 216, Department of Agricultural Economics, University of Wisconsin, Madison.

Bradburn, N. M., Rips, L. J., & Shevell, S. K. (1987). Answering autobiographical questions: The impact of memory and inference on surveys. *Science, 236,* 157-161.

Brookshire, D. S., d'Arge, R. C., Schulze W. D., & Thayer, M. A. (1981). Experiments in valuing public goods. In V. K. Smith (ed.), *Advances in applied microeconomics,* (Vol. 1) (pp. 123-172). CT: JAI Press, Inc.

Brookshire, D. S., Coursey, D. L., & Schulze, W. D. (1985). Experiments in the solicitation of private and public values: An overview. Draft prepared for L. Green & J. Kagel (eds.), *Advances in behavioral economics.* (in press).

Brookshire, D. S., Ives, B., & Schulze, W. D. (1976). The valuation of aesthetic preferences. *Journal Environmental Economics and Management, 3,* 325-346.

Brookshire, D. S., Randall, A., d'Arge, R. C., Eubanks, L. S., Stoll, J. R., Crocker, T. D., & Johnson, S. (1977). *Methodological experiments in valuing wildlife resources: Phase I interim report to the United States Fish and Wildlife Service.* Resource and Environmental Economics Laboratory, University of Wyoming, Laramie, WY.

Brookshire, D. S., Randall, A., & Stoll, J. (1980). Valuing increments and decrements in natural resource service flows. *American Journal Agricultural Economics, 62,* 477-488.

Brookshire, D. S., Schulze, W. D., Thayer, M. A., & d'Arge, R. C. (1982). Valuing public goods: A comparison of survey and hedonic approaches. *American Economics Review, 72,* 165-177.

Brookshire, D. S., Thayer, M. A., Tischirhard, J., & Schulze, W. D. (1984). *A test of the expected utility model: Evidence from earthquake risks.* Unpublished manuscript, University of Wyoming, Laramie.

Brown, G., Jr., & Mendelsohn, R. (1984). The hedonic travel cost method. *Review of Economics and Statistics, 66,* 427-433.

Brown, J., & Rosen, S. (1982). On estimation of structural hedonic price models. *Econometrica, 50,* 765-768.

Brown, T. (1984). The concept of value in resource allocation. *Land Economics, 60,* 231-246.

Brown, W. G., Sorhus, C., Yang, B. C., & Richards, J. A. (1983). Using individual observations to estimate recreation demand functions. *American Journal Agricultural Economics, 65,* 154-157.

Buggie, F. D. (1983). Focus Groups: Search for the right product. *Management Review, 72,* 39-41.

Burt, O. R., & Brewer, D. (1971). Estimation of net social benefits from outdoor recreation. *Econometrica, 39,* 813-827.

Cacioppo, J. T., Petty, R. E., & Stoltenberg, C. D. (1985). Process of social influence: The elaboration likelihood model of persuasion. *Advances in Cognitive-Behavioral Research and Therapy, 4,* 214-274.

Calder, B. J. (1977). Focus groups and the nature of qualitative marketing research. *Journal of Marketing Research, 14,* 353-364.

Campbell, D. T., & Fiske, R. W. (1959). Convergent and discriminant validation by the multitrait-multimethod matrix. *Psychology Bulletin, 52,* 81-105.

Carson, R. T., & Mitchell, R. C. (1985). *The value of clear water: The public's willingness to pay for boatable, fishable, and swimmable quality water* (Discussion Paper QE 85-08). Washington, DC: Resources for the Future.

Caulkins, P. P., Bishop, R. C., & Bowes, N. W. (1985). Omitted cross-price variable biases in the linear travel cost model: Correcting common misperceptions. *Land Economics, 61*, 182-187.

Cesario, F. J., & Knetsch, J. L. (1970). Time bias in recreation benefit estimates. *Water Resources Research, 6*, 700-704.

Cicchetti, C. J., Fisher, A. C., & Smith, V. K. (1976). An economic evaluation of a generalized consumer surplus measure: The Mineral King controversy. *Econometrica, 44*, 1259-1276.

Cocheba, D. J., & Langford, W. A. (1981). Direct willingness-to-pay questions: An analysis of their use for quantitatively valuing wildlife. *Journal Leisure Research, 13*, 311-322.

Coursey, D. L., Schulze, W. D., & Hovis, J. J. (1983). *A comparison of alternative valuation mechanisms for non-market commodities.* Unpublished manuscript, Department of Economics, University of Wyoming, Laramie.

Coursey, D. L., Schulze, W. D., & Hovis, J. J. (1984). *On the supposed disparity between willingness to accept and willingness to pay measures of value: A comment.* Unpublished manuscript, Department of Economics, University of Wyoming, Laramie.

Cronbach, L. J., & Meehl, P. E. (1955). Construct validation in psychological tests. *Psychology Bulletin, 52*, 281-302.

Cummings, R. G., Brookshire, D. S., & Schulze, W. D. (eds.). (1986). *Valuing public goods: An assessment of the contingent valuation method.* Totowa, NJ: Rowman and Allanheld Publishers.

Cummings, R. G., Schulze, W. D., Brookshire, D. S., & Gerking. S. D. (1983). *A note on comparing the elasticity of substitution of wages for municipal infrastructure: A comparison of the survey and wage hedonic approaches.* Unpublished manuscript, University of New Mexico, Santa Fe.

Daubert, J. T., & Young, R. A. (1981). Recreational demands for maintaining instream flows: A contingent valuation approach. *American Journal of Agricultural Economics, 63*, 666-676.

Desvousges, W., Smith, V. K., & McGivney, M. (1983). *A comparison of alternative approaches for estimating recreation and related benefits of water quality improvement.* (EPA-230-05-83-001). Washington, DC: U. S. Environmental Protection Agency, Office of Policy Analysis.

Dickie, M., Fisher, A., & Gerking, S. (1985). *Market transactions and hypothetical demand data: A comparative study.* Unpublished manuscript, University of Wyoming, Laramie.

Driver, B. L. (1985). Specifying what is produced by management of wildlife by public agencies. *Leisure Sciences, 7*, 281-295.

Driver, B. L., & Harris, C. C. (1981). Improving measurement of the benefits of outdoor recreation programs. In *Proceedings of the XVII Congress, International Union of Forest Resource Organization* (pp. 525-537), Kyoto, Japan.

Driver, B. L., Phillips, C., Bergersen, E. P., & Harris, C. C. (1985). Using angler preference data in defining types of sport fisheries to manage. *Transactions of the North American Wildlife and Natural Resource Conference, 49*, 82-90.

Edwards, S. F., & Anderson, G. D. (1987). Overlooked biases in contingent valuation surveys: Some considerations. *Land Economics, 63*, 168-178.

Eichner, A. S. (1986, Nov./Dec.). Can economics become a science? *Challenge*, 4-12.

Epple, D. (1987). Hedonic price and implicit markets: Estimating demand and supply functions for differentiated products. *Journal of Political Economics, 95*, 59-80.

Feenburg, D., & Mills, E. (1980). *Measuring the benefits of water pollution abatement.* New York: Academic Press.

Fischhoff, B. (1977). Cost-benefit analysis and the art of motorcycle maintenance. *Policy Science, 8*, 177-202.

Fischhoff, B., Goitein, B., & Shapira, Z. (1982). The experienced utility of expected utility approaches. In N. T. Feather (ed.), *Expectations and actions: Expectancy-value models in psychology.* Hillsdale, NJ: Erlbaum.

Fishbein, M., & Ajzen, I. (1975). *Belief, attitude, intention and behavior: An introduction to theory and research.* Reading, MA: Addison-Wesley.

Fisher, A., & Raucher, E. (1984). Intrinsic benefits of improved water quality: Conceptual and empirical perspectives. In V. K. Smith (ed.), *Advances in applied economics.* Greenwich, CT: JAI Press.

Freeman, A. M., III. (1979). *The benefits of environmental improvement: Theory and practice.* Baltimore, MD: Johns Hopkins Press.

Greenley, D. A., Walsh, R. G., & Young, R. A. (1981). Option value: Empirical evidence from a case study of recreation and water quality. *Quarterly Journal of Economics, 96*, 657-672.

Gregory, R., & Furby, L. (in press). Auctions, experiments and contingent valuation. *Public Choice.*

Greig, P. J. (1983). Recreation evaluation using a characteristics theory of consumer behavior. *American Journal of Agricultural Economics, 65*, 90-97.

Groves, T., & Ledyard, J. (1977). Optimal allocation of public goods: A solution to the free rider problem. *Econometrica, 45*, 263-291.

Gunn, C. (1979). *Tourism planning.* New York: Crane Russak.

Hammond, K. R., Mumpower, J. L., & Smith. T. H. (1977). Linking environmental models with models of human judgement: A symmetrical decision aid. *IEEE Transactions on Systems, Man, and Cybernetics, 7*, 358-378.

Hammond, K. R., Steward, T. R., Brehmer, B., & Steinmann, D. (1974). *Social judgement theory* (Report No. 176, Program of Research on Human Judgement and Social Interaction). Institute of Behavioral Science, University of Colorado, Boulder.

Hannemann, W. M. (1985). Statistical issues in discrete response contingent valuation studies. *Northeastern Journal of Agricultural Research Economics, 4*, 5-12.

Harris, C. C., Driver, B. L., & McLaughlin W. J. (1987). *Assessing contingent valuation methods from a psychological perspective.* Unpublished manuscript, Department of Wildland Recreation Management, University of Idaho, Moscow.

Harris, C. C., & McGown, M. (1986). *The propriety of applying economic methods to the allocation of public amenity resources: Paradigms, property rights, and progress.* Paper presented at the First National Symposium on the Social Sciences in Natural Resource Management, Oregon State University, Corvallis.

Haspell, A. E., & Johnson, F. R. (1982). Multiple destination trip bias in recreation benefit estimation. *Land Economics, 58*, 364-372.

Hovis, J. J., Coursey, D., & Schulze, W. (1983). *A comparison of alternative valuation mechanisms for nonmarket commodities.* Unpublished manuscript, University of Wyoming, Laramie.

Huston, T. (1974). *Foundations of interpersonal attraction.* New York: Academic Press.

Janis, I. L., & Terwilliger, R. (1962). An experimental study of psychological resistance to fear-arousing communications. *Journal of Abnormal and Personal Psychology, 65*, 403-410.

Kahn, A. E. (1966). The tyranny of small decisions: Market failures, imperfections, and the limits of economics. *Kyklos, 19*, 23-47.

Kahneman, D. (1986). Comments. In R. G. Cummings, D. S. Brookshire, & W. D. Schulze (eds.), *Valuing public goods: An assessment of the contingent valuation method* (pp. 185-194). Totowa, NJ: Rowman and Allanheld Publishers.

Kahneman, D., & Tversky, A. (1984). Choices, values, and frames. *American Psychology, 29*, 341-350.

Kidder, L. H. (1980). *Selltiz, Wrightsman and Cook's research methods in social relations* (4th ed.). New York: Holt, Rinehart and Winston.

Kleindorfer, P. R., & Kunreuther, H. (1983). Misinformation and equilibrium in insurance markets. In J. Finsinger (ed.), *Issues in pricing and regulation.* Boston, MA: Lexington Books.

Knetsch, J. L., & Davis, R. K. (1966). Comparisons of methods for recreation evaluation. In A. V. Kneese & S. C. Smith (eds.), *Water research* (pp. 125-142). Baltimore, MD: Johns Hopkins Press.

Kuttner, R. (1985). The poverty of economics. *Atlantic Monthly, 255*, 74-80, 82-84.

Ladd, G. W., & Zober, M. (1977). Model of consumer reaction to product characteristics. *Journal of Consumer Research, 4*, 89-101.

Ladd, G. W., & Zober, M. (1979). Comment. *Journal of Consumer Research, 6*, 85-86.

Lancaster, K. J. (1966). A new approach to demand theory. *Journal of Political Economics, 74*, 132-157.

Livengood, K. R. (1983). Value of big game from markets for hunting leases: The hedonic approach. *Land Economics, 59*, 287-291.

McConnell, K. E. (1980). Valuing congested sites. *Journal of Environmental Economics and Management, 7*, 384-394.

McGuire, W. J. (1969). Attitudes and attitude change. In G. Lindsey and E. Aronson (eds.), *Handbook of social psychology* (Vol. 2) (3rd Ed.) (pp. 233-346). New York: Random House.

McLaughlin, W. J., & Force, J. E. (1985). Planners and the planning process: Leaders, followers, partners? In *Foresters' future: Leaders or followers: Proceedings of the 1985 Society of American Foresters National Convention* (pp. 301-306). Society of American Foresters, Bethesda, MD.

Mendelsohn, R., & Brown, G. M. (1983). Revealed preference approaches to valuing outdoor recreation. *Natural Resource Journal, 23,* 607-618.

Milgram, S. (1974). *Obedience to authority.* New York: Harper and Row.

Mitchell, R. C., & Carson, R. T. (1981). *An experiment in determining willingness to pay for national water quality improvements.* (Draft report prepared for the U.S. Environmental Protection Agency). Washington, DC: Resources for the Future.

Mitchell, R. C., & Carson, R. T. (1984). *A contingent valuation estimate of national freshwater benefits: Technical report to the U.S. Environmental Protection Agency.* Washington, DC: Resources for the Future.

Mitchell, R. C., & Carson, R. T. (1985). Comment on option value: Empirical evidence from a case study of recreation and water quality. *Quarterly Journal of Economics, 100,* 291-293.

Mitchell, R. C., & Carson, R. T. (1986). *Using surveys to value the benefits of public goods: The contingent valuation method.* (Draft book manuscript). Washington, DC: Resources for the Future.

Musgrave, R. A., & Musgrave, P. B. (1976). *Public finance in theory and practice* (2nd ed.). New York: McGraw-Hill.

Nisbett, R. E., & Ross, L. (1980). *Human inference: Strategies and shortcomings of social judgement.* Englewood Cliffs, NJ: Prentice-Hall.

Novick, M. R. (1985). *Standards for educational and psychological testing.* Washington, DC: American Psychological Association.

Nunally, J. C. (1978). *Psychometric theory* (2nd ed.). New York: McGraw-Hill.

Payne, J. W. (1976). Task complexity and contingent processing in decisionmaking: An information search and protocol analysis. *Organized Behavior and Human Performance, 16,* 366-387.

Pratt, J. W., Wise, D., & Zeckhauser, R. (1979). Price differences in almost competitive markets. *Quarterly Journal of Economics, 93,* 189-211.

Radner, R. (1975). Satisficing. *Journal of Mathematical Psychology, 2,* 196-215.

Randall, A., Grunwald, O., Johnson, S., Ausness, R., & Pagoulatos, R. (1978). Reclaiming coal surface mines in Central Appalachia: A case study of the benefits and costs. *Land Economics, 54,* 472-489.

Randall, A. (1985). Methodology, ideology and the economics of policy: Why resource economists disagree. *American Journal of Agricultural Economics, 67,* 1022-1029.

Randall, A., Hoehn, J. P., & Brookshire, D. (1983). Contingent valuation surveys for evaluating environmental assets. *Natural Resource Journal, 23,* 635-648.

Ratchford, B. T. (1979). Operationalizing economic models of demand for characteristics. *Journal of Consumer Research, 6,* 76-85.

Rolandi, W. G. (1986, December). Knowledge engineering in practice. *AI Expert,* 58-59.

Rolston, H., III. (1985). Valuing wildlands. *Environmental Ethics, 7,* 23-48.

Rosen, S. (1974). Hedonic prices and implicit markets: Product differentiation in perfect competition. *Journal of Political Economics, 82,* 34-55.

Rosenthal, D. H. (1985). *Can accurate models of recreation demand be estimated if substitute prices are ignored: An empirical investigation.* Unpublished manuscript, Mimeo. Rocky Mountain Forest and Range Experiment Station, Fort Collins, CO.

Rosenthal, D. H., Loomis, J. B., & Peterson, G. L. (1980). *The travel cost model: Concepts and applications* (USDA Forest Service General Technical Report RM-109). Fort Collins, CO: Rocky Mountain Forest and Range Experiment Station.

Rosenthal, D. H., Waldman, D., & Driver, B. L. (1984). Construct validity of instruments measuring recreationists' preferences. *Leisure Science, 5,* 98-108.

Rowe, R., d'Arge, R. C., & Brookshire, D. S. (1980). An experiment on the economic value of visibility. *Journal of Environmental Economics and Management, 7,* 1-19.

Rowe, R. D., & Chestnut, L. G. (1983). Valuing environmental commodities: Revisited. *Land Economics, 59,* 404-410.

Schelling, T. C. (1978). *Micromotives and macrobehavior.* New York: Norton.

Schoemaker, P. J. H. (1982). The expected utility model: Its variants, purposes, evidence and limitations. *Journal of Economic Literature, 20,* 529-563.

Schulze, W. D., Cummings, R. G., Brookshire, D. S., Thayer, M. H., Whitworth, R. L., & Rahmatian, M. (1983). *Experimental approaches to valuing environmental commodities: Vol. II* (Draft final report for Methods Development in Measuring Benefits of Environmental Improvements). Washington, DC: U.S. Environmental Protection Agency.

Schulze, W. D., & Howe, C. W. (1985). Observations on the frontiers and fringes of the neoclassical paradigm. *American Journal of Agricultural Economics, 67,* 1035-1038.

Seller, C., Stoll, J. R., & Chavas, J. P. (1985). Validation of empirical measures of welfare change: A comparison of nonmarket techniques. *Land Economics, 61,* 156-175.

Sen, A. K. (1977). Rational fools: A critique of the behavioral foundations of economic theory. *Philosophy and Public Affairs, 614,* 317-344.

Simon, H. A. (1957). *Models of man.* New York: John Wiley & Sons.

Simon, H. A. (1986, Nov./Dec.). The failure of armchair economics. *Interview Challenge,* 18-25.

Slovic, P. (1972). *From Shakespeare to Simon: Speculations--and some evidence--about man's ability to process information.* Monograph 12. Eugene, OR: ORI Research.

Smith, V. K. (1985, April). Some issues in discrete response contingent valuation studies. *Northeastern Journal of Agricultural Resource Economics,* 1-4.

Smith, V. K. (1986). Comment 2. In D. W. Bromley (ed.), *Natural resource economics.* Boston, MA: Kluwer Nijhoff Publishing.

Smith, V. K., & Desvousges, W. J. (1985). The generalized travel cost model and water quality benefits: A reconsideration. *Southern Economics Journal, 52,* 371-381.

Smith, V. K., Desvousges, W. H., & Fisher, A. (1985). *A comparison of direct and indirect methods for estimating environmental benefits.* Unpublished manuscript, (Nashville, TN: Department of Economics and Business Administration, Vanderbilt University).

Smith, V. K., Desvousges, W. H., & McGivney, M. P. (1983). Estimating water quality benefits: An econometric analysis. *Southern Economics Journal, 50,* 422-437.

Smith, V. K., & Kaoru, Y. (1985). *The hedonic travel cost model: A view from the trenches* (Working Paper No. 85-W31). (Nashville, TN: Department of Economics and Business Administration, Vanderbilt University).

Sorg, C. F., & Loomis, J. B. (1984). *Empirical estimates of amenity forest values: A comparative review* (USDA Forest Service General Technical Report RM-107). Fort Collins, CO: Rocky Mountain Forest and Range Experiment Station.

Stynes, D. J. (1985a) *Simplifying the travel cost method.* Unpublished manuscript, Michigan State University, East Lansing.

Sutherland, R. J. (1982). The sensitivity of travel cost estimates of recreation demand to the functional form and definition of origin zones. *Western Journal of Agricultural Economics, 7,* 87-98.

Thaler, R. (1980). Toward a positive theory of consumer choice. *Journal of Economic Behavior and Organization, 1,* 39-60.

Thayer, M. (1981). Contingent valuation techniques for assessing environmental impact: Further evidence. *Journal of Environmental Economics and Management, 8,* 27-44.

Thayer, M., & Schulze, W. D. (1977). *Valuing environmental quality: A contingent substitution and expenditure approach.* Unpublished manuscript, Department of Economics, University of Southern California, Los Angeles.

Tinsley, H. E. A. (1984). The psychological benefits of leisure counseling (i.e., participation). *Society and Leisure, 7,* 125-140.

Tinsley, H. E. A., Driver, B. L., & Kass, R. A. (1981). Reliability and concurrent validity of the Recreation Experience Preference scales. *Education and Psychological Measurement, 41,* 897-907.

Tinsley, H. E. A., & Johnson, T. L. (1984). A preliminary taxonomy of leisure activities. *Journal of Leisure Research, 16,* 234-244.

Tinsley, H. E. A., & Kass, R. A. (1980). The construct validity of the leisure activities questionnaire and the paragraphs about leisure. *Education and Psychological Measurement, 40,* 219-226.

Tinsley, H. E. A., & Tinsley, D. J. (1986). A theory of the attributes, benefits and causes of leisure experience. *Leisure Sciences, 8,* 1-45.

Tversky, A., & Kahneman, D. (1981). The framing of decisions and the rationality of choice. *Science, 211,* 453-458.

Vaughn, W. J., & Russell, C. S. (1983). Valuing a fishing day: An application of a systematic varying parameter model. *Land Economics, 59,* 450-463.

Vickrey, W. (1961). Counter speculation, auctions, and competitive sealed tenders. *Journal of Finance, 16,* 8-37.

Walsh, R. G., Gillman, R. A., & Loomis, J. B. (1982). *Wilderness resource economics: Recreation use and preservation values.* Englewood, CO: American Wilderness Alliance.

Weiss, D. J. (1982). Improving measurement quality and efficiency with adaptive testing. *Applied Psychological Measurement, 6,* 473-492.

Footnotes

[1] Although some researchers advocate a broader perspective on economic analysis as a comparison of marginal benefits and costs (Becker, 1976), the dollar values generated for BCA with nonmarket economic valuations are often developed for comparisons with commodity values, thereby directly linking them to market analysis within the context of national economic development. In this context, the monetary values derived with nonmarket economic valuation methods are not merely the outcome of the application of marginalist principles; implicitly, they are proxies for market values. In light of their actual and intended use, values obtained with these methods and the propriety of that use require an evaluation of utility and consumer demand theories underlying BCA that is beyond the scope of this paper. It is important to note that concerns about the validity of the basic theories and methods applied in microeconomics increasingly are being raised, both by economists and noneconomic scholars (see, for example, Boulding, 1977; Eichner, 1986; Kuttner, 1985; Schoemaker, 1982; Simon, 1986; Thaler, 1980); the ramifications of these concerns for the soundness of values obtained with Economic Valuation Methods (EVMs) and that of BCAs, which rely on those values, are crucial but have yet to be assessed.

[2] See, for example, Rosenthal, Loomis, and Peterson's (1980) explication of the relation of values for nonmarket goods to prices for forest commodities.

[3] One reviewer of this paper suggested that a consideration of the TCM's assumptions are not necessary: "The issue of robustness appears (to) have been investigated by many and the conclusion is that it is not robust."

[4] The validity of this assumption, however, likely depends upon the kind of trip being taken. Recreation is typically viewed in experiential terms, with psychological benefits being obtained from all components of the trip (e.g., anticipation, trip planning, travel to and from the site, recollection), not merely from the experiences desired at a trip's destination (see Tinsley, 1984; Tinsley & Tinsley, 1986). These other components might be less important for short trips to nearby sites, but they are undoubtedly of major importance for long trips to a site far from an origin. Tinsley and Johnson (1984), for example, report evidence that travel is pleasurable and has value in itself.

[5] Among the reports of studies implementing the HPM and HTCM (e.g., Brookshire et al., 1982, 1984; Brown & Mendelsohn, 1984; Cummings et al., 1983; Greig, 1983; Livengood, 1983; Mendelsohn & Brown, 1983), some preface their empirical operationalization of the demand-for-characteristics approach with a cautionary note that their modeling efforts be used only for illustrative or exploratory purposes. This caution is based on concern over the success of these early modeling efforts: Greig (1983), for example, recognizes that the "predictive performance of the model...is relatively poor" (p. 95), and Livengood's (1983) hedonic price function included variable coefficients with unexpected signs.

[6] We would contend that, given that the "common man's" only experience with decisions about dollar values and expenditures is in the context of the marketplace, the use of monetary value as an index of preference is inescapably grounded in market and thus consumer behavior.

[7] One anonymous reviewer of this paper noted that "the attention paid to sampling considerations in most CV studies to date (is) appalling."

[8] As previously noted, Smith (1985, 1986) and others (Smith & Desvousges, 1985; Smith & Kaoru, 1985) have documented and stressed the role of the researchers' subjective judgements in implementing TCMs and HTCM; Mitchell and Carson (1986) also recognize the "necessarily problematic nature of...judgements (concerning the content validity of CV measures that)...cannot easily be evaluated by empirical or theoretical criteria...it is a matter of judgement" (p. 8-8).

[9] Our recommendation of this approach is not meant to be a frivolous one; indeed, a study is currently being conducted by agricultural economists at the University of Idaho to ascertain the comparative efficiency of private versus public management of national forests in the state of Idaho.

Part 6: Critique and Response

Blind Men and Elephants: Prospects for Integrating Disparate Approaches to Natural Resource Values

F. Reed Johnson
Economics Department
U. S. Naval Academy
and Office of Policy Analysis
U. S. Environmental Protection Agency.

The workshop on Integrating Economic and Psychological Knowledge in Valuations of Public Amenity Resources brought together scholars from a variety of disciplines to examine a proverbial "elephant." At times, I have wondered whether the problem may not be merely that the "blind men" are examining different parts of the "elephant," but different "elephants" as well. Nevertheless, my task is to identify the "major issues" relating to this workshop.

One strategy would be simply to point to the titles of the excellent papers that the workshop participants have presented. The Forest Service obviously had major issues in mind in designing the program. Another strategy would be to try summarize the consensus of concerns that emerged in the various discussion groups. The first alternative is obviously trivial and the second is impossible. I have reflected instead on what "major" might mean to each of the three groups participating in the workshop. I have also attempted to evaluate the prospects for integrating these disparate views on natural resource values, or at least for reaching some kind of accommodation.

Resource Values from Three Perspectives

The three groups broadly represented at this workshop are practitioners (i.e., natural resource program managers and policy analysts), academic economists, and academics from other disciplines. Each group has a different basis for their interest in natural resource values and operates within a different institutional and intellectual context. Therefore, what is important or relevant differs among (and to some extent within) these various groups.

Practitioners are generally bound by laws and regulations relating to their particular administrative or policy-making responsibilities. These rules may require balancing economic and other values (as the Forest Service planning process does) or preclude considering certain values (as the Clean Air Act does in prohibiting consideration of compliance costs). Sometimes decision-making rules neither require nor prohibit use of economic values, but pressures from the Office of Management and Budget (OMB), special interests, or internal goals create a demand for such values. The best example is the Executive Order 12291 requirement that regulatory decisions be accompanied by a Regulatory Impact Analysis, whether or not the statutory authority allows such an analysis to be used.

Careful use of economic estimates can serve to avert charges of arbitrary and capricious decisions. It follows that practitioners are primarily interested in credible, uncontroversial, low-cost methods of estimating natural resource values.

Academic economists are notorious intellectual imperialists. Whatever the limitations of data and estimating techniques, most economists remain unshakably devoted to the normative power of economic efficiency. No area of human (or apparently animal) endeavor or concern is safe from their intellectual picks and shovels. The fact that almost nobody else cares about efficient resource allocation does not seem to matter.

My economist colleagues generally have been attracted to natural resources issues by the intellectual challenge of measuring elusive nonmarket values. Most environmentalists harbor deep suspicions of economics and economists, but many natural resource economists are, in fact, closet "tree huggers." They believe that properly measured nonconsumptive values are often large enough to compete with commercial values and therefore correct benefit-cost comparisons will frequently favor preservation and conservation alternatives.

Whatever their priors may be about the relative magnitudes of nonconsumptive and consumptive values, academic economists have a specific set of intellectual tools at their disposal. These tools derive from standard economic theory and available quantitative methods and are designed to yield monetary measures of expected welfare changes. Like any other scientific paradigm, the economic paradigm identifies only particular questions as interesting and answerable. These intellectual blinders limit the realm of meaningful dialogue with sister disciplines. In particular, questions about nonmonetary measures of natural resource benefits are regarded as neither interesting nor answerable.

The third group represented at this workshop consists of academics from other disciplines--primarily psychology and sociology. Human experiences relating to natural resources are a fertile field in which to explore a variety of human perceptual and behavioral issues for such noneconomists. For example, Paul Slovic and his colleagues have written extensively on the importance of context in the formation and articulation of values. Because of the wide variety of disciplines and subdisciplines involved, generalization is difficult; however, Baruch Fischoff suggests that the concerns of psychologists and sociologists may be differentiated by the psychologists' preoccupation with "quirky" behavior.

These scholars clearly believe that noneconomic values are important to individual and social well-being. I detect no particular consensus on whether these values are just as important, more important, or the only important values relative to economic measures. However, noneconomists generally do not appear to be as intolerant as the economists.

Unfortunately, the institutional context of natural resource management tends to place noneconomists in a defensive and critical posture. They find themselves emphasizing the complexity of human responses to natural resources as a counterweight to the simplistic behavior of "Homo economicus." This emphasis limits the range of meaningful collaboration with the other two groups, who at least share a common concern for keeping explanations as simple as possible.

Perspectives on a Particular Problem: WTP and WTA

An issue discussed at length in the workshop may serve to illustrate the divergence of concerns among participants. The issue involves discrepancies in empirical willingness to pay (WTP) and willingness to accept compensation (WTA) measures of natural resource values. Practitioners fear that choice of one or the other of these measures leaves their decisions vulnerable to criticism by advocates of the rejected alternative. They resist use of either until there is a clear professional consensus on exactly what circumstances are appropriate for each. Practitioners generally have no interest in the conceptual squabble, per se.

The inconsistency between empirical estimates and standard theory are alarming to many academic economists. They see the problem as one of discovering an explanation consistent with standard theory or adapting the theory in a way that preserves the analytical power of the basic paradigm.

Other academics appear to regard the discrepancy as not at all surprising or even particularly interesting. They are prepared to offer a variety of possible explanations, none of which is likely to be relevant or useful for the economists. One can even detect a certain schadenfreude at the discomfort of the economists in this situation.

Assessing the Success of the Workshop

The different responses to the WTP/WTA issue are fairly typical of those observed for various topics raised in the formal presentations and informal discussions. Despite such different perspectives, was the workshop successful in integrating the various conflicting agendas?

I can respond with some confidence on behalf of two of the three groups, but can only speculate about the third. Putting on my "policy-analyst hat," I would have to respond that the workshop generally did not succeed in integrating my concerns. Discussions tended to drift off onto low-priority technical issues. I found little reassurance that resources invested in methods development have produced operational valuation procedures that can form the basis of standardized protocols. The academics could not even agree under what conditions sample sizes of 25 are acceptable. I was left wondering whether academics of any persuasion understand or care about institutional realities. Of the four declared purposes of the workshop, the first three relate to uses of methods, and only the fourth relates to technical improvements of methods. This emphasis was not reflected in the format or content of the workshop itself.

However, as an academic economist I thought the workshop was generally an integrative success. I was forced to look at what economists are trying to do from the point of view of interested and sympathetic noneconomists. Discussions piqued my interest in ways to adapt economic models to explain behavior that does not fit economists' conventional expectations. I sensed in this workshop more agreement than usual among the economists that there is merit in the research agendas of other disciplines.

I also sensed that the economists sometimes alienated noneconomists at the workshop by their failure to explain their concepts and jargon. The success of the workshop for the other academics depends on answers to some questions that I am not competent to answer. For example, did they understand that managers and analysts must have hard numbers that can withstand the unforgiving scrutiny of interest groups, the courts, and the OMB? Did they understand that fruitful collaboration with economists inevitably involves finding ways to adapt and extend economic models, not destroying them? Finally, did they nevertheless sense the genuine interest in their perspectives and even occasional glimmers of comprehension on the part of practitioners and economists?

Prospects for Integrating Approaches

The director of an interdisciplinary research project with which I was once associated used to worry about the problem of "interdisciplinary cross-sterilization." People have to spend so much time defining terms and explaining elementary concepts that little meaningful interdisciplinary research occurs. The result is that academics generally prefer to "graze quietly on their own turf." Straying into other pastures leads too often to frustration and squandered effort. Nevertheless, there are promising signs of new, fruitful collaborations between natural resource economists and scholars of other disciplines. Schulze and McClelland at the University of Colorado are an obvious example; Bishop and Heberlein at the University of Wisconsin are another.

It is precisely the demands of policy analysis that are motivating much of this collaboration. As we have seen, academic disciplines ask questions and formulate answers in a particular way. However, natural resource management problems rarely sort themselves out along established disciplinary boundaries. Research that is truly responsive to the requirements of policy formulation will usually have to draw on the strengths of more than one discipline.

Narrowly defined economic efficiency can provide only part of the information necessary to answer the question: "What is the best use of a natural resource?" As Schelling (1978) has observed:

> ...we can get carried away with our image of goal seeking and problem solving. We can forget that people pursue misguided goals or don't know their goals, and that they enjoy or suffer subconscious processes that deceive them about their goals. And we can exaggerate how much good is accomplished when people achieve the goals we think they think they have been pursuing. (pp. 18-19)

The effectiveness of goal-seeking behavior, and thus the reliability of the conventional economic model, is especially problematic in such nonmarket, relatively unfamiliar choice situations often associated with environmental and natural resources. It is in analyzing these choices and implicit benefits that economics can be informed by the rich hypotheses of other behavioral sciences. These other sciences can, in turn, be informed by the quantitative rigor and formal logic of economics.

Suggestions for a Future Workshop

A future workshop might well take advantage of the integrative framework provided by natural resource policy problems. Two or three management decisions could be presented by groups of practitioners to various economists and noneconomists in advance of the meeting. Participants would respond with papers incorporating their own discipline's perspective on the problem, supporting their analysis with empirical estimates where possible. At the workshop, discussions would focus on combining the elements of the various perspectives to construct as complete and useful an analysis as possible. Discussions would be chaired by resource managers who would ensure that the discussion addressed policy-relevant and institutionally appropriate issues.

This format would ensure that the "blind men" at least examined the same "elephant." Whether or not they are able to describe and analyze the "beast" in a meaningful and useful way would provide a convincing test of the possibility of integrating disparate approaches to natural resource values.

Reference

Schelling, T. C. (1978). *Micromotives and macrobehavior* (pp. 18-19). New York: W. W. Norton and Co.

A Camel Is A Camel Is ...

Alan Randall
Department of Agricultural Economics and Rural Sociology
Ohio State University.

The purpose of this workshop, as I understand, was to evaluate the progress and prospects with respect to the contingent valuation method (CVM), and to do this in a multidisciplinary social science setting. Nevertheless, the social science disciplines are not co-equal in this context. The underlying objective was to measure benefits and costs in the standard welfare-economic framework, which placed economists firmly in control of the agenda. Rather than a co-equal multidisciplinary exchange about valuation broadly construed, it seems that the purpose of this workshop was to find out what economists can learn from each other and from other social scientists about more effective use of the CVM.

Given the time and space constraints imposed necessarily on the commentators, I have discarded any ambition to provide a reasonably complete summary and critique of the proceedings. It would be absurd to attempt to summarize and critique a set of papers weighing at least 10 pounds in manuscript form plus at least 10 hours of split-session discussions, in a single-digit number of pages. Rather, I chose to elaborate just a few points worth considering at this stage in the development of the CVM research program.

Status of the CVM

I am pleased to observe that discussion of CVM has reached a certain stage of maturity. No longer are we asking "does CVM work?" and no longer is a simple theoretical assertion or some particular characteristic of a single data set cited as proof that CVM, generically, works or does not work. By now, a convincing body of evidence supports the notion that CVM seldom does badly and often works surprisingly well. Further, there seems to be widespread recognition that CVM includes a considerable variety of question forms and research procedures. Particular applications can be examined and critiqued for consistency with the welfare-economic framework, appropriate incentives for careful value formulation and unbiased value reporting, contextual validity, and competent research procedures for sampling, data collection and handling, analysis, and interpretation of results. Some applications will withstand this scrutiny, rejecting the pessimist's conjecture that CVM never works; other applications will fail, confirming that CVM, too, must submit to Murphy's Law--anything that can just conceivably go wrong will.

CVM Within the PPI Framework

I believe it is best to treat the welfare-economic basis of CVM as nonnegotiable. CVM is one technique for generating value estimates that can be interpreted directly in the potential Pareto-improvement (PPI) or benefit-cost analysis (BCA) framework. The PPI is a particular utilitarian solution to the fundamental problem of political ethics. It can be derived from a small number of simple ethical premises:

1. What the individual wants is good for that individual. This implies that all value derives from human preferences, and that individual preferences are not subject to review by other individuals or the group at large.
2. Individual valuations reflect individual preferences and endowments. It follows that those things preferred by the well-endowed count for more, under the PPI criterion.
3. Societal valuations are determined by simple aggregation of individual valuations.
4. A proposal is determined to be a PPI if the aggregate willingness to pay (WTP) of its beneficiaries exceeds the aggregate compensation demanded by its victims. The PPI makes no provision for the actual payment of compensation.

It is important to recognize that these premises implement a specialized form of utilitarianism, and that the PPI is therefore a particular system of political ethics. The PPI has well-established relationships with market prices and economic efficiency but, I insist, these relationships are secondary to the PPI's status as a system of political ethics. Thus, the PPI is not an attempt to impose the alien values of the market on those aspects of human existence that are customarily the agenda of policy.

None of this suggests that the PPI is a compelling criterion for public decisions. It is perfectly legitimate to argue that any one, or perhaps every one, of its underlying premises is ethically repugnant. But, unfortunately, that is also true of rival ethical systems. It is characteristic of ethical systems that none is universally compelling.

Nevertheless, I argue that the PPI criterion for BCA should be nonnegotiable: If it goes by the name of BCA, it must be a test of PPI's. Then, BCA is at least an unambiguous activity. Anyone who cares can expediently ascertain the ethical and welfare-economic underpinnings of any BCA that implements the PPI criterion. It is better to accept BCA for what it is and debate directly the issue of whether it should serve as a public decision criterion (in general or in particular cases) than to become embroiled in the ultimately impossible task of somehow modifying BCA to make it a compelling criterion for public decisions.

To use a metaphor, BCA is a camel. A camel may seem to be a thoroughly imperfect animal. A multidisciplinary team of critics might find fault with its appearance (the heavy eyelids, the sagging and protruding lower lip, the absurdly large feet, and the ridiculously small tail), its vestigial vocal range, its legendary bad temper, and its functional restrictions (e.g., it is totally useless in mud and water). A committee might suggest a substantial redesign, extending perhaps to the addition of fins and flippers for aquatic travel.

I would counsel against such a strategy. The camel is at least unambiguous; once the initial confusion surrounding the dromedary has been cleared away, everyone knows what a camel is. Also, the camel does have its own place in the broader scheme of things. Rather than a multidisciplinary effort to design the perfect animal, it seems more appropriate that the various thought-systems each develop one or a few animals consistent with its own fundamental premises. Within the basic outline for each animal, there may well be questions of design and execution that cry out for multidisciplinary solution, and that should be sought. Nevertheless, the fundamental premises should be followed faithfully, to produce a variety of unique but internally consistent animals. Then, it is entirely appropriate that there be rivalry among particular animals for particular functional purposes, but also a broader ecosystem in which various and diverse animals each have a niche.

My line of reasoning suggests that it is best for CVM to be performed within the PPI framework, recognizing that other evaluative systems may also be applied and may compete for attention in a complex and participatory public decision process. Thus, I argue that the PPI basis for CVM should be nonnegotiable, but that the PPI is itself noncompelling as a public decision criterion. The noneconomic social science disciplines each have a broad and legitimate agenda of their own. Nevertheless, in the particular context of CVM, it is best that they attempt to contribute by suggesting more effective ways to perform CVM within the PPI framework, rather than by telling economists that they really ought to abandon the PPI in favor of some alternative, but equally noncompelling, ethical framework.

CVM Values Are Constructs, but So What?

Several of the papers have mentioned that the values estimated with CVM are constructs: They are situational, contextual, and, to that extent, artifacts of the particular CVM device that measures them. I have no quarrel with this. However, some who are not economists and, more surprising to me, some who are economists seem to believe that this constitutes, in and of itself, some kind of flaw in CVM. To the contrary, all economic values are situational, contextual, and relative. There is no fixed point on some dollar scale that represents the value of, say, oil. Rather, its economic value fluctuates depending on underlying supply and demand conditions, inflation and the value of the U.S. dollar relative to other currencies, public and corporate policies in the net-importer nations, and the ability of the Organization of Petroleum Exporting Countries' coalition to achieve a consensus about goals and the methods for implementing them. Neophyte economists learn that one of the great virtues of price is its tendency to adjust rapidly to changing conditions, in so doing, transmitting information and relaying incentives for equilibrating adjustments.

The relativistic and contextual nature of price--and of value measures such as consumer's surplus, that might be measured with CVM--is a reality. For CVM, the issue is not eliminating contextual influences on CVM-generated values, but making sure that the inevitable contextual influences reflect the appropriate context. Those contextual influences that are mere artifacts of arbitrary features in a particular CVM design are troublesome; the fact that values are inherently contextual is not.

The Contingent Policy Choice Referendum

A recent development, the contingent policy choice referendum, holds considerable promise for "getting the context right" when the task is to estimate the benefits of environmental public goods. Traditional methods of contingent valuation have been based on a market analogy, even where public goods were at

issue. This has the advantage of consistency with the economic theory of welfare change measurement, but also the disadvantage of introducing a degree of cognitive dissonance by imposing a market analogy on a context that citizens are accustomed to conceptualizing in policy terms. Recent developments in understanding the referendum format and interpreting its results suggest that certain referendum formats offer the advantages of traditional CVM without the disadvantages.

First, we now understand that the market analogy is not essential for welfare change measurement in the PPI framework. The PPI is fundamentally a criterion of political ethics and its relationship to certain market-generated value measures is secondary. Second, analytical methods are now available for generating welfare change measures from discreet choice data, such as might be generated by referendum formats (Bishop & Heberlein, 1979; Hanemann, 1984; Sellar, Stoll, & Chavas, 1985). Third, it is now understood that certain referendum formats are incentive-comparable (Hoehn & Randall, in press). These developments establish the contingent policy choice referendum as a valid, and perhaps preferred, form of CVM. For evaluating policies that would change the level of environmental public goods, it has the particular virtue that it confirms and harnesses the ordinary citizen intuition that the level of such goods is typically a policy question.

Estimation of WTA remains a challenge for CVM. Empirical studies typically find a rather substantial divergence between WTP and willingness to accept (WTA). However, there seems to be no consensus as to the interpretation of these divergences. First, with quantity-rationed goods, economic theory suggests that WTP and WTA may diverge considerably in some cases. The Randall-Stoll (Randall & Stoll, 1980) analysis generates formulae for using observations of one measure to generate approximations of the other. It does not provide an argument that they are typically approximately equal. Thus, some (perhaps considerable) divergence between WTP and WTA is real, not an artifact of measurement error.

Second, some psychological evidence suggests that people are risk-conservative and loss-conservative. These characteristics would lead to relatively large values for WTA. However, there is a smattering of experimental evidence that, with repetition and learning, WTP and WTA tend to converge. Researchers appear to be in some disagreement as to whether large values for WTA, reflecting loss-conservatism, should be treated as valid for welfare change measurement or merely pathological responses that can be "cured" with effort and ingenuity on the part of the researcher.

Third, "market analogy" CVM formats to estimate WTA invite participants to individually accept (or reject) decrements in public goods in return for individual compensation. Probing of refusals to accept finite compensation reveals a tendency to recoil from "selling out" one's compatriots. Clearly, this third source of large WTA values must be treated as measurement error.

The contingent policy choice referendum offers the potential for estimating WTA in a manner that avoids this third source of divergence. A referendum format for WTA invites participants to cast one vote for (or against) a policy to simultaneously reduce public goods and the prices and taxes everyone pays. "Selling out" is not a problem, and one source of unambiguous measurement error is avoided.

In summary, for valuing environmental public goods typically provided by public policies, the contingent policy choice referendum appears to offer an important opportunity for obtaining value estimates in the appropriate context.

Requiem for the Reference Operating Conditions?

One may observe that the contingent policy choice referendum systematically violates the celebrated "reference operating conditions" (ROCs) of Cummings, Brookshire, and Schulze (1986). This is not surprising, because the ROCs are rooted fundamentally in the traditional, "market analogy" form of CVM. Given the mutual incompatibility of the ROCs and the contingent policy choice referendum, my inclination is to challenge the ROCs. Frankly, the evidence for the ROCs is mostly impressionistic, while the arguments for the contingent policy choice referendum have a sound theoretical basis.

I conjecture that the day will come when the ROCs are viewed not as the beginning of a new era for CVM, but as the end of the first era: The era when valid CVM was believed to require imposition of the market analogy regardless of the essential characteristics--exclusive or nonexclusive, rival or nonrival--of the goods and amenities subject to valuation. Future applications of CVM to public goods seem likely to develop in the direction of the contingent policy choice referendum. This approach offers the best of both worlds: desirable cognitive characteristics, and the generation of data that can be interpreted in PPI terms.

Concluding Comment

There is much that the other social sciences can contribute to the development of CVM. This potential contribution includes the body of methods and research results that constitute the core of each discipline, but also certain attitudes: an awareness of need for clear communication between researcher and respondent and the avoidance of cognitive dissonance; an alertness to the specifics of each application--the particulars of context and method that make it unique; a respect for the niceties of experimental method, sampling, and data handling--a respect sometimes absent among economists; and a willingness to challenge the market analogy whenever it seems inappropriate. These contributions will lead to improved CVM and more satisfactory BCA, that is, to better camels.

I am less sanguine about the kinds of contributions that amount to an attempt to reformulate CVM, BCA, and the PPI generically until they are no longer recognizable. My point is not that these things are currently perfect--far from it--but that the search of the perfect policy evaluation framework, the perfect animal, is foredoomed. Because no perfect animal exists, the other social sciences can play their part by helping to improve the CVM/BCA/PPI camel while, at the same time, each working on its own animals that coexist, and compete, with the camel.

References

Bishop, R. C., & Heberlein, T. A. (1979). Measuring values of environmental assets: Are indirect measures biased? *American Journal of Agricultural Economics, 61*, 926-930.

Cummings, R. G., Brookshire, D. S., & Schulze, W. D. (Eds.). (1986). *Valuing environmental goods: An assessment of the contingent valuation method.* Totowa, NJ: Rowman and Allanheld.

Hanemann, M. (1984). Welfare evaluations in contingent valuation experiments with discrete responses. *American Journal of Agricultural Economics, 66*, 332-341.

Hoehn, J. P., & Randall, A. (in press). A satisfactory benefit cost indicator from contingent valuation. *Journal of Environmental Economics and Management.*

Randall, A., & Stoll, J. (1980). Consumer's surplus in commodity space. *American Economic Review, 70*, 449-454.

Sellar, C., Stoll, J., & Chavas, J.P. (1985). Validation of empirical measures of welfare change: A comparison of nonmarket techniques. *Land Economics, 61*, 156-175.

Integrating Social Science Research in the Contingent Valuation Method: An Overview

Victor Brajer
Department of Economics
California State University at Fullerton

Ronald G. Cummings
Department of Economics
University of New Mexico

Over the past decade, interest in the contingent valuation method (CVM) for valuing nonmarket goods has increased immeasurably. Despite this interest, many researchers feel that development of the CVM by economists has been somewhat narrow, both theoretically and methodologically, and that the efforts of other social scientists can aid in further developing this method. Towards that purpose, a group of highly respected resource economists, psychologists, and other behavioral scientists were assembled at the Workshop on Integrating Economic and Psychological Knowledge in Valuations of Public Amenity Resources, held in Estes Park, Colorado, May 1986.

In this chapter, we summarize the presentations and discussions of some of these participants. Of course, this chapter is not intended to be a comprehensive review of all that was said at the workshop; for that, the interested reader is referred to the other chapters in this volume. Instead, our intent is to highlight the more interesting points raised in various papers presented at the workshop, and to critique them in terms of the current state of the art of the CVM, as we perceive it.

In a recent work, Cummings, Brookshire, and Schulze (1986)[1] examined the state of the art of the CVM, and made several general observations concerning previous CVM efforts. First, a lack of consensus was noted among researchers as to the priority of issues in CVM research that warrant further empirical focus. Past research efforts were seen as scattered and diffuse, with empirical applications outstripping inquiry regarding how individuals behave within contingent markets. In this regard, V. Kerry Smith (1986) argued that the relevant state of the art in CVM was one in which little could be said, quantitatively or qualitatively, about the implications of various problems (e.g., the familiarity problem) because no model of how individuals behave or respond existed in the CVM literature.

A second general conclusion reached by Cummings et al. (1986) relates to the differences between values based on "willingness to pay" (WTP) and those based on "willingness to accept" (WTA) compensation. With no compelling case having yet been made that WTP and WTA measures are related to "true" valuations, Cummings et al. (1986) clearly implied that more attention should be given to the collection and analysis of psychological and attitudinal data in future CVM studies. Further, Kahneman and Tversky's (1979) "prospect theory" arguments were found to be not only intuitively appealing, but also consistent with considerable empirical findings, and certainly worthy of further consideration. It was also concluded that any suggested "burial" of WTA might be premature, and additional research was needed to focus on explaining the differences between WTP and WTA.

Finally, Cummings et al. (1986) noted that CVM researchers had been defensive and apologetic in the past, due to the feeling that CVM responses were in some way inferior to hard market data. Overall, they concluded that it was time to replace apologies with a positive research agenda.

The workshop represented a significant step in addressing the bulk of these issues. New modeling efforts were initiated, the WTP/WTA disparity was examined in more detail, and the behavior of subjects in the contingent valuation interview situations was given careful consideration by many well-known behavioral scientists. In the following pages, we attempt to outline some of the more significant points and issues raised by the workshop participants.

At the outset, the work by Kaiser, Brown, and Davis served to set the tone for the workshop. They began by pointing out that amenity values are merely a subset of the many values recognized in socio-economic analysis. The key word here is "subset," which reminds us of the point of the whole workshop--that economic values are sometimes incapable of measuring the full range of positive and/or negative effects on individuals that may accompany changes in environmental quality. This fact clearly establishes the need for other social scientists in the development of the CVM.

This need for interdisciplinary collaboration in CVM research, stressed by Kaiser et al., lies at the heart of two other workshop papers. In the first, Boulding and Lundstedt offered an excellent comparison between economic and psychological ideas of valuation. In doing so, they made a point central to the spirit of the workshop, that the economist's view of value is limited in certain ways, and we (as economists) can learn some things from other social scientists (especially psychologists), regarding the notion of value. The totally different orientation assumed by economists and psychologists is cleverly and effectively pointed out by Boulding and Lundstedt through their discussion of the possibilities boundary. They note that "what an economist called an equilibrium, where economic man goes placidly and happily to the point of his highest welfare..., psychologists call 'frustration.' On a more general level, Boulding and Lundstedt note the importance of recognizing that "all data, and especially so-called scientific data, consists of evidence, not of absolute truth."

This point is also stressed by MacLean and Mills, who note the value-laden nature of what we call "hard science," as values "seep into science at many junctures, determining what to count as evidence, how to report findings, the bases for accepting or rejecting theories, and so on." McLean and Mills also offer a philosophical discussion (somewhat more specific than the Boulding-Lundstedt argument) through their examination of behavioral decision theory (prospect theory). Their main theme is that we have been less clear than we should about "distinguishing the normative from the empirical and understanding the relationship between them." In their consideration of the valuation issue, MacLean and Mills conclude that loss aversion and framing (two aspects of prospect theory) are totally acceptable as parts of the correct empirical account of behavior, and that "theoretical considerations should lead us to a more basic explanation, which can apply to a wider range of problems." Prospect theory, in their view, provides such a basic explanation.

In addition, MacLean and Mills' comparison between the psychologists' and economists' viewpoints reveals an interesting and important difference. When faced with an obvious disparity between WTP and WTA (which, from the standpoint of economic theory, should not have existed), economists in the past were quick to dismiss (deny) this disparity and to proclaim WTP as the "correct" measure (see Cummings et al. [1986] regarding the premature "burial" of WTA). Psychologists, however, accepted the disparity between WTP and WTA, and attempted to offer (in this workshop, for example) reasons for the difference.

Finally, MacLean and Mills, through their analysis of the Coase Theorem, raise the important issue (also made by Boulding and Lundstedt) that the economist's view is only one view of how people make decisions. The limitedness of this view, along with the confusion that can arise between the "normative" and the "empirical," has been revealed in the case of expected utility, for example, by the repeated violations of the theory observed in actual behavior, and the continued belief in the theory.

In these regards, the tremendous amount of empirical studies made in recent years may have had both positive and negative results. One beneficial aspect is that, today, the environment is given a "fairer" valuation, certainly a more careful one. The negative side, however, is that perhaps "too many" empirical studies are performed. Instead of developing a comprehensive theoretical and methodological base, attention in CVM research has focused solely on churning out value estimates. This is essentially the point stressed by Driver and Burch, who note the danger inherent in the overemphasis on empirical work in CVM research, which must be viewed as exploratory or in the development stage. Driver and Burch argue that such emphasis has resulted in greater specialization that has encouraged overly myopic disciplinary perspectives. They contribute two important points for future amenity resource valuation efforts: a reminder of the need for interdisciplinary research efforts and, perhaps more importantly, a discussion of the difficulties (e.g., overlapping and conflicting goals) facing federal and state land management agencies that will use these values. In regard to the first point, Driver and Burch note that a variety of valuation methods will probably be needed, involving various systems of accounts. Concerning the second point, they develop a comprehensive valuation paradigm, and in so doing, remind us of the necessary and difficult steps involved in actually valuing amenity resources.

One potential problem that Driver and Burch feel may be implied by these analyses is that policymakers may be asking for simple answers to complex valuation issues. The merging of economics and psychology may be of academic interest, but it also may lead to conclusions or answers that policymakers do not want to hear. This point leads Driver and Burch to call for the development of "social values," implying environmental valuation measures which, while perhaps eclectic or complicated, are based on comparable philosophical foundations, consistent accounting stances, and values preferably expressed in dollar terms.

In a similar vein, Kaiser et al. argue that two important issues still need to be addressed before extramarket valuation can be fully integrated into resource analysis. The first concerns the development of values that share the same theoretical and philosophical foundation with market values, and the second deals with understanding why individuals establish values for social services involving natural resources. While the second point, understanding why individuals establish values, is obviously a key question, it does not seem as clear why we want resource values that share a foundation, either theoretical or philosophical, with "market" values, given that the types of environmental goods being considered here fall more into the category of "public goods," which might be better allocated with a mechanism other than the free market. This is admittedly a departure from traditional economic thinking on valuation issues, yet was a point addressed by several workshop participants.

Brown and Slovic reach a similar conclusion, arguing that economic valuation is merely a subset of the types of valuation methods that can be employed for resource valuation. They observe that an economic measure of value (for example, a demand function) is but one context-specific measure of assigned value. More specifically, Brown and Slovic question the "truth" in economic valuations, which can be affected by the context of the decision situation. By examining context effects and the role of context, they offer explanations for why context might affect respondents. In doing so, they also examine the attitude/opinion forming process, developing a quantitative modeling effort to explain people's behavior in the CVM setting. The contextual ideas developed in their paper have implications not only for future CVM design and research, but also for more general economic issues as well, for example, expected utility theory. It would seem that the range of potential biases previously examined by economists is but a small subset of the various "context effects" that can be considered in valuation.

The issue of bias is explored in more detail by Mitchell and Carson, who in addressing the need for analyzing how people respond to the "whole interview situation" offer an exhaustive analysis of the bias problem in its many forms. In the process, they make several excellent points. First, concerning the "exploratory" nature of early CV studies: It seems that conclusions involving systematic variations in CV valuations to changes in starting points, payment vehicles, and types of information provided to respondents may have been unfounded. Reflecting the exploratory nature of early studies, many are methodologically weak, thereby rendering any conclusions obtained less robust. As a corollary of this first point, Mitchell and Carson note that many CV bias experiments were conducted with sample sizes too small to provide sufficient statistical power to reject the null hypothesis of no difference in treatment effects.

Fisher, McClelland, and Schulze offer the same two criticisms of early CV work. First, they point out that samples used in CV studies were often small and not representative of the population to which the value estimates were applied. Second, they note that economists' early CV studies were oriented more toward whether the method might work than toward producing value estimates that could be used in policy decisions. Harris, Tinsley, and Donnelly extend this idea further, noting that the number of statistically usable samples has been further reduced by anomalies of data such as nonresponses, protest bids, and outlier bids. They also point out the exploratory nature of past CV research, which emphasized the development of methods as opposed to descriptive or explanatory research.

Second, Mitchell and Carson, as well as Boulding and Lundstedt, seem willing to extend the concept of economic man, noting that people are motivated by norms of equity and helpfulness in addition to a desire to maximize their personal advantage. Further, in contrast to the traditional economists' view that changing one's valuation in the face of new evidence or information constituted a form of bias, they make a distinction between bias and misspecification, rejecting the concept of an "information bias."

Finally, in their analysis of the interview situation, Mitchell and Carson point out that shared meanings between people are problematic because meaning is subjective and contextual and that it cannot be taken for granted that what the researcher intends to convey by the research instrument's wording will be so understood by the respondent. Two points are relevant here. First, the importance of the context of the valuation situation developed by Brown and Slovic is again raised. Second, the importance of the sponsor (researcher) knowing exactly what he wants to value is implied.

Fischhoff, in particular, calls attention to the need for researchers to understand the relevant issues (what should be asked) in an interview. This point should not be understated, or taken lightly. Most studies concerning survey techniques carry the implicit assumption that there are few problems with the questions developed by the researchers, and more fundamentally, that the sponsors know what values they are trying to find. Therefore, while good questionnaire design is generally recognized as a prerequisite to a good survey, more study has been devoted to problems emanating from the respondents' end of the process. A related point raised by Fischhoff is that researchers must be careful that questions are not designed to deliberately elicit certain answers, as may be the case in many types of marketing-related or policy-related (political) questions.

Another crucial point noted by Fischhoff is the need to define carefully the variables being measured. Of course, this point is discussed by several of workshop participants, but its importance warrants particular consideration. For example, Driver and Burch note the importance of defining what is to be measured initially, arguing that much too little attention has been given in the past to clearly defining what specific good or service is being valued. They assert that a fundamental tenet of science is to clearly define variables. In addition, Brown and Slovic comment on the difficulty of accurately specifying a CV good, noting that the specific good at issue often serves as a symbol for a whole class of goods. The difficulties associated with ill-defined variables in CVM research are brought into sharp focus in the results of Fischhoff's review of 24 studies concerning the economic value of visibility. He finds a wide range of diversity in what risk management specialists and investigators have chosen as an appropriate variable or definition for the term visibility. Fischhoff suggests that this variability in definitions raises questions about the comparability of studies. The implications for judging accuracy of the CVM by making comparisons to either the Travel Cost Method (TCM) or Hedonic Price Method (HPM) are obvious.

The use of the TCM and the HPM, as alternatives to the CVM as methods for valuing nonmarket resources systems, are considered by Mendelsohn and Markstrom, who offer a basic, yet thorough, review of these methods. While their discussion is clear and comprehensive, it is not clear exactly how it fits into the overall theme of the workshop. The HPM, for example, relies on indirect market data, not survey results, and the reader is left unsure as to the role of the psychologist in the development of such methods. Mendelsohn and Markstrom's discussion of the TCM and HPM does lead us to an important point, however. It seems fair to say that in the past, economists working with the CVM would have found little problem in using measures drawn from the travel cost method or the hedonic price method as "best" estimates for market values (see Cummings et al., 1986). We have noted, however, that the parallelism between values derived from the TCM and HPM methods, and real market values has begun to come under sharp criticism. It is now generally recognized that such parallelism has yet to be firmly established.

If, in our search for a standard to be used in the analysis of accuracy in CVM values, we are to eschew values derived from these indirect methods, we should perhaps consider values derived from simulated markets. A class of studies in experimental economics, in essence, simulates markets. In this regard,

two striking features characterize the laboratory experiments conducted in this subdiscipline of economics: incentive-competitively mechanisms, which provide (theoretically, at least) subject valuations that fully reveal utility maximizing valuations for experimental commodities; and repetitive trials of the laboratory setting, which provide subjects required time and experience with the valuation process for informed revelations of preferences. Many behavioral scientists have expressed the need for laboratory experimentation. Harris, Tinsley, and Donnelly, for example, view this recent trend of redirecting CV research as clearly a step in the right direction for improving CVM valuation.

In two of the workshop presentations, pioneering work in the area of laboratory experiments is reported. Fisher et al. describe experiments conducted by Coursey, Hovis, and Schulze (in press) in which purely hypothetical and "semihypothetical" valuations are compared to those obtained in a Vickrey auction. Coursey, Brookshire, and Radosevich offer further extensions of this experimental work. In noting the obvious importance of these efforts, we must also acknowledge that the process of laboratory experimentation is still in its infancy. In future research efforts, refinements will likely be made, and anomalies, found to exist in results thus far, will be explained. The work of psychologists and other behavioral scientists will undoubtedly play an integral role in this process. As Brookshire et al. note, for example, the dynamics of the convergence process between WTP and WTA do not appear to be consistent with current psychological explanations of value, and require further investigation.

In addition to their experimental work, Fisher et al. also present several other important points. They offer a discussion of possible reasons for the WTP/WTA disparity and develop a model that addresses the problem. Of interest concerning the spirit of the workshop, as well as earlier comments by Mendelsohn and Markstrom, is that the model incorporates certain features of Kahneman and Tversky's (1979) Prospect Theory. In addition, Fisher et al. discuss the differences between WTP and WTA observed in laboratory experiments comparing private and public goods. The distinction is important because, ultimately, the public good experiments will have the most direct relevance on contingent valuation surveys designed to elicit valuations regarding public amenity goods and resources.

Gregory and Bishop also consider the disparity observed between WTP and WTA value measures. While also pointing out reasons for the disparity, Gregory and Bishop take a slightly different focus than Fisher et al. Specifically, they consider how policymakers should respond to the disparity (i.e., what does this difference between WTP and WTA imply for policymakers?). On a more general level, Gregory and Bishop question the use of a potential compensation test as a guide for welfare assessments (evaluations) of public policies. They note six limitations of the test, through which traditional economic measures of social welfare are seen to be extremely limited.

It is apparent that many of the papers presented at this workshop have referred to the "limitations" of traditional economic thinking concerning valuation issues. Some of the papers even do this quite indirectly. For example, Harris et al., through their excellent discussion of certain psychological theories (for example, hit rate analysis, utility theory, and various psychometric measures of validity), seem to underscore not only the wealth of ideas that exist within the domains of other social sciences, but also the "limitedness" of the traditional economic approach. Of course, giving attention to the work and ideas of other social scientists in no way implies that the role of the economist in matters of resource valuation has been diminished. On the "behalf" of economists, Mendelsohn and Peterson offer an insightful assessment of the economist's use of monetary valuation as a public policy tool. They critically analyze a number of common arguments (reasons) given for why monetary values should not be used by public policymakers. In every case but one, they find monetary values do have considerable worth, reinforcing the positive role the economist plays in the valuation process.

Further, the viewpoints of economists and psychologists are certainly not mutually exclusive. Brookshire et al. note that the two different approaches are not totally incompatible. Each discipline argues that it is impossible to separate the measured value of the good from the elicitation procedure through which that value is obtained. Also, both professions seem to believe that value asymmetry can and will disappear in a market environment.

The key result of this workshop, of course, remains the importance of questioning how people approach the valuation problem. Quite insightful in this respect is the presentation by Kleindorfer and Kunreuther, who through some specific case studies shed additional light on the problem, demonstrating at the same time the inadequacy of expected utility theory and the need for the inclusion of certain psychological and institutional considerations in the analysis. Kleindorfer and Kunreuther also question two basic economic assumptions: that individuals are well-informed and rational, noting that there is growing evidence that many firms and individuals are neither; and that individuals may use more simple heuristic procedures than maximizing expected utility to make choices. Fischhoff also makes this point, arguing that when respondents are faced with a complex question, a likely result of being overloaded by detail is insensitivity to some of these details. Further, Mitchell and Carson also recognize the possibility that people may use systematic rules of thumb or judgmental heuristics when making choices under conditions of uncertainty.

Although the problems studied by Kleindorfer and Kunreuther are fairly specific, their relevance and crossover potential to respondent behavior in dealing with CVM surveys is obvious. Important in this regard are the four hypotheses created concerning respondent behavior. Such work is a vital step toward addressing the need for a theoretical model regarding behavior. Finally, their conclusion that a key research agenda is one that encompasses monetary valuation but also other factors is consistent with the overall theme of the workshop--the need for multiattribute valuation.

The need for a decision-making approach that preserves the multidimensional character of the decision problem, instead of collapsing the decision onto a single scale (such as dollars), is argued by Schroeder and Dwyer. We agree with this assessment. Forcing respondents to express their responses entirely in terms of dollars puts them in an unnatural position, and perhaps frames the problem in a context in which economic reasoning is not perceived as legitimate. Public understanding and acceptance is a crucial factor in the presentation of alternative policy scenarios. We cannot help but note the similarity of this situation to that in a groundwater valuation project recently com-

pleted for a New Mexico Special Advisory Committee (Brajer & Cummings, 1986). In attempting to analyze New Mexico's water "future," we found that the general public could not adequately accept (understand) the nature of water shortage projection dates; that is, specific years in which current water supply and demand projections led to water supplies being totally depleted ("running out" of water). However, by developing water scarcity "benchmarks"--qualitative descriptions of the inevitable changes caused by the shifting supply-demand patterns on various institutions (i.e., changes in the economic, socio-institutional, and lifestyle characteristics in the affected areas)--we were able to convey information that could be understood and utilized in policy decisions. Information derived from CV surveys must be just as accessible and useful.

Overall, within the context of critical issues for future CVM research, a number of important points have been raised and discussed in the papers presented at the workshop. We have noted that the tremendous need for amenity resource valuation (as outlined by Kaiser et al. and Driver et al.) has led in part to one of the current problems in CVM research--the emphasis on empirical as opposed to theoretical work. This has resulted in an ad hoc approach to CVM research, described as a "chemistry set" approach by some CV practitioners. One major conclusion offered in Cummings et al. (1986) regarding critical issues for future CVM research was the need for modeling efforts that focus on individual behavior in contingent market settings. Several papers in the workshop have taken positive steps toward addressing this modeling issue, the importance of which cannot be understated. Such models can serve as the basis for formulating empirically testable hypotheses.

In addition, there seems to be a clear need to turn to laboratory experiments, and to other related social science disciplines. The workshop represents an important step in this direction. That the benefits from collaborating with other social scientists and decision theorists are of potentially considerable magnitude has been made apparent by the ideas and issues raised at the workshop. This in no way implies that the work of the economist is finished, however. Instead, resource economists working with the CVM are merely becoming increasingly aware of the implications of research in the various fields of psychology, particularly in the subdiscipline of cognitive psychology, for developing the CVM. We believe that a key challenge to economists in this regard is the identification of meaningful, measurable manifestations of cognitive and affective components of attitudes that can serve as variables. Adding to this challenge is the need for developing some meaningful index for attitudinal variables, which will allow their inclusion in quantitative analyses.

Another challenge to CVM practitioners concerns the issue of accuracy, which has only recently taken a center stage in efforts to develop the CVM. This issue, briefly mentioned by Gregory and Bishop and explored in somewhat more detail by Harris et al., remains unresolved in our minds. In the past, an "accurate" valuation of an environmental good was taken to be a market-analogous revelation of a subject's preference for the good in question. The necessity, or even the desirability, of the market analogy was questioned, however, by many of the workshop participants. Harris et al., for example, argue that the propriety of valuing public goods with approaches whose theoretical frameworks are based upon a market system that deals exclusively with private goods is questionable. From this line of analysis, they feel that a voting, or referendum, approach might be more appropriate, in terms of theoretical consistency. This same conclusion was reached by Hoehn and Sorg, who in developing another model of respondent behavior extended the traditional economic "textbook" model of optimizing behavior, and demonstrated, among other things, the desirability of a voting, or referendum, rule for obtaining "true" valuations.

Economists, of course, find it natural to frame the problem in an economic way, by focusing on the potential research costs required to obtain "accuracy" in CVM measures. Given, as we have earlier asserted, that laboratory experiments can provide a standard for accurate valuations derived from applications of the CVM (or, indeed, from any other methodology), the obvious question arises: Why would one ever wish to use the CVM; why not simply use the method which one knows will yield an accurate valuation--the experimental method? The response to this question is that laboratory experiments are costly relative to applications of the CVM, on the order of 3 to 5 times more costly (on a per observation basis). Given the substantial cost difference between laboratory experiments and the CVM, and the potential difference in the accuracy of value measures derived from the two methods, an obvious tradeoff is implied.

In conclusion, we note that over the course of the workshop, a variety of problems have been pointed out concerning the development and use of the CVM. Despite all of the problems, however, most CV practitioners seem to remain optimistic about the use of CVM. As Gregory and Bishop point out, "the results of the research conducted to date are sufficiently consistent to indicate that considerably more attention should be given to improving methods." Further, Fisher et al. note that the existing problems "do not appear to overwhelm the potential usefulness of CVM. Rather, these problems represent a list of design issues that need to be considered carefully when planning a CVM study."

We agree with these statements, and offer two final thoughts in closing. The first concerns some of the more "novel" suggestions made by Harris et al. regarding future directions for CVM research and the development of new valuation methods. As examples, they recommend the creation of a structure for leas-

ing public resources to entities in the private sector, whose actions could then be regulated, and they also call for the creation of a resource "supermarket," where a variety of public amenities could actually be sold. Given the myriad of problems involved in valuing public amenities, which have been alluded to in many of the workshop papers, we believe that the need for such imaginative and innovative thinking is strong. Lastly, recalling the reasons cited earlier regarding the tremendous need for resource valuation studies, we feel that it is important, amid all of the theoretical and methodological discussions, to keep in mind that the ultimate goal of the CVM is, in our opinion, an important and noble one--to make the most informed policy decisions possible concerning our scarce, and rapidly dwindling, environmental and amenity resources.

References

Brajer, V., & Cummings, R. G. (1986). Benchmarks for Water Scarcity in New Mexico's Future. In Dumars, et al. *State Appropriation of Unappropriated Groundwater: A Strategy for Insuring New Mexico a Water Future,* Albuquerque, NM: New Mexico Water Resources Research Institute and University of New Mexico School of Law.

Coursey, D. L.; Hovis, J. J.; & Schulze, W. (in press). On the disparity between willingness to accept and willingness to pay measures of value. *Quarterly Journal of Economics.*

Cummings, R. G.; Brookshire, D. S.; & Schulze, W. D. eds. (1986). *Valuing environmental goods: Assessment of the contingent valuation method.* Totowa, NJ: Rowman and Allanheld.

Kahneman, D., & Tversky, A. (1979). Prospect theory: An analysis of decisions under risk. *Econometrica, 47*(2), 263-291.

Smith, V. Kerry (1986). To keep or toss the contingent valuation method. In Cummings, et al. *Valuing environmental goods: Assessment of the contingent valuation method* (pp. 196-216). Totowa, NJ: Rowman and Allanheld.

Footnote

[1]Reference to authors imply papers in this volume unless a date is given.

Economics and Social Psychology in Amenity Valuation

Thomas A. Heberlein
Center of Resource Policy Studies and Programs
University of Wisconsin
Madison, Wisconsin

In this paper I discuss economic and psychological approaches to amenity valuation, from a social psychological perspective. The unique demands of amenity valuation have brought economists and psychologists together and the better we understand each other, the better we will be able to work together to advance knowledge. My hope is that this paper will further that understanding.

My discussion is based on the papers in this book and on the presentations and reactions at the Workshop on Integrating Economic and Psychological Knowledge in Valuations of Public Amenity Resources where these papers were originally presented. It is also based on over 10 years of my experience as a co-principal investigator with several economists on valuation and energy conservation projects.

One of the truly exciting things about amenity valuation is that it does require interdisciplinary work, as opposed to a multidisciplinary approach. In multidisciplinary research the two or more disciplines do their thing and the parts are linked together like a car body built in one division and fitted onto the chassis built by another. In interdisciplinary research, the skills of several disciplines are integrated into one product. To progress in amenity valuation, economists have turned to other disciplines, incorporating the procedures of sociologists and the theories of social psychologists. Because of this interdisciplinary synthesis, valuation of environmental goods is much better today than it was 10 years ago. It is my hope that by pointing out how disciplines mesh, or fail to mesh, will help individuals of the various disciplines work better together. If nothing else, I hope the discussion in this paper helps reduce some of the frustrations of interdisciplinary work.

Adam Smith, I believe, pointed out the importance of specialization. Sometimes it is better to call in a psychologist or sociologist rather than trying to become one. Better knowledge of how the allied social science disciplines can serve economics will help economists know when to call in a sociologist, psychologist, or social psychologist, and what might be expected of the results. In that sense, this paper might be thought of as consumer education for economists.

In this paper I compare social psychology and economics in terms of theory and method. Willingness to pay and willingness to accept discrepancy are discussed to illustrate the differences between the two fields; in doing so, additional sociological explanations for the discrepancy are suggested. I also discuss the key difference between the two disciplines over the conceptualization and measurement of value, and speculate about the causes, benefits, and problems of continuing cooperation.

Psychology is a multifaceted discipline. Some people do physiological work on animals, while others do therapy on people. In valuation work, economics draws on social psychology. Social psychology deals with individual social behavior and focuses on the social context of the individual. It loosely links sociology and psychology. Sociological social psychologists tend to emphasize the social context and the psychological social psychologists the intrapsych processes or "what goes on in people's heads." The former tend to be trained in, and found in, departments of sociology, and the later in psychology departments. For example, among workshop participants, Ajzen and Slovic are more psychological social psychologists, and Mitchell and I are more sociological social psychologists. For the remainder of the paper, I mainly compare and contrast social psychology and economics, with occasional references to the generic fields of sociology and psychology.

DIFFERENCES BETWEEN SOCIAL PSYCHOLOGY AND ECONOMICS

It is sometimes difficult for economists and social psychologists to understand each other because the two fields differ in terms of theory, method, data, and focus. Amenity valuation forces economists to understand the theory of social psychology and adopt methods and data of sociologists and psychologists, while retaining their own economic focus on valuation. This produces a true interdisciplinary product, but also creates misunderstanding because of the different perspectives of each discipline.

Theory in Economics and Social Psychology

To a noneconomist, theory in economics seems to be an overarching framework of propositions. It is highly mathematical, with propositions stated in functional relationships, and is exceedingly well-integrated. New conclusions seem to be derived from the linking together of parts of the theory. Unlike social psychology, theory in economics can be quantified and the concepts are well-defined. No matter what perspective is taken in economics, people generally agree on the functional relationships of models (e.g., the demand curve). In this sense, it is the envy of social psychologists.

On the other hand, social psychologists are puzzled by the testability of the economic theory, or of parts of the theory. The model for social psychology is derived from physics; observations about a phenomenon are collected and an explanation is invented. This explanation may be an absolute guess, in which case one may think of it as theory with a small "t." Some experiment is devised to test the theory, and if the data are inconsistent, the theory is rejected and social psychologists move on to some other explanation. Sewell (1952), for example, seriously damaged psycho-analytic theory with a single carefully designed test of toilet training practices of mothers, and personality characteristics of sons in Richland County, Wisconsin. He showed that, in spite of the central role of toilet training in Freudian theory, it had no demonstrable effect on personality when systematically measured in a large sample.

In this tradition, if data are found to be consistent with theory, the theory is not "accepted" but simply "not rejected." If a theory gives consistent results after a long period of testing, it becomes established. Theories that have avoided falsification become laws. It is interesting to note that the Theory of Relativity in physics is still just that, a theory, while the supply and demand relationship observed among humans by economists is deemed a law. From this it seems that economists view the economic behavior of humans as more regularly predictable than the behavior of the physical universe.

From a social psychologist's perspective, theory in economics doesn't appear to be falsifiable. Economists seem to spend little time testing and rejecting theory, and much more time quantifying the parameters. When data are inconsistent with theory, the data, not the theory, tend to be questioned. Social psychologists view economic theory as more of a framework for examining how people ought to behave as producers and consumers than a formally testable scientific theory.

Social psychology, on the other hand, has too many theories, for example, cognitive theory, role theory, stimulus response theory, the theory of cognitive dissonance, and attribution theory. There is so much theory, that compared to economics, there is really no theory at all. Social psychology is a rather loose set of ideas in a specific domain, that try to explain or predict individual behavior. There is no overarching framework such as in economics.

Theory in social psychology is seldom mathematical. Generally it cannot be stated in a set of formal propositions. The propositions that do exist are not linked together well. Because of the empirical nature of social psychology, the discipline frequently uses various statistics. Sociological social psychologists who build complex models on single data sets use quantitative analysis, but as a rule, mathematical models are not fundamental to social psychology.

Probably even more amazing to economists and other scientists is that social psychologists cannot even agree on conceptual and operational definitions of the basic concepts in the field. The term attitude is a fundamental component of social psychology. Yet, Fishbein and Ajzen (1975) define attitude as only one component of the more general use of attitude by some others in the field (including myself). Fundamental disagreements exist in spite of over 50 years of modern scientific work on the attitude concept, and lead to communication problems with those outside the field, such as economists.

Despite the lack of any broad theory, social psychologists are preoccupied with testing theory, or at least testing something. Ideas in limited context are operationalized and "tested" in contrived situations called laboratories. Once when I bragged that we social psychologists were looking for general laws that applied to all people at all times, I was put in my place by a distinguished demographer who noted it was important to show that something had happened at least once. Much highly toted experimental work in social psychology is just that, demonstration projects to show that something can happen at least once.

As should be evident from this somewhat cynical and certainly oversimplified discussion of both economic and social psychological theory, both economists and social psychologists have something to learn from each other. Possibly, the social psychologists have more to learn than the economists. Joint work in amenity valuation may be helpful in that regard. Perhaps economists will become more interested in testing and rejecting theory, and social psychologists will be more interested in developing a set of actual propositions.

Data and Method in Economics and Social Psychology

Some differences in the role of theory between the two disciplines are due to the data and methods necessary to investigate the phenomena of interest in both fields. Economists should be happy that we live in a society that keeps accurate records of economic activity. Many agencies and institutions collect and store data on the variables that most interest economists. Thus, economists often have large, complex, and interesting data sets to analyze. They seldom have to get involved with the "messy" work of actually collecting the data. As a result, economists do more secondary analysis than social psychologists. This may be why economists do not seem to pay a lot of attention to the source of the data. In secondary analysis, the analyst usually does not take much responsibility for the quality of the data because he or she did not personally collect the data. One simply assumes the data are accurate and moves on to the more interesting analysis, hoping, in some cases correctly, that complex analysis can overcome or compensate for deficiencies of the data. This attention to measurement is encouraged because economists often are interested in easily measured data. Finally, a focus on aggregates rather than individuals greatly reduces the errors in estimates due to measurement error, and increases in sample size can be used to offset the loss of precision in measurement (this applies only for random error, not systematic error or bias).

Social psychologists, on the other hand, most often collect their own data. They either design and conduct surveys or design and conduct experiments. When doing a survey there is a great concern for measurement. The paper is blank and one has to decide how, and then take responsibility for, constructing a measure. Thus, discussions of the realities of measurement are a major part of training in survey methodology for sociologists. Even sociological social psychologists who do secondary analysis pay a lot of attention to measurement. Part of this concern about measurement is because social psychologists use abstract concepts in their theories, such as alienation, status, and power, which are difficult to measure. These concepts are multidimensional and often conceptually loose. Indeed, the "theoretical" debates in social psychology often come down to measurement issues. Thus, much of the intellectual energy in social psychology has focused on measurement, while intellectual energy in economics has focused on analysis because of the tight theory and availability of secondary data.

Another outcome of this survey research tradition is that sociological social psychologists have a great concern about the representativeness of a sample. They want to make accurate generalizations. (The predictions that Landon and Dewey would win based on survey data continue to leave their mark.) Thus, when an economist generalizes to the entire nation based on a sample in one area of one city, we are shocked.

Psychological social psychologists usually collect their own data, but rather than doing surveys or secondary analysis of surveys, they conduct experiments. Adopting the strategy of the natural sciences, this group attempts to test theories of human behavior in laboratories. By eliminating extraneous factors, random assignment, and the introduction of experimental manipulations, one gains powerful ways of establishing causality and determining effects. A great deal of attention is paid to establishing the experimental situation that correctly operationalizes the independent and dependent variables.

In the case of experiments, the data are generally easy to analyze. Simple comparison of means between groups is usually sufficient. Thus, social psychologists are less interested in complex models to tease out effects, but rather more interested in designing unambiguous experiments to test theory. Psychological social psychologists are rather less concerned with representative samples than those that come from more sociological survey research traditions. They assume that, in the lab situation, one human being is a lot like another, just as biologists feel that one white rat, or cell, in a laboratory is a lot like another. Thus, those in the more traditional field of psychology tend to draw from convenient subject populations, for example, college sophomores taking introductory classes in psychology.

WTP/WTA Controversy as an Example

One of the most interesting findings in amenity valuation is the well-documented fact that the amount people say they are willing to pay for something (WTP) is much less that the amount they say they will take to give it up (WTA). According to Fisher, McClelland, and Schulze (this volume), this finding has been replicated at least 16 times in the literature since 1974. Indeed, in every case examined, WTA has exceeded WTP. The differences are not small. WTA is from 1.6 to more than 16 times greater than WTP.

The first study that showed this finding was conducted by Hammack and Brown (1974), the second by Sinclair (1976), and the third by Banford et al. (1979/1980). Based on as few as three replications, empirically oriented social psychologists would have no trouble saying that there is a real and demonstrable difference between WTP and WTA. One reason that they are easily influenced by these data is that they have no strong theoretical reason to think that these two values should be the same. Social psychologists feel that buying behavior is quite different from selling behavior. People have much more experience with one than the other; buyers and sellers have different roles in society and the social context of their behaviors are also different. Hence, social psychologists would expect the behaviors to be different. Because values are determined by behavior (the actual buying and selling), the values obtained through any method that approximates these behaviors should also be different.

Economists, on the other hand, have a theory, that WTP and WTA values should be similar (Willig, 1976). Rather than give up the theory or try to modify the theory, economists have looked for all sorts of bias to account for the differences. One argument, for example, was that the differences were based on hypothetical questions on surveys. Bishop and I, along with other social psychologists, used real money for WTP and WTA and showed that the difference persisted (Heberlein & Bishop, 1986). Finally, after 16 replications and 13 years of research, economists are beginning to believe the phenomena is real and are collaborating with social psychologists to search for explanations of the phenomena.

Economists are adopting both the method (experiments) and theory (loss aversion or prospect theory) of social psychologists. My concern as a sociological social psychologist is that economists are adopting both the method (lab experiments) and theory (intrapsych theories) of psychological social psychologists rather than a more sociological social psychological orientation. This criticism is, I hope, not motivated solely by disciplinary imperialism, but rather by a real concern that buying and selling, the behavioral basis of value, occurs in a social context, and that lab studies and formal intrapsychic theories may miss the key contextual effects that influence human behavior.

When confronted with the necessity of acknowledging the difference as real, Fisher et al. (this volume) have two explanations: strategic bias and loss aversion. It is interesting that the term strategic bias is used, rather than strategic behavior. When the questionnaire responses are not consistent with theory, economists, who prefer to believe the theory is correct, refer to the data as biased. Little empirical evidence in the CV literature suggests any large strategic bias (see Brookshire, Ives, & Schulze, 1976; Hoehn & Sorg, this volume). Indeed, in looking at free rider issues, Marwell and Ames (1981) showed that the only group of students who behaved strategically were graduate students in economics, thus suggesting that it is the economists rather than noneconomists who tend to think strategically. In their limited discussion of strategic bias, Fisher et al. (this volume) highlight the important role of experience in the process. This contextual effect of experience could be a key issue in the WTP/WTA controversy, and should not be neglected; but I believe, it is largely independent from strategic bias.

By adopting the second explanation, loss aversion or prospect theory, economists switch from using one formal theory to another formal theory. It would be convenient if people simply used a different metric when giving up things than when acquiring things. This, if true, would allow a simple mathematical conversion when moving from buying to selling. Prospect theory has some empirical support in the psychological literature and may explain these differences between WTP and WTA. Economists appear to be more comfortable moving from one formal theory to another without getting in the "messy" business of individual human choices. They appear to be trying to adapt prospect theory, which grew out of research on how people understand probabilities, rather than developing a new theory that specifically addresses the problem. This is apparently done with the hope that another theory will somehow resolve the paradox.

An alternative approach that data-driven social psychologists often take is to carefully examine the phenomena and ask, "Under what conditions does the phenomena occur and under what conditions does it not." The difficulty here is that there are currently no cases where WTP equals WTA. Fisher et al. (this volume) take some steps in this direction by looking at the case where the differences are "small" with WTA only two or three times as large as WTP and where they are "large," 10 or more times greater. They point to the key issue of "psychological commitment or personal involvement." However, Fisher et al. do not let this variable stand alone, but rather claim that it enhances loss aversion. I argue more directly that it explains a good bit of the loss aversion phenomena, without resorting to prospect theory.

A more sociological social psychological explanation could involve at least three components: experience, identity, and property rights. Fisher et al. (this volume) discerns the first two of the components, which might be brought together as a viable alternative to strategic bias and prospect theory. These three components will be much less attractive to economists because they are not included in a formal theory nor do they interface with economic theory as well as strategic bias or loss aversion.

As Fisher et al. (this volume) note, people have different experience levels in buying (WTP) than they do in selling (WTA): "Occasional sales of their old car or house hardly give experience comparable to the frequent purchases of food, clothing, and gasoline, etc." Thus, people have an idea of what they are willing to pay for something but not of what they are willing to sell it for. Bishop and I have argued (Heberlein & Bishop, 1986) that this is the reason that WTP measures are good indicators of what people will really pay in our experiments comparing CV with simulated markets, while WTA measures are much different. When people have more experience, what they say approximates what they do; when they have less, it does not. Apparently, as individuals gain more experience, WTP and WTA will converge. Indeed, the Coursey, Hovis, and Schulze (1986) experiment and the Brookshire, Coursey, and Radosevich (this volume) experiment show just that. People who have experience buying and selling do, as economic theory suggests, give the same value to WTP and WTA.

This still presents a serious problem for economic theory because consumers do not have experience with both WTP and WTA. This lack of experience will be reflected in CV studies that attempt to establish amenity values. Thus, while the difference can be erased in the lab, it still exists in the consumer world. For example, consumers have a far better idea of what they will pay to reduce acid rain than what they will accept for lower air and water quality from sulphur dioxide emissions. Even if we could give consumers experience in the research process, which is the true value--the one given with or without experience? Experience is important; it plays a role, and it should not be ignored.

Why does it take more to get people to give up things they own than they will pay to own them? The examples given by Fisher et al. (this volume) of medals for amateur athletes and the example discussed at the workshop, teddy bears in children's arms versus on store shelves, highlight a key aspect of the phenomena-identity. Identity recently has made a big comeback in sociological social psychology (see Schlenker, 1984). An identity describes the way a person defines himself or herself. These self-definitions are crucial for understanding human behavior. One's possessions define self. When giving up something, one is losing part of one's self-definition. The two examples where economists and social psychologists agree that WTP < WTA involve a substantial amount of self-definition. The athlete is defined by the medal. (Note that the example given by Fisher et al. [this volume] was of an amateur athlete). The amateur, rather than the professional, is doing the activity to express and obtain an identity; the professional, motivated more by money, should be more willing to give up the medal for what he "paid" for it (i.e., since it is less part of his personal identity). The child and the teddy bear is also an example ladened with identity. In early stages of child development, identity is particularly tied to dyadic relationships. The child gains a sense of self by the child-teddy bear relationship. The teddy bear on the shelf is not part of that relationship, while the teddy bear in the arms is. The loss of self-identity is linked to the difference between WTP and WTA. In some cases this price is high.

The role of identity is clear in our hunting studies (Fisher et al., this volume, Table 1). The ratio of WTA/WTP was 4.8 for goose hunters (Bishop & Heberlein, 1979), and 16.5 for deer hunters (Heberlein & Bishop, 1986). Elsewhere (Baumgartner & Heberlein, 1981), deer hunters were shown to have a much higher psychological and social commitment to the activity. Thus, with a much stronger identity associated with deer hunting, we would expect to see these differences. The goose hunters

have a stronger identity than other recreation groups, so we would not expect their ratio to be equal. Heberlein and Vaske (1977) showed that trout fishermen on the Brule River in northern Wisconsin, a classic trout stream, have a much higher level of psychological commitment than canoers, and canoers are more committed than those floating the river in tubes. I would expect that the WTP/WTA gap would be greatest for the trout anglers and lowest for the tubers, with canoers falling in the middle based on this discussion of identities.

The final sociological explanation deals with property rights. I expect that institutional economists can discuss this more persuasively than I, but it seems obvious that giving up ownership (private property) is different than acquiring something you do not already own, or being paid for something that is not in the domain of private property (WTA). For example, if we tell the farmer in Saskatchewan, who is plowing up potholes to plant grain, that he must compensate the hunters for the loss of ducks produced on the potholes, he will object based on his property rights. He owns the potholes, and no one owns the ducks. The duck hunter in the U.S. will not be able to state what he will accept in compensation from farmers because he does not think the ducks are private property and no institutional mechanism treats them as private property. Our society is oriented around the concept of private property; deep seated beliefs, values, and institutions revolve around the institution of private property. This may explain at least part of the WTP/WTA gap. When I talk to the farmer who will not sell his woodlot for market value, but would not replace it for half the price, I suspect that something associated with the predictability, power, and institutional support that comes with private ownership is influencing his decision.

Thus, while not completely discounting loss aversion as a intrapsych mechanism that accounts for part of the gap, I caution economists not to rely completely on this explanation, attractive as it might seem. Experience, identity, and private ownership, I think, play a greater role. They are, however, much less quantifiable than loss aversion, and would be much more difficult for economists to model.

In addition to adopting social psychological theory to explain the differences between WTP/WTA, economists are adopting the methods of social psychologists, namely the experiment. Brookshire and Schulze and their associates have moved to the laboratory. One experiment reported in this volume (Brookshire et al.) and one reported elsewhere (Coursey et al., 1986), examined the WTA/WTP issue. Both experiments examined paying not to drink averse substances and paying to drink pleasant beverages. The experience variable was manipulated in repeated trials. The two experiments taken together test the loss aversion hypothesis in contrast to the experience hypothesis. The findings support the experience hypothesis. In both cases, the WTP and WTA converge as people get more experience. The values also converge on WTP, although, in one case, prospect theory would suggest that WTP should converge on WTA. People probably have more experience paying for avoiding bads and obtaining goods and Thus, WTP continues to act as an anchor in spite of the prospect theory prediction.

These types of experiments can be done quickly and alternative explanations can be ruled out. New explanations can be tested. The analysis is straight-forward. Causality is established. In spite of the benefits, there are some cautions about experiments. The history of social psychology has shown that experiments often develop a "life of their own," and become inbred, ending up as far from reality as econometric models sometimes do. Meticulous lab work needs to be followed up with careful field testing. Labs also have an artificial nature and students sometimes play games for the "fun of it." Thus, the strategic over bidding of a single individual in the last trial fouled up the data in Brookshire et al. (this volume). This separateness of laboratories from real life context makes it difficult to test the identity and private property components of the explanation posited earlier, although clever experimentalists can overcome some of these difficulties in the laboratory. Further laboratory experiments, I believe, will aid understanding of the WTP and WTA gap.

Value as Key Difference Between the Disciplines

Despite the merging of economics and social psychology in amenity valuation and particularly in contingent valuation and explorations of WTP/WTA, there remains a conceptual and methodological abyss between the two disciplines. This abyss separates the two over the most fundamental premise: the conceptualization and measurement of the concept value. Our basic ability to work together is continually thwarted by deeply ingrained differences over this basic concept. Even when we acknowledge the difference and try to use the term in the same way as those in the other discipline, our years of training and effective professional socialization puts blinders on us and makes us revert to type. The purpose of this discussion is to again highlight the differences discussed in a number of the papers in this volume (e.g., Ajzen & Peterson; Mendelsohn & Markstrom; Mendelsohn & Peterson). The goal is to continue to try to get a light line across the abyss to be followed by a larger line, and then a cable until we might truly build a bridge, which will promote the free and easy commerce of ideas between economists and social psychologists about the concept of value.

At the workshop at Estes Park where these papers were first presented and discussed, one could see economists and psychologists falling into the abyss. Sometimes we may have even pushed each other. For example, an economist discussing seatbelt use described a situation where only a low percentage of people used seatbelts. After an intervention program where people would be rewarded for using seatbelts, the use rate dramatically increased. He argued that the people had changed their value about seat belt usage. The social psychologists in the audience winced noticeably. Later in the workshop, a social psychologist claimed "money has nothing to do with value." The economists in earshot exchanged wry looks of incredulity. When the two disciplines have such fundamentally different perspectives, it is difficult to see how we can ever work together effectively. Yet, for the advancement of knowledge in amenity valuation, we must.

The fundamental difference between the two fields is that economics treats value as an observable behavior that is isomorphic with some underlying disposition, while social psychologists treat value as an unobservable underlying disposition that, as often as not, has little to do with observable behavior. Simply

stated, economists think that value is behavior, and social psychologists think that value is attitude.

Value as Behavior

Economics has been blessed with a wealth of behavioral data. People have kept track of prices, whether a person has been employed or not, and how much money people earn. These are all observable behaviors, even if they may have been obtained by paper and pencil surveys for convenience. The business of economics has been to examine some structural variable, price, for example, and see how many people engaged in a behavior (i.e., buying) under various prices. On the basis of these observations, they have built models of human behavior. Mendelsohn and Peterson (this volume) note that "The positive part of microeconomics (see Milton Friedman) is trying to explain observable behavior. The theory has consequently evolved into a preoccupation with values which can be derived from behavior." Later on, they state more succinctly that "Monetary values are consequently behavioral values." They further claim that "The source of those values is a black box whose interior structure is intentionally ignored."

In amenity valuation, two of the principle methods, travel cost and hedonic pricing, have been built on the foundation of observable behavior. Travel cost examines visitation rates (an observable behavior) and distance (another observable). Hedonics examines consumer choices and statistically estimates the component of variance that was due to a particular attribute. As Mendelsohn and Markstrom (this volume) state, "Both methods attempt to reveal values by observing actual market behavior." It is no surprise that economists have moved to a behavioral approach to amenity valuation because by training, experience, and tradition their whole discipline has focused on behavior.

Value as Attitude

Values to a social psychologist are unobservable; they are attitudes, not behavior. From a social psychological perspective, "the value of any commodity, whether traded in the marketplace or not, cannot be directly observed" (Ajzen & Peterson, this volume).

Because attitudes cannot be observed directly, as behavior can, social psychologists prefer to have a number of behaviors or behavioral traces to infer attitudes. Responses to a questionnaire are behaviors. The physical check marks or the verbal responses are observables from which we try to infer the unobservables. Fortunately, new statistical techniques (e.g., LISREL) deal quickly and efficiently with multiple indicators (Joreskog & Sorbom, 1983; Long, 1976, 1983). We need multiple behavioral indicators because any single behavior is likely to be a flawed representative of the underlying disposition of an attitude.

It is no surprise that social psychologists' definitions of unobservables are inconsistent; because no one can see them, it is easier to disagree. Value has two related meanings. A value is a belief that some end, state, or process is preferable to others (Rokeach, 1970, 1973). Freedom, equality, and love of nature are broad values that influence other more specific unobservables that form the components of the attitude construct. The second way the word value is used is to represent the evaluative component of the attitude construct. The attitude object is either liked or disliked, or loved or hated to highlight the emotional component of the evaluation. Evaluation, suggesting that something is better or worse, is how values fit into the attitudes. One should pay more for things one likes (values more) and less for things one dislikes (values less). Thus, the evaluation component of attitudes is most like the economists' concept of utility.

To further articulate the attitude construct, it can be divided into three unobservable components: beliefs, evaluations, and behavioral intentions (or the cognitive, affective, and conative components, in technical terms). They are loosely related, but the functional form of the relationship differs across attitude objects.

Concerning any attitude object (e.g., a deer hunting permit or acid rain), one has beliefs that reciprocally influence ones' evaluations (e.g., "I like deer hunting"), and which reciprocally influence ones' behavioral intentions ("I think I'll go deer hunting"). The behavioral intention is not an observable behavior. One has not done it yet. Thus, it can have a reciprocal effect on beliefs. (Deciding to go deer hunting may make you consider how cold and miserable it is going to be, how much it is going to cost, or to check the probabilities of success.) This can, in turn, influence the behavioral intention ("maybe I won't go hunting") or even the evaluation ("if it costs that much, I guess I don't like deer hunting so much").

Contingent valuation is a behavioral intention. It is not a behavior. How much people say they will pay or accept is not necessarily what they will be observed to do. Thus, contingent values are unobservables. To make these into economic values, one must move from an unobservable to an observable, or from a component of attitude to a behavior. As Mendelsohn and Peterson (this volume) stated, "Thus, contingent valuation surveys have tended to measure attitudes, not monetary values." Ironically, from the social psychological point of view, the economist refers to value as behavioral intention, which is conceptually different from the two unobservables--value in the broad sense and the evaluative component of attitudes that the social psychologist refers to as value. Evaluations are seen as relatively stable and broad values as very stable. Thus, when the economist says people changed their value of seat belts when they increase the rates that they wear them in response to some incentive scheme, the social psychologist does not think the value is changed one bit; people still hate seat belts but now wear them because they want to win a prize. This is also why psychologists make the heretical statement that money (either the observable behavior or WTP, the behavioral intention) have nothing to do with value. They are related to value, but are conceptually separate, and the relations are not easily specified. Thus, Ajzen and Peterson (this volume) conclude that "we argue against the equation of willingness to pay, no matter how ascertained, with psychological or social benefits."

Economists have already made some strides in treating CV as a component of attitude. The frequent discussions of bias show a concern. It does seem that if economists are going to use an attitudinal variable in their models, they should treat it as such. This means that a good deal of attention should be paid to the Behavioral/Behavioral Intention (B/BI) linkage. It is not for certain, or in every case, that BI is a good surrogate for B. If BI and B are correspondent (see Ajzen & Fishbein, 1977; Ajzen & Peterson, this volume), one will substitute for another, but achieving correspondence is not always a simple task. Also, economists should take seriously the use of multiple indicators to obtain the behavioral intention (WTA or WTP). A multiple indicator procedure (e.g., LISREL) will give better estimates than raw scores from single-item indicators.

WORKING TOGETHER: CAUSES, BENEFITS, AND PROBLEMS

Some researchers have stressed the need for an integration of social psychology and economics in amenity valuation. The value premise continues to be that the integration of more social psychology into microeconomics generally would be beneficial for both disciplines, and that amenity valuation experience might provide a model for other areas in micro economics.

Clearly, economists have reached out to the social psychologists, not the other way around. The important intellectual questions that drive this movement are essentially economic, not social psychological. Economics had three deficiencies--measurement, data collection, and theory--that made it difficult to do amenity valuation without involvement of other social science disciplines.

As noted earlier, economists usually get data from a secondary source. In amenity valuation, such data usually do not exist. Economists were faced with the need to actually go out and collect their own data, to do surveys, and to measure psychological constructs. Few economists are trained in either survey research or measurement. The early studies in amenity valuation were done without benefit of involvement of the allied social science disciplines. The criticism of these, from within the economic community, combined with the acknowledged lack of skills to do better, forced economists to seek out colleagues in other disciplines for technical help on how to design surveys and measure attitudinal variables.

It is also evident from the papers at this workshop that the theoretical gap in economics has driven economists to seek more theoretical input from other disciplines. For some reason, the variables (e.g., WTP/WTA) in amenity valuation regularly defy economic theory. These perturbations have survived more than 10 years of measurement debates. Thus, economists have shifted their attention to risk aversion and prospect theory. I hope with the inclusion of the Ajzen and Peterson paper in this volume and the current discussion, economists will examine attitude theory and more sociological variables, such as identity. I am not sanguine about the motivating aspects of these areas of social psychology because of the measurement problems and their vagueness compared to economic theory. Amenity valuation would benefit from further theoretical integration, but I am not optimistic that it will happen easily.

Cooperation is a two-way street. Three reasons for cooperation are intellectual interest, money, and policy concerns. While amenity valuation questions being asked by economists are not mainstream social psychology, they are interesting. The question remains if people will pay what they say they will pay, or if after repeated trials WTP/WTA will converge. Thus, the intellectual aspect provided some motivation. A small part of the motivation may be to advance our own paradigms either in prospect theory or attitude theory, but view this as "frosting on the cake," and an outcome yet to be realized.

Underfunded as economists are, social psychologists are in even worse shape. When natural resource problems cannot be solved by physical or biological scientists, or engineers, and when the society must turn toward social scientists for help, who do they come to? Certainly not the social psychologist. No one ever sits in a room in Washington and says, "What we have here is a social psychological problem, so lets hire ourselves a social psychologist." For lack of a better term or label, most human natural resource problems are labeled as economic, not social psychological, and those funding the research turn to economists. Like all good scientists, economists try to couch the problem in their own disciplinary context so it is tractable with the tools at hand. Unfortunately, amenity valuation does not fit into traditional models. First, economists tried to be survey researchers and social psychologists. They and their funders were dissatisfied with the results and they came to social psychologists bearing money. (Not too much money, but just enough to get them involved.)

To defend my own discipline of social psychology, from an overly crass view that we are simply money grubbers, it would be appropriate to point out that policy concerns rather than simply research dollars pushed social psychologists into amenity valuation. Social psychology does not have the clear policy relevance of economics, hence, it is more difficult for a social psychologist to do policy oriented research and have an impact on decisions. This is particularly true in the natural resources area (as opposed to mental health or poverty). For many of us, these policy concerns motivated the interest of social psychologists.

It clearly seems to me that economics has benefited from this integration. However, the discipline of social psychology has yet to benefit from the integration, and possibly never will. Individual social psychologists are better off than they were before, but not through contributions to the discipline. The benefits to economics are clearer. First, a number of resource economists have become skilled survey researchers. Questionnaires are better designed, the samples are much more representative, response rates are higher, and item nonresponse is less. In 1973, Cicchetti and Smith, for example, reported a CV study of wilderness users to determine how they felt about congestion (crowding and contacts). The questionnaire itself was convoluted at best. The overall response rate was less than 50%, and of those who did return it, many skipped the CV question. Thus, with data on about one third of the original sample, Cicchetti and Smith went ahead to analyze the data and write an article and a book. I doubt either would survive professional review by resource economists today, because of the improved standards of survey research. Better surveys lead to more generalizable data and more accurate input for policy decisions.

I am hopeful that the eventual resolution of the WTP/WTA disparity, whether by formally introducing prospect theory and discussing kinks in the demand curve, or by formally integrating other social psychological variables into economics, will make a contribution to basic economic theory. It seems to me that basic theory in either of our disciplines benefits from running up against real world problems and the struggle for their solution. I am hopeful that one or more of the economists working in amenity valuation will extract the lessons for the rest of the discipline.

Social psychology has benefited from the association less than economics. Some research funding has been provided and the ideas of social psychologists are entering the policy sector. Personally, I feel that I have gained an appreciation for the elegance and complexity of economic models. Ten years ago, these models simply seemed naive. Today, I admire the formal specification and the guidance that they provide both researcher and practitioner. Social psychology, which has some intuitive explanatory power, falls far short on the formal characteristics.

In spite of these benefits, some continuing difficulties in our collaborative relationship remain. Most serious is the lack of publication outlets for social psychologists. The questions we are exploring together may be of interest to an important segment of economists, but they do not speak to basic issues in social psychology. Thus, most of the publication and conference opportunities are for economists. Co-authored or even single-authored articles in economics journals do not have the professional recognition for those of us not in economics departments or in the economics profession. Thus, the professional rewards for continued collaboration are slim. To keep social psychologists involved, economists must try to provide time, funding, and support (like "irrelevant" sections on questionnaires) to cast questions that are a disciplinary contribution for social psychologist, and thus provide needed data for articles prepared for submission to the social psychology or other disciplinary journals.

One of the great frustrations with economists moving into these new areas is watching them re-invent the wheel, inventing new terms, and ad hoc theorizing about attitudes, just as I am sure our economist colleagues grow impatient with our naivete about basic economics (What is a demand curve again?). Sometimes I wish one could call a time-out and economists could take one course in psychological measurement theory and practice and one course in attitude theory.

Psychologists have been trying to measure unobservables (e.g. IQ, personality traits, and attitudes) for more than 50 years. A substantial body of knowledge, quite formal and mathematical, has been acquired. The classic book on test theory by Lord and Novik (1968) should interest and excite economists with a mathematical bent. In it are formal (really) definitions of reliability and validity. None of the papers in this volume present a thorough quantitative discussion of measurement, although they discuss some of the philosophical issues well (see Fischhoft; Harris, Tinsley, & Donnelly).

Test theory has two types of error: random and nonrandom. Reliability is defined in terms of random error ratios, and validity in terms of nonrandom error. By including certain types of indicators, one can estimate the components of nonrandom error. Economists have invented all sorts of terms for types of nonrandom error (e.g., strategic bias, hypothetical bias, vehicle bias). A serious consideration of test theory and measurement modeling would possibly identify these sources of bias. A number of economists have worked on measurement models and integrating latent or unobservable variables into econometric analysis (see Aigner et al., 1981; Aigner & Goldberger, 1977; Goldberger, 1972, 1974; Hauser & Goldberger, 1971; Zellner, 1970). Formally adopting these techniques could benefit work in amenity valuation.

SUMMARY AND CONCLUSION

This paper began with the assumption that better understanding of the two disciplines--economics and social psychology--would improve our ability to work together, and tried to provide a framework to achieve this objective. The two fields differ in terms of theory (highly integrated and formally specified vs. loose and ill-defined), approaches to theory testing (quantification of parameters vs. empirical assessment and rejection), data (secondary vs. primary), and method (analysis vs. surveys and experiments).

The preoccupation with methods and measurement explanations of the WTP/WTA difference shows the influence of theory on economists. Explanations of the phenomena currently popular with economists focuses on psychological theories and strategic behavior. Three more sociological variables are proposed as alternatives. These include differences in experience when it comes to buying versus selling, the role of identity when acquiring or giving up goods, and the ideological and institutional role of private property. Integration of these variables in economic models will be difficult because of poor definitions and measurement problems.

Economists are making clear progress in understanding the differences between WTP and WTA by adopting the experimental method of social psychologists. Early results from these experiments point more toward the role of experience than the predictions derived from prospect theory.

The key and most problematic difference between economics and social psychology is the conceptualization and measurement of value. Economists view value as a behavior measurable through observation, while social psychologists view value as an attitude inferred through a variety of behaviors. Contingent values, from a social psychological perspective, are behavioral intentions that differ from either values broadly defined or evaluations (components of attitude). This form of amenity value is an unobservable, but is conceptually different from what social psychologists define as values. As long as economists take this view of amenity values, it would appear useful for them to take up the multiple-item indicator measurement procedures for unobservables.

The collaboration between economists and social psychologists has advanced economics by leading to better survey research and methodology and are now adopting psychological theories. Social psychologists have been motivated to collaborate because the questions are provocative (if not in mainstream social psychology), financial support is available, and the research has policy relevance. That relationship has done more to advance economics than social psychology. Continuing difficulties include lack of publication outlets and professional recognition for social psychologists, and the lack of a grounding in both attitude theory and latent variable measurement by economists.

References

Aigner, D. J., & Goldberger, A. S. (eds.). (1977). *Latent variables in socio economic models*. Amsterdam: North-Holland Publishing Co.

Ajzen, I., & Fishbein, M. (1977). Attitude-behavior relations: A theoretical analysis and review of empirical research. *Psychological Bulletin, 84*, 888-912.

Banford, N. D., Knetsch, J. L., & Mauser, G. A. (1979/1980) Feasibility judgments and alternative measures of benefits and costs. *Journal of Business Administration, 11*, 25-35.

Baumgartner, R. M., & Heberlein, T. A. (1981). Process, goal and social interaction differences in recreation: What makes an activity substitutable. *Leisure Sciences, 4*, 443-458.

Bishop, R. C., & Heberlein, T. A. (1979). Measuring values of extra-market goods: Are indirect measures biased? *American Journal of Agricultural Economics, 64*, 927-930.

Brookshire, D. S., Ives, B., & Schulze, W. D. (1976). The valuation of aesthetic preferences. *Journal of Environmental Economics and Management, 3*, 325-346.

Brookshire, D., Coursey, D., & Schulze, W. (1986). Experiments in the solicitation of private and public values: An overview. In L. Green & J. Kagel (Eds.), *Advances in Behavioral Economics*. Ablex.

Cicchetti, C. T., & Smith, H. V. (1973). Congestion, quality deterioration and optimal use: Wilderness recreation in the Spanish Peaks Primative Area. *Social Science Research, 2*, 15-30.

Coursey, D. L., Hovis, J. J., & Schultze, W. D. (1986). On the disparity between willingness to accept and willingness to pay measure of value. *Quarterly Journal of Economics, August*, 679-690.

Fishbein, M., & Ajzen, I. (1975). *Belief, attitude, intention and behavior: An introduction to theory and research*. Reading, MA: Addison-Wesley.

Goldberger, A. S. (1974). Unobservable variables in econometrics. In P. Carembka (Ed.), *Frontiers in econometrics*. New York: Academic Press.

Goldberger, A. S. (1972). Maximum likelihood estimation of regressions containing unobservable independent variables. *International Economic Review, 13*, 1-15.

Hammack, J., & Brown, G. M., Jr. (1974). *Waterfowl and wetlands: Toward a bio-economic analysis*. Baltimore, MD: Johns Hopkins University Press.

Hauser, R. M., & Goldberger, A. S. (1971). The treatment of the unobservable variables in path analysis. In H. L. Costner (Ed.), *Sociological Methodology* (pp. 81-117). San Francisco, CA: Jossey-Bass.

Heberlein, T. A., & Bishop, R. C. (1986). Assessing the validity of contingent valuation: Three field experiments. *The Science of Total Environment, 56*, 99-107.

Heberlein, T. A., & Vaske, J. J. (1977). *Crowding and visitor conflict on the Bois-Brule River*. Water Resources Center. Technical Report WIS-WRC 77-04. University of Wisconsin, Madison.

Joreskog, K. G., & Sorbom, D. (1983). *LISREL: Analysis of linear structural relationships by method of maximum likelihood, versions V and VI* (2nd ed.). Chicago, IL: International Education Services.

Kahneman, D., & Tversky, A. (1979). Prospect theory: An analysis of decision under risk. *Econometrika, 47*, 263-291.

Long, J. (1976). Estimation and hypothesis testing in linear models containing measurement error. *Sociology Methods and Research, 5, 2*.

Long, J. (1983). *Confirmatory factor analysis: A preface to LISREL*. Sage Publication.

Lord, F. M., & Novick, M. R. (1968). *Statistical theory of mental test scores*. Reading: Addison-Wesley.

Marwell, G., & Ames, R. (1981). Economists free ride, does anyone else? Experiments on the provision of public goods, IV. *Journal of Public Economics, 15*, 295-310.

Rokeach, M. (1970. *Beliefs, attitudes and values*. San Francisco, CA: Jossey-Bass.

Rokeach, M. (1973). *The nature of human values*. New York: Free Press.

Sewell, W. H. (1952). Infant training and the personality of the child. *American Journal of Sociology, 58*, 150-159.

Schlenker, B. R. (1984). *Identities, identifications, and relationships*. In V. Derlaga (Ed.). Communication, intimacy and close relationships. New York: Academic Press.

Sinclair, W. S. (1976). *The economic and social impact of the Kemano II Hydroelectric Project on British Columbia's fisheries resources.* Vancouver, British Columbia, Canada: Fisheries and Marine Services, Department of the Environment.

Willig, R. D. (1976). Consumer surplus without apology. *American Economic Review, 66,* 589-597.

Zellner, A. (1970). Estimation of regression relationships containing unobservable variables. *International Economic Review,* 441-454.

Incorporating Psychology in Contingent Valuation Applications

Lauraine G. Chestnut
Energy and Resource Consultants
Boulder, Colorado

The purpose of this paper is to develop some specific practical suggestions for contingent valuation (CV) practitioners based on the presentations and discussions at the workshop. As an economist and a CV practitioner, my plan for preparing to write this paper was to listen carefully to the suggestions by the psychologists and other noneconomists at the workshop and to think about how their suggestions could be used to improve specific CV applications with which I am currently involved. It sounded like a straightforward task, but not surprisingly proved to be more difficult. Even though a great deal of discussion at the workshop concerned the CV method, it was clear that full consideration of the comments and suggestions by the noneconomists means more than simply rewording our questions.

This paper does include some practical suggestions for contingent valuation practitioners, but first it is helpful to summarize the types of comments and suggestions made by the noneconomists regarding CV applications. It is also important to note that to some extent the economists have been listening to the psychologists and other noneconomists all along, and in many instances have been making efforts to address the concerns that have been raised.

SUMMARY OF COMMENTS BY PSYCHOLOGISTS AND OTHERS

This section provides an overview of the types of comments and criticisms made at the workshop concerning CV methods to help assimilate these comments for the CV practitioner. However, it is not a comprehensive review of all that was said at the conference and in the papers concerning the contingent valuation method; the reader is referred to other papers in this volume for the details. It is also not a review of the entire conceptual, theoretical, and empirical CV literature, but some of the basic issues are briefly discussed.

The comments by the noneconomists can be largely grouped into two categories. One category concerns how we ask CV questions, and the other concerns whether we should be asking CV questions. Because a large portion of the comments fall into the second category, assimilation of these comments is difficult. Even though the purpose of this paper is to present some practical suggestions for CV applications, it seems inappropriate to proceed with these suggestions without first giving some attention to the issue of whether CV methods should be used at all.

Ajzen and Peterson (this volume) summarized the purpose of CV. Economists are busy trying to put a price on public amenities, such as visibility and nature preserves, to be able to use cost-benefit analysis of policy decisions that involve gains or losses in these amenities. Cost-benefit analysis is an intuitively appealing and simple evaluation tool. Costs of a proposed program are tallied on one side of the balance sheet and benefits on the other. If the benefits exceed the costs, then the program looks like a good one. If the costs exceed the benefits, then the program does not look worthwhile. The trouble is in finding a common metric with which to measure the benefits and costs. Dollars have been the traditional choice. CV results also provide a measure of the welfare impacts of alternative policy choices, even if cost-benefit analysis is not used.

This underlying motivation for the CV application seemed to be well understood and acknowledged by the noneconomist participants at the workshop. The economists were not preoccupied with explaining that there is a beneficial social welfare motive behind their urges to define everything on earth in dollars and cents. This allowed the interchange to proceed to the issue of how to quantify values for natural resources. The troubling thing was that even though this common ground was established, considerable concern was still raised about whether CV methods are useful for this purpose.

The use of the market analogy makes a CV method different from more general survey research concerning attitudes, preferences, and opinions. A value comparable to a market price is elicited by positing a hypothetical situation to the subject in which a payment for the aesthetic resource in question would be made. The subject is then asked to estimate the maximum that he or she would be willing to pay in the context described. The market analogy is more than a contrivance dreamed up to get the subject talking about dollars, it is meant to simulate the circumstances in actual markets from which economists theorize that certain information about values can be inferred. In actual competitive markets, prices are believed to reveal the marginal value of a unit of the item to society, in terms of what other things must be foregone to have one more unit of the item. This applies to the producer and the consumer of the item.

Whether or not this underlying motive was fully understood by the noneconomists, some important questions were raised by the participants in the workshop about whether the average person can give meaningful answers to the kinds of questions asked in CV studies, and whether even accurate answers to the questions give the economist the information he or she wants.

These comments suggest some important things to keep in mind when designing a CV application. One is that respondents may have trouble saying what they would be willing to pay for something that they typically do not think about paying for. This is something that CV practitioners have been talking about for a long time, but the solutions have tended to be to contrive a hypothetical situation that is as believable and as familiar to the subjects as possible. For example, researchers studying the value of visibility in parks have typically asked park visitors what they would be willing to pay in additional park entrance fees to have a specified level of visibility during their visit to the park. Ajzen and Peterson (this volume) point out that this approach may be resulting in questions that respondents can answer, but not providing information that the researcher really wants. It has always been acknowledged that answers to this kind of question give information only about use values (values to visitors that are directly related to their park visit), but it may also be that the answers tell us more about values for park visits than for visibility. A related point, stressed by Brown and Slovic (this volume), is that context matters. CV practitioners have to consider the likelihood that values are context specific. This suggests that contriving a hypothetical context may make an easy questionnaire that people can answer, but may not give any information relevant to a policy question that is different than the hypothetical scenario. For example, values given in response to questions about willingness to pay increased entrance fees to have better visibility at a park may be quite different than what people would be willing to pay in increased prices or taxes whether or not they visited the park.

Noneconomist workshop participants suggested that when we believe that subjects would be unable to answer a direct, policy-relevant CV question for a given issue, we may be better off giving up on CV than asking answerable questions that put the issue in a different context. For example, suppose a decision has to be made about whether to require a power plant located near a park to reduce emissions to improve visibility in the park. For a cost-benefit analysis of this situation, the economist would like to have a control cost estimate and a welfare measure of visibility values that are potentially preserved or lost. The desired welfare measure is the change in income that would cause the same change in utility (well-being) as the change in visibility would cause, for visitors and nonvisitors. Recognizing that people may have difficulty answering such a question if put to them directly, economists began asking subjects what they would pay in additional entrance fees for park visits to have visibility at some specified level during their visit, expecting to find out something useful about the desired welfare measure (such as a lower bound).

Some workshop participants suggested that with this effort to formulate a question that subjects can answer, we may have gotten so far from what we would like to know that the answers do not give us any useful information. They suggested that we think again about the policy question behind these CV questions and see if we can put the relevant questions more directly to the subjects. This may mean approaching the analysis of the policy options without the welfare measure desired for cost-benefit analysis.

It seems that the major question that comes out of these concerns is whether CV results are so error prone and so vulnerable to misinterpretation that better decisions could be made without them. Agreement to an answer to this question did not emerge from the workshop and probably few minds were changed that came into the workshop on one side or the other of this issue. My personal conclusion is that we need to keep listening and trying to improve our CV methods and that we need to make every effort to maintain skepticism and humility in interpreting and applying our results. However, with these caveats in mind, I think CV can provide some useful information to add to the decision-making arena.

HOW PSYCHOLOGY HAS ALREADY BEEN INCORPORATED IN CV APPLICATIONS

One thing that was clear at the workshop was that an effective dialogue between economists and others regarding contingent valuation applications has been going on for quite awhile. This is not to say that all the problems have been recognized and solved, but it seems important to note the efforts that have been and will continue to be made to respond to some of the types of issues raised at this workshop.

Fischhoff (this volume) discusses the treatment economists have given to potential biases in responses to CV questions. These biases include starting point bias, strategic bias, hypothetical bias, and payment vehicle bias. By concentrating on the term bias, economists may have failed to communicate that these concerns are related to the recognition that context matters. For example, discussions of potential payment vehicle bias reflect a concern that people may respond differently if asked how much they would pay as an increase in their utility bills versus as an increase in their taxes.

Considerable effort has been expended in trying to fine tune the CV approach by minimizing these kinds of "biases."[1] However, the concerns raised by Brown and Slovic, Ajzen and Peterson, and other authors in this volume, suggest that we may be spending our effort trying to fine tune the CV while ignoring more fundamental problems. For example, maybe when we ask willingness to pay questions we are asking something fundamentally different than the welfare measure of value we are trying to estimate. It seems safe to say that everyone agrees that context matters; the important differences are in the specifics.

Another area where economists have been influenced by the perspective of psychologists and other survey researchers is in the presentation of information in introducing the CV questions. In the earliest CV work, researchers presumed that people know what their values for things are, and they just needed to find a way to gets subjects to reveal them. The dominant concern of the economist was that strategic behavior would occur: If the subjects figured out that the study results might influence the provision of a public good then they might try to influence the outcome of the study by overstating or understating their true values. Therefore, the purposes of the early CV studies were kept as obscure as possible.

Results of these efforts and reactions from other survey researchers led CV practitioners to conclude that the difficulty subjects have in putting a monetary value on some nonmarket good is a much more significant problem than potential strategic behavior.[2]

Efforts have been made to address the concern that subjects may have difficulty giving accurate estimates of the amount they would be willing to pay for a good that they have no experience in purchasing for themselves. Among these efforts are:

1. Use of an iterative bidding process or payment cards to provide an opportunity for the respondent to consider different potential amounts that they might be willing to pay.
2. Careful development of introductory information to explain the issues to the subjects and to give them some understanding of the need for these kinds of estimates of value.
3. Use of preliminary questions about why the good may be useful or important to them to get them thinking about how they may value the good before being asked dollar questions.
4. Development of referendum questions (also referred to as close-ended questions) that ask whether or not the subject would be willing to pay some specified amount. These questions seem to be easier for subjects to answer because they need only decide if the amount they would be willing to pay is above or below some specified amount. By including enough subjects in the sample and varying the specified amount across subjects, an average willingness to pay can be estimated.

SPECIFIC SUGGESTIONS FOR CV PRACTITIONERS

The suggestions offered here primarily involve ways of adapting CV questionnaires to take into account how people think about resource protection issues. In many cases, asking a CV question necessitates asking respondents to consider an artificial or contrived hypothetical situation. Taking into account how people think about these issues on their own sometimes means asking additional questions to help interpret and supplement the CV responses and sometimes means moving away from CV questions all together.

Referendum (or close-ended) questions have been used in several recent CV applications and are discussed by Mitchell and Carson (this volume) and others as one solution to several of the problems that arise in CV applications. Although this suggestion has already been made, some discussion of the advantages and disadvantages for the CV practitioner are warranted here, because some problems and limitations remain.

The primary advantages of the close-ended style question are summarized as follows:
1. By making a question that is easier to answer, less interaction with the interviewer is required, reducing the potential for interviewer bias, and allowing CV questions to be more easily incorporated into a mail questionnaire that must be easy enough for the respondent to complete on his or her own.
2. Deciding yes or no on bond issues for schools, parks, and other public goods is familiar to most people and may therefore draw fewer objections or uncertain responses.
3. Respondents may find it easier to decide whether their actual willingness to pay is above or below a given amount than to give an accurate estimate of the actual amount they would be willing to pay.

Due to the following problems and limitations of the close-ended style CV question, it is not necessarily always preferable to use close-ended rather than open-ended CV questions. Some problems regarding the use of the close-ended questions also have not yet been addressed in CV applications. Problems and limitations of the close-ended style CV questions include:

1. Larger sample sizes are needed for the analysis of the responses to derive a willingness to pay function.
2. The analysis needed to derive a willingness to pay function from the yes/no responses is more complex than with open-ended responses (see Hanemann, 1984).
3. Just because respondents find close-ended questions easier to answer does not mean that their answers are more accurate.

An example of the introductory information provided and the close-ended CV question used in a recent mail questionnaire concerning preservation of the State Nature Preserve at Illinois Beach State Park is as follows (Bishop & Boyle, 1985). The percentages of respondents who selected each answer are shown in parentheses.

What Value Do You Place On The State Nature Preserve At Illinois Beach State Park?

When it comes down to what people think is important, preserving land in its natural condition often has a hard time competing with other uses of the land. We sometimes talk of things that are important to us in terms of their dollar value (such as how much a building lot is worth), but it has been difficult to talk about what State Nature Preserves are worth in terms of dollars. In this first group of questions, we are interested in finding out the dollar value that you place on the STATE NATURE PRESERVE at Illinois Beach State Park.

We would like you to assume that a private foundation has been formed to preserve the STATE NATURE PRESERVE at Illinois Beach State Park. This foundation will provide funds to build an off-shore breakwater to halt the erosion of the dunes and provide funds for the day-to-day management of the State Nature Preserve. We would like you to also assume that the foundation will be funded by selling memberships.

The interpretive trails in the State Nature Preserve will be open to all visitors at no charge. Members of the foundation will also have the satisfaction of knowing that they are helping to preserve this unique and interesting State Nature Preserve through their membership fees. Access to the remainder of the State Nature Preserve will be restricted to scientific researchers.

While answering the questions in this section, assume that the foundation will be able to preserve the State Nature Preserve (including the dunes) at Illinois Beach State Park only if enough people like yourself are willing to become supporting members.

The foundation mentioned in this survey is purely hypothetical. Our purpose in discussing the foundation is to determine the value you place on the State Nature Preserve at Illinois Beach State Park. Your name will not be given to any group soliciting money.

If a membership costs $X per year, with all funds being used to insure the preservation of the State Nature Preserve, would you become a member of the foundation described on the preceding page? (CIRCLE YES OR NO)

(45%) YES----> Why would you become a member? (CIRCLE ONE NUMBER)

(11%) 1. It is worth MORE THAN this amount per year to me to know that the State Nature Preserve is preserved.

(3%) 2. I would pay exactly this amount per year, but no more.

(1%) 3. It is worth LESS THAN this amount per year to me to know that the State Nature Preserve is preserved, but I said yes to help preserve the State Nature Preserve.

(29%) 4. I DON'T KNOW what I would pay for a membership, but I thought the State Nature Preserve should be preserved.

(1%) 5. Other, please explain.

(55%)	NO---->	Why wouldn't you become a member? (CIRCLE ONE NUMBER)
(2%)	1.	It is WORTH LESS THAN this amount per year to me to know that the State Nature Preserve is preserved.
(4%)	2.	The State Nature Preserve is WORTH THIS AMOUNT OR MORE per year to me, but I said no because I would let others pay for preservation.
(7%)	3.	The State Nature Preserve is NOT WORTH ANYTHING to me.
(17%)	4.	I DON'T KNOW what I would pay for a membership, but I thought that this amount was probably too much for me to pay.
(25%)	5.	Other, please explain.

The parallel open-ended CV question would have been: What is the most you would be willing to pay per year, with all funds being used to insure the preservation of the State Nature Preserve, to become a member of the foundation described on the preceding page?

Bishop and Boyle (1985) asked some good follow-up questions to help in interpreting the yes/no responses to their close-ended CV question. It is interesting that 64% of the respondents who said they would pay the amount asked, also said that they did not really know how much they would pay, but that they think the nature preserve should be preserved. This suggests that these respondents wanted the nature preserve protected and may have seen their positive response to the CV question more as a way to express this preference than as a measure of how much they would actually be willing to pay for this protection. This is a question that needs further exploration in future CV applications. If a large portion of respondents are answering the close-ended CV questions as if they are asking whether or not they think protection of the resource (or whatever the issue is) is a good thing, regardless of the dollar amount included in the question, then we are misinterpreting the responses in the effort to derive a willingness to pay function.

Another area where the research tools of the noneconomists can be incorporated to supplement CV questions is in the use of attitude questions and nondollar scales. Recent CV studies (such as Bishop & Boyle, 1985) have used questions about general attitudes toward environmental protection to obtain more information about the subjects. This information is typically used in examining differences between subjects in responses to CV questions. Attitude questions and questions about participation of the subjects in activities that might be related to the public good have also been frequently used to introduce the topic and get the subject thinking about the good before asking the valuation questions, as well as obtaining relevant information about the subject. It is also possible that attitude questions and nondollar scales can be used to provide additional information about the value of the good itself. Alternative techniques for measuring attitudes and strength of preferences can be compared with CV results and may provide some useful cross checks.

Examples of one way that additional questions can be used to supplement CV questions are in a recent study by Energy and Resource Consultants, Boulder, Colorado, concerning the effects of an inactive mine site along the Eagle River in Colorado.

(Results of this study are not yet available to the public because the case is still in litigation, but I can discuss the questions that were asked in the survey.) Six features related to the mine can be seen from the highway and were illustrated on a map as well as briefly described in each question. The subjects were first asked if these features had any effect on their enjoyment of the area. The questions about three of these features were as follows:

Q-1. Colored rocks and soil are present in and around the Eagle River near map site #1. The water also contains hazardous metals that may affect fish, other water life and drinking water. Have you ever seen the Eagle River in STRETCH II on the map? (CIRCLE NUMBER)
1. NO
2. YES----> How does this coloration and quality of the water in the Eagle River affect your enjoyment of the area? (CIRCLE NUMBER)
   1. DECREASES YOUR ENJOYMENT
   2. NO EFFECT ON YOUR ENJOYMENT
   3. INCREASES YOUR ENJOYMENT

Q-2. At map sites #2 and #4 are the Eagle Mine's old and new tailings ponds, which contain ore tailings and some hazardous metals. Have you ever seen the old or new tailings ponds? (CIRCLE NUMBER)
1. NO
2. YES----> How do these tailings ponds affect your enjoyment of the area? (CIRCLE NUMBER)
   1. DECREASES YOUR ENJOYMENT
   2. NO EFFECT ON YOUR ENJOYMENT
   3. INCREASES YOUR ENJOYMENT

Q-3. Have you ever seen the elevated wooden tailings pipeline at the map site #3? (CIRCLE NUMBER)
1. NO
2. YES----> How does this pipeline affect your enjoyment of the area? (CIRCLE NUMBER)
   1. DECREASES YOUR ENJOYMENT
   2. NO EFFECT ON YOUR ENJOYMENT
   3. INCREASES YOUR ENJOYMENT

Subjects were then asked how much time they had spent in recreation activities along this stretch of the river in the past year, and were asked to estimate how much time they would spend in recreation activities if the river and the landscape were restored to the pre-mine condition. The CV questions were then asked in the following way:

Various possibilities have been suggested for the future of the Eagle Mine site and the Eagle River. Some people suggest doing nothing. Some suggest the mine structures, tailing ponds and roaster piles should be cleaned up, while others want them preserved. Some suggest a clean-up of the Eagle River and local ground water. Efforts to clean up the area or to preserve the current appearance may cost a substantial amount of money. To help us measure how important site preservation and/or clean-up is to you, assume the only way to fund these efforts is for the State of Colorado to pay for them from a special fund and for each of us to pay into this fund. Assume any efforts would be started immediately.

Q-10. What do you think should be done about the appearance of the old and new tailings ponds, other smaller tailings ponds, the roaster piles and the colored rocks and soils around the Eagle River. (Assume your recommendation would have no effect on water quality in the Eagle River.) (CIRCLE NUMBER)

1. DO NOTHING AND SPEND NOTHING
2. RETURN THE AREA TO A NATURAL LAND-SCAPE APPEARANCE
3. PRESERVE CURRENT APPEARANCE

What is the MOST you would be willing to pay each year for the next 10 years for your desired option, given that unless enough funds are raised no action would be taken? $_____

Q-11. What do you think should be done about the appearance of the elevated wooden pipeline? (Assume your recommendation would have no effect on water quality in the Eagle River.) (CIRCLE NUMBER)

1. DO NOTHING AND SPEND NOTHING
2. REMOVE THE PIPELINE
3. PRESERVE ITS CURRENT APPEARANCE

What is the MOST you would be willing to pay each year for the next 10 years for your desired option, given that unless enough funds are raised no action would be taken? $_____

Q-12. The tailings ponds and roaster piles contain hazardous metals. Some of these metals now end up in the Eagle River and may affect the quality of the water for human use and for fish and other water life. Even with a clean-up of the current contamination, severe flooding or other unusual events could cause future contamination of the Eagle River. Also, the Eagle Mine is filling with water and could, in the next 2 to 10 years, overflow, spilling hazardous metals into the Eagle River. What do you think should be done about cleaning up and protecting the water quality of the Eagle River in STRETCH II? (CIRCLE NUMBER)

1. DO NOTHING AND SPEND NOTHING
2. CLEAN UP CURRENT CONTAMINATION SO THAT THE WATER QUALITY IS THE SAME AS IN STRETCH I
3. CLEAN UP CURRENT CONTAMINATION SO THAT THE WATER QUALITY IS THE SAME AS IN STRETCH I AND PROTECT AGAINST FU-TURE CONTAMINATION OF THE RIVER

What is the MOST you would be willing to pay each year for the next 10 years to clean up ONLY the current contamination, given that unless enough funds are raised no action would be taken? $_____

What is the MOST you would be willing to pay each year for the next 10 years to ALSO protect against events leading to future contamination? $_____

The questions that preceded the CV questions serve several purposes. They get the subjects looking at the map and thinking about the site and how they feel about the effects of the mining before they are asked the more difficult CV questions. More important, they give some additional information with which to evaluate the CV responses. For example, if someone says that the features related to the mine decrease their enjoyment of the area and that they think it should be restored to its pre-mining condition, but they give a $0 response to the CV question, then there is reason to believe that this is some sort of protest response to the CV question itself, rather than a true zero value for restoration. On the other hand, if someone says that the features do not affect their enjoyment of the area and that they think nothing should be done about restoration, then this provides confirmation of a true zero value for restoration.

It is also important that in this situation subjects have the option of saying that the features related to the mine actually increase their enjoyment of the area, because some people find old mine sites interesting. Responses to these questions can help reduce the difficulty in determining which $0 responses are "true."

Rowe and Chestnut (1985, 1986) used a more complex ranking question in conjunction with a CV approach in a study concerning the effects of air pollution on symptoms of people with asthma. The health example is a little off our topic, but a similar approach could be developed for some natural resource amenities, especially when use of the amenity involves some expenditure on the part of the individual. After several groups of questions about how asthma symptoms affect the subject's expenses, work, and leisure activities, the following ranking and CV questions were asked:

Q-29. Here is a list of some possible benefits you might receive from having your asthma improve. Please take your time and rank them from most important to least important. Exclude any that are of no importance.

RANKING   CATEGORIES

Most important _____   a. Lower expenditure on doctors, hospitals, medicines, special equipment and services.

_____   b. Higher productivity at work or ability to get higher wages and salaries.

_____   c. More flexibility about where to live.

_____   d. Better chance to participate in desired leisure, recreation and social activities.

Least important _____ e. Less pain and discomfort.

Q-30. If federal, state, or local governments set up programs that could reduce pollens, dusts, air pollutants and other factors throughout this area that might reduce your Bad Asthma Days by half, but would cost you increased tax dollars, what would be the maximum increase in taxes each year that you and your household would be willing to pay and still support such a program?

$_____

The responses to the ranking questions and to other questions concerning the effects of asthma symptoms made it possible to evaluate the responses to the willingness to pay question. For example, it was possible to compare the willingness to pay response to the estimate of medical expenditures incurred by the individual and also see where the medical expenses category fell in the ranking. This allowed for the development of criteria for identifying potential problem responses to the willingness to pay question that went beyond the usual evaluation of zero responses. One interesting conclusion from this evaluation was that several zero responses were judged to be valid responses even though "protest" answers were selected in a typical zero-bid follow-up question, because the individual reported very few "Bad Asthma Days" and very low medical expenses.

Overall, about 80% of the responses to the willingness to pay question were judged to be reasonably consistent with the responses to the other questions. This suggests that the majority of the willingness to pay responses are probably useful for evaluating policies, but that a portion of the subjects have trouble with the willingness to pay question for one reason or another. These problems do not always show up as zero or very large responses. Efforts need to continue to find appropriate ways to identify and evaluate potential problem responses, without simply throwing out answers that do not conform to the researchers' expectations.

The ranking responses also provide a link between the willingness to pay response and an actual expenditure made by the subject, in this case, medical expenditures. It has been hypothesized that medical care costs are only one factor that might influence willingness to pay for improvements in health. The ranking responses give an idea how important medical care costs are relative to "nonmarket" concerns such as effects on leisure activities. A similar approach might be taken with regard to recreation at a park. Economic analysis suggests that the value of a visit to a park is at least as much as the costs incurred by the individual in making the visit. It might be possible to develop questions that explore the perceived value of a visit to the individual relative to these costs that are incurred. This may make it possible to estimate how much maximum willingness to pay for the visit could be expected to exceed the actual costs of the visit. Care needs to be taken to account for the fact that the costs are incurred to obtain the perceived benefits of the visit (i.e., to avoid a double counting).

A useful suggestion made by Ajzen at the workshop concerning the design of questions like these, is to use open-ended questions in a small sample pretest to help identify the items to be used in a ranking or similar question. For example, results of CV studies suggest that subjects value the preservation of parks for many reasons in addition to their own interest in being able to use the park. The following question might be used to evaluate the relative importance of altruistic and existence value motives that have been discussed in the literature. The items listed are, however, based on the reflection of researchers about why people might value parks for reasons other than their own use. This question could probably be improved by asking a small sample of subjects why they think parks should be preserved. The possible question is as follows:

Below are some possible reasons you may want national parks preserved even if you never visit the parks yourself. Please circle the number that indicates the importance to you of each of these possible reasons.

1. So that others now and in the future will have the opportunity to visit and enjoy these areas.
2. Because it is important to preserve our natural and historic heritage.
3. So that there will be areas where native vegetation and wildlife can live.
4. To allow scientific research on nature and history.
5. So that nature's beauty will be preserved for its own sake, even if no one ever goes there.

In several previous studies concerning parks or other recreation related resources, subjects have been asked to allocate their willingness to pay totals among different motives. These motives have typically represented what researchers call use value, altruistic value, bequest value, and existence value (e.g., Walsh, Sanders, & Loomis, 1985). The above question gives an alternative approach for evaluating the relative importance of these different possible motives in a way that subjects might find easier to answer. An interesting exercise would be to compare the results of these different techniques for measuring the relative importance of the possible motives.

Ajzen and Peterson (this volume) suggest that several psychometric techniques are available for measuring the strength of subjects' preferences. References for these techniques are included in their paper. The idea is that many different approaches could be taken to rate or rank alternative choices. These approaches do not typically result in value responses in dollars or in information that can be used to infer dollar values. However, if obtaining dollar values is not feasible for the issue at hand, these techniques provide the possibility of obtaining some value information. Also, it would be useful to use these techniques, where appropriate, in conjunction with CV type questions to obtain a broader base of value information. Comparisons of results of psychometric measurement techniques to CV results for the same issue might provide some useful insights and could potentially provide useful supplemental information for policy decisions.

References

Bishop, R. C., & Boyle, K. J. (1985). *The economic value of Illinois Beach State Nature Preserve* (Final Report). Springfield, IL: Illinois Department of Conservation.

Hanemann, M. W. (1984). Welfare evaluations in contingent valuation experiments with discrete responses. *American Journal of Agricultural Economics, 66,* 332-341.

Rowe, R. D., & Chestnut, L. G. (1985). *Oxidants and asthmatics in Los Angeles: A benefits analysis* (Report No. EPA-230-07-85-010). Washington, DC: U.S. Environmental Protection Agency.

Rowe, R. D., & Chestnut, L. G. (1986). *Addendum to: Oxidants and asthmatics in Los Angeles: A benefits analysis* (Report No. EPA-230-09-86-017). Washington, DC: U.S. Environmental Protection Agency.

Walsh, R. G., Sanders, L. D., & Loomis, J. B. (1985). *Wild and scenic river economics: Recreation use and preservation values.* Englewood, CO: American Wilderness Alliance.

Footnotes

[1]The term bias has been used because these are things that may cause the responses to CV questions to fail to reflect the "true" welfare measure of value being sought. It has been pointed out that bias may not be quite the right term because it implies a systematic error, either positive or negative, and it is not clear that a systematic error is always involved.

[2]One CV study that specifically tested for strategic behavior found evidence of it for only one respondent--an economics professor at a local university.

Concluding Remarks

Let Us Hear the Conclusion of the Matter

George L. Peterson
Rocky Mountain Forest and Range Experiment Station
Fort Collins, Colorado

B. L. Driver
Rocky Mountain Forest and Range Experiment Station
Fort Collins, Colorado

Robin Gregory
Decision Research
Eugene, Oregon

"The Preacher" concludes the Old Testament book of Ecclesiastes with a simple admonition: "Of making many books there is no end; and much study is a weariness of the flesh. Let us hear the conclusion of the whole matter: Fear God, and keep his commandments; for this is the whole duty of man." To some, such a conclusion might seem appropriate for a text on amenity resource valuation. At times, that subject seems almost religious. Different points of view are frequently argued with great enthusiasm, often based only on the will to believe. At such times, it seems that The Preacher need modify his words only slightly to make them applicable to our situation: "Let us hear the conclusion of the whole matter: Fear academic dogma, and keep its commandments; for this is the whole duty of amenity resource valuation."

Yet, the topic before us should not be one of religion, and our mission is not that of preacher. Rather, it is to inquire whether the commandments of the academic disciplines are useful, correct, and sufficient. Lacking the guidance of prophetic vision in the matter of valuation of amenity goods and services, we assembled thoughtful scholars to question the old ways, to explore and compare the tenets of different sects of behavioral science, and to seek better answers than those we have been taught. We examined the familiar ground with colleagues from different disciplines, hoping for new perspective and escape from the feudalism of dull and confining academic dogmas.

Having ventured far and returned from the quest, we hope to provide in this final paper some useful observations and conclusions toward constructive integration of economics and other behavioral sciences over the domain of amenity valuation. Our intention is to provide a brief critical overview of the book and the workshop that contributed to its production, to identify and discuss some of the important issues that survive, and to point toward an agenda for future research.

WHY?

The basic goal of the book is to promote better application of the concepts and methods of economic valuation in the broad sense of human welfare, rather than the more narrow perspective of monetary transactions. Neoclassical microeconomic theory is the basis for much of what has been done in the field of amenity resource valuation. This framework of theory is elegant and rigorous. Indeed, it is both a work of art and a powerful tool that performs well those tasks for which it is suited.

However, problems have begun to pop up. Questions are being raised about the adequacy of the assumptions and implications about human behavior. For example, does economic theory intend to describe or prescribe human behavior, or is it simply an exercise in logical reasoning? Help appears to be needed and available from other behavioral sciences in evaluating the behavioral assumptions and propositions of microeconomics.

The behavioral sciences have accumulated much descriptive information about human behavior, but economists are not generally familiar with this knowledge, and it is not well catalogued in the kind of theoretical framework economists prefer. Are the findings irrelevant to economic valuation, or is it simply a matter of high tariffs and language barriers that have hindered

interdisciplinary trade? Whatever the reasons for isolationism, we first need to define more rigorously the objectives of economics in application to amenity goods and services. Then we then can discuss more meaningfully how and whether other behavioral disciplines should be integrated with economics.

One area where help is needed is experimental design and measurement. In applications where theory intends to describe and predict behavior, we need to dig more deeply with experimental shovels into the field of behavioral assumptions. The behavioral sciences have accumulated generations of such experience, and it needs to be applied to explain consumer decisions in both market and nonmarket situations.

For many priced commodities, competitive market transactions assign monetary values that come close to measuring marginal exchange values. However, for nonpriced goods and services, as well as for significant price changes in private goods, markets fail to measure full economic values in the broad sense of economic welfare. Extramarket methods must be employed, methods that measure behaviors and behavioral intentions from which monetary exchange values can be inferred. Social psychologists and other behavioral scientists have a lot of experience in evaluating such exchanges, using surveys and other value-elicitation techniques that environmental economists only recently have begun to employ.

The potential for trade among the disciplines is not one-sided. While social psychologists know a lot about human behavior and have an impressive array of tools for experimental design and the measurement of behavioral and subjective phenomena, their theoretical framework is quite different from that of economists. Theory tends to consist of collections of specific behavioral hypotheses and propositions, or broad conceptual models that often are difficult to connect to observable phenomena. For example, Heberlein points out in his paper that social psychology needs help in developing rigorous mathematical theories and models of individual and group behavior, models from which behavioral hypotheses can be deduced and that are connected operationally to measurable things. Does the economists' approach to behavioral modeling offer promise in other behavioral sciences, or have the economists simply elected to study only those concepts that respond to such logical attack, leaving the more fuzzy aspects of behavior to others?

The motivation for interdisciplinary work between economics and other behavioral sciences comes from a real need to explain and describe puzzling aspects of human behavior from a problem solving point of view. Social decision processes often need to assign values to extramarket goods and services so as to allow examination of the tradeoffs among alternative resource allocations. For example, as a result of the Renewable Resources Planning Act (RPA) and the National Forest Management Act (NFMA), economic efficiency analyses of alternative resource allocations are now a required part of forest planning and land management. Traditional economics has had to reach out beyond markets to estimate monetary exchange values for public goods and nonmarginal price changes. Economists have thus begun to explore the domain of social psychology, because that is what has to be done to get the needed answers. Such efforts might be viewed by academic dogmatists as an invasion of enemy turf, but we believe a more constructive view is that economists are extending their hands across the fence in a request for help and an offer to cooperate.

The problem goes beyond economic valuation, however. The political process of social choice is not satisfied by economic efficiency analysis alone. Information is required about the social distribution of costs and benefits. Also, because people often choose to exercise individual sovereignty in expressing their own values rather than to have economic analysts measure it for them, we need to know the specific beneficial and detrimental consequences of proposed actions, at the personal as well as the societal level.

These needs create a mandate for integration of the knowledge and skills of several academic and applied disciplines concerned with value-related human behavior. The walls of academic feudalism must come down, and, indeed, they have begun to crack and crumble in remote corners of the kingdoms. Integration needs to be accomplished, however, without asking people to change their professions or to become experts in several disciplines. If, through integration, we were to lose the power of specialization, the breadth of integration would be of little value. Breadth offers efficiency in problem solving, because it reveals the best tools to use for a given problem; but without the depth of specialization, tools often are of poor quality, and the craftspeople who use them may lack excellence.

WHAT?

Our efforts to estimate economic values and describe the beneficial consequences of amenity goods and services led to the production of this text. We wanted to find different parts of the puzzle and see if they might start coming together. A number of topics that seemed most promising for integration were identified, and those topics then were organized into a set of proposed papers. Scholars from the various topic areas were identified, with an eye to representation of economic and "noneconomic" points of view for each proposed paper. We asked people with different bents to write papers together. In general, we tried to put economists together with noneconomists to create constructive tension, stimulate creativity, build new working relationships, and cause educational encounters among people who might not otherwise have reason to meet.

As we went about commissioning the papers, we were pleased that most people accepted willingly. To facilitate an efficient process for technical review of the manuscripts and to further stimulate constructive conflict, a workshop was organized. At that workshop, the authors presented their papers in general sessions and then exchanged ideas and criticisms in smaller group settings. The dialogue was exciting, and the feedback received by authors allowed them to improve their manuscripts. This text is the outcome of that process.

WHETHER?

What was accomplished, and how useful is it? As researchers and editors, we are pleased with the outcome. The papers are excellent, and the process was educational and good fun. How-

ever, it is clearly premature to try to judge the usefulness of the effort at this point in time. If the book and the process by which it was produced influence how people think, both over time and over a wide range of disciplines, then it will have proven itself useful.

In hindsight, the principal problem with the product is that there are some holes in the fabric of the text. Some important issues are missing, and some people whose points of view should have been heard are not included. For example, the psychology of individual decision behavior is not well covered. Microeconomic economic theory is, in one sense, an individual decision theory. Economic man is posited as a rational being whose preferences are described by utility functions with rather restrictive mathematical properties. Gains and losses are valued equally, except for income effects, and individual and aggregate demand functions follow from the utility functions through an assumption of utility maximization under the constraint of a limited budget. Values are assigned by, and derived from, the choices people make. There is little room for human frailty or noble aspirations. But, how do people really make their choices? Psychologists have much to offer on this subject, but the book fails to provide an adequate psychological critique of the economic model of human behavior.

A principal focus of the book is on value measurement, particularly the measurement of extramarket values through experimental, simulated, and hypothetical market methods. Economists and behavioral scientists alike have struggled nobly with the challenge, but in general our efforts leap beyond a fundamental problem that first needs to be resolved: We go quickly to the task of measuring things, without first having fully understood measurement itself or the exact nature of the thing to be measured. The physical sciences long ago recognized that measurement is a discipline in its own right, and much effort has gone into understanding the measurement process so that what comes out of it makes sense.

Measurement must begin with an operative definition of the thing to be measured. That is, the object must first be defined such that different magnitude states can be identified, observed, and compared. Too often in amenity resource valuation, we start measuring values before defining what we mean by "value" in terms that can be measured with quantitative rigor. We also often fail to define precisely the thing to which value is to be assigned. The result is that we get numbers that are reliable, meaning that "something" has been measured, but in all honesty we are often at a loss to state exactly what has been measured or whether two independent measurements have identified different magnitude states of the same thing and can therefore be compared.

Finally, the entire effort, including the text itself, might have been better if it had focused on a more specific applied problem--such as treating forests with pesticides, coping with acid deposition, or disposing of hazardous wastes--rather than simply addressing abstract topic areas. While the participants generally came away from their assignments with enthusiastic agreement that something useful had happened, they also felt somewhat frustrated, and many expressed a desire to follow up the Estes Park workshop with another meeting. In the second conference, they wanted to focus on how valuation of specific resources would proceed in an applied policy context. For example, how would social psychologists measure the value of a change in the population of spotted owls resulting from timber management that modifies its habitat? How would psychological methods and measurements differ from the economist's approach? Could an economist and a social psychologist working together come up with a better approach?

However, the text speaks for itself in presenting at least the seed of a new perspective on important ideas, and the workshop already has spoken for itself in successfully stimulating meaningful exchange between disciplines. Whether the seeds have been planted sufficiently well for trees to grow remains to be seen, and whether the fruit will be palatable will be decided over time by our peers.

A BRIEF SUMMARY OF THE MAJOR ISSUES

Questions About Monetary Valuation and Economic Efficiency

One of the most significant issues raised is already well known but some times not acknowledged. There is much confusion and misunderstanding about economic valuation. This confusion is not limited to the so-called "noneconomists." Economists themselves also seem to have diverse views on both the scope and accuracy of economic valuation techniques. Valuation is a complex subject that is difficult enough to understand even within its technical domain. The problem is severely aggravated by the inseparability of its technical, philosophical, and political aspects. Upon careful examination, disagreement on technical matters often can be traced to different political judgments or philosophical positions that underlie the technical arguments.

Monetary valuation in the context of economic efficiency, i.e., measurement of potential Pareto improvement, is but a small part of the larger domain of valuation of amenity goods and services. Monetary value is a limited concept of exchange that is dependent on supply, demand, competing substitutes, and consumer sovereignty. It does not necessarily convey either inherent worth or ethical wisdom. Air, for example, has no direct monetary value, but we can't live without it. Monetary value can be further subdivided into priced and nonpriced, cash and non-cash values. It also can be broken into marginal prices and nonmarginal values, and further comes unglued in terms of willingness to pay for rights not owned and compensation demanded for the loss of owned rights.

Too often, even economists think of economic efficiency from the financial point of view of a private firm, under the assumption of perfect competition and marginal transactions. Even that narrow perspective is complicated enough, but it falls far short of the domain of economic efficiency and potential Pareto improvement in the management of amenity resources.

To many people, economic value means economic impact, rather than economic efficiency. Balance of payments, income, employment, local expenditures, and tax base are what matter at the local level, where the real concern often is, "What's in it for us?" The important question here is one of distribution, not efficiency, and the underlying concern is equity.

At a broader level, most of us want to know the specific details of how a proposed plan affects us. Tabulations and sums of economic costs and benefits are relatively uninteresting to individual consumers, unless they also have access to more disaggregate information. For example, the proposed new comprehensive plan for my town may boast eloquently of economic efficiency and more jobs for the local community, but what really matters to me is that it calls for widening my street and the loss of the big silver maple tree in front of my house. In the same vein, there may be hidden consequences that are not apparent, such as carcinogenic atmospheric deposition from a new industry attracted to the town. If we act only on the obvious effects, the resulting decision may move us away from, not toward, greater welfare. We need to understand not only things we see, but also the things we do not see, and this may require extensive research to expose the beneficial and detrimental consequences of a proposed action.

Valuation also transcends the individual point of view and extends to the societal level. In our social choice we often define values that are inconsistent with expressed individual preferences. For example, individuals choose to smoke, but the Surgeon General requires tobacco companies to warn the customers of potentially fatal consequences. Individuals choose to drive under the influence of alcohol, but collectively we define it to be unlawful and impose severe penalties.

From the efficiency point of view, the focal questions are: When is monetary valuation appropriate, what questions does it answer, what does it mean from a personal and policy point of view, and what important human concerns does it include and exclude? The answers to these questions are not generally understood and merit additional attention. Too often, economic analysts and critics of economic analysis fail to realize that economic efficiency with its attendant monetary valuation is only one of several value constructs that should be weighed when making resource allocation decisions.

In addition to their role in market transactions, monetary values find a place in "benefit-cost analysis" (BCA), where the monetary costs and benefits of a proposed change are summed to test for potential Pareto improvement, that is, whether the change creates more aggregate economic value than it consumes, without regard for who gains and who loses. In theory, each of us might do such an analysis for every personal decision we make, although we seldom are so formal. BCA is most often done by governments in the execution of their responsibility for social choice.

However, BCA can be conceived at several levels of completeness and in practice often falls short of perfection. In an ideal BCA, for example, the monetary worth of all gains and losses, including extramarket and external changes, would be measured perfectly. Such perfect value measurement would avoid the distortions of imperfect markets, biased expressions, or strategically motivated political negotiations. The outcome would identify those changes that are most economically beneficial to society in the aggregate, i.e., that produce the greatest increase in aggregate economic welfare.

Such information is necessary, but insufficient, for optimal social choice. The distribution of the gains and losses must also be exposed, so that affected individuals can strive for resolution of equity through economic bargaining, political conflict resolution, litigation, or warfare. Assuming perfect BCA, perfect exposure of the distribution of consequences, and perfect institutions for equity resolution, monetary valuation would seem to be sufficient for optimal social choice. But perfection is lacking on all counts, and people simply choose to want to know about other things as well, even to act in ways that seem to be arbitrary. BCA and monetary valuation must be regarded as one set of potentially useful information in a complex mosaic of facts and forces.

Some critics of monetary valuation seem to imply that better alternatives exist without actually producing them. In such cases, the game of, "I don't like your way, so do it differently" becomes a stalling tactic, a search for the illusory perfect approach, an exercise in fault finding, or simply a power struggle. Many of the essays in this book suggest there is a better way.

The authors represented in the text generally do not support the extreme argument that monetary valuation is so riddled with imperfection that no valuation is better than monetary valuation. Neither do they excuse partial or biased efforts in cases where improvement appears to be possible. Critics from all sides need to avoid fault finding and direct their attention to searching for constructive alternatives.

Questions About Value Measurement

One of the limiting factors in BCA is an unanswered question about our ability to obtain credible monetary value estimates for certain kinds of public goods. Even the best extramarket valuation methods require people to think of the valued object in a context of exchange and exclusion. Often these are things that never have been experienced in such a context, and their nature may be such that exchange and deprivation are impossible or unthinkable. Is this an ultimate limiting factor on the appropriateness of BCA and monetary valuation? Are there some amenity goods and services that cannot or should not be so treated?

The extramarket elicitations methods of the economist require people to make choices in real, experimental, simulated, or hypothetical markets. In theory, the choices they make reveal their assigned monetary values. Are people sufficiently aware of their preferences to be able to give valid verbal or behavioral responses? Are values implied by hidden consequences or subliminal physiological responses different from those that are consciously assigned? Recent research indicates that economists' fears about specific biases in contingent valuation methods (CVM) may only be toying with the tip of an iceberg.

Such questions lead to another perplexing dilemma. Do real markets correctly reveal monetary values? What is a "correct" value, and how is it identified? Do "true" values exist, or is value simply a fleeting shadow of wavering contexts, never absolutely existing, and only meaningful in a relative sense? Is the purpose of extramarket valuation to simulate real market outcomes or to measure something more fundamental? If markets suffer from biases and context relativity, should economists try to emulate these biases and relativities, or should they aim at greater purity? Is it possible to frame extramarket methods so that market-equivalent answers are obtained, and if so, how are we to know when we can trust value measurements as being sufficiently specified?

There has been much concern about alleged biases in extramarket valuation methods, especially on the subject of CVM. Economists tend to attack this question in much the same way that they attack all questions: from a theoretical and (in a behavioral sense) hypothetical, point of view. Many papers on this subject discuss various forms of supposed bias as if they are known to exist, but social psychologists have been heard to ask (a) whether these biases are, in fact, known to occur or whether they are simply hypotheses, and (b) if they are real, what are the parameters of variation. They further ask to see the framework of behavioral hypotheses, i.e., the "theory," from which specific experiments can be designed to test hypotheses and estimate parameters. Are the alleged biases much ado about nothing, or do the experimental, hypothetical, and simulated market methods inject extraneous but harmfully systematic variation?

Economic theory does not recognize a serious distinction between an individual's maximum willingness to pay (WTP) and his/her minimum compensation demanded (CD) for a good. Except for income effects, gaining something has the same monetary value as losing it. Thus, giving something up is viewed simply as the monetary opportunity cost of changing the form of an asset. However, empirical experience with CVM consistently demonstrates substantial differences between WTP and CD, with CD generally the larger of the two. Is the observed difference simply an artifact of poor experimental design, or is the difference real? Is the pain of loss greater than the pleasure of gain, other things being equal, and are people therefore understandably reluctant to sell? If the differences are real, when is WTP appropriate and when is CD the best measure to use? And, is it possible to measure CD with any degree of confidence? All these questions sound more like psychology than economics, yet there has been too little psychological attention given to them. Thus far, most research by psychologists tends to be in a form that economists are prone to ignore.

Also entangled in the problem of measuring WTP and CD is the subject of perceived rights and endowments. Some rights are defined and protected by law while others, such as possession of certain narcotics, are nullified by law. Other rights are legal but are attenuated by the nature of the rights themselves. As with nonpoint air pollution, the right to breath clean air may be legally defined, but if it is impossible to identify the persons who take away the right, compensation cannot be obtained.

What about perceived rights that exist only in the minds of those who hold them but are not recognized by law? For example, someone who enjoys visual or physical access to another's private land may perceive it as a right, but it is really only a privilege. If the owner denies access, no rights have been taken, but the loss is still real. Economic theory recognizes such welfare change, but the law requires no compensation.

As mentioned earlier, CVM experiments often give reliable and reproducible results. Therefore, it is argued, "something" has been measured. When the numbers are larger, that "something" is larger, and when they are smaller, "it" is certainly smaller, but, what is "it?" Is it a monetary exchange value of "something," and if it is such a value, what is the "something" to which the monetary value is assigned? Is it a proposed change, a policy or action intended to cause the change, a belief about the efficacy of such a policy, a policy by which payment for the change is to be made, or a belief about who should be responsible for payment?

Social psychologists, for example, suggest that CVM responses may be attitudes or verbal expressions of behavioral intentions rather than assignments of value. The questions are sometimes sufficiently vague that the attitude objects or the intended behaviors are not adequately identified.

Perhaps such questions may be resolved through more comprehensive experimental design that incorporates psychometric attitudinal methods to specify objects and to separate attitudes from values. Indeed, from the social psychological point of view, "value" is not the simple thing defined in economic theory. Psychological value is a rather different and more complex thing that may itself be worthy of attention in the measurement of monetary values.

One of the most promising possibilities for improvement in value measurement is the psychologists' frequent reliance on multiple measures of the same thing to ferret out elusive magnitudes that cleverly avoid direct observation. The multiple item inventory is a case in point. Stating a question in several different ways serves two important purposes. First, it allows individually reliable responses to be constructed from the communality among the responses. Second, because different words with similar meanings are used, the question is more precise using semantic triangulation. Meanings are more likely to be pinned down in the mind of a given respondent, and they are more likely to coincide in the minds of different respondents.

Economists may reply that we are ultimately interested in aggregate scores, not individual scores, and that we obtain reliability by combining the scores of several individuals rather than by combining several scores for a single individual. True, says the psychologist, but of what meaning is an aggregation of several answers to different questions? Clearly, there is more dialogue and exchange needed here. Indeed, the question of multiple measures goes beyond psychology into physiology: What is to be learned about assigned value by comparing market behaviors, verbal responses, and physiological indicators? According to the authors represented in this book, there probably is quite a lot to be learned.

SO WHERE DO WE GO FROM HERE?

Economists, we believe, need to do a better job of defining their objectives when applying economic theory to amenity resource valuation and benefit-cost analysis of policy alternatives. Is their theory normative, descriptive, or simply an unattached logical structure, a pure work of theoretical art? They also need to reach out to social psychology and other behavioral sciences to learn more about what is known concerning human behavior and valuation, to develop better definitions of what people mean by value and value objects, and to design more effective experiments for testing hypotheses and estimating values.

There are some hopeful signs. The fact that so many excellent economists and other behavioral scientists agreed to participate in this effort speaks for itself. Several successful interdisciplinary partnerships have been working on these problems for some time, and promising new connections have emerged from our workshop. There are also several academic programs, including those sponsored by the National Science Foundation and the Sloan Foundation, that focus on problems rather than disciplines.

Economists are not the only ones who need to push for changes. Social psychologists and other behavioral scientists need to become more interested in valuation in the context of applied public policy. Many of the topics they study, or at least the way they are studied, are interesting from a scientific point of view but are not very relevant to the needs of policy analysts. It will take movement from both sides if more effective collaborative arrangements are to be successfully consummated.

Perhaps what is needed is more bright scientists with the courage to display an applied mentality, people who try to solve practical problems by combining the separate sciences of relevant disciplines, or people who, like good politicians and talented poets, keep their sights on practical problems while working between disciplines to build bridges over ivy-covered walls.

There are institutional problems, too, that inhibit such progress by encouraging academic feudalism. What is the incentive for working on benefit-cost analysis as a social psychologist? Who will publish your work? Surely not the economic journals. Perhaps the journals of social psychology? Not them either, unfortunately, because they are driven by the quest for excellence in specialization and purity within the discipline. There are interdisciplinary journals, to be sure, but will your department give them equal weight when tenure is at stake?

It is time for a discipline of applied behavioral economics, or applied economic behavior, with a faculty consisting both of economists and of other behavioral scientists and with a targeted agenda of policy application. This text is a celebration of the possibilities of that new science, and of the environmental policy improvements that could arise from its practice.

AUGUSTANA UNIVERSITY COLLEGE
LIBRARY